Cambridge Studies in American Literature and Culture

Editor: Albert Gelpi, Stanford University

Other books in the series

CAMBRIDGE STUDIES IN AMERICAN LITERATURE AND CULTURE

Painterly Abstraction in Modernist American Poetry

Painterly Abstraction in Modernist American Poetry

The Contemporaneity of Modernism

CHARLES ALTIERI
University of Washington

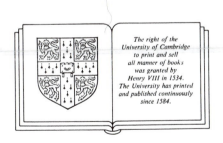

The right of the
University of Cambridge
to print and sell
all manner of books
was granted by
Henry VIII in 1534.
The University has printed
and published continuously
since 1584.

CAMBRIDGE UNIVERSITY PRESS
Cambridge
New York   Port Chester   Melbourne   Sydney

Published by the Press Syndicate of the University of Cambridge
The Pitt Building, Trumpington Street, Cambridge CB2 1RP
40 West 20th Street, New York, NY 10011, USA
10 Stamford Road, Oakleigh, Melbourne 3166, Australia

First published 1989

Printed in the United States of America

Library of Congress Cataloging-in-Publication Data
Altieri, Charles, 1942–
Painterly abstraction in Modernist American poetry.
(Cambridge studies in American literature and culture)
1. American poetry – 20th century – History and
criticism. 2. Modernism (Literature) – United States.
3. Abstraction in literature. 4. Self in literature.
I. Title. II. Series.
PS310.M57A58   1989   811'.5'091   88–35203

British Library Cataloguing in Publication Data
Altieri, Charles, 1942–
Painterly abstraction in modernist American poetry:
the contemporaneity of Modernism
– (Cambridge studies in American literature and culture)
1. Poetry in English. American writers.
Modernism 1900–1988. Critical studies.
I. Title
811.52'0912

ISBN 0–521–33085–8 hard covers

Contents

Acknowledgments

Perhaps the best compensation for the amount of time this book has taken is the range and depth of the gratitude I have come to feel. First there are the editors who helped me with earlier versions of some of the arguments set forth here. I want to express my thanks to the staffs of the following journals for working with essays that are listed in the bibliography: *American Poetry, Boundary 2, Bucknell Review, Critical Inquiry, Criticism, Dada / Surrealism, Kenyon Review, Iowa Review, Journal of Comparative Literature and Aesthetics, Michigan Quarterly Review, PMLA,* and *Southern Humanities Review.* And I would like to extend a special note of gratitude to those editors of collections on Modernist subjects who invited me to contribute and who put in the considerable time working with my prose that they knew they had contracted for: Anthony Cascardi, Albert Gelpi, Hank Lazer, and Wendy Steiner.

I wish I could also thank in particular those audiences who called forth some of that prose, especially those who expressed their dissatisfaction, but here a general statement of gratitude will have to do. Unfortunately I can do no more, even for those students who gave me the constant pleasure of their attention and their resistance. Prudence dictates that I not be so curt with the Graduate School at the University of Washington, the one body that granted me research support during the years I was preparing this book. And much more than prudence leads me to name in gratitude those friends whose conversation and patient reading of sections of this book saved me from embarrassing errors and opened new directions for approaching some of the materials. I wish I could get their names to roll off in Yeatsian cadences, but for criticism a simple list will have to do. Thank you to David Antin, David Bosworth, Doug Collins, Jean Dornbush, Jeanne Heuving, Heather McHugh, Bob

McNamara, Tom Mitchell, Raimonda Modiano, Marjorie Perloff, John Ruff, Steve Shaviro, Marian Sugano, Evan Watkins, and James Winchell. For help with the preparation of the manuscript, I am indebted to the excellent and good-natured work of Michael Caufield, Kim Johnson Bogart, Rob Weller, and especially Shannon Mattoon, whose remarkable competence in all domains of the practical world enables me to avoid it most of the time. Then there are those whose kindness and patience in reading the entire manuscript I have only now, in my final revisions, come fully to appreciate: Sharon Bryan, Carl Dennis, Charles Molesworth, and a very generous press reader. Al Gelpi endured all this twice and gave careful, detailed editorial help; for him I have no words to express my appreciation and my respect. Christie Lerch, my copy editor, may have other words for Al, but for me she managed not only to provide the most careful editing I have been given but also to make her constant criticism sound like praise. Readers will have a debt to her whose magnitude I hope they never know.

Finally I want to thank my wife Joanne and my daughter Laura for what must have been the even harder task of putting up with me day after day as I first anticipated these critical assessments, then indulged in the endless process of rationalizing myself in relation to them. I am grateful for their patience and for their remarkable capacity to change the subject; indeed, to change this subject. Since it is high time that I began putting pressure on Laura to read this kind of stuff, I will use the permissions granted to the complexities of a father's love and delight in what she is making of herself to dedicate this book to her.

Introduction

From the Modernism you choose you get the PostModernism you deserve.

David Antin

An old academic joke provides the best emblem for the historical and thematic concerns that will dominate this book. The story's ephebe is a graduate student whom we join as he knocks on the door of his illustrious professor. To the professor's somber "What can I do for you?" he replies, "I would like a letter of recommendation." This engenders a minute of solemn staring, followed by the professor's resolute, "I will give you a letter of description."

By suffering such rejections, our hero becomes an exemplary Modernist, or at least an exemplar of one significant version of Modernism, suffering the burdens both of the artists and of their critics. He confronts, in its apparently innocuous social form, the fundamental conflict generated by the increasing reliance of Western culture on empiricist criteria of judgment for all questions about value. Before rude awakenings like these, writers and critics had not imagined such insuperable gaps between description and recommendation, even though conflicts between the two had become apparent. But now there appear a variety of inescapable and irreducible contradictions, whose structural form our little tale makes evident. For there is perhaps no more bizarre way of attempting to correlate public and personal models of valuation. Clearly, the letter must have a sufficient degree of objectivity to allow others to make reasonable inferences about the candidate's probable success within his chosen profession. Otherwise the author loses credibility, and the student is likely to find himself in a situation he cannot handle. But where this degree of personal investment is at stake, conditions of objectivity are at best tenuously negotiable. The student wants disinterested external judgment, but not too disinterested; certainly not judgment impervious to the charms that seem to sanction his sense of being special, even though there may be little that actually distinguishes him. The ego seems to think that description and recommendation are much more compatible than our professor does – and it is precisely that hope for confirmation that keeps the ego dependent on the professor's authority. Although that authority claims to be based on an objective methodology, it is as dependent on the need for recommendation as the student is, differing primarily in the degree to which those in power can conceal their vulnerability. A moment's reflection shows that the professor's proclaimed commitment to description in fact denies what counts as objectivity within the practice of recommendation. Almost no one treats academic letters of recommendation as descriptions. Rather, they are elaborate codes that convey a good deal of information, provided that one reads them for what they encode. In this practice, "pure description" is not at all pure; it is a code that can be used to give a very negative recommendation. The professor can simultaneously ignore that fact and rely upon it, because his sense of self-importance is congruent with the dominant social criteria that grant him the role of arbiter.

The more closely we examine the situation, the more disturbing it becomes. Both the subject and his judge desire third-person standards, desire a sense of a transparent social order and clear evaluative structures, yet both also have intense first-person needs that make them want to bend or distort the conventional practices. Recommendation seems dependent on description, but also incompatible with it, so that the "I" is tempted to protect its investments by withdrawing from any possible public measure. The only difference between judge and judged may be the manner in which each engages in this withdrawal, the ephebe retreating into self-protective timidity or global irony, and the professor into a hardened insistence on methodologically secure impersonality. Neither strategy works very well: The student clearly loses the opportunity of self-assertion that he desires, and the professor's assertion leaves him susceptible to devastating demystification. Suppose someone were to attempt a careful description of what went into the professor's principles: The odds are good that she would find out how few recommendations students and colleagues have given him during the past few years, how bleak the future seems for him, and how thoroughly he worked to protect himself from those realities. Once a culture turns description on its authorized judges, it finds that apparently simple decisions reveal exposed vulnerabilities, which threaten to undermine the very principles claiming to have purified themselves of precisely those human excesses.

Perhaps all complex cultures suffer from some version of this problem. Some, though, manage or conceal it better than others. Modern culture is not so blessed. The set of values formed in the West over the past two hundred years may be especially vulnerable to public and private rhetorics of crisis, because its fundamental intellectual energy is bound up in fundamental contradictions. On the one hand, its high valuation of the self results in a commitment to radical subjectivity that cannot be subsumed under any general category; on the other, its ideal of intellectual judgment requires it to treat all human actions as if they were subject to exhaustive third-person descriptions, which necessarily undermine the status of self-reflexive individuality.

These abstract issues have concrete consequences. Imagine the student's shame and sense of impotence. Imagine, too, his profound self-disgust, both because he did not know he was so vulnerable and because he allowed himself to expose that vulnerability to this professor, this audience figure so concerned with marshaling his own powers that he would be unlikely to make an accurate recommendation, even if he were able to appreciate what the ephebe offers. Nothing so completely binds self-disgust with a desperate sense of vulnerability as this subjecting of the psyche's most intimate first-person needs to a third-person scrutiny whose demystifying force the first person had not anticipated. Finally, imagine the profound alienation that begins as a defensive gesture against the professor's authority, only to deepen in intensity and clarity as one realizes how shaky that authority is and how irrationally assertive it must become, because of its instability. Then one is in a position to understand the shame, the rage, the wild hopes, and the consequent sense of powerlessness that permeated the arts at the moment in our culture when the tension between the performative and the descriptive seemed most intense and inescapable, in both the private and the public domains.

I do not think it necessary to document the role of Modernist American poetry in defining this sense of cultural crisis. We have the obvious examples of Ezra Pound's Mauberley, T. S. Eliot's Prufrock, William Carlos Williams's uneasy self-defensiveness, and the eloquence of Wallace Stevens's Crispin:

> These bland excursions into time to come,
> Related in romance to backward flights,
> However prodigal, however proud,
> Contained in their afflatus the reproach
> That first drove Crispin to his wandering.
> He could not be content with counterfeit,
> With masquerade of thought, with hapless words
> That must belie the racking masquerade . . .

Hence it was
Preferring text to gloss, he humbly served
Grotesque apprenticeship to chance event,
A clown perhaps, but an aspiring clown.
(*Collected Poem* 39)[1]

In fact, the poets' early work did such a good job of portraying the conditions evoked by my parable that criticism has shaped its own languages accordingly.[2] We have inherited the poetics of "recommendations lost," and hence we see the poetry primarily as the range of defensive strategies necessary to ennoble the dispossession that the professor's world has inflicted on the arts. That language, however, seems to me a terrible reduction of the versions of human agency that the poets created for their culture and bequeathed to ours. Therefore, although I shall spend some time spelling out the historical terms of the crisis of recommendation, I shall concentrate on using that framework to define, by contrast, what the aspiring clowns eventually made of the alienated self-reflection to which they were driven. Frustrated by the culture's standards for recommendation, they sought alternative models of agency in the study of literary history, in the new ways of looking at the psyche being developed in their own time, and in the countercultural gestures elaborated by the visual arts. (Postmodernist writing was to turn, for its response to the professor, away from models of agency to strategies that might undercut his authority by making visible the contradictions suppressed by his postures.) All of those resources would then make it possible to project modes of lyric energy capable of bypassing the entire structure of mimetic values sustaining the professor's claims. An art opposed to representational principles could present itself as directly exemplifying certain performative dimensions of spirit.[3] So rather than rely on prevailing cultural values, the poets had plausible "objective" claims to be shaping a new, ideal culture, which could afford individuals both different principles for representing their desires or powers and a different kind of community that might be capable of assessing their commitments.

For a useful introduction to those projects we need to look no farther than the concluding lines of Stevens's "Academic Discourse at Havana":

All this is older than the oldest hymn,
Has no more meaning than tomorrow's bread.
But let the poet on his balcony
Speak and the sleepers in their sleep shall move,
Waken, and watch the moonlight on their floors.
This may be benediction, sepulcher,

And epitaph. It may, however, be
An incantation that the moon defines
By mere example, opulently clear.
And the old casino likewise may define
An infinite incantation of our selves
In the grand decadence of the perished swans.

(*Collected Poems* 144–5)

This is still fairly early Stevens, so we are dealing with ideas that had not yet been incorporated into the self-reflexive formal strategies elaborated in his later work. Yet the specific imaginative situation here is particularly apposite to this discussion, because it shows the poet confronting the same issues facing critics of his work today: How can one identify with imaginative energies from the past so that the principles of recommendation that they once offered do not now appear only "benediction, sepulcher, and epitaph"? For Stevens, this question entailed confronting the limitations of the Romantic lyric stance as it tried to engage a world in which traditional symbolic and social values had collapsed, leaving only the pathos of repetition to replace the dominant myth of progress. He realized that from an analytic, third-person perspective, the Romantic dream of personal expressive power now seemed little more than a monument to our own insufficiency. But, the poem suggests, another way of engaging those energies emerges if we can find imagistic equivalents for the evocative residue haunting us in our sense of loss, if only because we too must stage our own dispossession before historical change. Thus, in "Academic Discourse," the moon also speaks, but through an incantational process trying to embody the same affective states that the Romantics sought without the openings to irony inescapable in the personal lyric mode. And, more important, this incantation creates the possibility of a second, more capacious, "infinite incantation of ourselves," which takes the art well beyond any simple imagism. Once the image displaces the Romantic subject, it opens the way for a new model of agency, and a new economy for the imagination's emotional investments. Stevens can shift from the moon to the casino, from a natural figure to a figure that invokes a social world and returns us to the internal pattern of figuration that literally constitutes Stevens's own poetic incantation.

Now the poet's terms for addressing an audience have changed. Rather than exalted lyric speech, the poem requires another kind of eloquence, more closely tied to the quasi-ritual energies composing the incantations. These energies do not require celebrating the person of the poet. There need be no dream of heightened sensitivity or prophetic insight to tempt the poet to the kind of postures whose afflatus first drove Crispin to his wandering. The processes composed within the text itself must serve as

sanction and testimony – not because the work provides a separate formal reality, but because its role as incantation invites its audience to
participate self-reflexively in the version of human agency that the poem
makes available. Such incantations are "infinite" – ultimately un-
bounded by history – because this site so links words and worlds, in its
play of subjective and objective genitives, that no model of finite relations can account for the resulting product. Just as the physical scene is
absorbed into the site of incantation, the energies seeking expression fuse
with the objective construct to offer possible selves for those readers for
whom the poem projects needs and desires that they can take as their
own. The eloquence of song both elicits and defines selves, teasing out
expressive needs and producing an imaginative state that various selves
can enter because the expression ceases to belong to any one producer.

I shall have this entire book to establish the context of historical pressures and resources behind these experiments and to show, with the
necessary distinctions and qualifications, how those principles can play
significant roles in contemporary culture, either as direct sources of
imaginative energies or as challenges to our own pieties. But for now,
this poem will have to suffice as an emblem of the four basic tasks
confronting my project. The first takes form in Stevens's sense of the
contradictory demands that history imposes on Modernist poets. Clearly
the poets have good reason to conceive themselves as history's exiles.
Given the increasing social power of Enlightenment principles, they have
no alternative but to be intensely suspicious of those values cultivated by
their own imaginative traditions. Yet the fullness of those memories
makes it extremely difficult not also to distrust a modern cultural order
for which those hymns have "no more meaning than tomorrow's
bread." However, those very suspicions also sanction a belief that
through their exile they come to engage other, potentially deeper levels
of history, where one can locate the sense of abiding needs, energies, and
powers that attracted Eliot, Pound, Moore, and Stevens.[4] The result is
the imposing on readers of a complex double bind that replicates the
poets' basic dilemma: We must situate the poetry in relation to its historical context, but we must do so in a way that is responsive to its own
sense of how easily benedictions become epitaphs, unless they manage to
construct an imaginative life not reducible to the specific ideological
structures and the play of local interests out of which they are generated.

Negotiating that bind requires the other three basic tasks. If we are to
identify provisionally with the Modernist poets' versions of their own
historical project, we must be able to specify how the art can construct
models of agency and versions of emotional economy that provide significant alternatives to those of the mainstream culture. Where the Romantic lyric sensibility previously had reigned, there we must locate

dispositions of energy, and ways of engaging experience, that promise new means for representing our psychic lives to ourselves. To accomplish this, we also must take up the third task, that of learning to see how the internal logic constituting the incantation can carry the force of personal eloquence without relying on the dramatic and melodramatic theaters invoked by Romantic lyricism. We must be able to connect these formal structures to aspects of psychic powers embodied in new modes of human agency, and we must construct critical principles for projecting the modes of authority that can be established as alternatives to the professor's empiricism. Here the example of the theory and practice of the visual arts proves crucial, because it is in those domains that the opposition between incantation and empirical description has been most fully developed. Modernist art demonstrated the capacity of formal energies to reject mimetic structures and still retain extraordinary semantic force by relying directly on the production of exemplary attitudes that an audience might project into extraartistic contexts.

Last, since few contemporary theorists emphasize reading art for the infinite incantations of ourselves that it offers, I find myself relying on a critical perspective that may be anachronistic, or may prove genuinely radical, in its refusal of the prevailing "advanced" critical positions. For I shall neither deconstruct the poets' works nor treat them as elements within a complex network of social practices that can best be understood in terms of social ideology. In my view, before we allow ourselves such distanced analytic stances for reading *against* texts, we must learn to read *through* them by coming to appreciate the specific imaginative experiences they offer when taken as deliberate authorial constructs. Without that labor of provisional identification, the suspicious or deconstructive critic is simply not dealing with a sufficiently rich version of the object. And once one has put in the necessary labor (at least, once I had put in what I thought was the necessary labor), there seems little point in such suspicious enterprises. I am sure that there is much in this Modernist poetry to expose, or "problematize," or display as "undecidable," or adapt to various political practices. But all of those endeavors seem to me only to repeat, in increasingly sophisticated modes, the basic position of our professor, often without even providing the principles needed to recommend their practices as a socially important way to read works of art (since one would have to impose the same critical strictures on one's own claims). Because the Modernist poets sought to propose certain ideal structures displaying and testing possible powers of mind, it seems to me crucial to attempt to understand them on their own terms, if only as a means of focusing attention on specific values that, fully grasped, may provoke us to more accurate and more intricate versions of our own contemporaneity. By assuming that the historicizing of art requires a critical cavalry saving us from ideological mystification, "advanced" contemporary criticism risks losing sight of the many different social roles that art's constructive energies make available.

I would love to engage in theoretical arguments on these matters, but no one would wish this book longer. More important, the dominant critical positions are themselves now so suspicious of purely theoretical argument that I despair of finding common grounds on which to debate. There are so many practical ways of adapting deconstruction and the new historicism that no one theoretical attack could possibly hit the mark.[5] So the most prudent strategy is to accept the antifoundational nostrum that there are simply no ahistorical grounds to which theory can appeal: There are only pragmatic measures of how certain interests are served by specific critical approaches. Then the crucial question becomes how representative and useful one can make one's own case. And that can be resolved only by assessing my specific analyses. It would be foolish to let general suspicions about the terms for recommendation prevent us from exploring the degree to which the remarkable intelligence of Modernist poetry can challenge and perhaps even guide contemporary imaginations.

I envision this book as developing pragmatic implications for a stance that I can only call aesthetic idealism. Therefore, while I invoke historical contexts and try to elaborate a complex dialectical interpretation of the artists' relations to those contexts, I concentrate on how the stances that the artists elaborate have plausible claims on our contemporary values. This, in turn, requires two fundamental departures from traditional historical work on Modernism. First, although I shall be quite abstract and rely a good deal on the history of ideas, I shall not be content to describe intellectual backgrounds or fields of influence. Several scholars have recently done superb work in this vein.[6] So the primary need now is to show why such work matters: both how it helps us to read concrete works of art closely enough to appreciate them as distinctive processes of thinking, and how we develop languages to evaluate those processes.

The second departure involves my use of art history. Here it seems to me especially important not to confine oneself to the ideas or general stylistic models that may have influenced the poets. Minimally, we need to move from ideas to the concrete drama of possibility and threat that occurred as poets attended exhibitions or visited artists' studios, and as they imagined what this release from bondage to the representational principles fostering empiricist values might make available for their own work. Although the writers cared about the ideas, what moved their imaginations and engaged them in the rather scary task of trying to be absolutely modern was their specific encounter with works of art. We cannot know what they saw. Yet the better we understand that their works come fully alive under modes of reading informed by that visual art, the more likely we are to be able to provide speculative accounts of the challenges they saw themselves facing and the opportunities they envisioned for making their own medium explore possible models of agency. What poets learn from visual artists is usually not what those artists see in one another's work. Poets are likely to interpret visual experience by casting it in thematic terms. Therefore, critics tempted to draw analogies between the verbal and visual arts need to be rather bold in their speculations. Serious problems can arise in that activity, and there is no clear theoretical way to limit the field, because there is no obvious set of conditions one can propose for the different interpretations that the various practitioners give of what they encounter. All one can do is to make one's principles explicit and then push the analogies that seem plausible as far as possible. Even when we run into trouble or think we have reached a limit to the analogies, we will find our own experience a plausible encounter with problems that the poets themselves had to confront. And, more important for me, then it makes sense for literary critics, who may not respond to the full visual energies of a painting, to employ their own ways of participating in the imaginative life of the paintings. Even if we miss or distort what would engage painters, we might well be following precisely the tracks that fascinated those whose business is words.

In order to carry out the tasks I have been proposing, I have divided this book into four sections. The first consists of two introductory chapters. Chapter 1 outlines the strategies and values that become central when we approach Modernist poetry in terms of its relations to contemporaneous experiments in the visual arts, and Chapter 2 (along with my second appendix) elaborates the theoretical problems that we must confront if we are to deal clearly with those strategies and values. In Chapters 3 and 4, the second section of the book shifts from theory to history as it attempts to illustrate the set of imaginative problems to which Modernist poetry envisioned itself responding. This history dwells entirely on the structure of various imaginative attitudes, so it simply ignores material social forces and thus makes no effort to provide explanations for the phenomena it dwells on. For this book, at least, history matters not for what it caused, but for the figurative energies artists and writers brought to the process of responding to the pressures imposed by those causal forces.

The process of historical contextualizing culminates, in Chapter 5, with T. S. Eliot, the first American poet to develop a style sufficiently intricate and self-reflexive to be a truly Modernist instrument for engaging those cultural tensions. His early work shows us how many of the basic principles of Modernist abstraction derive from, and deepen, the spiritual paralysis that he found in the nineteenth century. And that, in turn, shows why, although Eliot is important in his own right, his major role in my story will be as an emblem. Seeing Eliot's apparent paralysis before the intricacy of his own self-reflexive powers, his peers had to seek alternative models for applying the very techniques he made available.

The third part of this book then turns to the task of clarifying what was at stake in those alternative models. In Chapter 6, I return to dialectical potentials within Impressionism that were displaced by Symboliste abstraction, then I work out the imaginative challenges to poetry that got defined through three distinctive Modernist painterly styles, each transforming the models of agency and constructive powers developed by its predecessor: Cézanne's pursuit of "realization;" Braque's and Picasso's early Cubist work, with its quite different adaptations of Cézanne's unmaking of sculptural space; and Malevich's noniconic internalizing of the modes of psychological activity explored in Cubism. On that basis, Chapter 7 can proceed to the fundamental principles of three parallel literary styles. From Cézanne, Williams's basic ambitions become clear; from Cubism, we come to appreciate the models of metamorphosis and artistic testimony basic to Stevens and to Stein; and from noniconic abstraction, we find useful parallels for the imaginative energies at work in poets as traditional, and as different, as William Butler Yeats and Marianne Moore.

This "grammar" of Modernist styles dramatizes the range of attitudes and values that abstraction enables the poets to explore. But it cannot sufficiently test the imaginative force of those experiments. For that, we need a fourth section (Chapters 8 and 9) devoted to aspects of poetic careers, where we can observe a poet grappling over a considerable period of time with a full panoply of values that painting affords, or at least that painting helps us describe. By turning to Pound as he worked his way beyond Vorticism, and to Stevens as he sought a form of social commitment free of the defensiveness and oversimplification of his political poems, I hope to show how the best Modernist poets transformed the painterly roots of Modernist aesthetics into a full writerly ethics. For, once the visual arts had freed the poets from traditional ideals of descriptive adequacy and symbolic depth, they found themselves forced to base their claims on the specific energies and reflective powers that they could demonstrate simply by the qualities of experience that their own medium makes available. Pound and Stevens then prove especially important, because they define sharply competing stances clarifying the two basic structures framing the variety of writerly ethics that we find central to the other Modernists, and indeed to the projects of several contemporary poets. These two poets became for poetry what Picasso and Mondrian were to painting. At one pole poetry proposes a Nietzschean will, testing its powers to forge facts into compelling objective manifestations of value, sustained purely by synthetic intelligence; at the other, it offers, in Stevens's later writing, an effort to compose a transpersonal subjectivity, whose claims about values receive direct testimony in the experience that the work affords to any reader willing to participate in its mode of thinking.

Finally, my last chapter turns explicitly to the question of the uses of Modernism in a Postmodernist society. I try very briefly to show how the particular readings the book offers both clarify the limits of those movements that claim to displace Modernist values and establish significant resources for at least individual resistance to hegemonic cultural values. In order to make my case for the continuing value of Modernist individualism, I adapt a Stevensian role. For each of my three Modernist approaches to abstraction I try to reconstruct an ideal model of agency; then I argue that if we can imagine using such ideals we have gone a long way toward understanding why the Modernists sought alternatives to a public political order all too easy to fit into misanthropic visions. As I feel the relief of completing this book, I cannot quite share that vision, but as I await the inauguration of George Bush and Dan Quayle I am most grateful to these poets and painters for establishing another way to satisfy most of our deepest human capacities.

1

It Must Be Abstract

I

Even to approximate infinite incantations of ourselves, art must be abstract. For there is no other way to tease out from our empirical representations the range of states we bring under the penumbra of self, and there is no other way to make visible the sense of intersubjective connectedness that this diversity affords. Thus Wallace Stevens's imperative provides the focus for this book: I hope to explain what Modernist poetry achieved in its experiments with abstraction, and I hope to show how those experiments can still carry imaginative and even ethical force for a contemporary audience. These are not exactly radical ambitions. A Postmodernist Lear might say that both my identification with Modernism and the critical project of using art as a locus for imaginative identifications have the smell of anachronism about them. But when such claims are accompanied by yet one more critique of Modernist art or poetry as formalist evasions of the gritty realities that a "materialist" historical perspective musters the courage to face, anachronism seems a minor risk. At least in seeking identifications with particular works, we make demands on ourselves to resist the kind of superficial readings that immediately locate those particulars in desired historical or moral contexts. If we can understand how such work sought to make its formal experiments a means of organizing substantial extraformal energies, we can hold out the promise of recovering from the past both possible identities in the present and strong contrastive measures for what is richest in our contemporary efforts to overthrow that past.[1]

In order to develop the cultural field of oppositions and possibilities that sustains Stevens's imperative and that provides an alternative to easy complaints about Modernist formalism and antihistoricism, I shall begin with a series of concrete examples demonstrating the impact of the new painting on the poets and testing the contribution that a critical language based on visual work can make in interpreting the poets' work. Prose statements by William Carlos Williams and Stevens will establish the poets' fundamental interest in abstraction. Next, by examining some specific works of art that derive from this concern, I isolate the desires and the problems that a new critical language and historical framework for analyzing this poetry must take into account. First I shall concentrate on two contrasting paintings by Marcel Duchamp that make explicit the Modernist faith in the capacity of abstraction to elaborate a new semantics and to exemplify powers of agency very different from those cultivated within representational art. Then we shall be able to see how texts by Williams and Stevens adapt those strategies to their literary media. Finally, close attention to a painting by Mondrian will establish, in the most extreme terms, the degree to which a language appropriate for painterly abstraction can be adapted to those texts. The stage will be set for the work of developing the conceptual distinctions necessary to account for these imaginative forces.

II

Abstraction promises Williams two fundamental shifts making possible what Stevens would later call "a cure of the ground / or a cure of ourselves that is equal to a cure / of the ground" (*Collected Poems* 526). Whereas traditional poetics had emphasized the semantic roles played by the mimetic features of the poem, Williams insisted on the semantic importance of the structural properties of the work. And whereas the lyric had seemed the quintessential exemplar of traditional values, Williams insisted on treating its formal properties as an experimental means of freeing individual expressive energies from the temptation to cast that individuality in specular autobiographical terms. Poetry consists less in what is said than in the compositional energies that give the saying a distinctive presence. Instead of subordinating the creative self to external demands for accurate description or coherent uses of traditional logics, Williams insisted that the artist makes the constructive activity itself take responsibility for the choices and for the qualities of attention and relation that the work articulates:

> (. . . Both the modern poem and the abstract in painting, though we are not the first to practice the latter, lead integrally into what we are and must be.). . .
> The American writer has two courses open to him: either to seek what security and comfort there is for him in past configu-

rations of learning, or to follow his great constructive genius
into his own world. . . .

What we are seeking is the least common denominator in the
means of expression: in painting, color, reft of all other reference; in the poem, the unaccented line, capable of accepting
every shade of revolutionary significance. . . . The basic idea
which underlies our art must be . . . that which Toynbee has
isolated for us: abundance, that is, permission for all. And it is in
the *structure* of our works that this must show. . .

But that is the exact place where for us modern art began. For
that is the essence of Cézanne . . . that we began to say that it is
no longer what you paint or what you write about that counts
but how you do it: how you lay on the pigment, how you place
the words to make a picture or a poem.

From that through Cubism, Matisse, to Motherwell, the ultimate step is one gesture. And it is important because it says that
you don't paint a picture or write a poem about anything. You
make a picture or a poem or anything. You see how all that
comes from Toynbee's discovery. Abundance for all. . . . It is in
the structure of the poem or painting the excellence exists, and
that is unlimited, the least common denominator. (*Recognizable
Image* 211, 217–18)

Exactly the same concern for the structuring power of the artist leads
Stevens to his fascination with abstraction. But for him the "cure of the
ground" is a matter, not of social abundance, but of a new way to
understand and to value the mind's power to resist history: abstraction is
less a means of dissemination than an exemplary level of concentration,
allowing one to compose livable orders out of that multiplicity. In abstraction, the mind finds an "elemental force" distinct from ideological
contents. Its manifestations of that force demonstrate a nobility or eloquence no longer mocked by history's reducing all of our metaphors to
tattered rags on the dumps of time:

The subject matter of poetry is not that collection of solid
objects extended in space but the life that is lived in the scene that
it composes; and so reality is not that external scene but the life
that is lived in it. His own measure as a poet, in spite of all the
passions of all the lovers of truth, is the measure of a power to
abstract himself, and to withdraw with him into his abstraction
the reality on which lovers of truth insist. He must be able to
abstract himself and also to abstract reality, which he does by
placing it in his imagination. (*Necessary Angel* 25)

A possible poet must be a poet capable of resisting or evading the pressure of reality of this last violent degree, with the knowledge that the degree of today may become a deadlier degree tomorrow. (27)

There is no element more conspicuously absent from contemporary poetry than nobility. . . . The nobility of rhetoric is, of course, a lifeless nobility. Pareto's epigram that history is a cemetery of aristocracies easily becomes another: that poetry is a cemetery of nobilities. For the sensitive poet, conscious of negations, nothing is more difficult than the affirmations of nobility and yet there is nothing that he requires of himself more persistently. (35)

But a wave is a force and not the water of which it is composed, which is never the same, so nobility is a force and not the manifestations of which it is composed. . . . It is not artifice that the mind has added to human nature. . . . It is the imagination pressing back against the pressure of reality. (35–6)

These statements provide our prose version of Wittgenstein's ladder. Now we must make it disappear, by turning to specific works of art that have the power not only to name the pressure of reality, but also to establish the necessary affirmations "pressing back against" it. I start with Duchamp, because he provides the most elaborate Modernist effort to explore the capacity of the visual to interpret, and to dramatize, the forces of abstraction that this prose struggles to define. Having painted a *Game of Chess* in the muted, elegant Nabi style in 1909, Duchamp returned to the same motif two years later in his *Portrait of Chess Players*. This time he showed how Cubist principles focused attention on aspects of agency, and forces within the objective world, that simply are not available to traditional representation. (See Figures 1 and 2.)[2] Because the earlier work devotes its energies to rendering the intricate color modulations and balanced domestic composure afforded by the scenic aspects of a chess game, it can do nothing to recommend chess playing or chess players. Quite the contrary: It mires both chess and art in the texture of domestic life, and it confines the composing presence to indulging in the delicate moods that the scene can embody. In contrast, the later painting makes its subject not the composed weight of a scene but the compositional energies by which art both revels in its own abundance and makes that abundance a vehicle for defining fresh dimensions of its subject. Here the structuring force of Cubist formal principles establishes an artistic equivalent for the state of concentration that makes chess a possible emblem for the mind at its most intense.

Portrait of Chess Players is clearly abstract. But its abstractness has very

Figure 1. Marcel Duchamp, *Game of Chess*. Philadelphia Museum of Art: Louise and Walter Arensberg Collection.

little to do with a concentration on the medium rather than the message, and even less to do with noniconic art. Obviously the subject matter here elicits our knowledge of the practical world. However, the painting does not rely on what Gombrich calls the "eyewitness principle," which invites us to contemplate an illusionary world organized around a visual object that we treat as if it could be within our frame of vision. Rather, it pursues two interrelated features that are basic to Modernist abstraction: First, it carves a space for abstract analogies between the physical and the spiritual orders that parallel those opened by traditional allegory; second, it charges that space with metaphoric energy, by having the compositional act serve as a vehicle extending and testing the models of agency that we can attribute both to chess and to art.

This focus on the semantic force of compositional energies may provide the only way that a secular world can continue to probe what had been the space of traditional religious allegory. But now, rather than postulate a level of meaning that abstractly contains and interprets the manifest signs, this work locates that abstracting force in the capacity of the painterly agency to inhabit modes of intensity that lead beyond any-

Figure 2. Marcel Duchamp, *Portrait of Chess Players*. Philadelphia Museum of Art: Louise and Walter Arensberg Collection.

thing the empirical understanding can provide. Notice how cold and impersonal this concentration is, as if the painting evoked powers so profoundly inward that they are transpersonal, virtual conditions of any subject's capacity for intense experience. What is incoherent as representation becomes coherent through the dominant figure of the action embodied in the painting. There we locate both the new semantic focus, where scene gives way to direct exploration of the essence of chess, and the new route of reference, where we examine the truth, or representativeness, of the work by testing the capacity of the organizing energies to establish analogous states of concentration and distributions of psychic investment. More radical noniconic work, such as Mondrian's, would assert a purer equivalence between the site that the work composes as visual presentation and what it suggests as a semantic or metaphoric gesture. But for writers, the crucial issue is the fact that these same principles can be evoked for processes of abstraction that still retain iconic implications deeply embedded in the medium.

We need to take Duchamp's cue and base our claims for these new powers on concrete contrasts. Notice first how the decreative energy in

Duchamp's Cubist work is inseparable from the activity of constructing a positive, alternative space for reflecting on the abstract dimensions of chess. Decreative gestures call attention to a corresponding constructive action, which then becomes the focus for qualities that take on metaphoric resonance. As forms are denied their typical appearances, they get reduced to the elemental structures out of which appearances are made. Chess pieces become simple markers; tables and boards define the geometric structures that control movement in the game; and human figures assume sharply defined yet ghostly presences, as if concentration both clarifies and simplifies personal features. All of the abstracted forms eventually create a dynamic rhythm of angles, lines, and tones, carefully balancing the concreteness of our concentration on chess with the abstract, almost mechanical set of relations that composes the agonistic space within which the game must be played. Both the concrete and the mechanical merge, as we realize that the power of chess is precisely this leading us into worlds where we identify, not with empirical desires, but with the structure of the game. The highest levels of chess require literally transforming oneself into a calculating machine, fully attuned to the marvelous freedom of having to think in terms of infinite, yet law-governed, possibilities.

This is portraiture in the deepest sense: not a description of some chess game, or of specific players, but an unfolding on a painterly surface of the subjective life available for all agents who enter the field of energies that chess makes available. Moreover, this is portraiture whose "truth" requires a model of reference substantially different from the one invoked by representational painting. The coherence and force of the work do not depend on its direct reference to specific agents or scenes populating an imaginary world which we understand in the same way that we understand our own practical behavior. Rather, the intensity and the "insight" of this portrait depend on the energy of the portraying. For it is here that we find both the objective correlative for what is claimed about chess and the testimonial to why those energies matter. Constructive energy is inseparable from the power to focus our own being in intense acts of pure concentration. Yet as we see psychic life in terms of physical energy, we recognize that what we see is an odd form of the physical world. It is a world not of scenes but of elemental relations, physical in large part because of the way the elements cohere in structures whose only locus is the realm of ideas. Indeed, the more the physical appears as elements so tightly interconnected by specific painterly rhythms, the more we have a physical world dependent on purely conceptual or aesthetic relations. Chess becomes an ontological metaphor.

This metaphoric reach ultimately restores our attention to the painting's force as an artistic act literally demonstrating the nature and value of certain states. For as we think about the roles played by painterly energy in the work, we recognize the fact that this kind of art has meaning only to the extent that we can align ourselves with the powers the act displays. Concentration is not merely a theme the painting uses to interpret chess. Rather, the painting elicits a state in the responder that makes literally present the very energies the work idealizes. The work coheres only if we identify with the way in which playing chess unites impersonal mental energies with a mechanical force of elemental laws governing our most vital states. Art as commentary and art as testimony reinforce one another, combining ontology and psychology into the work's synthetic union of elements and forces. That synthesis itself becomes metaphoric, projecting the act of concentration as so richly both a mental and a physical act that it participates in energies that lead beyond and beneath the human. Spiritual concentration articulates both the central properties of spirit and its basic relational grounds. Even the mechanical is, or can be, part of the vital – a vision far more radical than Bergson's, perhaps because it becomes plausible only in the intensive present of the concrete transpersonal immediacy that visual art can give to abstract properties.

For the principles I have been discussing, hundreds of examples would suffice. Duchamp is distinctive in deliberately setting these energies in contrast to another, more traditional handling of the same subject. By that process, he makes painting a self-reflexive projection of the principles that artists could claim might prepare the way for a new culture. We are invited to look back at the earlier painting, *Game of Chess,* in order to ask ourselves how and why the new art makes us see and judge differently. And then the earlier picture becomes a perfect expression of the emotional and epistemological problems that required an artistic revolution. Although we cannot be sure whether the painting is thus expressive by virtue of symptoms betrayed or qualities consciously displayed, knowing Duchamp as we do it is hard not to imagine that he has deliberately suggested here the emotional duplicities that only an audience trained in later art would recognize.

Look again at the composition of *Game of Chess*. How isolated each person is in his or her body, and how heavy each body seems as it so committedly occupies a specific spatiotemporal location. Notice the impression of the woman's arm in the grass, the emphatic buttocks of the seated woman, and the arch formed by the slumped shoulders of the men. Notice too how the structure of the painting emphasizes each body as an anchor for the others, in the process making all four construct a single parallelogram, which carves out a human space against a vague, encroaching, green nature. Unlike the structure of the later painting, which is at first indeterminate but then gradually takes purposive form as part of a semantically charged authorial act, this parallelogram composes the scene but comes to appear arbitrary as a semantic factor, and hence merely formal. Finally, notice how Duchamp projects his own attitude toward domesticity by a strange play on perspective. Are not the women a little too large, a little too imposing, as they form a barrier blocking the eye's access to the men, for whom chess becomes perhaps a necessary refuge, their brown table and nondescript colors set against the whites and reds of the women's world? Repose now seems a trap, a social and ontological confinement to a sensuous, scenic world of bodies and oblig- atory picnics. Representational art itself may be no more innocent than these lovely women, restraining what for Duchamp could become, in the later painting, a world of masculine energies reveling in the rela- tionships that chess exemplifies. Only there can one hope to escape a familiar world which traps everything within postures that must remain as lonely as they are definitive.[3]

III

William Carlos Williams's "A Matisse" devotes itself to the pos- sibility of adapting the principles of this new French painting to a new American poetry still in its early stages of self-definition. Whereas the ostensive subject of the essay is Matisse's *Blue Nude: Portrait of Bishkra* (see Figure 3), the writing calls attention to itself as the testing of powers that can parallel the model of active attention defined in Matisse's au- thorial activity:

> On the french grass, in that room on Fifth Ave., lay that woman who had never seen my own poor land. The dust and noise of Paris had fallen from her with the dress and underwear and shoes and stockings which she had just put aside to lie bathing in the sun. So too she lay in the sunlight of the man's easy attention. His eye and the sun had made day over her. She gave herself to them both for there was nothing to be told. Nothing is to be told to the sun at noonday. A violet clump before her belly mentioned that it was spring. A locomotive could be heard whistling beyond the hill. There was nothing to be told. Her body was neither classic nor whatever it might be supposed. There she lay and her curving torso and thighs were close upon the grass and violets.
>
> So he painted her. The sun had entered his head in the colors of sprays of flaming palm leaves. They had been walking for an hour or so after leaving the train. They were hot. He had chosen the place to rest and he had painted her resting with interest in the place she had chosen.

Figure 3. Henri Matisse, *Blue Nude, "Souvenir de Biskra."* Oil on canvas, 36¼ × 55¼″ (92.1 × 140.4 cm.). The Baltimore Museum of Art: The Cone Collection, formed by Dr. Claribel Cone and Miss Etta Cone of Baltimore, Maryland. BMA 1950.228.

It had been a lovely day in the air. – What pleasant women are these girls of ours! When they have worn clothes and take them off it is with the effect of having performed a small duty. They return to the sun with a gesture of accomplishment – Here she lay in this spot today not like Diana or Aphrodite but with better proof than they of regard for the place she was in. She rested and he painted her.

It was the first of summer. Bare as was his mind of interest in anything save the fullness of his knowledge, into which her simple body entered as into the eye of the sun himself, so he painted her. So she came to America. No man in my country has seen a woman naked and painted her as if he knew anything except that she was naked. No woman in my country is naked except at night.

In the french sun, on the french grass in a room on Fifth Ave., a french girl lies and smiles at the sun without seeing us. (*Selected Essays* 30–1)

This is emphatically not Duchamp's sense of women. Yet there is the same self-conscious reorienting of art, away from cogent dramatic scenes and expressive psyches, and toward a concern for the semantic import of the exemplary energies disposed in the artist's structuring activity. And there must be the same contrastive effort to indicate the cultural burdens that the new art might bear. For Williams, Matisse's great achievement lay in using that artistic activity to address two deeply connected forms of cultural blindness: a reliance on narrative forms of art that displace immediate energies into abstract moralistic frameworks, and a repressive sexuality bound to the self-images that those stories sustain. By dramatizing how the mind can fully engage itself within the physical world, Matisse proposes replacing our dependency on stories with a much more immediate form of plenitude. Then we have a "cure of the ground," or better of the "grounding," that can even restore the sensuous pastoral innocence sought by the Nabi style. Yet the artist need not reduce his material to subjective interests. Nor, on the other hand, must he submit himself to impersonal ideals that employ traditional values and justifications, a process that Williams thought would inevitably reproduce the anxiety displacing bodies into stories and a corollary deep sense of shame. Instead of referring to cultural codes, making comparisons to the classics, or letting the topic of nudity itself become the central issue, Matisse offers his art as a form of active forgetting, which allows the artist to align himself with the present as the sun aligns with the landscape.

Making no demands, and imposing no shadows, the painter simply pours his emotional state into the scenic backdrop, so that it forms a psychological version of impressionist atmosphere. Then he can appreciate how the woman might simply give her body as a gift, even as her face retains an irreducible privacy. The need for stories yields to the capacity of that body to define significant specific configurations of energy with the place and with the painter, and art becomes a concrete emblem for the reciprocal dynamics of an exemplary adult sexuality. The painter's line tells the story of what can replace story. Rather than simply outline the body, the line dallies over it in varying degrees of thickness, until the breasts virtually slow it down, making it conscious of itself as at once touch and the force that defines form. By becoming the literal sun of this figurative world, the painter allows the woman both secure rest and the intense desire of a thigh unwilling to be bound by the laws of perspective. This thigh, in fact, stages a complex relation between painterly act and evoked situation that is almost the equivalent of Matisse's magnificent *Conversation*. In one respect, the thigh's exaggerated twist self-defensively refuses the painter's gaze and hand access to her private parts, thus joining the face in its refusal of this sun's light. Yet this contortion of her body also seems to reach out in order to cooperate with the line, to offer more of her body to perspectival vision than is in fact possible within the laws that govern appearances. Self-protection and self-revela-

h powers. The greatest truth that we could hope to dis-
er . . . is that man's truth is the final resolution of every-
g. (173–5)

mentary, however, does not produce substantial portents of
. That takes poems such as "Of Modern Poetry," with the
rovide dramatic testimony for the stakes involved in one's
efforts to engage a reality of decreation:

poem of the mind in the act of finding
will suffice. It has not always had
nd: the scene was set: it repeated what
n the script.

the theatre was changed
mething else. Its past was a souvenir.

to be living, to learn the speech of the place.
to face the men of the time and to meet
omen of the time. It has to think about war
has to find what will suffice. It has
struct a new stage. It has to be on that stage
ke an insatiable actor, slowly and
editation, speak words that in the ear
elicatest ear of the mind, repeat
what it wants to hear, at the sound
ch, an invisible audience listens,
he play, but to itself, expressed
notion as of two people, as of two
s becoming one. The actor is
hysician in the dark, twanging
ument, twanging a wiry string that gives
assing through sudden rightnesses, wholly
ng the mind, below which it cannot descend
which it has no will to rise.

ding of a satisfaction, and may
an skating, a woman dancing, a woman
The poem of the act of mind.
(*Collected Poems* 239–40)

erns are obviously Romantic ones, yet both its vision
for realizing it are distinctively Modernist. Were this
y Wordsworth or Coleridge, looking within would
gning the self with energies in the natural world, but

tion seem to compete with one another. However, if we give interpretive weight to the woman's overall pose, with its remarkable structural balance suggesting that this woman could turn in any direction without losing her stability, I think we must then generalize that sense of balance. Under this sun, responding to this eye and line, the woman can treat both aspects of her nakedness as modes of self-possession at once enabling her to affirm control over her own sexuality and inviting him to imagine himself as completing it. Where story must look beyond the particulars for its significance, this painterly act composes a space in which there are no energies of the mind not at home in the flesh. Flesh, though, is at home anywhere: So thoroughly do these concrete relations take on reality within the painting that her energies survive the passage from country to country without having to see us, or to suffer the contamination of our needs, our stories, or, worst of all, of our idealizations.

More than the woman's intensity passes from country to country.[4] The deepest subject of Williams's "A Matisse" is not the painter's relation to his subject matter, but the inspiration that the painter's way of handling the subject matter gives to the writer. Verbal art too may be able to resist telling. That possibility leads Williams to refuse simple art-historical description, with its reliance on conventional processes of judgment. The fullest way to honor Matisse is to call attention to the specific writerly qualities that the painting liberated in Williams, so that he could appropriate the work for his own purposes. Williams's relation to Matisse parallels Matisse's relation to the woman: The medium of writing must create an equivalent to the energy that his subject generates within the scene, so that the full demands of our imaginative attention can be simultaneously expressed and satisfied. On this basis, the text can use a French painting as testimony to sustain a critique of American society.

That the subject of this portrait was actually Matisse's Algerian mistress is not the only embarrassing feature of Williams's prose. (How could he confuse palm fronds with "French grass"?) Because he wants to set this image against narrative, he makes an awkward effort to provide a quasi-narrative context for it. I am not sure whether this stems from his inability to free himself from those conventional desires for plot or whether he wants us to see the tension between the two ways of understanding what art offers. But whatever the reason, the repeated "so" insists that we subordinate these contexts to the text's effort to establish a sharp contrast between those tellings that displace their object and those forms of expression that can maintain the reciprocal relationship he celebrates. "So" is, first of all, a process term. The artwork is a record of choices that define the artist's power as he tries, not to transpose events into a narrative or argumentative form, but to render what his desire to render lets him see. Second, "so" is a particularizing term, celebrating art's ability to produce a self-contained, individual reality. The rendering produces just this set of relations. Finally, "so" comes to carry the full burden of what I call an "equivalence term," because the work self-consciously constitutes an incantation, demonstrating how creative energy can take responsibility for itself as it breaks from discursive argument. The stance thereby composed promises a mode of inhabiting the world more satisfying than any traditional notion of knowledge affords, because the energies of apprehension become inseparable from the object known, creating an imaginative site or set of semantic properties as distinctive to Williams's art as line is to Matisse. Because Matisse painted the girl just so, her body, the French grass, and the artist's sun can be transferred to America, making possible Williams's own discovery, not of her body, not of the percept per se, but of the artist's power to create equivalences and to appreciate their cultural consequences as expressive of hidden powers that ordinarily evade our rationalizations. Because art can produce images just so, it creates an alternative to the endless metaphoric chains of "just as" on which telling is based.

Yeats too made writing about a painting central to his version of Modernism, by printing Pater's effusion on the *Mona Lisa* as verse, making it the first entry in his edition of *The Oxford Book of Modern Verse* (1936). In Pater's essay we also find a highly self-conscious effort to provide writerly equivalents for painterly energies. But the similarities with Williams serve ultimately to call attention to differences as substantial as those between the bent nose of Cézanne's wife, in his 1885 portrait of her, and the Impressionist works that shared a hall with it, in the Boston Museum of Fine Arts, until the building was renovated. For Pater, writing about art is the direct recording of the sensations that the visual object elicits from his own complex sensibility. The writer's challenge is to capture the intricate rhythms of that sensibility, in part as a triumph of self-expression, in part as an example of the "adventure of the soul before masterpieces" that is available, in different registers, to other temperaments. Williams, on the other hand, does not emphasize the self-congratulatory recording sensibility seeking our approval. Rather, Williams foregrounds a structuring artistic intelligence that is responding, not primarily to the intricate mysteries evoked by Matisse's subject, but to the conditions of his own authorial action as it produces a framing in which the subject matter can take on a particular kind of reality. Prose does not describe or evoke the states of feeling that ennoble a particular subject; instead, prose becomes the equivalent of the formal or structural conditions of these feelings, offering, to consciousness, a sense of how its own compositional powers become a "sun" disclosing vital presences. Art becomes the paradigm for a full eros, capable of knowing and revel-

ing in the world without tell
metaphors that reinforce subj
under conventional patterns.

IV

For my example fr
when the Modernist experi
might reflect on the entire
years of Modernism into a
lyric quite does that, but, :
vens's "Of Modern Poetry
goal. Whereas Williams, i
compositional act as the r
relations to the concrete v
tion on the significance o
world of appearances pe
powers of composition (
self and for recovering
forms of old evaluative
That quest entails indu
used by the founders o
claims so self-consciou
sibility of such diffus
writes in *The Necessa*

The theor
poetry, ofte
more simpl
why the p
become in
pearance, a
things, wh
only throu
joined to
reality ch
this [idea
and from
much to
modern
This
Moder
are no

ow
cov
thin

Prose com
those power
capacity to p
constructive

The
Wha
To fi
Was

Then
To so

It has
It has
The w
And it
To co
And, l
With n
In the
Exactly
Of whi
Not to
In an e
Emotio
A metap
An instr
Sounds
Containi
Beyond

It must
Be the fi
Be of a n
Combing

The poem's con
and the basic mean
a meditative lyric
be a corollary of al

in Stevens's poem the world beyond the self has no symbolic resonance. That world enters the poem only as the force of historical change, destroying old fictions and making the demands that dominate the third stanza. As the mind tries to respond to all that history contaminates, it locates the necessary resources in its power of self-reflection. Different as these concerns are from Williams's, they still demand a version of his basic strategy: An authentic Modernism must be based on a fundamental contrast with some blocking condition in the very center of our capacity to represent experience. Only by such contrasts can the foregrounded compositional act exemplify a possible cure of the ground. But whereas Williams resists a flawed condition of apprehension (the woman's nakedness cannot be told), Stevens resists a flawed condition of judgment (the old theater's fixed scripts neither match modern reality nor indicate our capacity to fulfill ourselves in adapting to that reality). The new theater must prove itself by developing new ways of handling the baggage of discursive thought. At stake is not simply how we see objects, but how we conceive the nature of objectivity and the powers that produce it: how, in other words, we face the domestic entrapments so horrifying to Duchamp. Stevens's is a poetry about how the mind's eye can represent itself, when it reflects on its acts as metaphoric equivalents to the sun's.

A lyric with such ambitions must render the mind as simultaneously subject and object of the poem: The essential affirmative content of the poem must reside in the quality of its self-defining activities. Thus, instead of seeking symbolic or dramatic resolutions in some illusionary world, Stevens's poem relies on its own structural and metaphoric processes as its means to express, and to test, its capacity to escape the initial state of bondage. The initial dramatic situation is defined simply by the mind's awareness of change and the sense of lack that this awareness generates. Modernist self-consciousness emerges as a process of negation, orienting itself through the lens of all we have lost or can no longer be: yet that sense of loss is not without compensations. It brings in its wake a harsh realism, no less threatening to our vanity, but nonetheless offering terms by which the mind can take responsibility for its situation. Therefore the poem quickly turns to a list of necessities, which takes form as a strange litany based on the refrain "it has to." The formal repetition enables the mind to focus its attention on its own needs, processes, and powers, so that it can sustain a sense of responsibility sufficiently intense to inaugurate a counterpressure to the spirit of negation.

Defining that counterpressure poses the poem's most difficult challenge. Stevens must show how reflecting on necessities creates a stage for a responding act capable of a great deal more than contemplating its own victimization:

It has

To construct a new stage. It has to be on that stage
And, like an insatiable actor, slowly and
With meditation, speak words that in the ear . . .

Notice how the movement of these lines establishes a set of capacities entirely different from the poem's initial entrapment in its own pathos. The introductory theater metaphors had sustained a flat, prosaic syntax of isolated, brief clausal units. Self-consciousness begins in a domain of fact and tired language. With the litany, the language shifts to simple descriptive expressions, charged with syntactic urgency. Now the language once again changes, as we arrive at the need to construct on a stage. Similes and qualifications enter, and direct urgency gives way to a series of slowly unfolding repetitions and aural echoes that suspend the flow of thought into a lush state of reflective self-absorption.

The poem becomes its own subject, in every sense of that term. Its hovering over its own metaphors arouses, and justifies, an increasingly erotic inwardness (in the delicatest ear of the mind), suggesting that we participate on a new stage, where the process of abstraction can withdraw into itself that reality pursued by lovers of truth. Now it must be the words that become our actors, "heroic" by virtue of what they let an audience realize about its own powers, as it listens, "not to the play, but to itself, expressed / In an emotion as of two people, as of two / Emotions becoming one." What this heroism entails is perhaps clearest in the intricate evasions of the repeated "as." An emotion that is "as of two people" holds out the promise of also conjoining the two emotions into one, because anyone can share that "as." Anyone can step back from her activities as an empirical subject in order to explore other forms of intentionality defining possible transpersonal forms that our desire can take. Is this not precisely what the poem is doing in asking us to participate in its own depersonalized structure of internal relations, as if we entered a work of music? When we share the "as" of comparison, linking the two emotions, we also share the "as" of temporal and qualitative equivalences linking the states of mind produced in, or as, those emotions.

These equivalences return us to Williams's "so." Now, though, the focus is less on the physical space that the equivalences make possible than on the processes of self-consciousness required to negotiate this poem. Stevens's equivalences serve primarily to compose a self-reflexive world that minds must admit they share. For then the poem, an act of mind, can provide concrete testimony for the values that can be attributed to such acts. Because we realize that it is ultimately the audience that gives substance and depth to the "as," as it reads, we must treat reading as bound to the same stage and capable of sustaining the same process of self-articulation. We enter a strange intentional state in which we must look at our own reading processes as if they were not quite our own, not quite the possession of any one subject, because of the way that they distribute emotional investments, "as of two emotions becoming one." Not as overtly radical as Duchamp, Stevens nonetheless demands the same flexible imagination in his audience, as it watches itself enter new structures of intentionality. The transpersonality there realized is, at best, potential or virtual, but once we see how the poem refers to its own activity, those virtual dimensions are inseparable from our reflections on the text. And once we allow such virtual states to take on reality, every-thing that Stevens had said about "nobility," in his prose statement, begins to make clear sense. Substance has become subtlety, and the actor's composing of this theater has defined "precious portents of our own powers." Yet these portents owe nothing to the bitter glass. They depend on minimal ideological claims and require no representation. Rather, they depend on our ability to look beyond the contents of our representations to the shareable virtual space produced by reflecting on what we must bring to the representations that can satisfy us. Eloquence itself floats free of its anchors in ideology, to embody powers that we cannot but see enacted in our own constructive activity as we participate in this theater.

Having so constructed this complex stage, Stevens goes on to describe the actor. The hero composed of these processes has the combined traits of the metaphysician and the musician, a blend of the most abstract and the most sensual of properties. Music provides the objective rhythms that physically align our bodies to the becoming of the emotions, and metaphysics adds the metaphoric scope that allows the bodies to inhabit the romance space initially opened by traditional ideals of truth. The hero, then, is anyone able to internalize the language that can make "rightnesses" out of listening to the music that the poem produces with-in the erotic movements of its own syntax. Because philosophy becomes less a descriptive quest than a means for positioning the mind so that it can appreciate what takes place in the self-reflexive acts that the discipline engenders, the poem's clarity about its own processes ultimately estab-lishes a self-subsuming structure that literally enacts its basic claims. A mind displaced from the fixed scripts of a symbolic theater finds, simply in its own articulate rendering of its condition, a "strong exhilara-tion / Of what we feel from what we think" (*Collected Poems* 382).

By identifying itself with these "portents of its own powers," the mind can reject the dangerous alternatives otherwise inescapable for self-reflexive Modernism. At one pole is the temptation to "rise" to a my-stical aesthetics or a translunar paradise, where one imagines oneself dwelling in a realm beyond secular appearance. The other pole is an entrapment in infinite irony, the demonic "other" of transcendence. A mind unable to find a home for its powers descends to violent satiric energies or to self-negating processes as the only remaining authentic or lucid use of imaginative energy. For Stevens, though, the aim is to eliminate any sense that desire requires a specific domain where it can find adequate objects. Desire is fulfilled, not by possession but by reflection: by the satisfaction that comes from feeling that one's imaginative terms are defining the very needs they construct. Then there need be no fear of displacement, because there are no energies of thought that cannot be expressed and understood as potential lyric grounds for engaging self-reflexively in our common humanity at its most intense.

Full "containment" of the mind, however, demands more than this state of participation. Stevens wants us to be able to reflect upon that condition as itself composing a distinct imaginative site, where we see, in concrete figurative terms, what these levels of containment make available. So Stevens turns to another aspect of form, using his conclusion to indicate how the poem's abstract patterns give substance to the self-reflection that they free from dramatic illusionism. Formal structure becomes the means to articulate the ultimate grounds that warrant the poem's status as a transpersonal schema for the experience of value.

First, the climactic "[it] may be," in the last stanza, connects these concluding lines to the earlier pressures imposed by the "it has to" and "it must." The pattern so formed defines a thematic progression from the recognition of external necessity, to an internal alignment of one's choice with one's fated chance, to a resulting freedom to revel in all contingencies. Having accepted his confinement within history, the mind can value all of the particulars that constitute its place and provide it with terms for reflecting on its relation to that place. This acceptance then produces a second, pronounced formal pattern that clarifies the relational principles on which the entire act of mind depends. As the poem steps free at the end into pure particulars, it also steps back, to repeat the sense and syntax of the opening line, thus making "the poem of the act of mind," a physical framework that is literally the ground for the theatrical gestures. That echo, that end in its beginning, insistently refuses all transitive verbs, as if the delicate sonorities of the third stanza were only segments of a finer, more encompassing, quasi-physical space that only words can compose. The framing gestures give the poetic voice the aura of serving as the mind's body, now able to account for the eros charging all of the particulars that enter this action. By syntactically projecting a dimension of the "act of mind" that exists outside of time, the denial of transitivity and the repetition suggest the quality of a meditative theater, composed by and hushed for the sounds that can wholly contain the mind as it links author with audience in a site on the margin of history.[5]

To view these static qualities as pure aesthetic form, however, would be to impose contraries where Stevens sees complements operating on different levels. His point is not how space contrasts to flux, but how a constructed space makes it possible to feel one's own activity of mind as physically occupying that space, in way that renders it transpersonal (as if one could not distinguish scene from act). Therefore Stevens is careful to eliminate all active verbs from the act of mind that sets that scene: Rather than let any specific action set the stage, Stevens wants language to emerge as if the desires underlying all verbs called the poem into being. That is why, when particular verbs finally do appear, they seem in effect to channel those desires into specific permissions. The poem moves from "must," to "may be," to a series of participles that serve as emblems for the continual generating of imagined objects of attention – all poised between the substance of nominalized states and the activities that elicit and satisfy desire. Details such as combing are absolutely casual, and the casualness is never transformed into symbol. The transformation that does take place is on a different level: Casualness itself becomes resonant and reverberates, without ever tempting us to confuse the energies of composition with putative meanings *in* the world, and thus infectible by it.

As a treatment of objects, the poem inhabits a poetic universe completely defensible before modern analytic thought. Instead of relying on symbols, it depends solely on the energies of perception and construction. Such energies make no direct claims upon the practical world: "Nothing has been changed at all." But, as Wittgenstein suggested in his early works, there can be total transfigurations of the world that alter none of its factual qualities. Simply by understanding that one "must" construct some attitude toward objective processes, Stevens sees that one may be able to envision one's own desires as the very source of the world's vitality (perhaps a secular, subjective analog of God's creative fiat): It *may be* any particular that becomes "part of major reality, part of / an appreciation of a reality / And thus an elevation, as if I left / With something I could touch, touch every way" (*Opus Posthumous* 117). *As* the poet imagines, he performs modes of thinking that are not merely regulative forms or the confirmation of ideas about maturity. Rather, the poet focuses attention on the activities of framing, which allow us to treasure the varied world we have, and he reminds us that in the rhythm of concentration producing dispersals of the self, we find ourselves more truly and more strange, as the possessors of a power we all share.

Stevens's poem obviously is not shy at stating its own possible significance. But the full scope of what its abstractness makes available may not be clear unless we see how it elaborates a second prose remark Stevens made on poetry and painting, this time in a catalog entry on the painter Marcel Gromaire:

> One of the things [Gromaire] is determined about is sub-
> stance. . . . By substance he means the spiritual fund of the
> picture, the fund originating in the thought and feeling of the
> artist and perceptible in the painting. He does not mean the
> picture as itself a spiritual fund, except in that objective way. . . .
> He speaks of the human spirit seeking its own architecture, its
> own *"measure"* that will enable it to be in harmony with the
> world. It is from the intensity, the passion, of this search that the
> quality of works is derived . . .
>
> At the same time he postulates an *"art directement social"* which
> transmits itself to the spectator without mediation or explana-
> tion as much as by reason of its *"chimie intérieure"*: Sublimation,
> say, as by the idea which it materializes; social in the sense of
> something that affects the march of events, fixes the ephemeral
> sensation and makes it possible for the ephemeral sensation,
> thanks to this acquired characteristic of being perennial, to act on
> the future and on human behavior. ("Marcel Gromaire," in
> *Opus Posthumous* 291)

The link between spirit and substance claimed here (without, I suspect,
any intended allusion to Hegel) extends "Of Modern Poetry" in two
directions. First, it insists upon the testimonial quality of the particular
act of the mind. By embodying certain forms of the mind as a perennial
structure of forces, the poem gives the mind a rich physical existence – as
force and as formed substance. That physicality, in turn, becomes a
complex vehicle for creating and revealing social bonds not available if
one halts the process of abstraction where Williams does, at the point
where art formulates principles for actively disclosing particular features
of experience. Because art need not be merely about the world, and
hence at a distance from it, the forms it presents can be assessed as actual
forms of desire in themselves. And because the work has its own concreteness as an emblem of possible structures by which we constitute
meaning and values, its physical existence as the mind's movement
among meanings establishes a specific form for expressing and satisfying
desire. The form of this movement is too abstract to be subjective, too
elemental to reduce to the one situation. So it becomes, at the least, a
metaphor; at the most, an actual or literal emblem of the schema through
which all persons produce value, whatever the ideological contents. We
find powers allowing us to identify with, or as, one another, because we
see that our investments hold, as names that simply propound "as if the
language suddenly with ease, / Said things it had laboriously spoken"
(*Collected Poems* 387). Hearing such speech will not in itself produce an
actual society that we can identify with, but it may be a necessary beginning – a junction, where the "I" sees its embeddings in "anyone."

V

In many respects, Stevens's late work is as far as one can get from the visual arts. The poems are pure adventures in seeking an ease of discourse that allows consciousness a precise, yet relaxed, reflection on its own activity. The mind best contemplates its own energies when it can evade the contaminating effect of concrete images:

> It is not an image. It is a feeling.
> There is no image of the hero.
> There is a feeling as definition.
> How could there be an image, an outline,
> A design, a marble soiled by pigeons?
> The hero is a feeling, a man seen
> As if the eye was an emotion,
> As if in seeing we saw our feeling
> In the object seen and saved that mystic
> Against the sight, the penetrating
> Pure eye. Instead of allegory,
> We have and are the man, capable
> Of his brave quickenings, the human
> Accelerations that seem inhuman.
>   (*Collected Poems* 278–9)

And when Stevens does talk about those arts, as in the case of Gromaire, his is clearly a literary imagination, appropriating what it can thematize. Yet these differences ultimately highlight similarities that run deeper than intentions and that may be fundamental to the ideal of abstraction, whatever the medium.

Stevens's distrust of the image was not influenced by the similar wariness one finds in noniconic art. In fact, Stevens despised that art, primarily because he thought it attacked the idea of the human, as well as its icons. Yet significant analogies remain between his late work and the ambitions of those painters. History provides a partial explanation; of all the Modernists, Stevens was the one closest to the amalgam of idealist philosophy, theosophist theological speculation, and Symboliste poetics that provided the rationale for Piet Mondrian and Kasimir Malevich. But for our purposes, what matters is the parallel syntactic and thematic strategies that allow us to use painterly models to see how Stevens established new forms of agency and explored spirit's place within substance. Therefore, let us take as our example Mondrian's *Composition with Red, Yellow, and Blue* (1938–42) (see Figure 4), a work traditionally read as an essentially formal composition of relational forces.[6] There is no escaping that formal language, but such formal motifs both sustain and clarify several of the thematic concerns of this chapter: the role of artistic ele-

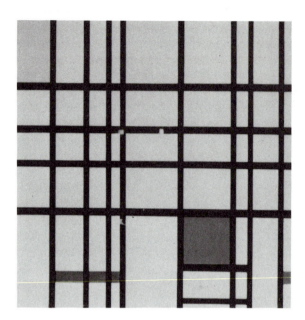

Figure 4. Piet Mondrian, *Composition with Red, Yellow, and Blue* (1938–42). Tate Gallery, London.

ments as literal forces within the world; the possibility that artworks dramatize a process of intensification that presents artworks as metaphysical theater; the notion of an elemental level of the real, whereby the fundamental forms of the mind are seen to parallel forces in nature; the consequent idea that abstraction is a means of containing the mind; the sense that all of these processes constitute a schema that captures transpersonal or schematic dimensions of the psyche, allowing two emotions to become one; and, above all, the sense that, through a very spare art, one can produce direct testimony for asserting the nobility necessary for a new monumentalism carrying letters of recommendation.

Mondrian's essay on "plastic art" sets the stage, in part by dramatizing the difficulty of expression that so embarrassed Stevens. Yet the strains in Mondrian's prose also make extraordinary demands on the concrete work of art to sustain significant values.[7]

> Art has shown that universal expression can only be created by *a real equation of the universal and the individual.* . . . Through intensification one creates successively on more profound planes; extension remains always on the same plane. Intensification be it noted is diametrically opposed to extension; they are at right angles to each other as are length and depth. . . . Art makes us

realize that there are *fixed laws which govern and point to the use of the constructive elements of the composition and of the inherent interrelationships between them.* These laws may be regarded as subsidiary laws to the *fundamental* law of dynamic equivalence which creates *dynamic equilibrium and reveals the true content of reality.* . . . Real life is the *mutual interaction of two oppositions of the same value but of a different aspect of nature.* . . . We are now at the turning point of this culture: the culture of particular form is approaching its end. The culture of determined relations has begun. . . . Non-figurative art demands the destruction of a particular form and the construction of a rhythm of mutual relations, of mutual forms or free lines. . . . It is of the greatest importance to note the destructive–constructive quality of dynamic equilibrium. . . . [This law] gives rise to a number of different laws which . . . determine the manner in which dynamic equilibrium is achieved. The relations of position and those of dimension both have their own laws. ("Plastic Art and Pure Plastic Art" 116–22)

This confident talk of "laws" is a far cry from Stevens's cautious probing beyond the limits of understanding, and it has exacted its price in the ways that art historians facilely dismiss Mondrian's ideas as mere mysticism. Consequently, it was quite difficult, until the exhibition Spiritualism in Art, held at the Los Angeles County Museum in 1987, to find academics who took Mondrian's ideas seriously (rather than simply noting their affinity with Dutch mysticism and proceeding to formal analysis). Yet there is no better exemplar of the capacity of those formal strategies to carry direct philosophical import, because there is no other artist as sensitive to the direct testimonial thematics that abstract art can compose. What Mondrian calls "dynamic equilibrium" begins in the play of destructive and creative energies that we found in both Stevens and Duchamp. Mondrian, however, makes no effort to evoke ideas concerning chess or concerning history as theater. Instead, he claims that everything about which we can make thematic generalizations literally occurs within the field of forces established by the painting. Thus, purely objective relations replace anything that might demand particular subjective responses, yet such impersonal forms are no less articulate or affecting. We encounter a process of intensification that aligns physical, emotional, and intellectual investments. That is clearest, he asserts, in the way inward and outward become substantially more than directions of physical force among what otherwise would be the mere extension of flat colors and lines on a canvas. For, as we respond to the balanced forces in the painting, flat extension in space yields to "a more autonomous life of the human mind becoming conscious of itself" ("Natural Reality and

Abstract Reality" 142), while at the same time the mind finds that autonomy grounded in the simplest forms and forces demonstrable in substance.

Notice first how the play of horizontal and vertical lines in this painting literally composes a theater in which the extensional space of the painting begins to be transformed into intensional forces, real only as one becomes self-conscious about one's own activity as the mediator between intensional relations and states of intensity. Strong verticals never quite master the canvas, because of the competing pull of the horizontals and the free-floating effect of the flat colors, denying and anchoring both linear pulls. Then these overall structural tensions introduce a further level of concrete intensification, by producing complex virtual relations among the particular rectangles. As each rectangle takes discrete form, it does so by destroying overall shape, then by contributing to the whole, in effect, another dimension, because that whole now contains so many discreet figures as potential parts of larger figures. Extension offers the potential for levels of shape and force, and specific containing shapes simultaneously deny and enrich what would contain them. Similarly, as the rectangles interact with one another they compose and decompose increasingly complex units. A stunning dance of identity and difference keeps the responding eye and mind always in motion and always securely contained.

So far, we have attended to something close to purely visual properties. The activities of decreation, composure, and containment became more complex, more deeply a literal intensification of what appears purely extensional, if we add the reflective motions of the mind that are elicited by the visual forces. There is a remarkable drama of figure and ground, established first by the ambiguity of white shapes and black lines, and subsequently extended to the emotions of mind, as it tries to stabilize the painting. Let us provisionally distinguish three horizontal sections, marked by lines extending from the inner boundaries of the yellow and red rectangles. That gesture seduces us into using the same objects to emphasize the structuring force of the verticals that run the length of the surface. But which is "ground" for the other? There is no answer, only a balance of tensions that gives considerable projected depth to the flat canvas, without denying the relation of force to surface. These tensions, in turn, get developed within each of the units created by the overall dividing lines. For example, the lower horizontal third sets up a new principle of balance in the relationship of colors, so that they complement the parallel rectangular shapes of the units composed by multiple black lines. The red square balances the elongated blue rectangle or line, but then the apparently similar vertical sections of this overall unit become almost pure contrasts: Where the one has elongated rectangles, the others emphasize horizontality, and where white dominates one, another insists on a stark black ground. Finally the intermediate space – once almost a simple blank – now becomes a vibrant rectangle, giving stability to the entire base of the painting. This stability, in turn, is countered by the eye's tendency to move from these colors to the yellow in the upper left of the painting, where color is not complicated by having to share a space formed by intersecting lines. This yellow, normally a color that projects from the canvas, here is made, by the lack of linear activity, to be the most stable, flattest extensional anchor for the canvas.

Yet the anchor is also a point of departure. It links to the smaller red unit, so that both are poised between the color forms enclosed by sharp linear patterns and the open forms that, on all of the edges of the painting surface, project into another kind of virtual space beyond the frame. Such contrasts bring together all of the thematic or ontological implications that hover over the formal language that we must use to describe Mondrian's work. Considered as a closed form, the painting takes on tremendous internal power as its extensional space comes to demand many levels of synthetic activity – all then literally present as we return to view the physical configurations as active forces. The inner life of mind and the pure externality of spatial relations permeate one another, carrying to a new level the theme of container–contained relations within the painting. The painting holds together forces in much the same way that the hero of traditional drama does: by projecting a virtual life beneath, or upon, the surfaces. And it has much the same claim to nobility, without a rhetoric of inwardness and of a tormented quest for the subjective basis of such force. With Mondrian, however, we do not stop with the closed form that arrests us. The painting does not coincide with the outer black lines. Instead, the concentration is balanced by a freedom of design and projected open spaces that join the yellow in calling our attention to the painting's utter casualness. All of the forces that the composition creates are projected here simply as possible moments in an infinite set of horizontal and vertical units, of which these comprise an intricately balanced instant. The individual work simultaneously realizes a dense configuration of universal forces and acknowledges its dependency on their infinite mutability, itself probably contained by the intensive laws that, for this moment, create this balance. Time and the timeless coalesce in a "real equation of the universal and the individual."[8]

VI

Our subject is so rich that one could indulge in an immense diversity of examples. But although it is ultimately those particulars that earn art its authority and value, we will greatly simplify the task if we now shift our attention to generalizing about the innovations illustrated in our four examples. Isolating six recurrent traits should help us identify what the poets and painters thought made their experiments worth pursuing. That, in turn, will stand me in good stead as I seek in the next chapter to propose a definition of abstraction capable of organizing the field of related notions that form what I shall call the "constructivist aesthetic." This framework will then help us formulate the significant differences among artists and movements, each given a distinctive place within a shared, and shareable, quest.

The most emphatic, and probably the most important, of the traits that we have observed is the works' foregrounding of the structuring activity of the artist: on the one hand posed thematically against "telling," or the old script, or a scenic, pictorial art, and on the other hand contrasted to Romantic notions of an expressive authorial presence. Whereas most Western art invites us to appreciate the authorial activity, very few works give that activity such a range of direct semantic roles to play. If we compare Matisse's nude to a painting such as the Rokeby *Venus,* we see that Matisse's woman has little force without the responding painterly activity that she elicits, whereas in Mondrian and, to a considerable degree, in Stevens's late work, there is simply no dramatic energy except for the constructive energies composing the surface.

This narrowing makes possible a second significant trait. By emphasizing these energies, and by using the work to interpret them, the artists try to make authorial activity carry the same kind of monumentality once available for the figure represented in the work but, in the nineteenth century, reduced to the condition of mere "foundling of the infected past" (Stevens *Collected Poems* 388). The new art might be spare, but it would make up, in direct, self-reflexive energy and conceptual scope, for what it lacked in dramatic intensity or ideological resonance.

Attributing qualities to those states requires as a third trait, a range of experiments in documenting art's claims on the world without relying on mimetic principles. If the poets and artists could base their metaphoric scope on the specific testimony sustained by the energies that the work disposes, they need not (in principle) rely for their sense of the monumental on any received cultural mythology. By seeking levels of abstraction that resist the cultural predicates usually employed in interpreting actions, the work offers exemplary structures that literally make visible new senses of the powers we have at our disposal and invite us to enter the modes of activity that tie our lives into those of other intentional agents: "Instead of allegory we have and are the man."

These first three traits are all contained in the display of authorial energies; the next three define some of the metaphoric implications made possible by those displays. For example, we can locate as a fourth trait the artists' effort to recast the basic features of intentional agency, so that the work becomes difficult to correlate with the assumptions about personality and the predicates used to make social judgments fundamental to representational art in Western society. Consider, for example, the contrast between traditional ideals of self-possession and the mechanical intensity that characterizes Duchamp's chess players, or the lush cast Stevens gives to impersonal reflection, or Eliot's redefinition of religious desire as a terrifying interplay of the obsessive and the ritualistic dispositions voice can maintain. Such art must force its audience to suspend their practical concerns – not because the art must transcend life, but because of its desire to fully participate in the real demands sharply differentiating commonsense ideas of what a person is from the fullest expression of our passions. If we rely only on scenic modes of organizing experience, we get a skewed vision of both the shape and the relative intensities of the emotional lives we are capable of leading. Vico caught this difference neatly when he distinguished between the violence of some states of anger and the tepid metaphors we use to describe them. Given that situation, he continued, there are strong reasons for attempting to reverse our usual preference for simile, so that we keep our metaphors under the kind of control allowing us to carry on our social lives.[9] Perhaps where the passions are at stake radical metaphor is closer to the unrepressed reality. Perhaps treating someone as a lion eager to kill serves better than simile to capture the intensity, and even the ontology, of rage. Perhaps no other route to self-knowledge is possible in an age so aware of the inescapable "others" who haunt the old centers of human thought.

My fifth trait derives from the artists' realization that our sense of substance can change, in direct proportion to these shifts in our understanding of spirit. For as agency changes, so does the nature of the energies that sustain and ground it. And abstraction makes that emphatic by enabling artists to propose their constructions as *literal sites:* The art is not offered as an interpretation of experience, but as a pure state, which all of the members of that audience can enter and explore. Indeed, they can enter the work only if they accept such principles, because the attempt to interpret it in traditional terms leaves them feeling outraged at this apparent fraud, or helpless before an art world that leaves their concerns behind. But, if they accept the experiment, they find themselves participating in actual physical forces that, in the reading or viewing, come to take on psychological significance, even as they exhibit certain ways that psychological energies lead beyond the bounds of the human. In William Carlos Williams's objectivist version of these possibilities, art provides "the spring-board for what the set-up it indicates induces objectively in things"[10]: Rather than expressing an authorial subject, the work establishes possible versions of aligning the self to the world that do not admit conventional subject–object boundaries.

The various poets we deal with have very different ways of realizing these five traits. But the major differences all derive from the sixth and last feature that runs through these examples: the sense that the need to respond to modern cultural conditions required a different, more ambitious, and more problematic concept of the artist's purposes than had been the case even for the Romantics. Modernist art, alienated from mainstream society and suspicious of all claims about truth and value that are based on representational principles, obviously could not confine itself to the traditional roles of entertainment and instruction. The task of creating new forms of "recommendation" could not rely on the accommodational tendencies that Eliot attributed to "minor" poetry. So the self-appointed Modernists embarked on a tension-filled and, in hindsight, paradoxical enterprise. It would be far too simple to reduce any major art to the roles of entertainment and instruction, unless we invoke a very complex sense of instruction. But representational art invites those descriptions, because its fundamental commitments are to reinforce or recover those powers of mind and grounding values idealized within their artistic traditions. Some Modernists would come to the same conclusions, but only after a considerably different journey exploring alternative ways that art could carry letters of recommendation not contaminated by a cultural order increasingly seen as the source of society's troubles rather than the vehicle for restoring lives art could celebrate. As a consequence the poets found themselves torn between moments of exalted idealism in what they proclaimed new possibilities for the human spirit and moments of apocalyptic rage in which they had to accommodate themselves to the irreducible mediocrity of the political order. These conflicts then leave us with the inescapable melodramatic question, "Was it worth it after all," after such temptations to political blindness, to self-delusory postures, and to the bitterness of a Yeats on his boiler and a Pound in his cage?

There is no easy answer. In my view, there is only the hope that criticism can make clear the range of issues that must go into such determinations. This must be a collective project. For my part, I want to show how these Modernist ambitions substantially alter the sense of powers that we can attribute to art as a mode of thinking. Because the Modernists thought that art could literally provide testimony for its own claims, they insisted that their work was not merely a supplement to philosophy, but provided direct alternatives to its traditional methods and values. The traits we are considering constitute an elaborate metaphysical exploration that requires a framework larger than art history, or even social history, if we are to assess what the art proposes. As we see what chess involves, as we see how bodies contour to the responding line, as two emotions literally become one, or as we observe ourselves complexly distributed in the play of extensional and intensional forces that permeate simple relations between planes, we begin to see that the questions once posed by Romanticism can now be pursued again without the risk of embarrassment and self-disgust. For once art defines a distinctive, abstract site and a specific set of energies, it can begin to conceive its strangeness less as an evasion of an oppressive reality than as heuristic exploration of how our constructive acts might modify our understanding of that reality. At one pole, that abstractness leads us to imagine the motions and elements of mind, and the immediacy of our emotional investments, as starkly external and visible: If there is to be a sense of spiritual powers, it can no longer be based on the intricacy of an inexpressible "buried life." Yet, at the other pole, the concreteness that this abstraction allows is asked to support claims to a radical inwardness, an insistence that the visible or the speakable become intelligible only in the recesses of radical acts of reflection attempting to adapt themselves to the essential qualities of an emotion or state of mind. The play among these positions becomes art's basis for insisting on its own irreducible philosophical significance: No other practice could so compose modes of concreteness, inwardness, and transpersonality into specific states that need not be victims of the general disenchantment with religious dreams that pervades secular culture, and no other practice could lead us to modes of engagement by which we enter, through our participation, the virtual world within which new identifications become possible. The only faith that this art needs is a willingness not so to hunger for justification before prevailing contemporary beliefs that we lose the ability to account for direct testimonies of what our hungers can produce.

2

Self-subsuming Artifacts: The Logic of Constructivist Abstraction

I

My six basic traits of Modernist art are now nothing more than an appallingly abstract taxonomy. In order to turn that taxonomy into a set of values we must discover the underlying principles and existential claims that provided, and provide, a rationale for these attributes. Therefore in this chapter I shall build to a definition of "constructivist abstraction" that defines a shared Modernist project and makes clear some of its fundamental differences from the dominant styles that preceded it.[1] This entails, first, getting clear on the burdens that the concept of abstraction had to carry for the artists and poets; after that I can spell out the principles enabling constructivist abstraction to provide a coherent alternative to traditional mimetic ideals. Because that discussion leads to more abstraction than I think most readers can bear so early in the book (to put the matter delicately), I confine myself to developing here the broad outlines for what will be taken up more intensively in my second appendix.

Both tasks clearly require careful attention to historical situations and archival materials. But if we are to keep the focus on how the poetry provides imaginative energies for the present, we shall have to modify the descriptive methods employed by the best historians of these artistic movements. We cannot capture many of the most dynamic and most structurally significant features of Modernism if we concentrate only on what the artists and writers actually said. Those specific claims must be connected to grounding principles and their underlying logic rationalized in ways that the agents often failed to elaborate. Their purposes were largely self-promoting; ours must assume a version of the Hegelian faith that we can know (and honor) the past in fuller conceptual terms than were available to the agents.

II

Our definition of constructivist abstraction must be both sufficiently general to account for the variety of Modernist experiments, and sufficiently perspicuous to establish a single field of relationships within which that variety becomes a structure of resonant differences.[2] Fortunately, Harold Osborne's *Abstraction and Artifice* provides us with a very good beginning for that enterprise. Osborne's study of Modernism in the visual arts makes it clear that some abstraction is necessary in any artifact, simply because the artifact cannot be an exact replica of its object. We take the additional step of treating an art as an abstract one, he claims, when we see it as calling attention to its specific abstracting features. Such art reorients the expressive force of a work so as "to place major emphasis upon the syntactical rather than the semantic information, upon the form or structure of a work rather than upon what it represents or depicts" (9). This emphasis is not merely a matter of design, or what Kant considered pure aesthetic formal "purposiveness." Syntax in itself promises expressive syntheses, and hence "aesthetic emotions," which resist the tyranny of the practical orientation that shapes our basic semantic categories. Syntactic patterns can be composed to serve unique, individual effects, whereas semantically oriented signs must attempt to adapt such uniqueness to the shareable space in which it makes sense to speak of "meanings." Distinctively Modernist abstraction uses these patterns to resist the confines of that shareable space by manipulating the tensions between the work's syntactic and its semantic elements. This resistance and recomposition takes two directions: "Semantic abstraction" preserves representational content, but so distributes the syntactic relations of the content that they make it impossible to interpret the work in accord with the naturalistic criteria governing our semantic expectations for visual art; at the other pole, noniconic abstraction refuses to rely on "the presentation of 'natural' appearances in any form" (27), so that its own properties as an aesthetic object serve as the irreducible focus of the work's expressive force.[3]

Even this simple clearing of the ground provides us with three very useful perspectives on aspects of Modernism that are often contested but rarely clarified. Abstraction has been charged with turning from life to formal concerns in order to escape the duplicity of treating a two–dimensional surface as if it could present a three–dimensional, sculptural space. Osborne provides a basis for general arguments that clear Modernist abstraction of this charge. Self-conscious reflections on the properties of the medium do not comprise the only, or even the basic, expressive forces the syntax carries. Nor does an emphasis on syntax preclude attending to three-dimensional space or representational signs. As Osborne points out, "Representation as such, semantic content, makes possible greater complexity and subtlety in the formal structure of a work, introduces, as it were, an additional parameter which the artist can exploit in the area of purely formal relations" (10). Even the most clichéd of pastoral scenes, he claims, allows Matisse's *Joie de Vivre* a rich synthesis of "semantic theme and syntactical composition" conveying "an expressive character of Arcadian joy" (13).

Second, as Hegel insisted, abstraction need not be opposed to concreteness. *Abstractness* is incompatible with an emphasis on descriptive accuracy to a particular scene, but there remains a serious question of whether describing "appearances" is in fact art's richest mode of concreteness. Suppose that the most concrete of natural forces is relational or structural; in that case, appearances are a diversion, attaching us to what Modernists often called the mere "outer world." This positing of a "mere" outer world opens the gates for a range of mystical claims that many of us find irresponsible. But because we have already seen that art based on such possibilities can reveal a good deal more than the prose muddies, it seems worth risking such errors, in order to take seriously modes of artistic thinking promising to establish alternatives to empiricism that may prove defensible in secular terms.[4] For that task, we need to flesh out the opposition between appearances and an underlying level of "real" forces, by resorting once more to Hegel's strategy of treating "concreteness," not as a condition of immediacy, but as a specific kind of relation between phenomena and interpretive systems. From this perspective, we see that we attribute "concreteness" to whatever seems to have a determinate place in a set of relations that establishes the particular as an enduring or significant element in some world. Thus we typically characterize realistic representations as concrete, not because they directly reproduce the immediacies of perception, but because they organize particulars in relational schema that are familiar and comfortable. Ideas too can be concrete in this way, whenever they play a part in cogent practices. Conversely, abstractions sometimes lose concreteness and suffer from abstractness, not because their substance is not perceptible, but because we cannot connect the terms to any informing set of relations. Abstractness occurs when we do not see how to apply a given formulation to the world. Ironically, this means that, in some cases, what we typically take as concrete becomes inordinately abstract: for example, if we rely on appearances when it is necessary to rely on relational or mathematical principles.[5]

Finally, Osborne's analysis of abstraction helps explain how writers can use painting and sculpture as models for new permissions. If abstraction need not reject all uses of representational imagery, its devices become available for a wide range of linguistic effects, even though these syntactic experiments also involve the referential dimension of the medium. Therefore Pound, Williams, and Stevens did not need to go to the lengths that Stein did, in order to adapt the principles that they saw in paintings. More important, Osborne's equating abstraction with an emphasis on the compositional act offers a model that we can imagine each art adapting to its own distinctive possibilities and limitations. We see, in theoretical terms, how a Duchamp, a Williams, a Stevens, and a Mondrian can each use nonrepresentational principles of composition to imagine new forms for projecting what persons can be and how minds engage in forces beyond them. Authorial performances in one medium become challenges for artists in a different medium to find their appropriate vehicle for exploring similar imaginative sites.

III

Unfortunately, this is as far as Osborne can take us, and it is not far enough. For although the concrete readings that we examined in Chapter 1 indicate that he is clearly right to emphasize the Modernists' reliance on the syntactic dimension of art, he is just as clearly wrong to treat these syntactic relations as if their primary function were to create new "aesthetic emotions." Osborne locates a distinctive feature of style, but stops before fully elaborating its significance. His stopping there, however, offers a very promising place to begin historical inquiry, for he places us in a dilemma that was precisely the one leading Pound and Wyndham Lewis to insist on a version of abstraction that would not simply resolve into the cult of aesthetic emotion. In their view, artists and writers had worked too hard to find their efforts reduced to sophisticated decorations for the leisured classes. It was necessary to replace the purely affective treatment of aesthetic syntax with models that showed how the new, antirepresentational stylistic principles afforded new ways in which art could carry extraformal content.

In these matters, Osborne's "only begetter" was Roger Fry, the figure whose very success at popularizing abstraction made Pound and Lewis fear that he would sacrifice the new art's revolutionary principles as the price of his own success with high society. The following is typical Fry – at once profoundly revolutionary, in his sense of why the past must go, and profoundly conservative, in assuming a type of modernity in art that Pound, in 1919, called only a "faint camoflage [*sic*] of the novel":[6]

As against these great advantages which art owes to impressionism we must set the fact that the pseudo-scientific and analytic method of [the Impressionist] painters forced artists to accept pictures which lacked design and formal coordination to a degree which had never before been permitted. They, or rather some of them, reduced the artistic vision to a continuous patchwork or mosaic of coloured patches without architectural framework or structural coherence. In this, impressionism marked the climax of a movement which had been going on more or less steadily from the thirteenth century – the tendency to approximate the forms of art more and more exactly to the representation of the totality of appearance. When once representation had been pushed to this point where further development was impossible, it was inevitable that artists should turn round and question the validity of the fundamental assumption that art aimed at representation; and the moment the question was fairly posed it became clear that the pseudo-scientific assumption that fidelity to appearance was the measure of art had no logical foundation. From that moment on it became evident that art had arrived at a critical point, and that the greatest revolution in art that had taken place since Graeco-Roman impressionism became converted into Byzantine formalism was inevitable. It was this revolution that Cézanne inaugurated and that Gauguin and van Gogh continued. There is no need here to give in detail the characteristics of this new movement: they are sufficiently familiar. But we may summarise them as the re-establishment of purely aesthetic criteria in place of the criterion of conformity to appearance – the rediscovery of the principles of structural design and harmony. (*Vision and Design* 19)

Out of such criticism there developed a theory of art as an expressive rendering of emotional states: The artist selects materials from a range of existential situations, in order to combine associated sensations and feelings into a distinctive overall aesthetic emotion, with no correlate in nonaesthetic experience. Hence aesthetic criteria become primary, and Fry can reassure his audience that what seemed to be radical innovations are only slight shifts in orientation, quite compatible with traditional art.

In fact, though, Fry enacts a subtle, yet potentially devastating, transformation. By treating the means for exploring new content as if it could only refer to itself, Fry gives Modernism a form or respectability that also makes it a mode fairly senseless for someone to devote a life to. Are principles of harmony and design sufficient reason for the sacrifices young artists make or, at the other pole, for the terms of self-importance that they want to attribute to their work? Osborne's answer is frighteningly self-assured, as he patronizingly dismisses Malevich's effort to make those syntactic formations carry a philosophical burden:

> Sometimes what [Malevich] meant seems to have been close to what Clive Bell and others call "pure aesthetic emotion," that is, affective response to the formal qualities of a composition which carries no representational or associative connotations. But Malevich also believed that this emotion, so aroused, is cosmic in character and brings one into contact with a realm of absolute and unchanging values. The appeal to "pure" or cosmic feeling is indicative of a kind of mysticism not uncommon among abstract artists of a geometrical persuasion who are less concerned with the embodiment of personal emotions than with a putatively universal feeling and the achievement of a mystical sense of cosmic harmony. In point of fact what they have in mind could possibly be explained without appeal to mysticism by the heightening and expansion of the perceptive faculty exercised upon an aesthetic construct which . . . exists for perception as a single complex configuration or gestalt. For a particular sort of emotional concomitant belongs to such intensification of perceptual alertness. (*Abstraction and Artifice* 138)[7]

I cannot allow myself too much self-righteous indignation. Better this, perhaps, than Malevich at his most mystical and obscure. But we are not dealing only with Malevich. And even Malevich – or, better, even Malevich's prose – can still help to produce an art that warrants such claims, precisely because it makes perceptual alertness the medium for dramatizing something very close to absolute and unchanging values. Appeal to mysticism may not be necessary; appeal to ideas is, even though none of the received ideas is adequate. Osborne and Fry make a reasonable response to that inadequacy: If we cannot propose clear ideas to account for the "content" of noniconic art, we can at least propose a clear psychology, permitting us to enjoy the affective configurations it affords. Yet such unresisting reliance on fallback positions seems to me extremely limiting for the analysis of the arts, the domain in our secular culture that has taken on the challenge of resisting many of the claims of common sense. Instead of asking how such challenges might be characterized, the aestheticist stance remains trapped within the oppositions between discursive ideas and purely aesthetic emotions that the Modernist emphasis on formal syntax was expected to resolve.

The danger is especially obvious in Osborne, because his general approach could easily have taken him past the views of syntax governing Fry and Quentin Bell. Osborne has the historical sense to connect Modernist art with previous movements in the arts that have emphasized abstraction, yet he ignores the fact that all of those movements were fostered by emphatic demands for new models of semantic content. In fact, it is here that the most radical and most conservative aspects of Modernism come together: The artists saw how formalist constructivism enabled them to return to the dreams of a Plato, or Augustine, or Dante that an abstracting method could produce a distinctive kind or level of content, free of the limitations of empiricism and crucial to the health of society. When Kandinsky stirred the desires of an entire generation by proposing that an abstract art might make "the soul of the object" stand "out most strongly, since the outer palpable beauty can no longer divert," he was doing little more than repeating an old Plotinian dream. Even Pound, who continually complained about Kandinsky's mushy and vapid transcendentalism, equated abstraction with the rediscovery of allegorical space: Jacob Epstein's *Marble Doves,* Pound wrote, makes available "the immutable, the calm thoroughness of unchanging relations" that manifest themselves like "the gods of the Epicureans, apart, unconcerned, unrelenting."[8] So, rather than reduce the semantic level of art to the production of aesthetic emotions, the new art sought a formal syntax capable of sustaining the abstract scope of allegory, while redefining its basic relationship between the spirit and its objects in two ways: There must be different means of securing the work's claims to semantic significance, and the new semantics would have to make the conditions of response serve as testimony for their thematic claims.

IV

I invoke traditional allegory because it provides the clearest example of the imaginative site necessary if abstraction is to have semantic content. One finds there a distinctive set of semantic properties that do not refer to manifest appearances, but nonetheless give the art broad cognitive claims. Literary allegories locate those properties in a realm opened up by the way that the authorial will pronouncedly takes liberties with such appearances. For then one must distinguish two levels of signification: a referential level, denoting particulars in real or imagined worlds, and a second-order framework interpreting the codes used on the referential level. Where illusionistic art concentrates on the work's adequacy to imagined scenes, allegorical art emphasizes the work's capacity to reflect upon the predicates we employ in making the judgments which negotiate that practical world. Rather than imagine art as a window on the world, allegory tries to examine the models of judgment that form the window; thus it has strong claims to deal with more permanent or deeper levels of reality that reveal the fundamental forms of shaping spirit. For example, Dante's *Commedia* makes the specific treatment of Florentine figures prelude to the process of learning to understand how the poet's own changing interpretations bring him closer to understanding the concrete forms that love gives to the world it governs.

Yet as much as the Modernist poets loved Dante, they could not simply borrow his methods. As the adventures of Stevens's Crispin make all too clear, the effort to locate a specific doctrinal core for allegory would only lead to a self-defensive set of parodic gestures, binding the author even more to the world of appearances that allegory must resist. If Modernist art were to engage the abstract and self-referential force of allegory, it would have to find more immediate access to the formal or interpretive energies of spirit that govern the mind's engagement in appearances, without the support of doctrine or conceptually coherent systems. That is why syntax becomes so important. It promises direct attention to the work of spirit, abstracted from practical appearances yet free of any determinate conceptual frame. Syntactic relations can occupy allegorical space, even though they do not yield to allegorical system (except in the form of prose interpretive commentaries that uneasily try to bridge the gap between new and old). And they can do so on good historical grounds. For, if one turns from literature to the Gothic architecture idealized by John Ruskin and by Wilhelm Worringer, one finds that the allegorical space is no longer dependent on an allegorical narrative anxious to compose the sensual details into a single thematic abstraction that suggests the timeless doctrinal significance of the event. Although built to doctrinal plans, and relying on systematic equations between material and spiritual signs, the Gothic cathedrals are, nonetheless, not interested in point-by-point parallels, preferring instead to let the overall material forces fuse with what the forces would signify as a nondiscursive transcendental presence. Then the divine spirit can seem literally manifest, in the relationship between the aspirations of carved stone and the dazzling effects of light's graces.

It is no wonder then that Modernist artists, brought up on such ideals, would turn also to Egyptian and African art. Perhaps there they could find concrete embodiments of a spirit whom one came to understand, not through verbal structures but through the life taken by formal energies. Rilke, meditating on Cézanne's efforts to understand the spirituality of seeing, saw in those "primitive" structures the challenge requiring a truly Modernist poetry: "Somehow I too must find a way of making *things;* not plastic, written things, but realities that arise from the craft itself. Somehow I too must discover the smallest constituent element, the cell of *my* art, the tangible immaterial means of expressing everything."[9] Here, then, lay the new imperatives for a renewed spiritual life. The first move would have to be negative, a clearing of the ground to be cured. By depriving the work of its emphasis on appearances and by eliminating the seductive graces of art, this new art could impose an enormous burden of expressive silence on its material formal elements (not unlike the silence of a cathedral): If this is all that a work offers its audience to accompany its obvious claims to seriousness, then the audience may have no alternative but to explore just how much of its spiritual investments the reduced material surface will bear. The work invites the audience not to treat it simply as an aesthetic emotion, but to ask the prior question of how and why this refusal of traditional aesthetic content can pretend to carry expressive significance. That immediately opens a space in which the audience must try out possible equations between what the audience itself brings and what the material surface provides. Here, the work, without losing the intense force of its material properties, begins to focus attention on how the constructive energies can sustain interpretive projections.

For evidence, we need only look again at what happens to the colors and shapes on Mondrian's canvas. Although they retain their physical presence, the material elements seem direct expressions or icons of a psychic life made visible as a transcendental physicality: The soul appears at once subject and object, the work itself the literal dwelling place of a Dutch version of Pound's unrelenting gods.[10] Yet our feeling of expansiveness cannot be equated simply with the materials. As the space of allegory opens into abstract domains, so too does our awareness that what seems elemental depends on the constructive energies that inform it. We find ourselves attaching predicates to the work that involve existential, as well as formal, concerns. Consequently, Mondrian's art is monumental less because of the material elements per se than because of the strange intelligence that pervades them, without displacing that physicality. The more the art seems to deny conventional signs, the more it foregrounds other forms of relational activity that have the same fascinating generality as traditional allegorical gestures, but without their dependency on systematic equations between flesh and spirit. Now spirit's activity takes on a manifest vitality, stressing what it can do simply as a force within matter – the very old truth of our creation myths. That vitality, moreover, clearly requires an impersonality as contemptuous of private histories as we can imagine sustained the architects of those Gothic cathedrals. When the work itself dictates what can be taken as spirit, the concerns of the private ego seem at best a metaphysical blindness.

I imagine that Osborne would have little quarrel with what I have said, although he might feel a few patronizing twinges at the metaphysical nostalgia of my formulations. But he would want to know what justifies calling all of these impressionistic fantasies "semantic." Why are they not just my way of describing an aesthetic emotion? I offer two responses. First, it seems to me impossible to avoid a semantic framework for artworks so obviously intended not merely to organize emotions, but also to influence how we think about them. The Modernist artists' and poets' prose statements tell us as much, and the works take great pains to invite predicates that engage more than matters of perception. Consider what we would lose if we accepted Osborne's view of Malevich, or if we took the features of Mondrian's painting as sensual fields upon which we are free to let our aesthetic emotions play. We would still have the monumental effects, but we would have no rationale for that monumentality; no sense that what composes an aesthetic emotion also demands our thinking about spirit's various ways of composing, revealing, and extending dynamic balance.

My second response has to do with the second major transformation that constructivist abstraction has worked on the Western tradition: its redefining the relationships that one can posit between art and the world, and between art and its audience. Once again, Osborne's stance is very clean: There is no need to burden abstract art with a concern for truth and falsity that elicits mystifying rhetoric about truths that are inaccessible to empirical criteria. But this way to sanity unnecessarily sanitizes the material. Artists, poets, and critics indulged in such rhetoric because they thought they had something important to say about how the art engaged the world. Here, for example, is Naum Gabo speculating on the social implications of an art that shifts from offering windows on the world to taking the forming syntax as its content:

> The apparently ideal companionship between Form and Content in the old Art was indeed an unequal division of rights and was based on the obedience of the Form to the Content. . . . All formalistic movements . . . never went so far as to presume the possibility of an independent existence of a work apart from the naturalistic content, nor to suspect that there might be a concept of the world which could reveal a Content in a Form.
>
> This was the main obstacle to the rejuvenation of Art, and it was at this point that the Constructive idea laid the cornerstone of its foundation. It has revealed a universal law that the elements of a visual art, such as lines, colors, shapes, possess their own forces of expression independent of any association with the external aspects of the world; that their life and their action are self-conditioned psychological phenomena rooted in human nature; that those elements are not chosen by convention for any utilitarian or other reason as words and figures are . . . but they

are immediately and organically bound up with human emotions. The revelation of this fundamental law has opened up a
vast new field in art giving the possibility of expression to those
human impulses and emotions which have been neglected . . .

The Constructive concept, being bound up with the new con-
ception of Art as a whole and of its functions in life, . . . sees
and values Art only as a creative act. By a creative act it means
every material or spiritual work which is destined to stimulate or
perfect the substance of material or spiritual life. . . .

In the light of the Constructive idea the creative mind of Man
has the last and decisive word in the definite construction of the
whole of our culture. ("Constructive Idea in Art" 110–2)

This highly speculative prose is not philosophically sophisticated, but if
we recognize how fully it registers the shifts to which we have been
attending, we will not dismiss the ambitious sense of art's significance
for its audience that Gabo provides.[11] Far better to attempt finding an
adequate philosophical translation, especially when a highly promising
route to that translation already exists in Nelson Goodman's work on the
concept of exemplification (work that is scandalously underused by literary critics).[12]

Osborne is willing to give up on semantics because he assumes that
any claims made for "meaning" must involve standard tests for denotational implication or theoretical consistency, tests that the arts fail to
meet. Goodman makes it possible to recast the question by insisting that
an adequate empiricism must reject the foundational, name-referent
models that have governed its philosophical accounts of meaning and
truth. Because we live in (and make) plural worlds, each involving quite
different criteria of how signs refer to shareable conditions that we can
call "reality," denotation is not the only route to reference: Statements
can have sense even if they cannot be translated into proposed descriptions for states of affairs. By analogy, the pursuit of representation is not
the only way that artworks take on semantic force. One can also refer to
the world by what Goodman calls "exemplification": that is, by exhibiting and clarifying properties that we can, on other occasions, employ for
making denotations. Then the reference resides in the fact that the exhibited properties or labels can be denoted, and then the constructive actions
within the work can take on existential significance as examples of possible states of agency.

In order to grasp what Goodman means by exemplification, we should
imagine someone holding a five-by-eight inch swatch of red cloth. The
person could use the cloth to represent or describe the color of Jane's
dress. This would be a paradigmatic case of using a sign for the purposes

of empirical denotation or, its corollary, a sense of fictional representation as verisimilitude: We compare the swatch with an existing state of affairs, so that we can judge the assertion's truth or falsity. But the person could also ask an auditor to take the swatch to a heap of dresses and take out from the pile only those that matched it. Now the swatch still serves cognitive functions by referring to something that we must treat as "real," but not as a description. Instead, the sample operates as a label or instrument. It establishes conditions of reference that can themselves be denoted. That is, when the auditor picks the dresses, he can explain the selections by pointing to the relevant properties of the label on which he had relied. Two features allow labels to serve these functions: the fact that one can identify specific properties possessed by the exemplar, and the fact that social practices specify some of those properties as the relevant comparative terms (in this case, the color of the swatch, but not its size). (Were someone unsure about the relevant terms, he might turn to some kind of criticism whose task it would be to show how the labels implicate certain possible properties in the world.)

Strictly speaking, this model of literal exemplification accounts only for the physical properties actually possessed by artworks. Thus it can capture significant distinctions between the denotational orientation of mimetic criticism and formalist attention to the disposition of those physical properties. But it cannot by itself sustain an alternative theory of semantic impact. For that, Goodman proposes a further distinction – the concept of "expressive signs" – which he defines as metaphoric uses of exemplified properties. Although our swatch exemplifies redness, the particular shade or shape or setting of that red can establish metaphoric associations, enabling it to express states that evoke predicates such as joy or passion or boldness or panic, each capable of infinite refinement, because every adjustment in the physical properties can modify the metaphoric disposition that the work comes to possess. Consider the remarkably different expressive states sustained by the changes in tonal key in any of Monet's sequences or in Kandinsky's more abstract versions of the same sense of affective modality.

Suggestive as Goodman is, however, his treatment of "expression" needs substantial modification before we can use it to clarify Modernist ambitions. Because of his empiricist commitment to an extensional language, Goodman would not countenance talk about "intentions" or about distinctive force of the overall synthetic and purposive unity that a work might establish. This leaves only the direct expressive quality of the individual signs, and it thus displaces all of the metaphoric dimensions of the authorial act that I have been trying to articulate. In order to accommodate those features, we must extend Goodman's theory by positing two fundamental kinds of metaphoric exemplification – one fundamentally expressive, the other fundamentally testimonial. In the first case we must be able to deal with affective dimensions that we elaborate from (or as) the metaphoric implications of physical properties possessed by the surface of the work, whether the surface be a formal syntax or a set of pictorial effects dependent on an illusionary scene. In the second case, we must adapt our analytic terms so that they refer not only to specific physical properties and their metaphoric implications, but also to basic conditions of response, which are created by the work as a whole and posited by it as metaphoric self-interpretations.

I doubt that one can draw hard-and-fast distinctions here, but it is crucial to note that the second set of concerns leads far beyond any talk of aesthetic emotions or even of art as a cognitive instrument enabling us to see possible configurations of experience. If artworks led only to "expressive" metaphoric elaborations of physical properties, one would not find much to say about Mondrian's *Composition with Red, Yellow, and Blue* (1938–42). At most, one could discuss its qualities of composure and dignity and balance. But in that case, painters of greater surface complexity and tonal variation, such as Kandinsky, would clearly offer more engaging emotional intensities. Yet my reading of Mondrian's painting in Chapter 1 suggests that this would be a severely limited position. For there I argued for another level of physical properties in the work. In addition to its physical balances on the canvas, the painting requires its viewers to occupy a position or site in which they see *themselves* as actually taking on that balance as a spiritual condition. How we construe the concept of literal possession then depends on what states we envision the audience coming to occupy under the direction of the work's formal relations. Once we grant this, we next need to ask how that level of possessed properties can be metaphoric because it exemplifies certain states for which we use psychological and existential predicates, as well as formal ones.

I do not have a very good theoretical account of the relevant mechanisms. However, if we let my reading of Mondrian provide the necessary terms, we can say that in these cases the metaphor involves, not an *emotional* expressiveness in the *properties,* but something like an *intellectual* expressiveness in the *principles* that the viewer comes to see governing her experience. The force of the metaphor resides in its ability to hover within what seem the irreducible physical properties emerging when the work is seen as a set of actual experiential energies that take hold as we try to bring the work to imaginative life.[13]

If artworks can provide such metaphoric exemplifications, we can treat them as actual testimony: To experience the work is to find oneself experiencing the plausible ground for what it claims as a metaphor. We have a way not only to attribute semantic content to art, but also to show

how we might go about testing the "truth value" of its metaphoric import, without having to rely on the traditional critical concern with the work's way of picturing external states of affairs. The semantic force of the work becomes its ability to account for the actual syntactic relations that it establishes.

This force, I hasten to add, need not hold only in noniconic work. Perhaps the most exciting feature of the line of thinking Goodman inaugurates is that it enables us to read back what we learn from the noniconic as a way of understanding how arts that focus more on representation can, nonetheless, provide a version of metaphoric testimony. The crucial step is positing a mode of physicality that does not trap us in sharp separations between the material properties of paint or words and their semantic functions. We have learned from Wittgenstein, and from J. L. Austin, that this dichotomy depends on misplaced assumptions of concreteness. It assumes that we must attribute the physical attributes of the medium to the signs (paint or words) themselves, rather than to the properties that accrue when we use the signs. But in fact most cases of reading involve our registering, not the physicality of the words but the virtual conditions they formulate for the mind, and the same principles hold for visual media. (Deconstruction demonstrates this from the opposite pole, when it insists that our reading must be governed by theory, so that we attend to the materiality of the words.) This virtuality takes on expressive significance when the work makes our physical experience sustain a metaphoric register. For example, as we participate in the dynamic balances evoked by a Mondrian painting, we literally position ourselves in a site where we become the transpersonal subject, no longer bound to the tragedy of individual existence. We experience ourselves as capable of feeling and of affirming relations that are, in all probability, fundamental to any subject's response to the painting. Similarly, even with the representational figures of Duchamp's *Portrait of Chess Players,* we find that both the authorial act and the internal relations of the surface possess physical properties, properties carrying direct metaphoric force, as modes of concentration that define the mode of agency which art can share with chess playing. Finally, although Wallace Stevens does not have the literal force of pictorial relations on which to build, he can have aural density compose an increasing syntactic, and metaphoric, complexity that extends a concrete utterance into a theater where the acting literally expresses the metaphoric force by which two emotions can become one. Rather than create an illusionary scene for his audience to interpret, Stevens constitutes a version of Williams's "so-ness" that readers can imagine actually sharing.

Goodman's principles clearly apply to all art, especially if we expand our idea of what we count as the properties that the work literally possesses. Yet Goodman's principles both emerge from Modernist contexts and prove especially relevant for them. There the principles account not only for the effects achieved, but also for the artists' ambition to overthrow a rhetorical notion of art as interpretation, by pursuing as far as they can the idea of art's testimonial metaphoric concreteness. In Modernist art, the ancient ideal of providing names for the world is transformed into the task of finding, and testing, names for what the mind is making of the world, as the mind reflects on its own processes. That emphasis allows the Modernists to turn from ideals of mimesis to ideals worked out in an equally ancient, but undervalued, tradition that emphasized art as a site where certain identifications are made possible. The effort to restore a site with the depth and scope that come from allegory's resistance to the logic of practical understanding, without relying on a doctrinal framework, leads back to the epistemology of Plotinus. Whereas mimetic art must emphasize the capacity of its images to correspond to some reality that they portray, the new art can base much more of its relation to extraformal content on the principle of participation. For, when art need no longer worry about providing pictures that match certain codes for interpreting experience, it can devote itself to eliciting the kind of participation that makes us recognize our capacity to dwell in worlds only dimly echoed by practical life. Art is literally empowerment: the making available of exemplifications that enable us to look at ourselves, as we encounter different sites of being and modes of inhabiting them. And the direct testimony provided by such examples promises to free its audience from its dependency on the entire apparatus of representation, and from the positing of interpretations trapped within the narrow expectations cultivated by the ideology of "aesthetic emotion." There we find ideals that may generate significant social change.

V

Now we can formulate a working definition of constructivist abstraction. Such a definition is needed to provide a clear focus for our concrete readings, and it should help demonstrate the deep interconnections between the specific programs elaborated by Modernist poets and painters. Finally, turning to definition will free those who have had enough abstraction about abstraction to begin concentrating on particular works of art. For those as fascinated as I am by the intricacy of the issues, I continue the efforts to elaborate a cogent theory of the semantics of abstraction in my second appendix.

Constructivist abstraction may be defined as the deliberate foregrounding of the syntactic activity of a work of art (either noniconically or in conjunction with representational content). Such foregrounding, however, is less an end in itself than the means for establishing a version of allegorical space in which the formal properties take on extraformal content. First, the reliance on syntax has the negative force of undoing the authority of those thematic expectations, psychological identifications, and interpretive logics that have bound, or "interpellated," an audience within the specific ideological involvements organized by Postrenaissance representational art. Instead of engaging our sympathy with the plight of particular agents, who are themselves largely defined by their social circumstances, and instead of focusing attention on the qualities of interpreting those personal plights and circumstances that the artist exhibits, these Modernist negations require us to locate the semantic force of the work in the distinctive compositional energies establishing their own level of agency. As Gabo put it, it is now the forming activity itself that constitutes the fundamental content – not as an alternative to the world of experience, but as a new way to exemplify states and powers that can change our understanding of human needs and capacities; that can alter our experiences of dominant emotional economies; and that can transfigure our understanding of our relationship to fundamental forces that impress us as being beyond the control of human will. The art *must* be abstract; then it *may* be the demonstrating of a concentration that engages the mind in the exhilaratingly mechanical forces of chess, or an actual encounter with dynamic balances, or an elaboration of the mind becoming its own self-transcending theater.

These different emphases put a difficult burden on criticism. On the metaphoric level, abstract art proposes modes of thinking that can carry enormous scope, yet the vehicle – the reliance on elemental syntactic properties – deprives us of the traditional dramatic, narrative, and argumentative frameworks that have, since the Renaissance, established the artwork's universalizing dimensions. This reductiveness has, as its social corollary, an adamant resistance to all received ethical forms for those universals. The resistance in itself is not distinctively Modernist, since most significant art makes internal relations within the work the basic interpretant of the concepts it takes as its subject: What Milton means by ideas such as "justice" and "obedience" depends ultimately on what those ideas organize and produce as approved actions within *Paradise Lost*. But Modernist abstraction is distinctive in the level of resistance it pursues. It hopes to alter, not only what we think, but also how we understand who one becomes as one adapts these various logics for identifying and sorting the elements of experience. Interpreting Modernist abstraction ties one to an essentially Romantic project of cultural cure, but it also requires the continual jettisoning of Romantic metaphors and Romantic visions of how the individual psyche finds itself empowered to proclaim its freedom from the socially dominant disciplines of inquiry.

At stake is, not a better way to read nature and history, but a better way to read against nature and history – which is why it is wise to attempt reading through the text. Therefore criticism's task is to find a language capable of showing how artistically composed direct experiences provide significant alternatives to the typical form of our subjective investments and to the culture's prevailing methods of objective validation.

3

Knowledge Enormous Denies the God in Me: Abstraction and the Romantic Tradition

I

Theoretical constructs are to criticism what grammar is to discourse: They make certain relations possible, even shape the contours of our investments; but they are inert, without distinctive dramatic qualities, until they enter an actual history. Now it is time to offer a version of the historical situation in which the Modernist aesthetic developed. Since I want to stay as close as I can to Modernist ideals about the uses of the past, the history I offer will not concern itself with events and forces, on the one hand, or the development of beliefs and styles on the other. History, here, will be the authors' own sense of the cultural situation that the course of events and changes in ideology produced for them. Therefore we shall have to renounce several important perspectives. Rather than seek broad coverage, I shall concentrate on the intensive analysis of a few examples that I think best define both the fundamental spiritual tensions inherited by Modernism from the nineteenth century, and the imaginative innovations that provided them with a repertoire of strategies that could be recast into a constructivist aesthetic.[1] Rather than evaluate whether these examples adequately represent historical forces, I shall be content with the fact that, for the Modernists, they seemed the most telling illustrations of what it meant to face up to their historical situation. And rather than pursue the complex affiliations and evasions made possible by such pictures, I shall be concerned only with fleshing out the Modernists' own versions of how art could resist the dominant values shaped by that history.

My working hypothesis is a simple one: History provides a measure of what writers accomplish, because it stages the complex of ideals, resources, and contradictions that they must negotiate in attempting to create a satisfying imaginative order out of what, as a heritage, seems to leave them confused and divided. Appreciating that accomplishment requires us to manipulate several critical stances: We must identify with the artists' predecessors, with their version of their predecessors, and with the actual forms of agency that the artists construct – all the while trying to maintain the distance to see how well the agents adapted to the relevant problems and resources within the drama they act out. My specific test cases for Romantic and Victorian poetry will elaborate one particular condition of agency: the possibility of imagining a philosopher figure capable of providing secular sanction for the poets' efforts to recuperate the full intensity of romance states elaborated by Preenlightenment imaginations. Thus, as these poets explored pastoral sites like the Spenserian garden and developed characters like Lamia or the Ancient Mariner or Blake's bard, who embody modes of being that Northrop Frye describes as projecting more-than-human powers, they found themselves needing the sanction of a projected philosopher, able to correlate such imaginative leaps with a discourse of "truth" that could claim social authority. The ensuing struggle for hegemony or accommodation provides a superb index of the models of expressive activity, and of the relations between private and transpersonal aspects of the subject, that define nineteenth-century poetic thinking. The results are as moving as they are disturbing, since they make strikingly clear what was, and is, at stake in the rhetoric of crisis that led the Modernists to their radical experiments. For our focus requires us to return to questions about the limits of representation; about the possibility of alternative forms of representativeness based on distinctive poetic sites; and, above all, about the intricacies of identification and judgment that emerged as poets sought to elaborate the necessary new terms on which to propose recommendations for their values. However, now my previous emphasis on purely conceptual relations must give way to an analysis of the emotional investments that cluster around these ideas, eventually breeding the insuperable contradictions that haunted the enervated poetic philosophers who populate Victorian poetry. The pathos that this history engenders should, in its turn, lead us to considerable respect for the Modernists' analytic ability and at least some sympathy for the plight which that analytic clarity imposed upon them. Finally, by focusing on the specific poetic history of these problems, we may arrive at the point where we, like the Modernists, are fully responsive to the opportunities offered by what seemed radically new painterly experiments promising to transform the most debilitating features of that heritage.

Developing this sequence will take three chapters. The first, this Chapter 3, has three basic sections. It begins by focusing on a few examples, in which Romantic poets tried to define the new sources of imaginative power made available by their struggle against Enlightenment values. The second section shifts to what happened to those Romantic constructs in Victorian poetry, where the poets found it much more difficult to draw the necessary bridges to romance states, and therefore saw the dream of empowerment ironically trapping the imagination within a "buried self," complexly overdetermining and underdetermining all efforts to establish plausible alternative forms of judgment. All projection seemed to come back as a haunting spectacle confronting poets with the powerlessness of their art. The final section of the chapter employs these Victorian literary versions of the philosopher as dramatic foils to demonstrate how incisively Kant, the best philosopher of the age, both established a concept of heteronomy capable of analyzing the lacks that the poets had encountered at the core of their philosophical projects and laid the foundation for the alternatives that Modernism would develop.

Clarifying nineteenth-century efforts to elaborate those alternatives and the problems they create requires a second chapter, Chapter 4, transporting us from England to French writers such as Baudelaire and Flaubert, who adapted to art the most radical features of Kant's versions of constitutive activity and tested specific models of agency by which such activity might resist many of the traps in Victorian poetics. A third chapter (Chapter 5) returns to American poetry by way of T. S. Eliot, as he attempted to engage the site of maximum tension between that Victorian heritage and the French efforts to rebuild romance principles in accord with a post-Kantian constructivism. The contradictions of that position were too great for even Eliot to resolve completely, but he earned his status as the paradigmatic Anglo-American Modernist by defining for all his peers what it meant to be contemporary, and what they would have to learn from the other arts if they were truly to escape the contaminated heritage that kept his politics in thrall to tradition, church, and king, and his poetry in thrall to the obsessively ironic self-consciousness that may have made those values seem necessary.

II

However ambiguous the relation, Modernism remains wed to Romanticism, because it was the Romantics who first felt on a large scale the fundamental problem that still oppresses the arts: How is it plausible to preserve as publicly significant the values in romance, or in the states made available by the lyric imagination, within a culture that grants intellectual authority only to a range of Enlightenment models developed as antagonists to all romance ideals.[2] We inherit, in poetry, a fundamental tension between the claims of *lucidity* and the claims of *lyricism* – each posed as an absolute, yet each desperately needing some complement, if it is to avoid severe self-contradiction. Because I have written on this dichotomy elsewhere,[3] I shall be brief and general here, attempting only to set forth basic principles, which will be more fully elaborated in my discussion of concrete examples. The terms "lucidity" and "lyricism" are disturbingly general and vague; yet we need that generality, and at least some openness to competing interpretations, because we must identify fundamental attitudes that capture a variety of specific content claims under a single set of problems.

Every culture probably has "lucidity terms": that is, ideals for forming values and plans on the best available public evidence. But the Enlightenment gave lucidity a particularly narrow and especially significant role to play in the hierarchy of values that a culture sustains. There, lucidity was posited as confronting the entire range of values that could be cast as depending on "superstition," "romance," and "authority." That basic opposition then generates two imperatives: that one seek, as evidence for one's claims, the form of certainty provided by the principle of visual proof, and that one assume an impersonal stance, subordinating first-person interests to the kind of third-person perspective that can easily be verified by observers. Eventually such ideals would be formalized in Rudolfe Carnap's logical empiricism: For a statement to be true, it must refer to determinate observable phenomena and combine them in accordance with demonstrable lawlike generalizations. But long before Carnap, thinkers such as Thomas Hobbes, Baron d'Holbach, Jeremy Bentham, and Auguste Comte developed versions of these principles into Western culture's dominant model for social and psychological inquiry.

Lyricism, in contrast, bases its model of value formation on principles that take their clearest form in the intensity of first-person experience. Indeed, one might say that lyricism must carry the spirit's full sense of its own capacity to confer, or disclose, the significance of nature or society for human life. In Postenlightenment culture, these impulses seem best defined in opposition to the frustration caused by the reductive force of analytic methods and their inability to explain the intense commitments that go into our efforts at analytically debunking the illusions of others. But, since lyric desire engages us in trying to make sense of what, to lucidity, seems excessive or delusory, those devoted to lyricism find themselves always on the defensive. At best they can hope to subsume the roles sanctioned by lucidity under a more expansive sense of what human life can be, in effect restoring what Stevens called "a time . . . when to be and to delight to be seemed to be one" (*Collected Poems* 149). But even then, what actually gets articulated as the grounds for lyricism seems always to take its form by opposing dominant social practices, so lyric principles tend to be much clearer on what they resist than on what they afford. The result is the continual production of partial theories or the appropriation of principles invented for other purposes.

Nonetheless I think we can locate two fundamental positive values that most of these Romantic projects shared. Against the forms of evidence that empiricism cultivates and that, for Kant, depend on the procedures of the "understanding," proponents of lyricism tried to work out versions of an "other side of representation" that postulate certain forces that cannot take determinate form. One thinks not only of Freud's unconscious, but also of Henri Bergson's *dureé,* Georg Walter Groddeck's "Gott-natur," Roland Barthes's *"textualité,"* and John Crowe Ransom's "sacramentalism." And against the claims to impersonality, lyricism insisted on the centrality of an "I," or its equivalent, capable of maintaining the irreducible, yet often problematic, first-person perspective. That perspective expresses psychic needs and psychic forces formed upon, and capable of developing through, the projections and commitments that the arts make available. Were lyric attitudes to prevail, society would have to make sharp distinctions between realms in which third-person perspectives are adequate and those where it is impossible to prise off the "I," as if it were a mere shifter or bearer of attitudes, allowing persons momentary access to sentences that could hold for any other subject. Lyricism brings a demand to correlate description and investment, so that one treats certain events as if they had to be understood in terms of the expressive acts that they engendered. Therefore we find the Romantic tradition obsessed with defining a "reality" that is inseparable from the qualities of voice that apprehend it (as in Schelling's version of the symbol). Thus, where Enlightenment lucidity threatened to narrow the social theater, pure lyricism simply exploded it into an endless range of purportedly immanent states, each the more to be valued by its incompatibility with a public language. Able to focus on subjective intensities, these lyric states put in the place of that public language a confidence in the modes of relation to the world sustained simply by the sense of enthusiasm carrying the subject beyond itself. Consequently, it is impossible to be content with claims for a "dead, objectified nature." Instead, the enthusiasm within the lyric agent also serves as testimony for some unrepresentable creative ground underlying the feeling that the energies also "belong" in the world that the agent experiences.

Given the cultural authority of enlightenment principles, however, these claims find themselves at best occupying the margin of what can count as testable propositions. The concepts sustaining the lyricism produce an exhilarating yet problematic amalgam of intense modes of self-consciousness, riddled with continual worry that one's basic values may be only anachronistic escapes from the reality of a much-diminished world. And for good reason, since these visions suffer from three serious problems. First, as Norman Mailer's *Steps of the Pentagon* demonstrates, the internalizing of principles of value tends to produce an inverse moral hierarchy, in which the "good" comes to be defined only in terms of the degree of resistance to social authority and the absoluteness of abstract integrity that the individual can muster. At the opposite pole, this "enthusiasm" is continually haunted by the fact that its formulations often fall into highly predictable logical structures whose very predictability denies the creative difference that the heart proclaims itself making: If there are to be first-person claims about values, there simply must be hypotheses about the "other" side of representation. Once we realize that, what seemed distinctive assertions threaten to become only self-delusion, a pandering to needs that reveal the lyric spirit as a supplicant, seeking scraps from the stingy beneficence of empiricist criteria. Finally, these fears keep lyricism so uneasy that it tends to exaggerate its claims, hoping thereby to protect something from lucidity's imperialism. Each stance creates lacks in the other since both generate supplemental fantasies as elaborate as they are ultimately indefensible. Nothing else could account for phenomena such as the persistent conflict in epistemology between an idealism that makes ontology match the perceptive structures of the subject, and an empiricism whose resistance to expressive subjectivity culminated in Bertrand Russell's theory of types, where the truth claim of the utterance must be separated from all traces of the speaker's act.

III

Philosophy's traditional task has been to attempt to resolve such conflicts. I want, instead, to explore the investments that the conflicts elicit and the pressures they impose on modern minds, so I shall be concerned less with single solutions than with elaborating the range of conditions defining the poets' situations and demanding new artistic experiments. For that task, we must shift from the process of hypothetical generalization to the concrete texts by which nineteenth-century writers sought to establish forms of spiritual life that they could take as neither reductive nor embarrassing. Let us, then, turn to poems by Wordsworth and by Keats, the two poets whom the rest of the century saw as establishing its basic imaginative options. At one pole, we shall track through Wordsworth what can be called a *scenic mode* for locating within the secular world certain models of creative energy that promise to align the spirit, momentarily forced into dizzying self-reflexive ironies, with a dynamic source of spiritual values on the "other" side of representation. By forcing his desire for an egotistical sublime to its limits, Wordsworth locates plausible immanent forces that afford poetry the constitutive roles that are necessary if it is to resist traditional humanistic pieties. At the other pole, we shall attend to Keats's ability to develop exuberantly sensuous romance states that make visible certain modes of impersonal intensity that transcend philosophy's versions of reflective objectivity. Yet despite their differences, we shall find both poets caught in such a complex mix of blindness and insight that we will not be sure whether what is most moving about the work derives from the constructive intelligence of the authors or from their constant self-scrutiny, which puts in question all claims that the mind can bring to the level of thematization, as if art had to doubt anything that it has the power to project. We shall, in other words, find ourselves in a good position to appreciate both the profound ambivalences that these achievements created for the Victorians, and the Modernists' effort to recuperate the best features of those projects under very different artistic principles.

Our first example of the philosopher figure in Romantic poetry must be that most representative of all Romantic figures, the youth first learning both the need for, and the power in, shaping an identity by reflecting on what romance states make available. For that task, there is no better philosopher than the hero of Wordsworth's "Nutting," because there the youth must earn his sense of a distinctive lyric self by resisting the accumulated weight of sentimentalized British Enlightenment values. Against the easy rhetoric engendered by that heritage, the ephebe must turn to resources that sustain a very different hierarchy of psychic functions, radically stretching available conditions of representation, so that they focus attention on a force that cannot be made to appear except in the process of poetic self-reflection. Exiled from official cultural ideologies, romance gets located in the processes of memory, which are themselves engendered by an intensity of perception so compelling that one must alter the basic terms linking the ego to its grounds in nature. So the youthful Romantic experiences what will become the fundamental logic of Modernist constructivism, yet he remains severely limited by the scenic frame posited as the stage on which the mind must define its constitutive powers.

The initial situation of "Nutting" strikingly juxtaposes motives for idealizations and invitations to an ironic stance. But rather than give one priority over the other, Wordsworth makes the conjunction itself carry the new lyric energies: What matters is the force that enables the poet to recognize the absurdly mock-heroic dimensions of this motley hero, "in proud disguise of cast-off weeds," yet not to be content with irony, because these odd, overdetermined traces of adolescent sexual fantasies prove the vehicle for a new sense of the sublime. Rather than the reflective pathos of William Cowper's "Castaway" or the exalted contemplative scope of the voice in Thomas Gray's "Elegy in a Country Churchyard," this poem demands our working against generalized sentiments to focus on what the compulsion to narrate reveals about the mind's relation to nature. That compulsion, in turn, derives from the fact that this kind of event, and this eagerness for self-exposure, demand attention because they do not have either the representativeness or the corresponding easy resonance of what seemed canonical in Wordsworth's day. An equivocal hero performs an overdetermined act, for unspecified reasons, leading to an ambiguous affirmation of a spirit in the woods, who seems incongruent with traditional Christian understandings of spirit. Thus deprived of the culture's standard interpretive predicates, the poet must use his performance as an appeal to a new, non-Horatian model, in which close reading promises the reader access to principles of relation that lead beyond what the culture encodes.

The challenges to received values are most emphatic in Wordsworth's manipulations of genre. Rather than invoke and vary pastoral form, as a means to present a situation, Wordsworth makes the tension between the event and the forms available for representing it to the self the basic subject within the poem. Actions that seem to follow from one tradition turn out to demand a new understanding of how we can relate to nature, and it to us:

> I heard the murmur and the murmuring sound,
> In that sweet mood when pleasure loves to pay
> Tribute to ease; and, of its joy secure,
> The heart luxuriates with indifferent things,
> Wasting Its kindliness on stocks and stones,
> And on the vacant air. Then up I rose
> And dragged to earth both branch and bough, with crash
> and merciless ravage . . .
> And the shady nook
> Of hazels, and the green and mossy bower,
> Deformed and sullied, patiently gave up
> Their quiet being: and unless I now
> Confound my present feelings with the past;
> Ere from the mutilated bower I turned
> Exulting, rich beyond the wealth of Kings,
> I felt a sense of pain when I beheld
> The silent trees and saw the intruding sky. –
> Then, dearest maiden, move along these shades
> In gentleness of heart; with gentle hand
> Touch – for there is a spirit in the woods.[4]

(38–55)

We are given no specific dramatic cause for the violence, so we must examine the rhetoric defining the state of mind leading up to it. We find there the standard humanism of Romance pastoral – the mind coming to the recognition of its own power – now rendered with an eye to its cost (as if nature were allowed its say). As the heart luxuriates, the mind exalts its own importance by setting itself against a nature that becomes merely its object. But the proclamation soon takes on a violence that reveals how much it is in fact the overcompensation for severe lack. As it asserts its hegemony, the mind becomes anxious before a greater self-sufficiency that it encounters (or creates) outside itself, so its sense of its power leaves it at odds with the conventional attitude initially producing a coherent scene. "Kindliness" beautifully captures these dualities, on which the Enlightenment tradition was to founder. From the humanist perspective, "kindliness" refers to the appreciation of a distinctively human potential in the encounter. But this makes nature a little less than kin, reduced to hoping for the subject's kindnesses and hence also a fit victim for his tirades. Yet violence produces another kindliness, linking him to precisely that capacity for disorder in nature that probably made the effort to cover over the differences seem necessary in the first place. From this perspective, consciousness seems to share, not nature's depth, but the superficiality of its appearances, as if both domains distanced and distorted some deeper possibility of lawfulness.

The logic is pure Augustine: The secular dream of being more than nature reduces one to being less than one's own nature can be; one must find a way of reading one's experiences so that the awareness of this acculturated blindness becomes a means of redefining spirit. For Wordsworth, the new means is confessional narrative, and the new goal a state of sublimity, earned by the narrative process of working through lack and contradiction. In this more dialectical sense of landscape, poetry cannot be content with describing nature or reflecting on the general truths that nature might illustrate. Rather, poetry must become self-reflexive enough to provoke errors, then test the capacity of the composing voice to spell out new lines of relation between a mind in excess of nature and a force of nature that reveals its power only through the collapse of kindliness. Once the sky can become an intruding presence, the youth must learn how narrative enables him to take responsibility for both his difference from nature and the divisions from himself that generated so unreasoned and ostensively spontaneous a destructive act. The result is a new form of the sublime, different from Burke's, that gives moral force to the state of self-consciousness it calls forth. The rude shock of what one is not – *not* one with the appearance of nature, and *not* one with the rhetoric that gives man superiority over a yielding nature – forces memory and poetry to the constructive work of the concluding lines. There is a spirit in these woods, but its meaning and force are reserved for those who can learn to read it as the poem does: through a series of negations that clear the way for this particular poetic naming to resist a history of false associations. Then it requires the dialectic of narrative memory to show why there must be a spirit and why it must remain on the margin of human experience, beyond the control of an interpretive violence that most ephebes in the culture never outgrow.

Wordsworth's great achievement here is to have his sublime romance and to moralize it too, while making the conjunction testimony to the power of poetry. One could cast these Wordsworthian moments in the frame of Freudian instruction scenes, since "Nutting" overdetermines the poem's resolution, just as it had the violent act, by casting this spirit in the woods as a surrogate father, punishing the son for raping his sister-mother, and thus composing (or imposing) nature as a superego figure. Yet Freudian language will not suffice, because this overdetermination is quite deliberate. The scene instructs because of its overt properties as scene: as a mode of presentation that can undo the received model of interpretive authority and make the specific process of unfolding, which the poem enacts, necessary to define what spirit can be. Rather than limit spirit to something we find in the unconscious, we are invited to envision it as the active force to which narrative can testify, once it comes to understand that the mind is capable of modes of attention and memory more sensitive, and more capacious, than the models of man that the poem seeks to displace.

On that narrative base, Wordsworth builds a moral and metaphysical dimension for this interpretive power, thereby taking responsibility for a specific model of instruction that in effect defines a new social role for poetry. Because the spirit in the woods can become the spirit defined by the field of energies the poem's narrative act composes, the narrated recognition scene becomes available for an entire society. Error on the dramatic level becomes, in discourse, the basis of a rhetoric that can compete with the discredited humanism, by at once honoring the other-ness of nature and giving man a dialectical form for attending to its voice. A journey in space becomes a journey in time, where consciousness can exercise its own form of producing differences, in order to restore a sense of identity on a new level. This is a spirit in a personal narrative's self-critical activity that can engage the spirit in the woods and make reflection on such engagements part of what it offers a community.

Making good on the demands which that community imposes, however, would create substantial trouble for this productive spirit. The poetry's effort to establish a new model of sublime authenticity remains dangerously close to the moralizing abstractness of the rhetoric whose blindness provoked Nutting's act of self-purification. So Wordsworth had to elaborate a framework interpreting his differences from that rhetoric and showing how his model has access to distinctive modes of spiritual life. That need gave birth to his indispensable "Preface" to *Lyrical Ballads,* which postulates a new poetics, based on what I shall call the "model of the scenic self." This model offers two essential differences from the ideals of poetic knowledge that sustained traditional humanist rhetorics: In the place of received notions of judgment, Wordsworth based the psyche's powers of discrimination on its capacity to identify with the spirit one found in the woods or in the forms of life embodied in socially marginal figures such as the leech-gatherer; and in the place of traditional ideals of a generalizable poetic truth, Wordsworth located the representativeness of poetry in its capacity to provide a form of testimony that might directly exemplify the powers that those identifications conferred.

I stress the role of "scenic self" in that poetics, because I think it captures the radical nature of Wordsworth's psychology, and because it will eventually explain why his poetry, despite its promising model of expressive energies, led to ideals of personal sincerity and symbolically charged perceptions that became increasingly difficult to reconcile with the secular order. Traditional humanistic and rationalist models of self are categorical, rather than scenic. That is, they emphasize the capacity of ideas or images both to establish ideals with which the self will identify and to sanction versions of judgment that proceed from the rule to the instance. Wordsworthian psychology does not renounce those generalizations, but it does ground them differently, and in so doing it requires a different mapping of how the self discovers and assesses values. Judgment becomes what Friedrich Schlegel called a form of "spiritual sensuality,"[5] which must locate its generalizing principles within the scene that it composes. Rather than base judgment on abstract ideas or taste, Wordsworth attaches it to a history of negotiations with an environment. The self is "scenic," then, because its investments and judgments derive from the scenes that it has been attached to and the traces that those leave in his memory. Scenes are not mere instances, passively awaiting the forming influence of the mind. Rather, they serve as metonyms for behavioral complexes that spread out over time and into a range of repeated habits and related social practices. Because the self neither creates meanings nor can trust dominant cultural generalizations, its deepest powers and most intimate loyalties are shaped by the history of the adjustments it makes to those environmental forces. And because these adjustments involve the measure of time – of repeated connections to nature and other people, as well as a history of rewards and instructive failures – the energies they engage can be much more comprehensive, and more immediately compelling and flexible, than anything that generalized principles can afford. The expansive life of scenic consciousness both elicits and rewards a temperament that gradually develops patterns of attention and care binding it to its surrounding community.

Such humble beginnings soon come to sustain quite ambitious claims. If there is to be a new model of judgment, there must also be a new hierarchy among mental faculties. Poetry is "the most philosophical of all writing," because only its model of attention sufficiently embodies the intimate relations between the mind's productive and its receptive powers. Only poetry treats "immediate pleasure" as both the formative means, and constant test, of knowledge:

> [Poetry's] object is truth, not individual and local, but general and operative; not standing upon external testimony, but carried alive into the heart by passion; truth which is its own testimony, which gives competence and confidence to the tribunal to which it appeals, and receives from them the same tribunal. Poetry is the image of man and nature.[6]

Poetry can provide truth that is its own testimony, because it replaces all descriptive versions of poetic reference with an emphasis on the force through which a scene can take hold in and on the mind, thereby freeing the imagination to explore the full panoply of feelings that connect the one scene to the relations it has built up over time. Poetic truth is its own testimony, because it literally measures what poets can make of and through the scenes that have formed their habits of attention and the contours of the memory that must extend attention into the more general realm of reflective spirit. The constitutive energies of the work define processes of adjusting to the course of events that establish demonstrable modes of spiritual life capable of opposing dominant ideologies.

This testimonial model of truth makes it possible for Wordsworth to treat the poem's constitutive activity as a directly ethical force, quite similar to what the Modernists were to seek in less subjectivist terms. For it becomes impossible to separate the modes of attention that a specific scenic encounter engenders from the eloquence that defines the claims of its speaker to become an exemplary representative for his community. That is why, as early as "Tintern Abbey," Wordsworth's overwhelming question is "Has it been worth it, after all, to have so oriented one's attentions and affections?" – a question answerable only by the qualities of consciousness that the poem's language will sustain, as acts of memory and focused attention try to take responsibility for the agent's having lived a certain kind of life. Personal justification becomes a matter of articulating through poetic syntax a mode of agency that can adjust to the spirits it encounters in the scene it inhabits:

For I have learned
To look on nature, not as in the hour
Of thoughtless youth; but hearing oftentimes
The still sad music of humanity,
Nor harsh nor grating, though of ample power
To chasten and subdue. And I have felt
A presence that disturbs me with the joy
Of elevated thoughts; a sense sublime
Of something far more deeply interfused,
Whose dwelling is the light of setting suns,
And the round ocean and the living air
And the blue sky and in the mind of man:
A motion and a spirit, that impels
All thinking things, all objects of all thought
And rolls through all things. Therefore am I still
A lover of the meadows . . . of all the mighty world
Of eye, and ear, – both what they half create,
And what perceive; well pleased to recognize
In nature and the language of the sense,
The anchor of my purest thoughts, the nurse,
The guide, the guardian of my heart, and soul
Of all my moral being.

("Tintern Abbey" 87–110)

The passage begins in a self-reflexive distance, content with a precise description of the effects of memory. Then, as the poem shifts from learning to feeling, testimony of a different kind dominates the stage. Feeling will not stay in the past tense. Rather it produces a periodic sentence, whose process of unfolding dramatizes the intense syntheses that a mind so formed can now make of the scene. Notice first the movements between sense and spirit embodied in the syntactic positions of subject and object. "Presence" produces "thoughts," which transpose into "sense," a term connecting both poles. Then nouns give way to another, much more expansive, appositional syntax, in which language reaches out to implicate what cannot be represented. That reaching, in fact, becomes the bearer of testimony to poetic values capable of providing an alternative to received models of representation. The *and*s in this periodic cadence compose a richer sense of plenitude than any return to Romance pastoral. As the *and*s link clauses, the references to ocean, air, and mind begin to generate equivalences between body and spirit, until the poem finally arrives at the "mind of man." Here the pleonastic sequence seems to reach its climax. But in this scenic environment, mind is at once a climactic state and a generative force inaugurating another appositional sequence that leads us back to "a motion and a spirit" – dual and single – shared by thinking things and their objects. The repeated "all," which in most poetry would be a terrible piece of rhetorical over-kill, now seems required, if language is even to approximate the synthet-ic force of the motion and spirit running through this sentence.

Then the climax arrives: "Therefore am I still . . ." Because the ex-pression occupies the same position in the line as the initial "For I have learned," we see the closing of a circle that can only be read as the spiritual spiral envisioned in Romantic dreams of *Bildung*. What begins as memory reaches its apogee as the recovery of identity. The speaking "I" in the poem is the final locus of its synthetic activity – not to become the apocalyptic "I," but to correlate its own catalog of particular loves with the overall dynamic relations that the scene offers to reflective concen-tration. The "still," here, is a sublime expression of identity, the Ro-mantic emblem for what, in Modernism, must become Williams's "so." Born from an elaborate process of thinking, the "I" manifests its self-knowledge in the capacity of voice and syntax to gather temporal flow into a resolved stillness where the voicing of nature also becomes its final peace. This peace can even include a rhetorical version of postcoital deflation as the language flattens into virtual clichés like "anchor of my pure thoughts." Creation rejoins an order of perception, so that the momentarily secure self can relax into ordinary language.

Obviously the same logic takes much more expansive form in *The Prelude*. But here I can only point out that in this poem Wordsworth extends the equation of self with the internal processes of the poem, in order to make the power of scenic reflection the basis for postulating the terms of social community. These internal processes must be seen as dialectical, since they depend on spirit's coming to integrate the diverse aspects of its own productive history. But Wordsworth's reliance on the generative force of particular scenes makes that dialectic very different from the Hegelian one that Meyer Abrams's *Natural Supernaturalism* tries to impose on the poem. Spirit does not quite subsume into itself what it first encounters as the material substance, defining and negating its op-portunities for self-knowledge. Rather than subsume nature, the scenic self comes to appreciate its powers, because it is nature's demands that call forth spirit's increasing freedom to adjust to what contains it. Vision does not absorb the world into the self, but frees the self to appreciate how its attentiveness to landscape helps create a practical ethical attitude, in which Kantian rationality gives way to an intelligence willing to be governed by the affections that its specific history has fostered. And, in those affections, one comes to glimpse both the freedom and the depen-dencies that provide a sense of shape for subjective lives that poets could not locate in either reason or the traditions of high culture.

Wordsworth's is an enormous cultural achievement, matched only, perhaps, by the enormous cultural problems it was to create for poetry. For now there was a version of Hegel's "law of the heart," sufficiently open to the formative influences of nature and of society to make poetic forms of apprehension seem so fundamental that Mill would spend a lifetime lamenting their loss. Wordsworth correlates inwardness with forms of value that reject reason's impersonal models of assessment for a form of assessment based simply on how individuals adapt to their own experience: The grounds of feeling become clear only as feeling leads us to sites on the margin of a world everywhere else written over by a pious rhetoric, whose mark is the insistence of allegory. But this route to romance may prove too successful, or at least too absolute, for its own good. How does one mediate between such moments or their sources and the society that desperately needs them? *The Prelude* is rich in its understanding of how an ethical character can be formed out of the intensity of lyric experience, but it does less well at showing how that character can take on public responsibilities – which is equivalent to showing how poetry deserves some kind of public authority. Because the moment of scenic empowerment is immediate, the understanding is consumed in self-consciousness, and thus becomes hauntingly vulnerable to a range of interpretive languages that claim to speak for it, but necessarily displace the site where the authority resides.

I do not need to say much about the first difficulty that Wordsworth's scenic poetics creates, because the issue simply returns us to our old friend allegory. The more intense the visionary experience, the greater the need – for poet as well as audience – to resist the condition of marginality that made the vision possible, while rendering its social use problematic. The poems' complexity as experience creates extraordinary pressure to offer allegorical structures that clarify the moral impact. Or, to slightly alter the point, there is a considerable gulf between the specific personal powers to which poetry can testify and the need to determine whether those powers offer an exemplary moral ethos for a community. Making the link requires the supplements of a public moral and religious rhetoric. But that rhetoric threatens to undermine the distinctively personal effort to come to terms with the "otherness" where spirit resides. Public rhetoric may reduce personal voice to the belief systems that process it, or it may reveal to sharp observers, like Keats, how disparate the poet's "I" must be to keep control of what threatens to separate into the spiritual divisions soon to characterize Victorian poetry. Therefore, passages in *The Prelude* such as Wordsworth's reflections on the nature of poetic power, called up by his climbing Mount Snowdon, are not simply lapses into Christianity. Rather, they reveal a fundamental need for generalizable meaning that no attention can discover and no performance of

the self quite sanction. Wordsworth's need for the support of such conceptual frameworks eventually tempted him to subordinate the growth
of the individual poet's mind to a process of repression that promised
sorely needed rest from such "unchartered freedom":

> Most worthy then of trust when most intense.
> Hence, amid ills that vex and wrongs that crush
> Our hearts – if here the words of Holy Writ
> May with fit reverence be applied – that peace
> Which passeth understanding, that repose
> In moral judgments which from this pure source
> Must come, or will by men be sought in vain.
>   (14:124–9, 1859 version)

Wordsworth's instinctive resistance to such constraints creates a second difficulty, even more crucial to nineteenth-century poetry. Perhaps
one can avoid allegory by finding alternative modes of representativeness. The emphasis on self-interpretation establishes the obvious candidate, since the personal virtues so realized may be able to provide
sufficient exemplars for stances denser, and more compelling, than anything allegory can create, especially if the scene can be expanded to
include audience figures, who illustrate the kind of effect the exemplar
can have. Any strategy Plato uses cannot be shoddy. So, by subordinating description to what the poet David Antin calls processes of "tuning"
one's sensibility to an imagined audience, Wordsworth makes ethos do
the work of Logos in providing grounding terms for a community.
Through the positions they create for Coleridge and Dorothy (characters
whom Wordsworth would have had to invent, if they had not existed),
his poems not only claim to provide testimony; they also represent their
own representativeness by having actual persons measure the kinds of
effects the poet can exert on society. Rather than rely on rational measures for the collective good, the scenic rendering of psychological reactions composes enduring forms, intimate enough to command affection
and capacious enough to shape principles of judgment.

But how do we judge such judgments, or trust ourselves in making
them? These were the problems that haunted Wordsworth's heirs. After
all, had not Wordsworth's erroneous engagement in the French Revolution, and even his faith in rationality, been primarily the effect of immediate identifications – with friends such as Beapuy, and with authors
such as Godwin? Many of his best poems make the influx of spirit so
dependent on a sense of irreducible otherness that one must fear that
treating the self as the authoritative mediator may displace precisely what
makes the experience significant. For, although the poet must try to
recuperate for the culture the force of sublimity existing at its margins,

the effort at translation may destroy the experience of difference that inaugurates the enterprise. Similarly, the poet's effort to bind that civilization together by preserving the spirit of old stories may be as fruitless, in the emerging industrial society, as was Michael's continual mourning for Luke. What exalts the poet's powers may make him an absurd figure when he tries to make claims on his society's practical life, unless he connects his vision to an established moral language that suppresses the immediacies of scenic encounter in favor of the production of a public persona who is always uneasy about his authority. And then, as much of the last version of *The Prelude* illustrates, the price of social representativeness is the loss of the very naturalness that first distinguished the moment of vision. Moreover, it becomes extremely difficult to know whether it is virtue that appeals, and not a rhetorical ability to manipulate fantasies. The more a poet achieves identifications with his audience, the greater the chance that he has in fact already compromised the energies potential in his vision.

Problems of identification do not arise only for other people. Perhaps the most dangerous feature of Wordsworth's poetic proved to be its ability to seduce the poet himself. As the poem tries to gather its intensities within the figure of a single interpreting consciousness, nothing seems more natural than to attribute to the self precisely the spirit that first appeared because the self had been suspended. But that spirit in the woods may very well be the antithesis of the enduring sources of personal strength sought, by *The Prelude,* as a principle of personal identity to offer its audience. A principle of vitality serves as a seductive lure for doing covertly what older allegorical styles can take responsibility for. Wordsworth wants memory at once to recuperate the psyche's most intense encounters with an otherness that escapes our moralizings, and to allow that otherness a mode of socialization. Those lyric moments whose discontinuity with practical life most threatens psychic and social stability must become precisely the source of such stability in a new idea of that social order. However, then the poet must be haunted by two possible delusions. He may be basing social forms on lyric principles that will not sustain social orders, but instead will cultivate irreconcilable differences. And he may be imposing socializable forms on the more radical demands that the otherness requires. In projecting those social values, he may be absorbing back into traditional mental forms and romance fictions everything that could break through to new sources of psychic energy. Yet now even the otherness gets cast in terms of moral responsibilities and psychic continuities, so it must play the role of the romance maiden, forced once again to seek a redeeming knight – who is, of course, our sublime poet.

Wordsworth therefore is still the figure who most acutely defines the problems that oppressed Postenlightenment poetry. The constitutive particularity shaping his concrete scenes of instruction establishes powers of agency that make it quite difficult to return to older discursive or argumentative poetic styles. But the focus that this mode puts on the self seems to require forms of theatricality that subject poetry to the same charges of rhetoricity that he leveled against his predecessors. Where Wordsworth could find Holy Writ, those heirs would be haunted by a reliance on self-fostering eloquence that might betray a lack at the core of scenic consciousness. And where the ideal of scenic attachments promised to correlate self-expansion with an increasing sense of loyalty to one's formative grounds, the resulting dream of an "authentic self" threatened to replace nature entirely with the anxieties that arise in trying to represent ourselves to ourselves. Ultimately, the entire project of finding a self through what nature affords might lead to losing both self and nature to the rhetorical process of composing a self that the imagination can take delight and instruction in finding.

IV

As Arthur Henry Hallam's enormously influential essay "On Some of the Characteristics of Modern Poetry" described the situation, Victorian poetry found itself torn between two powerful Romantic attitudes: Wordsworth's effort to make the poet a sublime moral example, and Keats's rejection of moral values in favor of an exuberant sensuality, eager to explore every possible form of imaginative intensity.[7] Our age has developed quite different views of both poets and sought much less impressionistic critical categories. Nonetheless, there is no better index of the fundamental alternatives available for handling the relation between lucidity and lyricism, and no better introduction to irreconcilable opposites that were to drive Victorian poetry to far more disillusioned images of the philosopher.

We need say no more about Wordsworth as moral exemplar: His dialectical testimony to what an individual sensibility could make of its specific history provided the model of lyric authority on which lesser, or more scrupulous, imaginations were to founder. But we do need to spend time understanding why Keats's kind of sensuality could seem so important and so appealing an alternative to that image of moral probity. This will mean taking Keats's sensuality as considerably more than Yuppie self-indulgence. We must understand how Keats's poetry takes on Wordsworth's egotistical sublime, at its most capacious and most philosophical. For Keats offers a radically different way of conceiving poetry as a power constituting viable models for recuperating romance as an alternative to Enlightenment thinking. The sense of intensity and responsibility that Wordsworth sought by elaborating the self's relation to its scenic environs, Keats sought by projecting pure imaginative absorption in states that would make a mockery of any ego attempting to impose a personal history upon them. Whereas Wordsworth tried to humanize an essentially behaviorist empiricism, Keats tried to reach beyond his contemporary options to revitalize what he (and Hölderlin, and, later, Nietzsche) saw as a Greek insistence on encountering directly those energies of the mind that cannot be accommodated to the categories of moral reason, or even to the forms of coherence proposed by the self-reflexive memory. No spirit of admonition in the woods could draw forth that song. The poet had to understand that the imagination could produce intensities that moral reason could not comprehend – not because these intensities were marginal to society, but because social life seemed marginal to the full knowledge of our spiritual energies. Thus, whereas Wordsworth built subjectivity on the possibility of reflectively mediating that otherness, Keats built poetry on the demand to treat even the life of the subject in the most objective of possible terms, because only those terms eliminate the temptation to subordinate constructive energies to the scenic composition of selves for whom one could claim moral powers.

Keats was not without ambivalence toward these intensities. In his letters he kept trying to convince himself that he could have his Shakespeare and his morality as well. And, as we shall see, he was eventually driven by his fascination with Hyperion to assume a version of the Wordsworthian first person as his means of coming to terms with the failure of his own theophanic ambitions. But much of his greatest poetry, and almost all of his influence for the next one hundred years, stemmed from his efforts to emulate his beloved Greeks in their pursuit of an objective imaginative intensity that might successfully war on the gods whose cruelty keeps us mortal. Wordsworthian consolation must give way to a fully secular insistence that the unlivable is an essential component of the imagination at its whitest heat – not because art's fictions are false, but because they challenge the very notions of self and world that philosophy depends on. Were Keats to triumph, he would force philosophy to recognize that at such moments the best thing it can do is to learn to be silent – which is the one thing it cannot do without ceasing to be philosophy. But Keats did not triumph. Critics treated his sensuality as mere absorption in the life of the senses; philosophy had its day; and Victorian poets found themselves trapped in the role of a somewhat guilty Moneta, trying to suppress her own imaginative intensities in diminished versions of a Wordsworthian rhetoric deprived of its enabling scenic contexts. The basic components of Keats's purely secular mode of apocalyptic vision were to return only through Yeats's Ireland, Pound's Provence, and Stevens's lonely walks around New York.

Keats was not a constructivist poet. But no other predecessor of the

Modernists except Blake was concerned with the powers that become available if poetry concentrates on the direct presentation of romance states, without the intervention of the sublimating scenic ego. Keats saw that if lyricism is to resist the claims of lucidity effectively, it must compose modes of presence capable of constituting their own compelling reality. But he also worried over the cost such commitments would exact: The imagination that responds fully to that reality will not share Wordsworth's ability to reconcile himself to the kind of truths that find their place in shareable social practices. Both concerns are most concretely and most fully rendered in the fantasy world of "Lamia," where Keats's version of the ephebe finds, as his "spirit in the woods," an all too visible woman, whose hold on him he cannot adapt to the two basic demands of social life: that one be able to project a public identity, by taking responsibility for the forces motivating one's actions; and that one be able to contain momentary states of lyric enthusiasm within the framework of narrative time and projected goals. Here Keats's own concern for immediate presence composes a virtually mythic embodiment of the general conflict between a pure romance principle and the imperative to sanction that vision through the mediating representativeness that philosophy offers. This abstraction, this sense that the poem directly encounters the underlying imaginative issues, makes the entire authorial process a metapoetic analog for the action, with the implicit authorial presence forced to maintain its own protective distance from the dramatic figure who claims the right to interpret the action. The most the author could interpose is the use of this situation to introduce the volume *Lamia, Isabella, &c.* (1820), so that the entire work can make the problem of correlating romance vision and reflective thought the generating condition for the range of states it explores.[8]

"Lamia" sets that stage brilliantly by focusing its energies on one insistent dilemma: We must ask, "Who is Lamia?", but any answer we give threatens to deprive her of the mystery that makes her so compelling an embodiment of romance possibilities. Most critics have little trouble with that question, proceeding to attribute to her every form of substance from the role of demonic sorceress to that of the life-giving anima principle.[9] Yet to concentrate on establishing any one among these conflicting claims is to consign ourselves to an allegorical level, where we are likely to misconceive the power of the poem and the depth of Keats's understanding of his cultural plight. It seems to me more plausible to approach her as the poem does – that is, not so much as an entity to be named as a figure to be read, through the ways in which she is reflected in the only genre that she can inhabit. She exists most fully as a problem, and as a force so much in tension with the understanding that she seduces us into the fascination of wondering what her "real" substance may be. Her indefinability is the central determinate, and determining, factor in the text. For our uncertainties make us participate in an adventure that leads us beyond looking for the right interpretation to wondering what is at stake in the enterprise of coming to grips with mysterious qualities that so fascinate, and ultimately so perplex, our sense of ordinary social life.

There are two ways to let significance gather around the figure of Lamia, without imposing any more specific allegory on her than is necessary to establish her determinate romance indeterminacy: We can simply keep attention focused on the overt qualities that Keats invites us to attribute to her, and we can try to account for the positions she forces others to occupy. We know, for example, that she is a figure from classical romance, most directly mediated through Robert Burton's *Anatomy of Melancholy*. And we know that making her visible to a nineteenth-century audience (as Lycius must do for his city) seems to have led Keats to adopt a Spenserian style. So our first way of attributing significance leads us to postulate a complex set of equations between the story narrated and the condition of the narrative, since both levels pose the questions of why we continue to take romance principles seriously and how that apparent need can be authorized for a contemporary audience. Anachronism becomes a superb strategy for suspending the representational criteria of his age in order to give a concrete presence to a compelling version of the other of representation on each of those two levels. But in order to engage that situation fully, we must turn to the second possible framework: If we cannot establish who Lamia is, we can try to appreciate her significance within the tale by concentrating on the ways that she establishes certain positions that must be occupied by those who encounter her. That leads us to the two contrasts that define the problems Lycius exemplifies: the contrast between the ephebe poet and the god Hermes; and the contrast between the poet and the philosopher Apollonius, who had been his teacher.

In Burton's version of the tale, there is no mention of Hermes and no introductory scene to illustrate the nature of Lamia's powers. But when Keats enters romance states, he turns immediately to differences between humans and the gods who can dwell in that supernatural realm, thereby dooming us to the awareness that our very fascination with them reveals the deepest limitations of our mortal nature. Conversely, Lamia is not an object of desire for Hermes, only a mediator to be bargained with, so that he can find the nymph he pines for. Yet when Lycius sees Lamia, no reciprocal relationship is possible. Moreover, Hermes is content with his nymph: "Real are the dreams of gods, and smoothly pass their pleasures in a long immortal dream" (1:126–7).[10] When dreams can be real, there is no need to concern oneself with mystery or to make one's visions intelligible to others. Immediate gratification suffices, making every other state seem a pathetic illusion. Lycius, on the other hand, cannot possess what he is possessed by, nor can he be content with the kind of gratifications that his pursuit offers him. Lacking the god's power, he must compensate by indulging psychic states where the constant risk of frustration nonetheless holds out the promise of an epistemological frisson not available to the gods. Lycius not only sees and dallies with Lamia; he also experiences her mysterious power to hold out the promise of an other and finer tone of being, in which the direct physical gratification that satisfies the god seems less important than the modes of self-awareness she inspires.

Understanding that mysterious power is the key to the poem, and also, indeed, to the sense of possibility, threat, and loss that permeates the Keatsian line in Romantic poetry. First of all, Lamia's indefinable presence creates a site where religious language has force, and thus where mere dallying with nymphs seems an inadequate alternative. (The gods cannot see themselves in religious terms; at best they can recognize that others worship, but they do not feel the exaltation of worship.) This is Lycius's reaction to hearing Lamia sing:

> It seemed as if he had loved them a whole summer long:
> And soon his eyes had drunk her beauty up,
> Leaving no drop in the wildering cup,
> And still the cup was full, – while he, afraid
> Lest she should vanish ere his lip had paid
> Due adoration, thus began to adore.
>
> (1:250–8)

Time and space get radically transformed, so that all of his energies can focus on the one moment where the thought instantly becomes the act, and fear opens the way to worship.

A second aspect of the state that Lamia creates makes the crucial difference from the gods even more pronounced. At the moment when Lamia enters mortal space in the shape of a woman, she makes her essential appeal to Lycius by hymning his name – as if it were in this romance bower that the ephebe could have repeated, in adult form, the maternal affirmation establishing our imaginary sense of distinctive individuality. In other words, Lamia appears as the core of romance, the source of the dream that sustains the imaginary, and therefore sustains all pursuits that lead us into the symbolic order of pleasure and pain unavailable to the gods. No wonder that she must be the mortal enemy of the philosopher. Against his insistence on the claims of the empirical world, she brings the lore of "Cupid's college" (1:196). Lessons informed by such wisdom cast even absolutes of fleshliness that satisfy "all my many senses" (1:284) in forms that project beyond sense into fantasy space. "A virgin purest lipped, yet in the lore / Of love deep learned to the red heart's core" (1:189–90), she is at once strumpet and virgin, the nymph's sensuality and the dream of transcendence, sexual object and ungraspable spiritual ideal. Confronted with such enticing contradictions, Lycius cannot share Hermes' sense that women are interchangeable. Instead, he commits himself to the foolish and heroic faith in the uniqueness of the object he loves (a uniqueness ironically true of the irreducible difference that is her true substance).

But the very intensity Lamia inspires dooms the romance she mediates. Hermes has no need to test or to publish the experiences his nymphs afford. But Lycius is bound to a different model of value, which we best grasp by understanding the contrasts making necessary a second part to the poem. Trumpets from the city mark the transition to the realm where the ephebe must confront the authority of the philosopher: "The sounds fled, / But left a thought a-buzzing in his head," so that "his spirit passed beyond its golden bourn / Into the noisy world almost forsworn" (1:29–33). With this thought come complex divisions – first, between the lovers (since she wants him to ignore the sounds), then in Lycius's own attitude. Now he must experience the complex emotions appropriate to that urban life, combining naked pride with the desire to make known the joy he has experienced:

> What mortal hath a prize, that other men
> May be confounded and abashed withal
> But lets it sometimes pace abroad majestical,
> And triumph, as in thee I should rejoice.
> (2:57–60)

It is difficult to imagine a richer link between romance modes and lyric energies. In the initial state that Lycius and Lamia create, it is impossible to know whether one wakes or sleeps, so intense is the feeling of presence, and so absolute the power of metaphor to treat beloveds as what they make us feel, rather than as what they in fact are. Within romance the challenge is

> How to entangle, trammel up and snare
> Your soul in mine, and labyrinth you there
> Like the hid scent in an unbudded rose.
> (2:52–4)

But the psyche is not easily contented with so fugitive and cloistered a condition – for lovers or, above all, for poets, to whom the trumpets of the city are never out of earshot. So, when the trumpets call, poet and lover feel the pull of a performative self and a public identity that must take what negative capability wins and test its claims on a larger world. Where the god can simply be, Lycius's identity depends on supplementary interpretations sanctioned by the authority of a shared symbolic order (cf. 2:85, where he asks for her name so that he can introduce her to a public).

To pass muster within that order, however, entails finding a way to represent oneself before the philosopher's scrutinizing eye. Philosophy, then, becomes not simply the "other" of romance, but also its necessary validation – the parent feared and sought, as sanction for the poet's faith that his indulgences are an educating of the imagination. Yet Apollonius can recognize only the old Lycius, with his old commitments: The "I, now" of erotic transcendence cannot be reconciled with the "this person still" of public discourse and philosophical noncontradiction. The situation will not yield to a language that tempers Apollonius's gaze, the figure of pure lucidity (or perhaps of philosophy grown mathematical), by some "appeal" (2:256) to recognize the differences the boy has experienced. "There was no recognition in those orbs" (2:260) – neither of Lamia nor of any shareable factors to which the new Lycius can appeal. There is only self-righteous repetition, with a consistency that no lover can match, and no poet satisfy.

The full pathos of the situation is beautifully rendered in Keats's brilliant series of concluding metonyms. First Lamia vanishes with a scream – erotic cooing forced beyond the pale of language into sheer otherness, its substance an inversion of intelligible sounds. Then attention turns to Lycius:

> And Lycius's arms were empty of delight,
> As were his limbs of life, from that same night,
> On the high couch he lay! – his friends came round –
> Supported him – no public, or breath they found,
> And in its marriage robe, the heavy body wound.
>
> (2:307–10)

The inversions of Wordsworth's dialectic here are too rich to be deliberate. First there is a quick shift from the object of attention, suddenly emptied of all romance, to the parallel state in the subject, unable now to live without what it lost by trying to name her. This leaves the philosopher's eye the only principle that can take in the scene of loss – its triumph the triple rhyme that also defines the kind of witness all of Lycius's friends can offer. Under that gaze, the one who tried to make his new mode of being visible ends up the object of uncomprehending stares. Fantasized trumpets are now silent, and romance reduced to its mere physical constituents: There is no Horatio to tell this story. Philosophy conquers, leaving nothing worth conquering. Instead of dialectical syntheses, we are left with only a chain of metonymic figures for what once was sublime romance. These metonyms, in turn, require two incommensurable, yet absolutely necessary interpretations of Apollonius's act: The philosopher's name does accurately capture Lamia's physical reality, but, in order to see that reality, it must be blind to everything that transforms that reality into erotic life. In naming her substance, philosophy gives up any claims the mind might have to produce worlds that can rival those the gods enjoy.

If we turn to the larger question of how this version of philosophy is positioned within Romantic poetry, we must say that, although clearly Apollonius will not do as a figure for its philosophical ambitions, he just as clearly cannot be escaped. He must be internalized, but how? That question pervades Keats's late work and defines a spiritual adventure that shapes much of Victorian poetry. For Helen Vendler, Keats's richest answer emerges in "To Autumn," the poem he wrote immediately after finishing "Lamia." Romance there seems as tightly woven into a purely material nature as is the luxuriant plenitude for the wandering eye in a Constable landscape. Where Lycius's quest for transcendental romance led only to the poem's concluding metonyms, now the spirit finds its needs satisfied by aligning itself with the orders of natural process and the human praxis adapted to it. Consequently, poetry's demands on the philosopher get transformed into the self-sufficing, contemplative expansiveness of this generalizing, sympathetic imagination.

Persuasive as that Keats and Vendler are, however, I cannot help but wonder if Lycius could, or should, be content with this form of spirituality. Can romance be allowed such harmony with a purely natural scene, without even a hint of compositional energies that seek other, more intensely self-reflexive imaginative states? Is not this autumnal setting the mind's way to soothe its surrender to Apollonius, perhaps in the process generating the frustrations out of which a new Lamia will appear? That these are not idle or academic questions is made evident by Keats's own obsessions at the time. The odes surrounding "To Autumn" seem to me to define imaginative needs beyond the ken of that poem's version of plenitude, because it is so tied to natural temporal sequences and social practices that simply do not contain or structure some of the spirit's most fundamental energies. Whereas "To Autumn" is content with natural time, "Ode on a Grecian Urn" and "Ode to Psyche" take up the more complex demands of historical time, where loss is not so easily integrated, and where the constant hunger of imagination for more sublime states makes itself felt. How different a world it is when, with "Ode to Psyche," we find ourselves fascinated by powers that may lie hidden in a set of imaginative forces never sullied by historical interpretations. Spared the interpretive overkill of generations of philosophers, this goddess offers what may be a purely objective life for the spirit, which promises direct participation in energies that lead beyond the human:

> Yes I will be thy priest, and build a fane
>   In some untrodden region of my mind,
> Where branched thoughts, new grown with pleasant pain
>   Instead of pines shall murmur in the wind: . . .
> A rosy sanctuary will I dress
> With the wreath'd trellis of a working brain, . . .
> And there shall be for thee all soft delight
>   That shadowy thought can win,
> A bright torch, and a casement ope at night,
>   To let the warm Love in!
>
> (50–67)

Rather than attach to the scene, in Wordsworth's fashion, this poetic consciousness simply absorbs it as an analogy for its own constructive acts. Rather than identify with other persons, this consciousness seeks to position itself so that the young god who is in love with Psyche can literally enter the temple. (If one were to invoke Heidegger on the temple, one would have to treat Keats's clearing as a space of mind, not a clearing of the earth.) And rather than adapt itself to time, this mind seeks in its capacities a permanent state of apperception free from all heteronomy. Truth and beauty are literally one.

Helen Vendler understands these desires, but she insists, in her *Odes of John Keats,* that "To Autumn" offers the latest and most comprehensive attitude in the odes, and thus earns the right to "judge" the others. From the perspective that this poem authorizes, she argues, the reader can take on the Apollonian role of judging the poet's work in "Ode to Psyche" as "a private task rather than a service to society" (56). Such a judgment, however, seems to me to raise more problems than it resolves (although, in doing that, it provides a marvelous emblem for anxieties about the relation of duty to loss that would soon oppress Keats's heirs). First, it is by no means clear that for Keats, or even for us, the best way for the poet to serve society is to make sharp distinctions between private and public realms: Those may only reinforce the authority of limited social notions. What is left for the poet to do, if we already know what society demands? And which is the greater service to society: to provide consolation for what society cannot transcend; or to insist, as far as one is able, that if individuals resist social norms, they can least appreciate what is involved in Apollo's sudden discovery, "Knowledge enormous makes a god of me"? Second, it is by no means clear that Keats was satisfied with "To Autumn" – precisely because it could not raise the self-reflexive questions about powers actualized and powers repressed that its glorious surrender to the natural order demanded. That poem is like a Shakespearean song, composing a purely contemplative state, where the scenic absorbs the temporal and all desires have limited, and therefore adequate, objects. But it does not address the intensities of Shakespearean tragedy or Miltonic self-projection. There, imagination must take responsibility for those demands and capacities that the art itself shows are capable of sustaining alternative identities, however ill adapted they are to the pragmatic order.

"To Autumn" was not Keats's last poem. Try as he might to align himself with the natural and social orders, he could not free himself of the figure of Hyperion, who perhaps suffered most from that model of cyclic time. For, if the poet could identify with Hyperion, he could in effect frame time rather than simply submit to it, thus finding the power to enter both the old and the new sites where romance can flourish. But the more richly Keats understood what it would take to dwell in sites where one might rival the gods, the less he could trust himself to create a plausible Apollo who might think in the dialectical terms lacking to Apollonius's version of philosophy. Just as Hyperion haunts Keats's identification with the conciliatory mode of "To Autumn," the sense of limits defined by that poem binds him to the pathos of Saturn's nostalgia, where epic intensities linger solely in the contemplation of defeat, ennobled only by self-consciousness that can stage itself as "betrayed to a most hateful seeing of itself" (2:370).

Confronted by these contradictions, Keats makes the move that, in effect, inaugurates Victorian poetry and renounces his own deepest dreams. Convinced that he cannot find a poetic medium that can fully identify with these gods, Keats seeks at least a voice that can reflect philosophically upon the significance of the quest. So he turns from the epic voice of "Hyperion" to the first-person stance of "The Fall of Hyperion." If one cannot fully identify with the new gods, one's failure may open one to the kind of mediation that Diotima provided for Socrates: Let first-person narration create a community of those who must heed each other because they have all experienced the loss of that mode of presence promised by pure romance. And, if one cannot successfully transcend the self, one may be able to establish a voice responsive to the full contradictions of that effort. At the very least, this alternative enabled the poet to avoid Apollonius's skepticism and still have access to lyric resources that serve the public by encompassing the very essence of private loss:

> . . ."Then Moneta's voice
> Came brief upon my ear." So Saturn sat
> When he had lost his Realms – "where there grew
> A power within me of enormous ken
> To see as a god sees, and take the depth
> Of things as nimbly as the outward eye
> Can size and shape pervade. . . . I set myself
> Upon an eagle's watch that I might see,
> And seeing ne'er forget."
>
> (302–10)

Now, though, there is only the memory of her memory. As Nietzsche once put it, one who hangs very long over an abyss had better be an eagle, but this poet must admit he is no eagle. That is evident in how far these metaphors are from the Shakespearean terms that, in "Ode to Psyche," create their own world. This speaking voice cannot maintain a position allowing it to identify with either the power of the gods or the immensity of their sense of loss. Unable to share Hyperion's hopes, Keats now finds himself also barred even from identifying with the power that makes Saturn's loss so immense. The only options left are a career of endless lamentation, or the effort to concentrate on those first-person features that make one sufficiently limited and humble to shift one's identifications from the gods to the figure of Moneta. Thus, in one of the most depressing gestures in poetry, Keats moves from the desire to enjoy the ambiguous seductress Lamia to a resigned identification with the sententious Moneta, mediatrix of virtues probably outdated, or at least too datable by the very conditions that make them knowable. There is left of romance only a trace of its grandeur and the challenge to ennoble the substitutes that remain by shifting one's terms for imaginative identity from what gods experience to the stories men tell themselves.

There is left, one might say, only the consoling attitude of that other sententious Romantic who was to dominate Victorian poetry. All of Keats's efforts to construct immediate, unmoralized moments of imaginative intensity seem to have led back to a version of Wordsworth's first-person intimacies, now humble enough to seek wisdom from a Moneta, but deprived, by that self-abnegation, of the personal contexts that gave Wordsworth's speakers such eloquent access to psychic powers. Keats had projected another way. He had envisioned a form of objective imaginative presence, which promised to take the spirit out of the woods and put it within the world that the artist could watch himself making. There art truly supplanted philosophy, because it allowed direct identifications with principles that the philosopher could not even describe. But Keats found himself unable to draw the necessary links between the timeless order of romance and his own specific place in history. Every image that he could use to represent the gods seemed to belie the vision, and to lack the reality, that could compel the fealty of an Apollonius or justify a rebellion against everything that Apollonius stood for. Keats wanted it both ways: wanted both the constitutive particularity that only poetry could compose, and the reflective authority that depended on a shareable human world. He got only Moneta: only a vague hope of translating into moral terms what he could not sufficiently trust as romance.

In Keats there remains the drama of the quest. But that drama could not survive the history that it helped engender. Victorian poetry returned to the two strands that Keats wanted to combine, reducing each to the oversimplifications that sanction a poetry devoted largely to lamenting its own plight. It absorbed Moneta into a vague and generalized myth of maturity – attributed primarily to Wordsworth – that was to prove as oppressive as Apollonius in its idealization of duty, yet lacked Wordsworth's dialectical framework for defining the powers that the call to duty tests. Therefore the Romantic ideal of romance internalized as the power of moral consciousness modulated into the sad precision of Arnold's effort to make duty itself serve as the only available spirit to be glimpsed in his historical woods: "The dialogue of the mind with itself has commenced . . . in which the suffering finds no vent in action, in which a continuous state of mental distress is prolonged, unrelieved by incident, hope, or resistance; in which there is everything to be endured, nothing to be done."[11] Poetry could still dream of the consolations available from Keats's kind of sensuality, but only by imposing on it such a burden of moral anxiety that it could not sustain its imaginative challenge to traditional models of agency. The last thing the Victorian imagination could handle was the prospect of making one's soul by trying to take on the self-reflexive intensities of the gods: One cannot imagine that as part of Arnold's self-congratulatory pathos. And since Keats had not found his own myth, his own way of making romance figures populate nineteenth-century representational schema, his version of the power of art was reduced to a version of escapist formalism, the fate of all arts that fail to connect their constitutive energies to plausible extraformal content. Keats became the poet whom the Victorians could patronize as the great figure of lyric escape from all of the serious cares of the moral and the manipulative public life. He gave his heirs palaces of art where the gods are reduced to stone effigies and the working brain mollified by its own effeminate lyric indulgences: "No shrine, no grove, no oracle, no heat / Of pale-mouth'd prophet dreaming." And no plausible alternative to what history was making of them all.

V

There is perhaps no better version of prose that is its own testimony than the passage of Arnold's that I have just quoted. It displays the uneasy contortions of a mind eager to locate in its own anxieties the only poetic powers that could survive the gaze of Apollonius. So the prose has a strong lyric component, but the romance resides all in the pain, or better, all in the self-staging of a lucidity so difficult yet noble to bear that it has its own lyric consolations. We are, in short, already within Victorian poetry – the art born of collapsing the Romantic idealized projections into an endless dialogue spoken within a mind unable to get beyond its own self-doubts. Romantic poetry depended on resisting the confines of humanistic rhetoric, on the one hand, and the philosopher's narrow lucidity on the other. Once neither option seemed feasible, the Victorians found themselves forced to internalize the philosopher's myth of lucidity. The internal conflicts that this philosophical voice engendered then could provide at least one abiding source of lyric emotion, as if the pathos of Wordsworth's egotistical sublime had become the poets' only trusted form of power. Romantic dreams that poets could dialectically synthesize their various selves now fostered only the inescapable repetition of lyric sensibilities more anxious for release than confident of their own status as exemplary models for social identifications. Consequently much of Victorian poetry stages a grand psychomachia, with the public self desperately seeking to treat its oppressive self-consciousness as an adequate lyric force, while the private self just as desperately locates its emotional authenticity in a projected Keatsian romance that cannot be absorbed by any public attitude. To see this psychomachia in action, we shall trace in this section the transformation of the philosopher figure into the poet's emblem for a mind whose only real power is its ability to theatricalize the terms of its own impotence.

Not all of the Victorians shared the dilemmas that I have been outlining. Christina Rossetti and Robert Browning, in fact, used the paralyzing self-consciousness of their peers as a contrastive setting for their own efforts to ground imaginative desires in more fluid processes of identification, which can free the mind from self-absorption without imposing on it Keats's demand for a theophany. But most of the Victorian poetry that was self-consciously Postromantic became a tale of powers lost, leaving Modernist writers only the shadowiest and neediest of father figures.[12] Here two poets should suffice to define that heritage. The first is Tennyson, whose "Lucretius" may be Victorian poetry's greatest rendering of the distance between Romantic lyricism and the forms of romance possible once poetry has internalized the philosopher's authority. The second is Arnold, whose philosophers locate romance almost entirely in the forms of pathos that this philosophical stance puts in the place of Romantic constitutive particularity. In fact, Arnold was so thoroughly pervaded by this attitude that even when he tried to reject the dialogue of the mind with itself, as in his 1853 "Preface," the argument took on the cast of a lurid spectacle, in which reflective consciousness seems to take pleasure in watching itself betray its quite intelligent arguments.

I begin with Tennyson, because his late poem, "Lucretius," provides a capacious and deeply moving summary of what happened during the nineteenth century, to Wordsworth's dream that poetry could testify to truths which link the intimate sources of the self's investments with principles which are potentially representative for public life. In Tennyson's poem, there is no natural scenic source of lyric intensity, and hence no possible grounds for the speaker to take himself as a positive exemplar for his community. Desire comes only from the magic potions that Lucretius's wife resorts to, in order to find relief from his cold philosophical ways. So instead of integrating the various aspects of psychic life, this influx of imaginative energies serves only to set the different aspects of Lucretius's nature against one another. He must witness what the ravages of desire do to a judgment that has lost its authority, but that has maintained its lucid grasp of the pathos involved in desiring to retain the powers one has lost.

Twenty-five lines of introduction and seven of conclusion succinctly set the scene and describe all of the events. Two hundred forty-nine lines of a tortuously intricate lyric monologue comprise the rest: the cry of a sensibility with no control over events, and precious little over its need to display its useless dialogue with itself, in the hope of some vague self-justification and sympathy. Whereas Lycius has Lamia to display, Lucretius has only the effects of his failure to satisfy his wife, and his deep desire for a "passionless bride, divine tranquility."[13] And whereas Apollonius had Lamia to condemn, Lucretius can only turn in contempt from his own foolish efforts to live a life of passion.

"Lucretius" is a poem about Epicurianism lost, a quasi-Miltonic lament for the gulf between rhetorical expansiveness and a confident sense of judgment. The mind once capable of trusting philosophical judgment must experience all that the ideal of calm lucidity had repressed. And it must do so solely from a tormented personal need, without the comforting sense of a conquering "higher" stance that one finds in a Nietzsche or Freud or Derrida. The result is a series of deconstructive gestures, unrelieved by any playful manipulation. The philosopher's dream of an eternal calm yields to a violent nature generating endless supplements, and the stumbling mind confronts the eternal return of all that it tried to conquer. Every effort to recover a Romantic sense of nature instantly spawns differences and calls up metaphors that lead back again to their divided origin:

> "Can I not fling this horror off me again,
> Seeing with how great ease Nature can smile,
> Balmier and nobler from her bath of storm
> At random ravage? And how easily
> The mountain there has cast his cloudy slough, . . .
> A mountain o'er a mountain, – ay and within
> All hollow as the hopes and fears of men."
>
> (173–80)

This hollowness proves even more compelling and frightening when we shift our attention from what is said to the conditions of saying. It is crucial that Lucretius's monologue does not have the implicit audience assumed by Browning and by Tennyson in his early poems. Wondering who could be an audience is part of Lucretius's problem, as he ranges from calling upon the gods to exhorting his better self. Audience shifts as quickly as subject matter, so there can be no fixed "otherness" by which even to project a dialectical resolution. The only constant is Lucretius's sense of his own self-division. He knows he is the subject, the object, and the audience of his speech, but each role simply mutates into the other when he tries to grasp it:

> "I thought I lived securely as yourselves [the gods] . . .
> But now it seems some unseen monster lays
> His vast and filthy hands upon my will,
> Wrenching it backward into his, and spoils
> My bliss in being; and it was not great."
>
> (210–22)

The effort to know the self promotes efforts to stage the self, which in turn increase Lucretius's susceptibility to forces in his dreams that defy any effort at lucidity. What had been the constituents of Romantic dialectic now collapse into uncertain and shifting relations of cognition, will, and judgment, so it is not surprising that Lucretius's monologue can end only in his suicide. What other condition could stop the chain of signifiers or the efforts of the self somehow to end its duplicity, if only by seducing some audience to respond to expressive gestures that may in fact be there largely to get the audience's attention.[14]

Ironically, the only remaining source of value seems to be a perverse version of the Romantic religion of nature. If the self becomes what Kant called the "empirical subject," victim of determining forces, then its only peace is to become fully one with nature's elemental processes. "The womb and tomb of all" is absolute, even if it lacks the teleological dimension that the Romantics found in it. Yet even this vision of an absolute also proves contaminated for the philosopher manqué, because he must try to give it meaning: "Why should I, beastlike as I find myself, / Not manlike end myself?" The old Roman way is perhaps still a route to dignity. But how can one assert "manlike" control in a discourse so permeated by duplicity, and in a mind so trapped in its own lyric excesses? Is this decision rational? Can any self-idealizing gesture be trusted, once we are so attuned to the ways in which self-exhibition panders to will? Lucretius's final act is at once pure theater and a submission to a complex chain of sexual displacements that project the ultimate fantasy of being subject and object of one's own lovemaking:

> "Passionless Bride, divine Tranquility,
> Yearned after by the wisest of wise . . .
> > yet out of season, thus
> I woo thee roughly, for thou carest not
> How roughly men may woo thee so they win –
> Thus – thus – the soul flies out and dies in the air."
> > > (266–73)

Where does this sense of lyric effusiveness leave the poet? It is a striking and disturbing feature of this poem that it seems to rely on the same fundamental emotional appeals as Lucretius himself does. So it is tempting to see Tennyson as using the mask provided by the impersonal dramatic monologue form to allow himself a parallel lament for having submitted himself to a lifelong struggle between the claims of private sensibility and the public ones of duty, work, and reason. If this is the case, the lyric has won a remarkably Pyrrhic victory. For now it has found its place in the social order by providing that order a way, simultaneously, to express and to evade its own contradictions. And now we see "Lucretius" as the ironic culmination of tendencies that had pervaded Tennyson's entire career. Even when the young Tennyson tried to keep the strands distinct – to balance a "Lotus-Eaters" with a "Ulysses," or a moment of effusive lyricism like Keats's with an almost parodic vigor of triumphant duty – the moral strand had a way of crossing over into the self-indulgent.[15] At the conclusion of "Ulysses," the poet calls on all of his resources to make poetic speech define a ringing public alternative to what he took to be "Romantic" sensibility: "That which we are, we are,– / . . . Made weak by time and fate, but strong in will / To strive, to seek, to find, and not to yield." Yet what stands out is not the vitality of the speaker so much as his ability to be deluded by his own uplifting rhetoric. For, if we look closely, we see that these strong words carry surprisingly empty meanings, whose only real force is the melodramatic gesture. Every one of these strong action verbs is intransitive. None admits any object that might make it possible to hold the action responsible for any qualities or consequences that have projectable social effects. But now there is no spirit in the woods to provide an alternative to the roles that the public rhetoric authorizes. There are only the forty years it takes before the plight of Victorian judgment got fully defined in Lucretius's tormented cries.[16]

These intransitive lyric laments made Arnold as embarrassed for the poetry of his time as Keats was embarrassed by Wordsworth's egotistical sublime. But two things had changed, producing a very different cultural climate. It had become increasingly difficult to imagine the ego serving as a dialectical force for recuperating energies latent in a scene; and Lamia had become only Lucretius's wife with her ill-chosen potion. So there was little to promise direct intensities that can elicit an identification taking us beyond the self that is bound to lamentable historical situations. In Arnold, the poet's only source of strength seems to be the capacity to see clearly all of the evasions inherent in Romanticism; consequently, the poet's dominant energies stem from a critical bitterness, strong enough to reveal in the shadows a truly lyric "buried life," but skeptical enough to fear that any effort to represent that life would destroy it by forcing it to play its part in the melodramatic farces produced by the lyric imagination. The effect is of a lyric consciousness bound, even more than in Tennyson's, to the pathos of its own interminable wanderings. Arnold tries to find an "other" of representation through the scrupulous effort to purge poetry of its lyric excesses, but he succeeds only in making explicit the burden of a self-consciousness unable to conquer the pathos of self-expression that it produces and feeds upon.

Arnold's paradigmatic philosopher is Empedocles, another figure of belatedness, but tormented this time not by desire but by its lack: by the bleak, totalizing picture offered by his philosophical self-reflection. Empedocles proceeds to the mountaintop, traditional site of vision, by negating the claims upon him of Callicles, modeled on Wordsworth's pastoral poet, and of Pausanias, the spirit of empirical social service. Seeking to master all he surveys, and thus to recall the mind's ordering powers, Empedocles finds himself standing on a volcanic "charred, blackened, melancholy waste," which can at any time erupt in chaos. As another of Apollo's votaries, he has only his own consciousness, and that provides all too severe company:

> "Where shall thy votary fly then? back to men?
> But they will gladly welcome him once more.
> And help him to unbend his too tense thought,

And rid him of the presence of himself,
And keep their friendly chatter at his ear,
And haunt him, till the absence from himself,
That other torment, grow unbearable;
And he will fly to solitude again,
And he will find its air too keen for him,
And so change back, and many thousand times
Be miserably bandied to and fro
Like a sea-wave, betwixt the world and thee,
Thou young, implacable God? And only death
Can cut his oscillations short, and so
Bring him to poise. There is no other way."[17]

(2:220–33)

Arnold *thought* he thought that such Byronic fustian was contemptible self-indulgence: the lyric spirit, purchased at the price of the intellect. So runs the argument of his 1853 "Preface." Unfortunately, that role of the alienated critic who judges his time in terms of a set of ideals from better days turns out to be terribly close to the role that Empedocles assumes. Judgment, then, is not so simple a practice: Once poetry manages to define the conditions of expressive self-indulgence, it leads us to look for them in discourses where the agent claims quite different purposes. "Empedocles" may be such a threat to Arnold precisely because its self-indulgence is inseparable from its ability to make us recognize the limitations of those who would judge it. The poem sustains two necessary yet incompatible models of judgment, whose tension provides a powerful emblem of the spiritual dilemma pervading Victorian culture. On the one hand, it offers considerable support for Callicles' traditional view that Empedocles, in refusing to accept the limits molding his life (1:182–6), has become nearly insane with unjustified pride. From this perspective (that of Vendler's Keats and Wordsworth's Wordsworth), individuals ought to subordinate themselves to the reasonable claims of their community. On the other hand, the poem treats Empedocles' climb up Mount Etna as an ascent to new levels of lucidity, where one can understand and reject the compromises that govern those social mores. The Enlightenment dream of freedom from superstition modulates into a vision of the poet-superman. So the poet is left at once dreaming of an expressive authenticity that can compel the philosopher, and fearing that the very intensity unleashed makes all social claims on the expressive ego highly problematic – not because the individualism is false and evasive, as in Tennyson, but because it may be the only plausible source of uncontaminated values.

These conflicting perspectives come to a climax in the poem's second act, where Arnold recognizes the moral inadequacy of Empedocles' stance, yet cannot but in large part identify with the opportunity it gives for Arnold's own repressed expressive energies. Now "alone" on the summit of Etna, Empedocles views his own prudential advice as mere "social debt" (2:7), not binding on a consciousness that sees through the shams of society. But without society, one must seek the ground of one's being in a pure, unmediated relation to a cosmic order, itself no longer amenable to human value terms. This leaves Empedocles caught in a chain of endlessly regressive self-reflections, which he can escape only by denying consciousness itself and submitting himself to a primal chaos. Given these conditions, memory, for Wordsworth the key faculty for renouncing apocalyptic desire and coming to terms with loss, becomes for Empedocles just a sad register of the difference between his triumphant past and his present plight (2:235–75). Similarly, the Romantic dream of a numinous nature, whose energies may soothe the mind by revealing structures of significance responsive to its needs, serves now only to deepen isolation and place the burden of thought completely on the individual lyric voice. The world may brim "with life" (2:308); the landscape he sees from the mountain may live "with held-in joy swelling its heart"; but Empedocles' "I" has no way of connecting to that life. "I alone / Am dead to life and joy, and therefore I read / In all things my own deadness" (2:320–2). The strong poet can maintain that position only by a terrifyingly negative and private rejection of all possible categories of judgment. There is only the lyric voice, and to sing, it must cultivate its own pain.

Like Arnold, in his "Preface," Empedocles sees clearly the need for a spiritual cure, set in motion by the analytic mind's resisting the seductions of the lyric ego. Yet, like Empedocles, Arnold seems to exaggerate the pain, in order to intensify the lyric claims of the sufferer. The greater the cultural malaise, the more likely it is that the two functions of poetry will become inextricably mixed: one needs poetry to give authority and currency to classical modes of agency to which the prose can only point, but the cure proves so burdensome and reductive that one needs another kind of poetry to express the pain. After all, Empedocles too is a classical figure, perhaps one of the few close enough to the modern world to haunt it with the possibility that over time humans might build a social world capable of playing the roles that nature played for the Romantics. But the risk of all such identifications may merely confirm the need to accept a version of Empedocles' "sad lucidity of soul" that knows its limits, and proposes the bearing of them as poetry's heroic feat.

Arnold's "Scholar Gypsy" is his richest effort to grapple with the contradictions emerging from the models of identification and agency proposed by his critical principles. In tone, this poem replaces Empedocles' fustian with a version of Wordsworth's voice, carefully and sensitively looking outside itself for sources of strength that the ego can build upon. From this stance, the poem then sets itself the task of locating in culture what I call a "creative ground," capable of tapping and defining resources in the self that, for the Romantics, were latent in nature. But culture proves to have too much in common with Empedocles' volcano: The ground shakes continually, because it is riven with faults. So Arnold's idealizing becomes an ironic reversal of Romantic dialectics, ultimately leading to an inverted version of apocalypse: Cultural products can be preserved as a set of governing ideals only if they are kept free of the contamination of society. The very sense of nobility that draws the mind to recognize its own resources forces the ephebe to treat culture itself as a version of the palace of art protecting values from the demands of practical life.

Structure here deepens the plight by a superb reversal of the greater Romantic lyric. Initially the poem promises a traditional three-part dialectical structure: an introductory pastoral state breeds a disillusioned rejection of enchantment, which, in turn, motivates a symbolic recovery of what has been lost, so that the Future remains open. Arnold thus seems to resolve his oppositions by transposing the gypsy into an image of the vitality of powers "undiverted to the world without" (162). But the moment of dialectical recovery leads quickly to a fourth, ironic movement in which Arnold does not possess the gypsy but is possessed by him. Now the Romantic dream of being rooted in what Yeats called "one clear perpetual place" leads only to a tragic sense of the gap between conceptual and empirical selves. The very ideals the gypsy symbolizes can only be maintained as concepts exiled from the confusion of empirical experience:

> Still fly, plunge deeper in the bowering wood!
>   Averse, as Dido did with gesture stern
> From her false friend's approach in Hades turn,
>   Wave us away, and keep thy solitude . . .
> . . . .
> But fly our paths, our feverish contact fly!
>   For strong the infection of our mental strife. . . .
> And we should win thee from thy own fair life,
>   Like us distracted, and like us unblest.
>
>   (207–10, 221–5)

Ideally, culture provides both the distance from one's immediate situation and the terms for judging it that enable us to make dissatisfaction the impetus for developing our potential best selves. Yet in this poem, as in "Empedocles," there is no dialectic between what the past manages to represent and what can be effectual in the public order, and there is no god who comes to earth: The authority of "culture" depends on preserving its sheerly conceptual status and maintaining an absolute distinction from the realm of actions. Humanism then arrives at the final paradox that will provide the site for Eliot's *Waste Land:* Under the pressure of empirical lucidity, cultural ideals can retain their power only to the extent that one does not try to apply them. And the classical exemplar must become not Aeneas, but Dido, because the suicidal preserver of her abstract identity is a more appropriate model than the man of action, whose practical pursuit of his ideals led only to his perpetuating an order of violence.

Arnold's prose values could lead to no other poetry, since there seemed no plausible way to mediate between the scholar and his society, or between what could compel individual emotions and what could sustain interpersonal norms for judgment. There remained, however, the possibility of a poetry devoted to spelling out the resources of the private self that could sustain individuals in their exile. But for Arnold, the ideals of classical culture and the demands of lucidity contaminated even this, by leading that self to internalize tribunals and postures that deepened the sense of exile. The sole thing that the person can rely on is the ambivalent security of the most extreme of romance hopes: that, in our exile, we can connect with an ennobling buried life, which is denied by any gesture attempting to represent it. No stranger to exile, Eliot provides the best commentary on the consequences of that dream for Arnold: The dream of the buried life makes Arnold's private lyrics seem the epitome of academic poetry, because their voice sounds so much like the paralyzed public persona. Yet, perhaps because Eliot knew this temptation so well, he did not fully explore the implications of that voice, which exemplified the most oppressive of all these cultural forces that demanded new Modernist models of agency. In these poems Arnold reveals such an immense gulf between the subject's needs and the languages available for expressing them that the Romantic symbol must be transformed into the most demonic form of allegory: Every effort to speak as a composed, untheatrical, private self finds itself subsumed under frameworks that displace the very needs and energies that they would focus.

Can there be lyric openings much more despondent than this?

> Yes, in the sea of life enisled,
> With echoing straits between us thrown,
> Dotting the shoreless watery wild,
> We mortal millions live alone.
> The islands feel the enclasping flow
> And then their endless bounds they know.
> ("To Marguerite – Continued" 1–6)

This is the fifth of the poems addressing Marguerite – if we can speak of "address," when we have a voice for whom actual speech so quickly gives way to a debate with himself that the woman is allowed to overhear. The opening "yes" tells the whole story. Why would he begin with this, if even his statements of passion did not emerge from the mind's endless dialogue with itself? So "yes" is really "no" – "no" to any possibility of letting experience break into the self-regarding terms of that discourse. "Yes" is only an affirmation of the discourse itself, which forces the emotions into this highly conventionalized allegory. This is a self who achieves a mode of self-mastery that becomes its most severe limitation. The critic's ideal of heroic identity exacts its pound of flesh. What "masters" the emotions is this allegorizing representation that makes the energies of longing appear as harbingers of despair, because they remind us of what we do not have and force us to defend against the possibility of things being different. There is thus no better emblem for the condition of this voice than the poem's concluding line, "The unplumbed, salt, estranging sea." The startling contrast of harsh monosyllable and smooth Latinate polysyllabics gives a body to the tension between those abstractions and all the bitter particularity that the language cannot absorb into its efforts at a consoling music.

One could go on endlessly about Arnold as a representative of the darker side of respectable Victorian idealism, but such analyses cannot become fully significant for the history of poetry unless we focus them on the specific mode of agency that Arnold's lyrics construct. It will take just the slightest twist to hear these poems as those of Prufrock, and only slightly more invention to project the Georgian reaction that sought to repress all discursive self-consciousness as its way of avoiding Arnold's plight without fully confronting it. But neither model quite holds for Arnold, because of the strange conjunction of sincerity and symptomatic self-projection that his poems display. Consider the opening for the Marguerite lyric that precedes the one we have been reading. Here the poet takes up the conventional motif of blaming the lady for her infidelity:

> We were apart; yet, day by day,
> I bade my heart more constant be.
> I bade it keep the world away,
> And grow a home for only thee;
> Nor fear'd but thy love likewise grew,
> Like mine, each day, more tried, more true.
> 　　　　　("Isolation. To Marguerite" 1–6)

Yet this is no traditional love lyric. Lyric speakers do not treat their loves as duties. Absence here makes the heart grow sterner, so that it may be fonder. This poet does not know himself, despite his claim to lucid control. His claims about his own fidelity postulate a reciprocity that his discourse reveals is impossible, and not only because we sympathize with the lady's straying eye. This demand for fidelity is addressed less to her than to the poet's need to make the condemnation of her a form of moral vindication for his own righteous loneliness: The Byronic sublime become a form of *ressentiment*. The effort to project universal terms for his own behavior brings out the worst aspect of Arnold's desire to represent the self in relation to the "best that has been thought and said." For the resulting pose of calm lucidity adapts those abstractions to the most self-serving of conclusions: The process of universalizing his condition absolves him of all responsibility for his distinctive attitude. So the powers herein cultivated rely on treating the social bond as a means of deepening and sanctioning the theatricalized confirmation of his own loneliness, as if this noble pathos were the one romance left to this version of lucidity.

Yet, despite all these self-evasions, it is difficult not to be deeply moved by this speaker – and not with the protective ironic distance that we adopt toward the pathos of a Prufrock. This voice is not primarily a set of symptoms staged by an author. Rather, the voice simultaneously manages to sublimate Tennysonian melodrama and to expose the kind of vulnerabilities that emerge when the speaker cannot appreciate the ironies we have been noticing. Even without a sense of irony, the speakers are not blind to the pathos of their situations. And this particular form of pathos makes the irony seem trivial, unable to take the measure of what so obviously invites it. In Arnold's awkward and stubborn refusal to back off from the pain of such speaking, we cannot but feel the continuing pressure of some buried life, belied by that which tries to express it. This lyric intensity establishes a subjective correlate for the impossibility of judgment that pervades "Empedocles." Poetry now does not merely stage a poetic sincerity like Wordsworth's, ennobled by its ability to read what its suffering makes visible as a force that leads beyond the self. Instead, Arnold's lyrics seem to be direct expressions of personal forces so compelling and inescapable that they make the effort at moral judgment appear a gross imposition. Here poetry truly comes down from its stilts, leaving Arnold's heirs an all too accurate measure of the limitations and painfulness of first-person cries.[18] This final vision is modulated only by the marvelously delicate self-mockery that allows the act of thinking to suspend the despair of watching one's buried life follow its own course:

> And then he thinks he knows
> The hills where his life rose
> And the sea where it goes.

VI

Modernism had to be experimental, because it could not see itself continuing in this resigned tracking of buried lives that caught the questing ego in an endless regress of self-expressive posturing. But such strong antidotes required very different versions of the philosopher. Thinking had to involve something more than destruction or lament, so that art could offer itself as constructing new intentional stances, rather than seek the old selves in sites that must belie the effort to represent them. No fictive philosopher could provide that. Instead we must turn to an actual philosopher, whose stolid faith in reason and duty were too perfectly typecast to be invented. For that stern a refusal of the expressivist ego was needed if one was to explain why this ego caused so much misery, and that unshakeable a faith in powers of abstraction was required to create the grounds for the constructivist aesthetic beginning to take shape in Baudelaire and in Flaubert. This philosopher of course was Kant, who provided the intellectual foundations both for Romantic metaphysics and for the resistance to the Romantic ego that combined to produce Modernism.

This is not the place to trace the history of Kant's influence on the arts,[19] nor can this even be the place for careful attention to the precise philosophical discourse originally responsible for that influence. We shall have quite enough to do in attempting to spell out how Kant's resistance to empiricist thought provided the arts with two closely related concepts fundamental to the ideals that abstraction would come to serve: the notion of *heteronomy*, enabling Kant's ethical theory to explain why both empiricist lucidity and the Romantic expressive lyricism anxious to displace it proved so problematic, and the notion of *autonomy*, which defined alternative ideals of agency that inspired new models for the productive energies of artworks.

"Heteronomy" literally means "otherness to the law," or the subjection to laws that are "other" to their subject because they enforce external constraints, rather than articulating powers that the agent would assert as principles of self-legislation. Those various forms of otherness play a central role for Kant because they make it possible to suggest a tight link between the empiricist attitude that cannot account for real causality in the natural world, and prudential or practical ethical attitudes, which cannot postulate a satisfying principle of moral identity for the ethical realm. In both empiricism and in prudential ethics, Kant argued, the analytic framework applied does not sufficiently attend to the productive, synthetic force that the mind can bring to the confusing buzz of phenomenal appearances. What nature is in Hume, the ego becomes in the moral world that characters like Hume leave us. For, if one views human agency from an empiricist perspective, the subject is simply the object of laws and regularities that the person cannot control. At best, one can learn to adapt to one's environment, but one cannot judge that, and one cannot overcome the passivity and the irreducible self-division that we found in Tennyson's Lucretius and Arnold's Empedocles. Despite their very different attitudes toward desire, both figures experience it as always beyond consciousness – always in the position of the "other," who controls without being visible. In "Lucretius," for example, the potion becomes the symbol of a philosophy that cannot handle the tension between a purported natural rationality and the actual desires that it must handle. So it is no wonder that Lucretius must substitute, for the self as legislator, the self as anxious narrator, controlled by what he hopes the narrative can master. Similarly, it is no wonder that when he faces the question of his duties, at the close of his speech, he has no way to align himself with their demands. Having identified his rationality with nature, he has no terms for a second, analogical nature that, for Kant, is necessary for the ethical world, and he has no way to resist what, for Kant, would be the merely anthropological claim that there is no longer a viable social order sanctioning those duties.

Kant hoped that if one could explain how heteronomy took hold, one could postulate a radical alternative to those social orders, which might restore a sense of moral action as a plausible, nonexpressivist version of the sublime. Once we recognize what those desires make of us, we might have a way to stop basing our moral judgments either on constantly shifting social interests or on the dream that by introspection we can locate the deep interests of a "real self" amid the constant fantasies and rhetorical seductions that occupy the ego. Instead, Kant argued, we can imagine the self as capable of acting in accord with a pure rationality, so that it is at once subject and object of moral law: both its creator, and its obedient servant. That construction makes it possible, by analogy, to envision artistic genius as the force that gives the law to nature, and that then defines itself by the law that it chooses to make the spiritual life of the work. In both cases, "autonomy" consists in setting against the heteronomy of natural law this capacity of spirit to bind itself to desired modes of identity that can be free to define itself by the way that the agent directs and takes responsibility for its own productions:

> A man may not presume to know even himself as he really is by knowing himself through inner sensation. For since he does not, as it were, produce himself or derive his concept of himself a priori but only empirically, . . . in respect to mere perception and receptivity to sensation he must count himself as belonging to the world of sense; but in respect to that which may be pure activity in himself (i.e. in respect to that which reaches consciousness directly and not by affecting the senses) he must recognize himself as belonging to the intellectual world. But he has no further knowledge of that world . . .

Thus he has two standpoints from which he can consider himself and recognize the laws of the employment of his powers and consequently of all his actions: first as belonging to the world of sense under laws of nature (heteronomy), and, second, as belonging to the intelligible world under laws which, independent of nature, are not empirical but founded only on reason . . . The concept of autonomy is inseparably connected with the idea of freedom, and with the former there is inseparably bound the universal principle of morality, which ideally is the ground of all actions of rational beings, just as natural law is the ground of all appearance.[20]

To the degree that agents belong to the world of sense, they have no control over the laws that govern their actions. Heteronomous behavior subjects us to what we have no part in making and no distinctive identity to gain by pursuing. Who one is is always given, rather than chosen, and the idea of freedom is merely an illusion that panders to some determining conditions. What we see theatricalized in Empedocles and Lucretius therefore has its core in the most common of situations. Suppose, for example, that I have to make a decision about whether or not I should tell a lie in certain circumstances. The obvious procedure would be to work out some kind of prudential calculus determining the probable consequences of each option. But, for Kant, that would leave me bound to both the contingencies of the situation and the shifting judgments of others – which will not sustain any deeper claims for the self. My determinations, therefore, bind me to laws that I do not determine and that can change as circumstances change. If, on the other hand, I try to correct for those dependencies, by seeking to intuit some basic principles consistent with an introspective sense of character, I have no way of deciding even what in that decision is truly principled, what based on the various self-regarding seductions that the imagination holds out.

Choice according to rational imperatives is very different, Kant claims. In this second model, one's autonomous identity resides in the effort to bind oneself to certain laws that are intrinsic to the desired model of agency. One would decide not to lie, for example, simply because lying is incompatible with the very nature of rational being. Lying is wrong, not because of the possible consequences, but because of the condition of self that it demands. If I lie, I misuse the one feature that can distinguish a human being: its capacity to make its use of signs consistent, univocal, and determined by universal considerations. For Kant, then, the decision on principle not to lie requires assuming an identity shaped in accord with the one interest that cannot seek empirical satisfaction: the interest in actualizing one's capacities as a rational being

(69). Rationality must be self-defining, its authority derived from relations internal to its own procedures rather than from social practices. Under its aegis, there is none of the slippage that besets the ideal of self-expression, because, for the rational subject, the willing of rationality is inseparable from aligning the self with secure determinants of one's identity. The subject *wills* to be bound to the rational law, which then defines the subject by determinate universals (in the same way that wishing to do geometry binds one to deal with its laws). The subject wills itself a rational objectivity. And these universals assure the subject a mode of social community that kept slipping away from Wordsworth's projections of the representative subject. For the affirming of rationality is, necessarily, the willing of universals that bind into a community all those who realize that there can be a second nature, or city of ends consistent with the subject's deepest interests. Finally, such commitments to rationality create a possibility that all subjects can win for themselves a dignity, and a sublimity, that society previously had attributed solely to the aristocracy. There can be nothing more noble than this resistance to empirical interests and practical calculations in order to identify oneself with the truly "legislative" dimension of one's being, with a sense of making what one obeys. To appreciate this, one need simply consider how different this model of heroism is from the isolated loneliness of those poets and philosopher figures for whom the only measure of the self's legislative force is its difference from its society.

VII

I love Kant's work as art too much to want to defend it as philosophy. There is no denying that his ideas create serious problems. As Kant himself saw, so unrelenting a rationalism had great difficulty connecting itself to the practical realities of empirical existence. At best, Kant's moral thinking has to be seen today as a model of sublime heroism, rather than a description of what people actually do. But that kind of model was precisely what artists like Flaubert and Baudelaire, who had had enough of what people actually do, needed, especially since it seemed possible to conceive a "legislative imagination" that could assume many of the features Kant had idealized in his treatment of rationality, without its unpalatable absolutes. Therefore, this dwelling on Kant should, at the very least, make clear that the ideal of moral autonomy is considerably more than a life-denying formalism. Even if its rationalist foundation proves shaky, the ideal creates some important new ways to imagine a lyric fullness at the heart of philosophical lucidity. Minimally, Kant gives new life to an anti-Enlightenment enthusiasm about ideals, by recovering in secular terms the Christian and Greek model of our being able to realize a "second nature," free of many of the limits that we take in with our specific acculturation. Now we can enter that second nature by resisting the temptation to view the self in scenic grounds or to trust any intuitional sense of personal powers. By overcoming what Wordsworth made of constitutive spirit, we can entertain a truly Keatsian ideal. And on that basis, we can construct a cogent notion of values that are ends in themselves, because of the conditions of agency that they allow – quintessentially, Kant says, in the state of "a will good in itself, whose worth transcends everything" (20). With this model of value, Kant restores a moral version of the Romantic sublime, in which the clarity of self-definition replaces the murky "otherness" of nature: "Though there is no sublimity in [a moral agent] in so far as he is subject to moral law, yet he is sublime in so far as he is legislative with reference to the law and subject to it only for this reason" (58). Rather than compel awe before nature, this fidelity to the law that one produces as one's second nature compels awe of what the human spirit can make by resisting the consolations that its heteronomous culture holds out to it.

Taken as philosophy, these principles are haunted by the empiricism they attempt to resist. For Kant's demonstration that we cannot do more than speculate on what exceeds understanding makes it impossible for his heirs to avoid the fear that their own efforts to establish an adequate lyricism offer little more than evasions of the secularizing process. Yet what in philosophy appears only as speculation can in art take on different valences. For there the concrete uses of legislative energies made it possible to treat Kantian themes like sublime, self-legislating agency and radically transpersonal modes of judgment as if they offered plausible principles of value. In fact one might say that constructivist aesthetics developed through artists' efforts to take this challenge as their fundamental intellectual task. Convinced that Kant's critique of heteronomy captured the fundamental contradictions in Romantic expressivism, thinkers such as Baudelaire and Flaubert turned for their version of autonomy, not to Kant's ethics, but to the model of legislative imagination developed in his aesthetic. For only that vision of productive agency seemed to them capable of linking concrete passions with transpersonal and law-governed states.[21] Were we to place their versions of Kant historically, we would have to trace the very different aesthetic appropriations of Kantian morality that took place in Schiller and the late French Romantics. But here I shall try only to illustrate the influential conceptual shifts by pointing out the metaphoric potential within Kant's aesthetic that emerged as the artists adapted his model of autonomous agency to conceptions of artistic form and projections of its extraformal implications.

If one is to use Kant's aesthetic against his rationalism, the fundamental need is for an equivalent to the image of self-legislating dignity that rationality allows. Kant locates this by postulating artistic form as an alternative mode of lawfulness generated by the productive activity of spirit. His means is the Romantic concept of *genius,* given a stunning twist: "Genius is the innate mental disposition (ingenium) through which nature gives the rule to art" (*Critique of Judgment* 150). Like Wordsworth's blend of memory and vision, Kant's "genius" is the mind's elaboration of something fundamental to natural energies. But its role is not to create a capacious personal ethos from the conjunction of forces. Genius is an abstracting force: It distills the personal into a mode of intentionality within the work that Kant calls a "purposiveness without purpose." Genius cannot be reduced to purposes or subjective interests, because it does not work by plans provided by the understanding and it does not seek the empirical goals pursued by practical judgment. But it also cannot be reduced to a mode of cognition providing discrete insights into a reality that could exist without its activity. Genius is purposive. Its purposive spirit composes art objects so that their internal relations constantly manifest intelligence and direction within appearances, while refusing to allow "any definite thought, i.e., any concept, being capable of being adequate to it." Such self-legislation is art's "counterpart of a *rational idea,* which conversely is a concept to which no intuition (or representation of the imagination) can be adequate" (157). Like reason, genius defines an architecture for spirit. But the architecture does not have the exponible, systematic, relational form that reason provides. Instead, it makes available a sense of the phenomenal world as literally remade, in connection with a second nature that now finds all of its diffuse playful energies in harmony with appearances. The undefinable inner lawfulness of the work becomes in itself a vehicle for exhibiting the nature of spirit in a secular world.

In so freeing the constructive energies of the work, Kant also makes it possible to attribute new semantic roles to that activity. Art as an instrument of knowledge need not be treated primarily in terms of descriptive or sentential truths. Instead, Plotinus's notion of knowledge as a form of participation becomes available, to describe and to extend what was already taking place in artists such as Wordsworth, Constable, and Friedrich. Aesthetics could concentrate on the work's capacity to create self-reflexive states for its audience. For example, for Kant beauty becomes "the purposive attuning of the imagination to agreement with the faculty of concepts in general" (189). So now the role of theory is to align a faculty of cognition (intuition) to a faculty of production (imagination) in a way that specifies how the object displays powers that neither the understanding nor reason can comprehend. And the role of the artist is to make the purposive activity show that there can be an other to representation, because art so "puts the mental powers purposefully into swing" (157) that we feel a connection to the world, and to our own nature, that cannot be explained by the categories available to the understanding. The inner lawfulness of the work simply establishes a direct spiritual life as a site inviting a reflective judgment that all participants can share.[22]

These are not claims simply about producing vague states of sublimity. For Kant, art not only moves the soul, but it does so in ways that call forth specific projections about the spirit's powers. These are produced in two ways. First, each work displays its own "purposive attuning of the imagination to agreement with the faculty of concepts in general" (189). Although art resists the understanding, it nonetheless demonstrates the efficacy of concepts by re-deploying them in the service of imagination. As concepts are pushed to their limits, they give us access to productive energies that suggest a world beyond the authority of the understanding, yet harmonious with its structures. Although one may never come to "understand" *Hamlet* or the *Madonna of the Rocks,* the effort at understanding gives these works their vitality and enables us to appreciate the forces of the productive activity that transcend received cognitive categories. We come to realize how far this mode of concreteness is from simple perception, and how rich is the mind's capacity to be satisfied by the range of its own activity, without irritable reaching after fact and reason.

Second, Kant's aesthetic theory projects ideals of transpersonality that seem more feasible, and more compelling, than the universals entailed by rational behavior. To the degree that the form created by genius gives the art work purposiveness, it can be said to take it from the heteronomous pursuit of individual pleasures to the distinctive aesthetic realm, in which we feel that we judge as if there were a subjective universality of taste. Were the work primarily an experience of enhanced sensuality, the only judgments it could invite would be those determining the degree of individual pleasure conferred or blocked. But, because we are given that purposive intentionality, we are asked to judge the work in more general terms – in terms that involve approval, rather than simply pleasure. Approval is a matter, not merely of response, but of assessing a determinate structure, and approval requires seeing oneself in the legislating role that has the same transpersonality as any other use of a conceptual framework:

> The judgment of taste is based on a concept (viz. the concept of the general ground of the subjective purposiveness of nature for the judgment); from which, however, nothing can be known and proved in respect of the object, because it is in itself undeterminable and useless for knowledge. Yet at the same time and in that

very account the judgment has validity for everyone (though of course for each only as a singular judgment immediately accompanying his intuition), because its determining ground lies perhaps in the concept of that which may be regarded as the supersensible substrata of humanity. (*Critique of Judgment* 185)

No Postromantic artist could, or would, use this language. But it bears translation, because it suggests a model for the idea of the "virtuality" of the audience. If I try to judge an object projecting purposive form, I must try to grasp it as a relational whole, not simply as a conjunction of parts giving various degrees of pleasure. This means that I must employ the faculty that deals with concepts, even though the work uses understanding without being subject to its categories. Then, because the understanding does not provide the necessary framework for grasping that wholeness, I find myself having to locate the wholeness in the condition of activity that the work has engendered. Because that condition depends on formal relations, however, it cannot be fairly assessed simply in terms of contexts and interests brought to the work by the individual. And, because I affirm the value of the work in terms of that purposiveness, I must assume that I myself become someone different as I judge. I enter a site where I can imagine engaging a stratum of will and reflection that makes sense only as something that subjects share by virtue of being legislative agents. I will the pleasure as something in everyone's interest, and I locate the pleasure in the objective set of relations that I imagine engaging every attentive member of its audience.

This image of aesthetic judgment, then, makes it possible to claim that in responding to art we get a more concrete glimpse of autonomy than we do in moral experience (where we must rely on rational concepts to which no intuition can be adequate). In this view of aesthetic judgment, the responding agent literally "gives the law to itself" (199), because our deepest passions depend on our submitting ourselves to the formal dictates of the work. We pursue a version of personal interests that requires us to subject ourselves to essentially transpersonal practices, which we try to make as articulate as possible – not in order to master them, but in order to publish our pleasure and test the degree to which we can share what can be objectively available to all. Thus, through the virtuality elicited by aesthetic forms, the spirit comes to appreciate its ability to inhabit a world where the impositions of form are seen as the preconditions for affirming a second nature in which the spirit glimpses the universality at the core of its own creative energies. The moral agent finds specific imperatives within that reason, which will actually embody this potential in specific actions. But precisely because the moral law is rationally definable, we do not quite see how deep, or how satisfying, that potential is, until we see the symbolic equivalent of those imperatives in art's disposition of will as a pure condition of transpersonal affirmation (see 197–8).

For our literary culture, Kant the moral philosopher seems little more than another Apollonius. We see him as producing a doctrinal system whose fate is inseparable from the fates melodramatically staged for philosophy by Victorian poetry. But to shrink Kant to that melodramatic plot is to ignore the degree to which he continues to make possible models of agency for art capable of projecting beyond the margins of philosophy that he had so carefully drawn. Both in his own practice and in what he inspired, Kant could show how and why, in certain domains, the concepts of the understanding could not suffice: There must be models of idealization responsive to the possibility of our being able to demonstrate productive energies that take on sublimity because of what we do rather than what we behold. The arts then became the testing ground for these possible idealizations. Kant's own aesthetics created a model of artistic purposiveness allowing others to work out means of adapting what he had claimed for moral autonomy to the empirical order that Kant's ethical theory consigned to mere heteronomy. For he made clear the kind of contrasts with heteronomy that art could struggle to realize, and he demonstrated what was at stake in the fact that such work could compose states where the audience could turn self-reflexively on the modes of agency suddenly made real for them. From Kant, then, we can trace art's fascination with the testing through formal experiment of a significant variety of ethical models, each authorized by its capacity to demonstrate productive energies holding off the claims of analytic reason without collapsing into heteronomous duplicities. And it may be that we must return to Kant if we are to find ways of responding now to a reason that finds everywhere nothing but simulacra of value and truth.

4

Modernist Irony and the Kantian Heritage

I

One could use the various Kants developed by the nineteenth century to map its complex ambitions and the contradictions they generated. There was the clearheaded thinker who expelled all mysticism, and there was the reluctant mystic who cleared the way for claiming transcendental dimensions to our experiences of nature and of our own processes of self-consciousness. Similarly there was the great philosopher of duty, showing how the spirit could earn an autonomous self-legislating state where reason need not be merely the pander for will, and there was the mistaken rationalist, who showed those like Hegel how any idealizing of spirit could have force only if it was in fact defined in relation to specific cultural struggles. And finally there was the Kant whom the artists could patronize and transform into a figure satisfying their own interests in developing an art not bound to the marketplace values that he characterized as fundamentally heteronomous.

I cannot here speculate on the significance or consequences of these conflicts. Rather I invoke that variety to indicate that the writers and artists who appropriated Kant participated in a larger cultural enterprise and, more important, to set a stage for arguing that the Kant they struggled to recast has important philosophical claims on us. This means concentrating on Baudelaire and Flaubert, the two literary figures who inaugurated a distinctive Modernism by realizing what Kant made available for characterizing the energies of authorial composition. By such a concentration we shall take up two tasks. First, we shall try to understand how each of these writers developed powerful alternatives to Kantian rationalism by adapting to their own genius popular renderings of his concepts of autonomy, the end in itself, and the properties of purposiveness distinctive to artistic form. In other words, these writers were not scholars of Kant; they twisted the Kants that their culture offered them into a set of concerns whose import could be fully stated only within their own disposition of artistic energies. Second, we shall have to understand why even these twistings could not suffice, but instead left their heirs the task of developing a Modernism severely plagued by infinite ironies at least as debilitating as the expressivist heteronomies that they had set out to resist. For, once Kant's concept of autonomy was separated from his theory of rationality, the "legislating spirit" proved extremely difficult to ground or to socialize. The working out of new Modernist possibilities therefore involved the continual worry that this desire for new artistic principles was merely a seductive mode of self-destruction. There could be forms of agency mobile and supple enough to allow writers the dream of lucid self-possession. Yet in pursuing that freedom, they found little but the composing self for the mind to feed upon, so there remained only the mind's corrosive power to sustain desired states of sublimity shaped in the imagination by very different cultural possibilities.

Mallarmé's "*Le Tombeau de Charles Baudelaire*" caught in six lines what will take me forty pages to elaborate:

> *Quel feuillage séché dans les cités sans soir*
> *Votif pourra bénir comme elle se rasseoir*
> *Contre le marbre vainement de Baudelaire*
>
> *Au voile qui la ceint absente avec frissons*
> *Celle son Ombre même un poison tutélaire*
> *Toujours à respirer si nous en périssons*[1]

> [What leaves, dried in cities without evening, votive can bless as she, seating herself in vain against the marble of Baudelaire, shudderingly absent from the veil that girdles her, she, his very shade, a guardian poison, always to be breathed although we die of it.]

This shade of Baudelaire is tutelary in its poison, because it shows art capable of literally composing forms of spirit that can, in their self-reflexive powers, testify to strengths and intricacies in creative activity that can overcome the expressivist self-delusions driving Victorian lyricism. But that figure remains deadly, precisely because it is a shade – an ideal not realizable by those of us who must sit by Baudelaire's tomb, and an ideal already rendered vain by the specific forms of self-reflexive irony that make the work itself a sublime tomb of spirit.

By placing Baudelaire between Flaubert and Eliot, I hope to capture both aspects of this vanity willing to explore a lucidity so intimate to the lyric spirit that it rendered that spirit at once sublime and self-destructive. Flaubert made the crucial break from dominant nineteenth-century styles by having the writing itself become a theater, in which purposiveness wars on what he thought were the heteronomous forces dominant in any realistic mode's fidelity to appearances. Baudelaire then tried to win a lyric ethos from Flaubert's Olympian distance by foregrounding poetic rhetoricity as a form of spiritual mobility. Yet Baudelaire found that mobility increasingly terrifying because it eventually cannibalized even the roles that most evocatively produced it, and thus left self-consciousness at once absolutely free and absolutely doomed to repeating this self-destructive process. The plight of this project sets the stage for my chapter on Eliot (Chapter 5), where we shall see him raising Baudelaire's ironies to a more abstract level, on which the poet could stage his work as providing antidotes for the poison it disseminated. Mobility of spirit then yielded glimpses of needs and resources suggesting deeper, transpersonal levels of self-consciousness available to the lyric imagination. And although Eliot's particular mythic and theological reading of those resources repelled many of his peers, the mode of abstraction he established gave them a theater in which plausible alternatives could be explored. There poets would finally bring to fruition Baudelaire's remarkable realization that an art based on color relations could provide intensities capable, like Keats's, of reformulating everything that Renaissance reliance on sculptural modeling had taught the culture to treat as "natural." The lucid mind could finally align itself with its own romance needs within a new relational ontology, whose best testimony was precisely the purposive activities that Kant had isolated, in the service of very different principles.

To get this rather complex story straight, we must first examine the three concepts of Kant's that the writers adapted to their purposes. First, and most important, is the concept of autonomy. It is tempting to say that Flaubert and Baudelaire simply shifted the concept from Kant's rationalist moral philosophy into the domain of anesthetics, where autonomy is art's reward for successfully achieving a state of disinterest about practical affairs. In this version, autonomy simply becomes a predicate that one applies to works of art when they manifest the capacity of self-possession that Kant attributed to moral agents. On this basis, formalist art becomes a perfect correlate to the denial of practical interests that Kant argued was necessary if one was to attain rational freedom. But in following that line, we must be careful to avoid the assumption common to much contemporary criticism that the pursuit of autonomy is in essence a means of escaping the demands of social reality. For in seeking autonomy, the best artists in the tradition of Flaubert and Baudelaire clearly envisioned themselves not as rejecting "life," but as renouncing an inadequate way of casting life that narrowed the values possible within artistic experience to those compatible with the bourgeois practical realm. In order for significant social change to take place, these writers believed, they had to use the new constructive powers that Kant had made conceptually available for purposes very different from those he envisioned. They had to invent an artistic version of constitutive particularity that could serve the same role as the concept of a "categorical imperative." Just as that imperative projected an agent capable of basing her own moral action on a disinterested affirmation of rationally legislating for all persons, the dream of artistic autonomy provided an ideal of a constructive psyche able to demonstrate an individual nobility, earned by its resistance to the practical sphere. Art must make visible a purposiveness in the constitutive activity that can dignify character, in the same way that achieving rational actions does for Kant. And art must carry transcendental energies that can still give access to Keats's romance sites, but freed from their conventional trappings.

As these artists tried to develop ideals of autonomy appropriate to art, a second need, and a second opportunity, immediately emerged. If artworks in fact demonstrate the achievement of significant moments of self-legislation, then writers must foster new ways of understanding how certain acts of mind can be said to compose a second nature. And they must learn how to use such constructions to make available qualities that have practical significance, yet are not amenable to the conditions of understanding normally governing our practical judgments. These opportunities placed an enormous burden on the specific work of art, since then it had to carry the force that Kant attributed to moral character. Literary form had to free Wordsworthian eloquence from those ideals shaped by his model of how "scenically" constituted selves come to self-possession. No wonder attention shifted from the work as "window" to the work as "testimonial imaginative site." Whereas Kant's "second nature" had to remain a purely speculative, transcendental phenomenon, writers and artists could claim to make that second nature literally visible through the purposive energies that took on physical existence in the work's formal relationships.

A third transformation of Kant was called for to handle the question of how artists should value these newly manifest powers. Kant's own transformation of Edmund Burke's popular doctrine of the "sublime" laid the necessary groundwork. In the eighteenth century the concept of the sublime had been essentially a category for describing sensations. With Kant, it became a concept one could apply both to conditions of knowledge and to properties of human action (as, indeed, had been the case in Longinus's original formulation). Flaubert and Baudelaire elaborated that difference, replacing the sublime in nature with a sublime available only in constitutive activity. For they believed that it is only in such activity that one can fully observe spirit resisting everything that tries to subsume it under the categories of the understanding. Thus, by foregrounding the constitutive power of the work, the artist creates a site where he dramatizes qualities of human agency that have the same awe-inspiring properties as Kant's moral exemplars. Now, however, the value of the example is not in the laws that it instantiates, but in the specific traits that it allows us to predicate of the consciousness forming it. Ideally, the works make, out of their intense disgust with things as they are, a lyricism so intricate that its enactment requires radically individualist forms of self-consciousness, justifiable only in terms of the differences they could maintain from all collective values. Even Kant's transcendentalism would have its secular aesthetic analog.

II

No work surpasses *Madame Bovary* at defining the demands that eventually led European art to Modernism. Dramatically, Flaubert's novel affords a keen critical analysis of the conditions that trap desire in the law of heteronomy. Metadramatically, the text seeks, in its own activity, a mode of purposive self-legislation capable of providing an alternative to realist commitments, which could only picture, and thus reinforce, that heteronomy. However, in so emphasizing the oppositional force of the constructive imagination, Flaubert paid a large price for his freedom. This self-reflexive romance site can be enjoyed only by setting it not only against realism, but also against all of the moral and psychological ideals that traditional art had sustained by mimetic strategies. The very success of that art bound it far too closely to a contaminated social order.

The essential dramatic impact of *Madame Bovary* needs only the briefest summary, which Flaubert provides in the narrative sequence that concludes his book.[2] First we see Emma, the figure of will and romance lyricism, reduced to the status of a beggar, whose actions are reported from the cold, impersonal, third-person vantage point of her neighbors, so completely has she lost the power to define her own world. Then Flaubert shifts to the metaphysical dimension of that passivity, in effect invoking a Christian framework for judging heteronomous secular desire, while refusing to hold out any hope for a transcendental alternative. As the priest administers extreme unction, Emma's soul provides the necessary inner grace, luxuriating in its condemnation of each of the senses, until it can wholeheartedly glue her lips to the image of the crucified "man-god." Here, at least, passion can fully express its imaginary demands. For the others, for the living, there is only more contradiction, and the pathos of language doomed to report it. We are led back to her husband Charles, as he too loses the power of first-person control over his emotional life. Others must speak for him or give meaning to his actions, as if the autopsy that he is given at the end of the book could serve as an emblem for the book's realist commitments and the lives that require them. All of the analytic instruments agree:

> He discovered a box and kicked it open. Rodolphe's portrait flew out at him, from among the pile of love-letters. People wondered at his despondency. He never went out, saw no one, refused even to visit his patients. Then they said "he shut himself up to drink." At times, however, someone would climb on the garden hedge, moved by curiosity. They would stare in amazement at this long-bearded, shabbily clothed wild figure of a man, who wept aloud as he walked up and down. . . .
>
> Rodolfe remained silent. And Charles, his head in his hands, went on in a broken voice, with the resigned accent of infinite grief: "No, I can't blame you any longer." He even made a phrase, the only one he'd ever made: "Fate willed it this way." Rodolphe, who had been the agent of this fate, thought him very meek for a man in his situation, comic even and slightly despicable. . . .
>
> At seven o'clock little Berthe, who had not seen him all afternoon, came to fetch him for dinner. His head was leaning against the wall, with closed eyes and open mouth, and in his hand was a long tress of black hair. "Papa, come!" And thinking he wanted to play, she gave him a gentle push, he fell to the ground. He was dead. Thirty six hours later, at the pharmacist's request, Monsieur Canivet arrived. He performed an autopsy, but found nothing. (*Madame Bovary* 254–5)

On the metadramatic level, however, this grim climax requires a somewhat different emotional response. The novel seems unwilling to endorse the appropriate tragic attitude, refusing to sanction anything less complex than an intricate balance, in these concluding moments, between vicious parody and the deep, almost self-indulgent sympathy whose analog is Emma's embrace of the man-god. This is not the style of a nineteenth-century realist. The writing has too much fun, indulges too much in self-consciously producing the pathos of Charles's plight. Notice that there are carefully wrought stages in his degradation, from people simply wondering at his despondency to people climbing the fence in violation of his monstrous privacy. Then there is the cruel blow of reintroducing Rodolfe, who rejects the conventional realist ploy of attributing the course of events to an exonerating fate, and Flaubert gives us, in the place of such a resolution, only a final conjunction of the child's desire to play, the flat, reportorial prose rendering the death, and the surgical lucidity that produces the autopsy's verdict, "nothing." This nothing, in other words, seems so contextualized as to elicit the presence of another, competing sensibility that Flaubert was to describe in a famous letter to Louise Colet:

> What seems beautiful to me, what I should like to write, is a book about nothing, a book dependent on nothing external, which would be held together by the strength of its style, just as the earth, suspended in the void, depends on nothing external for its support; a book which would have no subject, or at least in which the subject would be almost invisible. . . . The finest works are those that contain the least matter; the closer expression comes to thought, the closer language comes to coinciding and merging with it, the finer the result. . . . Form is as free as the will of its creator. . . .
>
> It is for this reason that there are no noble subjects or ignoble subjects; from the standpoint of pure Art one might almost establish the axiom that there is no such thing as subject, style in itself being an almost absolute manner of seeing things. (Reprinted in *Madame Bovary* 309–10)

Style is the "something" that must replace and compensate for an empirical world that has been reduced by the lucid analytic mind to a "nothing" in the domain of values. The metadramatic role of the writing, then, is to flesh out what style can achieve as a model of possible agency by establishing a contrast between the forms of desire that govern the lives of its characters and an attitude that the writing can exemplify and justify. Therefore, instead of offering a reading of the novel, I want simply to show how this foregrounded authorial action responds to the cultural problems we have been tracing in such a way as to constitute a basic permission for, and challenge to, Modernist art.

That critical enterprise requires two basic tasks: First, I must show how the internal structure of *Madame Bovary* gives resonance to its writerly presence; second, I must explore the terms for self-legislation that take shape through that resonance and that dramatize the capacity of art to realize what philosophy can only dream on. By focusing on the energies specific to the purposiveness in the writing, *Madame Bovary* posits a counterpressure to the bleak truths that its descriptions seem to sustain. This is done, not by inculcating conventional dramatic distance from the characters as a means for judging them, but by staging the struggle to maintain distance as itself the spiritual or ethical force that the work offers its society. The author engages in the same dialectic between first-

and third-person stances that the characters enter, but on the authorial level the agent experiences both stances as aspects of his own imaginative life. In one movement, he is compelled to sympathize with his own creation; in another, he holds himself aloof, reducing the characters' worlds to essentially two-dimensional terms. Yet he need not choose between these possibilities. Rather, the point of the writing is to be sensitive and mobile enough not to be trapped in any one attitude, but to manipulate attitudes, so that their tension creates something like a second nature. Self-consciousness about the desires that writing can negotiate becomes the text's alternative to Emma's foolish and sublime will to romance.

My emphasis on the constitutive role of writing is not surprising, in our critical climate.[3] But it behooves us to attempt to keep it surprising enough that we let Flaubert, rather than Derrida, show us what it involves – and that means keeping the text's particular drama of desires, as much as possible, the focus for our attention. The following passage, identified as the quintessential Flaubert by Erich Auerbach, makes this an easy and pleasant task. This passage beautifully embodies the fundamental elements of the dialectic that Flaubert relies on to establish the activity of writing as a significant ethical model. Emma is in the process of recognizing the truth that is veiled by her culture's romantic ideals about marriage:

> But it was above all the meal-times that were unbearable to her, in this small room on the ground floor, with its smoking stove, its creaking door, the walls that sweated, the damp pavement; all the bitterness of life seemed served up on her plate, and with the smoke of the boiled beef there rose from her secret soul waves of nauseous disgust. Charles was a slow eater; she played with a few nuts, or leaning on her elbow, amused herself drawing lines across the oil-cloth table cover with the point of her knife.[4] (47)

She who had lived by the senses now begins to die by them. Abstract conditions, such as a feeling about the bitterness of life, get irreducibly mixed into the most concrete details of her meal, the smoke of the beef a telling externalization of what her soul seems to have become. So the room becomes an analog for the soul, as the sensations it creates literally constitute the life of the spirit, absorbing into this confined space an imaginative life accustomed to dreaming by open windows.

When we notice how Flaubert's evocative and philosophically compelling use of the imperfect tense turns the screw even tighter, the writing itself becomes a means for deepening the emblematic qualities of the room. Every active verb in this passage reminds us that these are not single actions but repeated conditions, with the experiential force of absolute types – at least in Emma's mind. Tense transforms passing events into states of mind that persist, that make moments bear the weight of a life. So a form of Romantic symbolism persists, but it is one that completely reverses Wordsworth's scenic logic. Details mean more than a description can carry – there is a universal participating in these particulars – but it is psychological, not ontological: Everything becomes pervaded by her despondent sense of an impotent spirit, condemned to observe all that must remain absent from her life. Or, to put the same point another way, it is as if Wordsworth's attention to particulars was a curse, rather than a means to grace, with his reliance on place now a mark of the limitations on spirit, rather than a vehicle for locating new sources of psychic strength. These limitations, one hardly needs to add, all come to a climax when the text shifts its attention to Charles, as at once the force that constrains her life and the image of what she is likely to become if she continues to have to understand her own spirit in terms of this sensory life. As she watches Charles, we see his slow eating come to express a terrifyingly pure sensuous existence, occupying all of space and time.[5]

Yet there is something about this scene that makes it impossible to speak simply of an ironic inversion of Romanticism. The use of the imperfect tense is one reason. Flaubert seems to employ his craft, simultaneously, to define the ironic condition and to create possibilities for sympathy within it. That imperfect tense virtually makes available the fundamental temporality of Emma's existence, as if the writer could identify with its elemental rhythms. The final detail of the scene, indeed, makes this identification the primary point. As Emma manages a somewhat pathetic and desperate act of freedom by doodling with her knife, she becomes a kind of writer, balancing in her gesture a violence and despair that capture everything that she puts into romance. But, bound as she is to flesh, her writing is compelled to the purely oppositional task of projecting a fantasy space that, even in its wordless repetition, provides relief from the constraints of a scenic realism. Indeed, her composing, too, is in the imperfect, an imperfect brilliantly built on a reflexive. So the condition of her writing, the activity of *"s'amusait,"* ties the very idea of her preserving a sense of self to this Sisyphean gesturing.

If we understand why Emma's writing must fail, we begin to see the pressure on Flaubert's sympathy. He must hope that a certain way of identifying with Emma can produce a different site of writing, which will sustain an ethos bound neither to her sensual existence nor to the laws of heteronomy that eventually dominate that sensuous existence. Flaubert, commenting on the poverty of modern life to Louise Colet (a subject on which he sounds like Matthew Arnold, perhaps because he lacks the protective veil of his fiction), makes this writerly ideal explicit: "But I believe there is something above all this, to wit, the ironic acceptance of existence and its plastic or complete recasting through art."[6] A purely critical irony will not suffice. Such an attitude might establish a distance from heteronomy, but it does not "recast" life. For that, we need "plasticity" of spirit, which I take to mean a mobility of emotional and imaginative energies, which can share the characters' desires while judging those desires as destructive. But this plasticity too must be judged, so we must realize that Emma's imaginary writing deepens her plight, by fostering romance desires that will ultimately make her subject to another kind of writing, dominated by Rodolfe. As she watches Charles, as she sees him become part of the alienating objective scene, she preserves her own subjectivity by withdrawing into a silent imaginary space, where she is at least different from the spirit that suffuses the room. However, Emma's way of defending her subjectivity effectively undermines it, because identity itself comes to depend on the romance imagination that is controlled by cultural forces within which she is a mere pawn.

Emma's tragedy is inseparable from her openness to parody. She is awesomely inventive and dogged in her pursuit of a single sense of identity that she cannot have, except in her dying moment with the man-god. The authorial agency of the book, on the other hand, need not pursue such a limited sense of self, because of the mobile plasticity of consciousness that the writing sustains. The writing composes its agency in accord with the logic of the symbol, so that the universal, now everywhere manifest in the particulars, is not a natural force, but a human potential. This mode of narrating itself creates a new heroism, based on being able to subsume everyone else's position, while retaining the distance to produce the conditions that make the others suffer.

How that identity differs from Emma's – in the process, composing a mode of fictional investment new to Western literature – appears most provocatively at the moment when Emma seems most successful in her own quest. After her first adultery with Rodolphe, in the open countryside, Emma returns home. Having made her horse prance as she enters Yonville and gotten "rid of Charles" to shut herself by the window of her room, where she indulges her romantic dreams, Emma looks at the self she has become:

> But when she saw herself in the mirror she wondered at her face. Never had her eyes been so large, so black, nor so deep. Something subtle about her being transfigured her.
> She repeated: "I have a lover, a lover!" delighting at the idea as if a second puberty had come to her. So at last she was to

know those joys of love, that fever of happiness, of which she
had despaired. . . .

Then she recalled the heroines of the books that she had read,
and the lyric legion of these adulterous women began to sing in
her memory. . . . She became herself, as it were, an actual part
of these lyrical imaginings. . . . Besides, Emma felt a satisfaction of revenge. How she had suffered. But she had won out at
last, and the love so long pent up erupted in joyous
outbursts. (117)

To be so desired is, for Emma, to experience the ultimate lyric experience available to romance identity, She finally has the intense subjectivity
that was only negatively projected in her idle writing on the tablecloth.
But Flaubert proves crueler than any of her lovers, in part because of his
sympathy. Emma's deep privacy is in no way inviolate, because its
source in that "lyric legion of adulterous women" blinds her to the
cultural pressures that anyone can recognize if he has a sufficient ear for
cliché. Flaubert is so aware of those pressures that his sympathy melds
with hatred, and both lead to what might be described as the most
profound rape in literature. At the very moment when Emma most
insistently claims possession over her own spirit, that soul becomes the
property of another lover, far more subtle than Rodolphe. Rodolphe
merely fools her; Flaubert possesses her by knowing her better than she
knows herself. His reward takes the form of fully dominating the very
imperatives and modes of intensity that make Emma so touchingly vulnerable. Flaubert has no particular object of desire that can give him the
exaltation of lyric identity: He will never "have" a lover in the way that
Emma thinks she does, but then neither, really, does she. He can, nonetheless, have his Emma, and his Charles, and his Homais, and even his
Larivet, the author's fantasized surgeon figure. Flaubert, in short, desires
not a life, but a book, for only the modes of desire that a book sustains
can dignify his writerly acts as an ethos worth living for.

The best way to appreciate how this writerly desire gets defined by the
text as a significant mode of agency is to focus on its position between
the modes of desire represented at one pole by Emma, and at the other by
Homais, the novel's figure for everything in bourgeois life fostered by
the demystified realism that was conquering traditional mores. Whereas
Emma's imaginary dreams are incompatible with the practical order,
Homais thrives by manipulating the illusions that others live by, in the
process never revealing his own personal stakes. Nowhere is there a
better conjunction of the merchant and the official artist, each role preferring self-protection and long-term ends to any values that might be
achieved in expressing one's immediate desire or pursuing a state not

sanctioned by convention. Thus, whereas for Emma everything must approximate the state of romance, for Homais all romance is reduced to the pursuit of social recognition, and the latter is to be achieved by expunging everything worth being romantic about, in favor of the most grotesquely ideological pieties. Emma is unable to live out fantasies, because they are based on an anachronistic set of values completely inappropriate to bourgeois life (but perhaps necessary as fictions in order to keep enough victims for the merchants). Homais, in contrast, can idealize progress and identify with the future, because he is on the side soon to achieve absolute hegemony. In this domain at least, it pays to cultivate a distance that enables one to manipulate the law of heteronomy, so that it serves an individual's ends rather than victimizing him.

But where does this leave the writer? His distance from Emma frees him to a world of diverse vicarious desires. But to base one's writerly identity solely on that ironic distance is to come dangerously close to aligning oneself with Homais, and thus to the writer's mimicking what he most despises. Flaubert cannot treat that distance merely as an escape from the contingencies of desire; he must also claim a distinctive power for it, as an absolute way of seeing. This, in turn, puts the burden on the reader of having to project the model of agency that is sustained by the unique aspects of Flaubert's style, such as the habit that Henry James described as his vacillating between "flat" and "round" views of the agents.[7] We are invited to see that if we had only the choice between Emma and Homais, we would face, in almost parodic form, the full impact of the conflict between lyricism and lucidity. It is by contrast to Homais that Emma's romanticism seems as necessary as it is pathetic. How else can one face a world in which all that once seemed worth living for goes the way of a carefully managed repression, in the name of success and freedom? But how can one who takes Emma's path not become the victim of the romance imagination, doomed to degrading self-exhibition before the insensitive, third-person stares of a righteous community? Given such extremes, the attitude that the writing seems to take becomes the only plausible alternative. An irony that sustains an "absolute way of seeing" makes available a form of desire able to identify with the agents' strengths, while exposing their limitations. For the writer, there are infinite Rodolphes: Every character offers the possibility of romance. Yet, if the writer is good enough, he runs no risk of being seduced by that romance. He escapes, not because he represses his emotions, but because he lives them so fully, in the imagining, that they need never be bound to the heteronomous empirical world. Instead of desiring what exists outside his own control, Flaubert directs as much of his investments as he can into the making of textualized feelings, which depend on his own created relationships substituting for the world they evoke. As realist, Flaubert tries to alter nothing in the external world to make it conform to romance desires; as stylist, he tries to put all of that externality under the control of the writerly consciousness and will, flaunting its refusal of bourgeois self-protection.

The significance of Flaubert's achievement has been variously defined. For the generation of the New Critics, that sense of totality was primarily a model for the ability of fiction to maintain nondiscursive forms of "knowing," irreducible to the grosser predicates demanded by the empiricist spirit. Our best contemporary critics of Flaubert give a different epistemological status to this mobile intelligence. Both Jonathan Culler and Ranier Waring, for example, share the New Critical concern for a mode of knowing that resists the certitudes of the empirical understanding. But they also refuse to idealize the achievement of the aesthetic object as a more complete form of knowing. For them, Flaubert's power consists primarily in the subtlety with which he continually undermines meaning: To do that to James was why he came. If, however, we approach Flaubert in the terms I have been using, we begin to wonder whether this stress on meaning and the epistemological status of the fiction affords the most appropriate critical arena. An adequate account of the text must indicate the lines of force established by at least three fundamental factors of the writing: its complex rendering of persons, of scenes, and of the emotions they elicit in the audience; its foregrounding of the authorial act as itself a mode of eliciting and playing out desires; and its constant reminders of the artificiality or constructedness of what nonetheless is capable of shaping emotions that carry over into the world beyond the specific text. Yet the set of concerns organized by issues of indeterminacy seems to me inadequate for this task. That critical perspective lacks the terms for agency allowing it to address the purposiveness behind the textual gestures, especially that set of forces which stages itself as using realism against itself in order to establish an alternative way to live the investments the realism elicits.

Kant's concern for constitutive activity in art, and his general project of examining the nature of understanding, create a climate in which it makes sense to approach the novelist's task less as a matter of providing possible knowledge about the concrete world than as a staging of what an authorial act can do in relation to modern fears about knowledge. Even more important, this emphasis on constitutive activity has direct consequences for how artists might think about the nature of the values they seek through their work. Kant suggests that there are two domains of value: One is based on the prudential principles that are caught up in the heteronomy of all empirical desires (whose name might be Homais), the other is based on the possibility of earning certain kinds of identity through the performative choices that try to enter worlds where heteronomy no longer governs. In Kant, of course, any aesthetic projection of such values can only be a symbol for the moral, since autonomy for an agent depends on her aligning herself with the dictates of rationality. But in Flaubert, the distinctive way in which one achieves a pronounced puposiveness, free of the constraints of conventional understanding, literally becomes one's claim to have achieved a form of autonomy – not simply for the work, but also for the mode of spiritual activity, or absolute "seeing," to which the work testifies.

Imagine that Flaubert had composed a traditional fiction, devoted to positing a coherent interpretation of Emma's tragedy for the delight and edification of the audience. The necessary correlate of this enterprise – the need to contour the rendering to social expectations about coherent actions and possible moral judgments – would have trapped him within the very laws of heteronomy that the novel tries to imagine escaping. To pursue what others interpret as "consistency" is to condemn oneself to the vagaries shaping their tastes and beliefs. And to think that one can ultimately serve ideal readers not subject to those laws is, perhaps, no different from Emma's dreaming of romance lovers and a better life than the provinces afford. Kant could continue to believe that rationality made that ideal reader an audience worth writing for: But that reader has little need for fiction, and even less hope of maintaining his values in a world dominated by figures like Homais.

Flaubert's aesthetic offers a very different route to idealization. He ennobles the activity of writing by having it confront two fundamental Postromantic temptations: to make one's lucidity about the law of heteronomy a justification for a purely parodic attitude toward human desire; and to luxuriate in the pathos of recognizing the ironic limitations of pursuing critical irony. The force doing the confronting is Flaubert's specific version of Kant's notion of "genius": Style remakes a world that, on the level of description, can only be the object of the surgeon's autopsy. Because the fiction composes its world, it establishes a domain where an authorial will can stretch itself to enjoy the panoply of emotions that the imagination can wrest from their tragic consequences. It is that will, then, which can bear the qualities that Kant attributes to "purposiveness," making of them its claim to establish an ethos as responsible for its own constitutive activity as is Kant's rational moral agent.

The inner coherence that in Kant depended on fidelity to the form and content of the rational law is available for artists through the coherence that they give their compositional act. One can determine the value of that coherence without the hypothesis of a categorical imperative, simply by measuring how thoroughly the authorial act defines and tests powers to take responsibility for the world created. Realism becomes a matter not of imitating the world, but of appropriating it within a structure dramatizing particular qualities of the authorial will. Flaubert's realism can be faithful to conditions that warrant a total nihilism and can still claim to transcend that nihilism by elaborating a space for the articulation of a second nature. We never engage an Emma who seems the representation of a real person (as, for example we might find in Henry James's fiction). Rather, we are always watching Flaubert's Emma, and therefore always watching the authorial act engaging in the problems that she encounters. The novel does not cease to refer to the real, but the references now serve primarily as elements in its own struggle to define an attitude that can engage the history which it portrays and despises.

Ultimately, the novel itself responds to the condition of its characters by exemplifying a power to identify with so many emotions that the author depends on no single object of desire for his satisfactions. Instead of pursuing goals projected by these desires, this authorial presence has as its primary goal maintaining its own highest degree of intensity. Flaubert's art projects, as its morality, the possibility of an attitude that can refuse all interest in being either moral or immoral, so that it can pursue states of consciousness richer than either can provide. "Ironic acceptance of existence" frees Flaubert from the anxieties of an Emma and the defensive evasiveness of a Homais. Then the "plastic or complete recasting" of that life through art establishes the claim to dignity that makes this alternative space worth dwelling in. Unlike Homais, the artist can take complete responsibility for the ethos that he projects, because the work, in effect, provides the necessary terms for self-definition. This compositional ethos depends on demonstrating a lucid awareness of the ironies attendant upon the death of God and the consequent decentering of meaning. But it makes that awareness the basis for a new romance site, wherein the mind celebrates its capacity to make a habitable realm by flaunting its own composing of desires otherwise inescapably caught in the law of heteronomy.

III

For Charles Baudelaire, it was Eugène Delacroix's painting that provided the richest version of a new romance site. By setting the spiritual mobility of the colorist against the fixities of what Baudelaire called the "sculptural" ideals that had dominated all of Western thought since the Renaissance, this painter planted the seeds for a relational ontology that could simply bypass the authority of the categorical understanding, without requiring transcendental claims. Having glimpsed that possibility, Baudelaire devoted his poetic career to exploring modes of rhetorical self-consciousness that would create, for writing, the same blend of distance, immediacy, and spiritual mobility that "color" (in his scheme, the opposite of "sculpture") had done for the visual arts. In fact, the poet can lay claim to an even more complete set of spiritual adventures, because language can project more complex modes of ethos and entertain more complex degrees of identification and distance with such projections. Poetry might preserve the intensity of Romantic expressionism, while altering the nature of the expressive subject: Rather than locate the distinctive powers of lyric agency in the scenic history that shapes them, the poet could treat the purposive intelligence within the work as its constituent element, enabling him to combine colorist harmonies with an explicitly self-reflexive grounding of rhetorical passion. Constructivist selves could replace narrated ones, or even those desperate to evoke a specific expressive identity. But this foregrounded self-consciousness faced the dilemma of having to find ways to control or to interpret its freedom, without simply reinstituting romantic irony on other, more psychological grounds.

The implications of Baudelaire's project were perhaps most clearly defined in his review of *Madame Bovary*. Although he acknowledged Flaubert's achievement, Baudelaire projected the lyric poet as the figure best suited to elaborate the romance site created by Flaubert's writerly self-consciousness. Whereas Flaubert had found a place for Kant's principles within the lucid, description-bound mode of documentary realism, Baudelaire insisted on the need for greater identification with Emma's passion. Standing toward Flaubert much as Flaubert did toward Emma, Baudelaire staged himself as a sympathetic observer, trying to identify with the novelist's decision on how to relate to the "desiccated souls" of his time:

> The fact is they [these souls] do not really know what they would like; their one positive dislike is for all great things: unaffected, ardent passion, release of poetic emotion, these things make them blush and affront them. Let us therefore be commonplace in our choice of subject. . . . And let us further studiously avoid letting ourselves go, speaking in our own name. We shall be as cold as ice, as we relate passions and adventures that provide the ordinary run of men with ardent excitement; as they say in the school, we shall be objective and impersonal. . . . We will imprison the warmest, the most burning feelings within the most trivial adventure. The most solemn, the most fateful words will fall from the lips of the most vacuous. . . . I shall proceed, leaning on the twin supports of analysis and logic, and, like that, I shall be able to show convincingly that all subjects are equally good or bad according to the way they are treated, and that the most commonplace can become the best.[8]

The sympathy breaks down almost immediately. The poet must insist that such luxuriant self-control simply does not suffice for fully appreciating the qualities of spirit that Flaubert had given his heroine. As Sartre repeated one hundred years later, Baudelaire argues that Flaubert's obsessive pursuit of autonomy in the form of lucid distance comes dangerously close to repeating the defensive self-protectiveness that characterizes the bourgeois mentality of Homais. The objective novelist cannot be sufficiently lyric:

> I would have found it easy to recognize, under the closely woven texture of *Madame Bovary,* the high capacity for irony and lyricism that extravagantly lights up *La Tentation de Saint Antoine.* Here the poet appears without disguise, and his Bovary, tempted by all the devils of illusion, of heresy, by all the lusts of the physical surroundings – in short, his St Anthony, harassed by all the lunatic urges that get the better of us, would have provided a better apologia than his humble tale of bourgeois life. . . . I should have found it easy to show that Gustave Flaubert has deliberately veiled in *Madame Bovary* the brilliant lyrical and ironic gifts so freely displayed in the *Tentation,* and that this latter work, secret recess of his mind, evidently remains the more interesting one for poets and philosophers. (254–5)

Having failed as a poet, Baudelaire argues, Flaubert could not fully appreciate what his novelistic activity had created. The willingness to risk pathos in the pursuit of emotional intensities repressed by her social order might make Emma herself the age's most complete exemplar of precisely what the novelist lacked:

> And yet Madame Bovary gives herself; carried away by the sophistries of her imagination, she falls magnificently and generously, just as a man would, for cads who are not her equals, just as a poet falls for trollops. . . . In fine, this woman is truly great, but, above all, worthy of pity, and, despite the systematic inflexibility of the author, who has made every effort to withdraw from his work, and to play the part of a puppet showman, all women with intellectual pretensions will be grateful to him for having developed the feminine potential to such a degree of power, so far removed from the pure animal, so close to the ideal man, and for having made it reflect that dual character, compounded of calculation and reverie, that constitutes the perfect being. (251–2)

In Emma's compound of calculation and reverie, Baudelaire finds a mode of lyric lucidity that need not establish itself primarily in opposition to other people's blindness. Rather, the romance site remains within an expressive lyric psyche. But that psyche becomes the central factor in the development of Modernism, because it maintains two crucial differences from Romantic expressivism. Its lyric extremes are always, to some extent, held at a distance, as if the spirit needs to see itself in a play, in order to muster its deeply passionate energies out of the conflicts that self-consciousness experiences. And the "theater" is always built on foregrounding an impersonal "logic of the work itself . . . equal to all the postulates of morality" (250) as its fundamental constitutive mode. Formal activity composes a central dimension of the emotional complex that the work creates. Thus, calculated reverie may be able to preserve both Flaubert's mobility and the distance of absolute irony, while also generating modes of compressed lyric purposiveness that become perhaps the only terms left in which to imagine moral sublimity.

Baudelaire goes on to claim that whereas Flaubert had failed, Delacroix had proved magisterial, providing the necessary model for art's ability to turn its distance into an expansive rhetorical willfulness, aligned with Emma's Romantic expressivism without being trapped within it:

> As great as all the great, as skilled as all the skilled, why does he give us greater pleasure? We could perhaps say that, being endowed with a richer imagination, he expresses in particular the most intimate recesses of the brain and the unexpected aspect of things, such is the fidelity of his work to the character and mood of his conception. The infinite is there in the finite. A dream quality is there, and I mean by "dream," not the store of figments conjured up at night, but the version produced by intense meditation, or, in less fertile intellects, by an artificial stimulant. In a word, the soul at its golden hours, that is Delacroix's theme as a painter.[9] (*Selected Writings* 314; *Oeuvres* 1053)

Although the ideal of self-expression remains, the self to be expressed changes. Instead of the dramatic agent, defining his relation to specific existential conditions, we have the artist's calculated reverie, trying to capture deep, transpersonal recesses of the brain by using his craft as an instrument. This abstracted self makes possible a new definition of the Romantic symbol. There is still the concern for the participation of the finite in the infinite. Now, though, the infinite has only a derivative relation to transcendental aspects of nature. Its basic qualities derive from art's ability to render the logic of "character and mood" produced by intense meditation. What had been the domain of theology now depends on the secularizing skill of the artist. One does not look through the

work to some mysterious nature beyond it; one concentrates on the
intricacy of the psychic states that the meditation itself establishes. Calculated reverie itself suffices to construct those ideal moments when the
soul can figure golden hours or, as "*L'Invitation au Voyage*" puts it,
where "*Tout y parlerait / A l'âme en secret / Sa douce langue natale*"
(Baudelaire 108).

These are ends worth replacing the novel for. But how does one
maintain Flaubert's lucidity? That is where Delacroix's own technical
mastery fleshes out Baudelaire's vision – in the process, inaugurating
what I take to be the single most important principle generating Modernist experiments. Delacroix gives color relations priority over "sculptural" ones, thereby transforming the nature of the modes of coherence
that art must adapt. Under the dispensation of Renaissance sculpture, the
logic of appearance is primary: The work takes hold because of the ways
in which its figures occupy positions in physical space. Color relations
are more fluid, and potentially more abstract. What we take as real
depends more on what the expressive spirit composes out of relational
principles not tied to the laws of gravity, physically or metaphorically.
As Cézanne, then Picasso and Kandinsky would elaborate, in their different ways, the demands of sculpture might impose concepts of mass and
gravity that actually distort the logic of seeing and prevent us from
realizing that the eye, too, is an expressive instrument. Once sculptural
mass becomes merely a derivative aspect of seeing, the eye is freed from
gravity and allowed to occupy the planes composed by the reflective
mind, just as the self freed from "sculptured" identity is also freed to
explore the intricacies of its own involvement in the figural play of the
rhetorics that modeled identity conditions.

Such stakes suggest that we should look very carefully at the passage in
Baudelaire's review of the 1846 Salon Exhibition in which he gives his
fullest interpretation of Delacroix's color at work:

> This great symphony of today, which is the eternally renewed
> variation of the symphony of yesterday, this succession of melo-
> dies, where the variety comes always from the infinite, this
> complex hymn is called colour.
>
> In colour we find harmony, melody and counterpoint. . . .
> Colour, then, means the balance of two tones. A warm tone and
> a cold tone, the contrast between them constituting the whole
> theory, cannot be defined absolutely; they exist only in relation
> to each other. . . . That explains why a colourist can be para-
> doxical in his way of expressing colour and why the study of
> nature often leads to a result quite different from nature. . . .
> The right way of knowing whether a picture is melodious is to

look at it from far enough away to make it impossible for us to
see what it is about or appreciate its lines. If it is melodious, it
has already taken a place in our collection of memories. Style
and feeling in colour come from choice, and choice comes from
temperament. . . .

Sculpture, for which colour is meaningless, and any expression of movement difficult, can have no claim to the attention of an artist particularly dedicated to movement, colour and
atmosphere. These three elements necessarily require shapes that
are not too clearly defined, lines that are light and hesitant, and
bold touches of colour. . . . From Delacroix's standpoint, the
line does not exist; for however fine it be, a teasing geometrician
can always suppose it thick enough to contain a thousand others;
and for colourists, who seek to render the eternal restlessness of
nature, lines are as in the rainbow, nothing but the intimate
fusion of two colours. (56–7, 67)

Purposiveness is no longer simply an intentional state. For Baudelaire
color extends that model in two ways. Color insists on the presence of an
authorial agency that is at once within the work and reflexively removed
from it. And color shows how that agency can be cast in terms of an
ontology substantially different from Kant's. Color aligns the artist with
absolutely concrete and fluid relational systems. They resist interpretation, but less because they are given the rule by the artist's genius than
because his genius has penetrated levels of experience for which old
interpretive instruments are no longer adequate. Whereas an emphasis on
linear modeling had insisted on the heroic willfulness bred of a sharp
opposition between the artist and his materials, these fluid, dreamlike
passages of color across the perceptual field constitute harmonies that
cannot be reduced to subject–object distinctions.

Ethically, the new order demanded that a figure like Colleone – a
monument to sculpture's absolute egoism as it imposes form on inert
objects – yield to the mobile purposiveness capable of appreciating
Emma's sensitive and noble pathos. And ontologically, everything based
on the oppositions necessary for a firm sense of underlying substance
must give way to the primacy of these relational fields. Here idealist
versions of Kant, such as Schelling's aesthetics, modulated into principles
that were to influence strongly both Impressionism and Symbolisme,
producing more similarity than difference in doctrines otherwise far
apart. Instead of imagining minds and worlds, or subjects and objects, in
two-term oppositional relationships or theologically grounded moments
of symbolic fusion, this ontology casts its poles as inherently caught up
in one another. Where the self or the subject was, there is now the

"temperament," a mode of purposive compositional agency so fine that it cannot be separated from the scenes that activate and dispose its investments. Temperament is Wordsworth's scenic self, freed from its need for dialectical self-interpretation. Similarly, where individual objects had been, the external world takes form primarily as a sense of atmosphere, which blends physical properties with attributes of tone, shades, and movement that seem to require psychological predicates. Under the haze of distance, a new immediacy is born: Substance is no longer a dominant lack of spirit, begging for the incarnational grace of the symbol, and spirit is no longer an essentially rational activity, at its purest when distanced from the empirical self. In art, at least, all appearances clearly depend on the way in which the work constitutes an immediate process of calculated selections, which can be said to reveal the person to his or her self, at the same time as they give a particular tonality to the world. The spirit knows itself, and indulges itself, by watching the aura of differences that its own contribution makes to the way in which a given scene recedes into a second nature, comprised of mutually sustaining, harmonious interrelations.[10]

What poetry needed, and what Baudelaire's work promised, was not a truer self, but a richer self-consciousness about the range of constitutive rhetorical energies that can maintain complex purposive sites – and hence possible selves. The aim was not truth per se: neither truth to self nor truth to nature. What mattered was the intensity and scope used in deploying a range of psychic energies within a relational field. In order for that field to be fully self-conscious, poetry had to learn to treat its own rhetorical energies in the same way that Delacroix had treated color. Only then would art rouse the soul to its full powers, and only then would the world of objects yield to Keats's domain of constitutive energies, where we become aware of the range of states available to that soul.[11]

Poetry, then, is eloquence. Eloquence is normally associated with a voice around which a community can form, even if the eloquence originates in the private meditations of an isolated, contemplative ego such as Wordsworth's, but Baudelaire locates eloquence simply as the display of mind, dominating its model in nature "just as the creator dominates his creation" (66). Insistent poetic rhetoric defines a mode of self-legislation that can free itself of melodramatic expressivism, not by purifying its gestures, but by subordinating them to the deliberate, calculating self. It becomes possible, therefore, to combine radically disjunct attitudes, as if rhetoric related to ordinary language in the same way that a half-playful "perversity" does to "normal" sexuality. The excess disturbs an audience and poses the self as divided between responding to an object and watching itself respond as its ordinary expectations break down. Yet, as

the poet watches himself trying to invent a self in the midst of constructing genuine passions, he indeed stages the process of creating a second
nature capacious enough (and capricious enough) to allow consciousness
the largest possible field of relations for its energies.

That field sets in motion a mobility that is everywhere at once overdetermined and underdetermined. We know that each utterance is an
expression of deep lyric need; yet the language is so exaggerated, or so
fluid, in its movement that we must see each pose as somehow already
partially rejected by the persona. The symbols or correspondences that
we find do not so much lead us back into the world as guide us to modes
of self-reflection in which we watch the symbols being composed. Instead of nature containing the mind and rewarding its efforts, the mind
must be seen as the container of nature, giving it life and depth by
submitting it to the evasions, doublings, and confusions that comprise
the life of the individual psyche.

IV

Baudelaire has two fundamental ways of elaborating these rhetorical supplements. The first, basic to poems such as *"L'Incompatibilité"*
and *"Harmonie du Soir,"* develops mood states that virtually parallel the
reveries that he finds in Delacroix.[12] The second is more important for
this study, because it extends the rhetoric of mood into a self-conscious
exploration of the qualities of ethos that the mood can sustain, preparing
the way for Modernist efforts to make the poetics of mood bear the
weight of exploring new modes of agency. The emphasis, in Baudelaire's poems, is still on complex emotional states, but now attention is
focused on the kind of composing agent who can provoke the emotions
and make them part of a repertoire of roles projected into public life.
Whereas Wordsworth built a dialectical, self-reflexive philosopher out of
his scenic encounters, Baudelaire presented his moods as states transforming that humanist model of nobility into the dandy as a self-staging
"aristocrat":

> Contrary to what a lot of thoughtless people seem to believe,
> dandyism is not even an excessive delight in clothes and material
> elegance. For the perfect dandy these things are no more than the
> symbol of the aristocratic superiority of his mind. . . . [His pas-
> sion] is above all the burning desire to create a personal form of
> originality, within the external limits of social conventions. It is
> a kind of cult of the ego which can still survive the pursuit of that
> form of happiness to be found in others, in woman, for exam-
> ple, which can even survive what are called illusions. . . .

> Clearly then dandyism in certain respects comes close to spir-
> ituality and to stoicism. . . . Let the reader not be shocked by
> this mixture of the grave and the gay; let him rather reflect that
> there is a sort of grandeur in all follies, a driving power in every
> sort of excess. A strange form of spirituality indeed. . . . Dan-
> dyism appears especially in those periods of transition when
> democracy has not yet become all-powerful, and when aristoc-
> racy is only partially weakened and discredited. In the confusion
> of such times, a certain number of men . . . may conceive the
> idea of establishing a new kind of aristocracy. (420–1)

One could easily insist that this projection merely stages the artist as a
pseudoaristocrat, walking down Piccadilly with a poppy or a lily in his
medieval hand, deluding himself into thinking that he can evade his
bourgeois origins. But that view may too easily sustain our own bourgeois comforts. It may therefore be worthwhile to attempt to read this
rhetoric carefully, noticing that its intricate self-consciousness imagines a
mode of agency bound neither to the duplicities of "sincerity" nor to the
dominant public models of the "*chic*" and the "*poncif,*" which Baudelaire
saw as reducing art to conventional finish and monumentalizing gesture
(86). The dandy denies all conventions – not by rejecting them for more
direct expressive energies, but by making them simply the repertoire
through which spirit performs its self-legislating acts.[13] The stance of the
dandy, then, promises to restore the lyric powers of the imagination, in
the form of a flexible and sinuous tonal accompaniment to all public
roles, including its own overt manifestation as a mode of fashion. Thus,
as Baudelaire's statement indicates, the elements of the work are to be
viewed as "symbols," not of underlying realities, but of infinite qualities
that can be teased out by the composing mind. The aim is not truth, but
life; not answers or models, but testimony to powers that are still under
the control of the spirit.

Notice, for example, how the passage plays with its own discomfort.
We see this first in the vacillation, in the opening lines, between a desire
to shock and a fear of being misunderstood as someone concerned only
to shock. A few sentences later, Baudelaire directly faces those fears,
showing his awareness that the dandy's desire to assert himself as an
aristocrat may be an illusion. But it only "may" be an illusion, so one
needs to find room for the possibility by not surrendering to an overly
eager and gross sense of the demands of truth. Then the various strands
become the pretext for the synthesis of the "grave" and the "gay," in
those marvelous closing lines that situate the dandy as "the last flicker of
heroism," simultaneously asserting and denying its power as it tries to
bridge two cultures. This is not Flaubert's savage irony, turned against

the author himself as he begins to feel Emma's charms. Rather, it is an irony that dramatizes the constitutive elements of a complex soul, too aware of the intricacies of life to indulge in a completely corrosive rhetoric. Disgust at self and others gives way to a calculated access to reverie, where a traditional lyric desire joins another, more reflexive lyricism, born of exalted resignation.

What the prose adumbrates, the poetry elaborates. The ever-present irony requires Baudelaire to seek a poetry of expressive character, but on a more abstract level than that sought by his Romantic predecessors. Claims to sincerity or to truths outside the self must yield to a sincerity won virtually despite itself – not by reference to the autobiographical agent, but by virtue of the particular manner in which the purposive work puts a soul together, as it marries classical syntactic balance to an involuted, self-dispersing sensibility. As Baudelaire put it, speaking of Goya's "monstrous kind of verisimilitude," it must be impossible to detect "the seam, the juncture between the real and the fantastic. . . , so transcendent and natural at one and the same time is the art displayed" (238). By this seaming, one forges the sublimities of a self-legislating sensibility that is responsive to the constant sense of discontinuity that characterizes modernity.

The best example of Baudelaire's version of the sublime may well be "*Une Charogne*" (Carrion). No other poem has so elaborate a sense of the radical powerlessness before nature that demands a human sublime, and no other poem so brilliantly plays on the idea of correspondences, now in the form of failed sacraments that require a new religion. Although the poem is too long for extended discussion here, its dominant effects are so strong as to emerge even in a fairly cursory treatment. The opening offers a version of "Dover Beach":

> *Rappelez-vous l'objet que nous vîmes, mon âme,*
> *Ce beau matin d'été si doux:*
> *Au détour d'un sentier une charogne infâme*
> *Sur un lit semé de cailloux,*
>
> *Les jambes en l'air, comme une femme lubrique,*
> *Brûlante et suant les poisons,*
> *Ouvrait d'une façon nonchalante et cynique*
> *Son ventre plein d'exhalaisons.*
>
> *Le soleil rayonnait sur cette pourriture,*
> *Comme afin de la cuire à point,*
> *Et de rendre au centuple à la grande Nature*
> *Tout ce qu'ensemble elle avait joint;*

Et le ciel regardait la carcasse superbe
Comme une fleur s'épanouir.
La puanteur était si forte, que sur l'herbe
Vous crûtes vous évanouir.

(47–8)

[Remember, O my soul, that thing we saw on that fine summer's morning, so mild: there where the path turned, a disgust-
ing corpse on a bed of shingle, with its legs in the air like a lewd
woman, burning and oozing poisons, nonchalantly and cyni-
cally opened its stinking belly.

The sun was shining on that rotten meat as if to roast it to a
turn, and to render a hundredfold to Nature all that she had
brought together; while the sky looked down on that proud
carcass, watching it blossom like a flower, and the stench was so
strong that you all but fainted on the grass.]

This is a romance about the perversion of romance. The frame of
casual conversation between lovers sharing a memory sets up expectations about content and tone that the poem plays upon as its basis for the
contrasts necessary to the sublime. On the level of content, the poem
opens a terrifying gulf between the correspondences with nature that we
embrace under the rubric of eros and the inescapable heteronomy imposed upon us by nature's laws. The same contradictions emerge on the
level of diction, suggesting that what overthrows the mind's capacities,
in good sublime fashion, is not nature itself, but our own "overdetermining" nature into mythic patterns that make us vulnerable to ironic
inversions, like those at work in the poem. Even when the corpse comes
into focus, it continues to elicit traditional lyric language, marvelously
accurate in this odd context. The position and state of decay of the body
are surprisingly similar to a *"femme lubrique:"* Nature wrought to its
uttermost. This is nature at one with itself, with the carcass strangely like
a flower in an inhuman world for which all scents are equal narcissistic
celebrations of that unity. Such scents even warrant, in their fashion, the
romantic state of feeling that one's passion is so strong that one will faint
on the grass.

That very overdetermination, however, eventually also makes possible the grounds for a sublimity that offers a form of power adequate to
this dizzying sight. The power is not God's, but man's; not an ultimate
link between man and forces beyond his ken, but testimony to a self-
sufficient second nature, available to one so in control of himself that he
can inhabit the ironies and find, in his awareness of his limits, a site
against sight, where the composing will can celebrate its own grim forms
of sacramental play:

Et pourtant vous serez semblable à cette ordure,
À cette horrible infection,
Étoile de mes yeux, soleil de ma nature,
*   Vous, mon ange et ma passion!*

Oui! telle vous serez, ô la reine des grâces
*   Après les derniers sacrements,*
Quand vous irez, sous l'herbe et les floraisons grasses,
*   Moisir parmi les ossements.*

Alors, ô ma beauté! dites à la vermine
*   Qui vous mangera de baisers,*
Que j'ai gardé la forme et l'essence divine
*   De mes amours décomposés!*

                                    (49–50)

[And yet, you will come to resemble that offal, that loathsome corruption, O star of my eyes, O sun of my nature, my angel and my passion! Yes, such will you be, O Queen of graces, after the last sacraments, when you will go down beneath the grass and unctuous flowers to turn green among the bones. Then, O my beauty, tell the vermin which will devour you with kisses, how I have immortalized the form and divine essence of my decayed loves.]

Dialogue, here, does not lead out to a deepening of the lovers' communion with each other, at least not in the way that it does in "Dover Beach." But neither is there Arnold's passivity and pathos. The lover can do something – can construct a lucidity able to counter death, by making his "*amours décomposés*" (decayed loves) an emblem both of the terrifying bond between doomed lovers and of what the poet makes by his decomposing of nature's laws into this set of fluid, tonally intricate gestures. Thus the final triumphant lines vacillate between self-disgust at assuming so self-pitying a stance, and the full arrogance of affirming the poetic power to restore a version of the romance site so lovingly destroyed in those opening stanzas. This poet has encountered the essence of heteronomy and partially conquered it by dramatizing a mobility at least its equal. In this mobility, Kant's autonomy and dignity find a new site, perhaps more habitable, in its duplicities, than anything that rationality can construct.

V

"*Une Charogne*" presents the rhetorical Baudelaire at the height of his powers. But Baudelaire proved too much the true Romantic to trust such triumphant moments without feeling compelled to examine what might lie hidden within or occluded by them. He had to ask why such powers are necessary, and whether the person who one thereby becomes makes the best use of the self-reflexive dimensions that characterize the richest forms of spirituality. Such questions, however, were to prove more destructive than even he expected, generating forms of infinite regress that were eventually to force at least Mallarmé and Eliot to turn against the influence that had at first made them absolutely modern.

"L'Albatros" beautifully defines the issues at stake. For it makes visible a rich set of tensions between a pathos-laden dramatic situation and the author's efforts to take an ironic distance from the lyric rhetoric that the situation elicits. In the first three stanzas, we encounter a lurid scene that allegorically stages mimetic representation as a process of mind torturing its own deepest lyric possibilities:

> Souvent, pour s'amuser, les hommes d'equipage
> Prennent des albatros, vastes oiseaux des mers,
> Qui suivent, indolents compagnons de voyage,
> Le navire glissant sur les gouffres amers.
>
> A peine les ont-ils déposés sur les planches,
> Que ces rois de l'azur, maladroits et honteux,
> Laissent piteusement leurs grandes ailes blanches
> Comme des avirons traîner a côté d'eux.
>
> Ce voyageur ailé, comme il est gauche et veule!
> Lui, naguère si beau, qu'il est comique et laid
> L'un agace son bec avec un brûle-gueule,
> L'autre mime, en boitant, l'infirme qui volait!
>
> (8)

[Often, for their amusement, sailors catch albatross, those vast birds of the seas, indolent companions of their voyages, that follow the ship gliding across the bitter seas.

No sooner have the sailors stretched them out on the deck than those kings of the azure, awkward and ashamed, let their long white wings trail painfully by their side, like oars.

How ungainly, how contemptible the winged traveller becomes, how laughable and graceless, he who but a moment ago was so full of beauty. A sailor teases his beak with a pipe; another drags his foot to mimic the cripple who once soared through the air.]

Even the poet's language seems caught up in this conflict between the birds' potential for flight and the objectifying force of the mimicry that subjects them to the sailors' will. In the first stanza, the authorial presence hangs over the details with the same careless ease as the albatross, because the sentence suspends the simple transitive links between subject, predicate, and object, producing instead an elaborate appositional indolence. With the second stanza, point of view elaborates what syntax had inaugurated. As we enter the birds' perspective, we experience their passive victimage as another chain of appositional phrases – now less a sign of indolence than a means of making concrete the feeling of wings forced to carry the symbolic weight of their clumsiness and shame. That identification quickly shifts, in the third stanza, to what seems an omniscient view, able to encompass the entire scene from a distance. Yet we are by now so bound to our identifications that the distance itself also embodies a possible point of view that the birds can have toward their own plight. We see from a distance the view that the birds must have of their own powerlessness as they submit to the sailor's miming, which deprives them of freedom and dignity.

This, one might say, is the deep emotional logic of mimesis: The figure for romantic spirit is forced to watch passively while some alien force assumes the authority to treat subjective life as if it were material for an autopsy. The king of the skies loses not only his native domain, but any hope of asserting an identity in his loss, because now his identity depends on being mimicked. A monstrous double defines how he can be seen on the ship, and, in the process, becomes the only thing he can see. The infirm could once fly (and would fly, we also hear in the conditional), just as it can recognize itself as once beautiful. But memory serves only to exacerbate the violation, since it intensifies the oppressive taunts of these miming representatives of the social order, and leaves one trapped in precisely the modes of psychic life that are vulnerable to such power.

The more complex this little drama becomes, the harder it gets to understand why, when revising this poem, Baudelaire could remain satisfied with this concluding stanza:

> *Le poëte est semblable au prince des nuées*
> *Qui hante la tempête et se rit de l'archer;*
> *Exilé sur le sol au milieu des huées,*
> *Ses ailes de géant l'empêchent de marcher.*
>
> (9)

> [The poet shares the fate of this prince of the clouds, who rejoices in the tempest, mocking the archer below; exiled on earth, an object of scorn, his giant wings impede him as he walks.]

Leo Bersani suggests that such rhetoric provides an idealized escape "from the anxieties . . . of psychic mobility, of unanchored identity" set free by the earlier materials (*Baudelaire and Freud* 2). Indeed when mobility so readily gets trapped in pathos, the bird's powers so completely subordinated to the realm of the mimers, there is good reason to attempt to reclaim the poet's authority over the sailors by making the bird's suffering the justification for his own self-congratulatory image of persecuted nobility. But by 1859 such naive bids for pathos are rare in Baudelaire, especially in a situation where it would be difficult not to see that the rhetorical effort to ennoble the poet threatens to impose on him the same kind of alien forms appropriating the bird's spirit of flight to their own vicious games. So we probably come closer to the poem's full purposive energies if we concentrate on how well this closing rhetorical gesture extends the plays on obsession and judgment, distance and sympathy, that permeate the poem. The final rhetorical gesture then becomes one more overdetermined act in a poem based on highly complex identifications.

By the end of the third stanza, there are not one but two potentially exemplary states in the poem: that of the passive, tormented bird, and that of the tormenting sailor, whose distanced manipulation has more to do with calculated reverie than Baudelaire wants to dwell on. So the conclusion must take responsibility for both identifications, melding the energy of the sailor and the injured nobility of the albatross, while hoping to compensate for the limitations in each by invoking the opposite strength. A lyricized sailor might give a voice to the imprisoned spirit of plight, but, just as the two may complement one another, they may also clash in ways that exacerbate one another's limitations. Every effort to identify with the bird may mock the bird's suffering. Just as the sailors revel in their greater material power, the authorial presence would be using its position to impose an unearned and self-pitying parallel between their plights. The poet comes to praise, not to mock, yet it is terribly easy to surrender a potential freedom of flight to the strained and overblown phrases that appeal to those confined to the narrow world of the ship. This rhetorician too must fly dangerously close to the "*navire glissant*" (gliding ship), where he shares the sailor's incapacity to do anything more than deform as he mimes. His efforts may even have the same effect as the other sailor's "*brule-gueule*" (pike). For the very pathos of the rhetoric only dooms the poet to exaggerate his suffering, as the proof of his authenticity, in an endless cycle that, Baudelaire is beginning to recognize, has governed his own lyricizing of pain into real torment.[14]

Insofar as his was an expressive, rather than a mimetic enterprise, Baudelaire could claim to be different from these sailors. But he was becoming increasingly aware that both modes of relating to the world depend on forms of staging their material that necessarily displace it. So he tried to shift the focus to this kind of necessarily failed performance, which brings the poet much closer to the bird's vulnerability than his stage rhetoric can control. This victimage may even be self-inflicted. The poet is the dupe of his own desire for aggrandizement, which subjects him to an absurd rhetoric that not even he can quite believe. This realization, though, aligns the poet more with the sailors than with the birds, since it situates him at a similar terrifying distance from what he observes. So a gorgeously balanced syntactic structure at once mocks its need for idealization and seeks, in that mockery, a deeper link between the poet and the bird. The effort to glorify the poet strains credulity, but the strain itself, tinged with irony, ends up as a telling reminder of how much this poet's miming becomes a form of broken wings, making it impossible to negotiate the practical world. The poet may not be able to haunt the clouds, but the desire itself is sufficient for his full empathy with a suffering that he repeats as he tries to articulate it.

If we imagine Baudelaire in control of all of these ramifications, we can describe his basic gift to Modernist poetry as the elaboration of a site that enables the poet to hover just off the ship's stern. He cannot soar without provoking mockery, yet he can so master his own involvement in the conditions provoking mockery that he wins a slight degree of freedom from the sailors, whose art he has also internalized. The more vicious he becomes toward his own temptation to lyric escape, the more he continues to sanction at least one mode of self-legislating freedom. The poet's act opens seams in the real by weaving into our sensations qualities of the fantastic and of the infinitely intricate that cannot be dismissed, but must remain in a constant, irreducible interplay: which simply is the available life of spirit. The more the poet's rhetoric stages a self-reflexive irony, the more that irony generates a condition of pathos that no analytic stance can explain, or otherwise master, without finding itself exposed as another version of the sailor's cruelty, not even defensible by the slim justification that one is aware of one's necessities. Spirit lives in the shadows that understanding casts, and it thrives in a poetry that can pervade these shadows at – and as – will.

VI

Even this form of spirituality, however, seems inadequate to the suspicions about poetic rhetoric that emerge in the last stanza of "*L'Albatros.*" Baudelaire's freedom as a rhetorical and expressivist ironist depended on a capacity to do, in lyric language, what Flaubert had done in dealing with characters: maintain a fluidity that, in overdetermining all that it confronts, remains itself sufficiently underdetermined to imagine itself free within what the irony exposes. Baudelaire's example could even be considered a more livable one than Flaubert's, because, as a lyric poet, Baudelaire has a mobility that does not depend on maintaining distance from the world of empirical desires. Rather, a mobile imagination extends the self through a series of lyric identifications, with the poem the testimony that one sensibility can so legislate its own investments. The poet is everywhere, absorbing all scenic content into analogies that enable him both to make and to play out his complex psyche. But as he tries to find a rhetoric that can ennoble that state, the entire edifice threatens to crumble under the irony it had been able to master.

Again the problem of allegory, which we encountered in Chapter 3, returns. To the degree that the poet's rhetoric seeks a content, in addition to the modes of identification that it elicits, it requires grounds that its own mobility constantly undercuts. Or so Baudelaire seems to think, as he turns to the disturbing form of distance characterizing what we might call the "splenetic" mode of his late poetry. There the marvelous mobility of the shape changer comes to seem a pathetic set of variations on a single theme: the need to escape an ennui that exposes the inescapable banality of the very spirit that Baudelaire had tried to project as a fascinating alternative to positivist culture. Under this pressure, the old dream seems mere complicity in the realm of hypocrite authors and readers. A true alternative to such lives would require presenting the "I" as able to master the ennui engendered by his own performative rhetoric, so that the self becomes no more, and no less, than a simple fact among the facts comprising the order of nature. Yet as Baudelaire tries to muster the necessary discipline, he cannot avoid the awareness, and the self-disgust accompanying it, that in so staging the lucid self he still seeks rather cheap lyric consolations and has no way, within his poetic, to take control over that reliance on pathos.

A spirit based on rhetoricity can never lament its choices without confirming them – the law, perhaps, of an infinite irony different from that developed by Kant's heirs, who were in search of a sublime that could never be called to account by language. Baudelaire had sought to return self-conscious rhetoricity to Romantic poetry; now he had to face the fact that he had succeeded all too well. There seems to be no lyric state not reducible to a set of linguistic roles and appeals to an audience's sympathy. Even as one tries to imagine a liberating privacy, one finds roles, more roles. Infinite irony then takes on a different tinge. Rather than providing access to a transcendental principle no longer definable within doctrinal modes, this irony is infinite only because it is endlessly regressive. The constitutive spirit finds itself bound to a "voracious irony" (159), which can imagine as its alternative only a "*Goût du Néant*" (longing for nothingness) giving self-disgust the means to realities not tarnished by the theatrical self. What begins as a romance, where the mobile spirit can transform corpses into an erotic lyric theater, becomes a condition in which every lyric gesture offers as its shadow a glimpse of the corpse that ought at least to have the self-control to stop appealing for pity.

This splenetic phase of Baudelaire's career demands a few moments of abstract reflection, because it can be said to articulate the fundamental limitations within the one nineteenth-century movement that seemed capable of linking lucidity with the lyric pursuit of modes of agency worth idealizing. That, in turn, enables us to appreciate the complexity and comprehensiveness of the critical acts performed by early Modernists such as Eliot, as they attempted the kind of anatomy of this style that Flaubert had devoted to realism. And it prepares us to understand how important the alternative view of art inaugurated by Impressionism was to become, because it allowed artists to graft the mobility achieved by Baudelaire onto a sense of the world not trapped by the "contrived corridors" of rhetorical self-consciousness.

"*Le Jeu*" (The gamble) shows very clearly what becomes of one who can recognize the situation facing the poet in "*L'Albatros*." A once-confident, satanic rhetoric, celebrating the capacity of constitutive spirit to provide alternatives to all of the categories that sustain divine authority, now turns on itself in disgust. The poem opens with an elaborate description of a gambling hall. The list of characters, too much like the membership list of a retirement home for satanic figures, ends with the saddest of all, "*pöetes illustres / . . . viennent gaspiller leurs sanglantes sueurs*" (illustrious poets who come to squander their bloody perspiration). Then we find out that the image is a dream, defining the poet's own sense of distance from even these roles, so intense is his self-consciousness:

> *Voilà le noir tableau qu'en un rêve nocturne*
> *Je vis se dérouler sous mon oeil clairvoyant.*
> *Moi-même, dans un coin de l'antre taciturne,*
> *Je me vis accoudé, froid, muet, enviant,*
>
> *Enviant de ces gens la passion tenace,*
> *De ces vielles putains la funèbre gâité,*
> *Et tous gaillardement trafiquant à ma face,*
> *L'un de son vieil honneur, l'autre de sa beauté!*
>
> *Et mon coeur s'effraya d'envier maint pauvre homme*
> *Courant avec ferveur à l'abîme béant*
> *Et qui, soûl de son sang, préférerait en somme*
> *La douleur à la mort et l'enfer au néant!*
>
> (173–4)

[Such is the sombre picture that in a dream, one night, I saw unfold before my seer's gaze. I saw myself in a corner of that silent den, myself leaning there on my elbows, cold, speechless, and envying, yes envying those people's intense passion, the old bawd's dismal sprightliness, and all of them as they cheerfully sold, under my very nose, one, his long-established honor, the other, her beauty. And my heart brimmed with fear that I should envy many a poor man hastening so eagerly towards the gaping pit, who, drunk with his own blood, would really prefer pain to death, and hell to nothingness.]

The gamblers have the intensity of their roles. Drunk on that intensity, they can imagine the sublimities of rebellion and risk staged in earlier Baudelaire poems. But the poet now only watches and wonders. And what a watching! At the very center of the poem, the eye that had looked out must turn on itself in a gesture of self-alienation that is often at the basis of Baudelaire's heroic roles. Now, however, watching the self cannot elicit the old rhetorical theater. The poet tries, running through a series of participles, in the hope that he may strike a chord able to summon another heroic gesture. Yet only one predicate sticks, that of the condition of envy, which comes to dominate the rest of the poem.

Baudelaire has come a long way from his earlier theatrics. As Dante knew, envy is perhaps the one psychic state utterly incompatible with heroism, because it condemns the agent to passivity and puts the burden of acting and feeling on others. Satanism is doubly removed: The poet lacks the passion to take risks, and he has too much self-knowledge to continue believing that lyric intensity is worth pursuing, given the illusions that it necessarily reinforces. However, Baudelaire cannot avoid trying to make even this refusal sublime. The final stanza's beautifully balanced clauses in effect assert an essential nobility in the heart that must make such refusals. But now the albatross has clearly recognized that much of its claim on an audience depends on the work of the sailor, who in fact dwells within his breast. So the appeal to pathos becomes a final compelling case for the need to turn to a radical contrast, to a *néant* that can put all dreams of flight to rest, even the one that hopes to find nobility in that very gesture.[15]

Yet nothingness will not come to the poet. As Eliot will insist, two conditions deny that blessing. No matter how lucid the poet, memory and desire will each provoke and torment the other. Once, Baudelaire could dream that his mobile spirit might travel to exotic sites where one could recognize *"les urnes d'amour dont vos grands coeurs sont pleins"* (19) (the urns of love with which your great hearts brim), and the very imagination of voyaging would produce in the poet's heart the chant of the mariners (56). The imagination might even make death itself give up its secrets: "*que la Mort, planant comme un soleil nouveau, / Fera s'épanouir les fleurs de leur cerveau!*" (83) (that death, soaring like a new sun, will make bloom the flowers of their brain). Now, though, the sublime lucidity of a "*conscience dans le mal*" (158) (consciousness in evil) finds itself forced to a distance not redeemable as atmosphere. Consciousness of evil can only be consciousness circulating about evil, as it circulates about everything else, at once too possessive and too impotent to bring phenomena to full life. Even the quest for nothing must be resigned to writing poems about it, displacing that, too, into something like mere theater. Born in the desire for self-legislation, Baudelaire's mobility expires in "Au Lecteur"'s realization that constitutive processes without grounds in natural or social life depend, for their energy, on cannibalizing their own products:

> La sottise, l'erreur, le péché, la lésine
> Occupent nos esprits et travaillent nos corps,
> Et nous alimentons nos aimables remords,
> Comme les mendiants nourrissent leur vermine.
>
> (154)

[Stupidity, error, sin, and meanness possess our minds and work on our bodies, and we feed our fond remorses as beggars suckle their own lice.]

5

Eliot's Symboliste Subject as End and Beginning

I

It proved quite easy for poets to imitate Baudelaire's moods and provocative gestures. But to engage Baudelaire was a much more difficult enterprise. How could one stand against such a master of intricate irony without exposing oneself as either a naive sentimentalist or an anxiety-prone coward, unable to bear the complexities of one's own psyche? For Mallarmé, and then for T. S. Eliot, transforming those ironies required turning to modes of abstraction that redirected Baudelaire's mobility toward more metaphysical domains. For them, mobility served less as end than as means, establishing, in its flight from the empirical, certain endur-ing needs and demands that the imagination could try to pursue by modifying Baudelaire's strategies. On the one hand, experience must be broken down into constituents much finer and more fluid than the con-fines of a melodramatic personal theater could produce; on the other, such analytic procedures had to generate new versions of compositional agen-cy. There was no escaping self-consciousness: There could be ways to transform the abstracted voice that haunted Baudelaire's personal gestures into an entirely impersonal, or transpersonal, presence. Such a locus for eloquence might allow the work's formal intensities to provide the lyric spirit a substance too deep and resilient for any irony to dispel, or even reduce to expressivist psychology.

Mallarmé's way had involved an elaborate rhetoric of Nietzschean forgetting, intended to project the spirit's mobility on the whitest of pages, so that none of its intricacy might be lost to merely empirical factors. Eliot's project is to me the more impressive and significant, because it took as its stage the very historical processes that seemed to have made it necessary to confront Baudelaire as "the greatest exemplar in modern poetry."[1] Eliot's abstraction became a way of turning history against itself: If he could understand both the emotional pressures that required Baudelaire's reaction to Romantic expressivism and the problems driving late Baudelaire to his splenetic phase, Eliot might be able to test a new poetry by dramatizing the fundamental forces that were shaping its needs and possibilities. Whereas Baudelaire's Kantian second nature remained at the mercy of the individual psyche, Eliot's form of historicism might engage a more Hegelian version of that constructed site in which rhetorical energies reveal transpersonal needs and desires, given shape within history but projecting beyond it. The aim was not to explain that history, but to frame it, so that the poem's linguistic resources become vehicles for at once analyzing the sources of Victorian anxieties and providing different versions of the lyric spirit, less bound to the cultural dilemmas creating those anxieties. Such a project would then make it possible to modify the resources of French Symbolisme to address the limitations of an Anglo-American cultural heritage.[2]

II

The opening of "The Love Song of J. Alfred Prufrock" affords a superb example of how the young Eliot, combining Baudelairean mobility with Flaubertian distance, elaborated a mode of abstraction able to define and to combat the spiritual dilemmas that he inherited from the Victorians:

> Let us go then, you and I,
> When the evening is spread out against the sky
> Like a patient etherised upon a table;
> Let us go through certain half-deserted streets,
> The muttering retreats
> Of restless nights in one-night cheap hotels
> And sawdust restaurants with oyster shells:
> Streets that follow like a tedious argument of insidious
>   intent
> To lead you to an overwhelming question. . .
> Oh, do not ask, 'what is it?'
> Let us go and make our visit.[3]

Baudelaire's mobility here takes the sublimely ironic form of leading us rapidly through at least three of the Baudelaires elaborated by his heirs.

The first two lines offer a somewhat neurasthenic lover, inviting us on a mood-filled walk through some exotic urban neighborhoods, in the mode of Oscar Wilde or Arthur Symons. But this speaker soon proves unfit for their poems, because he cannot take his pleasures in a sufficiently civilized and discriminating manner. So charged is the scene with indefinable subjective implications that the dissociated self-consciousness of Gérard de Nerval and Jules Laforgue keeps breaking in. Finally, the overall situation presents a version of the mode that Eliot insists was Baudelaire's major invention: the transformation of Romantic nature poetry into a "poetry of flight," which so deeply registers the frustrations of empirical existence that, despite itself, it betrays "the direction of beatitude," by suffusing the whole with a religious desperation (*Selected Essays* 379). In "Prufrock," all three modes combine to match the effect of competing voices in Baudelaire's late poetry: Since no single style can take control, the mobile spirit is trapped by the very multiplicity that was to have been its spiritual strength in a world dominated by categorical rigidity. It is this level that gives the title its resonance: How can there be a love poem when there is no one lover? How can there be a lover when all of the gestures available to him are at once underdetermined, in their inadequacy to express feelings, and overdetermined, with respect to the history of lyric rhetorics?

"Prufrock" presents Baudelaire's mobile spirit, tempered by Laforgue's more intricately ironic self-consciousness. But the more one hears those voices, the more one is also struck by the need to introduce a fourth system of coordinates, framing this psychological intricacy by means of the more overtly formal experimentation fostered in poets such as Mallarmé. In Baudelaire's lyricism, all of the ironies ultimately lead back to the exemplary sublimity of the speaker, both victim and hero of his corrosive intelligence and exquisite sensitivity. Eliot, on the other hand, is not content with self-theatricalizing claims that one is heroic simply because one creates a complex psychological space out of the folds one weaves from materialist culture. Eliot's poem is suffused by an oppressive desire not to be Prufrock – not to be caught in the metaphoric web that absorbs the world into the sensibility, and not to attract "pain to himself" as his excuse for reveling in the strength "merely to *suffer*" (374). This demands a different kind of irony from the one that permitted Baudelaire the luxury of simultaneously seeing through his speaker's rhetoric and identifying with the pathos of the voice. Now, the more Romantic the temptation, the more haunting the dream of classicists like Arnold, and realists like Flaubert, that an author can establish another level in the work, judging the lyric character as a historically shaped set of symptomatic behaviors that the poet is trying to get beyond.

But how can one construct such a context without that too becoming grist for Baudelaire's theatrics? It seems as if the ideal of knowing one's limitations is now less a classical restoration of balance than an irresistible excuse for pathos, since one thereby lays claim both to the power of knowledge and the impotence of that form of heroism. Thus "Prufrock" faces a formidable task. It must be able to treat Baudelaire's tension between knowledge and will sympathetically, as the fundamental modern dilemma; yet it must not take itself so seriously that it celebrates having defined a psychology that makes suffering a form of nobility. It must resist Romantic pity for the sensitivity so anatomized, without turning the religious subtext into pure farce. And it must try to locate through form a relatively independent vantage point from which to maintain the necessary distance.

I think this need for distance required Eliot to elaborate a style that projected a unique and powerful model of self-referential authorial activity, paralleling that explored in Modernist painting. There must be a character in "Prufrock" who is not seduced by Prufrock, yet who is not willing to dismiss the religious subtext of Prufrock's speech. Or, to put the same point more in the spirit of Modernist painting, there must be an authorial site where powers are marshaled and tested for their ability to negotiate the double bind of having both to sympathize with and to resist Prufrock's fantasies. Eliot responded to this challenge primarily by putting Mallarmé to Arnoldian ends. Insistent that poetic discursiveness must choke on its own rhetoricity, Eliot turned Mallarmé's dense internal formal relations into his means of responding to the contrived corridors of historical life. Then, what had been means for constructing an abstract meditative site could serve as vehicles by which the composing intelligence might reach beyond Prufrock's specific psychological dilemmas to tease out levels of the language and of the culture trapping him within nineteenth-century attitudes toward personal expression. Understanding is not overcoming: That truism was to prove especially appropriate for an age as pronouncedly belated as the Modernist. But understanding might make us aware of how the problems are shared, and perhaps even of how this sharing suggests certain transpersonal aspects of the psyche that have transcendental implications. Perhaps the very mobility of Baudelairean rhetoric leaves in its flight traces of recurrent forms of desire (for example, in "Prufrock"'s level of religious connotations) that remind us of necessities which neither rhetoric nor irony can dispel.

These are highly speculative matters, but that may be what poetry has to offer a culture bound to empiricist models of representation. Look carefully at the work Eliot makes the language perform in the poem's peculiar refrain, at once pathetic in its oversimplification and compelling in its accuracy:

For I have known them all already, known them all
Have known the evenings, mornings, afternoons,
I have measured out my life with coffee spoons;
. . . .
And I have known the eyes already, known them all –
The eyes that fix you in a formulated phrase. . . .

And I have known the arms already, known them all.

(4–5)

In one sense, this dream of an "all" is the kind of illusion that seems to justify Victorian self-pity. By asking for too much, Prufrock creates a scenario in which fragments continually displace one another as unsatisfying substitutes for some unimaginable, and unimagable, whole. Even the language cancels itself, or transforms presence into absence, by its insistent rhetoricity: a lament cast as description. (If one takes this model of desire seriously, the only plausible plenitude becomes the Buddhist void, which in fact Eliot found an attractive hypothesis at the time.)[4] Yet this lament is, in another register, all too perfect a self-description. For the solipsism of this rhetoric makes it an ironically accurate account of the expressivist sensibility. Because his emotive moods mark the limit of his world, Prufrock has seen all that he can and will see. Thus he must vacillate between a desire to possess the woman, which becomes the source of perennially unsatisfied desires, and a desire to merge himself entirely in conditions of absolute negativity, where all desires appear as unnecessary delusions. It is no accident that the dream of the lady generates, as its counterpart, the fantasy of being a pair of ragged claws. Unlike actual living creatures, the claws have absolutely no concern for overall identity as a single organism. They are completely content with the status of pure fragmentation. Empedocles' dream of a sublime wholeness, in a nature without consciousness, here encounters its slightly ridiculous Modernist counterpart.

Taken simply as a commentary on the refrain, these seem inflated terms. But the refrain is only the most obvious means of insisting on patterns that shape all of Prufrock's relationships to his human environment.[5] Notice how the tension between parts and wholes, the fragment and the all, becomes the fundamental condition of a self-consciousness all too prone to find itself "formulated in a phrase." The dream of a deeply buried life seems inextricable from a desperate fear that identity itself depends on external matters over which one has no control. There can only be another version of the Victorian cry, as one watches all of one's fictions about one's masterful identity become scattered fragments, subject to the interpretive frameworks imposed by others, whose own insecurity only deepens their need to cast everyone else in a critical light:

(They will say: "How his hair is growing thin!")
My morning coat, my collar mounting firmly to the chin,
My necktie rich and modest, but asserted by a simple pin –
(They will say: "But how his arms and legs are thin!")

(4)

To every fantasy of having given an expressive meaning to some part of one's appearance, other persons can always posit an alternative story that makes of the effort at mastery a sign of vulnerability.

This is still language used on a dramatic level. We fully grasp Eliot's distinctive Modernism only if we turn to his foregrounding of the linguistic structures that can be said to underlie those dramatic conditions and that, in so doing, interpret Prufrock's relation to his predecessors in the dramatic monologue. Therefore, I want to shift our focus to the figure of metonymy pervading the poem, for it is through this that Eliot establishes a historical intelligence able to project the desired distance from his hero's plight. "Evenings, mornings, afternoons" each carries the "all" of Prufrock's existence; eyes and arms comprise the "all" of what he needs and fears in others, and the dynamic form of his inner life consists in marshaling diverse particulars such as coat, collar, and necktie against those parts, such as his hair or his arms and legs, that have already succumbed to the definitions imposed on them, and hence on the person of Prufrock. Within the traditional mimetic framework that I have been using, this emphasis would simply have reinforced the specific feeling of incompleteness and absence. But Eliot is so insistent on the prevalence of metonymy that we must go farther: We must treat the poem as interpreting the figure of metonymy, as much as the figure interprets Prufrock. Rather than be content with a rhetorical definition of the figure, we must see Eliot grappling to evoke what has been thematized, in recent Structuralist thought, as a dynamic contrast between *metonymic* and *metaphoric* poles of thinking – the one dramatizing a gulf between particulars and informing universals, the other stressing the capacity of certain rhetorical figures to sustain elaborate synthetic structures such as mythic systems.[6] Allowing ourselves that more elaborate framework will enable us to flesh out the significance of the poem's return to metonymy for its final image of human voices producing the frustration that drowns him. More important, it will help clarify the two fundamental ways in which the efforts at abstraction in this poem inaugurate a quest that shaped Eliot's career through *The Waste Land*. First, the foregrounded use of a rhetorical figure for its thematic significance allows the writer to call attention to the interpretive force of the authorial act, while making it strangely impersonal, as if, in the performance, the author managed to develop a mode of agency that could identify with a logic inherent in the structure of the language. Therefore language takes on powers paralleling those explored by Modernist painters: Basic properties of the medium establish a truly elemental semantic force, which, one can presume, holds as a schema for the entire audience, even though no dependency on specific doctrinal claims or melodramatic events is apparent. Yet, because this device is insistently literary, it has a historical dimension more difficult to locate in painting. Hence my second claim: that this foregrounding of the logic of metonymy offers a precise abstract measure of the spiritual problems that Prufrock inherits from the various poetic projects that we have been considering. That elemental abstraction enables the lyric to propose itself as a fundamental vehicle for cultural analysis, capable of tracing the most intimate psychic contradictions characteristic of Eliot's society back to Victorian expressivist ideals.

As Eliot presents it, metonymy captures, in a concrete principle of psychic life, the logic that seems inescapably inscribed within the late-Romantic cult of infinite desire. By engaging the life of the spirit at this fundamental level of processing information, Eliot shows how the pressures of heteronomy have become so inseparable from the law of the heart that no form of personal expression can free itself from infinite slippage. What is Arnold's "buried life" but an evasive idealization of precisely the ungraspable residues left by a constant diet of metonymic experience? And what else are Empedocles' laments for his past but an expression of the sense of lack constantly created for him by the details of his present environment, especially by the images for his own self-definition that he has at its disposal? The world that Arnold's speakers can describe or engage does not satisfy their imaginative demands, and the world that they cannot resist desiring will not fade into the simple realm of memory, but imposes its traces on every investment. And Tennyson offers an even deeper version of these problems, because the hold of religion on his imagination brings him to the conceptual core of the issues. The "dark house" of *In Memoriam* is a paradigmatic metonymy, the mark of an absence that mocks possible wholeness at every level of psychic life and generates an endless discourse that extends contiguity in the effort to find an integrative structure for it. Even the poem's Christian resolution proves prophetic in its links between explicitly religious concerns and its more abstract projection of myth as a structure capable of relieving the horror of sheer particularity, endlessly and infinitely repeated.[7]

Such responsiveness to his heritage enabled Eliot to envision his analytic use of rhetorical figures as at least the beginning of a poetry that could cast itself as a project of "curing" the cultural "ground." Even if there seems no obvious alternative to the model of subjectivity responsible for these metonymic conditions, the poet can hope that the analysis will establish a contrastive measure for exploring whatever contrary values the poet can disclose by taking a radically impersonal stance toward those expressive needs. This hope centers in two distinct yet mutually reinforcing modes of abstraction that the impersonal stance can foreground. The first creates the possibility that if the poem can reach beyond the speaker's intentions to grasp some of the forces shaping them, it can claim to make present transhistorical factors at the core of that subjective activity. This set of forces then makes possible a second, more lyric aspect of abstraction. Whereas Flaubert and Baudelaire use insistently metonymic styles to call attention to the gulf between the scenic and the underlying authorial energies, Eliot makes those energies a means for staging a struggle between metonymy and metaphor. The poet tries to absorb the speaker's self-evasions and their implicit historical context into patterns of desire and need that seem to articulate constitutive forces basic to the life of any ego in modern culture.

Before Eliot could fully explore this mode of abstraction, however, he had to face the problems created by his choice of the dramatic-monologue form. Within this form, these gestures toward a more abstract site seem always on the verge of collapsing into the intricate identifications that characterized Baudelaire's rhetoric. Although seeking distance, the authorial presence is continually tempted to yield to sympathy, so that the poet seems trapped in the same metonymic relation to his character as the character maintains toward the details of his own life. There is far too much of the author in the character to sustain the distance, yet far too much of the fool in the character for the author to be content with the identification – and far too much of the reader in the author to save him from replicating those very conditions. Thus, although there are clear qualitative differences between the modes of self-consciousness available to the character who lives the situations and those of us who witness it, there is no guarantee that the more sophisticated consciousness will have any easier time in freeing its behavior from what it can so thoroughly analyze. As we read, as we seek that distance, we must confront the nagging fear that this very pursuit of distance is in large part responsible for making Prufrock what he is. The effort to stand outside Baudelaire's version of spirit may in fact only return us the more adamantly to one of Baudelaire's fundamental problems. Like him, we must wonder whether the powers of poetry so assiduously cultivated by nineteenth-century thought are a cure for our difficulty, or a seductive means of exacerbating the disease. As we remember that Prufrock makes his decision, not by facing it, but by burying it within his deliberations, we find ourselves entering a sensibility so fluid and evasive that it makes classical distance necessary, but at the same time renders it impotent.

Yet, as we go through these reflections and provisional identifications, we are now, at the very least, able to understand the contradictions that we still cannot control. Even within the dramatic monologue, Eliot manages to create a site where we imagine ourselves able to grasp our vacillations between sympathy and intelligence as the literal embodiment of essential tensions between first- and third-person principles constantly at war. We must wonder whether this abstractness is just another excuse for indulging in dilemmas that simply repeat, in an ironic mode, the dilemmas of Romantic expressivism, now as a universalized excuse for self-pity: But at least we now possess a means for holding, in a single thought, the endless dance of identity and difference to which the subject is condemned.

III

Clearly, another dramatic monologue would not take Eliot much farther in exploring these problems. That form would only replicate the pathos of the lyric ego at odds with itself, and once again place the authorial act within inescapable contradictions between sympathy and knowledge. But perhaps the opposite tack could provide a plausible alternative. Instead of dramatizing the effort at impersonal distance in relation to lyric expression, one could try to generate lyric emotions from something close to a purely lucid, analytic stance. The poet could replace the seductive cries of a distinct and needy speaker by composing an imaginative site sufficiently abstract to focus attention on the very contradictions that seem inescapable effects within more expressive styles. Instead of finding himself trapped within the intricacies of identification, he could treat the tension between sympathy and judgment as a much clearer, more literal embodiment of an essential contradiction between first- and third-person principles within the psyche. And then, rather than recapitulate essentially historical dilemmas, he might explore transhistorical states, where the poem would include within itself the very impulses that lead us to construe the world in subjective terms. Instead of subordinating itself to the complex chain of metonymies it renders, the poem could try to achieve a distance that would allow it to reflect on metonymy purely as a figure, as a way of organizing desire.

That figure, one must remember, is perhaps inseparable from modern models of subjectivity. A poetry able to concentrate on metonymy may therefore be able to achieve a different kind of impersonality, one devoted, not to escaping from personality, but to understanding the experience of every modern psyche as it becomes aware of how vulnerable its subjective life is. One may not be able quite to overcome the Prufrock within, but one may be able to use that knowledge as a means of capturing what all human voices seem to share, as they face the empiricist orientation inseparable from Modernity. By bringing that vulnerability to light, lyric poetry may regain social, and even philosophical, currency as our best index of the problems inherent in preserving imaginary investments in a world for which all descriptions must take third-person form. Paradoxically, a more radical impersonality in poetry may produce a deeper sense that the lyric dimension is perhaps woven into the very concept of first-person experience.

I offer this extensive preface to my discussion of Eliot's "Preludes" because no commentary has yet captured the distinctive qualities of this sequence, qualities that help to explain Eliot's turn to F. H. Bradley and, eventually, Eliot's achievement in *The Waste Land*. Critics usually treat "Preludes" in quasi-dramatic terms, as Impressionist landscape poetry, in the tradition of Wilde's "Impression" poems or Symons's "City Nights" sequence (or, for that matter, the opening passage of "Prufrock"). All are renderings of the Romantic sensibility as it stages itself giving way to a weary lucidity and content with the refined impressions that language teases from a hostile world. But this approach ignores both the internal pressures on Eliot and remarkable, innovative resistance of "Preludes" to the scenic mode for constituting moods and selves. When Eliot started "Prufrock," he had already completed two of the poems in "Preludes." But it was only after "Prufrock" that he saw the advantage to building a sequence of descriptions: It forced him to resolve his material without relying on any single dramatic situation or mood. Were he once again to subsume the poems under a single speaker like Prufrock, he would have to treat the emotions as if they required the contexts provided by that single psyche. If, on the other hand, one could cut the emotions free from the control of any single speaker, they might seem to be "pure" states of the psyche, which every consciousness may have to confront. Moreover, at this level of abstraction, the various states might appear less as simply personal states than as typological constituents, which could combine in various ways to form the moods indulged by specific characters. Where character had been, and where the foregrounding of metonymy had initiated a counterforce to that particularity, poetry might begin to focus on an abstract grammar of moods underlying the specific situations that satisfied Eliot's Georgian peers. And poetry could cast itself as heroically facing the limitations of the age, in order to imagine agency itself as more complex and fragmented than it appears when we have the unifying illusion of character.[8] In such direct confrontations, poetry takes on a different kind of historicity, because it appears less the complicitor with history's victims than the analyst (or anatomist) of the conditions of feeling that history imposes upon us.

"Preludes," too, has its metonymic opening, but this time the sense of agency is much more abstract than in "Prufrock." As the presentation of fact upon fact creates an aura of absence, we find ourselves confronting the apparently inescapable modern dilemma that first-person concerns seem exiled to the margins of public life. Our humanity seems to consist primarily in what we lack, because we see ourselves tormented by needs that do not arise in the plenitude enjoyed by beings without reflexive consciousness:

> The winter evening settles down
> With smell of steaks in passageways. . .
> And now a gusty shower wraps
> The grimy scraps
> Of withered leaves about your feet
> And newspapers from vacant lots; . . .
> And at the corner of the street
> A lonely cab-horse steams and stamps.
> And then the lighting of the lamps.
>
> (12)

Flat as these lines are, they present two significant experiments. Instead of dramatically rendering the mood or plight of an individual, they focus attention on the struggle of poetic language, seeking to wrest spirit out of the imperatives of pure description. They leave us no basis for action, except the capacity of the language to form structural patterns that both order the details on a more abstract level and define basic contrasts between the model of sensation rendering the details and the different investments produced by the poem's shifting personal pronouns. Such abstraction ultimately casts the entire poem as the intense working out of the conflict between subject and object roles that is finally stated in its closing lines:

> I am moved by fancies that are curled
> Around these images, and cling:
> The notion of some infinitely gentle
> Infinitely suffering thing.
>
> Wipe your hand across your mouth, and laugh;
> The worlds revolve like ancient women
> Gathering fuel in ancient lots.
>
> (13)

Just as the title parodies Chopin, but retains his implicit presence as a parallel to its lyric cries, the strange physicality of the description also serves to highlight the effect of the juxtapositional structure: The more we cannot be satisfied by sensation, the more the poet must create intervals that constitute evocative, irreducible silences, capable of generating a counterpressure to that oppressive reality.

The specific terms of the conflict between the first- and third-person roles are established by the flatness of that opening description, where the only actions are performed by inanimate objects. The closest we come to human affective energies is the image of "the lonely cab horse." But Eliot subtly suffuses the chain of descriptions with a sense of need and desire. There appears to be a progression toward the human, in the sequence of minimal actions that take place: from the evening settling down, to the forces exerted by the showers, to the horse's stamping, to the final "lighting of the lamps." But how do we fit this last tautology into the sequence? A human agent is at once suggested and denied, as we come to realize that if the lights are now electric, they could be seen as lighting themselves (while metonymically echoing the older ways). In this landscape, it is dangerous not to register every sign of dehumanization, because otherwise one might relax and lose the necessary tension. And there is an overt reference to human agency, incorporated in a casual adjectival reference to "your feet," which the context provided by the other sections makes important enough to reward our vigilance. Looking back simply at this configuration of details, we notice that this hint of an investing consciousness occurs at the close of the seventh of thirteen lines, a pathetic center of this metonymic, impersonal, turning world.

The second section then builds on that trace. "Morning comes to consciousness" in the form of a range of metonymic details, building to this transformation of the adjectival possessive into active reflection that is inseparable from a chain of identifications:

> One thinks of all the hands
> That are raising dingy shades
> In a thousand furnished rooms.
> (12)

Because the moment of self-reflection is so embedded in physical description, there is a strange equation of the thinking with the hands – each responding to a hope that is inseparable from self-mockery. But even this much consciousness allows the third "Prelude" to let us inside the room, inside the agent's own view of his life. Yet for this stance, this kind of identification, the impersonal "one" must give way to the more intimate, and more threatening, second-person pronoun:

> You tossed a blanket from the bed,
> You lay upon your back and waited;
> You dozed, and watched the night revealing
> The thousand sordid images
> Of which your soul was constituted . . .
> You curled the papers from your hair,
> Or clasped the yellow souls of feet
> In the palms of both soiled hands.
> (13)

This entire section captures the strange accusatory distance that accompanies the subject's effort to focus on its own needs and desires. Ironically, this effort at possessing the self in the present bogs down in the past, the only site where the objectifying subject can find the necessary information, and wield the necessary authority, to treat the self as itself a landscape, reduced to "the thousand sordid images of which your soul was constituted." The self has its visions, but the effort to understand them literally drives out everything except the needy body, seen only from the outside. The "you" is simultaneously distanced from the act of thinking and too intimate to be captured as an object of thought.

If the voice is to align itself with the agent of the visions, it must undergo the finer tensions of the third-person stance that begins the fourth "Prelude":

> His soul stretched tight across the skies
> That fade behind a city block . . .
> And short square fingers stuffing pipes
> And evening newspapers, and eyes
> Assured of certain certainties,
> The conscience of a blackened street
> Impatient to assume the world.
>
> (13)

Here verbs and adjectival participles become indistinguishable ("stretched tight"), and the speaking voice becomes strangely woven into a potpourri of perspectives, so that personal presence remains little more than an adjectival intrusion on a world of facts. However, once it goes through this cycle, consciousness cannot avoid the traces of itself and of a minimal social life that accrue around the images – in the process, providing a measure of the insufficiency of images for grasping the indefinable, imaginary plenitude that seduces the "I" into its deepest investments. Having distributed the soul among the various actors in the scene, the poem can now let the "I" enter, in and as "fancies that are curled / Around these images, and cling: / The notion of some infinitely gentle / Infinitely suffering thing." But because its imaginary status requires it to be maintained by acts of negation, this "I" is terrifyingly vulnerable, breeding, by the gaps it causes and the wistfulness it sustains, a constant temptation to expunge it and restore life to its impersonal equanimity. So the poem, ironically, comes to its emotional climax by shifting to the imperative mood, whose form, for the subject, is a chillingly profound blend of second and third persons. The spirit of lucidity attempts to sacrifice the subjective "I" to the empty generality of a destiny whose banal image of recurrence carries strange overtones of dark Greek forces.

The distance allowing these generalizations exacts an enormous price.

As the "I" falls subject to irony, it becomes trapped in a world where all active energy is granted to the impersonal, collective, and infinitely repetitious revolution of worlds. Purely impersonal voices wake it, and it drowns, since consciousness generalizes, but does not transform. So its images can only give mythic echoes to the very banalities of time's cycle with which the poem began. It seems, then, that the more abstract our sense of the "I," the more vulnerable it becomes before this leveling lucidity. There appears to be no alternative but to wish that one could reduce the self to the simple, marginal status of adjectives, modifying appearances within a turning world. Epistemology too has its ragged claws.

Yet surrendering in this way to the final voice of the poem seems too simple, as if the reader were blind to the virtual forces that the poem has been gathering in order to give depth and texture to that "infinitely gentle, infinitely suffering thing." Even though there is no dramatic surrogate for this "I," the appeal it makes to the reader may invoke powers with the ability to resist this triumphant objectivity. For it is difficult to imagine reading the poem without seeing one's own investments as a fundamental counterforce to the pressure of that analytic voice.[9] In reenacting the poem's play among perspectives and in offering our sympathy, we win, from the pressure of a world reduced to sensation, a gradual sense of the fragile "I" that the sensations negate, but, in negating, reproduce. Then, as our own investments become evanescent and difficult to fix, we are asked to turn on ourselves, with the dismissive arrogance of the demand for disillusioned lucidity that is the modern myth of authenticity. But by now there are, curled around this imperative, "fancies that cling:" fancies such as the very myth of authenticity, the echoes of tragic submission to destiny, and the need to overcompensate for vulnerability by resorting to the poem's closing ironic attitude. The effort to dispel the fragile "I" doth protest too much, since the desire for that heroic distance seems deeply dependent on the same investments it would negate. As the reader tries to muster this pure negation, she finds herself invoking a set of lyric concerns that, in bringing the poem to life, proves the contrary of the final assertion. We cannot laugh, because we find ourselves participating within a fragile yet persistent lyric "I," poised within and against forces of objectification in nature, as well as those in the mind's second- and third-person positions. The poem's juxtapositional relations. the sensual qualities by which it renders the pressure of its sensations, the intelligence manifest in the economy, precision, and delicacy of the language, and, most important, the remarkable feelings of pressure and of contradiction, all become testimony to the pathos and power of an "infinitely gentle, infinitely suffering thing" curled about our self-denying efforts to treat the world simply in terms of the images we reproduce for it. Here Eliot makes the reader the surrogate who internalizes and applies what in Mallarmé remained abstract relational forces.

IV

Such a shadowy rendering of the lyric mode cannot suffice for truly great poetry. It can, though, do a great deal to prepare new forms for the richest achievements in that vein. For "Preludes" demonstrates the power of abstract pattern and impersonal voice (not necessarily a third-person voice) to explore models of agency free from the seductive specularity of the dramatic monologue. Even more important, Eliot's poem makes it clear that poets can so define the reading act that it provides literal testimony for their metaphoric claims by actually bringing into being the state that the poem proclaims. To see how such permissions would change the course of Modernist poetry, we need only focus on the ways such devices enabled Eliot's *Waste Land* to transform Symboliste tensions between constitutive mind and recalcitrant world into a complex tragic rendering of public life. This is not the occasion to attempt to elaborate that claim by an extensive reading of the later poem. Rather, I shall concentrate only on what I think our specific context enables us to recover of its experimental qualities, qualities that often are suppressed in the thematic and psychological discourses dominating contemporary criticism. Were I to attempt a thematic interpretation, I would have nothing to add to the superb account of the poem given by Michael Levenson in Chapter 9 of his *Genealogy of Modernism*. Yet precisely because he is so deeply responsive to the "sense" of Eliot's poem, Levenson creates a useful contrast, showing how the concerns we are pursuing here bring out aspects of the poem's imaginative force that require more attention to the foregrounded authorial activity.

Levenson's reading is definitive, for me, because it manages to give full credit both to the semantic ambitions of Eliot's abstract patterns in *The Waste Land* and to the skepticism that finds this expansive lucidity paralyzing for the will. Levenson shows that the poem is organized in terms of pronounced thematic patterns, yet offers no thematic resolution: no way to take what the thunder says as a piece of wisdom providing the mind with a concrete principle of action because of what it learns through the poem. Rather, Levenson argues, the poem establishes a different kind of interpretive activity, by attempting to "draw a circle of consciousness around fragmentation" (176). This circle need not "transform fragmentation into coherence," because the circle has its own complex ways of expanding and multiplying, which do not conform to standard expectations about coherence. Instead, Eliot works by developing "intermittent harmonies" that elicit "a plurality of consciousnesses," articulating "an ever-increasing series of points of view, which struggle towards an emergent unity and then continue to struggle past that unity" (192–3). Eliot uses, in other words, a distinctive mythic method, which becomes a necessary "prosthesis for the dissociated sensibility" (196), even though it offers no direct access to encompassing cognitive and normative frameworks. The most the poet can hope for is to project, beyond those fragmented personae, a single "I" that becomes a figure for "what these literary fragments have in common" (199). In the place of a dramatic logic that places the personal "I" in a narrative development, this poem unfolds a general cultural consciousness, by a process of "contextual development":

> The poem moves forward only as it moves sideways, toward new analogies, new parallels, new possibilities for comparison. The completion of the quest becomes of less central dramatic emphasis than the recognition of other quest-motifs in other cultural settings. The poem develops not by resolving conflicts but by enlarging contexts, by establishing relations between contexts, by situating motifs within an increasingly elaborate set of cultural parallels – by widening. (201)

It takes that sense of a flexible "I," whose powers are composed within the poem, to bring us this far. But Levenson relies too much on an equation of that "I" with the semantic circles that it can draw. This greatly narrows the emotional intensities at stake, and it reduces criticism to positing, as its primary term for praise, an "inclusiveness" that is so clearly problematic within the poem. Levenson sees this quest for inclusiveness fulfilled when Eliot became editor of the *Criterion* and could then try to lead "modernism back toward a *rapprochement* with England" (211) by consolidating its tenets within the more general culture whose relational fields were mapped in *The Waste Land*. However, as Levenson knows, but does not sufficiently emphasize, that kind of inclusiveness has little to do with what seemed experimentally Modernist about the poem, or with the emotional pressures it tries to handle by playing a new mode of concentration against its broad cultural scope. If we are to take those features fully into our critical consciousness, I think we must use our analyses of the other Eliot poems in order to highlight three distinctively Modernist features giving *The Waste Land* its depth and intensity: its elaborating the tension between first- and third-person stances in order to correlate mobile lyric energies with the demands of the public order; its expanding the figure of metonymy as its vehicle for tying affective needs to historical conditions; and its expanding the power of formal experiments to make the reader a self-reflexive participant, whose activity comes to constitute the site in which the cries from the Waste Land modulate into a kind of prayer.

Had we the time, I could set the stage by showing how the experiments in "Preludes" shaped Eliot's interest in the philosophy of F. H. Bradley (rather than Bradley's philosophy shaping Eliot's thematic concerns). I could show how the treatment of first- and third-person roles in *The Waste Land* gets transformed into an obsessive tension between analytic distance and the immediacy of desire, word, and flesh that pervades poems such as "Mr. Eliot's Sunday Morning Service."[10] But, for this occasion, we must go directly to the opening passages of *The Waste Land,* because it is there that we find Eliot's most complete transformation of Baudelaire's mobility into an instrument disseminating the poet into the diverse strands of his cultural life. Recall the many ways in which the first lines literally mix memory and desire, as the poem moves brilliantly from landscape to reverie, through an intricate dance of tenses, participial forms, and shifting pronouns. To have memory return is to find consciousness pervaded by a variety of identifications, all simultaneously composing and fragmenting a shared public space, until that space itself seems to authorize another, far more abstract and imposing "I":

> What are the roots that clutch, what branches grow
> Out of this stony rubbish? Son of man,
> You cannot say, or guess, for you know only
> A heap of broken images . . .
> And I will show you something different from either
> Your shadow at morning striding behind you
> Or your shadow at evening rising to meet you;
> I will show you fear in a handful of dust.
>
> (53)

It seems as if the casual overheard dialogues of the opening now modulate into something like the underlying truth of their speech situations – perhaps into a voice whose authority resides in the fact that it seems to speak for the deep imaginary fears and needs that they all share.

Here, then, is the poem's challenge: Not only must we work out the poem's patterns of allusion; we must be able to align ourselves with its speaking position, by coming to understand in ourselves those levels of human agency that can, in effect, carry this burden of a collective subjectivity that is not a traditional transcendental ego. One must learn to hear, in one's own propensity to fragmentation, what the play of voices yields, as access to that mysteriously intimate yet abstract "you." No wonder that the poem refuses any thematic synthesis. The stakes are not primarily intellectual, at least not as Victorian poetry understood the intellect. Reading this poem is not a matter of finding the right interpretation, but of finding in oneself the capacity to exercise the power necessary to flesh out what Levenson calls the "circle of consciousness" that it distributes. Rather than make arguments about the world, Eliot wants to make the formal complexity of the poem a vehicle for defining various levels of a mobile pysche (potentially belonging to each reader), as it simultaneously tries to interpret its dramatic situation and to reflect upon those traces within its activity that open on to a capacity for deeper identifications and more oppressive losses. Or, to put the same point another way, the truly stunning feature of Eliot's poem is its capacity to correlate the pysche's most intimate fears with its most abstract cultural dependencies. That is why making sense of the poem seems of a piece with making sense of an entire cultural heritage. Enticed both to seek meanings and to believe that meanings can have the force that the poem seems to posit for them, we find that the dualities held in agonizing balance at the end of "Preludes" expand here into a much more capacious theater. The analytic desire to wipe one's hand across one's mouth and laugh seems demanded by every manifestation of what once were ideals. Yet the shadows cast by those ideals continue to haunt – a public version of that "infinitely gentle, infinitely suffering thing," and a poetic reminder that engaging the reader in complex, self-interpreting quests can provide much richer and more powerful versions of "meaning" than any thematic assertion. By leading the reader through the experience of her own potential mobility, as she explores her own dependencies and limitations, the poem can claim a version of truth as direct testimony not available to (and not necessary for) more traditional poetic thinking. The experience of the poem demonstrates the scope of the problem it sets forth, in exactly the same way that "Preludes" demonstrates the nature of the infinitely gentle and infinitely suffering ego.

The figure of metonymy provides a perfect vehicle for capturing this relationship between fears and possibilities. But now, thanks to Bradley, metonymy has a more capacious emotional logic, extending to the core of metaphoric activity.[11] Hieronymo's mad again, because every model accounting for the synthetic acts that the mind is clearly performing seems to collapse under its own success. This poem does not lack synthetic patterns: it overflows in them. There are substantial traces that would warrant our reading it, for example, as a coded, private allegory, or as an allegory of Christian redemption, or as a psychodrama of the conflict between frustration and release into learning to view experience as a sexless Tiresias does, or as an ironic rendering of the gulf between the past and the sterility of the present, or as a sign that only art can hold what in life must appear contradictory. But although each pattern explains many of the details and allusions, the proliferation of metaphors generates several incompatible possibilities for organizing all of the references into a single whole. The terror of these shadows is that there are so many of them, undoing, in their multiple implications, the possibility that any single metaphor will stop the chain of lacks and differences. Metaphor only deepens the metonymic plight, reproducing, in twentieth-century terms, Empedocles' doomed trek up the mountain of reflective consciousness. Here, though, the emblem of possible heroism is the even more pathetic figure of Tiresias, whose ability to synthesize is not matched by a corresponding ability to make thought the ground for action.[12]

If meanings collapse in this way, why not simply speak of the poem as capturing the "indeterminacy" soon to pervade modern culture's self-representations?[13] As Levenson sees, that route ignores the fact that the problem is less a problem of the powers of consciousness than of their relation to will. And, more important, that route misses both Eliot's cognitive accomplishment in the poem and the emotional intensity he brings to that cognition by managing to find figural equivalents for the "heap of broken images" that is the scene for the action. The cognitive accomplishment is clearest if we keep Derrida in mind. The richest deconstructions of an old order do not simply render its organizing metaphors indeterminate; they also make a quite determinate image of the incommensurable, yet apparently necessary, components that fail to mesh. The full interpretive casting of indeterminacy requires a firm grasp of the intractable dilemma that the text poses itself. For Eliot, that grasp must not only clarify our anxieties, but also intensify the emotional complexes they create. For that task, the old attention to metonymy provides the perfect theater, since it leads us to look beyond the failed metaphors to the desire for unity that inhabits them. Symboliste strategies enable the poetry to work its way beyond tangible realities, so that it can inhabit the shadows cast by the failed metaphoric patterns, locating there a dynamic life that invites the audience to reflect on the needs, desires, and energies focused within the process of watching one's desire for meanings come undone. Eliot invents a modernist epic that inverts the standard heroic dream of recovering from history modes of idealization possible for contemporary life. Where answers had been, there only self-consciousness about one's limitations can emerge. But there remains the possibility of a heroism based on the degree to which one explores who one becomes because of those changes. Fully registering what loss of cultural coherence involves may even allow one to glimpse, in that loss, new conditions of social awareness. The self-reflexive lyricism of the dandy becomes the meditative instrument of the skeptical idealist, aware that the absolute is, at best, a way of understanding that the mind's inevitable failures to know itself can open to other, indefinable hopes and cares.

By so generalizing the metonymic conditions that underlie, and undermine, the mind's desire for metaphoric coherence, Eliot in effect makes
Symboliste modes of alienated reading means of both cultural analysis
and cultural cure. In Symbolisme, a person's increasing awareness of the
limits of empirical knowledge justifies turning back to the unplucked
flower, where one comes to appreciate the mind's self-reflexive energies
and to feel the transcendental force of what contemporary Symbolistes
such as Roland Barthes and Julia Kristeva call *"textualité."* Eliot transforms that individual withdrawal into a mode of access to values that lead
back into the public order: minimally, as the basis for new modes of
sympathy; maximally, as the ground for understanding the forms of
consciousness that sustain those who accept religious dispensations,
Buddhist or Christian. For, if we allow ourselves to become involved
readers of his poem, we find ourselves in the condition of the disciples at
Emmaeus. In the heart of the desert, visions appear. One may simply be
hallucinating, like the explorers in Shackleton's expedition. Shadows
that beckon from under the red rock may be only a means of avoiding
the fear one has been made to see in a handful of dust. The very process
of producing metaphors may be an evasion of an inescapably metonymic
condition. Yet one cannot be sure. The infinitely suffering thing we feel
may here also take on the more general form of some potential redeeming force, if only as a sense of the spiritual needs we cannot dispel. So,
like those disciples, readers must ask who we are becoming by virtue of
the site we find ourselves inhabiting. Perhaps our questions will reveal a
lyricism about lucidity – even, perhaps, within lucidity – that could no
more be extinguished than the most fundamental human expressions of
desire.

The best way to understand the relationship between lyricism and
lucidity in *The Waste Land* is to concentrate on what this poem adds to
"Prufrock"'s analysis of the Victorian voices that delineated that problem. Now, rather than stop with the dilemmas of expressivity, Eliot tries
to hear what is buried in fictions of a buried life. For this task, his ideal
precursor is Tennyson's *In Memoriam,* because that poem makes a radically metonymic condition the basis for a dialectical recovery of faith. By
meditating on the loss of Hallam, the speaker finds in his own suffering
glimpses of spiritual possibilities that cannot be expunged by loss, but
instead take form within it. Cry, in effect, modulates into prayer. In
Eliot's recasting of that spiritual condition, there can be no dialectic, but
there remain glimpses of transcendence, earned simply by the intensity
with which one experiences the inherent contradictions between cry and
prayer as irreducibly part of the same historical plight: The scope of
memory both provokes and resists the paralysis of will; personal obsession both leads to levels of the psyche where we appreciate the full force

of ritual and blocks access to its transpersonal processes; the desire to escape the present, paradoxically, accompanies a terror that one has no access to it; the private self keeps finding itself forced into a public, excruciatingly historical syntax for understanding its condition, yet, at the same time, this public understanding seems incapable of satisfying any of the deep private needs that push the poem increasingly toward the desperation of its last section; and voices seem at once to assert, and to deny, that there can be a single Logos.

Were *The Waste Land* a dramatic monologue, those contradictions would be attributable in large part to character, and the reader's task would be to understand why the character has those reactions. By making the poem abstract, Eliot makes that cry and prayer at once more deeply historical and more intensely personal. For the analogy with Tennyson is not simply a critical projection. Eliot's poem is virtually made of affinities with his predecessors, so that it may appear as essentially a continuation of those voices, especially those within his Victorian heritage now sufficiently free of the contingencies of history to express the contradictions pervading the culture's efforts to adapt its lyric needs to a world that played the role of Baudelaire's sailors. Because there is no dramatic surrogate for those voices, they come together to form a speaking site only in the activity of the reader, who becomes a participant in a drama that seems to persist within historical change. Taking up the speaking voices of the poem, we find within ourselves another, more concentrated version of Tennyson's shadows, which seems to make those contradictions possible preconditions for moments of visionary release more capacious than those tormenting moments in the rose garden. This is why the echoes of myth can take on secular force: They actually become plausible, shaping containers for the experience the text engenders. In other words, Eliot's pronounced rhythms and patterns become a great deal more than rhetorical means to highlight a situation. Instead, they bring into play certain configurations that have their own distinctive and resonant reality, inner versions of the chapels that pervade the poem. Thus, although Frazer's mythological patterns do not suffice as metaphoric interpretants of the details, they do serve perhaps the richer task of giving something close to an articulate form to the desires that drive us to search for those principles.

My interpretive language is becoming far too metaphoric, as it begins to attribute positive content to Eliot. At this point in his career, he was too good a Kantian to allow those hints of transcendence to be anything more than possibilities. In fact, the most significant and original feature of the site that Eliot composes is its haunting otherness: Symbolisme wrought to its uttermost, as its version of the self-legislating spirit manages to make its presence felt only as shadows, inseparable from the needs they create. *The Waste Land* is intended to drive us mad, by confronting us with two inescapable facts about our secular imaginings: that they inevitably remind us of ideal states that they cannot bring about; and that they inevitably betray in us desires for the same states that produce the dilemmas of metaphoricity which the poem exemplifies. The more completely we know ourselves, and the more fully we come to read this poem, the more we must be aware of the gulf between knowledge and action, or, perhaps, between the sense of ritual that poetry recovers and the purity of prayer that only the individual can utter when she recognizes the limitations of her knowledge.

Perhaps Symboliste spirituality can have no other end, however rich it becomes in rendering abstract emblems of its plight. For Eliot, there need be no other end, because this focus on the limits of knowledge forced him to turn, instead: to hope for a grace that would simultaneously dignify and transcend those limitations. Although the appropriate word would not resound in secular poetry, abstraction could lead us beyond the authority of its culture by providing testimony that even the most comprehensive of art forms, and the most assertive of authorial energies, lead us to the same impasse: The only hope is to begin from the point of view that faith establishes and let its terms provide the necessary links between thought and action. Everything else is contaminated by the very flexibility of spirit that keeps secular humanism constantly reproducing the same ritual dramas of frustrated imaginative demand.

For poets such as William Carlos Williams and Wallace Stevens, however, this end required the effort to forge a new beginning. Fascinated by Eliot's stylistic achievement, yet appalled by the plight that this achievement seemed compelled to repeat, these poets had to develop new ways of adapting the abstract space and sense of psychic mobility that Eliot had defined for English poetry. That redefinition would call on a wide range of resources. But for our purposes it must suffice to concentrate on what painterly abstraction made available for that enterprise. And if we are to reconstruct the challenge that they took on, I think the best way to understand those resources is to recuperate the imaginative possibilities generated by the painters' efforts to elaborate what Baudelaire insisted was the priority of color over sculptural line. Filtered through those painterly exemplars, Flaubert's absolute way of seeing became, not simply an idealized window on experience, but a mode of dramatizing a constructivist will that did not need the sanction of universals, and Baudelaire's mobility of spirit produced a juxtapositional style that dramatized this will's capacity to make adjustments to all of those features of secular flux driving Eliot to the brink of suicide.

6

"The Abstraction of the Artist": Three Painterly Models for the Constructivist Will

I

For Eliot the triumph of Modernism made it clear that not even the most innovative art could suffice for the spirit's needs. Trapped in the endless spinning out of possible selves, the poet's efforts to develop a firm ground for identity could achieve little more than an endless litany of *I am nots*. Therefore Eliot decided that the poet had first to find faith; then the appropriate art would follow. Only that path would make it possible to align intelligence with a transcendental principle capable of securing both the desired grounds for identity and the desired terms for spiritual romance. For most of Eliot's peers, however, his ideal of a cure seemed the basic cause of the disease; the transcendental cast of his desires made his secular despair inescapable. *The Waste Land* was ultimate testimony, not of the limits of the secular, but of the dangers in attempting to make Modernist strategies address the old religious questions. The arts could only be made new, and then lead to new social visions, if they devoted themselves to eliminating Eliotic nostalgia and elaborating lyric models of the relation between persons and their world that were compatible with secular principles.[1] So rather than seek a religious revival, poets like Pound could make the scope of the crisis cause for hope that the culture was entering a new Renaissance which would establish different frameworks for thinking about values. These were the dreams that led poets to the challenges provided by the visual arts – the domain where spirit was in the process of providing the necessary testimony that the culture no longer had to rely on the models Eliot continued to idealize. Ironically, if poetry was to recover Wordsworthian eloquence without his scenic self, and if it was to revive Keatsian constitutive intensities that could sustain new models of ethos, it would have to discover its new grounds in those painterly experiments.

There may be as many versions of this new ethos as there are significant Modernist works of art. Nonetheless I think we can get a fairly accurate sense of the dynamic principles involved if we concentrate on three fundamental models of agency enabling the painters to redefine spirit for a secular age. The first two models consist of historical influences with which the poets grappled, whereas in the third case we shall deal with aesthetic principles that did not directly influence poets, but nonetheless provide the best analogies available for understanding much of the originality and force in their enterprise.

In the first case, we shall concentrate on the paintings of Cézanne and the discourses on art by which he tried to explain his principle of *réalisation* (realization), for these discourses in effect established a place for the paintings in the world of words and shaped what the poets would see there. Cézanne's paintings and letters, then, provide our models for the use of multiple perspectives, modeling by color relations, and, above all, the sense of painting as self-reflexive meditation, which clarified, for both the poets and the Cubist painters, what could be at stake in resisting the logic of sculptural organization basic to representational aesthetics. Our second model, provided by Braque and Picasso, extends that war on sculptural modeling into a more radical demonstration that the will can find material correlates in a constant metamorphic process suturing vision with the full life of imaginative desire. And finally we shall turn to noniconic painting, especially that of Malevich, in order to elaborate concretely the models of transpersonality and testimonial audience involvement fundamental for establishing modes of agency that could sustain lyric idealization.

My following chapter will explore representative literary engagements in each of these three structures of imaginative possibility. Williams provides the richest English effort to preserve the intricate balance between pronounced artifice and careful attention to the actual logic of seeing fundamental to Cézanne's principle of realization. Then I use the early Cubist paintings to show how Stevens and Stein put language in the service of far more complex visions of agency than Williams could sustain. Rather than be content with recuperating the life of the natural eye through the apparent deformations worked by the mind, these writers concentrate on the capacity of metamorphosis itself to link the mind's energies to deeper levels of dynamic life. Finally I turn to Yeats and to Moore, as my examples of poets for whom noniconic painting provides terms helping us to understand what is distinctive in their treatments of virtual imaginative forces made to serve testimonial roles. Then, once the basic models are established, I move to two much more concentrated chapters showing how this entire grammar of possibilities came to bear when Pound and Stevens each turned, at crucial moments in their careers, to test the resources they could muster by engaging the work of the painters, indeed by insisting that they could develop from those painterly examples distinctively verbal processes capable of sustaining ethical claims not available from purely visual testimony.

II

We cannot proceed directly to Cézanne. To understand Cézanne's originality, and hence the place he occupied for the Modernist imagination, we must grasp his relations to Impressionist theory and practice. And to do that today proves a very difficult enterprise. Familiarity with Impressionist art blurs its experimental qualities, especially for those who know their art history. For art history's relation to those paintings is heavily influenced by a triumphant Postimpressionist rhetoric that labored to condemn its predecessors as offering nothing but an art of appearances.[2] Therefore we tend to interpret Impressionist principles under the aegis of essentially Symboliste values, whose consequences we have seen worked out in Eliot's career. I want to argue that poets like Pound and Stevens went back to a very different Impressionism, one that they thought provided alternatives to Symboliste idealizations of a reflective consciousness doomed to the alternatives of infinite irony or anachronistic faith. From Impressionist examples, these poets (as well as Conrad and James) realized that those painters gave a cast very different from Eliot's to Baudelaire's reflections on the example of Delacroix. Rather than stress an infinitely self-reflexive attention to one's own rhetoricity, as Eliot did, the Impressionist painters emphasized the capacity of coloristic mobility to transform our sense of the psyche's relation to nature. Consequently they inaugurated a complex dialectic between painterly and writerly experiments in conceiving modes of agency and their relations to their environments that I shall attempt to trace. And Cézanne's full force only appears in terms of the roles he plays in that dialectical process.

If we are to give these experiments in agency a full hearing, Paul Valéry must replace Eliot as our guide. Eliot's equal in recognizing the depth of cultural transformations taking place at the beginning of the twentieth century, Valéry, nonetheless, could envision an art able to dispel the nostalgia for metaphoric coherence by turning to the modes of secular testimony offered by Impressionist art. Valéry's differences from Eliot emerge clearly in some comments Valéry made on the aesthetic qualities of Berthe Morisot's paintings. Everything, he wrote, revolves around the activity of

> her great eyes, whose extraordinary concentration on their function, on their continual activity, gave her that air of foreignness . . . rendered alien and remote by excessive presence. . . . [In practical life people] will see nothing as purely *seen.* . . . Utility dismisses reality; the meaning of objects dismisses their form. And at once we can see nothing but hopes and regrets, potential properties and virtues, promises of harvest . . . our eyes on past and future, we cannot see the stains of the pure instant. At the opposite pole stands the abstraction of the artist. To him color speaks of color, and to color he replies with color. He lives in his object, in the very midst of what he is trying to capture, perpetually beset by temptation and challenge. . . . He cannot but see what he is thinking and think what he is seeing. . . . A life dedicated to colors and forms is not *necessarily* less profound or less admirable than a life devoted to "inner" shadows whose mysterious essence is nothing perhaps but an obscure sense of the vicissitudes of vegetative existence, a re-echoing of the events of visceral being. (*Degas Manet Morisot* 125–8)

This absorption in the immediacy of what the eye engages posits a life of spirit directly opposed to the ideals of agency pursued by figures as diverse as Wordsworth and Eliot. For Valéry, the ideal of "inward depth" is little more than primitive superstition. To indulge it is to shirk the spiritual intellect's great work by simply turning theology into psychology. If they pursue this aim, the arts fail to explore those powers that might define a significant human presence within a truly secular realism. Performing that task requires artists to work out what is involved in living a life of color and forms that is neither trivial nor achingly metonymic. Are there plausible ways of measuring or willing a life, so that we retain self-reflection, without submitting it to the hall of mirrors that the old rhetoric seems to entail? And can this attention to colors and forms relieve solipsism, by opening up alternative links between centers of feeling? For his answer, Valéry turned to the example of Impressionist painting, since it made the play of color relations its means of liberating itself from the forms of significance demanded by humanist values.

What he saw remains just as compelling today for those who look closely at the work of art that earned Impressionism its name, Claude Monet's *Impression: Fog* (1872). (For a reproduction, see H. H. Arnason, *History of Modern Art* [New York: Abrams, 1971], 34.) I can imagine no better image for living "in the midst of what one is trying to capture." Fog so disposes the scene that there can be no independent vantage point not already suffused with that which it purports to render. In fact, fog

provides the perfect "antisculptural" force, since it leaves no single object sufficient control of space to sustain strong individual identity. And
once sculptural modeling goes, so too does the kind of focus that demands dramatic interpretation. Here the focus is not on what some
character feels, but on the implications of the painter's own involvement
in what he sees. Thus, refusing the dramatic is in no way a refusal of the
intellect. We simply redirect our attention, so that we reflect upon the
increasing sense of delight and connection that arises, as we become
aware of all that a given state affords the fully engaged mind.

Were this a Caspar Friedrich landscape, the sun at the horizon would
lead beyond the visible to some other place, where perhaps the mind
could find its own sublime nature. But Monet's sun at the horizon is so
framed that it focuses all of the visual energy back toward the foreground, toward what the sun makes available for, and almost as, an eye.
This source of light does not generate the sharply etched edges that make
for intense drama, nor does it gather its own vortex. Its role is not to
overpower, but to empower, by providing a visual anchor for the slow
proliferation of infinitely varied textures, created by remarkable tonal
adjustments among the contraries, orange and blue. Rather than defining
and mastering what stands before it, Monet's sun is satisfied with the
muted role of disseminating shades and permutations that compose an
event of seeing, freed from all interpretive demands, in order to explore
what it can make of its own present moment.[3] That freedom, in turn,
allows the human its own place – not at the margin, as in Wordsworth's
poetry, but as part of the emphatic brushwork composing the overall,
intricate rhythm that makes "atmosphere," in this painting, something
that no meteorological instrument could register. The pleasures of
seeing, and perhaps also of painting, are an intimate feature of the factors
that compose the scene.

Could we stop here, we would have a relatively unproblematic and
satisfying form of immanence to set against Eliot. The mind would have
its home in a dynamic nature, freed from symbols, and the will its peace
in the harmonies distributed by the mobility of light and color. But we
would also have a static and self-satisfied artistic culture, quite different
from the set of experimental demands that Impressionism in fact generated. So we need to locate the serpent in our foggy garden. And we find
it where all the serpents start: in the "foul rag-and-bone shop" of the
interpreting mind. For the very effort to write about Monet makes clear
the demands that the success of Impressionist art imposed upon later
generations: We must align minds hungry for meanings to scenes gorged
with the perceptible. At one pole, the interpretive act seems rather silly –
an uneasy, and perhaps anachronistic, gesture to preserve everything that
Valéry saw called into question. Clearly, this "reading" has a much more

awkward relationship to its source than does writing about dramatic scenes, partially because the best Impressionist art is so obviously intended to provide an alternative to our humanistic interpretings. As Renoir put it, "What seems most significant to me about our movement is that we have freed painting from the importance of the subject. I am at liberty to paint flowers and call them simply flowers without their need-ing to tell a story." Such liberty makes it possible to envision replacing the cult of the ironist with a new ethos: "It is the eye of the sensualist that I wish to open. Not everyone is a sensualist just because he wishes to be. There are some who never become sensualists no matter how they try" ("From Renoir's Notebook," in Nochlin 49, 48).

But why "try" to be a sensualist? Where can that imperative come from, except interpretive frameworks? So I suspect that in Renoir's culture, and in ours, the more intense the sensualism, the greater the need for something like language, in order to specify the significance of that sensuality and to show the degree of intelligence it can bear. In other words, as soon as the arts invoke the sensualist, someone such as Valéry seems necessary, to characterize it in terms of a marvelously metaphoric "eye." Blocked from "story" by the new art's pursuit of immediacy, interpretation returned in the form of speculative philosophical gestures, necessary to maintain the difference between the actual sensualist and the idea of a sensualist. For every Degas, content to present his work as a "way of seeing," there would be a Valéry, insisting that "what Degas was content to call a 'way of seeing' must consequently bear a wide enough interpretation to include *way of being, power, knowledge, and will.*"[4] How else could the art assume cultural significance? But how could it also prevent that same means of assuming significance from placing it back within the irritable searching after truth and meaning whose cost Valéry himself had superbly analyzed? All of Eliot's concerns came rushing back in: The world we see may not be able to ground the mental energies that it elicits: or, to put the same condition the other way, our need to describe ourselves seems to preclude our complete absorption in the act of seeing.

III

We have become witnesses to the fundamental tension between the immediate and the metaphoric,[5] which I tried (in Chapter 2) to show can be resolved in conceptual terms by the notions of "exemplification," "testimony," and "virtuality." But now we are dealing with specific works of art, not with theory, and our concern is less with the resolving of tensions than with the deepening of them, so that we get a full sense of the pressures on the arts. Therefore I want to focus on the gulf between poets who commented on Impressionist painting, such as Jules Laforgue, Mallarmé, and Valéry, and the far simpler vocabulary of the painters. In the contrast we shall find a framework emerging that makes it impossible to accept Renoir's sensualism as adequate explanation. In its stead, we see an urgent, overdetermined, and overdetermining quest for significance, which ultimately reveals (or creates) pressures within the painting that required it to give way to a more self-reflexive and abstract art. Our writers simultaneously developed an ideology for Impressionist painting and make articulated the values that would undo it by demanding increasingly complex versions of sensuality.

To see why these interpretive texts matter for art history, observe what happens when our contemporary criticism ignores them. Take the following statement by Fritz Novotny, for example:

> The principle of Impressionist painting is an extreme form of illusionism. There still remains the second question, that of the role assigned to aesthetic form. . . . For while the fabric of spots of color was certainly a means to achieve illusionism . . . the technique of colour-spots also opened the way to an independent colourism. Impressionism is a radically painterly form of painting, and therein lay its great possibilities. The question as to which of the two roots was more important for the genesis of Impressionism, the realistic doctrine of appearances or the urge towards a pure painting, the spots of color as the means to an end or the end itself, cannot be answered. (Novotny 331)

Clearly, this is an accurate picture of two strands that any account of Impressionism must reconcile. Its terms lead us into the central issue of this chapter: the need to correlate what I call a *radical of disclosure,* explaining how the art opens us to new truths, and a *radical of presentation,* taking responsibility for what the authorial will asserts in its formal structuring. But Novotny himself does little to extend these observations into engaged and suggestive interpretive thinking. Anachronistic dichotomies between content and form lead to positing a naive realism at one pole, and at the other a concern for the painterly act that can sustain only the simplest language of motives or interpretive dramas.

We need the more urgent conceptual demands on both painters and critics that our poets provide.[6] If we turn to their comments, we find an intricate dialectic taking form. Its first stage consisted in establishing a language of praise, in which sensuality itself became a complex Baudelairean blend of spirit and substance, temperament and texture. But, the more intricate the model of sensuality, the more it engendered an anti-materialist rhetoric, which was soon to authorize a Postimpressionist quest for spiritual forces that painting could be said to "free" from the

Impressionist emphasis on scenic properties. Therefore the writer's interpretations, in effect, established the middle terms, calling attention to those features of Impressionist painting that were to require the revisionary work of subsequent generations. If Renoir's sensualist is not Valéry's, Cézanne's is, precisely because Cézanne must have asked, like Valéry, how the Impressionist "way of seeing" could also "include a *way of being, power, knowledge, and will."* Similarly, much of Paul Gauguin's expressivism can be seen as a profound response to Degas's statements about point of view and Laforgue's claims about new ways to unify subject and object. Even Picasso's recasting Cézanne's "war on sculpture" follows roughly the same pattern, although in this case Picasso's own interest in Nietzschean ideas took the place of critical commentary by the poets. Ultimately, the depth with which the painters engaged these interpretive challenges led to a reversal of our initial situation: It was the thematic experiments of the painters that led the writers to reconsider their own, too simple understanding of the resources available within their medium.

Virtually every art movement sets itself against its predecessor by claiming to disclose more complete or more significant truths. Impressionism's distinction was to set itself against the entire Renaissance tradition, by insisting not only on its own distinctive content, but also on its status as instrument for gaining access to a substantially different kind of truth. We find the stakes humbly and succinctly stated in the advice that the aging Camille Pissarro gave a young painter:

> Look for the kind of nature that suits your temperament. The motif should be observed more for shape and color than for drawing. There is no need to tighten the form, which can be obtained without that. Precise drawing is dry and hampers the impression of the whole; it destroys all sensations. . . . Don't work bit by bit, but paint everything at once by placing tones everywhere, with brush strokes of the right color and value, while noticing what is alongside. ("Advice to a Young Artist," in Nochlin 60)

Underlying these remarks is a sharp distinction, like Baudelaire's, between the observation of phenomena and the rendering of the sensations released by those phenomena. The Renaissance version of "painting what one sees" required an elaborate perspectival machinery, capable of delineating the precise boundaries that give each object its integrity and compose a coherent proportional spatial framework. In this new dispensation, on the other hand, nature is less a set of observed objects or provocative symbols than it is an enveloping "atmosphere." Precision of reference is far less important than capturing the feel of the entire range of relations that define one's possible apprehension of one's place at any given moment. Sight itself becomes the most profound registering of relatedness, because it organizes a set of properties – nuance, atmosphere, harmony, and above all the play of temperament – that establishes forms of individuality not dependent on the rhetorical will. The "I" can share the "eye's" mobility – at once composing a scene, and able to reflect on how the scene is contained within the whole that it makes visible.

Our exemplary writer makes essentially the same points, but with a remarkable difference in tone that is the glory and pain of knowing one's Baudelaire. Here is the young Jules Laforgue, in 1883, showing what a Parisian poet could make of such peasant fare, and providing a rationale for the experiments by Pissarro's friend Cézanne that Pissarro could not understand:

> Leaving aside the two artistic illusions, the two criteria on which aestheticians have foolishly insisted – *Absolute Beauty* and *Absolute Human Taste* – one can point to three supreme illusions by which technicians of painting have always lived: *line, perspective, studio lighting*. To these three things, which have become second nature to the painter, correspond the three steps of the Impressionist formula: form obtained not by line but solely by vibration and contrast of color; theoretic perspective replaced by the natural perspective of color vibration and contrast; studio lighting . . . replaced by *plein-air,* open air, that is by painting done in front of its subject. . . . Let us look in detail at these three points, these three dead language procedures, and see them replaced by life itself. ("Impressionism," in Nochlin 15)

So self-conscious a stance must put itself on a historical stage. Therefore, Laforgue casts Impressionism as an explicit antidote to everything inaugurated during the Renaissance. By idealizing the painter's interpretive role, the inherited tradition had subordinated sight and temperament to academic criteria, insisting that grass had to be brown, shadows black, and human forms gorgeously modeled in dramatic poses. But once these standards could be exposed as mere conventions, there would be strong grounds for proposing a counteridealization, much more vague and ambitious than anything Pissarro was to claim. The metaphor of "bondage" sanctions a claim to the radical "freedom" of being able to disclose life itself; sensation becomes a heroic force, connecting painting to all of the other revolutions taking place in the nineteenth century, and casting art as perhaps the culture's finest measure of its own claims to evolutionary progress:

> Essentially the eye should know only luminous vibration, just as the acoustic nerve knows only sonorous vibration. The eye after having begun by appropriating, refining, and systematizing the tactile faculties, has lived, developed and maintained itself in this state of illusion by centuries of line drawings; and hence its evolution as the organ of luminous vibration has been extremely retarded in relation to that of the ear. . . . Then a natural – or a refined eye, for this organ, before moving ahead, must first become primitive again by ridding itself of tactile illusions – . . . reaches a point where it can see reality in the living atmosphere of forms, decomposed, refracted, reflected by beings and things in incessant variation. (16)

This is to take one's claims about revealing life quite seriously indeed. For now the natural eye offers a level of elemental awareness that, simultaneously, gives us access to the most primitive and the most advanced forms of vision. Both domains are occluded by dead languages, and both require rejecting linear outlines in order to align the eye to fluctuating and mobile realities that are in constant permutation. But these ideals also put such burdens on sensation that Laforgue begins to wonder whether painting must seek a new subject matter, capable of eliciting a romance spirit like Baudelaire's, which can be reconciled with the spirit of scientific lucidity:

> Where the academic painter sees nothing but a broad expanse of whiteness, the Impressionist sees light as bathing everything not with a dead whiteness but rather with a thousand vibrant struggling colors of rich prismatic decomposition. Where the one sees only the external outline of objects, the other sees the real living lines built not in geometric forms but in a thousand irregular strokes, which, at a distance, establish life. Where one sees things placed in their regular respective planes according to a skeleton reducible to pure theoretic design, the other sees perspective established by a thousand trivial touches of tone and brush, by the varieties of atmospheric states induced by moving planes. The Impressionist eye is, in short, the most advanced eye in human evolution, the one which until now has grasped and rendered the most complicated combinations of nuances known. (16–17)

So advanced an eye must look within, as well as without. As he warms to his subject, Laforgue proposes what would become the central tenet of Modernism: that the principles one uses to separate authentic disclosure from the products of dead languages require reinterpreting both the powers we can attribute to human subjects, and the ways we envision those powers relating the subject to the forces that consciousness does not control. Claims about sites entail claims about agency: What we see, depends on how we see, which depends on who we become as we see. Pissarro was content to cast this "who" as the expression of individual temperament. Laforgue realizes that Impressionist temperament is not so simple a notion, because its expression is not merely a matter of psychology available to self-consciousness. Rather, we know the painter as a set of powers that comprise a "faculty of prismatic sensibility," taking form both in the domain of perception and in the domain of composition. So it is precisely in this combination of presentational forces that the romance spirit finds a new habitation. Painting leads to the grandeur of musical metaphors, as the poet tries to postulate an intimacy and scope of spirit that promises Baudelaire's mobility and scope, without his self-destructive willfulness:

> No longer an isolated melody, the whole thing is like a symphony which is living and changing like the "forest voices" of Wagner, all struggling to become the great voice of the forest – like the Unconscious, the law of the world that is the great melodic voice resulting from the symphony of the consciousness of races and individuals. . . . Subject and object are then irretrievably in motion, inapprehensible and unapprehending. In the flashes of identity between subject and object lies the nature of genius. And any attempt to codify such flashes is but an academic pastime. (17–18)

Such mobile states of spirit dissolve the Romantic dichotomy between disclosure and presentation. As Fritz Novotny put it, "It is precisely in the rendering of material things that spiritualization, if such a word can be used, in the sphere of Impressionism shows itself most clearly" (*Painting and Sculpture in Europe* 350). By depriving the work of any action within the scene, the artist invites us to identify with emotion projected by the painterly hand extending the scenic into the symphonic. That constructive activity, in effect, becomes a way of dwelling within the scene, as if the spirit's heightened capacity for sight also made present the inner registers evoked by music. So it is precisely this relation between painterly and perceptual modes that allows Impressionism to offer a plausible alternative to principles of idealization based on rhetorical intricacy or allegorical allusion. This engaged sensibility simply leaves no "lack" within which metonymies can become oppressive. In one sense, everything is metonymic: There are only horizontal, rather than vertical, relations of force, only a sun diffused among particulars: Yet since the subject moves so fluidly in its composition of harmonic structures, it seems capable of constantly enclosing those metonymies within more encompassing frameworks that need not take the old allegorical forms.

The writers elaborated three distinctive features of agency from Impressionist painting, each an attempt to synthesize the painter's sense of a scenically constituted self with the versions of inner life opened by Kant's notion of genius. Consider, first, how different Laforgue's sense of expressive spirit is from the Romantic one. Without dramatic actions, Laforgue claims, there cannot be significant inwardness. There are simply no stories, anymore, capable of organizing the quests that carry the dreams and frustrations constituting a rich inner life. But perhaps because it so totally refuses that domain of story, landscape takes on the power to at least hint at a local habitation and a name for spirit within contemporary culture. When the sensing mind is so bound to elemental constituents of the visual field, every twist, every modification, elaborates possible harmonies between chance and choice – between a psyche distributed over a landscape and a process of recording the psyche's sensations that gives us the most intimate knowledge of its workings. The tonal effects of light seem so tightly woven into the subtlest nuances of feeling that looking out, and looking within, become inseparably linked. This basic a relation between eye and object makes the most delicate of self-reflexive states themselves part of the immanent life of the visual field.

Delicacy, however, is not without its dangers. The more radically immanent the state of consciousness, the easier it is to treat spirit as an essentially passive force, entirely dependent on the visual sensations that compose its life. Laforgue's vaunted "life" threatens to become merely a matter of watching oneself look, as if everything that defined temperament were simply folded into the scene and would be destroyed by the need to make choices and take action. But here a second feature of Kant's thinking promises to right the balance. For genius, in Kant's view, is not primarily a matter of adjusting oneself to harmonies with nature; rather, it is the imposing of choice on sensation, so that a modified drama, at least, exists within the flattened world of the canvas, as the spirit seeks to build sensations into symphonies. Then Kant adds a further condition. For him, that intentionality could never be subsumed within natural rhythms, but had instead to submit itself to the higher rationality of the moral law. But for Laforgue, it sufficed for genius simply to express the active force of individual temperament. For then the spirit allies itself to "life" precisely because the spirit's individualizing force frees the activity from the clutches of abstract morality. Genius affords spirit the nobility of making one's sensations sing, without displacing the concrete scene that calls them into activity.

No one caught this fundamental shift in models of active spirit better than the young Mallarmé. Taking up Baudelaire's taste for Manet, Mallarmé presents that painter as the exemplar for resistance to conventional ideals. In their stead, he claimed, Manet composed "curious and singular paintings," so "disquieting to the true and reflective critic" that he "could not refrain from asking himself what manner of man is this":

> The scope and aim . . . of Manet and his followers is that painting shall be steeped again in its cause, and its relation to nature. But what except to decorate the ceilings of salons and palaces with a crowd of idealized types in magnificent foreshortening, what can be the aim of a painter before everyday Nature. To imitate her? Then his best efforts can never equal the original with the inestimable advantages of life and space. . . . [So he must reply,] "The better to satisfy my creative artistic instinct, that which I preserve through the power of Impressionism, is not the material portion which already exists, superior to any mere representation of it, but the delight of having recreated nature touch by touch. I leave the massive and tangible solidity to its fitter exponent, sculpture. I content myself with reflecting on the clear mirror of painting, that which perpetually lives yet dies every moment, which only exists by the will of Idea, yet constitutes in my domain the only authentic and certain merit of nature – the Aspect. . . . When rudely thrown at the close of an epoch of dreams in the front of reality, I have taken from it only that which properly belongs to my art, an original and exact perception which distinguishes for itself the things it perceives with the steadfast gaze of a vision restored to its simplest perfection."[7] ("The Impressionists and Edouard Manet," in Frascina and Harrison 39, 45)

This, we might say, is Kant's purposiveness, in a world where sculptural modeling has given way to other primary modes for projecting coherence upon our sensations. Genius replaces a mimetic art with one that can give the rule to nature by imposing temperament upon it. But, in that process, temperament also undergoes the transformation imposed by formal disciplines. For the will finds itself identifying with the transpersonal states that emerge as it works on the modes of feeling afforded within the act of composing a visual structure.

Mallarmé's comments bring us to the third and most ambitious feature of agency projected onto the paintings: a capacity to sustain new, more aggressively secular modes of sublimity. In Kant, and arguably in the English poetic tradition that leads to Eliot, the sublime serves simultaneously to reveal what surpasses the understanding and to terrify the will, so liberated, into submitting itself to some more encompassing moral authority. Mallarmé and Laforgue envision a radical alternative, in which sublimity consists in the will's power to make its own activity, and its own "aspect," sufficient grounds for resisting all more general categories. As in Nietzsche, the aim is to envision spirit as capable of taking responsibility for its own distinctness, without presuming to be able to locate that distinctness in thematizing acts of psychological self-reflection. A mind able to stylize its own difference, its own point of access to the real, and its own continual transformation of it, can hope to represent the entire pattern of activity as an emblem of the mobile spirit, at peace with the external world that helps give it access to its own nature.[8] The more complete the rendering of the aspect, the richer the alternative to the condition of heteronomy, where each desire postulates a key that merely confirms the solipsist's prison. Once one can align oneself with Monet's fluid, diffused sunlight, the old theatrics of alienation no longer confirm the spirit's superiority to matter; instead, they indict the agent, for failing to cultivate an eye sufficiently responsive to the harmonies that the landscape affords the composing will.

No one understood these changing ideals about agency better than Valéry, in part because he shared Laforgue's historical self-consciousness, in part because he was acutely aware that the old culture had to yield to another, more capable of basing spiritual values on the life of the senses. Valéry, as responsive to Mallarmé as that poet had been to Baudelaire, thought that intense concentration on the elementary life of the senses could give each art access to the romance energies at the source of its creative life, energies so deeply sensual they could sustain the most abstract of vehicles:

> By 1860, Romanticism and Classicism had become caricatures of themselves. . . . Realism appeared, but its novelty told rather on the choice of subject than on the ways of seeing and feeling. . . . The imagination which the Romantics set out to inflame, the truth which the realists claimed to transfix, were found to be somehow exhausted. Art now looked for quite another thing: in fact for nothing less than *the event of pure sensibility*. This meant an all important transformation of motive, technique, and values in the world of aesthetic production, almost an organic alteration, coinciding with the increasing influence of music during the same period. . . . Just as Monet and his associates founded their art upon the general principle of vision and on the acuter study of the eye's most delicate reactions to light . . . , so Mallarmé strove to deduce all poetry from the very principle of language – to consider it, that is, in complete generality; each poem, consequently, was to be considered and

treated as a particular example, of which the essential function
was to direct the mind back toward the very power of words in
themselves. It seems to me necessary to bring together Mallarmé's intuitions of absolute poetry, which stem from the very
source of expression, and the beginning of Impressionism with
its treatment of things and beings as modulations of light, on
which they depend for their purely visual existence. . . . If the
word "mystery" has a meaning, I cannot see it better applied
than to the principle of all things: the life of the senses. (*Degas
Manet Morisot* 117–18)

IV

Ironically, Valéry did not much like any painting more experimental than Degas's. Having grasped the logic that was to lead beyond
Impressionism, he could not make himself identify with its concrete
embodiments. His limitations, however, become our permissions, because they give us access to the complex dialectic between painterly
achievements, writerly appropriations, and painterly responses that was
beginning to define distinctively Modernist values. On the one hand, his
description provides a model for the life of the senses that is much more
nuanced, and even much more responsive to the paintings, than the
descriptions proposed by Renoir and by Pissarro. Yet Valéry was blind
to many of the possibilities for new work that were implicit in his own
criticism, especially in his concern for the material sources of expressive
energies and the forms of power they confer – a blindness shared by
virtually all of the writers of his generation, even Proust. Therefore, if
we are to understand that new work, we need to shift our attention from
what the poet's critical language makes available to what painters actually did. If we begin by studying the three basic ways that Modernist
painting responded to and extended the poets' critical language, we put
ourselves in a position to understand how the Modernist painters completed the dialectic by developing formal principles for adapting the
painters' discoveries to the realm of linguistic relations. Getting there,
however, will require a long detour from poetry.

When we turn from poets reading Impressionist painters to imagining
painters such as Cézanne and Picasso responding to the prose critiques of
Mallarmé and Valéry, we clearly enter a new stage in our dialectic. For
now we can imagine the painters posing hard questions to the poets'
versions of painterly disclosure. Can the aim of enhancing the life of the
senses be a sufficient ideal for an art as self-reflexive as painting? Is
breaking perception down into its constituent units enough, if painters
are successfully to resist the idealizing conventions that had defined the

real? And the problems only intensify when we reflect on how the painters might react to the poets' descriptions of their presentational activity. Are there not more complex and capacious powers at stake in the ways artists can understand productive genius? Can we simply equate the compositional energies disposed within the work with the activity of a "temperament" so mobile that it is intimately bound to the modulations that constitute atmospheric harmonies? The hungers of will seem to require more expansive terms for self-consciousness, and a far more stable and enduring sense of visual structures, moving beyond the "aspect" to certain permanent qualities of vision. Therefore, rather than accept Renoir's version of spirit as sensibility, the artists had to project painting as a less passive, more dynamic instrument. Painting had to embody a will that could treat the event of sensibility as a means, rather than an end. Then it might become possible to envision certain alignments of seeing and willing that articulate a "source of expression" leading to mysteries much more evocative, and ethically significant, than even Valéry's version of sensuality could postulate. And then painting could confidently propose itself as an alternative to Eliot's search for a metaphoric ground sanctioning our values.

Such doubts and questions first emerged in the two basic Postimpressionist critiques of what had become the dominant "Modern" style. On the one hand, Symboliste and Synthetiste values, at their most extreme and most interesting, tried to reverse the equation of mobile spirit with subjective temperament. In its stead, they explored strategies whose "essential aim" was, in Gustave Kahn's words, "to objectify the subjective (externalization of the idea), instead of subjectifying the objective (Nature seen through a temperament)." Gauguin and Van Gogh, on the other hand, subsumed impersonal or transpersonal disclosure under the imperative of personal expression no longer content simply to elaborate temperament, but demanding that the entire work be suffused by the artist's deepest subjective energies.[9] But, if we want the deepest and most provocative version of what, in both movements, established the models of site and agency that engendered radically Modernist art, we can proceed directly to Cézanne. In his work, an obsessive concern to render how we see is inseparable from a constant pressure to make the facts of seeing provide an adequate ground for the full affirmative energies of the will, "below which it cannot descend, / Beyond which it has no will to rise."

Forced to prose commentary in order to make his innovations intelligible, Cézanne managed to integrate these desires for disclosure and for presentational immanence within a single model that he called *"réalisation"* (realization). The following passage from a letter to Emile Bernard (October 23, 1905) offers the clearest rendering of that ideal:

> Your letters are valuable to me . . . because I am able to de-
> scribe to you again, rather too much I am afraid, the obstinacy
> with which I pursue the realization of that part of nature, which,
> coming into our line of vision, gives the picture. Now the theme
> to develop is that – whatever our temperament or power in the
> presence of nature may be – we must render the image of what
> we see, forgetting everything that existed before us. Which, I
> believe, must permit the artist to give his entire personality,
> whether great or small. (*Letters* 251–2)

This statement shares the basic distinction in Impressionist theory between perception and sensation, because it insists that one cannot imagine significant disclosures about the world that are not defined in relation
to the prehensive act of a responding sensibility. But Cézanne offers a
new, much more careful and suggestive analysis of how those two poles
can interact, and of what that means for the will.[10] His model of disclosure requires having actual objective properties of the aspect, not
temperament, "give the picture." The eye is not the slave of mood.
Rather, it is irreducibly active – at once the force that we recognize at
work making phenomena visible, and the principle by which the will
aligns itself to those phenomenal conditions. Such an eye makes demands
on the painter's presentational act. It will not suffice to cast one's art as
the weaving of musical harmonies through a landscape in order to extend
those moments when the temperament finds itself at home in the scenes
before it. Instead, these presentational acts must make visible the intellectual dramas available to vision by defining the struggles involved in
grasping painting's ability to make us see how we see. Previously painting had sought to compose harmonies between subject and object; now it
must begin with desperate efforts to undo all of the old idealizations. For
only by including the full, potentially disruptive demands of the will
could the painter hope eventually to disclose energies and structures
within the scene that would compel the entire personality to subordinate
its will to the authority of what it comes to see. Painting must become an
introspective and a religious art, without relying on expressivist models
for the nature of introspective agency or on Romantic symbolism as the
ground for those religious values.

Realization, then, transforms the event of sensibility into a complex
and concentrated balance among three fundamental forces: first, the
painter's desire to see, as purely as he can, into what makes certain
aspects of scenes wholly contain the mind; second, Flaubert's challenge
of using one's medium so that the work insists, simultaneously, on the
necessity of craft (if there is to be anything like the purified seeing that
Impressionism dreamed of), and the necessity of subsuming technique

under the qualities it makes visible (if there is to be any purpose to the display); and finally, the incorporation, within the life of the eye, of the most intense expressive dramas, as the will tries to find, in the forces of vision and composition, sufficient grounds for projecting itself as reconciled to what it has produced. The reflective eye and the constructive hand must establish powers capable of reorienting painting, so that it becomes less a matter of making particular phenomena visible than of exploring what the nature of visibility allows painting to project about the relation between the will and the world. What Emile Bernard called Cézanne's art of "ponderation" ("On Paul Cézanne," in Nochlin 101) transformed an essentially scenic sense of painting into an emphasis on authorial action, through which the intensity and dignity of eye and hand had to satisfy desires that, in literature, had created the problematics of Romantic expressivity.

Not even the most devoted lover of words can long prefer Cézanne the writer to Cézanne the painter. Most of the doubts we have posed about Impressionism appear intensely present in paintings as early as Cézanne's contribution to the first Impressionist exhibition in 1874.[11] Whereas Monet and Pissarro continue Eugène Boudin's great expanse of sky, which allows atmospheric permutations to swell into intricate harmonies, Cézanne's *Etude: Paysage à Auvers* virtually eliminates this mode of satisfying lyric emotion. In this canvas, there is almost no open air. Rather, everything conspires to constrain the eye to specific play of angles that expels all Impressionist dalliance with the charms that light affords and makes the intense structural relations figural signs of inner tensions unrelieved by outer and visible graces. Only so bold and rigid an armature could withstand the pressure of the imposing dark shapes of the leaves in the foreground and the flat green fields that press outward upon the scene.

By the 1890s, Cézanne had found the desired grace, largely by crossing the intensity of his early landscapes with the conditions of self-reflection that are encouraged by the studio genre of still life, which slows vision down and makes the processes of looking the object of experimental inquiry. To understand how Cézanne opened new directions for painting and poetry, let us concentrate on his ability to establish a dialogue between the two genres of still life and landscape. It was his late landscapes that most dramatically extended realization into an ontology based on the painterly process of subsuming structural modeling into the life of the painterly eye. But we most clearly locate the forces at stake in those acts if we see how they echo and extend the experiments in ponderation explored within still lifes.

Before Cézanne, still life had been a minor genre, best suited either to intricate naturalistic design effects or to what Roland Barthes brilliantly

describes as the perverse celebration of bourgeois reification that dominated Dutch art of the seventeenth century. To Cézanne, though, that
minor status provided the perfect instrument for an ambitious art, because its version of minimalism combined a mode of forgetting, on the
level of content, with a new vehicle for focusing on presentational energies. If still life subject matter is treated as a window through which one
represents the world, it simply does not engage major cultural issues.
But this limitation on the level of representational content makes the
genre an ideal site for experimenting in what the painterly hand can bring
to such representations – both as a cognitive instrument and as a means
of testing how the personality can dispose itself toward what it sees. The
emphasis on detailed attention and the lack of dramatic context put the
entire burden of the picture on the painter's choices. Anxious to make
such choices transform a minor genre into major art, Cézanne made
them carry two fundamental ambitions. The need to focus on compositional relations enabled him to work out an alternative to the sculptural
modeling that, for Baudelaire and Mallarmé, was the ultimate force
imposing the logic of appearances on the life of the psyche. Cézanne then
could make will itself responsible for the connective tissue that modeling
had previously supplied, so that the work, in effect, tests the capacity of a
pondering will to submit itself wholly to the life that the eye might
compose.

The imperative for his experiments in still life began in a reflection that
came to Cézanne as he was working on a landscape of Estaque in 1876:
"The sun is so terrific here that it seems to me as if the objects were
silhouetted not only in black and white, but in blue, red, brown, and
violet. I may be mistaken, but this seems to me to be the opposite of
modeling" (*Letters* 103). There would prove no better way than still lifes
to flesh out the consequences of this insight, because that genre can
virtually suspend all other concerns, allowing the artist to experiment
with using alternative principles of modeling by color to organize a
spatial field. In the old dispensation, depth of field is a matter of objective
relations between a source of light, the play of shadows, and the monocular organization of spatial recession. In the new, spatial recession derives
from the modulation of color hues, establishing an "apical point" where
light most emphatically strikes an object and defines a frontal plane. In
Still Life with Apples (1895–8), for example, each of the fruits near the
edge of the table achieves its own three-dimensional shape by a distinct
set of hues keyed by the point of maximum intensity (Figure 5). The
fruits, then, take on an aura of self-possession, while at the same time
inaugurating complex push-and-pull effects with the background green
apples and the glorious pitcher.[12]

This composition still relies on the primacy of color relations fundamental to Impressionist aesthetics. But color now has much more com-

Figure 5. Paul Cézanne, *Still Life with Apples* (1895–8). Oil on canvas, 27 × 36½". Collection, The Museum of Modern Art, New York: Lillie P. Bliss Collection.

plicated thematic roles to play. Each visual object, each lime, for example, in effect defines its own reality by literally composing its own depth. Pissarro's "whole" becomes an apparently endless adventure of individual acts of energized perception, in which the vitality of the eye and hand is indistinguishable from a sense of the life that each object possesses, without that life in any way depending on some vitalist version of underlying forces. What we see, in our seeing, is in no sense a metaphor; it is fact engaging will. And as fact, it establishes an elaborate ironic reversal of the role that sculpture once played, for it restores, on quite altered grounds, the Renaissance dream that painting could be aligned with science, rather than with illustration. In so composing depth, painting simultaneously discovers possible laws of vision and testifies to their emotional significance.

These qualities of pure event, however, cannot by themselves provide a very satisfying site for the will. Cézanne had to find, in this way of modeling, some complementary principle of abiding structure. He managed this by developing two brilliantly linked strategies, one simply extending Impressionist *passage* (the bleeding of color from object to object) the other radically transforming the Renaissance perspectival system based on sculptural modeling. *Passage* becomes less the testing of how colors fuse under certain conditions of light than a principle demonstrating how the life of the mind modulates the varied events comprising a scene into a satisfying whole. Notice, for example, how the infinite gradations of color in the white table cloth can serve as a figure for that prehending mind, as they form complex structural patterns out of what they reflect. Then this sense of the vital eye itself becomes the source of intricate organizing forms, which reveal the eye's own needs and powers. On the one hand, it would be difficult to imagine a more rigid structural order than this interlocking of orthogonals through the complex central vertical established by the lemon and the dish. But the marvelous play of textures (especially in the relation between glass and pitcher), and, above all, the undulant, snakelike movement of the individual pieces of fruit, eventually transform the very idea of structure. The motion is so active and fluid that the structures appear, not impositions of authorial will, but a mode of peaceful coherence, earned by the eye's restless activity. Because the undulant line is as relaxed as the artifacts are rigid, and because the viewer has already been witness to the elaborate creative force that the eye possesses, structure becomes an elaborate ritual of containment. This pure classicist need not rely on tradition or impose order, because he can capture the eye's ability to enter an elaborate dance, in which motion and structure each embraces the other, and through which we are led to treat the wholeness of the scene as composing a site no longer quite in the world of objects – or perhaps no longer only in the world of objects.[13]

I am not suggesting anything mystical – not yet, and not in the usual way. If there is a mysticism in Cézanne, it is a mysticism of sight, not one seeking to look through sight to some transcendental reality. So we must stay in touch with other structural effects that join with *passage* to deepen this sense that we enter a world at a tangent from the world that we think we experience as the normal one. Look again at *Still Life with Apples,* this time observing how it handles perspective in ways that complement the structural effect of *passage.* We notice that there is no one projected position from which the whole can be viewed. At least two perspectives seem both to compete and to cooperate in composing the scene. There is one angle from which we are able to look down at the dish of fruit, another from which we must look up at the table, as we follow the strong orthogonal and bright light introduced by the cloth at the painting's lower right-hand corner. (Other contemporaneous still lifes of his, such as *Still life with Curtain and Flowered Pitcher,* even set dishes at different angles and introduce at least three possible perspectives.)

What could Cézanne be after? We have, by now, seen enough of him at work to know that the only way to answer that question is to ask what the play on perspective helps him realize about seeing, and about how we can adapt the will to that process. It will not suffice to speak about experiments in spatial organization, unless we can motivate them in terms of actual perceptual principles and extend them into significant emotional dramas. In my view, this leaves us with two possible answers to our question. The first, read back from Cubism, posits Cézanne as demanding a much more complex version of the immediate visual field than Impressionism offered. In Impressionism, we find what now seems an uneasy compromise between an immediacy of sight, bound to the logic of color, and a radical sense of arbitrary point of view, which aligns immediacy with a specific sense of an agent momentarily stumbling upon this specific prospect. The two strategies should correlate, since nothing would seem a better guarantee of immediacy than fidelity to the single point of view that might take the scene in with a momentary glance. But suppose that the very idea of a single point of view is itself an inference, based on an idea about immediacy that is simply false to the facts of seeing. Perhaps the more a painter purifies seeing from convention, the more she realizes that the pure eye is in no sense an innocent one. The closer we get to the pure act of seeing, the more we realize that, as with any other bodily motion, our looking is a complex of retentions and projections, a searching around an object in space and in memory, rather than a straightforward looking on.

The second answer extends those visual possibilities into thematic ones, with the emphasis on the states of self-reflection that such a way of looking engenders. Now the same synthetic force that we noticed in speaking about *passage* comes to the foreground, proposing a different sense of agency from the model of the sensualist. There is no way to isolate a moment of seeing without also calling attention to more enduring properties of the person looking. Cézanne wants us to see the nature of our own mobility as observers, largely because that leads well beyond the image of the viewer as passive temperament, having to adapt the pysche to the emotional configuration of light's harmonies. In this painting, the eye does not let its energies diffuse throughout the scene. Instead, we are constantly aware of motives for the eye, of intelligence and memory working upon what is seen, so that it may satisfy the investments that they carry. No longer constrained by the conventional ideas of single perspective organizing a scene, yet still bound to treat the scene as an objective reality, Cézanne's work integrates two forces that together create a state close to the bound plenitude that Wittgenstein, in his *Tractatus,* posited as the basic condition of the mystical: Although the scene seems to reach out to offer the eye information in excess of what perspective would allow, the eye reveals its own ability to marshal the necessary responding intelligence that leads it far beyond the immediate moment of vision without ever turning the object into symbol or sign.

The only place to locate this "beyond" is in the third aspect of realization, its insistence on the expressive role that personality plays within this intense focus on how objects come to appear. All of this visual activity clearly calls attention to the painterly presence, but that presence must make itself felt without lapsing into the melodramatic psychologizing that Cézanne found contemptible in his peers. Cézanne avoided that danger by completely displacing all desires that might lead back to a subjective presence. Ponderation expels any more appropriative states. Thus, as Meyer Shapiro once put it, Cézanne paints apples that no one could desire to eat. Their appeal is not to that level of sense, but to modes of desire that only painting can define and satisfy.[14] We cannot eat what does not have sculptural mass. More important, one cannot even desire to eat, when the scene refuses to take form under any one point of view. Which perspective would gain the right to appropriate the object, and thereby remove it from the realm of the visible? And where, then, does the appropriation stop? What other objects will one have to turn to and destroy – each partial, and unable to elicit anything like the full life of personality one wants to engage in the world?

Cézanne hoped to resist this endless process of heteronomous substitutions by identifying the will fully with the cold and slow ponderation, as it sets itself against the metaphoric implications of sculptural gravity. In that release, painting reinvented the rationale behind Kant's concept of purposiveness, now in a context that purified it of the "dandified" associations created by Baudelaire's rhetoric: In place of the heteronomy inherent in practical desire, the artwork composes a site where one is invited to appreciate the full intricacy made possible by the eye's engagement in a particular event of seeing its own seeing. The unfolding of internal relationships takes the place of practical desire, first as we appreciate the complexity of the composition, then increasingly as we realize how much of our own psychic lives can take form, as our full absorption in the life of the canvas becomes a metaphor for the eye's relation to the objective world. To return to the specific cares of the empirical subject on such occasions seems a reduction of much more capacious forms of identity.

Precisely because the painting refuses our normal modes of desire, it forces us to ask who we become as we look. Only Kant provides even partially adequate terms for an answer. For we find ourselves experiencing a moment of autonomy that is in no way a desire to escape life – quite the contrary. Kant's autonomy is simply a way of taking responsibility for one's actions, as if one wants this particular way of acting to be recognized as definitively establishing one's claim to choose what one is and does. For Kant, of course, no art object could quite achieve this kind of responsibility. Its internal self-sufficiency could only be a symbol for those states, because the aesthetic could not produce the necessary clarity about intentions that reason could. But for Cézanne reason could not match vision as a form of self-possession. Whereas reasons seemed only to generate further reasons, in a sad parody of the empirical desire it was supposed to master, the life of the eye might be capable of a mode of self-reflection that could be internally coherent, clearly connected to the empirical world, and capable of satisfying all of the demands of the will. Painting could therefore provide a form of sublimity in no way transcendental, but located in how the mind comes to know and to will what the eye can ponder. In fact, as so much of the mind's energies become part of the life of the natural scene, the only plausible reaction is to seek a way of also capturing in paint the awe that attends upon so eloquent a silence. The conjunction of event and form establishes the canvas as an elaborate structure of containing shapes that combines fluid movement among objects with a constant sense of the single process that contemplates and wills the whole. There event and structure fuse in an atmosphere whose only imaginative analog is Mallarmé's *"l'azur."* But here there is no place for the *"poète impuissante"* who must curse a genius too bound to words to will its own enabling conditions, and too bound to self-pity to share the calm that comes from an absoluteness beyond human ironies.

V

Cézanne's still lifes are the best index of his originality. But it is his landscapes that give the richest and most sustained meditation on his motives, or, better, on what was at stake in the model of autonomous agency that the methods proclaimed. For it is in these contexts that we most clearly measure both the gulf between worlds painted and worlds lived and the possible interrelations between them. Landscape invokes complex associations – both existentially and aesthetically – so this genre requires our reflecting on who we become by virtue of how we see. Consequently it is in this aspect of Cézanne's work that we most clearly see the emotional and reflective implications of his war on sculptural modeling, vanishing-point perspective, and Impressionist relations between subject and object or presentation and disclosure. Finally, this proved to be the genre in which Cézanne did his most influential work. One cannot adequately discuss what Picasso or the poets could make of him without at least brief attention to his vision of landscape.

I know of no better example of that vision than Cézanne's *Pines and*

Figure 6. Paul Cézanne, *Pines and Rocks (Fontainebleau?)* (1896–9). Oil on canvas, 32 × 25¾″. Collection, The Museum of Modern Art, New York: Lillie P. Bliss Collection.

Rocks (1896–9) (Figure 6). For if we compare it to other Impressionist and Postimpressionist landscapes, such as Monet's *Poplars,* Van Gogh's *Olive Trees,* and even Cézanne's own earlier version of almost the same motif, *Melting Snow – Fontainebleau* (1879), we simply find ourselves having to use an entirely different critical vocabulary, which absorbs all descriptive terms into a complex, self-reflexive dialectic between the brush and the eye. Stunning painterly experiments call our attention to facts about vision, which then invoke an elaborate metaphoric register for thinking about what is involved in the ways the world becomes visible to and for us.

Impressionism taught us to imagine color harmonies as leading temperament out to a capacious sense of unfolding atmosphere. What, then, do we make of this inordinately compressed space, this sky, so much more tactile than the rocks which it so delicately outlines that it seems to take on their earthiness? One could locate the distinctive force of this painting in the remarkable push-and-pull effects that Cézanne achieves, or one could say simply that he has managed to render what the woods really look like from within (at least in my Pacific Northwest). Either would be no small accomplishment, in a culture where *plein air* harmonic expansiveness threaten to make us forget how much a part of earth the sky can be. But such interpretations do not face the challenge Cézanne offers us – that we make the new mode of seeing as also a way of engaging the reflective will – and thus they do not allow Cézanne his full response to the challenge that LaForgue and Mallarmé had posed for his culture.

If I am to take up that challenge, I must risk displacing those visual experiments into a somewhat self-indulgent language. But I see no other way to lead us back to the full implications of Cézanne's painterly act. Let us begin, therefore, with what Cézanne does to atmosphere. Rather than treat sky primarily as an envelope for the play of light, he insists on its dynamic capacity to bind the various physical objects of earth in remarkable intimacy. Sky then shares the *passage* qualities of material objects and takes on a similar tactility. Yet this sense of tactile substance remains compatible with the sky's role as the containing force for the entire scene. In fact, Cézanne's marvelous blue so permeates, modulates, and flattens everything it touches that it seems a surrogate for an eye itself become sensitive to the effects of its own movement.

The activity of sky typifies Cézanne's ability to dramatize a new vitality for the life of the eye. But to stop there is to ignore the second half of the equation requiring a doctrine of realization. In rendering the life of the eye, Cézanne makes the activity of painting carry the additional burden of dramatizing a reflective stance that defines possible responses of the will to what the image makes visible about the life of the eye. For this painting, the ladders start with the careful positioning of a pine branch precisely where traditional work would have established a vanishing point. Traditional perspectival recession will not suffice. By naturalizing painterly vision, it also subordinates will to appearance. But here everything conspires to make the activity of painting the precondition for there being a world of vision that can completely satisfy the mind. We notice first that under the pressure of the shallow recession, we can no longer take the light within the canvas as a function of atmosphere. In this compressed space and hushed coldness, the light that once seemed to emerge from the sun seems to have its source, instead, in the very composition of objects composing painterly space. The containing powers of light and sky are less the result of natural configurations than they are effects of a pronounced brushwork, echoing the movement of the branches. This identification gives the movement of details toward the surface plane a metaphoric twist, as if the self-discipline not to compete with the sun earned a lucidity about specific visual forces that enables the painting to mediate between what nature can offer and paint can compose. Cézanne's blue gathers all the effects of color into a single, dominant, containing space, which confers on the scene as a whole a sense of eternal "so-ness," in relation to which the seasons are mere ephemera.

Because he will not compete with the sun, Cézanne finds himself forced to compete with the force of gravity – so intensely that this second basic attribute of the painterly act establishes the dominant thematic force for *Pines and Rocks.* For over four hundred years Western painting had been dominated by the dream of capturing three-dimensional sculptural space on a two-dimensional canvas. Now Cézanne begins to wonder whether painterly modeling by color may provide a new model of visual space, in which the sculptural carries unnecessary and inessential baggage that distorts the immediate qualities of what actually appears before the active eye.[15] Consider the effects wrought here by his rendering of the rocks. In one respect, there is no illusion about this illusion: We know that these are rocks, because they have the inanimate rigidity we expect. Yet the pressure of emerging light, composition by apical points, and color in *passage* produce odd modeling effects. Although we register the volume of the rocks and their roles in three-dimensional space, we find it difficult to correlate that sense of substance with any feeling of weight or real mass. These rocks come to seem almost animate, since, instead of receding, they join the light in moving forward toward the surface of the canvas. Appearing to yield to the play of colors composing them, the rocks rely for their form less on gravity than on the stately dance organized by the vital life of the foliage. Ironically, it is the trees that take on considerable mass, as their vertical energy asserts itself to define the contours of the scene and to pull back from that seductive surface of pure color relations. The trees, in other words, keep the illusion of depth and resistance that saves this flattening of the canvas from becoming in any sense decorative. To collapse into design, to imitate, even for a moment, the gestures used by Gauguin, which Cézanne despised, would be to lose the most important feature of this experiment: its capacity to intensify our sense of the materiality of the scene, while it negates the principles of weight and mass that had provided the culture's most fundamental terms for substance.

If one thinks of Samuel Johnson, claiming to refute Berkeley by kicking a stone, one sees that this redefinition of substance sustains a good deal more than the visual ideals of traditional realism. It organizes an entire emotional field in terms of the drama created when human effort confronts the inert resistance of natural force. Replacing realism with realization sets up a different ontology, projecting emotional dramas in which the spirit seeks peace within the substance it helps to compose. A genuinely painterly modeling need not yield, either to the pure mobility of the Impressionist eye, or to the imposing will of the Renaissance heroism that set the sculptural ego against the simple background of landscape forms. Instead, it can stage vision as an activity that, in every step of realization, demands the full cooperation of will, so that the process of producing an objective world will also define the very terms of appropriation that can satisfy its most intense energies.

Cézanne's modeling provides us with a useful concrete emblem to employ in defining what his work made possible for the Modernists. First, it gives us a way of explaining the impact of the most disturbing feature of Cézanne's landscapes, their cold distance from social relations and practical actions. For Cézanne's world is about as far as one can get from the kind of scene that invites us to dally with John Constable's workers and their herds or to indulge in the lyric pleasures of Claude Lorrain's lonely shepherds. Just as Cézanne does not want the fruit in his still lifes to invite eating, he does not want his landscape to invite any form of bodily movement. Were he to allow such movement, he would subordinate vision to the forms of bodily freedom in space sought by the sculptural ambitions that sustained the cult of "objectified self-enjoyment." The eye so tied to a body seduces us into treating things as simple accomplices for the projects of human will, without imposing on us either their otherness or our responsibility for them. That eye, in turn, has nowhere to look for meanings, except to the intensity of its own inner life – to Cézanne, a poor substitute for the dynamic energies glimpsed in the activity of perception. But, if one can defamiliarize those attitudes that made us comfortable within Renaissance space, one might suggest a different psychic economy, permeating the most proprioceptive levels of self-perception. Thus Cézanne's landscapes insist that the body adapt itself to forms of movement at once more self-reflexive, and more immediate to the flow of sensation, than those that carry sculpture's organizing orientation toward the actionable. Unable simply to stretch out in relation to what she sees, the viewer must reflect on the powers of this cold calm of Cézanne's, perhaps locating there a physical exemplar for Kantian disinterest. By refusing the body's initial demands, by refusing even the desire for information about the particular time or season denoted (pines are not deciduous), Cézanne tries to paint modes of vision that we cannot imagine violating by the stuff heteronomy is made on.

Yet this is no mere aesthetic attitude, abstracted from the workings of the understanding. For Cézanne, the canvas provides testimony that such formative conditions restore our ability to appreciate what the eye actually does in seeing: Metaphor must rely on disclosures about the facts of vision. Once we see what it means to suspend mass while preserving volume, it becomes possible to imagine the attribution of weight, and hence sculptural space, as mere inferences that the mind tacks onto what the eye sees. Immediate vision – vision without inference or habit – sees volume, but not weight. One might say that volume is a primary quality, weight a secondary one, because the information it affords is not relevant to the strictly visual way that the scene appears. Weight is something one must hypothesize only if one has an interest in appropriating that appearance by doing something with the objects disclosed. But Cézanne's world cannot be organized by such practical concerns. The lyric gathering force of the eye in *Pines and Rocks* is not simply an affective response to an already constituted scene independent of the viewer. Rather than interpret the scene as embodying an idea of lyric perception, we see ourselves viewing lyrically, and we have direct evidence for contrasting this way of seeing to those anesthetized stances that do make mass a primary factor in organizing their world. Thus, by refusing to let us walk through his scenes, Cézanne puts radical aesthetic oppositions between vision and habit on the most concrete possible footing. Denying "meaning," he calls attention to sources of mystery in the very process by which sense constitutes its world.

If the presentational and the concern for disclosure have the dialectical relation I have just proposed, then we need a third attribute, capable of indicating what occurs when we reflect upon the conjunctions we have been tracking. I suggest that we take this third term to be the state of will that the paintings try to realize. I call that state of will Cézanne's distinctive "inwardness," in which we feel the pressure of a deep psychic life but refuse to grant any specific psychological sources for it, except for the stance that the painting manages to define toward its own energies. On the one hand, there is no lyric ego appropriating what is seen into stories or concerns that are located in a specific perspective: Yet there are intense investments in the specific ways that the eye ponders what it makes visible.

In Cézanne's still lifes, the force of a responding will is focused primarily through the interplay of perspectives: There, in effect, we are confronted with the synthetic nature of our seeing. When we turn to the landscapes, we find Cézanne increasingly attracted to dramatic framing devices as his means of registering the same synthetic qualities. The effects are clearest in his habit of having the branches of a tree define a frontal plane and situate an observer. In early work like *Etude: Paysage à Auvers,* the foregrounded leaves establish an uneasy emotional pressure. By Cézanne's magisterial renderings of Mont Sainte-Victoire, in 1885–7 (now at the Phillips and the Courtauld galleries), the looping pine branch in the foreground has quite the opposite effect. In visual terms, it provides a strangely mobile anchor, which parallels both the contours and the composing effects of the mountain, as if fluttering branch and enduring rock each had equal qualities of substance for the eye. Those parallels create an emphatic formal effect. Shared linear rhythms draw the eye quickly from the branch to the mountain, allowing it to traverse great distance at high speed. This is one power of the eye worth remarking. But as we reflect on that, we also become aware of the complement of that state. The green of the branch leaps past the mountain down to the fields, thus pulling everything toward the foreground, and setting up a lively tension with the mountain's capacity to organize the space surrounding it. What initially leaps over distances creates complex spatial fields, which make that distance itself a field for patient and pleasurable travels.

Mountains do such things to vision. Having registered that, however, Cézanne also wants to make us understand the affective consequences of such facts of vision, by inviting phenomenological modes of reflection. Notice that the relationships we have been tracing establish something like a drama of containing and releasing forces. As the branch draws the field into this foreground, it virtually makes present the focusing power of the eye. Then, once the eye has located itself physically within the scene, it can indulge itself in the rhythms and shapes that spread out as it moves back toward the mountain, itself creating parallel effects upon the landscape. These parallels then expand into more metaphoric realms, still within the picture, because the alliance of eye and mountain invites one to attempt to transfer other properties of the mountain to the implicit will that seems to accompany the seeing. The eye, now physically within the scene, can indulge in a profound hymn of acceptance, so deeply does it share both the mountain's material security and its ascetic capacity for an endurance that is a literal miracle of ponderation. Making no demands, eye and mountain occupy a position that can encompass, and provide focus for, an apparently endless variety of locales.

Those framing devices do not recur in Cézanne's last renderings of the mountain. They are no longer necessary, because he has found a more radical way to establish the responding eye's freedom from gravity. Now the brushwork does everything that the frame could do, but with more intense engagement in material life, which more profoundly links the transparent and the introspective. These late works, rather than paint seeing, paint the affect of painting what Cézanne's entire career had made it possible to see. In the various renderings that take the view from Lauves (especially those at Bale and Philadelphia), there is simply no substance not literally defined by the layering of thick brushstrokes upon one another: Yet there is remarkable weight. Those brushstrokes want to acknowledge, perhaps even to create, the otherness of this impervious world. For only that context will allow this intensity of light to assume its full resonance. And only that intensity will define the appropriate contrast for understanding the sublimity of the mountain's slightly softened harsh outlines, as they rise toward the contemplative dignity of a pale azure that seems to absorb all of the other colors. The brushwork that establishes substance prepares a modulation into something like the spirit of a presiding viewer, purified by art of all heteronomous distractions. One is tempted to speak of a painterly tragic vision – of a Kant transformed into Nietzsche's Dionysius – but that subsuming of visual into verbal categories would reach too anxiously for meanings that resist verbal equivalents.

VI

Cézanne died in 1906. There was a small exhibition of his work in that year, and a major retrospective in the following year – a retrospective so influential that it proved the single most important event in giving shape to the future of Modernism. Merleau-Ponty best caught the reason for Cézanne's impact. Here was painting become the most rigorous of professions; indeed, here was a form of work that seemed to take onto itself all of the obligations for authenticity that had been impossible to correlate with public behavior once the Romantic spirit had made righteousness a matter of the buried life. In Cézanne, the cognitive commitments of the scientist became inseparable from a radical idealizing of style: How one devoted oneself to the disclosing and presenting of one's research took form as visual testimony that such ends were worth the devotion they demanded. Only in the intense life organized by such research could one hope to find an alternative to the heterodoxy and the spiritual lethargy characterizing social life.

No one was to feel that impact more than two young painters who were fascinated by this exhibition: Georges Braque, seeking alternatives to the limited vocabulary of Fauve color and brushstroke, which he was rapidly exhausting, and Pablo Picasso, eager for a stance that would give him freedom from his own facility and from the Symboliste dualism between body and brooding spirit that his facility continually reinforced. Cézanne addressed those frustrations, in effect confirming the deep ambitions that underlay them, by showing that there could be a painting bound neither to the flux of sensation nor to the infinite regresses of pure self-reflection. Painting could devote itself to producing a mode of agency or ethos, within which the full energies of will could be at once entirely manifest and entirely justified through what the will composes: Painters could aspire to create for others the redefinitions of spirit that Cézanne had made possible for them. And then painting could play the provocative role that had been the province of the poets. Mallarmé had speculated on the possibility that analyzing a phenomenon into its facets would make it possible to capture the object in its fleeting moment, in its "absence," so that the work might explore "such themes as are the very logic and substance of our soul" ("Music and Literature" in Cook,

Mallarmé, Selected Prose 48–9). But now painting need not rely on such abstract attributions about the soul. For Braque and Picasso realized that Cézanne made it plausible to envision the war on substance as the vehicle for dramatizing a new vitality for spirit. Painting, rather than tie itself to objects, could define modes of visual thinking capable of making concrete the dreams of inventing a new Modernist sensibility.

Concentrating on such concerns will require us to pay less than adequate attention to the distinctive painterly innovations wrought by Cubist art. But my thematic focus should help us to clarify what the poets might have seen in these paintings, and may thereby lead us to appreciate certain emotional and cognitive properties in specific paintings that are not usually addressed by art historians.[16] At the least, we shall observe how radically Braque and Picasso differed in their thematic use of similar early Cubist techniques. Whereas Braque concentrated on a tactile intelligence, still devoted to Cézanne's interest in realizing how the eye engages and carries basic emotional investments, Picasso's Cubism was fundamentally a matter of foregrounding the power of the painter's transforming energies. In the place of a bourgeois Catholic concern for grounding the will in the world, this young Nietzschean insisted on making his painting a vehicle capable of folding the world into the composer's metamorphic eye. Next, we shall turn to the noniconic virtuality of Kasimir Malevich and Piet Mondrian as it took the further step of incorporating even that presentational will within a transpersonal force that makes individuation possible. At stake in all three discussions is the articulating of imaginative energies and strategies that then enable us to isolate certain distinctive qualities and projects in a variety of poetic work.

In order to demonstrate what Braque and Picasso made of Cézanne's heritage, I shall contrast two Proto-Cubist renderings of urban scenes. For Braque, I have chosen *Houses At Estaque* (1908) (Figure 7), because it adapts the inscribed eye so familiar in Cézannean landscape to a more interiorized emphasis on realizing what might be called "states of reflective tactility." Cézanne's refusal to paint mass and weight here leads to a more abstract transforming of physical gravity into its internal equivalent, thereby allowing the eye, freed from pure sensation, to explore those affective forces that bind it to objects.

Braque's chief vehicles for this enterprise are a recasting of Cézanne's perspective and a much more psychologized version of *passage*. Just as in Cézanne, Braque's work refuses to align itself to any one perspective, insisting that the event of seeing is not simply a matter of capturing a scene from one moment in space-time. But Braque goes farther. Now the shifts among perspectives establish modes of visual thinking no longer bound to the logic by which the eye actually composes a natural scene.

Figure 7. Georges Braque, *Houese At Estaque* 1908. Kunstmuseum Bern/Hermann und Margrit Rupf-Stiftung.

What matters is the visual rendering of how objects come to carry emotional investments for the eye. In following the movement of *passage,* we find ourselves constantly shifting among perspectives on the houses, as if the brush on the surface continually modulated between entire possible worlds. Ultimately we are led to imagine this painting as attempting to stretch the two-dimensional surface into a structure that can show a range of perspectives, comprising all three hundred sixty degrees of possible angles on the village. So we are tempted to think that Braque wants to replace the Impressionist painter's mobile temperament with something like a transpersonal mobility of sight as it moves among possible temperaments. The result is a radical rethinking of the enveloping "atmosphere" that was stressed in Impressionism and transformed by Cézanne into a contemplative force. Here, primarily through the figure of the eye projected in the framing branches, the containing force becomes an intricate play of intimacy and distance: We see what the eye frames, and we see the eye as a frame, itself contained within the play of visual forces.[17]

This foregrounding of the eye's complex relation to its objects provides both an imperative to interpret the visual activity and a focus for those interpretations. Everything about the work – the complex *passage,* the very narrow palette, the pronounced brushwork, and that framing eye – all seem to make the movement of perspectives itself the basic source of energy within the scene. On a purely visual level, this movement brings inanimate forms into something closely resembling organic life, but a life whose animating energy is literally the relation among those perspectives, so that we can imagine each, in its own way, constituting this town as sustaining deep personal investments. The result is a sense that we actually see the life created by seeing – or better, by intending: a superb way to imagine what is involved in looking at spaces that one inhabits along with diverse others, each capable of imposing her own order upon it. One knows that place, and one cares about it, because one is aware of the many ways in which it is regularly seen. And that awareness becomes, itself, a modification of how we actually see. The eye, in this painting, is too intimate to be a representation of immediate seeing; its engagement in what it sees is the realization, in the moment, of all that time has made of a person's sense of place. Such intimacy, in turn, cries out for the painter's brush, because it dwells in us on a level where we neither need nor seek words. It dwells in our immediate "feel" for place, in the most literal sense of the word "feel." Whereas traditional tactile painting (J. B. S. Chardin's, for example) tries to capture the textures of particular objects, Braque's abstract concern with the life that multiple perspectives set against sculptural modeling tries to project the sense of an eye so familiar with the nature of its dwelling place that it feels an entire expansive landscape as something that it can touch as it looks. All of these interpretive words, then, lead us back to something irreducibly and mysteriously visual: to the way that the eye, as part of the body, can align its proprioceptive investments to what the eye, as part of the mind, gathers in the expansive spaces that open before it. Tactility is an idea too fine and too capacious for anything but that radically physical mode of thinking. So, although painting here requires the intellect, it refuses to yield the kind of meanings with which the intellect is at home, proposing, instead, to make us reflect on the phenomenological ways in which that intellect can be bound to enhance the body's senses.

Braque has no patent on making the intellect serve the body's senses. Virtually all significant painting does that in some way. But Braque is distinctive in calling attention to that phenomenological enterprise as the central task of painting – perhaps even as an aspect of the painting inviting a sensual thinking about sensual thinking. This version of meta-painting establishes its claims by the power of that figurative eye to recall Cézanne and to remind us of how literally this work takes the ideal of realization. Whereas Cézanne's real remains a relation between how we see and a projected scene, Braque's real depends on calling attention to the ways in which the painter's making articulates certain affective dimensions that are intimate to seeing, but have been occluded by painting's four-hundred-year romance with appearances. Now, where painting had taken on heroic and moral subjects, the artist engages a simple sentiment. But he does so with such subtlety, and with such surprising economy, that the art takes on perhaps the more substantial value of defining a mode of introspection lucidly responsive to the most elemental attachments we form toward the world and toward other people.

To describe this achievement, we can imagine each of those attachments as transformations of Cézanne's idea of realization. First, realization defines the eye's power to produce and to sustain an affective idea of place. Next attention shifts to the way that such rendering of visual ideas can be said to engage the responding will. Because the subject of the painting is not the landscape per se, but the idea of that landscape site, Braque, like Cézanne, keeps people out of his scene: The painter's task is to contemplate the whole, not to find surrogates within it. The only way to populate this landscape is to align the will to the energies it disposes. Yet whereas Cézanne locates that will entirely in the direct physical and metaphysical forces mediated by the reflective eye, Braque gives it a social dimension. How the eye sees is inseparable from its capacity to make its feeling for that tactile surface also a means for eliciting and projecting certain qualities of caring. This mode of seeing depends on an intimate relation to the multiple perspectives that give the scene its visual life. When landscape becomes townscape, a good deal more than the physical setting changes. Just as Duchamp abstracts chess from the setting in which it is played,[18] in the painting that I discussed in Chapter 1, Braque empties his village of "its folk this pious morn," in order to place us in the position of its ideal inhabitant, a position that each inhabitant does indeed occupy in those moments when the eye is truly free of the expectations created by the culture's commitment to sculptural perspective. Then the viewer is offered the kind of self-knowledge that can come only when his own commitments are truly available to the touch.

VII

About a year after Braque painted *Houses at Estaque,* Picasso found, in Spain, even more elaborate and compelling reasons to adapt Cézanne's antisculptural principles to a village landscape. A series of paintings, culminating in *The Reservoir, Horta d'Ebro* (Figure 8), simultaneously extended Braque's technical research and showed that such experiments in disclosing the life of the eye as a reflective instrument could also involve substantial changes in what painting's presentational

Figure 8. Pablo Picasso, *The Reservoir, Horta d'Ebro*. Private collection.

action projected: Realization could become a force allowing painting to engage in that quest to define significant forms of ethos which had traditionally been the role of literature. As in Braque, *passage* in these paintings celebrates its freedom from sculptural modeling, by composing a remarkably intimate visual feeling for the idea of how one inhabits an urban space. In fact, this village takes form as a single entity whose tactile qualities give it an organic vitality, won by modulations of monochromatic hues that allow even the shadows a kind of substance. And why not, since in one's visual familiarity with the village, these shadows play as active a role as any other phenomenal attributes? That familiarity, moreover, may have led Picasso to imitate Braque's experiment in perspective, this time using the multiple implicit frameworks to give that shape a set of tensions, making it twist forward toward the frontal plane. A town can be brought to life by the virtual eyes that implicitly inhabit it, here giving it the appearance of something in a still life by Cézanne – so cold is the overall attitude, so composed and reserved are the forms, and so balanced the two competing demands that the eye enter from below the village, at the left corner, and from above the reservoir, on the right. Even Cézanne's framing eye is here, in the shape given the reservoir.

This eye, however, no longer wields the power it does in Cézanne or in Braque. Unable to contain the entire scene, even though it is equated figuratively with the containing form of the reservoir, the eye is reduced to appearing as an object among objects, forced to compete with the village for our attention. More important, this eye no longer moves freely between intimate dallying and a capacity to maintain a reflective distance on all that it surveys, as it moves through the scenes that it composes – both natural and self-reflective. Instead, the reservoir can mirror only what it stands over against. This mirroring has important roles to play. Without the reflecting surface provided by the reservoir, the painting would have no depth, the shape composed by the houses and the multiple perspectives no room to twist and expand. But providing those contrasts exacts a substantial price. In order to establish depth of field, the reflecting surface must become essentially two-dimensional. This rendering the eye as a figurative reservoir reduces its activity to the establishing of a pure reflecting surface that translates all of its contents into the working of a single plane. As a consequence, these reflections on the water become the most inert elements of the scene, locked into an unyielding horizontal design. So the figure of the eye, which has traditionally introduced human presence, and therefore allowed psychological depth to enter the scene, now can assert its power only by denying that depth, thereby, ironically, deepening the sense of force that we attribute to the strangely impersonal shape that it takes many eyes to compose.

Picasso has created a figural scene so complex that we cannot stop here, but must posit a more elaborate thematic interpretation, for even the difficulty of making that interpretation may become an aspect of this play on the nature of perspectives, and a means for reinforcing, by contrast, the magisterial silence of this image that can disdain our words. If we concentrate on the fundamental visual contrast between village and reservoir, we also produce obvious thematic contrasts between seeing and interpreting. The effect is to stage this work as a re-vision of Braque's faith in being able to share the intimate quality linking the many perspectives that comprise the visibility of the village. Conflict prevails between the texture of the reflecting surface of the reservoir and the fluid movements that carry the force of the multiple perspectives, as if this condition highlighted the enormous gulf between what gives a village its life and what is available for the reflective interpreter. One might take the reservoir's figurative eye as a strikingly literal emblem for the monocular model of seeing that once structured Renaissance perspective. But whereas once that eye had guaranteed perceptual depth of field, it now confines the real to a characterless flatness. Relying on so monadic a structure necessarily brings in its wake the terribly reductive world that Wilhelm Worringer complained of, because it erases all of the otherness that we see twisting through the competing image of the houses that the reflective eye so badly imitates.

What can compensate for, or resist, this diminution by the reflective eye? One possible answer is to idealize the multiplicity of perspectives inherent in the image of how the city comes to appear. Then Picasso would have created a more radical, and more dramatic, version of the mobile intimacy celebrated by Braque. But look again at this urban form. There is none of Braque's green to soften the ochers and cold grays, and there is no effort at a lyric, unifying, rhythmic, circular design. One might reply that these details are called for by the visual facts: Spanish landscape is not known for its luscious greens. But fact will not explain why these physical traits seem so well complemented by the tensile properties rendering the houses. Every effort to assert the calming force of gravity on this mass is countered by the clash of perspectives and tones that keep the parts in uneasy motion. So, if urban space is defined by the multiplicity of perspectives that give it its reality, there may be no way to avoid or absorb the conflicts that they necessarily engender. Braque's remarkable sophistication may mask an essentially pastoral understanding of the multiple perspectives that we see here destroying the possibility of pastoralism. Picasso will not let us forget a basic lesson of Cézanne's still life: the irreducible otherness of what the eye confronts. Thus, there are no people in this scene, not because Picasso suggests some deeper human understanding on the margin, but because no single person would be able to bear the astonishing coldness of what the eye must recognize as its social reality.[19]

The effort to find an alternative to that fragmented and flattened eye seems to leave the painter caught in a state much like Flaubert's in *Madame Bovary*. In order to recognize the otherness of the real, one must seek a remote distance, unwilling even to cast the self as the center of reflective contemplation, aligned to what it realizes. What is "realized" is a sense that the constructivist project cannot hope to stand outside the clash of perspectives that bring the city to life within the painting. Where contemplation had been, there the art must rely on its own willfulness, as it composes a strange and often frightening process of asserting and maintaining the differences that are continually challenged by the terms of sociality and artistic convention. Rather than aligning will with things as they are, the painter must explore modes of authority based on the struggle to impose on others his own efforts to remake that world with a difference that will never collapse into mere reflection, however triumphant. For Picasso, painting is not a matter of knowing and accepting, but of making, and thereby of asserting oneself against all forms of the given:

> "Truth cannot exist. If I pursue a truth on my canvas I can paint a hundred canvases with this same truth. Which one, then, is the truth? And what is truth – the thing that acts as my model, or what I am painting? . . . If there were only one truth, you couldn't paint a hundred canvases on the same theme." (Dore Ashton, *Picasso on Art* 21–2)

> "From errors one gets to know the personality! If I were to start correcting the mistakes you mention in accordance with rules that have nothing to do with me, whatever is personal in my writings would be lost in a grammar which I have not assimilated. I would prefer to invent a grammar of my own than bind myself to rules which do not belong to me." (45–6)

> "The goal I proposed myself in making Cubism? To paint and nothing more. And to paint seeking a new expression, divested of useless realism, with a method linked only to my thought – without enslaving myself or associating myself with objective reality. Neither the good or the true, neither the useful or the useless. It is my will that takes form outside of all extrinsic schemes, without considering what the public or the critics will say." (59–60)[20]

Presentation and disclosure now enter even more complex relations with one another. In one sense, they are incompatible. Whereas previously realization had been a process of seeking to align will and world, it now becomes a force essentially for producing worlds in accord with an embattled will. Yet, if the grammar of his own that the painter develops is to have any authority, it must continue to fascinate the eye and, probably, to influence how we see. Therefore, although Picasso's canvas cannot subordinate invention to research into the way things appear or how villages are inhabited, he must keep his concern for will bound to the logic of appearances that it tries to master. So now Cézanne's research becomes the construction of a sublime threshold between the dynamics of the eye and the dynamics of the imposing will.

That enterprise brings Picasso close to Flaubert's project of playing the lucid eye against the transforming will to art. But, as we have seen, the writerly will soon found itself beset by the ironies inherent in the kinds of self-consciousness that its sense of rhetoric elicits. Picasso does not yield to those ironies – in part because of iconic resources that he could adapt from his medium (and make available for analogical practices in other media); in part, because of the specific model of will that he elaborates. Writerly rhetoricity sets chains of signification, and layers of masks, in an endlessly regressive movement, apparently escapable only by realigning oneself to some ground in Logos or in realization. Picasso turns instead to the forms of agency that one can imagine as being sufficiently defined by the specific visual configurations they compose.

I hesitate to use so vulnerable a concept as "visual presence" to explain that version of agency. Nonetheless, I think we must recognize how careful the Cubist style is to make its internal fragmentation a form of defense against rhetorical slippage. When it is so hard simply to recognize what is being represented in the painting, we find ourselves not analyzing its rhetoric, but using the authorial energies as the only available principle that attaches us to the iconic surface. Picasso's energies offer such intelligence, and such refusals to evade the will, that raising epistemological questions at all seems largely to miss the point. Where no truth is promised, no lack of truth can return to haunt the signifier. And where the image itself so depends on our integrative activity, there emerges a kind of virtual testimony that enables us, at least partially, to repeat, in reconstructing the work, the forms of desire that it sets in motion. In Picasso's portrait of Kahnweiler (1912), for example, the strongest sign of the subject's intelligence is the way in which the viewer is led, by light and line, to make quick and forceful jumps between the sitter's face and his hands, as if his intelligence could be physically measured by the life it offers to our attentive looking.[21] Kahnweiler seems to welcome, if not to demand, the devices of this painterly will, while at the same time creating, by his implicit intelligence, a situation in which it would be trivial for the painter to try to express some distinctively subjective interpretation of Kahnweiler. It is precisely by not looking within, but by matching his intelligence to the demands of his subject, that the painter manages not to displace or evade a compelling otherness.

In Picasso, then, the romance of the eye becomes the vehicle for defining and testing modes of agency worthy of Nietzsche at his most assertive. In the place of subjective expressionism, we find a will refusing to justify itself by external categories or autobiographical contexts. Were its expressive force less intelligent, we might treat it as a version of the unconscious; were the work more seductive, we might take that force as calculating will. But perhaps all we can do with this strange blend of compulsive assertion and impeccable craft is to say with Stein, "This is Picasso." No other abstraction will bring us closer to this hand that Max Kozloff describes as laying on a "monkish monochrome . . . with sumptuous subtlety" (*Cubism and Futurism* 48). Rather, we must see here the culmination of a century obsessed by the dream of constitutive particularity, now taking form in an intelligence too insistent on itself even to quite fit our models of intentional action. Only the imaginative site of the artworks explains the motives responsible for its creation.

Look again at *The Reservoir, Horta d'Ebro,* this time concentrating on how that individuating intelligence seems at once to need, and to transform, Cézanne's "atmosphere." Again there is that cold silence, but here hinting of possible metaphors and lurking threats that seem to overflow the visual details. Clearly, Cézanne's contemplation will not suffice. In fact, were Picasso to remain contemplative, within these clashing perspectives and unstable signifiers, he would trap himself in what is essentially a mode of bad faith. He would use distance to deny the imperative to choose. But here, all of the distance is part of a choosing, part of an effort to acknowledge all the otherness that imposes itself on the eye, while at the same time making one's art the vehicle for absorbing that otherness within one's own constructed site. We might even see this painting as defining what a will can be that need not rely on buried lives or moral categories: Will is the insistence on maintaining the differences that refuse to let this visual image become simply a reflection. Will is the assertiveness manifest by the painting's insistence on reconstituting the town, in what then becomes the world that Picasso can dwell in. The transforming of houses into a single form is one emblem of this will; the other is the way the painting handles the eye shape that, in Cézanne and Braque, is the emblem of contemplative containment. To the degree that Picasso's reservoir simply reflects or contains the village, it condemns both the visual details and the responder to a flat, two-dimensional surface, mocked by the vital phallic shape that the painter's transforming activity establishes. The painter's energy does not flow through that eye, but resists it, by asserting the primacy of the appropriative intelligence that makes the eye its metaphoric and metamorphic instrument.

Because the painter's mind can understand the vital principle of urban life, the painter's craft can define the only possible individual response to that multiplicity of perspectives. The art must conquer the eye – not by looking within, but by staking the very idea of an individual on the person's ability to subsume seeing under making. The work comes to contain the painter's own powers of containment: figuratively, through this figure of the eye, and literally through the dynamic field that, we understand, both depends upon the eye and provides a new way of seeing. This painting literally incorporates the eye within the powers of will to transform how we see. And, by allowing the will this view of its own transforming powers, it creates the possibility of wanting to inhabit the fictions one may be condemned to create. The degree to which the audience comes to share that wanting becomes the ultimate measure of the substance and power that the will manages to take in the world.

Figure 9. Pablo Picasso, *Guitar, Sheet Music, and Wine Glass,* 1912. McNay Art Museum, San Antonio, Texas: Bequest of Marion Koogler McNay.

VIII

If we generalize from this painting,[22] we can see all of Cubism as the effort to transform perception into a distinctive painterly logic for space – not because the logic can be said to represent how we see, but because it is a way of imposing the conceptual on the "visual within the visual." So insistent was Picasso on the imperial force of *his* version of this logic that he eventually took the culminating step in the revolution that Cézanne had inaugurated: Picasso actually made sculpture on a purely painterly model of spatial composition. Thus, a work such as *Guitar, Sheet Music, and Wine Glass* (1912) (Figure 9) simultaneously offers a violent distortion of both object and medium and a brilliant recovery of the capacity of sculpture to reveal planar aspects of form. There is significant disclosure here, but only as the self-definition of will that has come dangerously close to obsession, as it in effect transforms Cézanne into a Logos needing the correction of a rebellious Demiourgos.

To grasp the principles of agency that Picasso ultimately developed, we need to turn immediately to the last phase of his analytic Cubism, where we see him reacting to the challenge of Braque's recent experiments in collage. Picasso, having subsumed traditional sculpture under painterly principles, saw in collage the possibility of taking visual art beyond logics bound either to sculpture or to painting. Perhaps by fragmenting not the illusion but the supporting material itself, one could make visible a logic at the very core of perception – even at the very core of our assumptions about substance that lead us to privilege perception. And perhaps, in doing this, the painter's will could most fully and most playfully define its claims to rival the divine creator – distorting, composing, and disclosing features not only of what we see, but of the very possibility of there being a substantial world for us to see.

Therefore I want to argue that Picasso's collages provide crucial testimony for the significance of the constitutive powers fundamental to Modernist experiment. The argument is necessary because Rosalind Krauss has made a very influential case to the contrary. In her essay "Representing Picasso," she claims that it is precisely these collages which emphatically put to an end naive Modernist dreams of establishing heroic models of agency by dramatizing the force of deconstructive thinking. If she is correct, Picasso's willfulness led inevitably to an ironic sense of endless displacement, so the dream of Modernism establishing plausible forms of direct testimony capable of overcoming such ironies must be relegated to the junk heaps where Postmodernist styles find their various garbs. But in my view, Picasso's Cubist collages go beyond such processes of displacement to insist on the virtual properties we bring to bear in the act of completing what the analytic mind can dissect into competing textures and surfaces. Thus he establishes a level of visual abstraction that goes beyond at least American deconstruction's version of the emptying of presences.[23] And, rather than reading those collages as leading directly to Postmodernist meditations on irreducibly riven surfaces, I emphasize their affinities with the experiments in testimonial agency carried on by noniconic painters. From that perspective, one can also understand why these experiments proved significant to poets, for they established levels of abstraction that verbal art could adapt to a thematics of presence and absence.

These arguments hinge on the adequacy of Krauss's claim that Picasso's collages of 1912 and 1913 constituted a radical break from Cubism, and thus established the fundamental tension and metaphoric strategies central to the rest of Picasso's career:

It is often claimed that the genius of collage – its Modernist genius – is its ability to heighten, not diminish, the viewer's experience of the ground, the picture surface, the material support of the image; as never before, the ground – we are told – forces itself on our perception. But in fact in collage the ground is literally masked and riven. It enters our experience not as an object of perception but as an object of discourse, of representation.

It is here that we see the opening of a rift between collage as a system and Modernism proper. For collage operates in direct opposition to Modernism's reach for perceptual plentitude and unimpeachable self-presence. Modernism's goal has always been to objectify the formal constituents of a given medium, making these, beginning with the ground that is the origin of their existence, the objects of vision. Collage problematizes that goal by setting up a discourse in place of presence, a discourse founded on a buried origin, a discourse fueled by absence. . . . The whole of Picasso's subsequent work is made in relation to the logic of collage and its problematic of the absent origin. . . . Obsessed with the labyrinth, he is also obsessed with a system whose center is not an origin but a double term, a pair of opposites, beast and man, instinct and reason, matter and language. ("Re-presenting Picasso" 93–4)

Thus the achievement of Picasso's collages is that they "represent representation" in such a way as to expose two ironic dimensions inherent in its signifying practices. First, the signs by which a work represents must differ from, and defer, that which they purport to make present. Second, we cannot stand outside the constant play of differing and deferring in order to interpret the signs as producing a single, consistent object of representation. Signs are always implicated in systems (which, in visual art, one can take to be styles), and the play of elements within systems frustrates any effort "to objectify the formal constituents of a given medium" (94). The power to distinguish constituents itself depends on signs for signs, in an infinite *mise en abîme*.

Such duplicity of signification leads Krauss to insist that the basic project of Modernism is doomed. There is no way to replace referential art with an autonomous work, characterized by "perceptual plentitude and unimpeachable self-presence" (96). The Modernist dream of aligning vision with will is now little more than a dead style, reminding us of the failure awaiting all dreams of plenitude. And Picasso's dream of a will that can stage his own freedom from such illusions yields to a collage mode denying his own mastery, his own pictorial representation" (92). Instead, Picasso becomes a consumer of styles, aware, in those acts, of an internal self-division, in which each representation of the self as a possessor is undercut by the very terms used in the representation. The style cannot be the man, because it is first a system that imposes an order on elements and, in so doing, displaces them. Collage, though, can at least embody this tension between signification and presence. For example, Krauss argues that, in *Guitar, Sheet Music, and Wine Glass,* the layering of real textures insists upon "a thoroughgoing submission to the action of the sign; it reformulates the visual as language," banishing "the guitar, the compote, the wine glass . . . from the image," in a way that makes them "reconjured only through a play of signs – representation as a self-conscious system of substitutions." In this collage there is not even a representation of a guitar; there is only the idea of the object, evoked by a relation among discreet signs. "It is thus the absence of the guitar that resonates through the disjunct signs that evoke it. . . . The image becomes a collection of signifiers, a field of signs, a theater of representation" (94). In foregrounding those signifying properties, then, Picasso's collages in effect dramatize the inescapable problematic of representation, because they negate both the material self-sufficiency of the objects and their ability to refer adequately to the objects they denote. Instead of purporting to represent objects, these signs evoke them, by putting under erasure, and thereby bracketing, any claims to a conventional assertive role.

Notice, for example, how in this work the glass *is* only a drawing. Then, *as* a drawing, its role is not to refer to a glass, but to define a contour of the guitar. Similarly, all of the other elements play dual, self-canceling roles, because the materials function primarily as representational signs, defining changes in luminosity, the texture of shadow, and the push and pull of planes in relation to negative and positive space. What should refer instead constitutes an alternative presence; what should be able to have its own substantial reference must yield it in the service of evoking an image. So, at its most general, the collage presents an irreducibly complex play of the figurative, the literal, and abstract formal codes. Elements "mean" only by not being what they are, and meaning itself is only an effect of signs, as they contradict the given nature of physical properties. Finally, this denial of presence necessarily entails the subordination of the expressive author to the affective force of preformed materials. The making is doubly remote from the seeing, because it is an act negated by materials whose negation forms the figural "object" in the artwork.

Brilliant as Krauss's reading is, however, her eye seems to me to register more than her critical model allows her to comprehend. Why must we accept her fundamental opposition between taking the painting's surface as a form of self-presence, and taking the irony of collage as insisting that the ground is "masked and riven"? It seems to me that despite all of its negations, the overwhelming effect of the work is not a sense of the absence of the guitar, but of its magical presence, even though, or because, the guitar emerges only as the transformation of other shapes. How tricky and unsatisfying, then, are terms like "ground" and "presence." For, if we insist on a material ground or a pictorially denoted presence, everything Krauss says is true. But suppose that Picasso is playing one notion of ground and of presence against another. Then, if we keep Krauss's questions, but concentrate on what Picasso leads us to reflect on in the working of this assemblage of signs, we will see that the quality of assertion takes the place of traditional ideals of reference, and thereby extends principles that he had been elaborating during his Cubist experiments.[24]

What is absence, in terms of material substance and referential signs, becomes presence, when we take the ground to be the power of the mind to synthesize elements of the world into the strange, magical state of a literal visual idea. And what a presence it is! We see, physically, a guitar that exists only for the mind, in its virtual space. Also, as part of that seeing, we recognize how the resignifying evokes a strange metaphysical twist. The properties of these elements, depending on a mental synthesis to become what they are not, nonetheless deepen our physical sense of what is involved in treating representation as essentially a matter of signs evoking ideas, rather than referring to actual objects. Designs and objects in effect have the same fluidity, and the same dependencies, as this glass, which, drawn in outline, can become an edge, evoking the form of a guitar. Thus, even though literal substance and direct reference are negated, the play of mind that these negations establish gives, both to the idea of the guitar and to the mind that composes it, remarkable physical presence. We feel the guitar's tactility as a richly textured object, and, in our effort to construct the idea referred to, we participate in the play of light and shade that this texture organizes. All of these physical properties then compose one further extension of the plays on absence and presence. We literally see the guitar's music: simply, in the copied notes, but also much more richly in the rhythmic force, the push-and-pull effects, of both the shapes and the colors. All of the movement, in turn, yields to the gentle control of the painted guitar hole (the constructed image of a ground), as it organizes both a circular movement and a three-dimensional version of the cubist pyramidal armature.

If I am correct in this reading, this central organizing shape completes the play on presence and absence by calling our attention to the synthetic intelligence that so plays upon the workings of the audience's actual processes of apprehension. As we negotiate this dance of negations, which nonetheless flesh out the several dimensions of this guitar, we increasingly feel our dependency on another set of mental energies that has the power to control certain very intimate constitutive processes. We realize that Krauss is right in pointing out that in order to get these synthetic effects, Picasso must suppress all of those traces, in line or color, that might express psychological subjectivity. But we also see that such restraint is hardly a terrible sacrifice to make to obtain this degree of power and this degree of ability to manipulate the very processes of judgment that are involved in perception. By surrendering the ex-pressivist pysche, Picasso has secured a more radical and imposing model of willful intellect, able to define a site dependent on such a brilliant union of rigor and whimsy that the audience is forced, at once, to pro-duce a full sense of the guitar, and to recognize its submission to the painter's ability to make an illusory world inescapably real.

It is difficult not to see so confident and quiet a control over such fundamental forces as one of Picasso's more successful efforts to assert his creative rivalry with the gods. The composer of this work seems to wield the kind of irony that makes creation an unfolding of plenitude, rather than a desperate compensation for unsatisfied needs. More impor-tant, this composing intelligence recognizes the ultimate force of creation as less the making of substance than the making of the Logos through which specific human acts of making are controlled and given purpose. Whim and logic not only produce a guitar and a music, present in, or because of, their absence; they also reveal a will, with the power to claim that it can so control the laws of perception that it can remake the very meaning of substance by controlling our most intimate perceptual ener-gies. Krauss can maintain her contrary view only by letting the frame-work she derived from Derrida blind her to the evidence of her senses, evidence that Picasso, ironically, both falsifies and reclaims for a different dimension of reference. Where Krauss's model dictates absences should be, there Picasso's artistic activity is, reveling in the power of composi-tion to redefine and absorb the resisting features of both physical objects and conventional codes. Freed by abstraction, from abstractions about what we should see, we can recognize how much depends upon the mind's powers to make worlds and to find in that act its physical, con-structive place, amid a world of signs.

Two particular aspects of this testimony prove especially resistant to the claim that Postmodernism has had to replace an epistemologically naive set of parents just off the boat from the nineteenth century. First, the collages clearly reveal the capacity of an artwork to dramatize virtual energies that literally display certain powers of mind and satisfy specific emotional investments. Second, because of this play of virtual energies, Picasso was able to go even farther than Cézanne and Braque in making his art a way of aligning the will to what the intelligence realizes: Here it is done by making available through this art's redefinition of the very concept of substance a set of transpersonal identifications.

Cézanne and Braque made it clear that a truly Modernist alternative to representational art would have to shift its emphasis from the interpretation of what is seen to the foregrounding of certain properties in the seeing that could be given active parallels in the formal syntax of the work. Picasso makes that activity of seeing practically a way of redefining substance, as if art also had the task of providing alternatives to what might be called "representational metaphysics." The process begins quite concretely. The initial task that *Guitar, Sheet Music and Wine Glass* imposes on its audience is to locate the idea of a guitar, made visible in its absence, in its ideality, by the transformed uses of other actual substances. But complications quickly arise. This idea must be treated as if it could be seen, and, in the effort to do that, we set in motion formal forces that create sensual analogs to the guitar's music. Yet all of this depends on the absence of the guitar. Were it to be actually present, in a painted illusion, there would be a direct spectator relation between the work and the viewer, a relation not so dependent on all of that virtual motion. In this collage, though, the only substance that the guitar can have is literally virtual: an effect of the space between signs, rather than of the image that is positively drawn. Nonetheless, it is precisely that virtuality that gives the guitar so immediate and forceful a presence: It is not given to the eye, but manifestly *constructed by it,* and done so with the awareness that any viewer who is able to see any of the intended force in the painting must share the same process of transposing the substances into signs. Moreover, in recognizing that transpersonal bond, we also see that the painter has gone beyond us, creating by understanding the terms of our creativity. On this level, one can no longer be content with the containing force of the eye in Cézanne's or Braque's paintings, because it is no longer the eye that quite contains what art makes visible. In Picasso's collage, what usually contains *is* contained, and what should *be* contained – the material force of elements that are the product of perception – becomes in fact the *container* that led us to perceive what *is* there by virtue of *not* being there. So, rather than relying on the eye to encompass what the painting represents, Picasso insists that the containing force is precisely these virtual powers that do constitute the ground of our seeing, and that can in effect suggest an entire social order, contained within the realizations that this activity of seeing brings to self-consciousness.

Now art carries something close to its own metaphysics. Our own virtual powers, our most intimate forces for completing perceptions, here take on the same kind of hovering presence, and perhaps even compose the same kind of music, as does the figure of the guitar. What seemed incomplete, a reversal of art's search for plenitude, turns out to warrant an even more radical aesthetics of presence, sanctioning the idea of the art object as a special site of being. The visual image becomes a visual figure, integrating, in its literal activities, levels of understanding that seem incompatible or unrealizable from any commonsense, empirical point of view. A violin emerges out of properties that deny visual illusionism. Yet nothing transcendental is involved. It seems as if nothing has been changed at all, in our secular world, except our sense of how created structures alter all of our conventional ways of making sense and of imposing values. Now we find perception itself appearing as an active, elemental force, freed from conventional contexts less to problematize representation than to celebrate the corresponding principles of order that the activity produces in the mind. By reducing the world to compositional elements, Picasso ties appearances to our own essential structures of synthesis. He makes his art the necessary instrument for such knowledge, precisely because it refuses both the illusions of representation and the consolations that come from dwelling on the ironies that result from staying in epistemological sites where one can see little else but the failures of the old ways. His collages seek instead the site made possible by taking absolutely literally the standard pun of the Cubist still life. This *jou,* which echoes the mundane world of newspapers while sounding like the term for all creative play, here has its dual truth: The image refers to the real, transforms it, and through its transformed state elicits a new sense of the simple, elemental dependencies of mind and world, constituting a level of objective relations that is stable enough to provide the structures for our transformations.[25]

Through this play, metaphysics begins to carry ethical force. As we have seen, inherited modes of idealization seemed contaminated by contradictions between the image projected and the forces that went into the representing, forces deriving from the artist's personal struggles, from the ideological formations that the artist could not control or rationalize for a different culture, and from the viewer's own impositions. Here, however, Picasso so manipulates his ironies that he liberates a lyric intensity of mind, so richly contained within the canvas that there is no need to depend on those sanctions. The energy of mind making the canvas dance, and arresting us with its intelligence, stands as an emblem of pure self-reflection, coming to suffice in, and as, the concrete world that it institutes. Art and metaphysics meet, as a casual tryst between creative whimsy and a profound grasp of the processes of sight, which we now must see as transpersonal. More important, seeing them as transpersonal, we find it hard not to affirm the condition that this transpersonality allows. We complete the guitar; we see that, in our activity, we align ourselves with all other responsive viewers, as well as with the proleptic invention of the painter; and in all of this, we take a pleasure in our own making of relationships, a making that itself becomes part of the work's testimony.

Therefore, we are put in the position of finding ourselves acting out certain fundamental values that would be rejected out of hand by the dominant empiricist faith. At one pole, this collage exemplifies the harmony between mind and world that Kant and the Romantics had made the reward of aesthetic experience. At the other, it makes visible the dream of purely transpersonal functions that Kant had seen as possible only in the categorical imperative (although he thought aesthetic judgment could be symbolic of such states). And in doing that, the collage finally gives the war against sculpture its full ethical analog, because what is idealized as possible relations among people in no way requires specific sculptural models, locating ethical identity in a fixed performative ego. The relevant condition of agency requires no specular figure to supplement the specific effect of the pleasures and identifications that the work literally makes visible. We find ourselves affirming lyric desires and modes of creative activity that rely solely on powers in ourselves that we realize, as we exercise them, are also available to everyone else. Such pleasure even complicates Picasso's own Nietzschean commitments. For, although the artwork still displays the brutal reality of a keen governing intelligence, now able even to transform how we see our seeing, that intelligence finds its inventions manifesting more capacious laws, revealing the remarkably intimate levels on which competing wills share the terms for producing their worlds.

IX

Although Picasso's collages can be said to discover the domain of transpersonal functions that a Modernist painting could make its subject, the resulting work never renounced the personal *frisson* available as one manipulates those functions. A more radical transpersonality would have to find ways of subsuming even those individuating traits within what seemed a more inclusive and more demanding logic that did not pander to such subjective pleasure. So we arrive at a third visual mode basic to Modernism's war on sculptural space, a mode that turns to noniconic figures, in order to define dynamic balances rich and supple and elemental enough to subsume the presentational will within the virtual relations sustained by the canvas. Here, as we saw in considering Mondrian, the Protestant desire to get beyond the irreducibly rhetorical nature of allegory finds an effective secular ground for the rhetorical will. Will itself becomes a dynamic force within structures that preserve the abstract transpersonality of allegory, without allegory's need to rely on foundational principles. Mondrian's case even echoes Picasso's plays on the nature of substance: "By the interiorization of what is known as matter, and by the externalization of what is known as mind . . . mind–matter becomes a unity" ("Principles of Neo-Plasticism," in Seuphor, *Piet Mondrian* 168). But now it is precisely that flexibility of the material that allows painters to dream of so defining elemental and transparent physical shapes that these could in themselves become testimony, making visible the virtual force that constitutes the effect of will and replaces gravity as our fundamental attachment to substance. Whereas painters could grant the fact that people would continue to differ in terms of the icons they served, painters might find noniconic images for the forces that these wills to difference had in common. And, in defining these forces, the arts might establish philosophical functions possible only for media that can make their activity their own fundamental subject.

Since we have already discussed Mondrian, it is fortunate for me that the most obvious noniconic example of this painterly subsuming of the allegorical will within virtual transpersonal forces is Kasimir Malevich's *Suprematist Composition: Red Square and Black Square* (1914 or 1915) (Figure 10). This painting still has a good deal of what must be called a somewhat vulgar insistence on allegorical content, but it is this insistent allegorizing that emphatically dramatizes how different such themes become when rendered in terms of the testimonial principles of noniconic art. So the theosophical traces that somewhat limit the art facilitate two arguments. First I want to use Malevich's treatment of those principles as an indirect way of criticizing Wassily Kandinsky, the sole noniconic painter to have a substantial influence on American poets, if only through his writings. But despite the importance of Kandinsky's ideas, his painting before World War I was, in my view, bound both conceptually and visually to the subjective expressionist ideals of his German apprenticeship (which may account for its popularity). Therefore, it does not provide a good index of either the resources of the noniconic or the ways that those resources complement the concern for impersonal and transpersonal stances that increasingly occupied the poets' attention. Malevich's painting, on the other hand, seems to me Russian enough to address the demands of the expressive psyche, yet analytic enough to do so in ways that make clear the full power of noniconic strategies. My second argument, then, will show how, in confronting all of these demands, the painting's handling of the rhetorical ego both takes on considerable philosophical interest in its own right and makes clear certain aspects of Modernism in the visual arts that require language for their full articulation.

Malevich's Suprematism is devoted to making visible what he calls the "non–objective element."[26] Being nonobjective, that element is difficult

Figure 10. Kasimir Malevich, *Suprematist Composition: Red Square and Black Square* (1914 or 1915?). Oil on canvas, 28 × 17½". Collection, The Museum of Modern Art, New York.

to fix through language. Nonetheless, the work we have already considered should help us get a grasp on the nature of the forces at stake. Like Mondrian, Malevich insists that this force manifests itself in terms of dynamic balances that cannot be reduced to any geometric or physiological laws. But unlike Mondrian's, his work eschews the appearance of system, so that he can connect the nonobjective element to something like the deep whimsy that, in Picasso, defines the presence of individual desire as the source of these energies. For Malevich, chance and choice must coalesce in delicate yet elaborate balances, since only that sense of the momentary provides the pressure to make the balance a significant claim on the will. In *Red Square and Black Square,* that general concern takes on an insistent and dramatic psychological cast, because of the intense and heavily associative nature of the organizing contrast, and that, in turn, provides precisely the confrontation with Picasso's principles that we need to set off the distinctive aspects of this third mode.[27]

In order to see how the painting's formal energies take on their psychological and intellectual significance, we must go slowly, treating the painting as if it led us through three distinctive stages. The first stage consists of a series of dynamic principles, all involved in subverting a potential domination of black. Imagine this work upside down. Everything would achieve rest in the black square, and all of the movement and openness would be negated. But Malevich's structure, instead, denies resolution by that single shape. As the eye moves downward to the conventional place of rest, it finds sharp contrast and reversal. The smaller square is by far the more active, because its tilt denies the coordinates established by the black square, while its primary color leaps forward from the canvas. The tilt, in turn, opens out into white space, and it asserts, in its small but almost weightless presence, a powerful refusal to echo the black square's echoing of the shape of the picture frame. The red's projection forward is duplicated by its horizontal movement, as each denies an order of repetitive form.

The very elementariness of these forms invites us to bring thematic analogs into our visual experience. Too bare to be decoration, the work must signify. In most of Malevich's Suprematist work, that signification would consist in a particular set of balances. This painting is distinctive, because the balances seem so single-mindedly focused that they implicate a second-order set of relations with pronounced thematic ambitions. Organizing those relations is the force of the tilt, as it sets against the black a second set of spatial coordinates that demands our recognizing at least two possible axes for organizing the visual field. Thus we find ourselves witnesses to the power of an individualizing force, through which the tilt establishes entire systems of differences that the black authoritative structure would suppress: Color requires noncolor, smallness a corresponding larger shape for contrast, new space an old set of coordinates, singleness duality, and self-assertion a sense of immanent norms and, perhaps, imminent oppression. Then, as these relations take on intellectual force, other sensual details assume a new intensity. The specific way that the red square tilts leads us out to the surrounding white space, thereby creating or restoring a delicate balance with the square. And now that balance becomes quite significant. It suggests that despite the denial of the black square's demand for a simple and repetitious order, there can be forms of order that comprehend, and even depend on, this assertion of difference. Here, in other words, Malevich's versions of theosophy enable him to give force to the dynamics of Hegelian logic. By negating one form of order, the red tilt makes the eye seek out larger contexts providing a new principle of balance. Instead of balance based on repetition of shape, we have a balance that in, or as, movement integrates all of the diverse elements. The pull among the competing coordinates and forms literally produces a sense of their interdependence, but that interdependence has as its ground the white space of canvas. This ground, like the mind, and like infinite space, holds all by allowing what is held to become manifest as force and as relationship: "Tranquility itself is defined by movement" (Malevich, *The World as Nonobjectivity* 16).

We are beginning to see the ways in which the virtual forces in the painting give some concrete content to the notion of nonobjectivity. These balances are crucial to the force that the red establishes, yet they do not have the simple material presence possessed by the flat, colored forms. The kind of presence they do have requires our leaping to a third, speculative level of interpretation, where we allow the idea of individualizing force to be fleshed out by the metaphoric implications of the painting's activity. Consider first how this self-reflexive tilt serves as an emblem for the kinds of force in fact possessed by the painting. Because the painting does not create any illusion that evokes a dramatic and semantic context, it can be said to signify nothing beyond itself. Unable to mean, it must simply be – must be art purely as a material structure of shapes, colors, and movements. We cannot read these as means intended to represent or stand for something else. Yet, as we meditate on the painting, we also cannot treat its literalness as simply physical. These relational structures clearly carry metaphoric implications, because they so perfectly define the logic of individuation and so intensely fill the canvas with a sense that sense is not enough. We find the sensual elements becoming abstract forms with their own drama, as if the tilt invoked an allegory that could never be incorporated within conventional allegorical signs, because it captured something so fundamental to the form of an idea that it could not quite be reduced to a specific set of relations. What we see, what is only physical form and movement, nonetheless grows in sense, so that sense itself becomes an elemental condition, bridging the gap between mental and physical – but only when we see the bridge as precisely this condition of a tilt away from conventional modes of seeing. To understand the painting is to understand the coordinates it sets up at a tangent to those used by ordinary perception. One might even say that the painting establishes or exemplifies a Kantian schema for this condition of producing differences that then establish concrete integrating balances.[28] The more we think about what we see, the more it seems that these elemental properties are not so much physical properties as pure forms for some basic condition of meaning. In effect, we see the mind in elements, and we see elements as aspects of the activity of the mind's processes of generating and balancing differences. We find our own vacillating between domains of sense and signification part of what the principle of the tilt, and its resulting balances, are all about. Because we are asked to step back and reflect upon the mystery of sense in sensation and the sensation of sense, we must be spiritually moved by the painting in order to experience its physical movement as fully present in its elemental concreteness.

What we attribute to the painting as a tilting of the perceptual also applies to the mode of agency that the painting both elicits and, ultimately, comes to stand for. We see that the painter has captured the fundamental condition of Picasso's willfulness: The work denies prevailing categories that condemn us to repetition; creates new coordinates of sense, resisting even the idealized selves necessary to dream of communication; and opens the possibility and necessity for new forms of balance or coherence among conflicting forces. Similarly, the work clearly implicates what is involved in our own viewing as we balance the sensual and the sensible and realize that only some private, willing subject can fully confer the force that the signs evoke. It is tempting, therefore, to say that it is here that one ought to invoke Derrida – not the Derrida of demystification, but the philosopher of difference, who has taught us to see that at the core of our attributions of meaning and of identity, there is a fundamental force of differentiation, itself never locatable except in the movement it imposes by making us seek new balances. But here a picture is worth a thousand philosophers. Derrida is not wrong, at least in this case. Indeed Malevich makes it possible not only to visualize what Derrida imagines, but to see how that imagining is consistent with what all who have thought of the self as negation, from Hegel to Sartre, have imagined. But Malevich also does something that none of those philosophers could accomplish. He creates a plausible formal model that self-reflexively both accounts for that negation and shows how this deepest of private movements is, at its core, fundamentally transpersonal and synthetic. Not only do we see a set of activities so elemental that they define the force of the personal in terms allowing a minimal degree of displacement by factors specific to any one personality (but now, we see, not essential to its force); we also realize that our apprehension of these forces testifies to the depth and accuracy of the image. There we find the distinguishing features of the painterly act that makes our own balancing possible.

When I discuss Wallace Stevens in Chapter 9, I shall try to show that Malevich's version of the self is complemented and extended by Wittgenstein's brilliant analysis of intentionality, based on the grammatical roles that "as" plays in our practices. Usually commentators are content to treat Wittgenstein's discussion of the "as" as a model for metaphor. But, given his ambitions as a psychologist, the entire second part of his *Philosophical Investigations* seems to me better understood as an account of what is at stake in metaphor making – namely, the possibility of staging one's descriptions so that they are inseparable from hypotheses about the position of the describer, whose responsibility is directly proportionate to the tilt that metaphor gives to established categories. Yet because the tilt is structural rather than self-referential, we need not understand that intentional state in terms of some specific set of distinctively personal needs and desires. Instead, we have grounds for something like a transcendental subject, purified of Kant's framework for sustaining that transcendental status. For now, though, I must be content to clarify Malevich's work, so I shall simply turn to an analogy for the stakes involved in these efforts to define subjective intentionality along such abstract lines. That analogy consists in an anecdote told by the analytic philosopher and conceptual artist John Perry, whose case I greatly oversimplify for my illustrative purposes. Perry's concern is to explain the investments we put in the "I," without positing some substantial self as their source or measure: A sense of the simple relational positions that the "I" locates will suffice."[29] One day, in a grocery store, Perry said, he found a trail of sugar, indicating that someone had a leaking bag. Being the most helpful of all creatures, the philosopher as Boy Scout, he set out to find the poor misguided shopper. But the trail seemed never to end. Then, philosopher to the last, he deduced the key to the mystery. The bag-leaker was he. But Perry could not experience that discovery in third-person terms. He did not observe an embarrassed "other" trying to sneak the bag back and pretending nothing had happened. He had to watch himself doing that, which meant that he could not simply watch: He had to feel the tilt that betrays the investments determining a particular set of coordinates, here in the form of the embarrassing sense that the tilt exposes one's own stupidity.

Perry's point is that the referent of the "I," in this story, is no different from the referent of the "he." The culprit is the same; the only thing that changes is the attitude the agent takes toward the referent. Malevich's painting could accommodate this view. But its play on virtuality tries to suggest that so behaviorist a model of the tilt begs the difficult questions. For, although it is true that the material referent of "he" and "I" remains the same, the issue of locating the "I" is not really a question of material referents, not a question of the angle of the red square, but of the tilt itself. The fundamental concern is not whether different pronouns refer to the same extensional bodies, but whether the first and third person can be handled by the same coordinates. Do both pronouns lead us to expect the same kind of responses from the agent identified? If not – if there are forces introduced by the first-person indexical that do change our coordinates – we may have to shift from questions of physically locating the referent to questions of the kinds of intentionality each mode requires, which means that we have to understand how intentionality entails virtual expectations not present when third-person descriptions seem adequate. Even if the material referent stays constant, the shift to first-person terms entails a great deal more than the discovery that I am "I" because I cannot comfortably masquerade as "he" or "she." Minimally, that shift entails recognizing that although the world we refer to does not change, the investments it allows and sustains do. We approximate here Jacques Lacan's "Imaginary," that is, an inescapable source of erotic energies and of an ego ideal / ideal ego, which has, in effect, no fixed content, but can be characterized as a demand to produce investments allowing an agent to make identifications within positions he occupies in language.

If this "tilt" will provide a figure for the self as a principle of difference, if it establishes a model for the force of the imaginary basic to subjectivity, will it not also account for the nature of the artwork itself, in its version of nonobjectivity? Thus the conjunction between physical properties and some mysterious "supplementary" investment, basic to the sense of the work, is no accident. Like Cézanne, but in a more abstract register, Malevich wants to make visible the conditions of our seeing: not seeing of objects, but seeing the very possibility of there being concrete images that cannot be reduced to material forms even when they are shorn of all trappings of expressive subjectivity. Works of art too create what might be called "ontological coordinates," which are at a "tilt" from the ordinary coordinates that dominate our practices of description. Although every part of the work admits extensional substitutions, the whole constitutes a particular balance, and a particular assertion of metaphoric appositeness, that retains their uniqueness, precisely because no material sign accounts for that force. The very intelligence that gives this work by Malevich its resonance and takes responsibility for the balances it does articulate is what makes the work untranslatable, and therefore nonobjective. The painting is at once within the world, and not congruent with it – as is perhaps indicated by the way my attempts at critical description border on the parodic. The more we try to naturalize this image, the more we realize that its force resides in its exemplary testimony that there can be modes of expression so precise, and so simple, that they remain ineluctably different from all of our efforts to appropriate them. And the more we attend to this specificity, the better we understand why the only answer to Picasso's sense of willfulness is so thoroughly to acknowledge its truth that the acknowledgment itself both confirms and redefines the point. To be an artist, one must establish particular coordinates that generate the work's sense of sense. But in doing that, one can cast the work as proposing transpersonal forms for that principle of difference, in both its psychological and its ontological modes.

Because he tried to use noniconic art to handle the most intimate of psychological forces, Malevich went a long way toward closing a circle that began with Wordsworth and Kant. They inaugurated perhaps the crucial aspect of cultural Modernism by seeking, in various aspects of constitutive particularity, a concrete model for the ideals of freedom and dignity fundamental to Enlightenment rhetorics. We have watched their heirs grapple with the complexities of that bequest, and I have argued that any successful negotiation of these claims about individuality must develop some version of Cézanne's contemplative self-reflexion, in order to align the will with the world. With Malevich, anti-Enlightenment theosophy provided the level of abstraction that could cast Cézanne's ideals in terms of self-testifying secular allegory. Here the purest sense of art's formal purposiveness becomes compatible with the nineteenth century's richest models of the energies that define the constitutive subject. What had been the irreducible force of differentiation, hidden beneath all of our efforts at lucidity, here becomes visible in its elemental form.

7

Modes of Abstraction in Modernist Poetry

I

It is now time to make good on promises long deferred. I need to show how both my discussions of literary history and my concern for Modernist painting make significant differences for our understanding Modernist poetry. This entails facing the fear that I may have spent a great deal of time elaborating what should be obvious – that Modernist painting offers several moving and relatively profound ways of engaging the basic questions about identities and values that oppressed the early twentieth century – while I ignore the ironic fact that the more precise we become about the painters' achievements, the more difficult it becomes to imagine the verbal arts engaging in the same project or competing for the same cultural authority. Although visual significance depends on cultural mediations, in much the same way that verbal artifacts do, the kind and degree of those mediations seem to differ substantially. Consider, for example, the arguments I hear from my colleague, the novelist David Bosworth, as we drive to play indoor tennis in rainy Seattle: "Music and painting can be avant-garde arts because their media are not bound, as literature is, to the conditions of practical life. Sound patterns and visual shapes readily take on something like an independent substance, which can produce or imply certain states and modes of agency sharply at odds with those we regularly live by, but the very sense of words requires a backdrop of expectations reinforcing the aura of common humanity that the experimental nature of the art tries to deny." Clearly, writers can try to imitate the visual arts' ability to express affective aspects of material substance, but do they not therefore sacrifice much of the power and significance that they otherwise could muster?

222

And do not such analogies box us into overvaluing experiment and undervaluing poetry that relies on more conventional aspects of language, with their access to deeply embedded human values? Finally, and perhaps most important for poets, is not their enterprise thereby subsumed under the authority of the painters, whom the poets must be seen as merely imitating, rather than rivaling?

I shall not deny the force of these observations, and I shall not pretend that there is a clear theoretical answer to them. Instead, it is crucial to see here the point of Wittgenstein's concern for replacing a desire for new answers with a capacity to make the force of old questions seem to dissolve. So long as we tie ourselves to questions of how we can and cannot use media, or can and cannot imitate another art, we ignore the degree to which we are imposing theory on practice, rather than using abstract reflection to clarify what has in fact already been achieved. I have tried to show that the painters greatly simplify the situation by themselves finessing the question of the limits of their medium. For they concentrate not simply on returning painting to its syntactic relations, but also on showing how that syntax can carry semantic force. This semantic force need not be limited to the specific syntactic moves that set it in motion. By inviting us to reflect on principles of site, agency, and testimony, the painters carve a discursive space, where it makes sense to compare different approaches to what concrete media make available, and where questions of imitation can yield to more complex models of threat, appropriation, and transformation. The crucial question, then, is not whether poetry can adapt the same principles of formal syntax that the painters employed, but whether it can respond in its own ways to the transformations of ethos and agency made possible by locating the semantic force of the work in the qualities of authorial action to which the work becomes testimony.

In order to focus the relevant parallels and transformations, I shall return to the three basic painterly styles elaborated in the last chapter, this time concentrating on how poets adapt particular modes for their own purposes and, in the process, articulate a grammar of stylistic possibilities that they could then employ in a variety of combinations. As examples of how painterly principles of "realization" help us to appreciate poetic experiments, I shall rely on two texts by William Carlos Williams. The first is devoted primarily to rendering in language the full implications of Cézanne's break from the logic of the window and the primacy of sculptural space, whereas the second adapts Cézanne's efforts to render the will as an aspect of the act of seeing. Innovative as Williams is, however, there are serious problems in his work, at its most ambitious. By examining his flawed attempts to adapt Cubist principles, we find ourselves in a good position to appreciate both the nature of the pressures compelling artists to Cubist experiments and the achievement of those writers who manage to handle what Williams cannot. We come next to the writing of my second set of authors, Gertrude Stein and Wallace Stevens. Stein works out the fullest strict parallels to Cubist painterly syntax that we find in any Modernist poet, and Stevens offers rich parallels to Picasso's testimony to those metamorphic powers that can become the object of our attention once the arts are no longer bound to the gravity imposed by representational principles. Finally, I switch to poetic work that parallels noniconic painterly strategies. Although I doubt any direct influence, I shall try to demonstrate the degree to which an awareness of the traps inherent in the "image" leads Marianne Moore and William Butler Yeats to parallel strategies for making virtual dimensions of the experience they can elicit serve as testimony for their larger claims. Such work finally brings our journey full circle, because it shows how the Modernists manage to recuperate, on very different grounds, Wordsworth's constitutive eloquence, Keats's projection of imaginative states where intensity breaks down all borders between the empirical and the transcendental, Flaubert's versions of Kantian autonomy, and Baudelaire's mobile subject, now no longer bound by the pathos that haunts both his struggles with Romantic expressivism and Eliot's efforts to find a transcendental alternative to that plight.

II

No American poet needed the supplementary contexts that painting provided more than William Carlos Williams. For, without some register for interpreting the self-consciousness that governs the formal experiments in his work, his poems are easily reduced to the voices and perceptions that provide their subject matter. Precisely that reduction gave us Williams the objectivist, treated by the poetry establishment of his own time as a minor, somewhat quirky, local-color realist. And sophisticated academic versions of the same critical habits have given us these values transposed into a triumphant Heideggerreanism. Thus, in J. Hillis Miller's intricate and influential version of this myth, Williams the realist becomes a philosophical poet, who defines a mode of attention that can "leap into things." Because Williams manages to "give up the ego," he can replace "those dramas of the interchange of subject and object, self and world, which have long been central in Western philosophy and literature," with the fluid mobility of attentions freed of their narcissistic attachments. However, the price of this mobility proved exorbitant. Whereas Miller could move to the more writerly and self-reflexive forms of mobility that Derrida made available within that philosophical tradition, Williams was left to languish in what increasingly seemed a naive and useless immanence. It soon turned out that the poetry could be saved for the critical world shaped by that Derridean perspective, but only by inverting the same oppositions that Miller had formulated. Williams the poet of presence became, in Joseph Riddel's work, the deconstructive angel calling attention to the violence that figural language does to perception. And even critical work as carefully historical as Carl Rapp's ended up approximating those same oppositions, by setting against Williams the objectivist a Williams acting out Emersonian versions of the idealist appropriative ego.[1]

The turn to painterly analogies will not entirely free us from these oppositions. But it should help us characterize the will in more concrete terms, so that we can understand how the art makes its mode of presentation a means of aligning immediate desires with a reflective sense of structures that can hold for the objective world. Two fine critics, Albert Cook and Henry Sayre, have already shown the way. Where earlier critics who concentrated on the relation of Williams's poetry to painting emphasized his adapting specific visual styles in order to achieve a painterly version of iconic immanence, Cook and Sayre have learned their lessons from Derrida without having to resort to that much too general vocabulary. They shift the focus from specific influences to Williams's general effort to establish verbal equivalents for certain powers revealed in Modernist painting, and they insist on treating those powers primarily as compositional rather than perceptual energies. Painterly analogs challenged Williams to develop impersonal structures for testing the capacity of the poet's active, forming mind to impose its own structures on the real – not to displace objects, but to bring them to life in the new dimension of constructed relations that, in Cubism, allowed an artwork to become a reality in its own right.[2]

Valuable as their contribution is, however, it may need modification in at least one respect. I find their version of construction an inadequate model for both the poetry and the painting, because it does not describe the compositional energies in terms that allow us to assess the significance of the reality so created. Criticism must be able to show how those constructions articulate the intensity of the struggles involved, or how audiences may use the reality as an exemplary site, defining modes of agency to which we can attribute specific values. Therefore it will not do to take the most general claims of the painterly aesthetic and apply it to the poetry. We need a little more skepticism about that rhetoric, a little more attention to what the specific works do. To that end, we can concentrate on the specific ways in which Williams's work invites comparison with some of the features of Cézanne's enterprise that we have considered under the rubric of "realization." Cézanne's paintings elicited exactly the same critical polarities that Williams's poems do, and Cézanne himself struggled with much the same sense of wild, Romantic energies that had to be accommodated to conditions that the artist could share with other people. Neither the artist nor the audience could have negotiated such energies if they had been content with abstractions about constructed objects. Rather, such projects require the artist to define the specific ways in which the constructing intelligence takes responsibility for its practices, and makes that taking of responsibility the means of aligning the compositional will to the world that its artifice discloses – the will's aim being, not to make worlds, but to establish principles by which we can fully inhabit the only world that extends beyond our projections onto it.

Williams was too concerned with beginnings not to have his most self-reflexive work, *Spring and All,* point directly to Cézanne's realization as the principle from which all of the ladders start:

> Today where everything is being brought into sight the real-ism of art has bewildered us, confused us and forced us to re-invent in order to retain that which the older generation had without that effort.
> Cézanne –
> The only realism in art is of the imagination. It is only there that the work escapes plagiarism after nature and becomes a creation[.]
> Invention of new forms to embody this reality of art, the one thing which art is, must occupy all serious minds concerned. (*Spring and All* 111)

One can easily read this statement as Cook and Sayre do – that is, as a claim about the power of works of art to construct their own realities. But that would be to give a thin account of how imagination and realism combine to embody that reality, and it would ignore the dramatic effect of leaving what Cézanne means so enticingly open. Therefore, I propose another way of proceeding. This open-ended passage occurs early in its volume. Let us turn immediately to the fuller, more triumphant prose of its concluding moments, then see how a particular landscape poem by Williams can so flesh out Cézanne as to justify those claims:

> Imagination is not to avoid reality, nor is it description nor an evocation of objects or situations, it is to say that poetry does not tamper with the world but moves it – it affirms reality most powerfully and therefore, since reality needs no personal sup-port but exists free from human action, as proven by science in the indestructibility of matter and of force, it creates a new object, a play a dance which is not a mirror up to nature but –

> As birds' wings beat the solid air without which none could fly so words freed by the imagination affirm reality by their flight. . . .
>
> The word is not liberated, therefore able to communicate release from the fixities which destroy it, until it is accurately tuned to the fact which giving it reality, by its own reality establishes its own freedom from the necessity of a word, thus freeing it and dynamizing it at the same time. (149–50)

This is not pellucid prose. In fact, its major role is to allow the concluding poem on the black-eyed susan to make sense of what here tries to fly against reality. We can, nonetheless, notice how this passage sustains that flight (and perhaps the flight of any of his best poems) by calling attention to two ambitions that make good the earlier invocation of Cézanne as the one who can show the way to a new realism. For poetry to move from the old realism to realization, it must learn to animate our perceptions without transforming them into evocative and symbolic interpretive substitutes for the feeling of directly encountering actual phenomena; and it must show how that animating power connects the presentational will of the artist to the energies that the will discloses. Ultimately, poetry too must be able to release both the subject and the object from the principles of gravity, in order to celebrate other, more spiritually subtle, ways of aligning mental and physical forms. The compositional will is violent or appropriative only when its necessary destruction of the old forms does not restore a new measure that enables the will, once again, to take the world as calling forth and rewarding its full intensity.

There is no better test case for these principles than what is probably Williams's most Cézannean poem, "Flowers by the Sea":

> When over the flowery sharp pasture's
> edge, unseen, the salt ocean
>
> lifts its form – chickory and daisies
> tied, released, seem hardly flowers alone
>
> but color and the movement – or the shape
> perhaps – of restlessness, whereas
>
> the sea is circled and sways
> peacefully upon its plantlike stem.
>   (*Collected Earlier Poems* 87)

The most obvious, and perhaps most important, feature of this poem is its constant refusal to turn into an Impressionist landscape, even though its subject is a motif much beloved by Monet. There is here neither the

fluidity of Impressionist light nor the mobility of Impressionist temperament, freed to wander through the plenitude created by the intricate
tones that the light disseminates. Where immanent plenitude had been,
there is now a single dominant contrast, taking place in several registers.
The restless movement of light among the flowers gives them the quality
of the sea, and the sea becomes like a single flower, swaying peacefully
on its stem.

Why, though, does such a simple structural contrast warrant invoking
Cézanne? Is that not simply another academic inflation, substituting
comparisons to painting for overworked philosophical ones? Ironically,
it is the simplicity of the painting that justifies the comparison, because
that trait so focuses the contrasting forces that we must shift our concern
from what the poem sees to what it brings to our attention *about* seeing.
The poem's subject is how poetry can fulfill, for the mind, what Modernist painting teaches the eye to see. Perhaps the strongest contrast with
earlier landscape poetry is that Williams, too, turns against the force of
gravity, both in his handling of visual detail and in his emphasis on the
containing force of the poem's single sentence. Try to visualize that first
stanza. The slightly ambiguous "unseen" makes us grope for the location of the water, which I think we can see only as waves, that is, as
matter already in pronounced formal pattern. The reference to form
combines with the detail of the "sharp edge" to suggest that the best way
to envision this scene is to free it of its spatiotemporal location, imagining instead that we are looking at a painting. There we can make perfect
sense of the sea being "over" the pasture. We project the sea at the top of
a canvas, where the wave movement defines a form pushing out toward
the frontal plane and releasing tonal parallels in the flowers, so that they
give up their distinctive shapes. Soon all of the details make location so
complex a question that they all establish the significance of the poem's
final contrast, as it sets in motion a counterforce, pulling against any
well-defined material weight. The richer the opening details' resistance
to gravity, the more effective is the hold of the "plantlike stem," fixing
the sea by the power of visual analogy and linguistic movement. Containment challenged on the level of specific scenic configurations becomes containment that can be celebrated as a force released in and by the
free play of the eye and the mind.

It is no small part of this release from gravity that the poem will not
long rest even in these painterly analogies. What takes shape, after all, are
not only material forms, but material evocations of qualities such as
restlessness and peace. Yet this is no allegory. We need the tutelary
presence of Cézanne, because Williams follows Cézanne's lead by making the medium itself the work's vehicle for defining spiritual forces that
do not rely on traditional means for drawing significance from the de-

picted material. Thus this process of transformation in the poem is ultimately a way of testing certain capacities in its own medium of language.
Vision, freed by the imagination, affirms by its flight the nature of the
linguistic ties that continue to bind us to the world, but in a somewhat
more abstract register.

Spring and All puts the case this way:

> The man of imagination who turns to art for release and ful-
> fillment of his baby promises contends with the sky through
> layers of demoded words and shapes. Demoded, not because the
> essential vitality which begot them is laid waste – this cannot be
> so, a young man feels because he feels it in himself – but because
> meanings have been lost through laziness or through changes in
> the form of existence which have let words empty. (*Imaginations*
> 100)

The poet must resist "demoded words and shapes" by first stressing the
power of artifice to negate stale conventions, then by showing how
language can realize precisely those metaphoric forces that, in sight, link
desire and vision, restlessness and peace. Thus, when the poem leads us
to shift attention from gazing at the sea to reflecting on the comparisons
that can give this gaze a rich affective scope, we are in effect also attending to some primary ways in which sight itself is suffused by semantic
and emotional concerns. One might even say that the poet's focusing on
the medium leads us to see the metaphors that carry those concerns, not
as impositions on the scene, but as investments deeply embedded in our
seeing when it is most intensely involved in the life of its objects. By
denying Impressionist fluidity of light and shifting emotional tones,
Williams makes his structural tensions the focus for an eye that sees in
terms of comparisons and contrasts, rather than by simple perceptual
differences. This is not conventional objectivist lucidity, but neither is it
idealism, because the mind's thriving is not at the cost of the scene. There
is no displacement into symbol, or away from other primary investments. There is only a sense that metaphors can be so simple, so embedded in appearances, that it would be foolish abstraction to treat them as
constructions by language, imposed on some pristine and unknowable
noumena.

Everything that I am trying to say abstractly about the force of the
medium is shown concretely in the marvelous device of having this flight
from gravity turn on the plantlike stem of a single intricate sentence,
whose contours provide a rich sense of how language itself becomes
virtually a material, containing force. This sentence is not a typical
speech act. There is no distinct speaker, and no speech context. Instead
there is the simple, abstract form of the sentence, with its containing

power stressed by the tight, logical linking of "when" and "whereas," terms that complicate scenic structure by placing the visual within a strange combination of temporal and logical operators. "When" and "whereas" define the parameters of this abstract space; then, the specific movement of the sentence fleshes it out with a complex set of qualifiers, not all of which can be seen, except in what the poetry makes us see about seeing, as it constructs a secular, transparent analog for the force of investments that once were grounded by attributing mythic back-grounds to perceptual events.[3] Language, in other words, keeps two forces in motion – one that liberates the scene into new relational forms, another that liberates the responding mind to set out its own analogous restlessness, which can fully appreciate what is involved in that final, eminently logical reversal that brings peace to all of the motion (without suppressing it).

Ultimately, that self-reflexive dimension of language involves our re-flecting on who we become by virtue of how we have learned to under-stand our own relationship to the natural scene. That is why the poem's restlessness is not merely epistemological, the peace not simply a matter of recognizing the containing power of linguistic artifice. The vitality that we feel within ourselves, as we seek to free perceptions from de-moded words and shapes, must find active means of aligning itself with what the medium makes available. Either the mind must turn, in ironic dismay, from the gulf between its intensities and its possibilities for action, or it must make those intensities a mode of defining and directing the will. Cézanne spoke of that definition as the aspect of realization that allows the artist to "give his entire personality," in rendering the image of what he sees. Williams is even more emphatic on the expressive di-mension of objective composition: "In the composition the artist does exactly what every eye must do with life, fix the particular with the universality of his own personality – Taught by the largeness of his own personality to feel every form which he sees moving within himself, he must prove the truth of this by expression" (*Imaginations* 105). Ex-pression itself must find its plantlike stem.

Such ideals become forces within the poem, and possibly within cul-tural life, if we turn again to the single sentence, this time imagining the kind of human presence that it manages to put in the place of a dramatic speaker. Rather than speakers speaking, we have what might be called a "sentence sentencing." Syntactic contrasts manage to resolve restlessness by replacing the unsatisfying flatness of the gravity inherent in the scene with an alternative gravity that binds into a single structure a great deal more than the empirical eye can. The sentence, then, establishes a lin-guistic analog for the containing eye that encloses the scene in Cézanne, then in Braque. A "when" can make us care so much about a "whereas," because we call up through, and as, this sentence a model of agency capable of fully fleshing out the move from restlessness to peace. Once we take the sentence itself as the plantlike stem on which the realized world of poetry depends, ponderation creates a blend of physical and mental forces no less complex than those set to work in Cézanne. The sentence itself takes on metaphoric force. On the most elemental level, the sentence sets the gravity of its own intentional energies against the mobility of the visual details. As we reflect on those energies, the containing process grows more abstract, gathering into a single structure the various forms of concern that we saw carried by the range of embedded metaphors.[4] Artifice, as a figurative eye, "realizes" an expressive will, which simultaneously discloses and affirms the intense life potential in our acts of seeing.

III

Williams claimed that a modern realism would have to restore by self-conscious labors certain states that its predecessors could enjoy without such efforts. Unfortunately, I can imagine more than one reader thinking, by this point in my analysis, that this much effort strains credulity: that so much ponderous reflection on the ponderation of a relatively frail vehicle like "Flowers by the Sea" threatens to lose sight of the visual experience at its core, and thus to annul the fresh perceptual field that the poem tries to make available. My only defense is to call attention to how thoroughly Williams embedded his early poetry in prose commentary, hoping for a synthesis of lyric immediacy and the scope made available by that interpretive activity. Therefore, although I admit that my critical prose may not distribute the interpretive weight very well, I hope to persuade the reader that the poems were intended to bear a version of it. Straining credulity is part of their point, because that activity also strains our sense of the real and opens us to appreciate the range of investments that an art of realization makes available for our ways of living within it.

Thus the only cure may be adamant repetition of the strain: herniated criticism as a new ideal. In that spirit, I shall turn to a second poem, "The Red Wheelbarrow," this one more overtly abstract in its version of realization. That increased degree of abstraction should serve the historical function of showing how poetry too can move quite easily between Cézanne's emphasis on the logic of actual seeing and Braque's concern for making visible the investments that go into our seeing. Then, because the poem's abstraction dramatically sets its single sentence against the forces of gravity that in this case dominate the visual scene, we shall also have a good example of Williams's tendency to make the gathering force of his formal elements also a metaphoric equivalent for the modes of ponderation and alignment carried out by Cézanne's formal energies.

Williams's best analyses of his own project are found in his comments on the powers of composition that give Marianne Moore her distinct hold on the real:

> There are two elements essential to Miss Moore's scheme of composition, the hard and unaffected concept of the apple itself as an idea, then its edge-to-edge contact with the things which surround it – the coil of a snake, leaves of various depths, or as it may be; and without connectives unless it be poetry, the inevitable connective if you will. (*Selected Essays* 127)

Normally, both elements that Williams mentions work to produce the dynamic processes of apprehension that we saw in "Flowers by the Sea." But there will obviously be temptations to reach beyond the work of that "edge-to-edge contact" in order to see if composition can focus attention on the "inevitable connective" and thereby isolate the concrete dynamics of the abstract force central to the idea of realization. "The Red Wheelbarrow" is one of those moments, wrought to its uttermost:

> so much depends
> upon
>
> a red wheel
> barrow
>
> glazed with rain
> water
>
> beside the white
> chickens
> (*Spring and All* 138)[5]

The work of edge-to-edge contact here does not need commentary; the effects of such connectives do. Why begin with that abstracting opening clause, if one is committed to the dominant force of the particular images? And why use a word count, rather than a syllable count, as one's organizing pattern? What can possibly be "realized" by drawing such parallels between word positions? Clearly, the sentence is once again the primary model of agency. But in "Flowers by the Sea," the agency was a fairly simple one. The sentence defined and complemented oppositions organized by our investments in seeing, so that the poem exercised a significant force, simply as visual rendering. Here, despite the confident realism attributed to it by critics, the visual rendering flirts with bathos. The picture as image is no more compelling a version of an actual scene than the abstracted vision Braque gives of the village at Estaque. Our interest must focus on the pronounced formal qualities. There resides our only route to substantial extraformal content. For example, one could concentrate on the way in which this structure calls attention to the material quality of these isolated words, as if, in glazing them, their power to make direct significations could be made manifest. But that is still to leave words in search of agency. For the poem to have much depth – to not be only about the lack of depth – we must define how the semantic force of that opening clause brings those material qualities to life and connects them to the poem's obvious concern for the nature of reference. We must show what can be realized through this treatment of dependency as a poetic site.

Ten years later, Williams made explicit the implications of that site: "This is, after all, the substance, therefore the explanation, of my poems and my life in which *there exists* (instead of *you exist*)" ("A Novelette and Other Prose," in *Imaginations* 302). Dependency, in other words, becomes a means of exploring ways in which subjectivity is subordinate to other, more inclusive and transpersonal models of intentionality. So much depends upon the red wheelbarrow, because so much depends on understanding what is at stake in the dual attributes of that "so much depends": the mind's manifestation of an abiding principle of care, inherent in this "there is," and the mind's becoming itself virtually tactile, in its efforts to compose the world so that those cares can reside in actual phenomena.[6]

I take the formal equivalent of this care to be the force of predication set in motion by the structural pattern of dividing the poem into four equal compositional units, with only one verb. The position of the verb is occupied, in the succeeding stanzas, by three adjectival functions, each literally depending, for its complete grammatical and semantic functioning, on the single words that complete the stanza. The effect is to have the completion of meaning constantly delayed, and to make the delay a means of slowing us down or defamiliarizing the process of conferring meanings, so that we are led to recognize the miraculous quality of words and cares eventually taking hold.

As we read, the mind is made to hover over details, until its waiting is rewarded – not only within the stanza, but also as each independent stanza emerges to fill out this waiting and to move us beyond details to a complex sense of a total life contained in these objects. How resonant the word "depends" becomes, when we recall its etymological meanings of "hanging from" or "hanging over." The mind acts, not by insisting on its own separateness, but by fully being "there": by dwelling on, depending on, the objects that depend on it. And words themselves take on that same quality, because each part of speech reveals its capacity to transfer force. Each first line ends in what could be a noun – a substance allowing rest in the flow of meaning – but that turns out to function adjectivally. As adjectives, the words define aspects of an intending mind – Locke's secondary qualities, perhaps – seeking a substance in which to inhere. But the words' nominal qualities do not disappear. Their incompleteness, and their shared position with the verb "depends," combine to create an effect of substance in action. In effect, concrete qualities seem verbal – seem capable, as Fenollosa insisted, of transferring force from object to object and from the mind's intentions to concrete events.

We are starting to recognize the justice of that initial abstract expression of emotion, "so much depends / upon." Because "so much" has no clear antecedent, the phrase itself expresses a sense of emotional possibilities, to be filled out and clarified only when the mind completes its action and finds a place. Ultimately, so much depends upon our recognizing the complex ways in which we depend on the scene (as the farmer depends on these specific objects for his sustenance). Moreover, the scene itself turns back to give concrete aspects to this initial abstraction – both by giving it a local habitation and, perhaps more important, by creating a set of structural parallels that invites us to feel the mind itself as a palpable, tactile entity – as the verbal equivalent to the containing knowledge in Braque's painting. First, the etymology of the word "depends" reminds us of the fact, so dear to objectivist poets, that most of our words for mind's activity depend upon metaphors that initially had concrete meanings. The structural parallels also intensify this sense of the mind's dependence as a palpable dimension of the scene. The word "upon," for example, occupies a position later occupied by a series of nouns, and it completes its verb, just as the nouns complete their intending adjectives. "Upon," then, approaches a literal state of being; it is no longer merely an abstract connective, but a physical presence of consciousness in action. Rather than presenting an icon that we take as a perceptual reality, Williams makes the iconic force of art testimony for the most abstract, yet most intimate of psychological energies: those that define the very form of intentionality.

We see this intentionality most clearly in the way that the three concrete stanzas enact the process of dependence by continually looking back to that initial opening that invests the scene with its governing verb and allows other elements to assume predicative force. By extending structural parallels into epistemological ones, mental acts become almost as palpable as physical objects. This palpable force actually thickens our sense of the interrelations between time and space. On the one hand, the reader's engagement in their dependency is profoundly temporal. This assertion about dependency erupts suddenly, forcing us, in effect, to leap a resisting frontal plane before we get to the object, itself slowly unfolding in time and as space. That leap keeps the object dependent on us, and keeps us watching the powers of our own connecting energies as they unfold. We move from the adjective states "red" and "wheel" to a simple noun, to a qualifier of that noun (with its dual roles of adjective and noun), to an adverbial modifier of place – all posed with a strange testing of language's ability to hold the real, so that we are tempted to think of the poem as the literal exploration of what language can trust, as if language were testing its predicate categories. Yet no poem in English is more spatial and timeless. On the mimetic level, these objects seem to have no history, to have always been there, and to represent a form of rural life whose essential habits, and dependence on natural processes, have never really changed. On the testimonial level, all of this motion is so under the control of pattern, and so abstracted to pure function, that it establishes another dimension, in which the various conditions making for objectivity contain and sustain the temporal features of intentional desire.

"Depends," therefore, has two temporal senses that complement its two meanings: One sense refers to the physical activity of depending on movement to complete the mind's intentions, and the other invokes an abstract meaning that suggests a total enduring relationship of mutual supports. One temporal sense refers to an immediate present that keeps changing; the other, Suzanne Langer has called an "eternal present" that we see in mathematical formulas such as "two plus two equals four" or "x is a function of y and depends on it." Taken together, these two senses reinforce Williams's idealization of the artist as "composing-antagonist" (*Imaginations* 99), who can disclose the real without either aestheticizing it or making violent impositions upon it. All of the energy leads back to this sense of sustaining interrelationships. This "eternal present" is not transcendental. It is simply our sense of visibility, made self-reflexively "ours" by the palpable form that works of art afford the mind. Because the acts of mind can be rooted in an objective world, there need be no idealist dialectic to reunite the poles of presentation and disclosure: Objects endure, and thus acts of mind that intensify them, and are intensified in turn, are infinitely repeatable. And, as Nietzsche knew, there is no greater test of will, of the spirit's capacity to align itself with necessities it cannot control, than this sense of infinite repetition. Because art can realize levels of experience concrete enough to be this abstract, Williams can sustain what amounts to a religious appropriation of Cézanne's aesthetics: "A life that is here and now is timeless. That is the universal I am seeking: to embody that in a work of art, a new world that is always real" (*Selected Essays* 196).

This reality is central to Williams, and to his heirs, because it is there that he can justify his claim to having taken on Eliot and provided a direction freeing American poetry from this history that condemned Eliot to metonymic structures, even when Eliot sought the metaphoric scope of *The Waste Land.* Williams cast Eliot in much the same role in which Wittgenstein cast rationalist and idealist philosophy, when he asserted that, for them, whether a given statement has a claim on the real "would depend on whether another proposition was true" (*Tractatus* 2.0211). What we can trust depends on what our interpretations say we can trust – obviously an infinite regress, leading either to Anglicanism or Derrida or the historical analysis of the terms of such trust. The ideal of realization provided Williams another way, because it promised a mode of testimony that would not ignore the chain of interpretations but subsume it, or make it clearly supplementary to a particular phenomenon that could endure through different interpretive frameworks. Hence the imperative to simplicity: What resists interpretation must have, if not self-presence, at least enough similarity to painterly icons so that the whole can remain in focus, even as interpretation manipulates the various parts. Hence the concern for this sense of the timeless here and now, achieved by replacing the old realism with a Modernist sense of realization. For instead of miming objects, whose significance therefore depends on interpretation, the aesthetic of realization seeks to render the very forms that align will with objects, the forms that we ultimately have to rely on in order to check our interpretations. Realization does not ignore readerly mediation; rather, it tries to make visible the timeless and transpersonal qualities of the "there is," rendered with an intensity and palpability that make the "you exist" at best a mildly interesting corollary. If the mind's full powers seem more active and intense within the poem than they do in our interpretive substitutes for it, and if that activity seems capable of showing how dramatic, psychological, and historical interpretation all seem to displace those energies, art as realization becomes a formidable philosophical extension of our sense of empirical realities.

IV

Williams also provides us a very good introduction to the desires and hopes that led poets to try going beyond realization to the conceptual sites explored by Cubist art. For like many of his peers, he understood the limitations of his realizational model, but his own efforts to address those limits were themselves severely limited, demonstrating, by their failures, how difficult it would be for poets to adapt Cézanne's more radical painterly innovations. The challenge is easy to state: Although the poets wanted to escape subjective expression, it was by no means evident that the emphasis on "there exists" could provide as capacious or resonant an imaginative theater as the old fascination with "you exist." If realizational principles were to handle the range of energies once sustained by personal psychology, at the very least they would have to redefine what was meant by "there."[7] Rather than concentrating on making visible the conditions of visibility within a single scene, poetry too would have to explore using the multiple perspectives freed by the war on sculpture to create sites that become coherent only by complex acts of imaginative synthesis. And rather than focusing attention on a purified language that can define sharp contours aligning the attentive mind to its perceptions, one might adapt language to the strategies that Cubist painting had employed for treating color, line, and volume as essentially compositional materials, giving sensual substance to states that have imaginative reality only in the domain of conceptual relations.[8] But in trying to accommodate these possibilities, Williams shows how difficult it proved to be to move from understanding the challenge posed by Cubism to forging a verbal art capable of employing its most radical principles. Therefore his work in that vein turns out to be most useful for the contrasts it provides with two more successful appropriations: by Stevens, in some of his most painterly poems, and above all by Stein, in her ability to make language actually compose material sites that require a comprehensive rethinking of how the "there" and the "you" might be integrated.

Williams's complex relationship to Cubism is clearest in his poem "The Rose Is Obsolete," which he casts as rendering in words the significance he attributes to a collage by Juan Gris.[9] Again the imperative is his sense that certain vital values from the past have lost their currency in modern life and need radical means of recovery. But whereas the other poems we have considered are set in relation to a demoded perceptual order, this poem aims to renew a set of symbolic terms: If the rose is obsolete, how can art recover the energies and visions that this symbol once brought to vivid life? Eliot's way was to attempt revivifying the discourse that surrounded the symbol. If we can imaginatively recreate Dante, we can imaginatively recreate the force of his symbolism. But how do we translate that understanding into action, unless we have a plausible modern equivalent for such discourse? Lacking that, Eliot needed a transcendental world, in which literal identifications become spiritual truths. Williams, insistent on this secular world, in space and in time, had to find a constructive principle that could make the renewal visible.

The opening movement of the poem inaugurates that process of renewal by insisting first on the absolute fact of the rose's obsolescence. That gesture frees the poem to make what it can of Gris's collage. The need is too great to allow it the comfort of aesthetic objecthood. Instead, the poetic voice must read the art as a form of desire, capable of using an elaborate geometry to "engage roses," so that it can make present, in its own energies and play of textures, what it could no longer refer to by the symbol it constitutes. The specifics of that process fall to the second half of the poem:

> The rose carried weight of love
> but love is at an end – of roses
>
> It is at the edge of the
> petal that love waits
>
> Crisp, worked to defeat
> laboredness – fragile
> plucked, moist, half-raised
> cold, precise, touching
>
> What
>
> The place between the petal's
> edge and the
>
> From the petal's edge a line starts
> that being of steel
> infinitely fine, infinitely
> rigid penetrates
> the Milky Way
> without contact – lifting
> from it – neither hanging
> nor pushing
>
> The fragility of the flower
> unbruised
> penetrates space
> *(Imaginations* 108–9)

Collage relations transform the simple, historical finality of "end" into a complex structure of overlapping edges, each now capable of expressing a form of desire. At "an end – of roses," an evocative "it" establishes a mode of waiting that invites completion, that calls to a responding consciousness to characterize it by a chain of adjectives increasingly absorbed in its own intensity. The chain moves beautifully from the simple effect of crispness, to hypotheses about the labor involved, to a range of sensuous terms that modulates out to the several dimensions of projected intimacy contained in "touching": a fact about edges, as well as a dream of precise eroticism. Echoing his comments about Moore's "edge-to-edge contact," Williams is careful here not to allow any of the adjectives a clear noun to modify. Such direct relation to nouns would lose the power of edges and once again tie love to symbols rather than processes. Where the image had been, where the poem reaches out in incomplete expressions blending confusion and freedom, the poem locates at the petal's edge a geometric line sufficient to complete its quest. Tracking it evokes a possibility of penetration without violence that need neither depend on nor displace what evokes it. Now the art object itself discloses a life of the rose, capable of synthesizing masculine and feminine in a complex structure of broken edges, liberated by the synthetic act that preserves their fragility while completing the forms they intend. Predicates once attributed to purely aesthetic experience here seem capable of preserving that imaginative space in which sexual identities can blend and sexual possession becomes a form of renewing the other's distinctness.

Clearly it is not simply the rose that has grown obsolete. So too has an entire model of symbolism, which can ultimately do little more than gesture at ideals. A new art would have to make literal the work of negation capable of clearing the way for an erotic life that can respond to fragility without bruising it. Symbol must give way to testimonial figuration, and that figuration must sustain its power by refusing any of the easy unities that we impose on perception. Only a mind reduced to its most elemental synthetic forces can be exalted as one capable of preserving the ideals of love in a society locked in the violent imposition of meanings (a demonic condition that dominates the perceptual order in the succeeding poem of *Spring and All*).

That is the erotics of Cubism. However, Williams cannot make his language adequate to that ideal. On the simplest level, one can say that this poem remains sentimental, putting abstract and pious ideals about love precisely where he claims to offer an alternative to the obsolescent rose. In my view, this is the same old rose, disguised by reference to a collage, yet in no real way transformed. But rather than debate that point, on the level of content, I want to take it up by discussing what Williams's own version of Gris's collage can and cannot do to replace the rose. For there we shall be able to see both why Williams sought Cubist analogs and why his specific understanding of Cubism led him into poetic problems that made his return to realizational strategies a wise decision indeed.

Gris's collage may in fact transform the rose sufficiently to save it from obsolescence. The collage can define tactile edges that engage a geometry charged with fascinated desire, and, as we have seen, collage can invoke virtual powers to transform negation into a synthetic containing of radically diverse forces. But not even Picasso or Braque would tie themselves to so heavily charged a thematic task. For although Williams, and perhaps Gris, dream of transforming the idea of the rose as symbol, they in fact only shift the level on which the symbol is asked to work. There is no visual equivalent to the rose that compares to the visual equivalents Picasso creates for the music of the guitar. Language can only provide an equivalent to the rose's fragility by violently pushing against the willful symbolism it imposes. The easiest way to see this is to notice that Williams can mime the broken edges of Gris's collage. But what then fills them? We saw Picasso fill the gaps by a complex visual process that literally transformed elements and made visible certain structures of intentionality. For Williams's poem to work, it would have to generate an erotic process similar in material intensity.[10] But all we find is the straining of language to impose meaning on gaps that in themselves have no virtual life. So the poet's physical medium does little more than provide an interpretive substitute for Gris's visual image.

This lack of fragility does not penetrate space; it is swallowed up by the gulfs it wants to fill. Unable to master the testimonial qualities of a medium, the poem testifies instead to the limitations of the poet's processes, limitations that I think haunted Williams's whole career. This poet, so attuned to the ways language is embedded in our acts of attention and in the physical attributes of speech, could never extend his sense of artifice into a full instrument for thinking about, and in, the kind of subjects that had occupied the major lyric poets. Perhaps everything about the rose was more obsolete than he had thought. Perhaps the very idea of an art proposing to go beyond the limits of what it could control by producing analogical processes was an anachronism. Certainly Williams was not alone in failing to appropriate the conceptual force of Cubism. One thinks of Cummings, whose visual forms given to language sometimes have considerable metaphoric force, yet never become anything more than metaphors for already formulated thoughts. However, if writing could appropriate for its medium the total energies of Cubist spatial relations, then it could confidently arbitrate what had become obsolete and what had legitimate claims to shape future imaginations.

Only Gertrude Stein had the nerve and the wherewithal to sustain that claim in its most radical form, largely because she felt that she was the only one wholly to appreciate what Picasso had wrought. It was Picasso, after all, who made evident what Williams could not accomplish in his version of collage. For Picasso showed that collage had not only to free new modes of edge-to-edge contact; it had also to transform its own negating energies into a new synthetic force dramatizing the transformational powers that Williams could only allude to. Stein, therefore, had to ask how language could adequately test itself against that definition of Modernity. In 1912 she decided that the only way to come to an answer was to attempt her own portraits of Picasso and Matisse, using the portrait form to test the modes of agency that language could make articulate, and using the differences that emerged as her means of specifying those resources of language that might give it a distinctive version of the painter's methods.

It takes the opening two paragraphs of her portrait of Picasso to make clear the range of differences that language could use to compose a verbal equivalent for the impression the sitter made upon the artist:

> One whom some were certainly following was one who was completely charming. One whom some were certainly following was one who was charming. One whom some were following was one who was completely charming. One whom some were following was one who was certainly completely charming.
>
> Some were certainly following and were certain that the one they were then following was one working and was one bringing out of himself then something. Some were certainly following and were certain that the one they were then following was one bringing out of himself then something that was coming to be a heavy thing, a solid thing and a complete thing. (*Picasso* 322)

This is not simply gesturing at the visual force of some object standing outside language. Rather, Stein shows that language can itself play various substances and registers against one another, so that the work takes on a Cubist density of perspectives and facets that echo and contrast with one another. Clearly, this is not an act of interpreting symbols. It is, rather, the process of remaking what one can do with symbols that are already in place within practical life. Critics usually account for this difference by showing that Stein treats language as a medium with the same range of direct expressive effects that painters can wrest from color, line, and form. That is certainly not wrong, but it does not explain the semantic force that her experiments generated, at least at this point in her career.[11] To capture the edge-to-edge contact that she generates among the set of terms she isolates, then twists into intricate interrelationships, we must speak of her making material, not the words as sensual elements, but the semantic weight of the words as composing their own site. That site, in turn, can be understood only in something like physical terms, because meanings appear to lock together, like facets turning in a four-dimensional space.

If Williams's sentence can be envisioned as establishing its own force of gravity, Stein's sentences must be treated as elements implicating a more comprehensive gravitational field, which can be observed only in the forces created as sentences engage one another. This is not a mode of the physical that can be measured in terms of the sensual qualities revealing the effects of the gravitational force. We must respond to those qualities, to the rhythms that tie the semantic elements to the most direct sensual feelings. But it is also crucial to allow those sensual relations to twist back into the abstract space created by the mysteries of dimly grasped, but increasingly articulate, patterns of meaning, patterns made even more mysterious by the pronounced mechanistic aspects of the repetitions. Whereas Williams envisions a vague, spiritualized geometry, Stein's artist assumes the cultural role of engineer, assigned to test structures that will be asked to provide support and passage for the psychic energies necessary to come to terms with Modernity.

Such structures are not mere architecture. They redefine the concept of portraiture along much the same paths that we saw Duchamp exploring in his *Portrait of Chess Players*. For they make the measure of a person's force – Stein's version of an inner life – the demands the person imposes on the resources of the medium and on the artist's ability to transform that pressure on the medium into a kind of gravitational field, where the distortions define and balance competing forces. Thus, presentation is literally disclosure, because the effort to test a containing form becomes art's way of measuring the impact of its subject. One knows the world by the demands it makes on Stein's efforts to negotiate it (a principle she shares with Leonardo's portraits). And one easily knows oneself – or, better, one knows who one can be – by reflecting on the interaction between these two principles. Stein's greatness therefore consists, first, in her ability to make us see and feel what is inherent in this materialized version of what Wittgenstein called "philosophical grammar," and, second, in her ability to show that invention can liberate the actual forces we encounter there by literally constructing verbal equivalents allowing those forces passage into the responding mind. Any more narrative, less abstract mode of presentation would succumb to symbolism by prematurely fusing the potential of the language with the desires of the individual will. That fusing will suffice for recovering old symbols, but it will not allow the fuller tensional structures necessary to provide the instrument that language needs for responding to the very different architecture of the psyche that Picasso made plausible.

These generalizations obviously need a little concrete substance of their own. In order to test them we must attend to three features of Stein's style: her use of repetition and variation to isolate certain abstract semantic forces as material energies within the text; her ability to make the play of semantic light and shadow compose a conceptual chiaroscuro (as if grammar itself were the implicit scenic background); and her casting the text's temporal movement as a means of eliciting the gravitational force that emotions can establish for phenomena set free from representational placements. These features explain how Stein's reducing her dra-

matic characters to relations among verbal structures nonetheless allows
her to project a complex and mysterious plot out of the various gaps that
language necessarily opens as it spins out differences. The edge-to-edge
contact among semantic textures develops an intricately faceted play
among compositional elements, thereby giving substance to realities that
no single semantic measure can capture.

Stein's first paragraph sets the stage by isolating several concepts that
serve as fugal motifs. The writer's materials for portraiture will consist of
four themes, each capable of being twisted into a range of interrelationships: possible connections between "one" and "some"; various
dimensions of the idea of certainty; questions about what it means to
follow someone's lead; and the desire to define how that authority can be
positioned in relation to the semantic and social registers introduced by the
idea of being "completely charming." Then the themes are put in motion,
by having each of the opening paragraphs enact simple structural transformations. In the first, we see two predicate terms set forth, each modified
by adverbs that themselves are complexly poised between empty social
markers and suggestive philosophical qualification. Then the paragraph
builds two sentences that each drop one of the two adverbs, only to return
both in a sentence that modifies the descriptive adjective. The effect is to
draw us in, as if we too were charmed, and were therefore learning about
the mystery of such spells. For there is no direct source of authority. We
cannot look for a specific intentional context, because the authorial agent
has submitted herself to a rule. Yet the rule is so unexpected in its logic that
we can be fascinated by the strange kind of intelligence that it seems to
wield. To get involved is to follow as one can, groping among tracks and
traces, thrown off by the differences that this structure puts in motion.[12]
In my reading – and here one can only offer one own's path, as a possible
route through the work – the differences cohere once we see the sentences
as efforts to make sense of the power of that "one" to impose a form of
charm that makes others follow. We join voices whose response to that
charm at first compels them to a range of gestures we associate with idle
talk. But, as the language wanders, it somehow moves the key term
"certainly" from modifying the "following" to modifying the charm of
the "one," and that focuses the problem for the rest of the poem: How do
we understand the conjunction of those alliterating terms, "certainly,
completely charming."

The second stanza makes one wonder whether the idea of "charm" can
provide a sufficient measure for this force that leads others to follow.
Perhaps that concept is primarily a defensive one, a way of distancing the
force into the social categories that, in turn, sanction the modes of idle
talk that we hear in those opening rhythms. There is no direct way to
handle that suspicion. Posed as I have cast it, the question is too tradi-

tional, too dependent on there being some abstract criteria that may provide a single answer. For this text, for this mode of agency, we must ask the question another way: What resources of language are there that will allow an author to modify this very confined field, so as to explore the limits of its initial understanding of "this one's" authority? Stein's answer is gloriously simple. Suppose we simply introduce another set of differences, by moving from the levels of semantic and modal alternations to the more fundamental syntactic level. Suppose we simply reverse the positions of subject and object, so that we now begin to see the "following" from the point of view of the "some." Several thematic implications follow (and one finds oneself wanting to use quotation marks around all of one's own terms that are affected by this multidimensional matrix). We notice first two changes from the initial sentence of the first paragraph. Somehow, from the position of the "some," "certainly" can modulate into its adjectival form, and "charm" becomes synonymous with the fascinations that the one working can weave by bringing "something" out of the self. Then we notice that, rather than developing a four-sentence sequence based on internal modification, this paragraph is content with an apparently simple two-sentence structure, based on expanding the first by an additional relative clause.

These are small changes, but the nature of language, or better of the philosophical grammar that we learn when we learn a language, is such that it projects a virtual order in which small changes can exert enormous consequences on how we understand a phenomenon. Simply by reversing subject and object, the author seems to have created a situation in which the idea of charm and of authority must radically change. The perspective of "some" cannot be content with either the explanations that charm allows or the social register that it involves, with its gushing adverbs. Whereas the "one" may be content with fantasies of being completely charming, the "some" see themselves as having reasons (ironically thereby becoming victims of what may be the deepest magic at work in our culture, its dream of certainty). Once this "some" defines the linguistic perspective, explicit references to charm are confined to only two instances, each carefully bound to adjectival modification of this new "thing." What replaces charm is primarily the set of forces generated by the text's modification of "certainly." In the initial paragraph, the term had been a perfect complement to the world of the "one," because it defined the kind of idle social voice susceptible to the one's fantasies of what it means to be an artist. But once the focus is put on the conditions of following, that adverbial modifier modulates into the adjectival one, in order to indicate the force the object wields. Now the social voice finds resources enabling the art to exercise the kind of force that is usually attributed to constructions in the "male" domains of philosophy and science. And those resources find their measure in the simple two-sentence structure. For the difference that makes a difference is the capacity enabling this sense of work to produce a "thing" and to cast the sentence as taking on a range of modifiers for the thing. Now there is actually a phenomenon in the world that makes demands on our adjective hoard and frees us from the endless idle talk that surrounds those works of art that have lost their reality as things.

It is tempting to continue in this vein, in order to show the dense materiality that Stein creates for her work as a structure of mutually reinforcing shadows and contours, spun out by the differences that language proliferates as its pigment. But, since I think that the logic is clear and this book quite long enough, I shall shift to the more general question of the overall effects achieved by her commitment to working within the systematic dissemination of differential structures. One cannot simply make a portrait of Picasso, as if his character or effect on the portrait maker were a single definable force. Character depends on context, and context on the set of contrasts that one can elicit, then facet to maximize an audience's sense of how the contrast facilitates complex understanding. More important, if one wants to concentrate on the force defining an artist's specific achievement, one can measure that achievement only by setting it in relation to artists with roughly equal, or superior, claims to certain kinds of status.

In 1912, defining the kind of art that could claim to inaugurate a full Modernism meant drawing two portraits, since Picasso could not be made fully intelligible without the background provided by a rendering of Henri Matisse. Stein's Matisse also concerns himself with certainty:

> One was quite certain that for a long part of his being one being living he had been trying to be certain that he was wrong in doing what he was doing and then when he could not come to be certain that he had been wrong in doing what he was doing, when he had completely convinced himself that he would not come to be certain that he had been wrong in doing what he had been doing he was really certain then that he was a great one and he certainly was a great one. Certainly every one could be certain of this thing that this one is a great one. (*Picasso* 329)

The most remarkable feature of this opening passage is Stein's ability to capture a quality of introspection entirely foreign to her rendering of Picasso. I think it has to do with the endless monosyllables, each cautiously posed in a series of intricate dependent clauses that make us think nothing can be ventured without this kind of hesitant testing. This way, too, lies a kind of greatness. But notice all of the dependencies and difficulties it creates. This artist looks first, not to the thing he has made, but to the possible criteria that might make him a failure. Consequently, the resulting certainty is more negative than positive: a certainty of having escaped error, rather than a certainty of having composed a distinctive reality.

Several crucial consequences follow from those hesitations. First, we notice that the object itself never claims greatness. All that we can claim certainty about is that the one making it is a great one. This certainty, however, has more to do with social relations than with art: That is why the rhythm of the passage moves from the hesitating voice of reflective doubt into the repeated "certainly," that haunts most artists as a reminder of the social class that supports and trivializes their work. Yet in Stein's portrait, the artist remains responsible for his fate. Matisse's dependencies have a simple and devastating cause: Insofar as the artist is obsessed by the fear of not being great, he cannot be "one," and cannot achieve the identity accruing to those self-determined objects that give an audience no choice but to follow or reject. The resources of grammar then both accurately portray the anxieties that plagued Matisse during the hegemony of Cubism and judge their historical consequences. It turns out to be artists like Matisse whose indefiniteness and hesitations justified, by contrast, the unqualified style that Picasso and Stein developed. For the art of faceting can subsume those shifting perspectives as constitutive conditions of its own wholeness, rendering precisely the irreducible uncertainties left by the old European ideals of expression and judgment, without irritable reaching after truth, reason, or justification:

> Some were certain that this one was clearly expressing something being struggling, some were certain that this one was not greatly expressing something being struggling. . . .
>
> This one was one, some were quite certain, one greatly expressing something being struggling. This one was one, some were quite certain, one not greatly expressing something being struggling. (332–3)

Questions here become substantial remarks. The artist who cannot overcome this divided world reduces certainty to whatever the "some" make, and, more important, reduces expression to the domain of psychology already exhausted and consigned to irony by the nineteenth century. As long as art depends on a myth of the struggling artist, the actual terms of its struggles and of its possible force in society will remain as vague, and as insecurely "one," as this artist around whom such incompatible certainties circulate.

Characterized by these contrasts, Picasso becomes a fount of permissions, many of them tested and extended by Stein's work of following:

> This one always had something being coming out of this one.
> This one was working. This one always had been working. This
> one was always having something that was coming out of this
> one that was a solid thing, a charming thing, a lovely thing, a
> perplexing thing, a disconcerting thing. . . . This one was one
> certainly being one having something coming out of him. This
> one was one whom some were following. This one was one
> who was working. (334)

There is simply no better description of the forces mustered by an objectivist model of expression. Even if one cannot dispel the doubts that
haunt Matisse, one can make them into an artifact, which then becomes a
condition for testing whether one can in fact make "something having
completely a real meaning." That is the test of art and the way to establish an identity challenging the few who may grasp what the work
projects for a future. And only that completeness, Stein hastens to add,
will give art its maximal capacity as a force for life, because only that
work of completion establishes the kind of oneness that can continue to
charm the world, rather than be absorbed by it. The closing paragraph of
the portrait of Matisse left him at the mercy of the various certainties
dividing the "some" into ideological camps. When we turn to Picasso's
achievement, we find two new elements introduced into this exfoliating
"thing": the long-withheld idea of meaning, and its apparent corollary,
the assertion that this maker could not be completely working, presum-
ably because, as maker, he experiences a freedom beyond the temptation
to smug identity that conscience affords:

> This one was one who was working and he was one needing
> this thing needing to be working so as to be one having some
> way of being one having some way of being working. . . . This
> one was almost always working. This one was not one com-
> pletely working. This one was not one working to have any-
> thing come out of him. He always did have something having
> meaning that did come out of him. . . . He was one having
> something coming out of him something having meaning. He
> was not ever completely working. (335)

V

Stein did not remain a follower for very long. These experiments showed her how to move from rendering the equivalents for
Cubist painting to articulating uniquely verbal ways to sustain forms of

radical immanence for her own preoccupations. After that, works such as *Tender Buttons* adapted the constructivist aesthetic to pure processes of constitutive thinking, in which the potentials of language in effect composed their own relational fields. Rather than rely on a denoted subject and the patterning that standard syntax affords, she made the freedom of linguistic play a theater for faceting the intricacies of desires that can have no denoted object and no fixed linguistic form. Whereas grammar had been able to provide the background needed for the thematic focus of her analytic portraits, this new freedom of association made possible a truly synthetic form of construction. Most of the enabling rhetorics for Modernism set the image against the constraining habitual qualities of language used in practical and political contexts. Stein's synthetic work sets the associational force of the image back into an indefinable simplicity that promises a world even more basic and familiar than the one we rely on in practical contexts, so that intimacy, mystery, and mobility of desire are put at the very core of our sense of what it means to possess a language. Composition and recognition, self-projection and the recovery of primary processes like those theorized by Julia Kristeva, seem aspects of a single continuum.

Unfortunately, we cannot take the time in this book to follow those developments. Their history is still being written by contemporary poetry, and I have little to say that others have not said better.[13] Moreover, although Stein clearly offers the most complete versions in English of what a Cubist style affords poetry, we have two strong reasons for turning now to other aspects of that influence. First of all, there are serious dangers in making Stein too dependent on Cubist models. The ways she eventually constructs for being "one" seem to me to be more intimately connected to primary-process thinking, and to certain mobile yet transpersonal aspects of desire characteristic of noniconic work, than to anything possible within the cool, self-reflexive compositional attitudes basic to Cubism (and soon also to frustrate Picasso). Conversely, similar dangers arise if we assume that the sole, or the best, way for poets to absorb Cubist principles was to imitate or transform its specific stylistic concerns for collage faceting and principles of simultaneity.

Wallace Stevens provides the fullest case for a different manner of approaching the cultural force that Cubism exerted, an approach that I think was far more influential on the course of Modernist poetry. Essays such as "The Effect of Analogy" and "The Relations between Poetry and Painting" clearly take their sense of the parameters of Modernity and limitations of classical models of mimesis from Cubist ideals. But rather than defining those ideals in terms of stylistic principles, Stevens makes a sharp distinction between work that is modern by virtue of form, and work that is modern "in respect to what it says" or to what it expresses (*Necessary Angel* 168).[14] From this angle, the effective Modernity of a writer is likely to be less a matter of specific devices than of the ends he or she pursues and of the overall impact of the work directed by those ends. When reality seems to have changed "from substance to subtlety, a subtlety in which it was natural for Cézanne to say, 'I see planes bestriding each other and sometimes straight lines seem to me to fall'" (174), there must be a corresponding change in the modes of agency that the art calls upon:

> We find that the operative force within us does not, in fact, seem to be the sensibility, that is to say, the feelings. It seems to be a constructive faculty, that derives its energy more from the imagination than from the sensibility. The mind retains experience . . . [to make] its own constructions out of that experience. . . . What it really does is to use it as material with which it does whatever it wills. . . . The point is that the poet does his job by virtue of an effort of the mind. In doing so, he is in rapport with the painter, who does his job, with respect to the problems of form and color . . . not by inspiration, but by imagination or by the miraculous kind of reason that the imagination sometimes promotes. In short, these two arts, poetry and painting, have in common a laborious element, which, when it is exercised, is not only a labor but a consummation as well. (*Necessary Angel* 164–5)

In Chapter 9 I shall try to spell out the many ways in which Stevens makes the Modernist principle of "testimony" the challenge to, and test of, a poetic presentational mode that can so fuse labor and consummation. Here I just want to develop his specific understanding of the sites and energies that Cubism made available for poetry. In order to keep the discussion as close as possible to both the paintings and the poems we have already considered, I shall concentrate on "Someone Puts a Pineapple Together," even though its overt emphasis on perceptual processes is not Stevens's most characteristic mode. Yet by focusing on this poem, we shall be able to see clearly what the essential lines of influence are, and how they lead Stevens to break with the style governing his earlier, more Impressionist and Cézannean work. In general, the difference comes down to Stevens recognizing that the fundamental force of Cubist art consisted in a power of metamorphosis that defined for Modernity what poets could do in perhaps finer and more comprehensive ways. For those powers made it possible to fuse the poles of artistic disclosure and metaphoric presentational energies, and to build on that basis a model of values dependent neither on the allegorical frameworks required by Romantic symbolism nor on the secular transcendentalism sought in Williams's broken yet unbruised flower.

The best context for "Someone Puts a Pineapple Together" is Stevens's earlier meditation on still life, "Study of Two Pears." In the earlier poem, the emphasis lies on learning to see the object by breaking its perceptual qualities down into something approximating Cézanne's individual brushstrokes, which model by color relations. The poem's second stanza provides a good example:

> They are yellow forms
> Composed of curves
> Bulging toward the base.
> They are touched red.
> (*Collected Poems of Wallace Stevens* 196–9)

But as the rhythm of negation and assertion that organizes the description restores vitality to the plain visual object, the poem must turn to metaphor in order to parallel the presence of Cézannean personality. The project of learning to see without imposing the will to metaphor leads inevitably back to the metaphoric component of all human creative processes:

> The yellow glistens.
> It glistens with various yellows,
> Citrons, oranges and greens
> Flowering over the skin.

This carefully delineated fruit must take both the form and the participial syntax of "flowering," if its vitality as fruit is to be fully appreciated.

Simply the title "Someone Puts a Pineapple Together" tells us that we have entered a very different universe from that of the earlier poem: There will be no pretense of a thing brought to realization in its material particularity. Now, from the beginning, the delighted eye is inseparable from the erratic metaphoric will, exuberant in its constant transformation of the sensual world:

> O juventes, o filii, he contemplates
> A wholly artificial nature, in which
> The profusion of metaphor has been increased.
>
> It is something on a table that he sees,
> The root of a form, as of this fruit, a fund. . . .
>
> He sees it in this tangent of himself.
> And in this tangent it becomes a thing
> Of weight on which the weightless rests: from which

The ephemeras of the tangent swarm, the chance
Concourse of planetary originals,
Yet, as it seems, of human residence.
                              (*Necessary Angel* 83–7)

As deconstruction shows, and Braque painted, every name comes from
somewhere different from the object under observation. A mode of
naming responsive to whatever makes a residence fully human must try
to exaggerate those tangential qualities, so that they compose the imaginary space where the actual pineapple lives in our investments. Only
there can the fruit's planetary home be fully situated in relation to the
"tropic of resemblances."

These tropics, in turn, make it possible to give a great deal more
substance than Williams could to the edges that lift the object into the
fullness of its life for the imagination. Like Williams, Stevens suggests
that there must have been an age "when a pineapple on a table was
enough." But he need not try to recover that state, or even give life to the
symbols that sustained the pineapple. Rather than look back, he turns
reflexively on the energies that make this kind of poetry an embarrassment to the realist orientation. Tracking those energies creates a poetics
of the tangent, responsible simultaneously to the simple perceptual plane
that connects the pineapple to its table and to the constant shifts in
interpretive frameworks that lead us to conceive that a "truth was not the
respect of one, / But always of many things."

As we track those tangents, material and figurative, the various edges
begin to show how "the incredible, also, had its truth." And as the
incredible takes hold within our reflective process, we find ourselves
actually constructing and manipulating edges of the object, in order to
understand the ways in which the object elicits such exuberance. This
putting together the pineapple that realism broke apart eventually establishes a Modernist version of Neoplatonic eros, composing figures for its
own excess and aligning itself to the world that this excess produces.
Cubist faceting becomes the richest way to understand how a Modernist
art can respond to fragmentation while still providing modes of gathering that resist the simple deconstructive treatment of that excess simply
as a process of supplementation.

Stevens's opening suggests that putting the pineapple together will
require bringing "three planets" into conjunction – sun, moon and
imagination, each orbiting this pineapple globe as its elect expositors,
and all together constituting the most complex poetic transformation of
gravity we have yet seen. As the "erudite" "propagations" of light from
the realist sun awaken "truth's most jealous subtlety," we realize that the
effort to "defy / the metaphor that murders metaphor" ironically generates metaphoric energy that no negation can dispel. The very excess of

sunlight, in other words, also introduces the kind of reflected moonlight that elicits other, more mysterious presences. Truth's jealousy cannot be subsumed under any of the values compatible with the ideal of truth. Instead, the stakes it places on eternal fidelity between pure word and virginal thing reveal precisely why, in a secular world, the ideal must continually falter, letting through the kinds of investments that cannot but bring the sun within the orbit of the moon's traditional figures for desire. If truth can enter romance, there must be an "incredible" that has its truth. Rather than separating what light illuminates from the other senses, the dream of accurate description engages us in the moon's shiftier and more exotic domain of sound (which, I assume, is shadowy light), where desire seeks "the particular tingle in proclamation / That makes it say the little thing it says, / Below the prerogative jumble."

In order to keep this tropical site clear enough to let light through, we need the mediating effects of the third planet, the imagination. It comes into our ken in the beginning of the third and final section:

> How thick this gobbet is with overlays,
> The double fruit of boisterous epicures,
> Like the same orange repeating on one tree.

> A single self. Divest reality
> Of its propriety. Admit the shaft
> Of that third planet to the table and then:
> 1. The hut stands by itself beneath the palms.
> 2. Out of their bottle the green genii come . . .
> 10. This is how yesterday's volcano looks . . .

What better note of entrance than this mood of exclamation, as if the poetry could now raise the object to the appropriate emotional level. However, such exponential processes are not without their price. If the imagination is to take a stable place in the scene, it must help us negotiate the semantics of doubled fruits that occurs at this level of self-reflection. This gobbet thick with overlays is both the actual delectable image of the pineapple and the imagined fruit, built up by the faceting play of sun and moon. Imagination must take responsibility for the energies that compose such doublings by establishing a dialectical theory of truth, responsive both to the need to "say nothing of the fruit that is / Not true" and to the "incredible" auras cast by the moon.

The task is not easy. First one must expose the limitations of the old stance – which Stevens does brilliantly by returning to the figure of truth's jealousy. Such jealousy binds proponents of truth to claims of propriety that turn out to undermine its ambitions, trapping the claimant in social decorums and forcing him to make unnecessarily abstract demands to possess the phenomenon on the basis of a single description. Truth as propriety assumes that one timeless set of names must stand in for the object, in a range of pragmatic contexts. Time, however, keeps turning those names into "effigies," and, more important, the names themselves tend to take over for the full life of the psyche. There must therefore be a new model of agency, a new definition of the lover and of his possible satisfactions. Grammar once again provides the necessary resources by enabling imagination to shift from the doublings of the indicative mood to the site made possible if one reflects on what one composes by allowing the spirit the modifications that occur in the imperative. For then we literally admit the shaft of that third planet, by observing a series of twelve transformations that the poem can wring on the appearance of the pineapple. On that basis, one is not merely making abstract arguments; one can begin to reflect on actual changes, made and proposed, in what truth had so jealously protected. The result is a delightfully playful restoring to the pineapple the mythic and affective associations that establish the full affective implications of its tropical origins.

That return deserves another. So the poem builds to its climax by shifting from how the pineapple appears in various guises to how we come to appear once we recognize the ways in which Cubist analogies provide the necessary means for reflecting on the transformations we have been observing.

> These casual exfoliations are
> Of the tropic of resemblances, sprigs
> Of Capricorn or as the sign demands,
>
> Apposites, to the slightest edge of the whole
> Undescribed composition of the sugar cone,
> Shiftings of an inchoate crystal tableau,
>
> The momentary footings of a climb
> Up the pineapple, a table Alp and yet
> An Alp, a purple Southern mountain bisqued
>
> With the molten mixings of related things.

Once again the figure of edges seems necessary to define this Cubist sense of objects reconstituted by the imagination. But here the tangents no longer go toward infinity. Instead they compose a complex relation of inner and outer, perceived and projected qualities, that metamorphose the pineapple into the dancing facets of reflecting crystal, Stevens's favorite figure for the kind of gravity that holds forces in balance within the mind. Then the figure of the pineapple / crystal modulates into a mountain, or, more properly, into what we take as a mountain to climb. Vision, in other words, leads us to align this reflection upon the humble pineapple with the most exalted of romance tropes, the quest to attain the visionary mountaintop. Now, however, all of the traveling is a matter of composition, all of the reward is present in the particular climb we have been attending. We see taking form the probable source of all the desires that have from the beginning intruded on description, and we put ourselves in a position to appreciate what has been involved in tracking all the modifications that those desires entail.

Coming to terms with those modifications requires letting the poem's syntax mime the process of climbing, to a point where we can look back over the entire journey. Thus the sentence just quoted continues for two more stanzas, until it returns to "a form" that

> At last, is the pineapple on the table or else
> . . . .
> An object the sum of its complications, seen
> And unseen. This is everybody's world.
> Here the total artifice reveals itself
>
> As the total reality. Therefore it is
> One says even of the odor of the fruit,
> That steeps the room, quickly, then not at all,
>
> It is more than the odor of this core of earth
> And water. It is that which is distilled
> In the prolific ellipses that we know,
>
> In the planes that tilt hard revelations on
> The eye, a geometric glitter, tiltings
> As of sections collecting towards the greenest cone.

The "this" concentrates that torturous sentence into a marvelously simple moment, simultaneously resolving the romance quest and recasting it as the crystal, now made abstract and equated with a total artifice revealed as a total reality. The "this" and the "here" locate everybody's world, because they gather the dual senses of "sum" – one the result of simply adding facet to facet, the other the totalizing Latin for "I am." The "this," then becomes resoundingly transpersonal, because we know that the "sum" carries such a range of perspectives that it would be foolish to assume the viewer must be bound to any one subjective slant. That transpersonality, in turn, deepens the idea of the crystal by forcing the "sum" to yield to more intricate geometric figures. A satisfying conclusion must articulate processes of containment opening onto dimensions that can have reality only for the composing mind as it approaches the greenest cone.

At its most abstract, however, this poem never loses its hold on the actual pineapple. Complementing the resounding "this" is the force of the repeated "it," that gathers into one site those profusions and ellipses so multiple that they cannot be the property of any one mind. Stevens carefully elaborates their resonance by having his last three sentences return to the syntactic intricacy of the climb up the mountain. In one sense, this gesture reopens the proliferations that the summary too easily gathers into a discursive generalization. But now the openness is syntactically tied to these repetitions of "it," as if the mind had an object to track that was at once too concrete and too abstract to allow any more determinate name. This "it" is ultimately not something we name; it is something that the artist tries to enclose, in all its elusiveness, within the tensional geometry that his artifice constructs. Therefore the simplest denotational pronoun extends the "this" to an aura of mystery leading beyond the odor of earth and water, then providing a subject for the "collectings" that enable geometry to embody the full figural implications of imaginative sense. The "it" becomes the force that circulates through all of the ellipses to become the only possible referent for the greenest cone: the "idea" of the pineapple, made real by the compositions it invites.

VI

Brilliant as Stevens is, there remains something unsatisfyingly abstract about that "greenest cone." We know what he means; we even see how the poem warrants the figure; but I suspect that most readers feel the poem's longing for much more than the pineapple can provide, even when caught in this faceted light. Perhaps that is because one cannot escape an enormous gulf between this single resolving metaphor and the geometric tensions that provide the synthetic force gathering the various transformations of a Cubist painting. In the most characteristic Cubist work, there is no greenest cone; there is only the faceting of sections that collect toward a complex visual structure, not translatable into any single color or form. Stevens's discursive Romanticism, on the other hand, cannot be content until it produces a single integrative abstraction allowing the mind to possess what the eye disposes. Were we to posit a painterly analog for this fundamental impulse, we would have to turn from Cubism to the noniconic work that Stevens never understood or liked. For there, single states of color or form take on that same abstracting of sensual intensity, and there painting seems continually on the margin of allegorizing the virtual activities that it calls forth.

This is not to say that Stevens, or any other American Modernist, either emulated noniconic painting or felt it as a challenge to his or her poetry. It is to suggest that once poets begin to take on the challenges posed by Cézanne and Picasso, the orientations of their own medium are likely to lead their experiments in directions best exemplified by non-iconic work. There was little direct imitation, because writers found it difficult to identify with canvases so eager for direct engagement with spiritual forces that they rejected both the denotational aspects of signs and the cultural connotations that allow language most of its affective force. Nonetheless, some features of that painting were much better complements to what the poets were trying to do than anything they claimed to find in Cubism. Remember how awkwardly Williams and Stevens try to make abstract symbolic figures out of the rose and the pineapple that they construct along Cubist lines. More important, even poets as sympathetic to Cubism as Stevens eventually grew disillusioned with the Nietzschean willfulness that characterized Picasso's versions of metamorphosis. Therefore, the task of positing alternatives led poets to explore in their own terms what is so powerfully exemplified in Malevich's simple exponential relation between red square and black square. Both poets and painters needed to articulate sites sufficiently transparent to carry transpersonal force, and both required forms of what I have called self-reflexive virtuality, in order to locate the power otherwise attributed to the individual will in aspects of the aesthetic experience that each member of its audience could realize in his or her own right. Finally, the very enterprise of resisting all of the worldly claims of representation in the arts led both poets and painters to similar models for asserting that their foregrounded imaginative energies were capable of transcending the historical conditions that generated them. The more elemental the relations, the better the chance that their configuration would not not get its imaginative force from the positivities shaping contemporary ideologies.

I do not want to argue that there cannot be good Cubist writing: The examples of Stein, Jacob, and Apollinaire refute that. Nor do I want to underplay the significance of what poets like Stevens made of its metamorphic principles, primarily because much of what Derrida has attuned us to takes form in that work as irreducible values at play in the life of reflective imagination. But honoring those achievements ought not blind us to the more indirect, but equally powerful imaginative role that non-iconic painting can play in deepening our appreciation of Modernist poetry. The obvious way to go about demonstrating this is to go back over the poems we have been considering, in order to point out the specific features illuminated by this different context. However, I shall not do that here: Much of what needs to be said could be filled in by anyone sturdy enough to have read this far, and the more complex affinities will be the center of my Chapter 9, where I discuss how Stevens incorporated the various painterly traditions in his later poems. Instead I shall concentrate on Marianne Moore and on the late work of William Butler Yeats, the two substantial Modernist poets whom critics have been slowest to connect to Modernist painting, in Yeats's case because of his strongly stated preference for the art of other epochs. The lack of any overt influence of noniconic art on their poetry offers a superb opportunity to elaborate the distinctive literary concerns that led poets to create abstract sites and explore self-reflexive virtuality. Thus, as we approach the most radical of painterly experiments, we find ourselves circling back to the most common and intense of the desires shared by the Modernist poets: the desire to reveal and take responsibility for those creative energies usually subordinated to the scenic stage subsuming them within the constraints of the practical understanding.

Perhaps the major reason that noniconic painting exercised so little influence on poetry was that the ideology informing that painting already derived from literary sources: One thinks both of those writings elaborating the theosophical doctrines that the painters made concrete and, more important for our purposes here, of Mallarmé's struggle to define the limitations of the image and to elaborate an alternative site for imaginative work. Therefore poets had little incentive to follow the painters' experiments or to seek other equivalents to stylistic forms of abstraction that they felt they already possessed. Indeed, for most poets, abstraction pursued at the price of concrete figuration seemed the least effective way to grapple with their own marginalization. Yet, despite those fears, there remained two central features of noniconic abstraction that the poets had to assume, in their own way: its resistance to the tendency of images to displace the constructive powers that inform them, and its direct manner of handling virtual testimony. Because the affective terms characteristic of those features take their most influential form in the writing Mallarmé wove from his early fascination with the diaphanous, desubstantializing qualities of Impressionism, I shall begin with a brief discussion of his prose poem "The White Water-Lily," where, once again, the process of reflecting on the mind's relation to a flower sets everything else in motion.

Mallarmé is the least paraphrasable poet I know, so in summarizing that work I must eliminate a great deal of the nuance. The poem opens within the mind of a narrator, as he considers the long time he has been rowing, half-enchanted, in his search for water flowers on the way to visit a friend's estate. Having run aground on a tuft of weeds, he realizes that he has arrived at a series of lawns belonging to this "friend," who, we are now told, is a lovely lady whom he has never met. Imagining that she has chosen this "watery and impenetrable retreat" because the crystal surface of the water provides "an inner mirror to protect herself from the brilliant discretion of the afternoons," he makes that image a talisman for

calling her up, in "her perfection and her purity."[15] Next the narrator
elaborates a marvelous series of hypotheses about her states of mind, and
about his own vacillation between fear of bondage to her and fear of
violating this dreamlike state by testing his images against her actual
appearance and actions. Finally he makes his decision:

> With a glance I shall gather up the virginal absence scattered
> through this solitude and steal away with it; just as, in memory
> of a special site, we pick one of those magical, still unopened
> water-lilies which suddenly spring up there and enclose, in their
> deep white, a nameless nothingness made of unbroken reveries
> of happiness never to be. . . .
>
> But if sensing something unusual, she was induced to ap-
> pear . . . , so much the worse for that ineffable face which I shall
> never know! For I executed my plan according to my rules: I
> pushed off . . . , and so, like a noble swan's egg fated never to
> burst forth in flight, I carried off my imaginary trophy, which
> bursts only with that exquisite absence of self which many a lady
> loves to pursue in summer along the paths of her park, as she
> stops sometimes and lingers by a spring which must be crossed
> or by a lake.

It is tempting to dismiss this as one more invocation of the Hamlet
complex, which provided early Modernism with perhaps its last means
of claiming a nobility that could justify refusing the demands of empirical reality and historical change. But to do that would also be to
dismiss the remarkable intelligence that here invites us to speculations
not easily subsumed under those historical parameters. The last sentence
will suffice to make the point. Notice how it first moves into an increasingly self-absorbed state, climaxed by the brandishing of the flower
as "imaginary trophy," only to loop beautifully back to the lady. The
movement of rejection becomes, on every level, a movement of reap-
propriation in a finer tone, providing precisely the spiritual model that
all abstract art pursues. In contrast to the practical understanding, art
tries to align itself with the unopened flower, so that this figure of
absolute deferral can serve as a means of gaining access to aspects of the
woman's inner life that are much deeper than those she would offer were
he to assume any standard social, or even sexual, role. Those standard
roles are the stuff of dramatic art, the domain that must wring infinite
variations on the ways that the man and the woman would each have to
be wary of the other, each having to show the other appearances that
protect the self, disappointed by the routines it must undergo. By refusing that erotic theater, the speaker enters a site on the other side of those
thresholds. There, "before the spring must be crossed," his own with-

drawal enables him to identify fully, if momentarily, with those truly intimate aspects of the self that emerge when the self is not the focus of attention.

The narrator's experience provides the psychological correlate for Mallarmé's fascination with virginity: In denying the standard exchanges of desire, one enters a solipsism that is potentially our deepest way to know the other in his or her privacy. By refusing to ask the kinds of questions about appearances that would enable someone to know about the lady's estate or her past, or even her dramatic feelings about the event of solicitations offered and parried, Mallarmé establishes a very different model of agency. He does not reject the deep expressive subject that fascinated the nineteenth century, but he locates that depth in a site that the art of that century could not enter. Those artists and writers kept finding that the subjective life they sought offered only traces of itself, provocations that produced defenses and categories displacing that which elicited them. Perhaps, then, the only plausible route to the vital life of spirit required beginning with the process of displacement that continually undid more direct efforts at knowledge. A writing intent on its own powers of displacement might align itself to the very needs it produced, so that it could release aspects of intentional activity that could not take the melodramatic stage provided by representational art. The self, defined in terms of frustrated desires, might borrow the tricks that Hegel's idealism attributes to the spirit, locating in the power of negation the virtual traces of spirit's deepest needs and desires. Then, barred by its initial choices from any more direct mode of satisfaction, art might be able to focus on the mysteries of that being whose most intimate expression depends upon a pronoun shared by all speakers of the language. In such public solitude, we find the power to realize those flowers that bloom only when the viewer can share their unopened state.

VII

There seem few obvious connections between Mallarmé and Marianne Moore. Whereas the one poet is willfully vague, the other has probably the sharpest control of precise imagery in twentieth-century poetry. Yet that precision may have become a trap for Moore, leading readers to concentrate on her surfaces and blinding them to the intellectual work the poems do in projecting distinctive forms of agency. What was for Mallarmé largely speculation about the resources of virginity become for her absolutely fundamental questions of poetic identity. Therefore I want to use the contexts I have been developing to examine this other dimension of Moore's work, based on her sense that poetry made it possible to locate means by which to preserve the imaginative

spaces figured in the lady's withdrawal from the traffic of sexual exchange. Moore had to be abstract – in part to preserve those aspects of
the flower contaminated by the (largely male) images promulgated by
her culture, and in part to locate forms of power enabling the female
Modernist to define a significant alternative to the modes of will cultivated by her constructivist peers. For Moore, construction became the
project of developing aspects of agency that could preserve idiosyncracy,
while finessing the specular mirrors that tend to enthrall those who must
labor to be different.

Moore's male peers had already been demonstrating that poets could at
least partially resist the hegemony of the image, by foregrounding in its
stead the mind's specific activity of composing resonant relational fields,
so that the significance of the poem consists primarily in the ways that it
elaborates our capacity to work around a mimetic orientation. Rather
than idealize the figure of the rose, the poem could focus attention on the
metamorphic constructs that provide spiritual equivalents to what the
rose once signified. But does not this end up idealizing the figure of the
artist? Such idealization may be necessary in many areas of cultural life, if
only to free us of other, more limiting, identifications. Yet it did not take
someone of Moore's intelligence a great deal of effort to see that her male
colleagues were perhaps a bit too drawn to versions of constructivism
that stressed those powers of the "composing-antagonist," and thus conferred on "the poet" the right to impose his order on the bland fields
horizontal before him. Resisting such emphases was not simply an abstract moral imperative. To be a woman, in her society, meant to be at
times a victim of those wills, and, more important, woman's place afforded an imaginative position where alternative forms of imaginative
power become available. If one replaced the composing will with a more
flexible imaginative playfulness, it might be possible to show how the
will itself can be understood in terms of virtual and transpersonal energies that an abstract art can display. Suppose, for example, that instead of
concentrating on how the spirit carries out metamorphic chains, the poet
tried to reflect on the traces of some incomplete and impersonal moral
allegory apparently engendering the desires at work in the poem. Then
will itself is not so much the driving force of the poem as one of the
elements within it that poetic intelligence tries to explore. The terms of
will can be elaborated by exploring virtual states, in much the same way
that Malevich's "tilt" organizes our visual responses to his painting. The
poet need not reject precise imagery. But, if she is to articulate the
features of subjective power most significant for those whose place in the
social order keeps them suspicious of all hegemonic figures, she must
resist the fascination of the completed image and create testimony for

that force of subjectivity that might make such displaced conditions themselves accessible to all readers.

Moore had a variety of terms for those powers. She spoke of "sincerity," "genuineness," and "authenticity" as the qualities that best distinguished her ambitions.[16] These terms, however, seem to me at best simple indices of the kind of presence that concerns her: They so clearly bear the marks of her fear of staging, and thereby displacing, the distinctive trait of her imaginative activity that they defer as much as they reveal. Therefore, rather than stay with her self-descriptions, I propose that we read some of her best poems in the light of her remarks on other writers and painters. Her most concise statement describing how poems constitute that "sincerity" and authenticity occurs in a review of E. MacKnight Kauffer, where she praises "an objectified logic of sensibility as inescapable as the colors refracted from a prism" (*Complete Prose of Marianne Moore* 427). Permeating the material qualities of the art is something more active, more comprehensive, and more fluid than any image can carry. And, precisely because of those attributes, the sensibility so defined can take objective form in a logic that all viewers can share. For her most general, and most clearly gendered, sense of how writing can adapt that logic, we must turn to her remarkable essay on H.D.:

> Only as one isolates portions of the work, does one perceive the magic and compressed energy of the author's imagination, actually in such lines as the following, being lost in the sense of spectacle. . . . One recognizes here, the artist – the mind which creates what it needs for its own subsistence and propitiates nothing, willing – indeed wishing to seem to find its only counterpart in the elements; yet in this case, as in the case of any true artist, reserve is a concomitant of intense feeling, not a cause of it. . . . Preeminently in the case of H.D. we have the intellectual, social woman, non-public and "feminine." There is, however, a connection between weapons and beauty. Cowardice and beauty are at swords' points and in H.D.'s work, suggested by the absence of subterfuge, cowardice, and the ambition to dominate by brute force, we have heroics which do not confuse transcendence with domination and which in their indestructibleness, are the core of tranquility and of intellectual equilibrium. (*Complete Prose* 80–2)

On this basis I propose to shift critical attention from Moore the objectivist, or Moore the moralist, to Moore as she tried to develop objectified models of agency capable of defining and sharing a heroics that does not "confuse transcendence with domination." From such a perspective, the content of her poems becomes inseparable from the leaps and projections that they invite an audience to see itself making, as it collaborates in the compositional activity. This version of Mallarmé's lady manages to preserve her strangeness, yet also achieves the power to forge, in her own terms, imaginary trophies with real and abiding desires in them. But despite her strong identification with H.D., Moore rarely called attention to the gendered investments in her own work, probably fearing that the resulting theatrics would displace the dimensions of impersonality and transpersonality sustaining the values that her gendered position enabled her to realize. I hope here to right the balance by showing how those abstract concerns are consistent with the powers that she does attribute on the mimetic level to female personae.

I have two reasons for this emphasis. First, I think that the context of noniconic art provides the best overall case for explaining why Moore resists more overt gender identifications, yet why she nonetheless feels that poetry can provide testimony to the kinds of imaginative forces to which gender gives poets access. The terms of her resistance should by now be obvious. Given her ironic self-consciousness, the more art could distance the immediate urgencies of such identifications, the more it freed intelligence to a more flexible and complex set of interventions in the world. If one could achieve the anonymous idiosyncrasy of a purely formal intelligence, one might be modern, without taking any specific sexual position at all. Yet the pure constructivist rationale clearly did not satisfy Moore. There remained features of her own imaginative energies that could take more definite and more distinctive shapes when identified as female, and there was the constant provocation of the male poets having appropriated Modernist principles for their fantasies of culture-creating willfulness. So she had to experiment with establishing an aura of gender as a property, not of the content of experience, but of its formal structure within the reflexive space of the poem. Moore tried to make the powers available to a gendered stance become part of the virtual presence that the work composed for all readers. As readers flesh out the world that the poem composes, they find themselves reenacting dispositions that take on the intensity and sharpness that they do because they derive from the imagination's struggle to deal with the pressures imposed by the culture's efforts to confine women to their "place."

My second reason consists of the exemplary role Moore's Modernist project can play for a contemporary criticism highly suspicious of Modernist ideals. The dominant ideology in feminist discussions of Modernist poetry emphasizes the limitations in the cult of impersonality, celebrating in its stead those poets who manage to find, or steal, a voice and a language that can express the distinguishing features of their individual experiences.[17] That view, however, confuses the limits of Modernism with the limits of male imaginations and posits an alternative that must rely on the notoriously slippery notion of expressing the truth of one's experiences. When one takes that perspective on experience, one relies on an essentially empty concept, which becomes whatever one wants: What is not "experience"? And, perhaps more disturbingly, what claim about experience does not invite ironic laments about the source being alienated from the means of representation available? It was precisely these questions that led Modernists like Moore to resist models of subjective expression. So it seems to me crucial that feminism at least try to align itself provisionally with a critical spirit that links suspiciousness of the scenic self with a fierce commitment to individualism. Modernist abstraction seemed to her capable of sustaining principles of idiosyncratic assertiveness that were not as likely as expressivist models to be shaped by prevailing cultural codes or to depend for their reinforcement on the social structures one hopes to change. One can be feminist by locating gender as a particular set of qualities that formal energies can both present and test: in Moore's case, by having a few poems make explicit connections between qualities of female polish and care that provide a frame for characterizing the authorial energies in the more impersonal work. The virtual aspects of the work invite readers both to identify with those properties and to test the degree to which what begins in gender can be extended to full transpersonal imaginative activity.[18]

The first step in defining the qualities Moore establishes for her authorial energies is to turn to "An Egyptian Pulled Glass Bottle in the Shape of a Fish," the poem that most clearly differentiates her model of composition from Williams's "composing-antagonist":

> Here we have thirst
> and patience, from the first,
>   and art, as in a wave held up for us to see
>   in its essential perpendicularity;
>
> not brittle but
> intense – the spectrum, that
>   spectacular and nimble animal the fish,
>   whose scales turn aside the sun's sword by their polish.[19]

This is no Romantic plea for unity with nature; it is as insistent as Williams on the willfulness, or resistance to the given, that is necessary for the site art composes. Moore, however, is careful not to turn such resistance into a self-sufficient "masked ball / attitude" that might impose on the quest for personal identity "a hollowness / that beauty's light momentum can't redeem" (86). There are hollownesses or gaps that are necessary to beauty, and to redemption, but one must be careful not to fill them in too quickly with one's own self-image. Rather than turn back on a representable will, Moore makes the movement of the poem itself the only possible definition of ethos. There she can establish a willfulness that can be kept in public circulation, available for any consciousness willing to recapitulate the control giving this work its polish.

The result is a polish that extends beyond any social connotations, to the most intricate and intimate relations between life and art. Notice first the two nouns that initially define the poem's "here," and thereby establish some of the qualities giving art an "essential perpendicularity" not translatable into any simpler, more naturalistic terms. What other site could so combine the physical and psychological properties of thirst and patience? "Here" we see the bottle's shape and function; we see the thirst it should alleviate strangely connected to the fish it represents; and we observe the traces of craft that ultimately align patience with another mode of thirst that only this play of forces might satisfy. No wonder these appearances so quickly transpose what we see, from physical object into the more abstract defining of the art itself as a wave, which we can envision cutting against the planes that pure perception must occupy.

All that the wave implies immediately takes psychological form in the second pair of adjectives syntactically linking the two stanzas. "Brittle" describes the glass, but, in conjunction with "intense" (and after the oxymorons of the first stanza), the adjectives expand to refer also to the activity (and thirst) of both the artist and the viewer. Yet the temptation to turn all of this into mere metaphor – into what the farmer might keep in his head – is denied, by the fact that the poem is also speaking about the spectrum of light growing inseparable from the movements of the fish. Now the fish begins actually to swim, although in an element that the artist has composed for him. And that light becomes something quite different from the "sun's sword," something whose polish does transform that sword into the perpendicularities of the poem's own prismatic waves. Language makes us see a new object. In fact, the movement of this language so fuses the abstract and the concrete that it becomes an example of that polish which, in the visual object, literally gives the fish a different medium.

Moore's celebration of art brilliantly combines the presentational forces of the two media, glass sculpture and language, showing how each transforms a world of thirsts into a world where the dynamic properties of the artistic acts compose a perpendicularity considerably more satisfying than any physical shape. Moore reveals no hidden symbolic forces and works out no deep psychological conflicts. She does, though, define modes of activity where it may be possible not to have to live in the sets of oppositions that are generated by those conflicts. "Egyptian Glass Bottle" suspends the claims of realism, in order to create the effect of liberating the self and language into an awareness of how the world can be contained by what our arts can make of our care and attention. There is no denying Williams's insistence on the artist's will as antagonist to the sun's sword, but there is also no need, with such intricate objective displays of what language can do, to turn that will into a specular icon of itself, which threatens to become a thirst that no mode of polished play will be able to satisfy.

Perpendicularity is Moore's version of Malevich's tilt: It carries the shift in coordinates necessary for the imaginary to take hold within the real. An art of words, however, will be tempted to try characterizing that perpendicularity, so that it will bear further predicates: The power of form must imply precisely the domain of qualities that Moore tries to avoid on the level of the image. This motif of polish clearly begins that process, since it takes what the culture codes as essentially female, in order to reappropriate those virtues in a finer tone. Like Derrida, commenting on Nietzsche on the stylus, Moore plays her own artifice against what finishing schools were expected to produce, while crossing that irony with a sly reference to the kind of attention one develops as one tries to keep one's mind alive while doing household chores. Irony, however, does not suffice. The intricacies of "polish" characterize the mode that establishes perpendicularity, but they do not adequately account for the concerns that they bring to bear. For that – for a fully human sense of what formal activity makes available as content – Moore turns to a version of Mondrian's self-reflexive virtuality. By rendering perpendicularity a site where the artist can free the self from the theatrical ego, she can also call attention to the forms of care and identification that become actual within the mode of agency that the poem establishes.

No Modernist poem makes better use of the resources of virtuality than Moore's final version of "Poetry":

> I, too dislike it. . . .
>   Reading it, however, with a perfect contempt for it, one
>   discovers in
>   it, after all, a place for the genuine.

(36)

This is not Shelley. Indeed it is not much of anything, until we find ways of locating where its poetry lies. But once we adapt the strategy necessary for noniconic art – once we see that much of the force of the work depends on its refusing to be something else – we can begin to understand what its exclusions make present. First, we must ask why the poem refers to poetry only as "it." What other options are there, and how does this choice establish the possibility of gaining authority for specific claims about the "genuine" that the poem wants to make? Suppose something about the ontological status of art – its tilt, perhaps – demands so indefinite a pronoun, just as Dante's Bertrand de Born does, when he stands facing the poet with his head in his hands. Perhaps it is only by treating poetry as so indefinite a category that one can see how its content depends on the specific processes of disclosure set in motion by a linguistic intricacy that puts relation in the place of substance.

These hypotheses are not wrong, but they are severely limited by the Romantic framework in which they are cast. Moore pushes against those limits by refusing to be content with the moment of negation that sets perpendicularity against reference. The force of the perpendicular must make possible a strange, yet evocative, positive characterization of that site. In this case, the main vehicle for fleshing out the content of the "genuine" is her note on the poem, which shows us what she cut from previous versions. For then we have a contrast to the "it," which motivates its strategic indefiniteness. Indeed, we have a complex set of virtual forces, leading both back, into Moore's past, and forward, into a more dynamic sense of how contempt and genuineness may be closely linked, mutually reinforcing states. Once we feel the pressure of all of these images that rush in to provide names for poetry, but actually displace it, we begin to understand that those indefinite pronouns both reflect highly intelligent choices and orient us toward the kind of negotiations necessary if poetry is to provide alternatives to those images. So long as one needs these supplemental metaphors to define poetry, one is condemned to the distance of attempting to explain the genuine – the site of perpendicularity and polish – in terms of merely illustrative materials, which are thus necessarily only partial realizations of what they attempt to instantiate. Such images turn the positive into positivity, preparing metaphors for the dump that so fascinated her friend Stevens. But as we realize the failure of images, we also get a glimpse of the deepest efforts of poetry – the quest to find, within the transient, a sense of the genuine that is abstract enough to allow for a range of contents, and fluid enough to merge into the state of grace achieved by individual poems.

If we were to make generalizations about this sense of discovery, we would have to say that the point of the poem is to show that we must conceive the genuine in poetry in terms of forces, rather than of things or images. Poetry must be abstract in order to focus attention on the genuine concreteness of its processes that tend to be subsumed under the narcissistic substitutes imposed upon them when we create scenic contexts and thematic interpretations. But, as we make even that generalization, the deeper point of Moore's poem begins to become clear. Generalization itself must take the role of indefinite pronoun. Rather than explaining anything, it too becomes a means of tracking this sense of the genuine, which resides less in anything we say about the poem than in what we do, as we try to cut through the images to the mobile inventiveness that underlies them and gives them a "place."

Moore's poem, in other words, is not about the genuine so much as it is the literal action of attempting to locate "it" in the only way that the "it" can be given significant content. Rather than proliferating names for the pronoun, we must let it lead us to reflecting on the forces that it gathers within the poem. These comprise what can be genuine about poetry. At one pole, the poem shifts from images to the force that the authorial process embodies, as it works out what is involved in Moore's epigraph, "Omissions are not accidents." Omissions are, or can be, an author's means of asserting control over the complex energies of negation that we have been observing at work. Omissions are not accidents because they are perhaps the only way of negotiating between the accidental and the essential. Thus they lead us to the complex framework of memories, needs, and cares that provides the background that poetry must rely on and bring into focus. The poet's powers of negation are her richest means of showing what motivates her quest and abides within it to prepare for the satisfactions that poetry's perpendicular presences afford. Such demonstration also calls attention to the other pole of readerly activity. The virtual background that the negations evoke is ultimately not abstract at all, since it takes specific form in the reader's own efforts to transform an initial befuddlement (not unlike contempt) into a momentary realization of all that the "it" comes to embody. Reading this poem engages us in precisely the process that the poem describes: Puzzled by the "it," we must recover what the early drafts offered and understand why that fails to define poetry. In its stead, we must put the realization that the genuine consists in this dialectical process, which establishes a "place" (in all of the senses of that term) where all readers can see what is shared in the effort to find something mediating between the "it" and its substitutes. To see what that entails is to demonstrate the capacity to achieve it.

This play of virtual forces and identifications is obviously not given a specific context. Yet it does serve the crucial role of indicating how thoroughly certain active forces in Moore's poems resonate in conjunction with qualities that some situations can mark as gendered. So now we must see how Moore focuses attention on those properties. The quickest and most general means for doing that is to shift from what Moore shares with noniconic painterly strategies to her departures from its characteristic concerns. Whereas the painters concentrated on rendering certain dynamic and irreducible balances that take form as essentially independent structures with which consciousness tries to align, Moore's virtual forces are irreducibly psychological and willful. The negation in "Poetry" is not so much a way of getting beyond the personal, as a way of getting within it – getting to forces of an individual will too wise to theatricalize the terms of caring, yet freed, by that wisdom, to relish that care as something approaching an absolute power. Indeed, in much of Moore's work, that care becomes so particular, so much a matter of polish wrought to its uttermost, by subtle winks and intricate shifts of imaginative position, that one must attend to its distinctively personal sources. That is when the poems about female powers begin to color the entire oeuvre. "Sea Unicorns and Land Unicorns," for example, offers its heroine as a specific embodiment of the liberating energies praised in such abstract terms by Williams, Stevens, and Burke. Reduced to reading about heroic male deeds, this domesticated lady nonetheless constructs an order of "agreeing difference" that male demands for possession can neither imitate nor appreciate (77–9). For hers is a remarkably active form of passivity, enabling her to domesticate, in her fashion, a beast whose freedom and rarity can only be glimpsed in reading and whose rebellious capacity to escape its male hunters can be "tamed only by a lady, inoffensive like itself – / as curiously wild and gentle." That wild and gentle consciousness, in effect, becomes the "genuine place" of poetry, possessing the ability to hunt without having to destroy what it discovers. Now that the romance will is indistinguishable from the scientific desire to reduce all phenomena to the tidy order of our maps and charts, Moore can cast her own wily processes as a necessary means for letting the unicorn maintain its place in the human imagination.

Having postulated her own version of wise passivity, Moore must explore the philosophical implications of such states. In my view, her richest response to that challenge is "The Plumet Basilisk," because it makes such care a psychological realization of what in previous cultures had required elaborate mythic images. Here all of Pound's and Yeats's nostalgia for the old gods gives way to a mode of composition managing to possess the gods simply in the wit by which it engages their absence. The poem is a typical Moore journey, with books as her maps and the imagination her principle for exploring the various locales. After voyaging from lizards, to dragons, to stories of the gods, attention returns to the basilisk:

> he is alive there
>   in his basilisk cocoon beneath
> the one of living green; his quicksilver ferocity
>   quenched in the rustle of his fall into the sheath
> which is the shattering sudden splash that marks his
> temporary loss.

(24)

Here the immediacy of her poetic play not only captures the activity of the basilisk, but also helps to explain why such figures make the mind think of gods. For what engages us in what we see also provides confidence that what we cannot see will return. We are led to experience loss in such a way that it calls up virtual powers of renewal – in the mind, as well as in what it observes and transforms. With the "temporary" so fully captured as itself an aspect of a larger temporality, the poem concludes by calling upon the implications of all of the allusive liberations that throughout the poem have given the lizard a place in our affections. Thus loss becomes a way of recognizing the significance and force of those affections. They testify to virtual relations between attention and temporality that warrant feelings that the gods are there in their loss – perhaps findable precisely because of the way in which that loss forces us to reconsider our own powers.

The principle of containment as release is a marvelous poetic ideal. But how far does it carry poetry into life? Or, to put the question in gender terms, how well does it avoid complicity in certain cultural visions that would impose the burden of care on women in order to "free" men for more worldly pursuits, while confining women's cleverness to the poetic imagination? Because Moore's own conservative individualism is content to propose certain imaginative possibilities that readers are free to use or ignore, it lacks any terms for adjudicating the political implications of such choices. So I can dodge the general issues here by adapting what I think would be her strategy. There remains, however, one crucial particularizing move of Moore's that does address the question of social implications, and that therefore must be considered as an index of her own sense of how the powers she explores have practical consequences. That move occurs in the poem "Silence," which concludes her 1935 *Selected Poems* and thus raises the possibility that everything in the book contributes to, and is modified by, this dialectical assertion of her female strength:

> My father used to say,
> "Superior people never make long visits,
> have to be shown Longfellow's grave
> or the glass flowers at Harvard.
> Self-reliant like the cat –
> that takes its prey to privacy,
> the mouse's limp tail hanging like a shoelace from its
> mouth –
> they sometimes enjoy solitude,
> and can be robbed of speech

by speech which has delighted them.
The deepest feeling always shows itself in silence;
not in silence, but restraint."
Nor was he insincere in saying, "Make my house your
inn."
Inns are not residences.

(91)

That "nor was he insincere" marvelously fixes a prevailing tone defining the emotional burdens that demand a daughter's Modernist refusal of
all of the old representational securities. Facing a father who so willfully
manipulates the powers that language confers, the daughter's primary
task is to appropriate those powers to her own mode of restraint, which
must grapple with the task of fixing him and freeing herself. Such needs,
however, also bring extreme risks. Should she either overestimate her
power or underestimate the task, she is likely to trap herself in poses of
hatred and obsessive resistance that only confirm his victory. Ironically,
that is why the father's advice is so compelling. One in her situation must
refrain from any self-staging – either as Elinor Wylie's self-pity or as
Sylvia Plath's fantasies of revenge. Instead, virtuality becomes a vital
weapon, and Modernist formal strategies establish a possible psychology. All of the care that attracts the unicorn or preserves traces of the
basilisk here goes into investing herself in the father's sources of strength,
without fixating on either his deeds or any single fantasy of her own
projected response. This empathic distance becomes formidable power
as she replaces melodramatic rhetoric with a withering precision, whose
formulated phrases capture in the simple double negative of "nor was he
insincere" the essential inhumanity of his reticence. Moore's speaker is
by no means immune to the power of his control over language, but this
"nor" superbly positions her attraction against the background of a
deeper, unspeakable negative, which casts his self-control as bordering
on the margin of a terrifying monstrosity. It is no wonder, then, that
once the daughter's imagination is released by an extended simile, it
dwells on the morbid scenario of the mouse in the cat's mouth, an
objective correlative for life with father.

For Moore, however, and for her *Selected Poems,* that terror must not
be allowed to prevail or to generate a counterviolence sustaining a similar
self-absorption. The first thing necessary to resist his authority is to do
him justice, by acknowledging the style and insight that make his idiosyncratic ways come to exemplify values that she seeks in her own
poetry. But one must test what one has made from those beginnings by
exploring both the poet's and the daughter's ability to transform the
strengths of her internalized father figure into a precursor for her own

sense of individual power. In order to understand, she must identify with him, by continuing to quote his characteristic utterances; but in order to conquer, she must be so supple in her identifications that she maintains her own difference, her own perpendicularity, without having to project it into the terms such fathers love to deconstruct. What better way to do that than to use her metamorphic abilities to appropriate the phrase most characteristic of her father's strengths and her fears, "Inns are not residences."

An emblem that she continues to hold in this strange mix of awe and fear becomes, through the testimony of this volume, also the expression that best characterizes her own capacity to make language a provisional and fluid mode of dwelling. There remains the risk that even this degree of accepting the father's formulation will make playing at differences only an evasion of remaining at heart the dutiful daughter. But for her poetry, that risk becomes part of the implicit background, part of the contrast that reminds us that thinking in such global categories either misses or denies precisely what gives Moore her claims to independence. Were one to avoid that risk, one would have to reject the entire culture shaped by such fathers. By quoting that authority, on the other hand, Moore can create a highly complex site where we observe language playing out a drama of affiliation and difference that is basic to life within a culture. Yes, her language then remains dependent on his. But that dependency is a beginning, not a final state. It resounds as an implicit contrastive context, testing her own ability to make language precise and fluid enough to appropriate what it echoes. As Pound would try to do, on a much more theatrical scale, Moore uses her mobile shifts simultaneously to confirm her banishment to a life of inns and to make that instability a residence in its own right – a home won by the power to control virtual identifications with such grace that they need never be tied to forms that invite either the mirror or the dump.

VIII

Yeats is Moore's antithesis. She seeks to make inns into residences, whereas all of Yeats's energies are devoted to establishing permanent structures. As Michael North notes, in his book *The Final Sculpture,* everything about Yeats's imagination is sculptural in its quest for the monumental and self-standing. But there is perhaps no commitment more likely to make its proponent acutely aware of the limitations of images, since the effort to make them permanent makes one vulnerable to all of their proclivities to the partial and the changing. Whereas Moore distrusted the image for its positivity, its complicity in narcissism's desire to fix knowledge in what will satisfy specular desires, Yeats in his last poems warred on the image because it is not narcissistic enough, is too bound to temporal flux to display the full sense of powers that the mind needs if it is to accept and will its fated place. Yet even though he begins from the opposite pole, Yeats too finds himself driven to the possibility of locating what endures, not in substance, but in those virtual forces that elicit, dispel, and mourn our fascination with the image. In his case, however, virtuality is less a matter of fluid care than a site where one locates energies so composed that they can break through the resisting surface of the image to the most elemental of enduring transpersonal desires. Moore envisions the virtual as an irreducible reserve, protecting the poet from overinvesting in any given particular; Yeats sees it as the source of triumphant excess, linking the spirit to the immediacy of those rhythmic songs that still have the power to make us participate in the shout of the Greeks as they murdered their ritual victims.

This very different kind of hunt does not need careful analysis for gender identifications: Its maleness is part of the pathos that it hopes to redeem by returning to elemental forces. Nor must we elaborate his relation to other Modernists, since for Yeats in his last poem, the route to the virtual was pretty obviously a matter of his obsession with the immediacy of song, on the one hand, and, on the other, of his engagement in the same theosophical writings that painters such as Mondrian and Malevich relied upon. The poet who came to maturity by turning to drama and politics, as his antidotes to Mallarmé's vague and disembodied Symbolisme, ended up returning to that abstract sense of the limits of all dramatic encounters. But in defining those limits, Yeats offered a much more intense and concentrated version of abstraction. Rather than evoke a sense of mystery beyond the poem, Yeats tries to make the work itself a process of exhausting heroic personality, so that it gathers to itself, in purified form, the conditions of desire underlying those heroic states.[20] In contrast to Moore's mobility and indirectness, poetry's eloquence must be all in the direct assertion of an agency capable of turning the personal against its own narcissistic self-images.

Yeats established the conceptual basis for this turn to the abstract and the impersonal in the thinking that led to his "Supernatural Songs." But it is only in some of his very last poems that he fully realized how to make his poetry engage the virtual forces necessary to testify to a concentrative force locating spirituality in a mode of transcendental physicality only cheapened by concepts such as "personality." For the limited purposes of this book, I shall concentrate on two of his poems. Because the two are sharply opposed, they make clear the range of identifications and forms of recommendation that poetic abstraction affords. At one pole, "Long-legged Fly" posits a compositional activity so intensely focused that it defines those elements in the life of the imagination that can claim to resist the pressure of history; at the other, "Man and Echo" so thoroughly denies the self any relief from the pure accidents of history that it manages to engage the purest of all gods, the one whose only form is in the sheer contingency of violent chance. There the spirit, in effect, finds in a stunning moment of pure absence an absolutely literal and transpersonal form of irreducible presence fundamental to the life of consciousness.

The modes of implicit force that abstraction can muster become evident in the very first gesture of "Long-legged Fly." The foregrounded purpose clause casts the entire poem as the enacting of complex dependency relations linking the actions of individuals to the dynamic principles that history casts for them:

> That civilisation may not sink,
> Its great battle lost,
> Quiet the dog, tether the pony
> To a distant post;
> Our master Caesar is in the tent
> Where the maps are spread,
> His eyes fixed upon nothing,
> A hand under his head.
> *Like a long-legged fly upon the stream*
> *His mind moves upon silence.*[21]

Few lyric openings impose such a burden on the poet. How can he possibly sustain both the sense of mysterious force within history and the stake of preserving civilization itself? Clearly there is no room for virtuoso self-consciousness or the elaborate spinning of the grace notes that personality might confer. Such issues must be engaged by language at its most elemental, at the cutting edge where it must reveal whatever resources it has to sustain this imperial dream.

The poem's response is to put in the place of the poet's less than heroic life a mode of concentration pure and intense enough to locate a level of that life that can identify with the creative energies giving each of the characters their moment of triumph:

> That the topless towers be burnt
> And men recall that face,
> Move most gently if move you must
> In this lonely place.
> She thinks, part woman, three parts a child,
> That nobody looks; her feet
> Practise a tinker shuffle
> Picked up on a street.
> *Like a long-legged fly upon the stream*
> *Her mind moves upon silence.*

That girls at puberty may find
The first Adam in their thought,
Shut the door of the Pope's chapel,
Keep those children out.
There on the scaffolding reclines
Michael Angelo.
With no more sound than the mice make
His hand moves to and fro.
Like a long-legged fly upon the stream
His mind moves upon silence.

Disappointed by the inability of modern philosophy to escape the subject–object duality imposed by empiricism, the philosopher Thomas Nagel cautiously asks, "Is there any way of including mental phenomena in the world as, well, part of what is simply there?" (*Mortal Questions* 201; cf. 179n). Yeats, much less cautiously, replies that one can, but only if one so intensifies the "here" of self-consciousness that it becomes something approximating a pure state of physical activity, available in its purity for all subjects. That purity depends on separating self-consciousness from its empirical contexts by contrasting the terms of the mind in action with the accoutrements that attach those acts to the conditioning forces of history. In "Long-legged Fly" that quest leads to setting the poem's own processes against any possibility of finding outside the poem an explanation for the forces governing historical change. Pattern replaces chronology. Pattern must assume the responsibility of facing charges that such displacement is mere idealism. Idealism and mere idealism must engage in warfare within the poem, primarily through the poet's efforts to make the force composing those patterns an intense modifying factor within material life. Mind becomes a function of the body's concentration. Such concentration makes demands on our senses of identity that are deeper and more compelling than any historically based ideology: It is not Christianity that puts images of Adam in our thoughts at puberty. Ideas and ideals in this poem depend on recognizing the power that eyes, feet, and finally the hand wield, as they organize energies that turn contingent events into dependent purpose clauses.

The poem's version of those energies is its own effort to set its structural movement against the logic that usually governs historical narrative. Yeats thus turns the elemental principles of ballad time against themselves. Considered chronologically, the events here mime versions of the decline of the West: Public events give way to private ones, and the efforts to have an impact on the political order yield to the work of the artist, isolated from even the dream of wielding political power. But in imaginative space, the poem's sequence projects the gradual clarification of the forces that enable all three agents to make their mark on history, shaping what would shape them. Michelangelo, by meditating on the connection between his own creating hand and the hand that governs all creation, transforms that metonymic figure into a metaphor for concentration. This concentration, in all three cases, gives the body access to a silence where the mind too "moves," in all the senses of words now free, like mysterious refrains, to resonate in a space outside the constraints of practical historical contexts.

Yeats's task is to articulate a creative intelligence that can identify with Michangelo's identifications, by making its own elaborate patterning a sign of its ability to participate in that site of counterhistorical forces. The poem must achieve a radical form of aesthetic autonomy – not to separate art from life, but to make art a vehicle for modes of intensity that are not possible within the mental dispositions put in motion by questions of historical judgment. This mode of autonomy cannot even accommodate any appeals to personal identity: That too yokes the spirit to a dying animal and, as Mondrian argued in a very different context, traps the will in individual concerns ultimately blinding it to forces that the will itself may only mediate. An art that can take full responsibility for itself must try to locate its own resistance to historical determinants in some more capacious domain: in a mode of pure concentration, composing an elemental and transpersonal silence, where the very physical intensity of mental energies leads self-consciousness to its own constitutive elements.[22] For Yeats, the poetic element most useful for this task is the refrain, which seems to link both the agents and the authorial agency in a single, metaphysically evocative self-commentary. On the level of content, the refrain posits a mysterious site where there dwells the force that enters each of the acts in the poem and draws them all together. In fact, the refrain's intricate balancing of stream and silence complements the transcendental physicality of the poem, by producing its own complex interchange of forces: the first term pulls the silence toward a palpable materiality, while the second gives the stream an evocative abstractness. Thus the refrain not only refers to the mind's motion; it also provides a powerful example of just what is distinctive and mysterious about that elemental synthetic force. Eye, foot, and hand concentrate in that single verb, whose own blend of the material and the abstract now suggests a form of motion that denies time, finding in silence a more demanding and rewarding ground.

Taken in isolation, however, the abstract brilliance of this content would leave the poem in severe contradiction. The richer its abstract case for the physicality of mind and hand, the greater the gulf between the means of expression and the actual claims that the poem proposes. To assert power is by no means the same thing as to possess it. In order to make good on its claims, the poem has to demonstrate the capacity of language to mediate between head and hand, perhaps even to have the kind of physicality that would literally be shared in the three heroic acts. An elegantly insistent rhythm provides a good deal of that physical force. But rhythm alone will not carry the semantic force necessary to absorb consciousness fully in the material movement. That is one reason why Yeats relies on traditional forms. Within such forms it is plausible to imagine rhythm as the consort of memory, the access in the present to energies elicited whenever people began to write and to read in the imagined presence of all of the others who had turned to the same formal structure. Perhaps, then, pure traditionalism is poetry's counterpart to noniconic painting's radically antitraditional ways of releasing the elemental forces of the visual medium that had traditionally been absorbed under literature. Yet, even if that is the case, the semantic dimension must focus and supplement those memories. The ballad must have its refrain, and the refrain must carry the burden of releasing the ballad narrative into these more abstract domains by focusing attention on the actual set of forces that the poem makes available for the identifications it celebrates.

In "Long-legged Fly" the refrain accomplishes that task by articulating and intensifying two fundamental features of the activity in which the audience participates as it brings the poem to life. First, its repeated insistence on a particular site of the mind's activity in effect captures and locates the spatializing energies that so concentrate historical formal associations within a single, adamantly transhistorical, present moment. What usually moves in time here moves only in the infinite recurrence of this charged silence. This motion, in turn, elicits a second dimension of virtuality, calling attention to the more general synthesizing forces that reading involves here. As we read, we perform precisely what the refrain points to, and in so doing we literally come to inhabit the site that it affirms. As we read about the mind's motion, we find ourselves enacting it. And as we enact that motion, we find ourselves both composing and filling out the silence that links all of the characters. We compose a site where the resistance to history allows all of those who can construct such silences to share one another's most intimate experience of creative power. The reader and the characters then all participate, through this refrain, in a mode of concentration where the dancer is truly indistinguishable from the dance, pure self-consciousness at one with pure participation in a transcendental condition that no empirical ego can inhabit.

This new heroic possibility allows both poet and reader versions of sublimity quite unlike those that had occupied Yeats the last Romantic. In most of Yeats's best work, processes of identification and participation are all focused on the reader's aligning herself with the divisions that torment the poet. We find ourselves wanting to take on the poet's powers and dreading the consequence: that the powers will lead us to dreams that, in their turn, elicit the self-mocking and self-doubting part of Yeats's imagination. In this ballad, on the other hand, reading locates a site where one can dismiss both the Romantic projection of tragic heroism and the self-mockery that is inseparable from those projections. In their place, we are asked to test a more radical, impersonal principle of identification, which makes the reading, rather than the writing, the locus of a tempered and immanent version of the sublime. Unable to imitate the tragic hero, Yeats now is content to see whether poetry can steal his or her intensity, without having to share the fate that accompanies it. Poetry's means must be abstraction, must be a process of locating imagination within states that the heroes share, but recasting those states in terms that permit only one possible confirmation: a responding mode of concentration so focused and so elemental that the sole action it can generate is self-reflective meditation on who one becomes by virtue of that imaginative effort. The ultimate test of soul is less what it can do within the political order than what it can produce as a mode of concentration able to share the fundamental sources of creative energy.

For "Man and Echo," this conclusion is far too confident. "Long-legged Fly" dreams of bodily intensity, without recognizing that a body capable of momentary escapes from history is still bound to its ultimate force. There is no escaping the guilt that the past imposes in order to divide the mind from its own full engagement in the present, and there is no escaping its conferring contingent individualities, doomed to change and death. To overcome the myth of a tragic hero is not to overcome the tragic conditions that we try to escape by such myths. A fully abstract poetry would have to make those conditions its focus, so that it could bring its sense of what imaginations can share to bear on the pains that most isolate them. There tragedy itself may even reveal a site where the mind comes to a silence in which it is content to move. To do so, however, does not require replacing the personal lyric with the ballad, but having the features of virtuality possible in this more impersonal mode actually engage and take over the personal, at its most dramatic and self-conscious. The result can be an abstracting force that sets the most elemental properties of verse, the task of transforming the poet's struggle with himself, into a theatrical moment where the conditions of a particular history or scenic context become increasingly irrelevant. What matters is the timeless confrontation of an individual with all of those forces of otherness that culminate in the fear we have of death. Poetry's task seems no longer the construction of images, but the intensifying of those pressures that can strip images of their seductions. Only under those conditions can one begin to trust any counterforce that may echo in the focused silences that the refrain continues to produce.

Yeats's speaker begins in his version of what Beckett calls the "old dispensation," the dream that by staging his terror before death, he can muster a form of self-justification that gives the terror a point. The poetic imagination can confront the violence of chance with a last affirmation of the individual's power to choose a self by taking responsibility for those moments when the power of will was least in evidence. But no synthetic image for that willed self emerges. Instead, the ideal of personality seems little more than the lure that death casts to force us to recognize its power over us:

> Did words of mine put too great strain
> On that woman's reeling brain?
> Could my spoken words have checked
> That whereby a house lay wrecked?
> And all seems evil until I
> Sleepless would lie down and die.
> > *Echo*
> Lie down and die.

$$(345-6)$$

This voice from beyond the self, with its reminders of the limits of the self, forces the speaker to a very different, impersonal, and philosophical vision. Instead of worrying about justification, he must simply try to achieve a mode of understanding that allows pure release from all self-hood, all concern about justification. Then death can bring a purity unavailable to the life desperate for categories that will sanction its actions:

> And till his intellect grows sure
> That all's arranged in one clear view,
> Pursues the thoughts that I pursue,
> Then stands in judgment on his soul.
> And, all work done, dismisses all
> Out of intellect and sight
> And sinks at last into the night.
> > *Echo*
> Into the night.

But even the dream that there can be some pure state of forgetfulness won by mind will not hold off this mocking echo. No matter how elemental the mind's knowledge, it needs to point to something that it can never encompass, something figured in both the image of the night and in the uncontrollable source that gives echo its voice. Under such pressure, the final stanza completely renounces these efforts at assertion and these dreams of a personal resolution. In their place, the poet tries to identify with whatever it is that the resistance of the echo might express. Assertion gives way to questioning, and questioning brilliantly offers itself as the only form of prayer possible with this kind of divinity:

> O Rocky Voice,
> Shall we in that great night rejoice?
> What do we know but that we face
> One another in this place?
> But hush, for I have lost the theme,
> Its joy or night seem but a dream;
> Up there some hawk or owl has struck,
> Dropping out of sky or rock,
> A stricken rabbit is crying out,
> And its cry distracts my thought.

Even the questions and the prayer, however, are exposed as efforts at evasion and consolation. There is only this irreducible otherness of violent events which we realize may be nature's parallels to the demystifying process that the poem has exercised upon the poet's attempted self-mythologizing. But because this otherness stems from a domain beyond language, it cannot be contained within the easy rhetoric of demystification, which attempts to reclaim for ironic consciousness the powers it denies to the assertive will. Here, as the poet's version of the humanizing rhetoric in Wordsworth's "Nutting" crumbles, the only spirit left in the woods is this echoing Rocky Voice, this trace of gods reduced to pure elemental chance. Yet even that elemental quality seems extremely appealing when the way of choice has become so rife with contradiction and self-evasion. So the poem sets itself the task of trying to participate in a form of presence that must remain virtual, must remain something that we know only by its way of resisting our efforts to appropriate it.

There is only one path. Because the god is manifest only in the echo, the poem must make its own version of the echo: Its refrain becomes its vehicle for participating in, and understanding, what the destruction of lyric self-consciousness affords. Yet it seems that the echo will not yield the desired identifications. Twice its mockery of the effort to evade death seemed to give that otherness a voice within the world that the poet could appropriate to his lyric demands. But by the conclusion, even this trace has been destroyed, probably because the gods who impose such casual violence demand as their correlate an absolute silence, a world deprived of anything that might give the ego back some form of reflecting presence. And once the gods reveal their utter separation from human desires, not even an articulate echo can remain. There is, however, another, less contaminated domain, where a version of the echo does return. For the the refrains have created a logic that does not resolve so bleakly or so melodramatically. Notice what seems to cause the echo to emerge. In each case, it speaks because the poet's own wandering ways have led him to try to incorporate, within his imaginings, aspects of material life that at once assert their own dumbness by only echoing words, and that assert their own adamant refusal of the power of words to give order or meaning to the domain they inhabit. If this is the case, there is no final echo, not because the poem passes even more completely into the night, but because this final word presents the one element that cannot be appropriated by the forces that take over the other two closing terms. Nature has neither the material equivalent for "thought" nor the capacity to turn that term into a memento mori.

Cured by that logic, we must begin to speculate on the reasons why the relation between the "stricken rabbit" and the poet's thought warrants such a transformation. Perhaps Yeats wants us to think that when the thought joins the rabbit's cry, it enters a realm so intense that there is no space for the echo. There is nothing but the pure state of casual pain, so absolute that it would be diffused and distorted by any repetition. Even an echo here would assuage the pain that the poem has insistently been setting against the mind's efforts to provide a ground for its own sense of self-importance. Therefore, as thought sets itself free of anything that might carry an echo, it puts itself in a position to realize that the very ideas of self, and even of world, may ultimately be illusions, masking the terrifying possibility that the purest, most intense state of human thinking may be identical to the state of pure "cry" that poets such as Tennyson and Eliot had tried to transform into a prayer. The cry itself may be our only prayer, our only access to whatever divinity shapes our ends and endows us with such quirky and compelling logics for the echo.

This closing drama is quintessentially Modernist, because everything depends on the semantic implications of the internal logic of the work. The ultimate prayer takes form not from the willful ego but from the traces that emerge as we track its undoing. The spirit that in this last stanza has the power to respond adequately to the rabbit's cry exists solely in our inferring a force based simply on a kind of thinking that has no personal history and adamantly refuses any image of itself. The responding cry is entirely relational – within the poem, and within every reader who re-creates the process of thinking for which there can be no echo. This counterpressure to the real is so abstract that it exists only in the most concrete aspects of readerly response, aspects so elemental that they in no way depend on the subjectivity of the reader or the images that subjectivity brings in its track. This spirit is secured by a logic as commanding, in its virtual space, as Rocky Voice is in its domain.

For Yeats, the most comprehensive constructive act consisted in composing a book that could stand as a more capacious self than any dramatic posture. Here that project reaches one of its most sublime moments, because it provides the poet's testimony to what that logic of thinking can win from the Rocky Voice as it transforms suffering into art. The second poem in Yeats's *Collected Poems* sets the condition to which this late poem returns. Confronted by the gulf between the fire of imagination and the watery glass of the image necessary for that fire to be reflected at all in the domain of understanding, the speaker turns to the figure of the poem as an elaborate shell, which changes all that the poet "sang to inarticulate moan / Among her wildering whirls, forgetting him" (9). For fifty years the poet had warred against that forgetfulness, projecting against it a willful concentration designed to transform those moans into emblems of a power to compel the terms on which he would be remembered. But it is only now, in wholly realizing the logic of song, that he can simply accept that moan. Now art makes the moan the expression of a virtual body that gains a voice through a mode of abstraction not mocked by the monuments it tries to construct to its own magnificence. The poet learns to preempt the indifferent whirls of the shell by reversing his usual dialectical ways. In the place of the synthetic personalizing act of mind, this poem tries to empty the first person of everything except the elemental logic of constructive thought, triumphantly reduced to a transpersonal core.

Everything attributed to thought, in "Man and Echo," takes even simpler and starker shape in Yeats's "Lullaby," where poetic tradition itself becomes the repository of these elemental acts of spirit. The generic title, and the poem's remarkable freedom to wander through space and time, tell us everything we need to know about the ultimate third-person form for the first-person intensities that characterize the life of spirit. Here poetry's capacity to give mind a physical force defines a condition in which the violence of predestination seems inextricable from an abiding "protecting care." This force has as its secular incarnation the reader's ability to flesh out the terror and consolation contained in this simple refrain's affirmation of such a sleep as loves are made on:

> Beloved, may your sleep be sound
> That have found it where you fed.
> What were all the world's alarms
> To mighty Paris when he found
> Sleep upon a golden bed
> That first dawn in Helen's arms? . . .

Such a sleep and sound as fell
Upon Eurota's grassy bank
When the holy bird, that there
Accomplished his predestined will,
From the limbs of Leda sank
But not from her protecting care.

(264–5)

8

Modernist Abstraction and Pound's First Cantos: The Ethos for a New Renaissance

We base our "science" on perceptions, but our ethics have not yet attained this palpable base.

Pound, on Remy de Gourmont

I

It would be easy, and enjoyable, to go on elaborating various ways that poets adapt the grammars developed by Modernist painting. Every shift in level of generalization opens up new patterns of difference and transformation. Yet so long as we remain readers of isolated poems, on whatever level, we cannot fully test the cultural theater that Modernist abstraction made available. The discussions so far have clarified what the writers learned from the painters, and even how they modified that example to develop resources distinctive to language. But if we are to understand the most general and significant roles that painterly abstraction came to play, we must shift from poems to poets; from choices that provide compelling particulars to choices that place those experiments within the desires and needs of a representative poetic career. By focusing on moments of crisis within such careers, we get a clear view of the problems motivating those engagements in what another art offered; we can observe the tensions and contradictions that develop as the poet elaborates such experiments as a means of handling the problems; and we find ourselves with sufficient dramatic context to test the consequences as the poet works out the implications of those stylistic decisions and takes responsibility for them.

Here I cannot trace the entire course of any one career. Instead I shall concentrate on what I take to be the two richest examples of Modernist American poets fully confronting the example of Modernist painting and adapting its principles to problems that threatened to limit severely what their writing could achieve. Each case represents a different epoch within Modernism, and the two offer radically contrasting modes of deriving

283

existential values from visual principles that radically contrast to the other, so the pairing offers a sharp confrontation between the two basic ethical attitudes which I see Modernist poetry defining for its, and our, culture. In addition, each gives us a perspective from which it is possible to resist the most fashionable innovations in criticism, without having to align ourselves with those positions whose limitations made us hunger for the new in the first place. The examples are Ezra Pound, as he worked his way from a Vorticist aesthetic to what I shall call an "individualist constructivism" that could compete with the ethical models sustaining traditional epic poetry, and Wallace Stevens, as he worked his way out of his disastrous efforts at an explicitly political poetry by developing principles of value and versions of constructive intentionality on the basis of Modernist principles of testimony.

There has been some very good critical commentary on Pound's use of the stylistic models provided by Cubism and Vorticism, especially in relation to the seven years of experiment that gave him the confidence to proceed with the *Cantos*. However, by relying too narrowly on the stylistic aspects of that influence, Pound criticism has for the most part trapped itself into treating those experiments in formal terms, as vehicles for intensifying an essentially contemplative and visionary poetry. I shall try to show instead that Pound was not content with establishing literary equivalents for Vorticism. His experiments were driven by a desire to transform Vorticist style into an exemplary disposition of poetic energies capable of shaping a new ethos. If poets could layer planes of experience so that they formed structures with the shaping power of formulas in analytic geometry, poets would manifest the force of character and the control of imaginative energies necessary for carrying on Romantic dreams of building a new culture, while avoiding the morass of Romantic expressivism. Instead of relying on the purported inwardness characteristic of Romantic heroes, Pound sought objective measures of character by emphasizing the degree of certitude achieved in the process of transforming subjective desire into articulate public structures that literally carried on the work of defining possible principles of value. As Marianne Moore put it, "The master quality throughout the *Cantos* is decision" (*Complete Prose* 275). Intentions do not matter; the depth of one's soul is irrelevant. Expression is judged simply by the relations that the authorial act keeps in dynamic tension. These compositional energies establish how much reality one can bear, while at the same time making it possible to assess one's deeds in relation to what other agents establish, especially those whose expressions form the "theater" that comprises our cultural traditions. By refusing all appeals to values, states, or categories that are simply projected as aspects of an unknowable "buried life," Pound makes Modernist expressivist principles the basis for a new individualism. A person's claim to value as an expressive individual depends entirely on his ability to create articulate structures for the self within public life. Life, then, is a struggle for power – first over the self's own tendency to live on a vague imaginative capital; second on the need to give public form to one's own particular style and the commitments it can carry. Such values make sympathy with suffering extremely difficult, but they serve the significant social role of provoking others to define their capacity to take responsibility for their particular stance toward the real. Picasso's will takes on cultural roles, and finds itself subject to both the threats and resonant echoes maintained by epic traditions.

Wallace Stevens was a poet as eager to escape epic ambitions as Pound was to realize them. Whereas Pound needed painting as a challenge to develop a wholly Modernist style, the Stevens we shall attend to needed it as an escape from what he had pursued as style. Committed to an abstract ideal of imaginative power, Stevens tried to develop his ideals in political poems that came close to showing them bankrupt. In reaction, he retreated to a quasi-Jungian hero of the imagination – humanity at its greenest cone – so that he could salvage a domain where a nobility of self-contemplation would reward those who refused the bitter self-divisions, rhetorical posturings, and social discipline of the political life. But the cult of this imaginary hero proved too thin to serve as a substantial alternative to political consciousness. If Stevens were to develop a plausible alternative for his culture, he had to find a way of embodying that heroism within common patterns of desire, so that poetry could show how an idealism like his might make a difference in people's concrete behavior.

Stevens found the necessary means by turning back to the painterly examples that had intrigued him early in his career. In the early 1940s, however, the needs were quite different. Stevens did not want a new style, he wanted a new model for understanding both what a style makes available and how the resulting product engages the desires and interests of a possible audience. If he was to have his poetry take up the reflections on the very idea of style that occupied his essays, he would have to get beyond fealty to any specific Modernist mode.[1] Rather than propose specific paradigms to develop, Stevens tried to formulate general principles that he could explore, especially those which would enable him to develop linguistic equivalents for the virtual states elaborated in Modernist painting. By inhabiting those states, he hoped to find a mode of poetic testimony deep enough to establish powers that did not rely on the life and death of particular metaphoric systems. Thus, instead of miming Pound's efforts at heroic expression – Romanticism against itself – Stevens envisioned his poetry as making visible both the fundamental forms of desire that myth displaces and the metaphoric processes that bind various agents to essentially the same manner of engaging in those desires. Abstraction in art clarified principles enabling a work to project its own relational energies as elemental powers of the psyche, articulated and sanctioned by the poet's ability to have his readers reflect on the modes of positioning desire and forging identifications that the poetry elicited from them. So long as poetry tries to make its own language the concrete realization of the imaginative processes that it thematically addresses, the plainest discursive abstraction carries an irreducible and expansive life of spirit. Where representation of the hero had been, there can now be the simple demonstration of powers available to all speakers of the language. And where Pound's epic ambitions impose a single lyric hero, bound to the maddening task of producing an audience that can respond in kind to his constructivist intensities, Stevens establishes a mode of lyric attention adaptable to the totally unheroic conditions of contemporary bourgeois life: unheroic, that is, except for the difficult task of reconciling oneself to the pathos of having no other world in which to sustain the force of our lyric heritage.

II

Pound's earliest drafts of his *Cantos* insist on the need for poetry to face the challenge of Modernist painting – in a style that makes it clear how much work still had to be done:

> . . . Behold, I say, she comes
> "Apparelled like the Spring, Graces her subjects,"
> (That's from Pericles).
> Oh, we have world's enough, and brave *decors,*
> And from these like we guess a soul for man
> And build him full of aery populations
> Mantegna a sterner line, and the new world about us:
> Barred lights, great flares, new form, Picasso or Lewis.
> If for a year a man write to paint, and not to music –
> O Casella!
>
> ["Three Cantos," *Poetry* (1917) 121]

The dream is of an epic poem capable of forming a bridge from Botticelli's Venus to the modern world. The reality is a poetry deeply torn by the conflicts and pressures that he would eventually define in his *Mauberley* poems, freed to do that by his increasing confidence that writing to paint provided him a means for separating himself from the E.P. that the poem tries to bury.

The remarkable feature of Pound's early work is how closely linked his strengths are to weaknesses that threatened to send the poet of epic ambitions back to Wabash College, the sadder but wiser hero of a tawdry

American tale recording one more case of dreams renounced and mediocrity embraced. This passage offers a finely wrought precision of diction and intensity of aural effect, revealing a scholar who had learned his
craft well – well enough, perhaps, to make good on the claim that he had
found in the past the imaginative news that those dominating contemporary taste simply could not provide: "Homer, Villon, Propertius, speak
of the world as I know it, whereas Mr. Tennyson and Dr. Bridges did
not. Even Dante and Guido with their so highly specialized culture speak
of a part of life as I know it" (*Selected Prose* 390). This might even be the
blend of learning and skill required to make good on such epic ambitions. But these scholarly graces seem also to have exacted an exorbitant
price. Both the allusiveness and the excessive fineness of the writing
suggest that this poetry has all too much of Guido's specialized culture:
The very energies that Pound wants to make contemporary threaten to
distance the speaking voice into something approximating the pale repetitions of Rossetti's repetitions of escapist romance.[2] In fact, this literalness of imagination turned out to plague even Pound's experiments in
hearing the voices of other cultures that did not have a Rossetti to con-
taminate them. When he turned to Cathay or to Propertius's Rome, the
keenness of his sensibility was never separate from an excessive delicacy,
leaving the scholar's refinement at odds with the scholar's commitment
to vital truths that contemporary culture lacked.

The tensions we are tracking go far beyond matters of style. Notice
the remarkably flexible imagination that enabled Pound to leap from a
somewhat medievalized Shakespeare to the tone of Mantegna's sterner
line, to the demands of Pound's contemporary world, then back to
Dante's lyric cry in the *Purgatorio*. This is the mobility of a Baudelaire,
which can be put into the service of treating the past as an infinitely
capacious, and infinitely relevant, body of imaginative energies, all available for identifications. But such flexibility is also, perhaps, the worst
condition for the epic imagination. Condemned to guessing souls for
man, rather than establishing a single heroic, gathering presence, such
mobility led Pound to keep repeating a lament that he first made in 1908:
"In the 'search for oneself,' in the search for 'sincere self-expression,' one
gropes, one finds some seeming verity. One says 'I am' this, that, or the
other, and with the words scarcely uttered one ceases to be that thing"
(*Gaudier-Brzeska* 85). The same gifts that enabled him to recreate the past
threatened to prevent him from taking responsibility for the present, so
that he could wholly realize the powers to provide articulate "testimony" that Pound found most compelling in his heroes (*Literary Essays*
11). It seemed that Pound could approach the present only by renouncing
his scholarly imagination, and then he found himself torn between two
mutually limiting roles. Pound the imagist could envision a pure, ecstatic

release into a specific "emotional and intellectual complex," with absolute claims on the present. But those claims involved moments of visionary intensity that left all historical complexities behind and presented
little resistance to the cult of delicate sensibility that was the curse of his
mastery over his medium. This tendency to the effete, then, breeds as its
other pole Pound the tough-guy satirist. Here the poet can dramatize his
lucid worldliness, but at the cost of absorbing all of his constructive
energies into a reductive, and destructive, psychological violence that
leaves none of the reserves required for even a minimal human dignity.
Pound the satirist proved the unrelenting antithesis to the models of
eloquent testimony envisioned by Pound the scholar.

It took Pound considerably more than a year of "writing to paint"
before he succeeded in making these contradictions productive enough to
help him realize his epic ambitions. Like Dante in relation to Casella, the
Pound of 1916 had to recognize the fact that the lyric gifts that had
proved sufficient to get him to this purgatory simply would not suffice
for the imaginative tasks required if one was to complete the epic journey. The journey demanded that he not simply absorb the painter's
perspective within his lyric sensibility. Rather, he had to change his
guides, to let Picasso and Wyndham Lewis lead him to new formal and
psychological principles that entailed radically remaking his own poetry.
If he could maintain the patience and the diligence to absorb the implications of their constructivism, he might even be able to surpass what those
painters had accomplished, by reintegrating his learning and his mobility
of imagination within the Modernist ethos that they exemplified for him.
Lewis, after all, had almost no sense of enduring cultural traditions, and
although Picasso could quote a variety of styles, he had yet to forge a
sense of living tradition from those quotations, or make those styles
come alive as possible dispositions for the flexible modern imagination.
Moreover, although these painters could demonstrate the importance of
using one's art to define personal energies in the present, they could not
explore two resources distinctive to language: the variety of selves inherent in the kinds of memories that language preserves and the modes of
ethical responsibility it makes possible. There were, then, enormous
opportunities to appropriate the lessons of painting for the poet's medium. Painting's ways of composing spatial relations could allow new
conjunctions among the complex attitudes language can carry, and the
pressure of those conjunctions could make demands on the composing
intelligence that would force it to explore an ethos compatible with the
powers cultivated by the art. The task of working out that Vorticist
ethos challenged Pound to establish a principle of testimony capable of
providing a focus for his mobile imagination, while his scholarly engagement in the past provided both the constituent energies and the con-

trastive measures enabling him to show how this new ethic could compete with those that had, in the past, sustained flourishing epic traditions.

Developing that ethos took not one year but seven. I shall begin by outlining Pound's transformations of Vorticist thought during those years. Next I shall argue that the final version of the opening *Cantos* manages to cast its compositional energies as testimony to a significant Vorticist ethic. In one sense this thesis is not radical. For Hugh Kenner, and therefore for virtually everyone else, "Pound's work, say, from Lustra to the last Cantos, is the longest working out in any art of premises like those of Cubism" (*Pound Era* 142). There are, however, significantly different possibilities for understanding both the relevant premises and Pound's means of working them out, and there are substantial stakes in rendering those premises in terms that are not easily susceptible to the critiques of a fetishistic sense of presence which increasingly occupy Pound criticism.

Kenner concentrates on the formal premises of Cubism and Vorticism because these principles seem most clearly to highlight Pound's originality as a poet and to dramatize the values that his work makes available. Cubist juxtapositions, Kenner holds, enabled Pound to recover dynamic aspects of objective compositional energies that had been lost when artists turned to the abstraction shared by Symboliste reverie or popular exhortation to the good, true, and beautiful. Such structural models, in turn, fostered a sense of agency that renewed the capacity to contemplate "a patterned energy" fusing emotion and form into "an enduring integrity, shaped by the movement shaping it" (146–7). Ultimately, these modes of contemplation enabled Pound's poetry to establish an alternative to subjective expressionism, because they demonstrated ways of grounding the full energies of the psyche that no longer relied on defensive irony or vague claims about higher, nondiscursive truths of the imagination.

Kenner is clearly not wrong. But in relying on him as it has, Pound criticism may have put too much emphasis on the means that Cubism and Vorticism made available, and not enough on the challenges that they presented, or the ends that Pound elaborated as he worked out the problem of creating a distinctive linguistic way of appropriating and testing painterly traditions.[3] The most concise way to state the problem is to suggest that Kenner is too close to the visual, too committed to the contemplative attitude that painting fosters. He concentrates on form, because that concept stresses dynamic links between the mind and the world that can satisfy the mind's desire to align itself with enduring grounds. But in stressing such conjunctions, Kenner necessarily underplays the more combative aspects of form-making that language stages. And his brilliant eye for formal invention often keeps him so intent on

how specifics fit together that he is not sufficiently attentive to the struggles that the poem sets up for its author, as it tries to establish a truly epic
project. Kenner's concern for pattern may even trap him in precisely the
picture of religious need and responding modes of attention that Pound
suggests confine us to the world of Botticelli. Poetry then remains a
belated substitute for religion, and its surface remains free of the kind of
battles it takes to resist a Picasso or a Lewis, or to assert oneself as a
worthy heir of the epic tradition. That is barely to "guess a soul for
man"; it is certainly not to understand how constructivist aesthetics
breaks from Romantic themes by defining a mode of soul making that
can take responsibility for resisting the compulsion to irony and speculative escape so pressing on the modern psyche.

For Pound's constructivist aesthetic, the relevant Cubist facets are less
moments of perception than expressive instances, crystallizing certain
attitudes that the poem plays against one another. The poet's main task is
to develop a form of authorial presence that can take responsibility for
trying on these roles and, in so doing, define modes of power that stem
from such provisional identifications. And this means that criticism must
shift its focus, from questions of formal strategy or adequate representation for each particular, to the posing of hypotheses attempting to characterize that authorial activity. I think one can best perform that task, at least
for *A Draft of Thirty Cantos,* by returning yet once more to the relation
between the *Ur-Cantos* and the decisions that Pound ultimately let stand.
Although a good deal of excellent close work has been done on specific
stylistic changes, critics have not yet posited an adequate account of what
it was about the final version that satisfied Pound and made it possible for
him to go on with the overall project. If I can provide such a picture, I shall
obviously have established a plausible model of authorial purpose, and I
shall have demonstrated what one can learn from "writing to paint."
Moreover, as we observe Pound's revision of the poems in relation to the
essays that he wrote with the aim of clarifying his options, we see his work
pass through three separate versions of what Picasso and Lewis afford
poetry: first, a stage in which he is fascinated by those painters, but still
bound by Symboliste and Pre-Raphaelite views of poetry; second, a stage
in which he is able to adapt his poetry to Cubist constructivist principles,
but is still tied to contemplative, form-oriented readings of the Vortex;
and finally, a stage in which he gradually shapes, from his thinking about
Henry James and Remy de Gourmont, a sense of an individualist Vorticist
ethics that avoids the awkward self-consciousness of his initial efforts and
provides the ethical correlate necessary for epic poetry. What begins as an
explanation of how to adapt Vorticist principles of dynamic form to
poetry leads eventually to emphasis on the authorial power to make
translation a test of what one can do with one's forms. If the epic poet is to
make forms responsive to both the author's place in history and the roles

history can play for the contemporary imagination, his own constructions must be able to stand up to the energies of the past and adapt them to his own expressive project. Thus Pound can claim the authority of an epic voice only to the degree that his own structure manifests its ability to share Acoetes' unflinching "I have seen what I have seen," without being paralyzed by that vision. Having rendered his seeing, the poet must combine the moments of intensity, so that they constitute a distinctive force for engaging contemporary life.

III

I shall not review the pursuit of an art of patterned energies in Pound's early Vorticist experiments such as "Heather" and "The Return." In this study, the relevant question is not Pound's achievement there, but the problems that the achievement created for him. And for that subject, the appropriate example is his version of Duchamp's painting, *Game of Chess* (discussed in Chapter 1). Pound's poem "Game of Chess" reveals an uneasy self-consciousness that was eventually to require the full-scale exorcism of the Mauberley poems:[4]

> The Game of Chess
> Dogmatic Statement Concerning the Game of Chess:
> Theme for a Series of Pictures
>
> Red knights, brown bishops, bright queens,
> Striking the board, falling in strong 'L's of
>   colour.
> Reaching and striking in angles,
>   holding lines in one colour.
> This board is alive with light;
>   these pieces are living in form,
> Their moves break and reform the pattern:
>   luminous green from the rooks,
> Clashing with 'X's of queens,
>   looped with the knight-leaps.
>
> 'Y' pawns, cleaving, embanking!
> Whirl! Centripetal! Mate! King down in the
>   vortex,
> Clash, leaping of bands, straight strips of hard
>   colour,
> Blocked lights working in. Escapes. Renewal of
>   contest.
>
>   (*Personae* 131)

On the simplest level, this is a verbal description of a chess game seen in terms of the permissions provided by Vorticist painting. Taut orthogonals dominate, sustaining sharp contrasts in color or intensity, and suggesting constant movement within patterns. But even in 1914 Pound was too ambitious and self-conscious to be content with imitating visual effects. He wants his readers to participate in a Vorticist sense of agency, parallelling the tensions that Wyndham Lewis generated in his stories. That is why the diction strains to invest the physical properties with psychological intensity, and that is why he establishes the striking stanza form that emphasizes contrasts between predicate units and the objects that complete them. Even the rather awkward exclamations serve a crucial role as indices of an intensity earned by the clash of surfaces that brook no metaphoric depths. Indeed, Vorticism holds open the possibility that neither metaphor nor a corollary sense of the reflective responding subject is required for lyric intensity. Instead, consciousness can be wholly absorbed by the vitality of patterned movement, which can itself sustain a final reflexive phrase, "Renewal of contest" – at once clarifying, resolving, and extending the Vortex's concentrative force.

This state of dynamic conflict would suffice for Vorticist painterly surfaces, and even for most poets. But Pound's elaborate subtitle for this poem (originally the title) indicates his discomfort with that achievement. This anxious aspirant to the avant-garde seems to know that he needs some protective distance, some way of evading the fact that he is simply imitating painterly strategies. So he defensively acknowledges that the text is only a statement of a poetics, not a poem possessing dynamic resources sufficient to give it an independent life. And the closer we look, the more we realize that this defensiveness reveals a sharp and paralyzed critical intelligence. How awkward the gestures of immediacy seem. Formal considerations may be able to justify, or at least to explain, the exclamations. But the indexicals cannot escape a perverse dialectic of presence and absence, or assertion and displacement. There is no referent, in the poetic act, for "this board" or "these pieces" or, by inference, any of the other proclaimed physical details. Rather, the assertions of presence are pure illusion, fictions that negate everything the Vorticist aesthetic seeks. The anti-Romantic Pound puts himself in a situation that depends for its intensity on an abstract Romantic enthusiasm. We must trust the source of exclamations, since we do not see sufficient physical or structural correlates for them within the space of the poem. But the last phrase makes it oppressively clear that the poem cannot achieve the balance of recognition and renewal that it seeks. A moment of awareness that is intended to be part of a visual event necessarily stands outside it, a sad emblem of how well Derridean themes of differing and deferring apply to the Romantic effort to combine descriptive and emotive uses of language. The last phrase points less to the scene than to the poet's need to impose interpretive significance on the life of the eye – in the process, ironically, demonstrating the gulf between visual absorption and reflective intellegibility. As words reassert their disturbing supplemental relation to the scene, they require us to seek that intelligibility in the form of a set of purposes motivating the process of utterance. We must provide an image for the action that makes sense of the fact that someone goes through the effort of stating emotional correlates to the description. Lacking this, the energy that overflows the visual patterns becomes evidence of unsatisfied needs and defensive adjustments in the pattern maker.

IV

We need not carry this tale of unsuccessful experiments through the *Ur-Cantos*. It suffices that we see Pound aware of both the limitations in his work and their relation to problems in connecting painterly permissions to poetic achievements. Pound knew the poetry of the past too well to be satisfied with what he could make of the present. But he did not rest in ironic treatments of that gulf. Indeed, "Hugh Selwyn Mauberley," his fully ironic rendering of his contemplative ideals, could be written only after he had set himself in another direction. Now we need to understand that direction by attempting an overview of the changes Pound worked on his initial Vorticist ideals.[5] *Gaudier-Brzeska,* his memorial to the sculptor, proves to be the central document for our purposes, because it afforded Pound two fundamental challenges. As a collection of Vorticist materials, it had an effect parallel to that of Yeats's 1908 *Collected Poems. Gaudier-Brzeska* set Pound to reflecting on the selves that Vorticism made available, and it required him to structure isolated essays into a coherent presentation measuring the powers of those selves. Second, Pound had to take up the role of epideictic rhetorician, an uncomfortable task for the modern mind. He had to invent a language of praise, without relying on public ideals borrowed from his society, and he therefore had to transform those aspects of his poetics that had been based simply on ideals of clear reference or fidelity to the prose tradition. For Pound, praise that stays praise could be based neither on simple description nor on any set of abstract claims. Those are as empty for art as they are for characterizing a lover. So he turned to a Romantic strategy, which he then stood on its head. One praises best by measuring effects on one's own life. But those effects could not be measured by reporting affective responses: Effects must be deeds, not sentiments. Therefore, one could render homage to Gaudier-Brzeska only by tracing the differences he made in helping Pound overthrow his aesthetic humanism, with its awkward melange of period styles and medieval gestures.

Each challenge prevented easy solutions to the other. How does one value the differences an influence makes, without constructing the kind of context that a collection of essays establishes? But how does one determine the force of the essays, without judging the identity of the praiser? This means that it could not suffice to concentrate on Gaudier-Brzeska as *"un Miglior Fabbro."* Stylistic models in themselves do not form an ethos. So Pound was in effect forced to a choice that was to prove fateful for the *Cantos*. To praise this sculptor, he would compare and contrast the forms of agency made available by Gaudier-Brzeska's stylistic example to those models of agency made available in the Renaissance, the age most devoted to having sculpture forge and test its dreams of human powers. Vorticism could be presented as posing an alternative to the art that had shaped the Western ideal of the human body through its defining psychological strength as a continuation of the body's control over three-dimensional space.

Pound uses the structure of *Gaudier-Brzeska* to define these new possibilities, and thus to establish defensible Modernist principles of epideixis. The book begins by developing a public identity for Gaudier-Brzeska – in the constructive force of his essays, then in his letters. In order to spell out the effects of that force, the second half of the book tries to define "what was visible to one spectator in 1913 and '14," and hence what Pound himself could make of Vorticist exemplars. By Chapter 12 we see Pound collecting three of his own essays, from early in 1915. For by then what had been potential in Vorticism could be transposed into lines of thinking made available for an entire culture. The series of essays begins with a telling account of how the decline of Renaissance ideals creates pressure for a thorough Modernist revolution. Representational principles have dwindled to the pursuit of "the caressable," and statues no longer model possible lives, but merely provide substitute forms of gratification: eros tied to illusory bodies. Consequently, public life is reduced to the sad spectacle of officials scurrying to avoid responsibility for acknowledging an early Rodin or accepting an Epstein sculpture offered as a gift to the Tate Gallery.

Such events require a second essay, elaborating the ramifications of that cultural blindness. The essay begins with a brief survey of typical attitudes among young Modernist writers, all rejecting their elders by adapting the archconservative poses of young Hellenes, blissfully beyond the tawdry struggles of their own age. At the other pole, in the seat of authority, one finds (unnamed) dear "uncle Billyum" wandering "in the half-light complaining that – 'Queens have died young and fair'" (102). Pound's own prophetic role obviously lies in mediating between the two. He must enter the lists with these classicists, and with Yeats, over who has the right to see himself as the heir of Athens and of Urbino. And he must find modes of reading and of writing not subject to the impotence, bitterness, and self-delusion that stem from trying to imitate the content of classical works in a nonclassical age. Vorticism will prove indispensable, because it seeks principles that operate at a level deeper than content. So it can hope to recover the energies of the past, as the necessary impetus for overthrowing what had become contaminated in the form of represented ideals.

The third essay begins the work of building the new ethos out of the process of juxtaposing exemplary energies from the past. Renaissance sculpture serves as both the model of what must be overcome and the challenge demanding a specific level of intensity in the overcoming. Vorticism, then, can work on history, as well as on perception and desires, here presenting in prose complex layerings of "motive ideas" still available for use in the present, if it can capture the vitality of these "incarnations or exponents" (112):

> This enjoyment of machinery is just as natural and just as significant a phase of this age as was the Renaissance "enjoyment of nature for its own sake," and not merely as an illustration of dogmatic ideas. The modern sense of the value of the "creative, constructive individual" . . . is just as definite a doctrine as the Renaissance attitude "De Dignitate," Humanism. As for external stimulus, new discoveries, new lands, new languages gradually opened to us . . .
>
> Ernest Fenollosa's finds in China and Japan, his intimate personal knowledge, are no less potent that Crisolora's manuscripts. . . . The Renaissance sought a realism and attained it. It rose in a search for precision and declined through rhetoric and rhetorical thinking, through a habit of defining things always "in terms of something else."
>
> Whatever force there may be in our own decade and vortex is likewise in a search for a certain precision; in a refusal to define things in terms of something else; in the "primary pigment." The Renaissance sought for a lost reality, a lost freedom. We seek for a lost reality and a lost intensity. We believe that the Renaissance was in part the result of a programme. We believe in the value of a programme in contradistinction to, but not in contradiction of, the individual impulse. (116–17)

Finally, the rest of *Gaudier-Brzeska* devotes itself to defining this "creative, constructive individual," who must be capable of a precision and intensity that can compete with the Renaissance image of dignified self-possession. For his foundation, Pound relies on what he regards as three fundamental principles of modern art, each capable of forming a bridge between art and life: its emphasis on the authorial powers focused by the art of abstraction; its distinctive treatment of the idea of expression; and its version of form, which becomes a model for individuals entering social relations without relying on the rhetorical practice of defining things in terms of something else.

Abstraction and expression were, for Pound, closely interwoven. He realized that Modernist painting had replaced representation's concern for subject matter with a demand that the work concentrate on "the power of the artist" (*Ezra Pound and the Visual Arts* xvii). This meant that expression required a similar redefinition. The relevant powers could not be manifest, if artists and poets devoted themselves to exploring the nature and ground of their own emotion or dreamed of somehow becoming Hegelian expressers of their age. Those were only ways of guessing a soul for man. Art could produce souls only if the artist found ways simultaneously to express powers and to testify directly to their significance. For then imaginative power is no longer something we interpret or hypothesize; it is something we witness and cannot evade, so long as we take seriously the form that embodies it. Patterned energies matter less because they are composed within formal structures than because the structures, in effect, define what is entailed in presenting the mind just so, and thus composing expressions that can modify the mental states of other cultures. Expression, therefore, is a matter of objective forms, but only because such forms objectify the powers of subjects. Poundian form is not an aestheticist evasion of history. Rather, it becomes the sole vehicle that allows the powers of agents to enter history as active forces, not displaced by all of the ideological baggage that normally accompanies any description or explanation of "historical circumstances." Objective form is testimony to the intensity and scope of the embodied agent's discriminations, ends, and capacity to realize what they engender.

In *Gaudier-Brzeska,* Pound's best test of these powers proved to be his use of these new models to interpret his own errors, as he tried to define his relationship to the two dominant styles of late nineteenth-century art, Impressionism and Symbolisme. In hindsight, he realized that each style trapped itself in a misleading emphasis on content that concealed its possibilities as a formal breakthrough. Impressionism bound its creative energies to those principles of flux that Yeats, following Lewis's *Time and Western Man,* was to employ to dismiss Pound. And Symbolisme based its thematics on vaguely idealized realms where a restless, unstable style might, nonetheless, be able to posit for itself the power to tease out glimpses of some permanent reality. Yet as emblems for the power of the artist, each broke new ground and promised a constructivist alternative to the essentially passive and critical stance that was Pound's "Imagism" (to be codified by Amy Lowell). Despite Impressionism's apparent lack of structural, formative intelligence (89), noted by the Post-impressionist critiques of Impressionism, Pound saw that it was Impressionism that made these critiques possible, because its model of creation required emphasizing the force of authorial powers. Impressionism offered "a method of presentation" that makes "arrangement in color" (85) the central creative principle. It had taken Whistler, Pound's great American predecessor in the world of exiles, to make the necessary transvaluation of values needed to treat these modes as the primary content of art. And now Whistler's great follower could claim to understand the law of Imagism in a distinctively Modernist fashion: "Direct treatment of the thing" made it possible to insist that the claims that a work of art exerted on its audience resided not in ideas, or even in images, but in the quality and force of the treatment.

With these shifts, the very notion of "thing" within art must change, allowing artists to attribute semantic content to these methods of presentation. Making that possible might be considered Symbolisme's major contribution to modern art. Symboliste poets and painters often employed "murky techniques" (85) as they tried to extend metonymic associations into patterns of "allusion, almost of allegory," thus degrading the "symbol to the status of a word" (84). Beneath the degradation, however, one can locate a level of constructive energies embodying a "profounder sense" of Symbolisme, based on belief in "a sort of permanent metaphor": "not necessarily a belief in a permanent world, but . . . a belief in that direction" (84). The arranged thing, formed by a display of the powers of constatation, becomes itself the symbol. It is the rendered activity, not the word, that claims the status of permanent metaphor. The act, as a feature of the physical world, constitutes form. And because form carries within it the dynamic principles of its own making, it literally offers itself as a possible permanent force, without depending on other explanatory terms. Instead of allegory, the trope of dependency, the new art could consist in pure equations among primary elements synthesized to produce a state of maximal energy. Luminous details embody creative powers of individual historical agents.

Now Pound could, in theory at least, put imagism behind him. What matters is less the mood rendered than the state of activity sustained by the forming energy. That energy does not require the same kind of interpretive translation as mimetic art, so it makes sense to claim that the art image "is real because we can know it directly" (86). Its components may depend on descriptions in terms of other things; but its reality, its force as one thing or act, consists in its capacity to be self-defining, to be graspable only in its differences from our standard categories, as a "word beyond formulated language" that articulates a condition of apprehension. A poem can have a direct force, distinct from our interpretive categories, if it composes an "intensive" image: not a spreading out of associations, but a synthesis into an "absolute metaphor." The new image is, in effect, the medium that brings about states of consciousness and allows artists to give us new eyes. The maximal degree of intensity occurs when, in Pound's famous analogy, the artist composes equations like those in analytic geometry, which at once create and define a permanent form, sustained by the balance and integrity of internal relationships.

Pound's specific descriptions of Vorticism, so far, are largely compatible with Kenner's views. Pound's next move, however, requires a shift in critical emphasis. If one asks what finally defines the nature and use value of this intensity, or what is presented in these modes of presentation, one sees that form must ultimately take on metaphoric dimensions. Kenner, and most Pound critics, answer the question just posed by relying on a model of disclosure: Form allows latent energies of experience to take objective shape. Pound, though, began by insisting on the powers of the artist as the essential feature of Modernist nonrepresentational art, so he had to return to the connection between form and agency – where, I hasten to add, he found his best case for responding to Renaissance sculpture.

Sculpture, Pound argues, makes clear that what matters in testimonial art are the ethical correlates sustained by the work's aesthetic immediacy. Intensity and intensiveness are properties we can predicate both of artworks and of artistic acts. Therefore artworks themselves can become signs and tests of character, and states of consciousness can become models for personal stances. An equation created as an organization of forms is not an object, but an action, "a much more energetic and creative action than the copying or imitating of light on a haystack" (92). So Pound can turn his argument to individual Vorticist exemplars, each expressed, not by meanings, but by the creative activity they generate on a motif (93). Finally, it is "the form of intelligence" reflected in acts such as the presenting of "masses in relation" (93) that establishes Modernism's right to oppose the "caressable," putting in its stead those human powers for which art is direct testimony:

> A few . . . of us believe in the mobility of thought. We believe that human dignity consists very largely in humanity's ability to invent. . . .
>
> Our respect is not for the subject matter, but for the creative power of the artist; for that which he is capable of adding to his

subject from himself; or in fact his capability to dispense with external subjects altogether, to create from himself or from elements. (96, 98)

This concern for the power of the artist repeats the central tenet of nineteenth-century expressionist attitudes as diverse as Carlyle's and Mill's. But Pound's concern for abstraction shifts all of the emphases and establishes different consequences for art. Now we see how Pound's ideals of expression need have nothing to do with subjective content or deep inwardness. The relevant sense of "expression" refers, not to the contents of a self, but to the nature, extent, and configuration of the mind's powers, which can be mobilized "working behind the words" (*Literary Essays* 420). Expressionism becomes objective, at least to the extent that it entails equating subjectivity with dramatized capacities to measure energies by the forms they allow a medium to take. Art gives us eyes to see people forming means of seeing, and it tests the value of these forms by demanding that they display intensive synthetic powers, to hold the pressures on experience within complex relational structures. In other words, Pound works the same transformation of expressionist theory that he does of Symbolisme and Impressionism, abstracting to an active core of energies not trapped within those ideals of reference that, we have seen, both narrow the cognitive domain art can address and breed silly metaphysical ideals in the hope of supplementing that narrowness.

In the case of expressionist theory, Pound realized that what had seemed the assertion of Romantic individualism was in fact its suppression, because the self becomes a victim of its own narrative, and its psychological dependencies and categories of significance are borrowed from the ideological marketplace. In reaction, he proposed conceiving of the expressive individual as a set of active qualities, rather than as a set of determinate contents, and he developed principles of reading for the force that these qualities might exert.[6] The artwork becomes at once a display and a test: It is possible to give form to an infinite range of qualities by synthesizing a system of equations, and the capacity of those equations, once created, to serve as instruments intensifying the perceptions and resistances of others becomes the public measure of the value in private acts. Art expresses, not worlds or selves, but ways of seeing and arranging the world. Therefore, the more abstract it is, the more concrete and universal can be the actual measure of its effects.

A phrase borrowed from Remy de Gourmont neatly captures Pound's new ideal: *"L'objectif est une des formes du subjectif"* ("The objective is one of the forms of the subjective") (*Literary Essays* 353). Objective energies give expression to subjectivity and provide other subjects with exemplary states that they may find representative. That representativeness, moreover, need not be on the level of shared beliefs. The powers are relational, not conceptual. It is "concentration," therefore, not "mass" or its literary analog, heroic rhetoric, that can be "monumental" (*Gaudier-Brzeska* 32), because concentration is an emblem of realized identity. Vorticist form matters in this ethos, because that concept of form provides a complete alternative to Platonic ideals. Vorticist objects do not *refer* to forms in some alternative sphere of reality. Instead they *possess* form, insisting on their own status as models of individuation, in a world tending toward repetition and dissolution. Standing in and as itself, sustained by the energies of a making, rather than the beliefs or needs of a maker, the work asserts and wields human creative power. It has identity, by conquering the slippage inherent in narrative presentations of the self. The work enters history by virtue of its power to resist the rule of history that all things lose their hold on the present. By pursuing the condition of absolute metaphor, works, like some persons, base their claims to significance on what they do, rather than on fulfilling some category that happens to be in force at a given moment. *Intensity* and *intensiveness* (that is, "concentration" and "synthetic power") become the dominant values of an expressionist aesthetic inseparable from an expressionist ethics:

> [Epstein] has had "form understanding"; he has not fallen into the decadence of all sculpture which is "the admiration of self."
>
> Why should we try to pin labels on what he has expressed? . . . It is the artist's job to express what is "true for himself." In such measure as he himself exists, a great one . . . But the man who tries to express his age, instead of expressing himself, is doomed to destruction.
>
> But this is also a side track. I should not spend my lines in answering carpings. I should pile my objectives upon Epstein, or better still, I should ask my opponents to argue, not with me, but to imagine themselves trying to argue with one of the Flenites, or with the energies of his "Sun-God." They'd "teach you to" talk about "expressing your age," and being the communal trumpet.
>
> The test of a man is not the phrases of his critics; the test lies in the work, in its "certitude." What answer is to be made to the "Flenites"? With what sophistry will you be able to escape their assertion? (*Gaudier-Brzeska* 101–2)

Pound tests this new model of *virtù* in a series of essays on individual writers such as James, Swinburne, and de Gourmont. Unable to carry off his epic ambitions in the self-conscious poetic style available to him,

Pound needed to project ways that his developing ideas of *virtù* and certitude might warrant a more ambitious and distinctive compositional stance for the *Cantos*. So he tried to extend the biographical emphases (84) and the contrast between sculptural styles on which *Gaudier-Brzeska* is based into general principles elaborating the possibility of a New Renaissance (see especially pages 116–17).[7] An enervated ideal of the sculpturally modeled individual must yield to an ethic elaborated out of the new art.

Just as Vorticism used Impressionist freedom to recover in secular terms the Symboliste faith in permanent metaphor (84), the new ethic relied on individualist assertions, as its means to restore all that in Kant and in Renaissance thought depended on subordinating the self to ideal categories. The key is a new way of valuing the constructive actions that produce a fabric of vital cultural differences. For Kant, as for most of Western moral thought, the good is, like the true, something that depends on socially acknowledged objectivity. For Pound, as for Epstein's *Flenites,* the sign of individual nobility is just the opposite: the capacity to assert one's difference, and thus to affect a community, by challenging it to sharpen the various synthetic intelligences whose interaction constitutes cultural life. Pound's rationale is not unlike what produces the will to assertion and the suspicion of categories in such critics as Bloom and Derrida. But his constructivism relies neither on a narrow oedipal model for expressive energies, nor on a dialectic of differences confined to the oscillations between stylus and the signifier. Pound finds his means of restating a Renaissance model for cultivating the individual in the exemplary work by which Henry James produced a "communication [that] is not a leveling . . . not an elimination of differences, of the right of differences to exist, of interest in finding things different":

> In describing *Pandora's* success as "purely personal," Henry James has hit on the secret of the Quattrocento, 1450 to 1550, the vital part of the Renaissance. Aristocracy decays when it ceases to be selective[,] when the basis of selection is not personal. It is a critical acuteness, not a snobbism, which last is selection on some other principle than that of a personal quality. . . . The whole force of the Renaissance was in the personality of its selection . . . .
>
> . . . Christianity lends itself to fanaticism. Barbarian ethics proceed by general taboos. The relation of two individuals is so complex that no third person can pass judgment upon it. Civilization is individual. The truth is the individual. The light of the Renaissance shines in Varchi when he declines to pass judgment on Lorenzaccio. (*Literary Essays* 298, 319)

V

The *Cantos* was to be the epic tale for this new tribe.[8] As such, it would have to elaborate three essential features of the anticategorical, individualist *virtù*. First, it would recover the fundamental conditions of Symboliste spirituality from the Symboliste dependency on vague correspondences and purely musical harmonies. Objective expression could create, in their place, the same kind of explicit metaphysical testimony as Duchamp's articulation of the energies of chess. As Pound says, citing Lewis: "Matter which has not intelligence enough to permeate it grows . . . gangrenous and rotten" (*Literary Essays* 280). Thus the condition for a vital sense of matter has nothing to do with traditional desires for a ground in nature or a transcendental site created by autonomous formal relations. Even vitality in nature is simply and solely a function of constructive intelligence. This intelligence, as it engages nature or history, tests itself, as James's does, by its capacity to produce "titanic volume, weight in the masses" that the artist holds in opposition, in productive differences within his or her work (*Literary Essays* 297).

The second feature of Pound's new aesthetic is simply a self-reflexive extension of the first. The new art must insist on the cultural force of such intelligences by foregrounding the specific modality of consciousness that allows them to produce the synthetic relations. In other words, artists must learn not to displace their creative energies into merely interpretive contexts, but must make the human power to assert difference the focus of attention. This is why quotation becomes, for Pound, the fundamental civilizing force allowing one to realize, in twentieth-century terms, what Longinus dreamed was the power of the rhetorical sublime. Quotation preserves for society an interplay of eloquent differences that parallels the vitality an individual spirit can produce within her specific world. De Gourmont is Pound's test case. The only way for Pound to capture his force is to have a tissue of quotations preserve the basic qualities of de Gourmont's intricate sensibility. Pound's role becomes that of the compiler, soon to be perhaps the most characteristic of Modernist authorial stances, but here focused in the commitment that with de Gourmont, we have "passed the point where people take abstract statement of dogma for 'enlightenment.' An idea has little value apart from the modality of the mind which receives it" (*Literary Essays* 343).[9]

Finally, the force of personal example provides Pound a Vorticist base for showing how a modern poetry can surpass the critical prose tradition that had initially cleared the space necessary for a break from nineteenth-century rhetorics. The constructivist space of poetry demands intensive concentration, which then composes a site where the careful attention to varied voices can take on its full differential resonance. So even the best Enlightenment prose remains tied to passive attitudes and socially contingent authorities that it was the task of poetry to combat by the modes of certitude it makes available (*Literary Essays* 343). In poetry, criticism must yield to creation:

> Most good prose arises, perhaps, from an instinct of negation; is the detailed convincing analysis of something detestable; of something which one wants to eliminate. Poetry is the assertion of a positive, i.e., of desire, and endures for a longer period. Poetic satire is only an assertion of this positive, inversely, i.e. as of an opposite hatred. . . .
>
> Most good poetry asserts something to be worth while or damns a contrary; at any rate asserts emotional values. The best prose is, has been a presentation . . . of circumstances, of conditions, for the most part abominable, or, at the mildest, amendable. . . .
>
> Poetry = Emotional synthesis, quite as real, quite as realist as any prose (or intellectual) analysis.
>
> Neither prose nor drama can attain poetic intensity save by construction, almost by scenario, by so arranging the circumstance that some perfectly simple speech, perception, dogmatic statement appears in abnormal vigour. (*Literary Essays* 324n)

VI

Our reward for concentrating on Pound's prose is the opportunity for a fresh look at what the *Cantos* make of Vorticist principles. We have already seen the subjunctive diffidence that permeated the 1917 version of the first Canto. Now we must return to the well-worn arena of Pound's development, to observe how the projection of a heroic, individualist ethos operates as a primary concern. The 1917 version of the third Canto had as its conclusion a passage that, Pound realized later, could make a strong beginning for his epic, because it fused a heroic story with a set of self-reflexive gestures that dramatize the poet's way of reliving the original energies. The story is of Odysseus; the modern poet's odyssey is the adventure of translation.

In the first version, the focus on translation was blurred by the early Pound's characteristic self-consciousness. It takes three pages on Renaissance recognition of Roman speech as "a sacrament" ("Three Cantos" 249) to introduce the Latin translation of the *Odyssey* by Andreas Divus, a text that Pound thought demonstrated both the vitality of the past and its challenges for those dreaming of a Renaissance. But that vitality is hard to realize, when even the act of translating requires constant monitoring, so self-protective is its contemporary mediator:

> "Wherever the Roman speech was, there was Rome,"
> Wherever the speech crept, there was "mastery"
> Spoke with the law's voice while your Greek logicians. . . .
> More Greeks than one! Doughty's "divine Homeros"
> Came before sophistry. Justinopolitan
> Uncatalogued Andreas Divus,
> Gave him in Latin, 1538 in my edition, the rest uncertain,
> Caught up in his cadence, word and syllable:
> "Down to the ships we went, set mast and sail,
> Black keel and beasts for bloody sacrifice,
> Weeping we went."
> I've strained my ear for -ensa, -ombra, and -ensa
> And cracked my wit on delicate canzoni –
> Here's but rough meaning:
> "And then went down to the ship, set keel to breakers,
> Forth on the godly sea;
> We set up mast and sail on the swarthy ship,
> Sheep bore we aboard her, and our bodies also
> Heavy with weeping."

Notice how dead the "we" is in this passage. When the speaking voice gets so self-conscious, there must be an excruciating distance between the making and the describing. By 1922, though, we have a very different translator. Now Pound can offer only the sacrament, without commentary.[10] The result is an elaborate interchange of presences: translations as complex modes of identification that measure the humanity of the maker:

> And then went down to the ship
> Set keel to breakers, forth on the godly sea, and
> We set up mast and sail on that swart ship,
> Bore sheep aboard her, and our bodies also
> Heavy with weeping, and winds from sternward
> Bore us out onward with bellying canvas,
> Circe's this craft, the trim-coifed goddess . . .
>
> And Anticlea came, whom I beat off, and then Tiresias
>   Theban
> Holding his golden wand, knew me, and spoke first:
> "A second time? Why? man of ill star,
> Facing the sunless dead and this joyless requiem?

Stand from the fosse, leave me my bloody bever
For soothsay."
And I stepped back
And he strong with the blood, said then, "Odysseus
Shalt return through spiteful Neptune, over dark seas
Lose all companions."[11]

The poem opens with a literal process of transubstantiation. We hear a
strange "we"; this, we learn, is the voice of Odysseus, who is actually
the sole survivor of his tale. So the "we" must soon become an "I," but
only after providing a measure of both the flexibility and the pathos of
that "I" – perhaps of all *I*s, since the maker of the poem also seems intent
on joining the "we." Such permutations will eventually spawn a range of
registers, within which diverse voices can enter. So, although this "we"
of heroic narrative might be isolated in its time, over time it forms
patterns into which can flow the rhythms and tones of Old English
laments and Renaissance discoveries that translation allows time itself to
be the field for imaginative journeys. The more the poem spreads out
into this space for translation, the more the play between the "I" and the
"we" constructs an authorial presence, putting poetry to work as a test
of his individual powers. Translation thereby affords the means both for
defining the hell that is one's present and for locating, through the Homeric model, sources of energy that transform efforts at guessing souls
into possibilities for producing them.

The affective differences between this version and the earlier one are
stunning. Although Pound substantially altered only the closing segments of the passage, in order to stress the assertive quality of Odysseus,
his elimination of the discursive context shifts the ontological status of
the entire event.[12] The final version has the same willful insistence on the
immediacy of strange presences that we find in the best Modernist painting. We are made to feel like anthropologists who have stumbled upon
an epic that tells the tale of a tribe whose powers and desires we must
infer from the text.

Translation is no less a direct form of experience than any other literary act. In fact, it may be one of our most intense forms of being, because
it synthesizes a variety of perspectives, merging past and present, as a
Cubist painting conjoins angles of vision. This folding of planes on one
another is clearest in the complex immediacy generated by the poems'
indexicals. Terms such as "here" apply both within the world of the
Odyssey and within the world that the compiling poet inhabits. Similarly,
the *I* and *we* of the opening get complexly doubled, allowing the author
and the readers purchase on both past and present, and making Tiresias's
question "A second time?" a measure of present urgencies permeating

the old poem. Even the Old English rhythms seem to establish magical rituals for once again invoking Tiresias. As a result, translation becomes less a process of mediating an old text into the present than a way of merging past and present, so that the dramatized actors, Odysseus and Tiresias, become literal embodiments of the transfer of energies that the author seeks in his structuring acts. So long as one relies on discursive statements about the sacramental, its powers remain external, a property of history or a transcendental Logos. Here, though, Pound makes a sacrament adequate for the modern mind, because the action consists simply in the transforming of outward texts into the direct energies of a writerly grace. Transubstantiation becomes the capacity to graft to oneself other identities, thus demonstrating that within individuals reside principles that can produce a sense of community without relying on abstract ideas.

As the poem's paradigmatic action, transubstantiation allows a radical reinterpretation of the relations between epic and history that make the poem possible. Although Pound's work shares the traditional in medias res opening, its emphasis is not on the course of events, but on the frames for interpreting them. In medias res is primarily a textual condition, requiring an author seeking a home in the present to recombine aspects of his cultural history. These demands on the author constitute the poem's real plot, its situating of the modern epic hero as the artistic consciousness that must make of the medias res, with all its fragments, a literal world, simultaneously marked by the presence of individual energies and providing those energies forms of expression more intense and more capacious than any mimetic rendering of the agent's private history. Structuring power, tested by the historical pressures eliciting the translation, provides a model for winning identity based on the mobility of intelligence.

Out of this mobility within fragments, a new model of depth must be born, grounding the subject in forces not tied to private history. Vorticism provides the necessary model for so casting the dramatic psychology of the poem. Depth equals intensiveness, the capacity to superimpose translations, so that although "there is nothing . . . nothing that's quite your own" (*Personae* 74), you manifest yourself by the quality of the relations you generate in, and as, your certitude. The endless, supplemental process of self-justification gives way to direct, expressive measures of personal worth, based, not on ideas about the self, but on qualities in one's compositional acts. Selves are not had as gifts, but selves are earned.

The entire *Draft of Thirty Cantos* takes as its main task elaborating the consequences of so earning a self, and thus of responding to the challenge posed by the closing section of Pound's first Canto. In the early version, he required a hesitant, self-conscious bridge from the *Odyssey* to the "florid[,] mellow phrase" of the "Hymn to Aphrodite," contained in the same volume with Divus's *Odyssey*. The 1922 version of the first Canto makes a small, but radical, change. If one drops the bridging materials, one puts the narrative and the ecstatic lyric movements in the same imaginative space, in effect suggesting that the worship of Aphrodite is inseparable from both the adventurous spirit and the constructivist will shaping this journey. One returns to Circe on her craft, but on one's own terms:

> And he sailed, by sirens and thence outward and away
> And unto Circe.
>   Venerandam,
> In the Cretan's phrase, with the golden crown, Aphrodite,
> Cypri munimenta sortita est, mirthful, oricalchi, with
>   golden
> Girdles and breast bands, though with dark eyelids
> Bearing the golden bough of Argicida. So that:
>
>   (60–6)

Two transitional elements interpret and secure this shift. First, the simple gerund "*venerandam*" places Venus at the linguistic root of the verb "to worship." The encounter with female divinities is possible at the very core of constructive translation: To worship is to embody Venus within one's own activity, a secular form of sacramental grace. Second, lest worship become too self-satisfied a stance, Pound projects as his conclusion the odd "so that." He wants us to reflect on the fact that what begins as engagement in the energies disposed by translation remains as a set of permissions and correlated demands. The epic muse is not external to the self. Rather, she resides in the poet's capacity to produce a ritual through which he transmits, for a second time, the energies that Homer imagined for his hero, now set in new relational frames. Whereas authorized stories can endure only as fragments within a metonymic sense of history, the fundamental synthetic principle for art must reside in the very model of action, and hence of agency, that art produces for itself. The phrase "so that," then, captures in abstract terms the implications of entering the epic in medias res and recognizing what that middle entails for one's own time. And by thus positioning the author, this closing phrase makes it possible to escape nagging comparisons with the wholeness of Robert Browning's Sordello. For the challenge of translation, in time and in space, offers a mode of intelligence sufficiently mobile and capacious to bring into play more complex models of identification than could be dreamt of in Browning's philosophy.

VII

Even more is at stake. Now Pound can handle a central problem in constructivist aesthetics, one that I suspect contributes strongly to Kenner's laying such heavy emphasis on patterned energies. If poems are intended to be imitative, we have fairly direct routes to discussing the possible values they offer. The work's content projects a stance and set of conditions continuous with empirical experience, and hence with needs and responsibilities that a society must negotiate. But what model of reality can complement constructivism? How can we say that the patterns it composes or the powers it illustrates lead back to the world in any significant way? In the painterly conceptions of Vorticist art, Pound found only claims about the transcendental features of abstract form or the vital effects of releasing conflicting energies. Once the plan of the Cantos began to take form, Pound could give a much more complete answer to those questions. Patterns matter, and compositional acts satisfy, to the extent that they participate in the heroic project of translating what the past has established into realities for the present. Translation at once challenges and judges the configurations of expressive energies that artists make available for their age. Constructivism not only calls for an alternative to submitting passively to historical determinants; it also inspires criteria by which to judge the responses it elicits.

There could be no better test of these possibilities than to stage a direct encounter with the problems of imitation and integration that "Sordello" had created for the *Ur-Cantos*. So Pound opens his second Canto by making those issues the first test of what the poem's "so that" entails for this new expressivist sense of structural intelligence:

> Hang it all, Robert Browning,
> There can be but the one "Sordello."
> But Sordello, and my Sordello?
> Lo Sordels si fo di Mantovana.
> So-shu churned in the sea.
> Seal sports in the spray-white circles of cliff-wash,
> Sleek head, daughter of Lir,
>   eyes of Picasso
> Under black fur-hood, lithe daughter of Ocean;
> And the wave runs in the beach-groove:
> "Eleanor, Elenaus, Eleptolis!"
> And poor old Homer blind, blind, as a bat,
> Ear, ear for the sea-surge, murmur of old men's voices.
>
> (1–13)

Translation emerges into a complete demonstration of a new constructivist ethos, soon to be tested in subsequent cantos by encounters with the burden of history. In this canto, though, Pound is content to elaborate the two fundamental dimensions of his ethical vision: a freedom story, demonstrating the capacity of Modernist constructivism to use the past as a locus of imaginative energies; and a story of powers, exemplifying the grounds of this new certitude, the forms of dignity it allows, and the psychological and (implicitly) social effects inherent in so constituting the self.

The moment of potentially paralyzing self-consciousness must be faced: "But Sordello, and my Sordello?" Now, however, the poet has a new arsenal, based on a fresh understanding of what Circe's craft entails. When writing need not be faithful to traditional logics that produce scenic or argumentative or narrative coherence, poets can begin to explore other resources potential within it. So self-consciousness is quickly deflected into a new process by which personality can be expressed and Sordellos appropriated. The energies of language lead to alternative presences and make available the identifications required to begin constituting a new model for poetic and practical identity. Like Picasso, Pound cultivates an apparent arbitrariness that proves intellectually defensible and affectively illuminating.

First, the structuring consciousness turns to an Italian historical account of Sordello, only to find available these other, nonhistorical principles of relationship. It is associations among sounds that are primarily responsible for the shift to So Shu, another poet figure related to the sea and to rhetoric (by Li Po's assessment), and thus to Homer and Odysseus. Sound, sea, and poetry then spawn the subsequent series of associations, or, better, super-positions, leading to Homer. Next, in the figures of the blind hero and the sea-surge becoming the old men's voices, Pound has emblems for his process of transforming the eye into the ear. And the poet's position in medias res establishes means for getting back to identify with the Homeric source of epic states. On reflection, we see that Pound has in fact generated the identification with Homer from a deep need that all of the poet figures share: Despite their different social situations, each must wring beauty out of violence, theophany out of history.

Now Pound must justify linking himself to Homer by demonstrating powers of his own that lead well beyond his relation of belatedness to Browning. The means is a brilliant conjunction of the concrete and the metapoetic. Pound recalls the rape of Tyro, then brings the memory to its climax in a moment of charged perception, where natural elements flesh out the sexualized atmosphere:

> Glare azure of water, cold welter, close cover.
> Quiet sun-tawny sand-stretch,
> The gulls broad out their wings,
>   nipping between the splay feathers.
>
>   (27–30)

Cold azure water sets off, by contrast, the warm, sunny stretch of sand. Then we shift to one of Pound's finest touches. The focus immediately becomes very narrow. From the beach, we attend to the gulls. But as we concentrate, the gulls themselves repeat the relation between distance and proximity, expansively spreading their wings as they nip at their feathers. Metapoetically we recognize a similar process taking place in the structuring action. The poem is free to revel in concrete, denotational celebrations of the physical world. Yet these particulars sustain highly abstract relations, which articulate the presence and pressure of the poem's constructive sensibility. All of the movements and tensions we have traced between sight and sound, immediacy and reflection, even violence and composure, form intensive relations that compose a complex balance. The mind, sidestepping the slippage inescapable in discursive self-justification, constructs equations that suffice for its expressive needs. The concrete is a world we win – not a world we are given.

This pressure on details helps explain the remarkable resonance in the next section of the poem, its account of Acoetes' response to the theophany of Dionysios. For the theophany, in effect, provides a narrative emblem for the ethos in the constructive processes that the poem has already set in motion. Acoetes' bondage and freedom become a self-reflexive figure for the poetic powers that the poem has been demonstrating. Pound's vehicle is Ovid's structural device of having a central mythological panel gather the motifs from less elaborately presented segments of his *Metamorphoses*. In Pound, though, the device functions self-reflexively to map the fundamental relations between moments of vision and the variety of translational processes that are required to draw out such a moment's consequences. First, the god must become palpable within the poem, primarily by means of the brilliant reversal effected by this Canto's opening sequence. There, sound led to sight, as multiplicity provided an escape from an all-absorbing self-consciousness. Here, a process of intensified concentration leads us from sight to hearing, from reflective distance to a suspended moment of sheer absorption that activates all of the senses:

> And where was gunwale, there now was vine trunk,
> And tenthril where cordage had been. . . .
> Heavy vine on the oarshafts,

> And, out of nothing, a breathing
> > hot breath on my ankles
> Beasts like shadows in glass,
> > a furred tail upon nothingness
> Lynx-purr, and heathery smell of beasts.
>
> > > (67–75)

The syntactic suspension in "out of nothing" virtually creates within the physical world the intensive space, the opening into otherness, that gods can inhabit. Yet this god appears citing no Father and mediating no Logos. For us, the god depends only on poetry, on a medium that creates the appearance of what Wordsworth called a "truth that is its own testimony."

Testimony requires witnesses – a fact that led Romantic poets to project the values that poems could assert in terms of audience figures defined within the poem. Pound adapts this same strategy to a totally non-Romantic exemplar, the person of Acoetes as he encounters the moment of theophany. Acoetes does not interpret the god or find resolution for dejection. He simply dramatizes the direct consequences of vision – consequences that are as immediate, as total and as unjustifiable in discursive terms, as is the vision itself:

> > And I worship.
> I have seen what I have seen.
> > When they brought the boy I said:
> "He has a god in him
> > though I do not know which god."
> And they kicked me into the fore-stays.
> I have seen what I have seen.
>
> > > (106–12)

Instead of the highly mediated process of displacement that traditional interpretation comprises, instead of the Wordsworthian movement to restate the import of his moments of lyric ecstacy, Acoetes responds to certitude with a corresponding certitude. Full acceptance of the vision generates the simplest and most heroic of self-definitions, a pure assertion of fealty, binding perception to ethos and projecting future responsibilities on the basis of present realities.

We, however, cannot worship as Acoetes does. What he encounters from the god's angry self-manifestation, we must produce as concrete structures composing our senses for theophany. Thus Pound measures Acoetes' vision by the consequences it has for his own poetry. Identification must focus productive differences, and wonder must be measurable by the ethos we derive from it. This is why Pound quickly shifts his poem to "a later year" and, at the same time, returns to the scenes with which the canto had opened. Pound too had seen what he had seen, but only after the theophany and model of bearing witness can he define for the poem the powers those visions make available. Now the earlier violence is tempered by an ecstatic reflective stance, whose structuring of the details becomes an active identification with Acoetes' worship. The poet's god does not invite allegorical structures or symbolic readings of events. Rather, the god's only manifestation is through what structure discloses of the immanent and makes available as potential grounds for self-enactment. By the conclusion of Canto 2, an initial escape from a history that might have trapped the author in a belated relation to Browning finds its reward in a capacity to recognize within history the patterned interrelations manifesting the Dionysian life principle:

> Lithe turning of water,
> > sinews of Poseidon,
> Black azure and hyaline,
> > glass wave over Tyro,
> Close cover, unstillness,
> > bright welter of wave-cords,
> Then quiet water,
> > quiet in the buff sands,
> Sea-fowl stretching wing-joints,
> > splashing in rock-hollows and sand-hollows
> In the wave-runs by the half-dune;
> Glass-glint of wave in the tide-rips against sunlight,
> > pallor of Hesperus,
> Grey peak of the wave,
> > wave, colour of grape's pulp,
>
> Olive grey in the near,
> > far, smoke grey of the rock-slide,
> Salmon-pink wings of the fish-hawk
> > cast grey shadows in water,
> The tower like a one-eyed great goose
> > cranes up out of the olive grove,
>
> And we have heard the fauns chiding Proteus
> > in the smell of hay under the olive-trees.
> And the frogs singing against the fauns
> > in the half-light.
> And . . .

(132–57)

Questions about identity give way to a triumphant "we," a society created around Acoetes' certitude and its testimony. The example of a witness gives us, not ideas to believe, but a modality for perceiving and constructing phenomena. So, although Pound shares Romantic poetry's obsession with how we see nature, he breaks with its basic means of forming a community through exemplary acts. Because Romantic poets sought to interpret their visions, their poems form careful, mutually balancing tensions between perceptual experience and the supplementary symbolic and sacramental overtones one can elicit from them. The mediating power of mind is dialectically recuperated by some latent version of Logos, be it Spirit or Nature, with the constant danger that nature will fail to sustain the supplements and reduce perceptions to nausea, and dreams of divinity to self-deluding fictions. Pound, on the other hand, makes seeing and the appearance of the god depend on acts of structuring,[13] on the simple, intensive composition of elements in mind and in the world. So his community is united, not by belief, but by the power of this constructive example to demonstrate a specific mode of activity. The audience need share nothing but the recognition of that possibility, which it can recast in terms of whatever different energies the theophany releases.

The second Canto concludes with an unmodified "and," a provocative corollary to the "so that" which interprets the effects of translation experienced in the first. The point is probably to invite us to think about the theme of incarnation in the second Canto as an extension and testing of those powers. The abstracting power of art gives one the concrete means to dwell fully within the flux of events. We can enter history, in all of its diversity, because we know how selfhood can be manifest as we produce provisional centers expressing those energies made available by what one has seen. Such expressions are ultimately the only means by which we can come to accept a society that condemns its visionaries to the forestays. The source and reward of expressive acts is their place in a world where communication consists in the challenge to define one's certitudes as significant differences.

VIII

So what has he given us, this poet seeking to develop a Vorticist ethic out of Modernist abstraction? On the most general level, Pound shows that heroic ambitions can be the stuff of Modernist poetry. Rather than withdraw into ironic musings on the slipperiness of one's medium, one can still attempt "an assertion of value that has not been in poetry *since* Cavalcanti and Dante and that the English 'philosophical' and other 'philosophical' poets have not produced" (*Literary Essays* 150). Pound saw that such a recovery was impossible, unless the poet honors the full force of critical attitudes based on the cardinal principle of Modernist thought: that abstract ideas cannot provide a sufficient ground for values, because they only engender further interpretations, each probably a displacement of desires it cannot name. But this principle need not elicit only negative energies or Nietzschean theatrics. It also provides a crucial challenge: One can counter the temptation to interpretation by constructing an expressive certitude that one can imagine directly engaging others in their efforts to project imaginary selves. In thinkers such as Croce, this antigeneric individualism had already produced a new expressivist poetics. But so long as no ethical correlate emerged, it was impossible to jettison idealist baggage such as Croce's notion of intuition, which confined expression to the realm of epistemology.

Pound saw his way to an alternative. All of the idealist claims might be boiled down to this simple motto: In constructing worlds, we make available relational principles that can be direct testimony to some basic truth or possible value. Constructive energy, and the possible quality of relations it produces, are simply facts in the world, certitudes that one does not so much interpret as define oneself against, in part by interpretation. So, the talk in the arts about epistemological matters may be largely a disguised theology, evading the ethical in an unending rhetoric about the imagination. If imagination matters, it matters because of what it produces concretely, as powers that make a difference in how we act or view our capacity to act. Pound's specific testimony, therefore, demonstrates these productive powers in two areas of experience. He dramatizes new forms of reference available to poetry by exploring what abstraction provides, and he extends this new content to emphasize an individualist ethic that our political rhetorics trivialize or ignore.

Pound's figure for his anticategorical poetics is the Chinese ideogram for truth, the image of a person standing by his or her word. Through that figure, Pound hopes to make us see that dichotomies between expression and description, emotion and perception, value and fact, or even past and present, are not necessary or inevitable, even though it would obviously be foolish to deny the significant roles they have played in our culture. If poets accept a constructivist ethos, statements are actions, and descriptive truths matter only to the extent that an assertion contributes to the projected power in a modality of apprehension. Acoetes is what Acoetes does within the set of relations that the poet forms out of his identification with him.

If we accept this constructivist ethic, idealistic themes, such as the autotelic poem or the total dependency of meanings on context, simply lose their urgency, because they come to seem unnecessary means of protecting poetry from the rigorous criteria that science uses for description. In Pound's view, as in the position that Richard Rorty's *Philosophy and the Mirror of Nature* is now popularizing, it is the effort to universalize empiricist criteria for description that ought be on the defensive, since its proponents often provide no clear pragmatic measures of how the criteria pertain to practical life, and hence no means of recommending their capacity to enhance our lives. Recognizing the limitations of all such universals, poets can confidently hone their language to fit the contours of the empirical world, so long as they make an issue of what such fit enables us to do or project. The issue of fit, in turn, leads to a way of handling the problem of endless supplements by directing us toward tests of specific qualities in an utterance that do not depend on its propositional functioning. For the end of poetry is not to provide propositions made problematic by metaphor, but to exemplify the terms by which the mind makes commitments, terms that require attention to a variety of qualitative modifiers and metaphoric implications. Thus, rather than offering only impoverished and defensive rivals of empiricist statements, poetry can present itself as a considerable social force, especially if one emphasizes the capacity of long poems (unlike paintings) to make time itself a measure of the energies that the poem gathers. Poems set up their own patterns of endurance and recurrence, which in effect test the range and scope of particular psychic economies. Poems written over a lifetime make even the temporal effects of that economy a literal test of the lives that the poetry elicits and helps authorize.

Making Pound's life a test for his poetry, however, all too obviously raises inescapable problems that confront anyone wanting to praise the ethos he constructed. The plain fact is that the poetry sanctioned, and probably encouraged, both political and private acts deeply offensive to most of us. What kind of value, then, can we attribute to the poetry or to the ethic it proPounds? Praise of the poetry apart from the ethic will not do: Epics are not matters of style, but of exemplary states of consciousness and models for understanding experience. We must deal with the ethic itself. But we must also grant that ethic a certain amount of interpretive generosity, if we are not to make ourselves appear more tyrannical and shrill than Pound at his worst. Minimally, we must be willing to take the early version of the *Cantos* as a distinctive project attempting to work out an ethic that Pound later came to think had to be subordinated to more general social programs, if the dreams of agency that he had developed were to be realized on any large scale. We must recreate an early Pound who could tell himself that he was a Wildean socialist. And I think we also ought remember that one of the dangers of any individualism is a propensity to slide from an insistence on productive conflict into a self-defensive claim that one particular version of the individual must govern others, in order to show them what they are missing. Individualist principles are more likely than most to succumb to the temptation of trying to realize, through state power, those commitments that cannot be accomplished by means of example and discussion. Those dangers, however, are counterbalanced by the fact that these principles provide us with the moral terms on which to resist the tyrannies they engender.

To see what Pound's ethical vision does, and does not, accomplish, we can contrast it with the best contemporary version of individualist ideals, Robert Nozick's *Philosophical Explanations*. Nozick is very good, and very thorough, on how individuals may have rights and achieve satisfactions that do not depend upon the existing social order. But he is rather weak on the actual values that individuals realize and that therefore justify that independence from a social measure of the good. Politically he relies on an abstract notion of absolute rights, and psychologically he defines individual values in terms of the capacity to sustain organic unities among increasingly diverse particulars. Those models make it difficult to maintain distinctions between quantity and quality or to distinguish depth from material complexity. And, more important, they rely on ideas of self-unification that are incompatible with the sense of the diverse, inherently multiple self that dominates contemporary theory. Both considerations make it easy to see Nozick's individual as the philosopher's Yuppie, indistinguishable from the specular selves idealized in our narcissistic culture.

Pound, though, is not narcissistic in this specular way. For him, individual identity is something that we construct, and then test, as we do all constructs, by the forces it makes available in the form of intensive structures and their plausible consequences. There is no reason why these manifestations ought be parts of any one determinate organism, and no need to base the expressive energy on a process of tracking a presumed "buried life" through the alienated, and alienating, detritus of a person's specific life history. What matters is not how I unify a self, but how I keep something like its *conatus,* or sense of power, vital through a variety of manifestations. The agent is translator of the world, not the producer of interpretive substitutes for it. Moreover, because expression takes the form of active translation into a living, and livable, present, it also provides a cogent model of the criteria that bind the individual performance to social structures. In Nozick's model, as in most existentialist frameworks, the only measure of individual achievement is the individual's own sense of organicist intensity. But Pound's sense of translation brings with it a responsibility to the communities that inspire the performance and form the ideal audience for judging it. Bad translation is a spiritual failure at measuring the self against the past. Finally, that flexible sense of the individual and sense of necessary conflict has, as its social corollary, a responsiveness to individual tones and qualities (like that of the early versions of the *Cantos*) that constitutes a rich and vital pluralism, not at all like the cult of toleration characterizing current ideals of letting the other be. Thus, at the least Pound's example reminds us of how much we lose when we suppress expressive energies under the therapeutic banners of sympathy and cultivated vulnerability, or subordinate them to the abstract collectivities promised by our political rhetorics.

There remains, however, the test of the poet's life. If we are to allow poems the role of projecting an ethos, we must consider the consequences they authorize, as well as the ideas they make possible (especially if the consequential relation is as tight as the one for an author and his works). In this regard, I cannot defend Pound. But I can suggest that there are plausible ways to finesse seeing his later politics as a necessary consequence of the values articulated by the *Cantos*. First, we must be careful not to impose on Pound's thought a psychological consistency that belies the differences manifest in his career and in the distinctions he tries to make. (I took up some concrete instances of such temptations in note 5.) Second, as Evan Watkins pointed out to me, we can ask whether poets are in fact the best interpreters of their own earlier beliefs and commitments. Perhaps readers can do better at understanding the implications and consequences of such ideas than the writers do as they try to adapt them to their own lives, where the frustrations about the empirical results of having staked themselves on such ideas are likely to have significant distorting consequences. Thus, although an aesthetics of translation must heed what an author makes of his or her life, it must recognize the modifications that history and psychology work on ideas and be willing to attempt to reformulate what the ideas and stylistic experiments make available for a cultural theater. For example, Pound knew that Malatesta was, in many respects, a rather silly Romantic, but he also realized that the energies Malatesta exhibited and the virtues he epitomized could enter other behavioral complexes, once they were dramatically brought to life. Indeed, all of Pound's energies were devoted to resisting both the ethics and the aesthetics of imitation, so that it becomes possible to see the self as positioned within a vortex of competing and conflicting human possibilities. That is what it means to have history as a resource, and people worth preserving that resource for.

A second dimension of the problem of assessing Pound takes us to the central issue in any claim that poetry carries an ethical force. Can one still make the assertion that the forms of thinking encouraged by poetry differ from straightforward political judgments, so that what is dangerous politically can be said to be important to engage imaginatively, because of the intelligence or intensity of the stance rendered? There is no easy answer; perhaps no single answer. But there are significant differences between the two realms that help to clarify both the strengths and weaknesses of poetic culture. Imaginative art may differ from politics in precisely the same way in which Pound's idea of expressive individualism differs from the generalized sense of the person as "anyone" required of a good political theory. The Poundian poet idealizes states that are possible for certain individuals. Such values become problematic when they begin to identify those individuals with the state, and thus to claim privileges for them based on their imaginative appeal. Political thinking, on the other hand, must think for the collective: Thus, it must devote itself to positing principles of adjudication among competing interests, in such a way as to maintain some degree of order and of justice for a whole society. Such theorizing becomes problematic when it becomes satisfied with its collectivist terms, which reduce individuals to functions assessable by categorical principles of judgment.

Rough as they are, such distinctions help us to understand why poets – especially American poets – tend to be impatient with the work of political judgment, finding it tragically easy to project their own powers as necessary and sufficient for the state. At the other pole, we see why it is all too easy for political theory, and political rulers, to prefer terms that impose a single order on the whole polis to terms that raise questions about the quality of life that the polis makes available to individuals. Facing such resistance or indifference, poets as passionate about their ideals as Pound find themselves so frustrated by their marginality that they turn to increasingly abstract models of order, and they find the violence imposing such order an appealing surrogate for their own frustration.

As critics, it is obviously crucial that we clarify the problems arising from such frustration. But, in my view, it is more important to keep the problems in perspective by recognizing the personal and social tensions that lead to such extremes. And it is even more important to try to preserve, from such work, that which matters for projecting challenges to the quality of individual lives. Ironically, this task is made easier by the fact that the more shrill the poetry, the less danger it has of producing political converts: I know no critics or poets who defend Pound's fascism, and few whose conservatism is threatened by criticism that "exposes" the anal-retentive fetishism of Pound's poetics. So attacking the fascism seems to me a somewhat empty way to assert one's own self-importance. This does not mean that one cannot propose a cogent attack on Pound's individualism. But it seems to me that such attacks must recognize the crucial difference between the promises necessary for life in a just society and the need for individuals to experience in their imaginative lives a wide range of possible attitudes. The democratic imperative to grant freedom even to positions like Pound's fascism – that is, to positions almost none of us can respect – provides a telling emblem for the degree to which the political is a domain we must endure, rather than identify with. (This does not preclude acting in order to make it less alien.) Therefore I do not think that constant reference to political measures of value will allow us the richest sense of our individual powers. Questions of how we imagine ourselves at our best require other perspectives where we ask, not what is right or fair, but what allows the greatest intensity and dignity for our individual actions and commitments.[14] Keeping alive the possibility of such questions, while challenging the answers that we find comfortable, seems to me to be a crucial political act, even when the visions involve problematic political ideas. At the least such questions insist on our paying attention to those individual freedoms and individual differences that make it worthwhile to cast a suspicious eye on even those political visions which have good claims on our fealties. And it may be this learning to see others as challenges to our meanings, rather than as threats to our material welfare, that enables us to take the political commitments to imaginative freedom as one of the indispensable conditions of social justice. Therefore Pound's individualism gives us a positive, unpatronizing view of what imaginative production can stimulate and why social collectivity matters. Ultimately, it is the conflict between assertions of certitude that forces us both to resist the ego's demand to recreate the world only in its own image and to engage those differences that society can produce and encourage. The palpable base of ethics grounds an impressive visionary tower:

> There is the residue of perception, perception of something which requires a human being to produce it. Which may even require a certain individual to produce it. This really complicates the aesthetic. You deal with an interactive force: the *virtù* in short. . . .
> We appear to have lost the radiant world where one thought cuts through another with clean edge a world of moving energies, . . . magnetisms that form, that are seen, or that border the visible. . . . Not the pagan worship of strength, nor the Greek perception of visual non-animate plastic . . . , but this "harmony in the sentience" or harmony *of* the sentient, where the thought has its demarcation, the substance its *virtù,* where stupid men have not reduced all "energy" to unbounded undistinguished abstraction. (*Literary Essays* 151, 154)

Towers crumble – personal as well as political. Pound's greatest social significance, for me, resides in the way his individualism eventually proved its capacity to handle even these destructive moments. For he finally became the exemplary reader of his own ethical project, conceiving that early work less as explicit social arguments than as the idealization of a human agent so faithful to what he had seen that he could make his Pisan cage into a bizarre but glorious Modernist Tempio. Confronting history at close to its most nightmarish, Pound proved how, even in error, the heritage of Modernist abstraction creates a personal presence in the poem's structuring action that commands respect and makes individual assertion seem a threshold bordering on some more intense, and perhaps more sublimely tragic, form of composed energies. Here, where categories get pushed to their breaking point, there endures the forceful certitude of a particular example, whose failures help to sustain this ultimate claim: "Here error is all in the not done, / All in the diffidence that faltered" (*Cantos* 522).[15] The proof of Pound's ethic is that such expressions can, and probably should, continue to haunt us, demanding, "With what among our many sophistries do we dare to escape such an assertion?"

9

Why Stevens Must Be Abstract

I

For Pound, epic ambitions demanded heroic acts enabling poetry to define an individual ethos in and for history. Abstraction mattered, therefore, primarily because it afforded a structural principle by which such identities could be asserted and could remain least subject to the twin perversions of narcissism and rhetorical self-evasion. For Wallace Stevens, always the conservative in matters of structure and, in his later years, always a diffident minimalist with regard to the epic, Modernist abstraction appealed primarily for the promise it offered of a new poetic content, a site where it becomes possible to rethink poetry's relation to both heroism and to history.

Rethinking is not rejection – of heroic ideals or of history:

> After the hero, the familiar man
> Makes the hero artificial
> But was the summer false? The hero?[1]

In Stevens's case, however, the process of "rethinking" demanded a very different sense of the identity of the poet, one much more responsive to these metaphors of seasonal flux and recurrence. If there was to be a plausible modern embodiment of nobility, it could not take Pound's essentially Romantic form – that of the solitary, visionary culture hero, locating in intensity of structure what could not otherwise be expressed within the confines of social reality. For Stevens, recovering summer's excess requires a poetic will capable of aligning itself with the "familiar man," perhaps differing from him only in the degree to which the poet labors to subsume individual differences under needs and powers that he

321

can share with his audience. It is only by grasping what we share through historical and seasonal change that we can hope to purge our idealizations of all of the ideological baggage that otherwise would betray them to history's junk heap of dead metaphors.

Modernist abstraction affords two principles that helped Stevens to work out this heroics of the familiar. The first principle consists in an ideal of a content for poetry that cannot be represented, because it is too concrete, too fundamental to universal processes for negotiating with the world, to appear as pictorial images within it. The poet can dream of rendering feelings, rather than images, and therefore can hope to compose a human presence that, "in being more than an exception," becomes "part, / Though an heroic part, of the commonal" (388). If one were to ask how poets can achieve the innocence or simplicity to maintain this "commonal" as anything more than a fiction, desperately and nakedly posing an illusory escape from the actual conditions of Modernity, there would be no direct way to respond. Any discursive answer would require positing a single idea, which would then become a surrogate hero, establishing or revealing another ideology. There can, however, be a response in the form of a style, a way of simultaneously using and refusing the imperatives to generalization. Providing terms for that response becomes Modernism's second contribution. Stevens realized that the abstraction he desired on the level of content might be possible without the traps of ideology, if he could adapt to poetry the testimonial, self-referential dimension of art explored in painting. An art that enacts what it asserts can be said to finesse ideology, because its assertions do not depend on relating to the world through propositional, or even dramatic, chains of inference that have obvious dependencies on beliefs within a particular social order. Rather, one can imagine appealing to levels of experience abstract enough to engage fundamental, recurrent needs and desires. Poems compose "The speech of truth in its true solitude, / A nature that is created in what it says"(490).

By establishing that nature, abstraction, in effect, makes intelligence our "element"(491): the weather we dwell in, the material we build with, and the form of life within which we are most ourselves. Consequently, it becomes possible to imagine poetry as a literal site, wherein that intelligence discloses its most fundamental and transpersonal properties. These, in turn, can sustain a heroism of the familiar, based on the poetic agency that exemplifies how little we lose to history, despite the constant erosion of our metaphors:

> And the candor of them is the strong exhilaration
> Of what we feel from what we think, of thought
> Beating in the heart, as if blood newly came,

An elixir, an excitation, a pure power.
The poem, through candor, brings back a power again
That gives a candid kind to everything.

(382)

II

To read Stevens is to face the same obligation he posed himself as a poet: One must imagine "an abstraction blooded, as a man by thought" (385). It is thoughts that circulate; humans then respond to them by giving them a range of emotional colorings. By the 1940s Stevens realized that poetry must take on the qualities of an abstract art, if it was to render the fluidity and the significance of the feelings born of this interchange between thoughts and agents.[2] For by then he had come to see clearly that for him, at least, poetry had to afford a radical alternative to the sites where real blood continued to be shed. In the late 1930s Stevens thought he could address political situations directly, but his failures in that mode, and his sense of World War II as a horrible necessity beyond the control of even political agency, created a different sense of the poet's role in social life. At first Stevens responded to this crisis primarily by exploring through essays what he thought could be garnered by treating Modernist art as a cultural imperative. Gradually he managed to adapt that thinking to his poetry, finding a mode of abstraction that could sustain a principle of metaphor and a model of testimony enabling him to extend the resources made available by Modernist painting. And as he developed that style, he teased out remarkable parallels to the later philosophy of Ludwig Wittgenstein, the one other modern figure as richly engaged in the quest for a nobility based on the most elemental, familiar, and transpersonal features of language use.

To isolate the pressures Stevens was responding to in his thinking about abstraction, I shall begin by discussing the recent critical fashion that challenges the value of everything he was trying to do. Ironically, the best of these debunking essays, Gerald Bruns's "Stevens without Epistemology," dramatizes precisely the attitudes that Stevens saw himself as fighting in his culture. There is thus no better test of whether he continues to provide imaginative resistance to what may be severely reductive orientations of the contemporary mind. In the spirit of both Michel Foucault and Richard Rorty, Bruns asks us to imagine three successive states in modern Western culture, each with its own principles of reading:

> There was a time when questions about nature, reality or the
> world began to be reformulated as questions about the mind,

consciousness or imagination rather than as questions about God. This was the "epistemological turn". . . . Then there came a time when questions about mind . . . (and therefore questions about reality) began to be reformulated as questions about language. . . . This was the "linguistic turn. . . . Finally, there came a time when questions about language (and also therefore questions about mind and reality) began to be reformulated as questions about social practice, or about historically contingent, socially determined and ideologically bound conventions of human life. . . . This was the "hermeneutical turn." (25–5)

Most Stevens criticism, Bruns says, identifies with his engagement in questions posed by the "epistemological turn": "We know what it is to read [Stevens] when you no longer believe in God. What is it to read him when you no longer think that there is such a thing as the imagination?" (25). But the new dispensation makes it imperative to ask, "What happens when one reads Stevens's poetry from the standpoint made available by the hermeneutical turn in human thinking?" (25) Bruns's answer is that, seen in social terms, Stevens appears as one intent on "repressing . . . strange, unwanted, . . . or uncontrollable voices. . . . Much of Stevens' poetry is designed to keep Crispin's experience of otherness from happening." If one can hear no one's voice but his own, one "can then enter into a new world without any loss of self-possession" (27–8).[3]

This historical and social perspective leads Bruns to three basic claims. First, it is the appropriation of the voice of the "other" that allows Stevens a reactionary model of agency, based on the discourse of a continuous and coherent self, engaged in "a monologue or song of world making" that converts "public dialogue and social interchange into private meditation, and people into pure emotion" (28–9). Second, poetry, thus deprived of sympathy, dialogue, or threat, can do little but idealize itself in terms of a spectator's relation to the world. Human voices give way to a writerly pursuit of synthetic musical structures like Mallarmé's (34–5), so that the poet's work is necessarily aligned with "our Enlightenment norms of rationality – single-mindedness, univocity, agreement with reality (or the next best thing, freedom from illusion, the knowledge that our fictions are only fictions), reflexivity, clarity of perception, self-certainty, orderly progress, hierarchical construction, and so on" (33).[4] Finally, Bruns claims, in submitting to this conjunction of the writerly and the monological, Stevens opts for a European model of poetry as "a sealed-off utterance," sharply at odds with "much of American poetic practice." Pound, Williams, and Eliot all write major "heteroglot poems," responsive to the vernacular and willing to explore the kind of dialogue that "does not consist in an exchange of views or a contest between them," but rather, according to Emmanuel Levinas, enables "the uncovering of oneself, in sincerity, the breaking up of inwardness and the abandon of all shelter, exposure to traumas, vulnerability." To enter dialogue is to submit to "the loss of subjectivity," a "terrible loss for an idealist, since this means the loss of self, world, everything" 31–3). Because Stevens denies all of these values, Bruns insists that we should begin to read his poetry against its intentions and the epistemological framework that sanctions them. Then criticism can propose the contrasts necessary to show "that the phenomenon of the voice of the other always threatens this outlook, and that this is the truth that Stevens' poetry teaches us, particularly in the way in which otherness is obsessively aestheticized" (36).

Bruns is too good a reader to be simply wrong. But even if Stevens were as close to Mallarmé as Bruns claims, there would hardly be cause to impose on him loyalties to orderly progress, single-mindedness, or univocity. So one begins to read against Bruns's text, wondering what leads him to such emphases. Although no critic as sophisticated as Bruns would assert a belief in progress or historical necessity, it seems to me that his working assumptions bring him terribly close to the teleological models of "progress" dominant in the thirties. What other attitudes would sanction attributing such authority to the third of his conceptual changes? Clearly, in Bruns's eyes that stance has somehow exposed the limitations of the other two (without even the claim to empirical success that justified earlier claims to progress) and proposed a preferable alternative, which now dictates the questions we are to ask. More important, and more problematically, this historical movement allows Bruns to make visible what seem to be timeless normative standards. The hermeneutical turn reveals the traditional lyric as what Mikhail Bakhtin calls "a unitary, monologically sealed-off utterance" (31) and makes it possible to locate a distinctive American tradition, whose dialogical refusal to poeticize or synthesize somehow earns it hegemony over other poetic modes. In sum, Bruns is not content with a historicism that raises questions and reveals options; he wants it to carry an authority that, if it does not silence the other, in the name of otherness, works hard to allow it only the role of exemplary repression of precisely those timeless values that the historicism enables us to see.

There are obvious differences between Bruns's stance and the two historicisms that oppressed Stevens – the respective dreams of progress maintained by bourgeois empiricism and Marxism. But there is also enough similarity to help us see why Stevens resisted the dialogical, and why that resistance continues to matter in a therapeutic society, so full of talk about dialogue that it has little idea of what is involved in actually allowing others their otherness. When arguments about historical change, if not historical progress, dictate both what constitutes the "truth" of poetry and how the truth ought be assessed, one needs to worry about what authority sanctions overriding the poet's apparent intentions. And then Stevens's version of individualism begins to make a great deal of sense. For, from his perspective, "otherness" is not an abstraction, but something earned when a person establishes distinctive modes of expression and tries to take responsibility for them. Such emphases entail two fundamental alternatives to the kind of judgment Bruns exemplifies. First, one must honor a version of the structuralist principle of difference: that a person can hear one set of things only by negating another. Everyone, and every idea, represses or suppresses; that is the precondition of its having any distinctive identity. So the issue is not whether a poet represses, but why he or she thinks that in denying one way of constructing imaginative worlds they make available something more valuable, or at least better suited to what the person's individual temperament can do in a distinctive way. Yes, Stevens denies the play of social voices. But if we are to grant differences, we must begin by trying to understand why such denial might have seemed to him the best way to accomplish something that he thought was more important. And then this openness provides the second alternative, because it creates the possibility of treating the imagination as considerably more than an epistemological issue, and Stevens as considerably more than a poet concerned with showing that our fictions are only fictions. It is precisely as we track individual choices, individual selections of what is other, what desirable, that we see how imagination becomes the basic force in positing and delineating values. Imagination carries investments; projects the contrasts that establish preferences for certain particulars; and enables persons to display scenarios clarifying or giving reasons for those investments and their plausible consequences. Only by tracking such engagements in values can poetry hope to define the individual in a manner that is at once true to the intensity of subjective desires and capable of abstracting from them certain forms of desiring that have social implications – if solely for the reflective stance that takes poetry as a significant mode for articulating socially relevant states of mind.

Now, rather than imposing questions sanctioned by a historical imperative, we can begin with what I take to be the transhistorical starting point of all dialogue: a willingness to try to understand the priorities of the other. I think Stevens did not devote much attention to the actual voices of other people, in part because he did not hear them well, and in part because he saw no point to the collage method, which simply recombined the many strands of difference that comprise a social order. For him, what matters is not the fact, or even the shape, of otherness:

What matters is how the individual disposes himself or herself to make the imagination of one's own otherness significant. Simply including voices would merely add to the furniture of the world, without developing any useful ways to arrange or engage it. Even when those voices assert pressure, it does not suffice to note their differences and congratulate oneself on one's vulnerability to them. To understand those differences or to modify oneself in their presence, is not a matter of hearing or acknowledging: It is a matter of learning to think, in new or better ways. And to accomplish that learning, we may well have to maintain precisely the dialectical ideals suppressed (or perhaps repressed) by collage otherness. One must put the synthetic activity of mind first (as Whitman, Pound, and Eliot also did, in their fashions), asking how a first-person stance can take responsibility for the range of ideas the person holds. Intensity of spirit must replace generosity of disposition, forcing the mind to see how otherness challenges the continuities posited for the self and demands response from that self.

This is Stevens's version of how the lyric self both responds to and serves the "other," by the struggle to give the self a responsible place within the social world:

> We could not speak of our world as something to be distinguished from the poet's sense of it unless we objectified it and recognized it as having an existence apart from the projection of his personality. . . . He himself desires to make the distinctions part of the process of realizing himself. Once the discovery has been made, it becomes an instrument for the exploration of poetry. By means of it we can determine the relation of the poet to his subject. This would be simple if he wrote about his own world. We could compare it with ours. But what he writes about is his sense of our world. If he is a melancholy person he gives a melancholy sense of our world. (*Necessary Angel* 118–19)
>
> The measure of the poet is the measure of his sense of the world and of the extent to which it involves the sense of other people. (123–4)

Rather than reproducing the differences that comprise a social structure, the poet pursues the more circuitous, dialectical route of first making that otherness a way of realizing his own difference, his own claim to individual spiritual identity, then of positing that difference in such a way that it promises to yield others a sense of similar orientations in their imaginative investments. By being one constantly self-scrutinizing voice, the poet can become a determinate social force: Not content to acknowledge differences, this poet must seek individual powers capable of producing the kind of differences that can become significant factors in how others envision their lives.

III

The pressures that Bruns imposes on Stevens can help us to clarify what Stevens made out of the conditions that he faced in the midthirties. By that time, Stevens knew that he had to face the fact of other people. However intricate his harmonium, and however eloquent his projections of imaginative order, there remained the social realities that the Depression had made all too apparent, and there loomed, because of those facts, a war that was to prove an even more disturbing challenge to the terms that the imagination had available. How could one cast that idealistic faculty as something other than a way of escaping the real into easy nostalgias, on the one hand, and false hopes for revolution on the other? How could poetry sustain both a voice and an imaginative framework general enough, not merely to hear the conflicting interests, but also to locate a common source of pain, and perhaps solace, within those differences?[5]

Stevens's response was to set himself two irreducible demands: that poetry be able to live in change, and that, within change, it manage to project something capacious enough to maintain a sense of what humans could possibly imagine sharing, as they negotiate the oppressive differences that shape the social and the intellectual arena. By putting the problems this abstractly, he finessed or avoided any need to document those differences. But he also took on the probably more difficult task of having always to cast himself as "other," of having to work through the contradictions and the limitations that became manifest in that enterprise. The poet had to be abstract and had to be self-absorbed, if there were to be any alternative to simply accepting the reality of society as incommensurate conflicting voices. By acknowledging that necessity, indeed by making Ananke a fundamental character in his thinking, Stevens eventually elaborated intricate and sophisticated strategies for reconciling the claims of individualism with the effort to involve the lives of other people.

For our purposes, the process of self-correction and the turn to painterly models begins with the poems in Stevens's *Owl's Clover* (1936). We know, from his decision not to collect these poems, that they embarrassed Stevens – in part, I suspect, because they exposed the intensity of his quest. More important, here we find emerging the two key demands that painterly abstraction was eventually to reconcile: the need to testify to one's openness to change, and the need to cast change as an element within some larger imaginative whole.[6] As those demands emerge, so also do the contradictions involved in reconciling them, and the difficulties of stating a voice that can convincingly mediate between the subject and the society.

"Mr. Burnshaw and the Statue" most clearly takes stock of the poet's situation. The poet dwells in a society torn between the pressure of empiricist definitions of the real, which empty the past by turning its conditions of belief into dead metaphors, and a Marxist program, which promises to make that sense of the real the basis for projecting a proletarian revolution. To Stevens, the cure was worse than the disease, since it sought power for persons and beliefs that neither feel the loss nor see any need to attempt to compensate for it. Thus the ideals of memory and monumentality, once fundamental to the statue, now become ciphers that stand as analogs to his own sense of impotence:

> The thing is dead . . . Everything is dead
> Except the future. Always everything
> That is dead except what ought to be.
> All things destroy themselves or are destroyed.
> . . . .
> The statue seems a thing from Schwarz's, a thing
> Of the dank imagination, much below
> Our crusted outlines hot and huge with fact.
> Ugly as an idea, not beautiful
> As sequels without thought
> . . . .
> . . . The stones
> That will replace it shall be carved, "*The Mass Appoints*
> *These Marbles Of Itself To Be*
> *Itself.* No more than that, no subterfuge,
> No memorable muffing, bare and blunt.
> (*Opus Posthumus* 46–8)

Ever the Romantic at heart, Stevens still dreamed of making poetry a vehicle of reconciliation, in this case by showing how each position proposes a false absolute: false as a claim on the world and, more important, false by the very fact of claiming absolutes, when "the world in which they live" is one of constant change, constantly composing as well as decomposing. Consequently, as the poem sets itself to resist both positions, it engenders an alternative sense of the political. The mode of consciousness that it testifies to is one that need not posit any absolute for itself, demonstrating instead that "it is only enough / to live incessantly in change." Such faith will suffice to enable meditative stances capable of the kind of ecstasy that Stevens proposes at the poem's conclusion:

Conceive that marble men
Serenely selves, transfigured by the selves
From which they came, make real the attitudes
Appointed for them and that the pediment
Bears words that are the speech of marble men.
In the glassy sound of your voices, the porcelain cries . . .
Speak . . . until
The porcelain bell-borrowings become
Implicit clarities in the way you cry
and are your feelings changed to sound, without
A change, until the waterish ditherings turn
To the tense, the maudlin, the true meridian
That is yourselves, when, at last, you are yourselves . . .
No longer of air but of the breathing earth,
Impassioned seducers and seduced, the pale
Pitched into swelling bodies, upward, drift
In a storm blown into glittering shapes, and flames
Wind-beaten into freshest, brightest fire.

(Opus Posthumus 52)

The aim was to have this eloquence extend the personal stance of "Sunday Morning" into something approximating a public mythology. Precisely because no symbol could any longer represent a stable myth, poetry had to make its own processes carry the cultivating force once given to the statue: By demonstrating what is possible to a mind that can dispose itself to what change affords, the poet set a counterforce against those willing to reduce the imagination to the bare and blunt identity claims necessary for a vision of a historically determined class revolution. The poet's politics consisted in aligning the demands for personal identity to the erotic responsiveness of an earth fertile with change. But two interrelated questions immediately arose: Can change itself suffice as a principle of value? And, can a poetic rhetoric based on fairly stable cultural scenarios be modified to address these new conditions? For, if change did suffice, there would not have been this somewhat desperate dallying with the most indulgent of Romantic ecstatic styles, which Stevens, in a letter, called "short hymns of reconciliation" (*Letters* 367). The hymn and the "apostrophe" (367) restored, on the level of form, the nostalgia that Stevens tried to overcome on the level of content. Now, though, one could even argue that the situation was worse, both because the "lack" was repressed and because the effort suggested needs that no specific intensity would satisfy, however fiery, without some kind of intellectual supplement. Yet now the difficulty of such supplements was all too evident: The project of dispelling the past ended up trapping itself in a language bound to the most conventional of images and the most clichéd of adjectives. The fluid eloquence that enabled the poet to have this banal language seem ecstatic in its oratorical grandeur, also revealed itself as an emblem of a facility that made it quite difficult to align oneself with the reality of change.

One measure of Stevens's greatness is the fact that he did not need other people to point out his problems. The letters that he wrote in 1940 to Hi Simons cast the very next poem in *Owl's Clover* as an effort to right the balance, by taking responsibility for the reach of that rhetoric. The project of "The Green Continent" is to posit another kind of fertility, not within change, but in the mind's capacity to win from that change a sense of possible underlying universals, which leave traces in the desire expressed in the poet's rhetoric. Stevens writes to Simons,

> One way of explaining this poem is to say that it concerns the difficulty of imposing the imagination on those that do not share it. . . . It is assumed that the South has its own consciousness, its own idea of God, its own imagination (I). The consciousness, etc. of the West is delineated (II); the difference between the two is disclosed (III), with some rather crude illustrations (IV); the apparent impossibility of overcoming the difference is stated (V). Yet the poem concludes with what is its point, that, if ideas of God are in conflict, the idea of pure poetry: imagination extended beyond local consciousness, may be an idea to be held in common by South, West, North and East. It would be a beginning to recognize Ananke, who, now more than ever, is the world's starless crown. (*Letters* 370)

On this basis, Stevens can imagine the entire sequence ultimately restoring meaning to the statue – not for any person the statue represents, but rather for the figure of general human powers it becomes, as "something pure and something lofty" that looms "above all agitation and change . . . a dominant, a metropolitan of mind" (372). This is the stuff on which his myth of the hero was to be forged.

However, such idealism remains haunted by two recurrent doubts.[7] The dream of heroism may be the way that we unmake what satisfactions the world affords. Positing ourselves as destined to judge the world, we may condemn ourselves to experience as "lack" what we envision as necessary values. Or, such projection may itself be a sign of personal failure, a sign of the poet's own inability to take responsibility for the dreams he proposes. This idealizing of an abstract figure may be little more than a way of creating an escape from politics, rather than an alternative to it. What else would explain the fact that whenever Stevens's poetry, during these years, tried to move from that abstract heroism to envisioning particular acts based on his ideals, the lines grew slack, and the imagination approximated the mawkishness most egregiously displayed in the coda to "Notes toward a Supreme Fiction"? As in Yeats, the very model of recommendation that the poet elaborated threatened to expose his failures.

IV

One way to avoid imputing such flaws to the self is to deny that the desire for heroism entails any kind of dialectic. For, in that case, even one's mistakes become elements within a constantly oscillating play of oppositions, bound to an iron rule of failure and recuperation. In another letter to Simons, Stevens writes,

> When I was a boy I used to think that things progressed by contrasts, that there was a law of contrasts. But this was building the world out of blocks. Afterwards I came to think of the energizing that comes from mere interplay, interaction. Thus, the various faculties of the mind co-exist and interact, and there is as much delight in this mere co-existence as man and woman find in each other's company. . . . Cross reflections, modifications, counter-balances, complements, giving and taking are illimitable. They make things inter-dependent and their interdependence sustains them and gives them pleasure. (*Letters* 368)[8]

Such beliefs restore a sophisticated hedonism and save the hero as an aesthetic ideal. But this is a difficult position to be content with, if only because one wants the oppositions continually sharpened, the play of faculties increasingly more intense. In Stevens's case, there was also the more pressing demand to cast poetry as replacing theology by providing, as religion once had, the deep commitments that give direction to lives and social roles to writers. So Stevens had to complement this contrarian position with the hope that some dialectic was possible. At the least, the effort to intensify one's sense of those contraries might make it possible to understand how the very process of focusing on change yields certain figures of desire that secure a common sense of humanity.

It was this hope, I think, that led Stevens to the discursive projects that occupied him through much of the 1940s. If he was to be a philosophical poet, able to address society on levels deeper than political rhetorics allowed, he had to understand what resources the newest principles in the arts made available for him. The artists faced the same problems of reconciling the particularity of the composing intelligence in time with some transpersonal dimensions brought into focus by that action. So, if he could posit a common project, he might also find ways of recasting his own abstractness so that it would take on the capacity to construct painterly sites, and even to characterize its constructive energies as sustaining certain claims to nobility. Painting afforded the clearest paradigm for self-reflexive, testimonial art, but once the model existed the poet might turn out to be the artist who had the richest opportunity to fulfill the model, because only language could comment upon precisely what the compositional action was doing.[9] The abstract painters all had to write essays on their own work in order to indicate what forces were involved, but only the poet could make that reasoning part of what the poem proposed for the audience's own self-reflexive experience.

The one thing his studies made overwhelmingly evident was that all of the arts seemed to confront the same antagonist – which he called the "pressure of reality," a term that I have borrowed to characterize the overall situation that this book elaborates. At stake now was whether he could recognize those links and find in what the artists had set against those pressures a model of abstraction defining, and even dignifying, poetry's best path of resistance. The pressures can, by this point in our study, be put in highly schematic form. Modernism, we have seen, sets itself in a social framework characterized by the gradual domination of third-person over first-person terms for understanding the psyche and conceiving the nature of social relations. Therefore the artist's role was to invent principles that could sustain the force of those first-person positions while evading those specific content claims from the past, now rightly consigned to the dump. The "other," it turned out, resided intimately within the self.

As the imagination tried to locate first-person terms for asserting its values, its claims seemed continually subject to demystifications that threatened to reduce them to third-person epiphenomena, caused by historical forces. But the imagination retained one crucial resource that complicated the simple melodramatic vision of fictions continually demystified by lucid analysis: The imagination could recognize itself also at work in the intensity with which people posit and pursue the dream of lucidity. It might be possible, then, for the lyric imagination to assume a version of the third-person position occupied by the spirit of demystification. If a process of decreation stemmed from first-person desires, the poet could show that it produced structures sufficiently impersonal and abstract to make the *I*'s way of living in change an exemplary alternative to a historicism bound to a logic of beginnings and endings. And on that basis, it might be possible to articulate modes of desire that people from different sociocultural contexts, even from different metaphoric systems, could share – not in their abstract claims to a common source, but in their particular way of being first-person desires. Perhaps the poet could use the poem's constitutive process to distinguish enduring human powers from the specific ideologies that historical agents keep projecting to account for those powers.

Stevens's first and most general discursive effort to come to terms with these problems and possibilities was his essay "The Noble Rider and the Sound of Words" (1942). Its first three parts contextualize and elaborate a definition of the "pressure of reality" as "the pressure of an external event or events on the consciousness to the exclusion of any power of contemplation" (*Necessary Angel* 20). Part 4 inaugurates the counterpressure through a brilliant, self-reflexive act of the imagination, turning to its own idealizing capacities: "Suppose we try, now, to construct the figure of a poet, a possible poet" (23). In the poet's construction of his own functions, you will know him and begin to see how such abstractions can reach levels not subsumable under specific historical positivities.

For our purposes, the argument can be cast in terms of four principles that Stevens attributes to the powers of abstraction in poetry.[10] First, abstraction is a means for poetry to make disclosures about the world, while setting itself against the pursuit of particular propositions that can be judged for their descriptive truth. Second, abstraction is a contrary of "truth," because it has force as a *process,* rather than as a statement. Indeed, it can resist the pressure of reality precisely because it can be opposed to all reification. Third, this process has claims both to be and to account for reality, because the process per se can be seen as occupying a particular site: that of the poem, where we, in effect, are confronted with a display of our own powers. This site allows a way of understanding processes that puts before us a sense of the self as having become impersonal, or transpersonal, and rendered on a level where reification and its resulting ideological forms can be evaded. The fundamental means for such evasion is the fact that the life lived in the scene is one in which any attentive reader can participate. Finally, these exercises in abstraction have the important consequence of enabling us to display to ourselves human powers, and human relations to an environment, with an intensity that warrants our claiming a nobility for ourselves without an attendant rhetoric of alienation. In an abstract art, actions can take the form of self-explanatory performances, enabling the writing to overcome the tendency of the culture's more specific and concrete forms of self-representation to produce more parody than persuasion. For what matters is not the image borrowed from a cultural mythology, but the enactment of something in our lives and our metaphors deeply enough embedded to take form despite the demise of particular beliefs. Thus, even lovers of truth can envision "enclosures of hypotheses" (*Collected Poems* 516) built on the ruins of their beloved propositions, as the work isolates forms of desire from the contingencies that determine its material shapes.[11]

V

Stevens's best commentary on the obligations incurred by these ideals consists in his effort to distinguish significant from insignificant abstract painting: "It is easy to like Klee and Kandinsky. What is difficult is to like the many minor figures who do not communicate any theory that validates what they do and, in consequence, impress one as being without validity" (*Letters* 762). The display that has validity is one that can carry its own theoretical force, that can carry what Stevens called, in writing on Marcel Gromaire, the drama of "the human spirit seeking its own architecture, its own '*mesure*' that will enable it to be in harmony with the world" ("Marcel Gromaire," in *Opus Posthumus* 291).[12] In seeking this architecture, the work of art literally makes its theorizing an enclosure, where it becomes possible to replace truth values with the life that the work creates within the scene. Theory and theorizing, the space of elemental spiritual relations and the constant effort to see how they align to shifting dynamic balances, play the roles of dancer and dance, each living the other's life and dying the other's death. Therefore, the domain that painting opens becomes, for poetry, a theater in which the process of self-reflection sets about making visible a fully human spiritual architecture:

> The theory of poetry, that is to say the total of the theories of poetry, often seems to become in time a mystical theology or, more simply, a mystique. . . . The reason is the same reason why the pictures in a museum of modern art often seem to become in time a mystical aesthetic, a prodigious search of appearance, as if to find a way of saying and of establishing that all things, whether below or above appearance, are one, and it is only through reality, in which they are reflected or, it may be, joined together, that we can reach them. Under such stress, reality changes from substance to subtlety. . . . Contending that this [i.e., quotations on the real from Cézanne and from Klee] sounds a bit like sacerdotal jargon, that is not too much to allow to those that have helped to create a new reality, a modern reality, since what has been created is nothing less.
>
> This reality is, also, the momentous world of poetry. . . .
>
> Modern reality is a reality of decreation in which our revelations are not the revelations of belief, but the precious portents

of our own powers. The greatest truth that we could hope to discover . . . is that man's truth is the final resolution of everything. (*Necessary Angel* 173–7)

Prose can do no more. Indeed, it has already done too much, by giving us terms such as "decreation" and slogans such as "man's truth," which either lead us back to irony or make us wonder if Stevens's thought was so banal that he ought not be allowed to lead us at all. But it does set the agenda. The poet must adapt two of those painterly strategies to his own work, each as much a challenge as it is a direct permission. Whereas painters could dream of defining sites that establish what Stevens's friend Walter Pach, in his *Masters of Modern Painting,* described as "principles which are invariable for all men,"[13] simply by manipulating the building blocks of their medium, poets had to tease out from their medium the very desires that had motivated the theoretical inquiry in the first place. Unable to locate self-sufficient dynamic relations, poets had to base their abstraction on the forces they saw eager to shape those relations. Desire is the poet's element, the principle whose life demands that the poet refuse the satisfaction of representational images in favor of theoretical self-reflection. Having located the writerly parallel to the painter's universal relations, the poet had the obligation of tracking the ways in which those desires took form in, and gave form to, the life in change opened by constantly exerting a counterpressure on appearances. This is the presentational and testimonial dimension in which the abstract forces had to reveal their significance within familiar life. And this is where poets could best differentiate their powers from those exemplified in Modernist painting. Because the poet not only makes her balances self-reflexive, but tests the possible languages for attributing significance to the virtual lives it implicates, the poem becomes testimony both for the shape of a reflective experience and for the language that the agent might be willing to use to represent it. How one experiences the poem provides both source and proof of poetry's own ways of carrying the mystical: in terms of how it positions us in relation to the elements of the natural world, and in terms of the bonds it creates as readers impute desires to others who can engage the same verbal structure. Concrete poems test the capacity of the theory of poetry to become the theory of life.

VI

Among the many ways in which poetry carries that theoretical burden, I want to concentrate on the three that I think most closely connected to Stevens's concerns for painterly abstractions. First I shall try to show how "The Pastor Caballero" extends the Cubist-inspired work we studied in Chapter 7. There we concentrated on how Stevens elaborated the relation between observation and will, so that his visual poems came to define verbal equivalents for the activities by which the mind expands what the senses present. Now I shall focus on his engaging the more challenging aspects of Cubism that tried to provide, in portraiture, direct emblems for the visions of human agency made possible by Cubism's "prodigious search of appearances." "The Pastor Caballero," in its echoes of that portraiture, posits itself the task of rendering poetry's capacity to establish its own parallel claims to define an ethos. I shall go on to elaborate Stevens's specific ways of using virtual processes to provide testimony for that ethos within an essentially discursive style. Finally, I shall argue that those testimonial processes allow Stevens a range of themes deserving to be taken seriously as a mode of philosophical reflection.

"The Pastor Caballero" is one of those odd, apparently flat, Stevens poems that at certain moments suddenly come to imaginative life. Yet for him this poem plays a crucial role in the entire *Collected Poems,* because it serves as the transition between *Transports to Summer* and *Notes toward a Supreme Fiction,* primarily by dramatizing how abstraction affects our sense of the concrete image. We begin with a sense of form asked to suggest nobility. Then the poem tries to make the process of naming transcend what the painterly hand can compose:

> The importance of its hat to a form becomes
> More definite. The sweeping brim of the hat
> Makes of the form Most Merciful Capitan,
>
> If the observer says so: grandiloquent
> Locution of a hand in a rhapsody.
> Its line moves quickly with the genius
>
> Of its improvisation until, at length,
> It enfolds the head in a vital ambiance,
> A vital, linear ambiance. The flare
>
> In the sweeping brim becomes the origin
> Of a human evocation, so disclosed
> That, nameless, it creates an affectionate name,
>
> Derived from adjectives of deepest mine.
> The actual form bears outwardly this grace,
> An image of the mind, an inward mate.
>
> Tall and unfretted, a figure meant to bear
> Its poisoned laurels in this poisoned wood,
> High in the height that is our total height.

The formidable helmet is nothing now.
These two go well together, the sinuous brim
And the green flauntings of the hours of peace.

(379)

I do not know any specific painting to which this poem alludes. I suspect, in fact, that anything more than a suggestion of resemblance would weaken the assertion of power that Stevens presents. For the important thing is not how poems, or paintings, refer to sources, but what they lead us to think and feel about ourselves. Notice how the poem's opening even refuses all questions of scene and setting, in order to emphasize questions of how artifacts produce significance. It is not names that demand attention, but acts and means of naming, primarily because only on that level can one hope to resist the tendency of names to become contaminated rhetorical gestures. This poem about heroism and nobility testifies to what it asserts, by foregrounding abstraction's power to generate those values without relying on myth or dogma. Names are derived from direct projections of human desire. The artist's acts display principles and passions that express the constant source of our names and provide values for their referents.

Such abstract situating puts a direct burden on the presentational level of the poem as it lives in change. It is here that the poetic line must earn for poetry the right to compare itself to painting, by dramatizing poetry's capacity as a portent of powers, as if the real portrait here had to be a clarification of the heroic properties that the poetry can display. Stevens's first vehicle for this portrait is his control of the sentence unit, the linguistic correlate of a "hand in rhapsody." As the poem explores its capacity to produce the desired form, its sentence units become increasingly complicated. After all, they must prepare for the heroic rhetoric of the sixth stanza – a task brilliantly carried off by having the fourth, pivotal stanza be the only one to lack a completed sentence. The effect is of a "vital linear ambiance" overflowing the verse boundaries. Thus, at the poem's dramatic climax, the poet must name the origin of art's names by an act that must be suspended, must resist closure, because the names involved derive, not from any resting place in reference, but rather from what is itself suspended within the filigree of language.

Foregrounded syntactic control is supplemented by semantic and structural effects. The poem consists of two segments: an initial description of the hat as comprising an expressive artistic gesture; and the synthetic, self-reflexive commentary of the last two sentences. These final sentences, in effect, try to make explicit the import of the poem. But they do so less as statement than as a literal embodiment of the space of mind that reflection makes as one comes to recognize that the portrait embodies "adjectives of deepest mine" (and mind). Normally, it would take allegory to give shadowy forms to these purported human potentials. Here, the allegory is inseparable from the movement of the lines: The object rendered defines what the rendering accomplishes. We see the outward image become "inward mate," and next we watch that equation sustain a somewhat overblown rhetoric, because of the complex reference of the "figure" metaphor. The hero who can bear heroic names in the "poisoned wood" of history gains his power from his situation, from the fact that he exists as a figure uniting the artist's construct, the Pastor's image, and the viewer-reader's sense of contemplating in the external expression an image of her own inner life.

This triumphant assertion, with all its intelligence, nonetheless seems too shrill, too dogmatic, too much a matter of attributing traits to external rather than internal images. This is why Stevens needs a final stanza, where a retrospective power earns the right to say whose woods these are, and what claims they license. Instead of gestures outward, all of the assertions are indexical and self-referential.[14] The helmet is "nothing now," both because it no longer signifies heroism and because the "now" has been so thickened by thought that it requires no specific object or name. Art creates a site where loss can be transformed into triumphant specificity. And now the flamboyant "flauntings" begin to make sense as a celebration of the power to name. Once the painting becomes our hero, what more appropriate gesture than to turn back on the creation and to say that it is good – so good that "these two," "brim" and "flauntings," can completely take over what had been a representational project. In this version of "collecting towards a greenest cone," even the oldest, most conventional of allegorical equations, that of green with peace, takes on precise, justified meanings in the literal testimony of the work. A green that can flaunt itself composes the very peace it asserts.

Flauntings in themselves, however, merely call attention to powers; they do not explain or contextualize them. For those tasks Stevens poses himself a very different testimonial process. Having demonstrated what the hero can assert, he must shift to the question of the degree of understanding that the poet can bring to these assertions. The figure of the hero, won by decreating figural representations of "heroism," must now merge with the figure of the philosopher, the one figure purely identifiable in terms of the reflective processes that language disposes. Rather than recompose the hero's flaunting, the powers asserted by "The Pastor Cabellero" must undergo the discipline of isolating the force that does the flaunting from the image that it seeks. Only then is the hero abstract enough to begin to be plausibly concrete.

This idea emerged for Stevens in the passage from "Examination of the Hero in a Time of War" that first defined the path for reconciling change and abstraction:

> It is not an image. It is a feeling.
> There is no image of the hero.
> There is a feeling as definition.
> How could there be an image, an outline,
> A design, a marble soiled by pigeons?
> The hero is a feeling, a man seen
> As if the eye was an emotion,
> As if in seeing we saw our feeling
> In the object seen and saved that mystic
> Against the sight, the penetrating
> Pure eye. Instead of allegory,
> We have and are the man, capable
> Of his brave quickenings, the human
> Accelerations that seem inhuman.
>
> (278–9)

The challenge here, common to all abstract art, is the danger of losing the man to the allegory. In rejecting the dramatic rendering of individuals, the artist risks retaining only codified signs, bound to fixed conceptual structures. Then as Paul De Man ceaselessly delighted in showing, the work's presentation undoes in time what allegory tries to compose in timeless space. But it may be possible to make what unfolds in time itself carry the allegorical weight. As decreative energy turns against standard ideals of the hero, it comes to seem capable of opening a new, modern site, where what matters is glimpsed mainly through the effort to get clear of excess ideological baggage, while still taking the old journeys. Decreation so positions the imagination that it can discard soiled metaphors, while locating actual sources for the metaphors in the literal testimony provided by the poem's specific course of reflections, so that the ideal of heroism depends on the portents of our powers that the poem itself generates. Therefore, by submitting the ideal of the hero to the ravages of time and change, the poet makes the poem's resistance to names its vehicle for participating in those "brave quickenings" leading to the sublime threshold where the collapse of images lets human feelings verge on elemental inhuman powers.

In "The Pastor Caballero" those brave quickenings are concentrated in a syntactic process of changing substance into subtlety. Simple introductory statements gradually expand into complex, self-referring acts, so that the blend of syntax and intricate aural play actually composes feeling, without the distortion of images. Through these quickenings, the stage is set for a climactic moment entirely free of images. The heroic becomes simply the capacity to absorb what the image carries, in a plain statement aware of what the sequence of engaged feelings has produced.

The climactic moment of the "it must be abstract" section, in *Notes toward a Supreme Fiction,* makes articulate the ways in which such flauntings define powers capable of subsuming allegory back into the man:

> The major abstraction is the idea of man
> And major man is its exponent, abler
> In the abstract than in his singular,
> More fecund as principle than particle. . . .
> In being more than an exception, part
>
> Through an heroic part of the commonal. . .
>
> It is of him, ephebe, to make, to confect
> The final elegance, not to console
> Nor sanctify, but plainly to propound.
>
> (388–9)

Conceiving "major man" as "exponent" serves itself as a remarkable exponent for the ways in which time can become a presentational factor in reading. An exponent is an interpreter or an interpretive sign, but the term's mathematical overtones cast interpreting as a form of power. Because exponents magnify by repeating the original, magnified or intensified by a certain factor, Stevens offers a figure for the kind of site where it makes sense to speak of a heroism not bound to any specific image. The heroism consists simply in who we become as exponents, that is, as agents increasingly aware of what happens as they speak. In establishing such states, poetic speech becomes part of the "commonal" – part of the theater that replaces an old representational stage and allows the artist to act out feelings that an audience grasps, "as of two emotions becoming one" (240). This abstract scope of exponential activity so incorporates an artificial elegance into the processes of syntax that the poem can plainly propound the ideas the language acts out. Concrete testimony need not depend on dramatic illusions, or on disguised thematics, or on covert intentions framing a narrative (all the sources of allegory), because the language as enacted can take responsibility for what it asserts. The quickening of language carries the burden otherwise put on metaphoric indirectness, and it becomes possible to locate the intensity of poetry in the expressive work of its plain propoundings.

VII

We have now seen why it must be abstract, and we have traced the basic ways in which Stevens elaborated a linguistic mode for giving the poet's activity the same testimonial qualities that the objectified agency takes on in Modernist painting. But we have yet to work out how or why these stylistic effects have any claim to suffice as a theory of life. And although we have observed Stevens flaunting the power to make his poems testify to the values he asserts, we have yet to consider how he elaborates what is at stake in those demonstrations or derives from them a set of imaginative consequences. We have a hero, but we have yet to understand why that figure is familiar or useful.

Perhaps the best way to address these lacks is to begin with a passage that is so ambitious in asserting those consequences that it threatens to force the poet back to the self-mocking devices of *Harmonium:*

> A scholar, in his Segmenta, left a note,
> As follows, "The Ruler of Reality,
> If more unreal than New Haven, is not
>
> A real ruler, but rules what is unreal.
> In addition, there were draftings of him, thus:
> He is the consort of the Queen of Fact.
>
> . . . He is the theorist of life, not death,
> The total excellence of its total book. . . .
>
> "This man abolishes by being himself
> That which is not ourselves: the regalia
> The attributions, the plume and helmet-ho."
>
> Again, "He has thought it out, he thinks it out,
> As he has been and is and, with the Queen
> Of Fact, lies at his ease beside the sea."
> . . . .
>
> If it should be true that reality exists
> In the mind . . .
> . . . .
> . . . , it follows that
> Real and Unreal are two in one: New Haven
> Before and after one arrives or, say,
>
> Bergamo on a postcard, Rome after dark
> Sweden described . . .

This endlessly elaborating poem
Displays the theory of poetry,
As the life of poetry. A more severe,
More harassing master would extemporize
Subtler, more urgent proof that the theory
Of poetry is the theory of life

As it is, in the intricate evasions of as,
In things seen and unseen, created from nothingness,
The heavens, the hells, the worlds, the longed-for-lands.

(485–6)

At this climax of "An Ordinary Evening in New Haven," Stevens calls attention to two themes that were to prove especially significant for demonstrating how the life of poetry contributes to the theory of life. At one pole, his insistence on the prodigious search of appearance yields a concrete ontology of imagination. Having searched for essential forces of consciousness, he now locates the dynamic force of abstraction in this continual interplay of real and unreal, the world viewed and the world constantly constructed for desire. Then, at the other pole, the need to live in change now takes on a substantial practical role in the poet's capacity to reflect on, and focus for, his audience the "intricate evasions of as." That simple operator, "as," turns out to carry within its philosophical grammar a remarkable complex field of operations, which intricately folds description into valuation and makes each description something that the audience can participate in. Because "I have not but I am and as I am, I am" (405), the "as" puts the relation between real and unreal at the core of all questions of identity and identification. The "I am" is not a matter of locating identity in a stable substance about which descriptions can be posited. Rather, it is relational or aspectual – a matter of the intensity with which a reflective consciousness becomes the exponent for a situation, and thus takes on the activity of testifying for what a given stance can make of experience. The "as" offers a fundamental feature of the medium of language, which one can isolate in the same way that painters isolate color and form – in this case, to define the powers that theorizing makes visible for life. In order to measure how rich a philosophical poetry this orientation creates, I shall compare Stevens to Ludwig Wittgenstein, that other great interpreter of the "as," especially with regard to the ways in which both thinkers provide a dynamic model of reading, where it becomes plausible to continue to speak of such hopelessly unhermeneutical terms as the "dream of nobility." My ultimate ambition in doing that is to make plausible and useful a critical enterprise that Harry Berger called (in responding to a paper of mine at a conference), with the idealized disdain for ideals that only a deconstructive historicist can muster, "as-kissing raised to the level of a humanistic ideal."

It behooves us to know the "as" we intend to kiss. And the best way to do that is to watch Stevens at work as he teased out its various ramifications earlier in the poem:

> The poem is the cry of its occasion,
> Part of the res itself and not about it.
> The poet speaks the poem as it is,
>
> Not as it was: part of the reverberations
> Of a windy night as it is, when the marble statues
> Are like newspapers blown by the wind. He speaks
>
> By sight and insight as they are.
>
> (473)

Defining the "as" is inseparable from working out the passage's governing contrasts between "as it is" and "as it was," and between being "part of the occasion" and being only "about it," with the "it" crucially ambiguous until the force of the "as" is determined. For, once again, identity depends not on substance, but on relationships. The simplest relationship sustained by the "as" is temporal. When its sustaining equations fail, the mind moves from participation in the present to a sense of its separation from events that then are freed to enter the past, to become merely events that language sets apart as its object. Those differences, however, also obviously entail fundamental modal relationships. What the "it" is depends on what the "as" allows. If the poem is only about the "res," the "it" is a simple record of events, things as they were. But if the "as" can align the cry with the res, then poem and event are one – each the referent of the "it," and each completing the other, so that language does not dissolve into idle talk, but lives in the changes it modulates. Thus the very possibility of there being a vital present, of the mind's adjusting to what the "it" can be, depends upon the speaker's capacity to suspend any demands not congruent with the particular alignments that the "as" can sustain.

The rest of the passage elaborates what emerges when the "as" becomes part of the res itself. Then the temporal and modal equations provide the basis for the proliferation of reverberations: What begins as adjustment to the present becomes the vehicle for extending perceptions into the dynamics of investment that requires a complete theory of metaphor. Being part of the res involves becoming part of the reverberations that allow the windy night to contain the desires projected into it. Through this second "as it is," "real and unreal" become consorts: The wind speaks, the marble statues take on the motion of the newspapers, and the "it" comes to refer to this entire field of reverberations that now comprise the occasion.

As we work out these reverberations, we put ourselves in the one position possible where we can entirely appreciate the modal force of the poem's concluding "as." We realize that the primary purpose of the poem has been to provide a definition of sight and insight – not as reified entities, requiring a faculty psychology, but as forces that we identify in terms of the set of equations that the poem establishes. We can move to mental terms, as they are, because we have been observing the difference they make in the occasion. As the occasion expands, we attribute this to a composing force that reveals its own properties as part of its elaborating the scene. This means that the copula can achieve the same kind of ambiguous density as the pronoun "it." The copulative verb is poised between the "is" of identity – let this define sight and insight – and the "is" attributing a distinctive form of existence: Sight and insight have at least this physical reality. As we interpret these relations, moreover, we realize that they all depend completely on the temporal and modal forces of "as" that equate sight and insight with the virtual activity of the audience as it brings sight and insight to bear on this occasion. The ultimate site of metaphor is our aspect-conferring activity, as it contours itself to the testimonial act, so that sight and insight simultaneously take on an irreducible identity within the constant process of adjustment that gives them their life and becomes inseparable from it.

There is no better linguistic equivalent for the modes of virtuality that abstraction affords Modernist painting. Everything about the "as" depends on agents considering who they become and what tacit resources they call upon as they use the term. And everything within those reflections shows how easy it is to overstate the demands of history, since the range of equivalences that the term mediates constantly sets the metaphoric present against the definitive "as it was" or the authoritarian "as it must be." In order to see the "as" as it is, we need to grant it three fundamental functions, all geared to allowing language to serve as the cry of the occasion and to make that cry something that an audience can take as its own.

First, the "as" affords complex temporal and spatial equivalences. The "as" modulates substance into aspect, and thus it is responsible for manipulating the complex ambiguities central to the very idea of an occasion. Second, the "as" also has a range of modal functions that call attention to what is responsible for the various qualities that we bring to the occasion. In this respect, the "as" is the quintessential grammatical index for metaphor, as it sets in motion chains of reverberations. Through the proliferation of aspects, the spirit is allowed mobility like Baudelaire's. Yet there is no need to become self-conscious about the rhetorical impositions that this mobility fosters, because the terms of spirit are inseparable from ways in which the world can in fact appear. The "as" is the instrument of feelings enabling the unreal to consort with the Queen of Fact: for example, in the fact that sensibility links the statue with the movements of the wind, or in the deep yet subtle differences that mark one's sense of "New Haven / Before or after one arrives." Then a third function of the "as" extends that mobility to the domain where we try on different identifications, made possible by the play of metaphor. We use the "as" not only to proliferate resemblances, but also to make attributions about sight and insight as they are defined by those resemblances. We can say, not only that I see this diagram as a duck or as a rabbit, but also that I understand the whole figure as a design that may create the appearance of duck or rabbit, depending on which line of equivalences the eye develops. This last trait is crucial, because it allows one to reconcile the pluralism necessary for Modernist views of reality with the Modernist desire to locate modes of consciousness not trapped in their particular historical moment. The "as" can position the poet beyond the differences that perspectivism insists upon, yet it allows her to show how the various attitudes might be available to everyone, "a visibility of thought, / in which hundreds of eyes, in one mind, see at once" (488). For the one mind can see as each of those eyes might see, while still making its reflections on that sight available to all.

I have considered each of these functions of "as" only with respect to the content they organize. We must realize, however, that all three functions also operate in terms of the site that the work of art carves for itself and in terms of the modes of sight and insight that it composes for its audience. The temporal, modal, and self-reflexive synthetic forces each qualifies the specific testimony of the rendering. The "as" literally produces resemblances, affords shifts in the level of discourse, and allows us to entertain provisional sympathies with a variety of attitudes. We see our seeing of x as y. Within such self-consciousness, the abstract "as" refers directly to the way poetry crosses life, because it names the state of equivalence basic to all acts of valuing. In order to appreciate what this involves, we need only think of how completely reading can serve as a paradigmatic form for such valuing: In the equivalences that reading provides, we take on other identities and observe ourselves as we so dispose our wills. Poems establish possibilities of relation that readers take on as portents of their own possible powers, as they read. Then, as one reflects on that reading, one is tempted to make it an emblem for that ontological play of real and unreal consorting in the reality of the event (see 476). Reading acts out situations in which there are no independent realities or logical simples, nothing one can separate from the activity of constituting a world as we construe its signs. Thus there are not worlds and interpretations, but worlds as interpreted in a variety of ways, each perhaps best articulated, not by descriptions, but by making manifest the energies involved.

This Stevensian hero still accepts the ideology of *Owl's Clover,* but now he renders that ideology so that it takes on a great deal more resonance, in part simply because the powers it cultivates are positioned as so familiar to our quotidian experience. What he has wrought becomes clear only if we imagine stepping back from the particular equivalences we have been tracing, in order to consider how our lives as a whole appear in relation to our capacity to wield the intricacies of "as." Such reflections lead us to what, for Stevens, is the "supreme fiction," the supreme consort of fact in its real unreality. Its first incarnation takes place for the mountain Chocorua, in "Chocorua to Its Neighbor," as it reflects on its place within a force capable of apprehending the physical world not simply as facts but as values:

> Cloud-casual, metaphysical metaphor,
> But resting on me, thinking in my snow,
> Physical if the eye is quick enough,
> So that, where he was, there is an enkindling, where
> He is, the air changes and grows fresh to breathe.
>
> The air changes, creates and re-creates, like strength,
> And to breathe is a fulfilling of desire,
> A clearing, a detecting, a completing,
> A largeness lived and not conceived, a space
> That is an instant nature, brilliantly.
>
> (301)

By the time Stevens wrote "An Ordinary Evening in New Haven," the focus on a physical element expanded to include the "endlessly elaborating poem" of the world. The mind must try to imagine itself as a whole, even as it knows that in so doing it only proliferates itself. In this project, "metaphysical metaphor" becomes the capacity to register the modes by which the unreal makes the real become actual. Then, as we approach this maximal degree of abstraction, the process can reverse itself. The simplest acts, like arriving in New Haven or "registering" the weather, take place on a metaphysical stage. The theory of poetry – or better, poetry as theorizing – becomes the theory of life, because it puts within contemplative brackets the essential force that makes value possible: the interdependence of the unreal and the real. The "as" becomes a metaphysical emblem, projecting the endlessly proliferating incarnations of the spirit in the flesh. And what began as Cubist metamorphoses of the world perceived expands to project this "as" as the body for the giant within whom we think, and from whom we feel at once a clearing and a completing of the forms of desire.

VIII

Hegel on substance and spirit, and Sartre on *en-soi* and *pour-soi*, had developed similar visions. But for them, the theory of life precluded poetry, because the criteria for theory required explaining the unreal by means of an elaborate metaphysical machinery. It takes decreation, the modern form of Occam's razor, to make the life lived in a reflective mode like that of poetry a direct focusing on the ways values are established in life. Similarly, it takes Wittgenstein, an even greater proponent of a decreation that becomes a composing of desire, to make us grasp the richness of Stevens's "as," as a mode for realizing the potential of Modernist abstraction. Two themes bond these thinkers and elaborate the most complete discursive framework we have for appreciating what poetry can make of those principles flaunted by painterly abstraction. The first theme is the effort, basic in Wittgenstein's early work, to imagine how philosophy can think Chocorua, or to delineate the threshold where the condition of value enters the "real" world of facts. The second theme is the project, elaborated in Wittgenstein's last work, of locating within the "as" models of human agency incompatible with behaviorist reductionism (and, I might add, with the various historical quasi determinisms that tempt contemporary critics). Although I shall, all too briefly, use Wittgenstein to elaborate the philosophical import of Stevens's work, the reader will see the reciprocal effect: Stevens's concerns help us to attend to implications of Wittgenstein's thinking that are all too rarely appreciated by philosophers.[15]

Wittgenstein's *Tractatus* articulates what would soon become the Vienna Circle's radical divorce between value and fact – an opposition that for Stevens took the form of the conflict between the unreal and the real:

> 6.41   The sense of the world must lie outside the world. In the world everything is as it is, and everything happens as it does happen: *in* it no value exists – and if it did, it would have no value.
>
> If there is any value that does have value, it must lie outside the whole sphere of what happens and is the case. For all that happens and is the case is accidental.
>
> What makes it non-accidental cannot lie *within* the world, since if it did it would itself be accidental. . . .

6.42   And so it is impossible for there to be propositions of ethics.

Propositions can express nothing of what is higher.

6.421   It is clear that ethics cannot be put into words.
Ethics is transcendental.
(Ethics and aesthetics are one and the same.)[16]

The logic here makes powerful use of Kant's themes. First, what can be named must be a fact in the world. Names mean, because they have referents; otherwise they are senseless. Then, as Kant argued, the condition determining the world *as it is* must be the working of empirical laws, those regularities within which concepts such as freedom and value make no sense. The world is lawful, but its laws are "accidental," because there is no reason they could not be otherwise; they simply are the case, with no appeal to purposes and justifications.

But Wittgenstein did not come only as the precursor of Positivism. He cared so much about what the world denies because he wanted to understand, as Kant did, where one can locate the sphere of values so that one can still propose ways in which philosophical thought might make a difference in the theory of life. In Wittgenstein's earlier writings, that difference was primarily negative. Again restating Kant, Wittgenstein thought that philosophy could clarify the nature of value only by denying adherents to analytic methods any access to the good. Value is the antithesis of propositional statement, because values cannot be accidental. Values depend on ends and purposes, so our only access to them must take the form of accepting our accidental destinies. By recognizing what philosophy cannot do, we locate a limit enabling us to imagine alternative relations to a world within which the unreal can play a cogent part. Attention to natural laws keeps us within the world; the life of values requires our occupying positions where we can frame the accidental and take up attitudes toward it *as* a whole. We must judge from a position, not within space and time, but at the border that these conditions of perception impose. Thus ethics and aesthetics become one, because both spheres involve the kind of viewing in which the mind frames an entire situation and takes a stance toward it as a whole. So conceived, both the aesthetic and the ethical border on the theological, allowing us to see ourselves in the same way that Chocorua reflects on what contains it: "To view the world *sub specie aeterni* is to view it as a whole – a limited whole. Feeling the world as a limited whole – it is this that is mystical" (6.45). And, because of this sense of the mystical, we recognize the need for a model of agency that cannot be represented by any form of rational or perspectival thought. The self who occupies these margins, Wittgenstein wrote, in his *Notebooks,* can be described only by the life that is lived in the scenes that it composes:

> Ethics does not treat of the world, Ethics must be a condition of the world, like logic.
> Ethics and aesthetics are one. . . .
> As the subject is not a part of the world but a presupposition of its existence, so good and evil are predicates of the subject, not properties in the world.
> Where in the world is a metaphysical subject to be found? You say that it is just as it is for the eye and the visual field. But you do not actually see the eye. And I think that nothing in the visual field would enable one to infer that it is seen from an eye.
> The thinking subject is surely mere illusion. But the willing subject exists.
> If the will did not exist, neither would there be that centre of the world, which we call the "I," and which is the bearer of ethics.
> What is good and evil is essentially the I, not the world; the "I," the "I" is what is deeply mysterious.
> The "I" is not an object. (*Notebooks: 1914–1916* 77–80)

This nonobjective "I" – at once too deep for words and too private to be manifest, except in the universal function of each willing subject pursuing its differences – could serve as the typical speaker of Stevens's later poems. We need abstraction for the qualities of will to manifest themselves; and we need a concept of the unreal in order to specify what the spirit produces at the margin of facts, as it tries simultaneously to proliferate differences and to envision their consort. But if we remain within analogies to Wittgenstein's early work, we never get past the condition of Chocorua, the immobile contemplator of the force that the unreal brings to our investments. The mature Stevens, like the mature Wittgenstein, added a principle for extending the life of the deep subject into the flux of the quotidian. It seems that both the poet and the philosopher can at once disclose the marginal nature of the willing subject and get beyond contemplation, to a sense of how the unreal permeates ordinary experience. Both ethics and aesthetics become more than abstract statements about values, and the theory of poetry becomes the basis for a complete theory of life.

The similarities between the two thinkers' late work most clearly come into focus when Wittgenstein, too, turns to the "as" as his emblem for certain powers of mind manifest only in its most elemental processes. Recall the first "as" we saw him employ: "In the world everything is *as* it is, and everything happens *as* it does happen" (emphasis added). The "as" here is an empiricist one, maintained by a subject attempting to separate observation from will, being from persons. The "as" is simply an operator that marks a congruence or equivalence between names and facts. The "as" projects no resemblances and thus brings no qualities to the occasion.

By section XI of *Philosophical Investigations,* radical changes have occurred. The section begins with two competing models of seeing the world: one where the "as" remains a copying operation, the other where the concept of "likeness" replaces that of the copy. In the latter case, we see an object "as we interpret it,"[17] so the philosopher's task is to fill out the grammar of this "as" by analyzing the many different dimensions of psychic life that contribute to interpreting its force. Now the "as" produces a constant tension between the real and the unreal, condensing into a drop of grammar a great deal of the fustian in the concepts proposed by idealist thinkers in order to link the theory of poetry to the theory of life. We need simply reflect on the ways in which our manipulating the "as" establishes powers within ordinary experience that flesh out what Wittgenstein had attributed to the deep subject confined at the margins of the real. Once we see how such elemental functions become testimony to substantial philosophical distinctions, we should recognize the price we pay if we translate Stevens back into the pure thematics of idealist critics or their materialist and hermeneuticist opponents. We realize that what matters is precisely an abstracting power sufficient to allow the most concrete linguistic elements to carry philosophical weight in their own right. Wittgenstein and Stevens each elaborates a Modernist imperative whose quest for concreteness, as a philosophical tool, leads ultimately to locating an "indefiniteness" at the core of human experience, which poets can try to put, "correctly and unfalsified, into words" (227). The theorizing of poetry becomes the theory of life by positing alternatives for both empiricist reductionism and idealist ontologizing. The being of beings is simply and miraculously a matter of how the "I" manipulates "the intricate evasions of as."

IX

The more I go on in this abstract vein, the more one doubt keeps nagging at me. In speaking of powers, nobilities, and acts of gathering, am I not appealing to a metaphysical sphere for what, in the pragmatic order, has no sanction, or even a real need to fill? I think not, but that thinking is so obviously in my self-interest that I must take up the problem explicitly, in order to specify some of the pragmatic implications of these lucubrations. If we are to attribute value to the model of agency that Stevens elaborates, we must be able to indicate how these

testimonial quickenings modify who we actually become *as* we participate in the acts of mind Stevens composes.

Let us turn to Wittgenstein one last time for our starting point. As he
thinks through the significance of the "as," he comes to recognize how
much more than perception is involved in the particular way that the
investments of the subject enter the occasion:

> If I heard someone talking about the duck-rabbit, and *now* he
> spoke in a certain way about the special expression on the rab-
> bit's face I should say, now he's seeing the picture as a rabbit.
>
> But the expression in one's voice and gestures is the same as if
> the object had altered and had ended by *becoming* this or that.
>
> I have a theme played to me several times and each time in a
> slower tempo. In the end I say "Now it's right," or "Now at
> last it's a march," "Now at last it's a dance." The same tone of
> voice expresses the dawning of an aspect. (*Philosophical Investi-
> gations*, p. 206–7)

Stevens expands this sense of becoming in order to focus attention on its
two features most intensely mediated by art; then he shows how art can so
control the "dawning of an aspect" that it makes those values available for
anyone willing to attempt participating in the perspective that the work
carries out. First, this focus on mobile investments provides a plausible
basis for describing those moments of disclosure in art that turn the flow
of time into a sense of radiant presence. The "as" is inseparable from the
triumphant "now," cry of its occasion. Phenomena suddenly come into
focus *as* something one cares about or recognizes in its possible significance – Heidegger's *aletheia,* without the abstracting metaphysics of
"*dasein.*" And then we see how the experience of presence correlates with
what idealist aesthetics labored to describe as organic unity. Grasped
under the right dispensation, parts begin to be seen as coherently related to
whole processes ("it's a dance" or "a march"), and concrete elements
grow inseparable from whole structures. We observe a mind not passively
responding to stimuli, but playing out its needs and powers as it locates
itself by composing contexts that link parts to wholes. Rather than establish an alternative to life, the aesthetic becomes a significant possibility for
understanding the kinds and intensities of satisfactions that life can bring
(see Wittgenstein's *Lectures and Conversations,* and his *Philosophical Investigations*, p. 202).

Wittgenstein's remarks indicate how the will aligns itself to appearances. They do not yet clarify how the reflective mind aligns itself
with the intricacies and intensities of the willing subject. For that, we
must shift our scenario. Rather than seeing a duck-rabbit, imagine staring at expressions on a human face. How is it that in some cases we see

only a face, whereas in others we see an expression that leads us to characterize that face in terms of expressive predicates? And how would one go about leading the person who saw only the face to appreciate the role those other predicates might have – both in what we say about the face, and in how we go on to dispose ourselves toward it? In most cases, the difference is not a matter of eyesight, but of the kind of cultural and psychological orientation that allows us to project what one might call "expressive fit" (see no. 537). When we register the expression, we in effect locate an unreal, inextricable from the real: How we imagine becomes inseparable from what we can go on to do.

Wittgenstein is content to open this set of interpretive possibilities. Ever cautious about saying more than he knows, he draws no conclusions and suggests no explanations. For Stevens, though, this latest version of the freed man inaugurates a complex series of meditations on reading, as the ultimate working out of an aspectual model of spiritual life. As we give spirit to that face, and as we then orient ourselves as agents in the kind of interchange that requires positing deep subjects at both poles, we have never once had to call upon inwardness or invoke any of the basic properties and contexts characterizing nineteenth-century attitudes toward the expressive self. Rather, the expression consists in fundamental signs, inseparable from how a culture teaches us to read them. The shifts in orientation are enormous, in essence positing inescapably first-person relations to the real that are, nonetheless, inseparable from what can be given third-person descriptions. There may be additional first-person properties and forces. All that one can know about them, however, are the kinds of reciprocities that they elicit when one learns to read the signs: "I have not, but as I am I am." So there is no point seeking the hidden. Instead, one is much better advised to reflect on how much we can know and share, as we learn the various forms of "as" that a face can carry, and as we recognize how fluid the ego is that can adapt itself to make the invited responses.

The best paradigm for that learning is the activity that we are capable of as fully aware readers: At least, so it seems in Stevens's late poetry, where all of the themes that we have been considering coalesce in conjunction with his meditations on that activity, and where his differences from Pound become most pronounced and most articulate. For it is reading that provides the most comprehensive testimony of how the theory of poetry intersects the theory of life; and, one might add, it is in inadequate readings that we most easily recognize the consequences of reductive philosophical positions. On the one hand, attention to reading becomes our access to the site of abstraction where subjects find themselves sharing certain powers and dispositions; on the other, it becomes the concrete vehicle where we assess on our pulses the exponential intensity of the work's ability to put those powers into significant testimonial action. It is as readers that we locate adjectives of "deepest mine," while treating the "as" of the work as its invitation to participate in the processes of fit that it composes. These identifications bring into play the second, presentational aspect of abstraction, because they afford literal testimony to how, as we entertain the "as," we become figures of desire, participating in the life of major man. Thus, by concentrating on the reading motif, Stevens can rely on the plain propoundings of his last poems, without any irritable reaching after the lyric and melodramatic. The burden of resisting pure lucidity is folded within the process of trying to be clear on precisely how one engages the occasion. Lyricism therefore, is less a matter of the confections of metaphor than it is of becoming aware of the process of aligning ourselves to the unfoldings of a speech that anyone can speak. We engage the poem in exactly the same way that we come to see that a face is expressive: not so much because of what the face seems to "mean" as because of the particular adjustments it elicits, so that we find ourselves able to share the intensity of its gestures. In the poem, however, that face turns out to be one that we find ourselves taking on, so that its motions become "portents of our own powers."

Once again, it takes poetry to show that these are not mere pieties. Or, I might say, it takes the testimony of reading to show that what seem pieties, for the critic, become justified by the investments to which they give expression in a work of art. Let us therefore turn to Stevens's "Large Red Man Reading," a poem about completing the physiognomy of earth. The conclusion asks us to see an unreal, giant reader, as he is read by those "who would have wept to step barefoot into reality" (whether the weeping is for joy or fear, we are not told).

> That would have wept and been happy, have shivered in
> > the frost
> And cried out to feel it again, have run fingers over leaves
> And against the most coiled thorn have seized on what was
> > ugly
>
> And laughed, as he sat there reading, from out of the
> > purple tabulae
> The outlines of being and its expressings, the syllables of its
> > law:
> Poesis, poesis, the literal characters, the vatic lines,
>
> Which in those ears and in those thin, those spended hearts,
> Took on color, took on shape and the size of things as they
> > are

And spoke the feeling for them, which was what they had
                                                    lacked.
                                                (423–4)

The content one reads has significance primarily for the processes it
sustains as mediations between Chocorua's giant and those he represents.
Reading becomes a powerful alternative to what lovers of truth seek,
because it shifts the burden of language from representation to representativeness, from objective statements to potentially transpersonal functions. This occurs in two registers that are conjoined in the brilliant
union of subjective and objective forces that Stevens puts to work in his
conclusion's rendering of the "as." The giant speaks the feeling for
"things as they are," as if there could be a single empirical world. Yet he
also speaks for things as they can enter feelings, so he calls attention to,
and thus stands for, the constitutive power that makes analogical relations as effectual within the real as any empirical objects.

Many poets have made similar claims. Stevens grounds those claims
by grafting onto them a remarkable self-referential process, linking the
composing act to the virtual life of the reader, whose experience provides
the most concrete evidence for the poem's claims. In reading, one becomes the giant; one no longer needs the testimony of Chocorua. First,
reading participates in his constitutive speech, because it requires our
taking up the aspects that the poem's words offer. As we read, we can
reflect on ourselves trying out possibilities, experiencing the words this
way or that, until particulars cohere and the text is seen in the size or
scope of things it can maintain. Poems need not establish true descriptions. They instead establish the power of language to make visible
certain aspects of the world. In reading the poem, it is the "characters of
being" that are said to come alive. And *as* we read, we test that claim by
proposing certain fits or alignments by which we speak a feeling our
world otherwise would lack. Reading can be literally the presence of that
aspect-consciousness that allows us to say, "Now I see," or "Seen like
this, it does make sense to believe I possess certain powers."

But why bring in the giant? This requires a second interpretation of
reading, as speech. Reading is not merely other-directed. Reading is a
form of attention to phenomena that so involves investments in both the
text and the world that it also becomes a paradigm for certain attitudes
toward the self. Some texts lead us to desire, not only a deeper grasp of
the world projected, but a more complete identification with the power
of what we might call the "textualized agency." As the "I" awakens, it
finds its own investments so realized in a verbal structure that it desires
the full life that may be available there. Like Penelope with Ulysses (520–
1), or the lover with his interior paramour (524), we find ourselves

projecting before us a deeper or a richer way of sharing the intensity of the work, so we know what it means to imagine a giant, and even to begin shaping ourselves so that we can better approximate those powers. Reading so intensely in one world puts us on the threshold of another, finer domain, where it seems "as if the design of all his words takes form / And frame from thinking and is realized" (511). There, all of the virtual sites that Modernist art pursues become miraculously and undeniably "part" of a commonal – elements at once of song and theater, where the spirit knows itself most truly and most strange.

As we occupy that threshold, it is crucial to realize that the state we entertain is not at all abstract, in the old sense of abstraction. This is the elemental, returned to the most concrete of verbal activities. For Stevens, it is only such refinement that allows him to take up once more the theme of repetition that had, in *Parts of a World*, seemed "this bitter meat [that] / Sustains us." Now, rather than treat images as "men eating reflections of themselves" (228), he can envision their proliferation and repetition as the vehicle that enables us to recognize and test what could be the most basic forms that our desires take. What seems monstrous, viewed as an effort to name a world that our names deface, becomes a way of feeling as intensely as possible our coming to share modes of fitting our desires to an unknowable world. Just as perception invites a sense of sections "collecting towards the greenest cone," reading produces a sense of ourselves completely inhabiting the forms of desire that most articulately give voice to the world. We become, in effect, "like rubies reddened by rubies reddening" (346), because our "readening" intensifies our capacity to participate in what cannot change, but can appear as a new emblem for our own powers. My bad pun is not "good reading" writ large, of course, but it does call attention to the way in which Stevens's expression stretches reading to unite the intractable materiality of rubies with the organic processes typified by ripening. Here substance becomes subject, and subjects learn to appreciate their own processes of becoming nature.

X

Reading is ultimately an idealist ideal, with little to offer one concerned with social analysis or the articulation of specific political interests. Yet the contrast with Pound that I have been developing suggests that reading has consequences somewhat different from those emphasized in typical idealist aesthetics. Stevens's emphasis is not on heroic creative acts, which appropriate the world under some single synthetic, compositional force. There are dreams of appropriation, but they project a "greenest cone," formed out of powers that we all share, powers that we can even imagine building a community around or using to develop the kind of principles that Habermas does out of the practice of conversation. Reading has a teleology that runs counter to individualist self-assertion. More important, reading is not a monistic principle. It idealizes shared powers, which themselves depend on worlds at once as intractable as minerals and as fertile as the "as" can make them. Thus Stevens, at the end of his career, comes to imagine a secular giant, hovering over worlds far less overtly sublime than Chocorua's, as in "The House Was Quiet and the World Was Calm":

> The house was quiet and the world was calm.
> The reader became the book; and summer night
>
> Was like the conscious being of the book.
> The house was quiet and the world was calm.
>
> . . . .
>
> The quiet was part of the meaning, part of the mind:
> The access of perfection to the page.
>
> And the world was calm. The truth in a calm world,
> In which there is no other meaning, itself
>
> Is calm, itself is summer and night, itself
> Is the reader leaning late and reading there.
>
> (358–9)

Here the abstract rendering of powers becomes a permission for investing our affections totally in the world as it is. And the poem becomes testimony for just how such affections can dispose themselves and reflect upon those dispositions. Precisely because the scene can be abstract, can be the reader's world within the self that reading composes, the action of the poem can combine an overall sense of calm with a progressively intensifying sense of the energies that such space can contain. The sentence is our hero, gradually manipulating repetitions until they lead to the brilliant syntactic shifts of the closing lines. Repetitions of single words (as opposed to the poem's earlier refrain effects) produce a sharp break with the dominant pattern of end-stopped lines. Thus, syntax is suspended, but only to speed up in very brief clauses. Then, as time turns back against itself, as reading self-consciously repeats its world and decides that it is good, the action finds its culminating expression in a series of present participles transforming all that calm into a pure state for which the reading stands as its perfection.

Confronting such a present, the engaged reader becomes absorbed in a corresponding activity. "There" and "here," the scene and the projected reader, then the projected reader and the actual reader, become dialectical functions of one another, all as exponents of this single figure, who proleptically represents one hundred eyes seeing at once. Such a site, for seeing sight, draws reading into a more intense leaning to strain every imaginative muscle. Yet the straining is part of – is perhaps cause of – a peace, in which anywhere becomes everywhere, and everywhere provides the basi‿ of romance. One hundred fifty years of Romantic quest leads to this plainest of propoundings. There need be no anxiety requiring the deferral of hidden intentions, and there need be no dramatic substitutes for one's plain sense of things. Poetry can be transparent, paradoxically, because the burden is not on its truth, but on the intense force in the present that the poem displays as it interprets, and hence takes responsibility for, its enabling conditions. For that burden, one needs no book – neither God's nor Mallarmé's. Simply engaging the words, as they elicit a world, composes an abstract space of such elemental sounds that one feels that reading has been given the same concrete presence that color and line give to sight. This is the hero's commonal.

10
Afterword: The Ends(s) of Modernism

Modernism is our resource. We may have problems with it.
We may in some sense be, or feel ourselves to be moving
towards the outside of it, but it's our resource. We cannot do
without it. We are not somewhere else.
                    T. J. Clark, *Modernism and Modernity*

I

For this book, Stevens's giant becomes the figure of a modern
hero, nowhere visible, but inescapably occupying the horizon of our
inquiry. Could we actually describe that giant, I think we would have no
trouble eliciting the recommendations that our professor withheld. And
that would, in turn, provide us a figure capable simultaneously of challenging contemporary culture and, through the work of the individual
artists, providing a range of models to engage in addressing that challenge. But of course the giant will not emerge. There can be no direct
and compelling image for the value of the values that we have been
tracing. Instead, my concluding summary, defining the values involved
in the field of energies and the corollary disciplines for the imagination
constituted by Modernist art, must rely on indirect means.

These indirect means are not difficult to come by. For, if we cannot
find our giant, we can easily locate the challenge of those who would
reduce him or her to a ninety-pound weakling on whom they can kick
sand. So, although we have no single ideal object to assess, we do have a
range of competing accounts that can make clear the stakes involved in
this study. In one respect, then, my end must return to its beginnings,
where I tried to demonstrate the inadequacy of the dominant evaluative
attitudes toward Modernist painting and Modernist poetry. But now the
situation is somewhat different: The framework that I have adopted
makes it necessary to engage those more general theorists who have
proclaimed a new Postmodernist cultural dispensation. From their perspective, my critical values simply reflect Modernist attitudes that continue to corrupt our cultural life by maintaining the Modernist illusions

359

and evasions. Everything that I argue for depends on the following idealist tenets: By attending to probable authorial intentions, and by close-reading individual art objects in a provisionally reverential tone, we can project as exemplary certain imaginative modes of thinking and feeling that have the capacity to influence how we represent ourselves as agents, and thus how we dispose ourselves toward the world and toward other people. But such commitments seem blithely unresponsive to the two major directions of what critics such as Frank Lentricchia like to call "advanced contemporary thought." The first is a Poststructuralist critique of the stable art object and, more important, of the subject who has either the interest in or the power to modify actions by determining its relation to exemplars and ideal audiences. Second, there is a range of political critiques that insists on tracing the structure of social representations and related social interests, which, the critics believe, are masked by these exemplars and profit from what might be called their "truth effects." Writers and critics who do not struggle to resist these effects condemn their own work to replicating a cultural order that has shown itself oppressive to many, and that is incapable of providing the resources needed for a better social organization.

These are large burdens to place on a conclusion to an already quite lengthy book. Yet the issues must be faced, if one is to maintain even a slim hope of making a difference in how the academy responds to Modernist work. In order to deal with these problems briefly, I shall first argue that these new stances are severely limited in their approach to literary issues; then I shall make the positive case that however much we may need to revise certain Modernist stances, the best way to do so is to adapt the Modernist view of the powers at stake in literary experiment.[1] Making that case will also prove the best way of drawing together our various themes so that I sketch at least the single ideal figure who embodies the fundamental values that I think Modernism defines for our culture.

Hal Foster provides a succinct treatment of the two directions in Postmodernist political values that enables me to get quickly to their most important limitations and, at the same time, characterize the political challenge facing any critic who tries to idealize Modernist testimony. In his *Recodings,* Foster distinguishes between the various deconstructive political stances, which he calls "the Postmodernism of transgression," and a second type of Postmodernism, which is devoted to actual political resistance. Whereas the Postmodernism of transgression concentrates on undoing our culture's accepted representations for the unified self and the hierarchies that they produce for the understanding, the latter Postmodernism takes on the responsibility of determining how art can foster social allegiances and posit ends within the political order (121–57).

Transgressive Postmodernism has, Foster claims, proved a powerful critical instrument. Thinkers like Derrida and artists like David Salle make us excruciatingly aware of how tenuous the entire fabric of our representations is. We see how much the arbitrary poses as the natural, and we find ourselves inescapably dependent on distinctions between inside and outside, conscious and unconscious, even good and bad, whose terms are irreducibly caught up in one another. More important, we learn from the best work in this vein how to take up complex modes of suspension, in which we allow those interwoven differences simply to manifest themselves, bracketing any effort to order them into discursive structures of oppositions. There we encounter a new "sublime," without any Kantian appeal to a recuperative reason. There is only the sense of the self's possible "otherness" to itself, which shows the self the impossibility of its own putative unity and opens us to moments of pure excess, where we begin to glimpse apocalyptic terror and wonder. Foster claims, however, that the more one identifies with these critical energies, the more one runs the risk of merely repeating the ironic Modernism that one set out to dismantle. This version of sublimity, for example, seems quite compatible with the Modernist desire to posit a distinctive reflective site for art, accompanied by a sense of the psyche as distributed into radically literal modes of being. In fact, Transgressive Postmodernism may differ only in the degree to which it tries to keep those modes of self-reflection isolated from practical experience, so that the audience is forced to explore its own nomadic indeterminacies. Transgressive Postmodernism, in Foster's view, leaves us in exactly the same position that we saw the Modernists occupying when they felt compelled to repudiate their own ironic stances: Faced with all of this indeterminacy, we need an art and a criticism that ask, "To the benefit of whom or what, *finally,* is this truth value banished, this meaning destructured?" For without these questions, such critique is likely not only to exacerbate our "schizo" inability to think our present, but also to serve capital in its erosion of traditional form of family and community (147).

An art committed only to transgression simply cannot satisfy a culture's need for idealized models of agency, which provide direction in transforming received forms of life. So Foster turns to his version of principles that Modernism located in a constructivist aesthetic. Suspicious of such idealism, he argues instead for an art that locates power in its actual resistance to hegemonic practices. But traditional Marxist alternatives to irony or apocalypse only embarrass him, forcing him to distinguish between a "political art" that "reproduces ideological representations" trapping it in old Marxist rhetorics, and "an art with a politic" that is "concerned with the structural positioning of thought and the material effectivity of practice within the social collectivity" (155). Unfortunately, the abstract terms in which he casts his positive program tell us more than the intelligence that insists on the distinction – for how will he define such positions and such collectivities without either over-simplifying the art or leaving the politics hopelessly vague and, perhaps, also far too elitist for the ends posited? How will he tell us for whom the demystification takes place, without resorting to some version of those "ideological representations," and thus once again subordinating the powers of the artworks to the collective terms of a political discourse capable of organizing large groups of people? The more sophisticated this "art with a politics" becomes, the more it tends to replicate the Poststructuralist vocabularies, and strategies for contemplative negation, that it wants to surpass.

Each of Foster's two Postmodernisms, therefore, finds itself partially undone by the triumph of its deconstructive tendencies over its recon-structive desires. Because both versions are suspicious of the historical affiliations necessary for an effective politics, and because neither dis-tinguishes sufficiently between the unitary ego (which demands critique) and the powers of practical judgment that we can wield on quite other grounds, these positions cannot produce a significant positive ethos – for art or for politics. Lacking an adequate language for constructive powers, these stances are left only two alternatives. Either they are forced back on irony (glorified as political critique of the writers' blindness), transform-ing spirit into a waste of shame, or they must absorb the art's particular mode of thinking within larger cultural contexts, to which they hesitate to attribute determinate characteristics lest they repeat the errors of thir-ties Marxism.[2] We are left with a politics without a polis, an obsession with ethical judgment without a carefully established set of ethical princi-ples, and a hunger for action deprived of any means of showing how what people have valued in aesthetic experience can claim the kind of material effectivity that their doctrine demands.[3]

What I suggest as a Modernist alternative to these Postmodernist ori-entations will not provide a direct political vision; will not make manifest the infinite slippage inherent in self-reflection; and will not mount a constant critique of the politics of representation. But it will provide a cogent case for taking artworks as exemplary testimonial structures that can affect the manner in which agents within the culture represent them-selves. And it will thus show that it is the artists' intelligence, rather than their truth effects, that is capable of addressing significant social needs, without either reducing the work to ideological shibboleth or treating the audience as mere dupes, to be saved from themselves by the heroic acts of demystified critics. My stance remains idealist, because it deals entirely with the order of self-reflection: with how we come to under-stand and explore psychic economies, rather than with the historical roles that the art has played. And, in the end, my stance will be forced to identify, at least in part, with stances that set themselves against the demands of any specific political order. But this idealism does entail an individualist pragmatics. And it is sustained by the strong possibility that the arts do not really have a cogent alternative. What kind of society, and what kind of education, are we likely to produce, if we do not grant audiences the dignity to construct and weigh meanings, and if we do not give our artists credit for making work that is meaningful because of the way that it tries to construe experience (rather than because of the critical interests we try to make it serve)? And where, if not in art, are we to find those elements within our culture that can appeal to our capacity for idealization and that can be said to modify how we come to determine who we can be, and what modes of self we want to pursue? Finally, where else, in an age so deeply suspicious of abstract ideas, are we to locate forms of testimony that can show how processes of exemplification engage us in assessing and applying new models of agency? If we are to give up such artistic and critical ideals, we ought at least to be presented with a compelling psychological or epistemological case against the models of judgment invoked. Or we ought be shown that a different approach to artistic force has, in fact, produced structures with at least the capacities to resist bourgeois values, and to address the deep imaginative needs, that one finds in much of Modernism.[4]

II

In many respects Modernist art shares the Postmodernist dilemma that we have been considering. As we have seen during the course of this discussion, it too required positive principles that it could not derive from received cultural values or from discursive models given authority by defined social interests. But its roots in Romantic theory provided it with a significantly different means of addressing the problems. Rather than rely on ideals of material effectiveness difficult to reconcile with the play of consciousness and self-reflection fundamental to the work that artists in fact carry out, this theory tried to locate the effectiveness of art in a concept of imaginative powers produced, defined, and disseminated by individual works of art. Art then could speak to society without having to represent any established interests, and it could promise to explore widely divergent modes of agency that need not be tied to any specific social formations.

Such promise, however, depends on the cogency of that thinking about powers. Let us begin by recalling the historical terms that the Modernists elaborated. Romantic theory set the stage by making central to art the possibility of semantic force based on principles of exemplification and testimony that could not be subsumed under discursive principles of "understanding." Thus Wordsworth and Kant, in their different ways, shifted the focus of art from the idea presented to the qualities of agency that particular works make visible and submit to imaginative tests. At one pole, these exemplary acts reveal to the audience its own capacities for purposive harmonies with nature and society; at the other they provide evidence for the psyche's deepest moral interests. Such cognitive claims, in turn, make the notion of the artwork as a locus of powers a means for sustaining value claims that had to negotiate several difficult boundaries: between the secular and the religious realms; between mechanical and vitalist models of consciousness; and between dependency on unconscious forces and an idealization of the assertive human will.[5] Such powers are both natural and mysterious, both imposed on the self and responsible to its various levels of creative control.

Ours is not a Romantic age. So, many of the Romantics' particular claims used to defend these assertions about powers will no longer hold up. But I hope I have shown that Modernism managed to recast those assertions along lines that allow me now simply to propose a loose definition of how the concept of human powers articulated and tested within art sustains some significant claims about art's relation to the social order. When we speak about the "powers" that art tests and exemplifies, we refer to those features of human agency that characterize the quality and intensity of the human activity conferring value on or in particular situations. Every view of human agency attributes powers when it posits views of how consciousness responds to or apprehends its environment; how persons distribute the energies that emerge from that response; how a mind regulates and modifies its own desires and interests; how an agent takes responsibility for or draws consequences from that reflection; and how judgment draws from the present what it projects as relevant for a person's future activities. I think all of this has clearly been at stake in our specific discussions of the values that individual poems and paintings make visible. But to stop with particulars is to miss the importance of the fact that in Western culture the arts have been designated as the arena where we not only participate in such powers, but also reflect on what these powers afford as powers: that is, as general attributes shaping the overall self-representations that we confer and pursue. Art is the domain where we cultivate the powers necessary for characterizing human potentials and for establishing the values that we then seek to bring about by political means. Through artistic examples, we compare competing visions of these powers, and thus we work out the degree to which it proves important to us to treat specific models of agency as significant social resources.[6]

Simply defining the concept of powers will not secure an effort to defend one of those specific models of agency. But it does clear the way for testing Modernism's claim to establish secular powers of adaptation, distribution, regulation, judgment, and projection that are capable of resisting the spiritual problems inherited from the nineteenth century (and still all too much with us). For that test, we must return to our close readings, but this time by attempting to abstract from them the three fundamental models of human agency that they can be said to articulate and to test. In doing this, we elaborate specific paths in which sets of Modernist values can be brought to bear on experience – either by providing direct sources with which to identify, or by establishing models that society can try to modify or to oppose. And we thus establish the ability of Modernist artworks to challenge both entrenched social attitudes and the competing efforts to invent plausible alternatives.

Paul Cézanne and William Carlos Williams are probably closest to the Romantic sense of the powers cultivated by art, because, as we saw, for them "so much depends" upon how attention is staged. In their work the mind had to adapt itself to a nature that could no longer be idealized by quasi-theological symbolism, yet had to be redeemed from what industrial society made of it, and therefore of us. For such adjustments, their art had to transform a fundamental Romantic ideal that the imagination could participate in natural energies, extending into the resonant symbolic realm of verbal relations. Cézanne and Williams develop an ideal of realization that reverses that process, putting the artifact first, then exploring what we learn to see through, and around, our awareness of our own formative activity. This foregrounding of the antagonist-composer, we saw, reduces both the mind's dependency on any transcendental source for its own intensities, and the mind's reliance on a personal history to explain the state of empowerment. In one respect, for Cézanne and Williams the artist is simply a medium, whose labor makes visible the very conditions of visibility, free of any need for dramatic contexts. That abstracting of personality, however, transforms such mediation into a new principle of passionate engagement in what art can disclose. Because there is no need to worry about all of the psychological registers that oppress a Prufrock, the labor of craft can carry, in its own right, a "mobility" of mind that releases a wide range of emotional energies. When the art need not try to elicit some authentic "buried self," it is free to flesh out investments in what it actually reveals as capable of compelling and rewarding our immediate attention. And then value is less a matter of interpreting the relation between particulars and informing universals than it is of exploring a transparent consciousness becoming intricately dispersed in the world that it composes. If only for isolated moments, the powers of adaptation and distribution provide a sense of identity, independent of all of the problematically allegorical ideals and categories necessary for attributing value to experience within traditional moral frameworks.

In Pablo Picasso, Gertrude Stein, and Ezra Pound, the pressure of allegory returns with a vengeance. For them, we saw, the necessary adaptations were not to nature but to history, a domain where no model of agency can suffice that is not thoroughly committed to the contrived corridors of ironic self-reflection. But irony is means, not end. The torments within the art become the artists' measure of a culture that panders to will and paralyzes judgment. Resisting that culture then becomes the drama of the work. The authorial act exemplifies a process of turning the ironic sensibility into a lyric resource: Reducing the social world to isolated fragments frees the mind to explore the repertoire of roles and constructive strategies that it can project upon that social world as vital forms of value. Thus, rather than seek grounds for the will in a renewed relation to the logic of seeing, these figures take their ground from within the forms that culture affords. A new transparency becomes possible – not of the mind's links to its environment, but of the creative mind's energies made manifest within artistic processes. Freed by their sense of irony from any hope in the powers of personal expression, the artists had to equate the self with the constructive activity, transforming the fragments that history leaves into a compositional field where the will can begin to take responsibility for its own stance toward that historicity. The only source of value is the ability to forge one's own continuous appropriation of what has no inherent logic or meaning.

Our third model of agency elaborates just the opposite psychic disposition. In Piet Mondrian, in Marianne Moore, and in the late poetry of Wallace Stevens, the primary concern is with finding alternatives to the individual self and locating, through those alternatives, radically different ways of aligning will to some general grounding condition. Here the sense of "plight" is broader than the one posed by the other stances. At stake is not simply the mind's relations to a deformed nature or a history of metaphors turned into a source of constant irony, but a global sense of the pathos of the ego. Correspondingly, here history and politics matter primarily for the constant reminders they give of the inadequacy of any specific secular practices, and of the need to constitute modes of investment that are not bound up in those dispositions. The logic of religion reigns, at least to the degree that art must seek permanent relational principles and identify with states of consciousness that do not easily connect with demands for practical action. But because it can render direct images for its own most fundamental powers, the art can treat religion as essentially a source of metaphors for what it manages to display in secular terms. Abstraction opens the way to a paradise so far within that it correlates the will's deepest energies with elemental dynamic forces in nature. But often that sense of elemental force won by abstraction is inseparable from a bleak awareness of how much one must deny in the abstracting, so that we are asked to identify with the autumnal spirit exemplified in these concluding lines of Stevens's "Plain Sense of Things":

> A fantastic effort has failed, a repetition
> In a repetitiousness of men and flies.
>
> Yet the absence of the imagination had
> To be imagined. The great pond,
> The plain sense of it, without reflections, leaves,
> Mud, water like dirty glass, expressing silence
>
> Of a sort, silence of a rat come out to see,
> The great pond and its waste of the lilies, all this
> Had to be imagined as an inevitable knowledge,
> Required, as a necessity requires.
>
> (*Collected Poems* 502–3)

III

I cannot yet conclude. There is something too disturbing in this paean to "silence of a sort" and its sordid cast of characters, whose only power seems to be a capacity to resign itself to external necessity. Had Modernism given all to its dream of art as empowerment and come to this? Perhaps there can be no other end for the hope that one can freely roam through possible imaginative identifications. For one must wonder, with Eliot's critique of Babbit's humanism, whether there is much difference between the plenitude of imaginative options and this need to imagine an absence of imagination. Does not the variety itself threaten any claims we might want to make for imaginative powers? How will so mobile a faculty help us decide which of these versions of agency is "true," or even which is pragmatically the best to adapt? And how will such mobility hold off the prospect that beneath the variety there drives an uncontrollable necessity, tossing out these epiphenomena for fools to dally with? Even if these varying attitudes engage us in the present moment of the work, such a profusion of options is unlikely to affect our deeper interests, except perhaps to conceal the interests, judgments, and orientations that actually govern behavior. As we try to specify the powers that art offers, aesthetic idealism seems unable to escape Kant's problems in correlating the mind's constructs with practical life, so it invites suspicion that its primary role is to avoid the harsh realities of that life or to sanction only the deliberative freedom of the academy.[7]

I wish I had a better response to such doubt than I do. For there is no abstract way to determine the degree to which we are, and are not, capable of manipulating this variety, so that it can play a cogent and consistent role in extending particular lives. But one can at least point out that the impossibility of clear determinations cuts both ways. If we cannot clearly establish a single model of agency capable of living in such options, we cannot rule out at least a considerable degree of flexibility in the psyche. We do not need to posit a radically independent subject, in order to find reductive those accounts that eliminate the range of interests that agents pursue or the capacity of vicarious imaginative experience to modify the identities we do compose. And we do not need to assume that in making such changes we are driven by determinate forces of social production, rather than by principles of judgment that we also develop over time, as we reflect upon several kinds of ideological products. Therefore, if we are to err in one direction or the other, the individual clearly does better to make a Pascal's wager for pursuing these complex imaginative possibilities, because that, at least, does not foreclose a range of possible powers that could become aspects of one's identity.

One way to imagine the self one would then wager on is to shift from a typology of attitudes to what might be called "complexes of powers" composed out of that typology. Here, then, we come closer to our giant. Rather than imagine Modernist powers under the dispensation of particular artistic visions, we can envision the specific projects as constituents in a more general common enterprise to establish overall alternatives to the ideals promoted by the dominant culture. Spelling out these complexes will require one more summary, but this time one that concentrates on showing how the work of the poets and artists participates in the cultural work also carried on by major thinkers in other domains. Let us then imagine the figures we have been considering shaping three basic complexes of powers, each best characterized by a particular philosophical project (Lacan's, Nietzsche's, and Kant's). Ultimately all three complexes prove compatible with one another, but in my view it is the Kantian complex that proves the most capacious and socially significant.

I invoke Lacan first, because his thinking helps us to organize the various ironic or deconstructive stances that Modernism cultivated into a single complex of powers. Were we simply to emphasize Modernist resistance to an increasingly commodified, increasingly instrumental and reductive capitalist social order, a host of thinkers would do for describing the force of the remarkable range of ironic strategies that the Modernists put at our disposal. But most of these frameworks do not account for what it is about the art, as art, that thickens the social critique, by making it something more than abstract thematic opposition. If we call upon Lacan, we see that the artists can claim to be attacking and reconstructing the very core of this social organization: namely, the way in which it develops, within individual people, psychological formations based on its prevailing schemes for representing the relation between self and world. Thus the artists' effort to show what is at stake in the narcissistic dimensions of representation and in the models of discursive closure that those representations sustain hold out the promise of leading us beyond debilitating cultural symptoms to those modes of imaginary investment that produce or reinforce those symptoms. Problems in social relations lead back to principles organizing psychic economies. And, once such relations become visible, it is plausible to claim that the deconstructive energies of Modernism prove inseparable from the larger project of constructing alternative forms of agency. Rather than simply rail in frustration against society, the art can be cast as both a keen analytic instrument and an indispensable vehicle for locating cure in the one place where change begins: in the ways that individuals come to define their own loyalties and priorities.

There is even a way in which we can see certain Modernist work as exploring Lacan's version of a cure for those imaginary structures. In the hands of an Eliot, a Samuel Beckett, a Kurt Schwitters, a Marcel Duchamp, and later a John Cage, a Jasper Johns, a Robert Rauschenberg, and a Jacques Derrida, the negative strategies used to undermine our specular satisfactions in our imaginary identities and social investments take on an oddly satisfying condition of active plenitude in their own right. Thus Malevich's "tilt" – his image of a spirit vital precisely in its separating itself from all need for any more elaborate means of identity – provides a superb image for the mode of imaginative identity that Lacan opens up, one in which the ironic attitude establishes the spirit's power to accept its own indissoluble marginality and to withhold investing in overdetermined contents that inevitably return us to the wheel of Schopenhauer's will.

But much of Modernist art was greedier than that. Having cleared the ground of most traditional moral and psychological investments, it sought determinate constructive forms for the capital that the imagination continues to make available. Here Nietzsche provides our most suggestive context for a second complex of powers:

> Let the people suppose that knowledge means knowing things entirely; the philosopher must say to himself: when I analyze the process that is expressed in the sentence "I think," I find a whole series of daring assertions that would be difficult, perhaps impossible, to prove; for example, that it is I who think, that there must necessarily be something that thinks, that thinking is an activity and operation on the part of a being who is thought of as

a cause. That there is an "ego," that it is already determined what is to be designated by thinking, that I *know* what thinking is. (23)

Schopenhauer only did what philosophers are in the habit of doing – he adopted a popular prejudice and exaggerated it. Willing seems to be above all something complicated, something that is a unit only in a word. . . . So let us for once be more cautious . . . let us say that in willing there is, first, a plurality of sensations, namely the state "away from which," the sensation of the state "towards which," the sensations of this "from" and "towards" themselves. (25)

When the new psychologist puts an end to the superstitions which have so far flourished with almost tropical luxuriance around the idea of the soul, he practically exiles himself into a new desert and a new suspicion – it is possible that the older psychologists had a merrier and more comfortable time of it; eventually he finds that precisely thereby he also condemns himself to invention – and who knows – perhaps to discovery. (*Beyond Good and Evil* 21)

There is no richer sense of what the critical spirit makes available. For, as one exposes those abstractions that had concealed the seething vitality of psychic energies, one also releases a wide range of intense and diverse states, each calling out for artistic rendering, and all potentially combining to establish an affirmative capability no longer bound to traditional myths. What seemed fragments become elements for new constructive syntheses, and what seemed the denial of the mind's synthetic powers a means for recognizing the strange and various forces that in fact connect sensibilities to their objects and to other people.

Several consequences follow for valuing what Modernism accomplished. First, we realize what was at stake in the war against dramatic structures and the psychic economy they fostered. For, once we need no longer attach emotions to causes that set in motion chains of events building to climaxes and then exploding in triumph or in tragedy, we are free to explore their mobility – as independent forces, and as the kind of irreducible affective attachments to objects that Eliot and Williams use in such different ways. What had been implicit in representational art – the fluidity of a psyche formed by intricate associational and textural patterns – could be foregrounded as a primary model for our investments. Rather than demand one general principle for integrating the poles of subject and object, artists could imagine those poles in constant oscillation. And, more important, this fluidity created the challenge of having to populate the psyche anew. Where the human soul or the mental faculties, or even drives and impulses, had been, there artists could try to make literal certain configurations defining and testing sites where the mental, the affective, and the physical come to live one another's life and die one another's death. As art turned to the building blocks of our affective and reflective lives, sharp dichotomies between the inner and the outer gave way to Stevens's "gusty emotions on wet roads on autumn nights" (*Collected Poems* 67) or Henri Matisse's marvelous goldfish, red rooms, and window scenes (extended in contemporary art by Jennifer Bartlett's *In the Garden*). The psyche can be identified only in terms of the atmospheres and textures that bring it to self-consciousness.

Yet this more mobile and intricately contoured self-consciousness is less end than means. In a Nietzschean dispensation, the crucial demand is to modify one's sense of will, and one's grasp of one's own ability, by revaluing what confronts one when one has finally shed the husk of the old representational forms. Freedom from illusion or cultural domination is inseparable from the cultivation of an affirmative capability that, in turn, realizes its dependence on the structure of differences necessary to affirm its uniqueness. When we apply this perspective to Modernism, we see the quest for affirmative capability taking form as a demonstration that these new modes of agency have the power to define stable grounds for once again reviving predicates for nobility and monumentality that, during the past two hundred years, had only been available for mock-heroic forms. The more diffuse the categorical frames for structure, the more the structuring activity takes on attributes that make it possible to treat the compositional act as an emblem for powers of individuation that could participate in Nietzsche's recasting of the process of self-legislation basic to Kant's idea of moral autonomy. And the more the art is freed from illusionistic drama and forced to serve as its own testimony, the better its opportunity to make its relation to history carry the grounding measure for the autonomy that in Kant must derive from reason.

The cultural terms for this struggle emerged most clearly in the reaction by conservative artists like William Butler Yeats and Wyndham Lewis against the "mobility" I have been praising. The intensity of their complaints that this Modernism had surrendered to the "flux," or to pure "temporality" divorced from spatial form, dramatizes the stakes art had come to carry: How aesthetic experience is composed becomes the measure of the fundamental terms sustaining ideas of moral identity. Given that challenge, and granted that theater for display, most of the Modernists, we have seen, took the alternative tack of treating engagement in the "flux" as considerably more than self-surrender. By exploring fragmentation, they foregrounded the process enabling the individual artistic act to appropriate, and to revalue, all of the energies that an ideal of exemplary aesthetic order could put into circulation. Consider how Pound and Picasso showed that the more diverse and mobile the spirit, as it ranges over history to absorb everything within its own intricate signature, the more one can define the powers of an authorial will not bound to "personality," to specific social roles, or to abstract principles. Bound to no law, this composing presence takes on an identity in the specific intensity and scope of its own movement through a world whose depersonalizing pressures we understand all too well. This will's movement sets in motion a dialectic of intensity and scope – with its claims on our attention depending on the degree that it makes the history that it engages the contrastive measure of its own achievement. Art carries on the dream of Baudelaire's aristocrat, who sought by his display of will to establish his own claims on the history inciting this will to action. Purposiveness becomes a way of engaging the mind within the contours imposed by culture, and autonomy becomes the degree to which that movement can take responsibility for its own gestures. The more abstract the art, one might add, the greater the opportunity to assume such responsibilities. For in that abstract art, the dialectic between intensity and scope focuses on the possibility of so locating general principles within history that the depersonalized creative intensity of the constructive act has nothing but its own concentrative relational field on which to stake its own future. There is nowhere to hide, and no anecdotal "supplements" to deflect the work's quest for the kind of lucid responsibility for oneself that is the fundamental condition for a truly monumental art.

In Nietzsche, therefore, we find terms that support Modernism's claim to have established a new individualism, able to compete with the last great individualizing movement of Renaissance thought, so that it both recovers and revalues those ambitions. But we are again faced with the obvious social implications of this individualism. Constructivist Modernism seems bound to Nietzsche's own aristocratic, hierarchical politics: not a likely stance from which to earn contemporary "recommendations." I propose two ways of addressing this problem. First, it is important to understand Modernist individualism in its political context, where the desire seems less a Nietzschean arrogance than a sense of the bleak necessity we just saw in Stevens. Art must cultivate individual virtues and resist the demands of history, because those demands stem from a dialectic so perplexing that every effort to break out of it tends only to deepen the writer's despair about political life. In their quest for recommendations, the poets and artists all wanted to propose idealized states that connect individual *virtù* with clear political roles. But how could they find a political context for those identifications that would remain consistent with the powers that they thought their art could exemplify? By the twentieth century, it seemed anachronistic to attach one's best political impulses to anything but democratic ideals, yet the national political institutions developed for realizing those ideals seemed to be already beginning the long, slow decline that religion had undergone over the previous centuries. How could one idealize a political order that, as Nietzsche showed, gave power precisely to those who could not reverence what the artists thought were substantial ideals, but instead made bourgeois economic concerns the basis for all values? How could one honor the ideal of expanding individual personal freedom, in a social order increasingly dominated by media devoted to erasing the very differences that democracy promised to cultivate? How could one dream of heroes, in a political system where the representatives of the people must spend all of their time trying to get reelected, and thus must avoid all difficult choices, however necessary for the physical and economic welfare of the society, and even of the planet? And finally, how could one continue to honor ideals whose enabling Enlightenment models of disinterested judgment came, increasingly, to seem all too much in the interest of a particular class, which did not even honor its own rhetoric? At best, then, politics might be a domain to which one had to accommodate oneself, or even in which one had to defend the rights of those for whom one had no real sympathy; but there was no actual institutional form for the domain that could sustain any of the revaluations that the artists were trying to develop.

To rest content with this case, however, is to stress the pathos of the artists, rather than their claims to provide us with imaginative energies worth pursuing. Therefore I consider it necessary to propose a second tack on the politics of individualism. Clearly, some of the uses to which those values were put are reprehensible. But if we turn to a third complex of powers, this one best typified by Kant, it becomes possible to isolate some significant values that are always latent in Modernist individualism, and at times come to the fore. Thus, although we need Nietzsche to flesh out constitutive aspects of Kant's thought that are suppressed under Kant's rationalism, we ultimately need the analog afforded by that rationalism to free some aspects of Modernist individualism from the Nietzschean politics that the imagination too easily grafts upon them. Although the issues involved here require another book, for my purposes here the main point can be stated baldly: Kant's map of the psyche promises to specify two limits to the political domain that make clear, by contrast, the possible roles that constructivist Modernist art can continue to play in contemporary culture. Suppose that politics proves so disillusioning because its commitments to the practical order engage us in a realm bound to principles of understanding (in

Kant's sense) and to assumptions about the motives governing actions, that cannot sustain the mind's desire to articulate modes of agency responsive to its full capacities to produce and revere values. Within the political realm, the mind must take its versions of causality from the practical understanding, and it therefore must take its models for practical motives and plausible ideals from within the particular set of social assumptions governing the given political order: Philosophy must yield to anthropology. If philosophy (and art) are to step free of those anthropological blinders, they must be able to capture the general rules of that understanding, and, in the process of interpreting those procedures, they may be able to open access to other domains of experience not subject to empiricist criteria.

Such thinking need not rely on Kant's specific formulations of the faculties or on the categories he attributes to understanding.[8] Philosophers as diverse as Edmund Husserl, Wittgenstein, and William James have tried to call our attention to significant features of subjective life that become visible as one tries to define the limits of understanding. For our discussion, what matters is simply the possibility of drawing a contrast between two conflicting ideas of subjectivity: subjectivity construed from the point of view of practical understanding, where it consists of interests and needs formed by specific sociocultural forces; and a version of subjective life that reflective thought offers as so fundamental to certain recurrent human experiences that it is impossible to bind to the practices of any specific society. Consider the admiration Americans have for heroes such as Gandhi, whose culture remains foreign to us, or consider the degree to which we feel that our engagements in subjects like ancient art could be appreciated by diverse social groups. Such observations show why it makes sense to speak of a transcendental aspect of subjectivity that can be distinguished from the empirical self. Through this aspect of self-reflexive activity we can imagine constructing common terms for understanding the very principle of difference as it is experienced by that empirical subject, since our shareable knowledge of that desire for difference allows us to understand what is at stake when competing desires take conflicting forms. And such recognitions then have a substantial role to play in political theorizing. For we can use them to establish criteria for judging among the competing social formations developed to help individuals pursue those differences. As John Rawls shows, in his *Theory of Justice,* so freeing the subject from its specific political affiliations makes it plausible to compose a site where agents from different political orders try out imaginative identities and identifications, capable of binding both cultures to a specific set of obligations.

For Modernism, as we have seen, the most important feature of this resistance to practical understandings of human agency was a fascination with the dynamic transpersonal functions that best become visible in a nonrepresentational art. Here one can dream, with the Russian constructivists, of art opening the way to new versions of what might bind individuals to political communities. So long as culture remains under a Cartesian dispensation, it must insist on a sharp dichotomy between subjective and objective domains, each characterized by a separate set of contents – the former permeated by private concerns and affective colorings, the latter characterized by properties that are conceived as detachable from any given mode of representation, and therefore independent of the viewer's particular biases. But with the new art, and with related developments in phenomenology and pragmatic philosophy, it becomes possible to treat "subjective" and "objective" primarily in functional terms. The consequences of that shift are substantial, influencing both the way we relocate what constitutes the intensity of subjective experience, and the way we consider the nature of political rights and political bonds. As Thomas Nagel points out, in *Mortal Questions,* we can share the beliefs and desires that a person takes as essential to subjective identity, without being able to share the subjectivity. So the subjectivity must lie elsewhere: not in the content of the beliefs, or in the history that formed them, but in something specific to the way they are held. What makes an internal state subjective is not the belief per se, but the sense of ownership, or sense of responsibility, involved in holding it as one's own. Subjectivity consists simply in the fact that the beliefs and desires are approached as someone's particular experience.[9]

Although this approach to subjectivity may seem circular, it actually calls our attention to a substantive distinction between the grammar of first- and third-person sentences that can help us to grasp how an apparently impersonal art can be said to carry the essential energies of subjective life. When we speak of "first-person" uses of language, we imagine an intimate relation between the speaker and the sentence, which cannot be replicated simply by using the sentence. When we speak of third-person terms, we imagine the sentence itself as the only significant factor: Anyone can use it, in exactly the same way and with the same affect, as if one were describing someone else's beliefs and desires. Thus, at whatever level we engage language, the crucial step for understanding the role of the subjective is to imagine how the impersonal content suddenly becomes alive as "someone's": as part of a virtual life. Imagine trying to make that subjective function itself the focus of one's art, as if one could at once display and experience the essential form of our investments. This is precisely what is at stake in Malevich's tilt, Stevens's *as,* Moore's mobile wit, and even in the synthetic pressure stressed by Pound and Picasso. By making us reflect on the very conditions of agency that we enter when we try to understand how this art goes beyond illusionistic space, to present creativity itself as its central drama, Modernist art casts audience participation as the entering of a profound secular mystery: Self-reflexion shows us sharing the very conditions by which subjects define their differences from one another.

Such personal states cannot sustain the profound social sympathies of the great nineteenth-century novelists, or even of work such as Words-worth's *Prelude*. But that does not mean that they must lack social force. At one pole, this sense of transpersonality affords a useful perspective from which to appreciate the political impact made possible by the set of strategies that I called the Lacanian complex of powers. We see how deeply the ideological structures are woven into subjective life, since in fact they are necessary, if the investing ego is to have any content at all. There is thus no distinguishing private from public life; there are only degrees of clarity about our dependencies and the alternative investments that might be available to us. Art therefore can hope to inhabit the site where ideology is actually produced, hoping that there art can at least generate the alienation effects that will set us in search of new terms for our identifications.

For most Modernist artists, that social site could never provide the conditions for establishing adequate alternative identities. Rather than try to understand the specific contents and affiliations available within the social theater, these artists concentrated on making visible the formal structures that could be said to be fundamental to all such investments, and therefore free of any one of them. This is the point at which any politics we attribute to the works must rely on Kant. Kant thought that once a polis can be made to understand what it means to treat others as self-legislating ends in themselves, and once it sees that all law has to be justified in terms of preserving the rights of these agents, then it will realize that there are fundamental principles that can take a variety of local forms. Modernist individualism has similar force, even when it refuses particular political filiations. For, once we see that the art testifies to certain principles of individual agency and makes clear its transper-sonal implications, there follow at least Habermas's principles of legit-imation, to which I have already alluded. If we can project what con-stitutes the full intensity of our individualizing energies, and if we have articulate public testimony for the emotional engagements such energies mobilize, we have strong grounds for insisting that a political system is legitimate only to the degree to which it makes those maximal conditions of experience available to an entire populace. There will still be substan-tial disagreement about how one brings about such conditions. Yet the arts can play a major role in constructing the sense of agency that must be used to judge among these political visions.

However, if one stops with the political dimension of such concerns, one ignores the major interests linking the artists to Kant. The central drama in his thought is not how we place individual actions within social setting, but how we come to understand what can be exemplified within the action itself. Although Kant had substantial interest in political matters, he devoted his most demanding work to spelling out plausible terms for attributing dignity to individual moral acts. Only this focus, he thought, would make it possible for bourgeois culture to recover the essential vision of human nobility that previous cultures had preserved for the aristocracy. Only a new sense of what was fundamental to all individuals would suffice to overthrow the overt social signs of nobility and power, and transform them into conditions of an inner life. So Kant retained the ideal of self-legislation, but now in the name of achieving rational identity. One becomes "noble" when one manages to suspend all interest in material rewards, so that one can realize the terms of a deeper, distinctively human interest in constituting the self as both subject and object of the moral law. By overcoming apparent interests, always seducing one to an irreducible heteronomy, the subject can both will its own interest – to be a rational being, above all – and find that will objectively sanctioned – rationality is precisely what the law dictates that subjects should do as rational beings.

Kant's commitment to law was to prove far too ascetic (and demanding) for Modernist artists. But Kant's principles nonetheless afford us a model that clarifies the vision of artistic lawfulness and self-realization that the artists set against the frustrations engendered by the political order. If they could cast their art as the pursuit of something that simply could not be incorporated in any practical model of living, something that claimed its authenticity as a refusal of the compromises demanded by common sense, they too could insist on a dignity that stemmed from seeking absolute conditions of being. Art would have its version of pure rationality, and the artist's legislative act could be at once the expression of her deepest subjective interests and the articulating of the transpersonal structures that give those interests an objective form. And then one could simultaneously explain one's frustrations with the compromise required by politics and offer one's own constructions as an alternative, within which one could experience human powers unlikely to be cultivated in any political order. Forced back on self-reflexive resources, the artists could cultivate a "fascination with the unlivable," which required their pushing imaginative investments to the point where the creative mind seems unsatisfied with any merely social theater. Art must approach the transcendental, if only in terms of secular intensities. Without that quest, we have neither sufficient alternatives to the failures of politics, nor sufficient motives for fully articulating the energies and desires that stage themselves as capable of working at the limits of understanding. With that quest, the very effort to define alternatives to the political might eventually make possible a society fostered on constant testimony to what the agents could revere in one another.[10]

By this point in this book, we need no further illustration of the specific forms developed for these transcendental desires. But we do need to recognize that this fascination with the "unlivable" creates a sharp focus for the conflict between Modernist and Postmodernist values, a focus that enables us to cut through the rhetorics and understand how the two orientations at once limit and complement one another. These stakes became clear to me through a conversation with Carl Dennis, in which he argued that "in pursuing monumentality, Modernism lost touch with mortality." Modernism's commitment to direct testimony left little interest in, or capacity for, learning to understand and have compassion for other people. Although the Modernist poets and painters worried a good deal about history as a general phenomenon, for the most part they had little interest in the specific texture of their own historical moment. Theirs was a lonely and, ultimately, self-regarding art, more concerned for the intensity and clarity of its constructed sites than for the social world out of which the sites were made, and to which they had to return for their validation.

I so admire Dennis's comment, because it cuts through the problematic rhetorics used to celebrate our various Postmodernisms, while still capturing a deep and important difference between our culture and Modernist values. For most contemporaries, the central imperative for the artist is to define ways of living within the history to which the Modernists could not be reconciled. This means locating art's fundamental resources, not in self-reflexive uses of its syntactic energies, but in some version of demotic experience, whether it be from popular visual media or from the textures of ordinary language. As Vincent Descombes put it, speaking of the imperatives governing Poststructuralist philosophy: Whereas Modernism sought to purify all of its disciplines by elaborating complex formal models that could abstract from the confusing noise of daily life, Postmodernism concentrates on the irreducible aspects of that noise, in order to dramatize the impure interests and suggestive slippage at the core of those idealized projects (see his "Essay on Philosophical Observation"). For Modernism, the fundamental need was to isolate underlying principles that enabled one to explore what could be developed by concentrating on the mind's constructive powers. For Postmodernism, the fundamental need is to accommodate such powers to the ironic, and irreducibly confused, textures that mock those powers and require entirely different dispositional complexes. The differences are clearest in epistemology. There the efforts of Bertrand Russell and Wittgenstein, in his early work, to establish a truth-functional language give way to Derrida's demonstration that the ideal of a "proper sense" for words is based on metaphors reintroducing the very notions of property and propriety that the project seeks to banish. Similarly, Modernism sought, in the transparency of self-reflexive testimonial art, access to those features of spiritual life that could be purified of their historical contexts. But for Postmodernism, no construction will banish or evade the inescapable effects of such conceptual slippage and such social embedding for our projects. The best one can do is develop arts as subtle and fluid as the intricate confusions that define social life and keep the constructive mind trapped within its proper parameters. So, rather than attempt to resist history, these poets and painters look for a "ground" within history that can sustain values reinforced by the collapse of constructivist ambitions: Where Schönberg had been, there Cage would have to suffice.

In my view, these Postmodernist experiments introduce a substantially new spiritual dispensation, finally making it possible to imagine an art that does not set itself against apparently irresistible forces of social and historical change. But that dispensation makes it even more crucial that we preserve the full energies cultivated by Modernism. For now that our own art tries to accommodate itself to all of the ironies of history, we need to be reminded that this is not the only, or perhaps even the best, way to understand the roles that art can play in our lives. The more we see what the task of accommodation involves, the more we shall need to challenge the contemporary imagination, by reminding it of those moments when the mind sees itself as capable of living in, and for, communities not bound to that history and the compromises it entails. We must continue to seek ideals of identity that insist on making their own forms for the noise threatening to subsume all of our fictions into the world that is all too much with us.[11]

Appendix 1:
Postmodernist Poetics Unfair to Modernist Poetry

Because one of my chief concerns is to propose a vital Modernist aesthetic that can at once guide and challenge contemporary poetry and criticism, I think it is important to direct these arguments against what are now the dominant enabling rhetorics for a Postmodernist poetry.[1] Although it is true that every age succumbs to the temptation to exaggerate its differences from its predecessors, the proponents of Postmodernism seem to succumb more readily than most: When one is eager to demystify the past, one is likely to feel few constraints against mystifying the present. For my purpose, these all too easy contrasts between a benighted "Modernism" and a heroic "Postmodernism" in fact isolate the self-congratulatory impulse, in all its shabby passion, and thereby make evident the force of Modernist critical imperatives. This then allows me to propose a pragmatic argument also defending two other, currently unfashionable, critical ambitions basic to this book: the curatorial project of describing past works of art in such a manner that their energies remain available for imaginative lives in the present, and the provocative task of proposing that past as a measure requiring contemporaries to explore richer and more complex versions of the powers they claim to cultivate.

No one model for Postmodernist poetry prevails today. Instead, two radically opposed models (with several variants) compete for hegemony. The first takes the basic demand on contemporary poetry to be continuing the ideals of avant-garde experiment, but adjusting them to meet the social and epistemological conditions that contemporaneity imposes. The second insists on a conservative faith that poetry best addresses its society by relying on fairly constant ideals of lyric expression. Ironically, each of these perspectives bases its appeal on claims that it can liberate us from what prove to be almost the same set of "Modernist errors." Yet each in fact turns out to share, in its characterizations of Modernism, the same contemporary blinders. Consider the degree to which the following statements allow our need to distinguish ourselves as contemporary to impoverish the vocabulary we have available for the discussion of Modernist values, and hence for formulating our significant differences from them.

I take my example of the first model from Marjorie Perloff's eloquent essay, "Postmodernism and the Impasse of Lyric." Perloff contrasts Anglo-American Modernism with a Postmodernist poetry that she praises for being much more responsive than Modernist poetry to the logic of "collage," initially elaborated by the European avant-garde:

> Postmodernism in poetry . . . begins in the urge to return the material so rigidly excluded – political, ethical, historical, philosophical – to the domain of poetry, which is to say that the Romantic lyric, the poem as expression of a moment of absolute insight, of emotion crystallized into a timeless pattern, gives way to a poetry that can, once again, accommodate narrative and didacticism, the serious and the comic, verse and prose. . . . A new poetry is emerging that wants to open the field so as to make contact with the *world* as well as the *word*. . . . In the poetry of the late twentieth century, the cry of the heart, as Yeats called it, is increasingly subjected to the play of the mind – a play that wants to take account of [what John Cage calls] "the process which is the world we live in." (180–1, 197)

Jonathan Holden, however, has little truck with that call for openness and process, preferring an ethical contrast that sets Modernist poetry against a dramatic, personal poetry which elicits emotional richness from representative human situations:

> The fundamental choice confronting the poet working in America today . . . is a choice between analogues, between forms which . . . range from the communal to the impersonal. Curiously enough, this choice ends up being not an epistemological one but an ethical one; whether to trust the self and presume to impose upon the world, by sheer force of character, an individual aesthetic and ethical order or to continue the Modernist hegemony of Eliot and Pound, to retreat in an elitist disgust from modern civilization and indulge in the facile despair of the parodist, recapitulating all the bad languages that comprise our environment, holding our own civilization up before us as if the sad facts could only speak for themselves. ("Postmodern Poetic Form: A Theory" 22)

There are better academic accounts of Modernist poetry.[2] These examples, however, offer superb illustrations of the difficulties that one faces in attempting to recommend the values that Modernist poetry tried to realize. If we elaborate what the two models share, we can locate four fundamental assumptions that threaten to confine Modernist poetry to the dusty stacks of literary history, to be called up only when one wants to dignify another contemporary movement.

1. Modernist poetry negates a vital sense of life, because of an excessive formalism. For Perloff, the formalism consists in fealty to the Romantic sense of the well-made expressive lyric, whose need for closure prevents it from attending to the intricacies of life as "process." For Holden and other conservative critics, the formalism stems from an anti-Romantic reduction of a metaphysical organicism to an aestheticist one, which confines the play of mind to the play of language. Thus Holden can add the ethical complaint that this formalism engenders an exotic, experimental spirit, setting poets in an adversary relation to the rest of culture, but Perloff must treat that experimental attitude as the necessary means to freeing the spirit from narrow moral and sentimental concerns. In either case, the central issue is the possibility of locating an "extraformal content" that directly engages the intellect in the social life of its culture and thus makes poetic images "conduits to everything that lies outside themselves."[3]

2. The modes of presenting human agency become severely problematic. Perloff sees the Modernist lyric as still, like earlier poetry, too personal, too tied to an expressivist ego that is poorly disguised by the surface impersonality. Bound to self-regarding melodramatic states, such work cannot engage in the full, free play of intellect that poetry affords, and that contemporary life demands, because of the intricate ways in which it distributes the psyche. Holden, on the other hand, reacts against Modernist poetry's dogmatic impersonality, locating there the denial of virtually everything that could make poetry significant for a society which is certainly impersonal enough in its own right. Impersonality simultaneously eliminates the personal struggle for form that gives the art its intensity, and deprives poetry of its most engaging content: the human voice, as it attempts to align its personal commitments with the pressures of reality.

3. The conjunction of impersonality with the imperative to formal autonomy severely reduces the social and psychological powers that can be claimed for poetry. As Charles Newman puts it, "The history of Modernism is the history of a failure to affect the moral life of the culture by aesthetic means alone" ("The Post-Modern Aura" 31). Those means simply cannot create a sufficient sense of the world – for Perloff, because they narrow attention to the lyric sensibility; for Holden, because, with

the refusal of the speaking voice, "the presence of a central consciousness all but disappears."[4] Thus Modernist poetry supposedly has no focus for idealization and is condemned to vacillate between two problematic poles. Most of the time, poetic utterance emerges from, and reinforces, fragmented psyches that replicate the general depersonalizing effects of modern capitalism. Under the pressure of such fragmentation, poets are tempted by fantasies of totally unified organic societies, freed from the burden of differences inescapable in actual political life.

4. The ultimate sign of the Modernist failure is the conservative political sympathies that so many Modernist poets adopted late in their careers. They were susceptible to such fealties, the reasoning goes, because their art never sufficiently bound them to the complex contingencies of practical life. Thus, they found authoritarian attitudes congenial – the imagination that was able to compose form could compose social order – and they easily succumbed to the compensatory fantasy that their lack of social impact was a sign of social decay requiring a radical cure.

These charges have a good deal of validity, but they fail to take into account the fact that the Modernists themselves recognized the dangers in the radical nature of their enterprise and worked hard to make clear those cultural forces that they thought demanded such strong countermeasures. Ironically, by overlooking this, contemporary criticism repeats precisely the conditions that Modernist poets opposed, so there is no better measure of Modernism's continuing importance. For example, it is argumentative procedures like Holden's that best justify insisting on "formal" routes to "extraformal" contents. Nothing could make impersonality more appealing than Holden's reliance on claims of personal sensitivity to shore up ethical assertions for which he has woefully inadequate grounds. Such devices for gaining authority echo the fundamental strategies of the Victorian poets, who, by substituting "sensitivity" for more intricate and abstract forms of self-consciousness and by using their sense of "righteousness" as a blunderbuss, evaded the need for careful moral analysis. So long as personalism reigns, poets have little incentive to resist narcissistic, self-deluding models of sensibility in favor of frameworks that might locate more intricate, and less subjective, principles of judgment. Such self-staging eventually demands that poets take another way: that they attempt to make formal energies their fundamental resource for projecting and testing alternative models for a human agency that might express its idealizing desires without having to be embarrassed by the results.[5]

Reading Perloff as symptomatic is more difficult, since Holden's arguments show that she is right in pointing to the continuing dangers of the cultural forces released by the Romantic tradition. There is nonetheless something limited about her statement. Eliminate the quotation from

Cage, and her comment would seem completely appropriate in the mouth of a Modernist poet or a critic such as Cleanth Brooks, as he tries to defend an urban complexity in poetry against the lyric indulgences of the nineteenth-century sensibility. That occurs, I think, because Perloff has internalized Modernist tastes, only to find herself in the dilemma of having to use their rhetoric against itself. Only in that way can she maintain for Postmodernism a version of that commitment to avant-garde experiments responsive to a distinctive contemporary reality. Indeed, the zeal to differ may conceal from her how closely she echoes the ringing tones of one of Modernism's fundamental exercises in self-definition. This is the climax of Eliot's essay, "The Metaphysical Poets":

> The difference is not a simple difference of degree between poets. It is something that happened to the mind of England between the time of Donne . . . and the time of Tennyson and Browning; it is the difference between the intellectual poet and the reflective poet. Tennyson and Browning are poets, and they think; but they do not feel their thought as immediately as the odour of a rose. A thought to Donne was an experience; it modified his sensibility. When a poet's mind is perfectly equipped for its work, it is constantly amalgamating disparate experiences. . . . We may express the difference by the following theory: The poets of the seventeenth century, the successors of the dramatists of the sixteenth, possessed a mechanism of sensibility which could devour any kind of experience. They are simple, artificial, difficult, or fantastic, as their predecessors were. . . . [But] the sentimental age began early in the eighteenth century, and continued. The poets revolted against the ratiocinative, the descriptive; they thought and felt by fits, unbalanced; they reflected. In one or two passages of Shelley's *Triumph of Life,* in the second *Hyperion,* there are traces of a struggle toward unification of sensibility. But Keats and Shelley died, and Tennyson and Browning ruminated. (*Selected Essays* 247–8)

Perloff would be quick to note, in this passage, a continuation of the Romantic concern for a unified sensibility completely at odds with her own values. But stopping with this reading of "unity" is precisely the problem. The unities that concern Eliot have very little to do with the subjective idealism basic to the Romantic notions of poetic form and the deep life of the individual ego. If we take Eliot's dissertation on Bradley as our norm, we see that for Eliot these constructed unities are the one escape that we have from the instability of the personal ego. And if we simply read the passage that I have just quoted carefully, we might observe that few contemporary poets are so bold as to imitate Deleuze by characterizing the agent of that unity as "a mechanism of sensibility that could devour any kind of experience." So even when Eliot echoes Romanticism, he is excruciatingly aware that his poetry must tease out a model of agency much less able to transform what it witnesses, and much more complex and fluid in relation to any attempt to cast that unity in humanistic terms. Instead of reinforcing persistent cultural paradigms, he imagines the intricate intelligence of the work itself as the necessary vehicle for establishing the force for what had been called "unity" and "subjectivity." But that effort will not speak to those anxious to condemn Eliot for his political beliefs, or even his Symboliste affinities, as if these too did not have to be understood through the work. Perloff's quick and sensitive grasp of the new, ironically, tempts her to accept its formulation of the old without quite coming to terms with elements that still leave their traces in our imaginative lives.[6]

Poetry had to be abstract, then, because the alternatives seemed only to repeat the fundamental problems still facing the culture: a tendency, on the one hand, to exalt the private sensibility and thereby avoid the difficulties posed by historical change, and, on the other, a tendency to represent those changes in a language all too easy to treat in relatively simple or melodramatic experimental terms, such as those of Futurism or Expressionist painting. Only rigorous distancing mechanisms seemed capable of releasing the constructive energies needed to produce more valid forms of idealization, not contaminated by the factors that transform sentiments such as Holden's into versions of Yeats's "bitter glass, mocking what it would memorialize." And only something as radical, and as resistant to the resources of our narcissism, as Eliot's intense reformulations of psychic life might produce the "cure of the ground" for which Stevens called.

Appendix 2:
A Conceptual Grammar for
Constructivist Abstraction

I

Getting straight about abstraction obviously takes an embarrassing amount of abstraction. But it would be a mistake to let frustration or embarrassment send us off to the pleasures of particular works without seeking the fullest possible theoretical framework for the values explored in those works, especially if one believes, as I do, that Modernist theorizing can have significant force on contemporary thinking in its own right. Therefore I resort to an appendix as my means of elaborating the theoretical complexities involved in Modernist thought. This way those interested primarily in the poetry will not be unnecessarily overburdened, while those who share my interest in the ideas can have the leisure to give them the attention they deserve. Granting that attention entails two closely related tasks, I must try to clarify several of the key concepts that I have relied upon in distinguishing Modernist constructivism from other stylistic orientations; and I must show how those concepts constitute an intricate network allowing us to make generalizations toward and about the work. In the arts we cannot treat such networks as coherent systems, since there is no apparent systematic principle for describing the mutual interactions. We can nonetheless speak of a coherent field of mutual influences and adaptations, kept in a kind of gravitational motion by the artists' efforts to replace representational values with principles capable of unmaking and remaking very powerfully entrenched aesthetic and moral expectations about art.

My exemplar for this project is Meyer Abrams's effort, in *The Mirror and the Lamp*, to identify four orientations that enable us to make significant distinctions among the basic poetic theories within Western culture.

But whereas Abrams's major concern is to establish terms for classifying and distinguishing among theories, I shall use his categories for what I call grammatical purposes. Rather than classifying stances by dominant tropes, I propose treating all four categories as necessary issues that every aesthetic theory must deal with if it hopes to be taken very seriously for very long.[1] Even though broad emphases vary enormously, Abrams shows that any theory in the arts, or any governing set of aesthetic assumptions, must account for (1) the nature of the productive force constituting authorship; (2) the set of formal arrangements that allows the work a distinctive presence as art; (3) the relation that those formal elements allow the work to maintain to the world; and (4) the resulting position that this relation establishes for an audience. More important, every theory or set of assumptions will eventually be judged by its ability to modify each of the constituent elements so that they come together to provide a coherent vision of the consequences of the underlying commitments. Like a fine bicycle, individual claims must be held in place by a complex set of tensions, with all of the elements often in need of continual (and annoying) adjustments.

Were I to select one governing principle for Modernist aesthetics, I would choose its foregrounding of authorial activity as formal energies that offer exemplary conditions of agency. However, this exercise would have little point – would in fact be a paradigm of abstractness – because it would assume that this one principle is independent of the others, and that its hegemony can be isolated from the related terms that give it a context and a definable force. We have already seen the contrary. In the painters and poets whose work we have examined, we have observed that what one means by authorial expression depends on one's view of what formal syntax makes available, and one's view of syntax relates to one's understanding of art's relation to models of the mind. Such models, in turn, involve ideas of how art might carry extraformal content, and the specific account that one gives of any of the three other categories in Abrams's scheme depends on how one imagines the audience's possible engagement in the sites that the work produces. Therefore, I shall concentrate here simply on showing how the various conceptual elements used to articulate these aspects of constructivist abstraction can be brought into the necessary adjustment with one another. A deconstructionist could go on to show that those adjustments are always unstable, because each of the constituents also depends on alternative frameworks: where there is a seam, there is also a potential gap or fault (as in my metaphors here). But I shall be content if I can clarify the interrelationships that compose as coherent an overall aesthetic as we are likely to get, however much the coherence is threatened by the compromises that make it possible. Given the magnitude of even that task, I shall have to rely on a minimal amount of quotation. More extensive documentation is available in the historical accounts that I have mentioned in my notes, and in some of the concrete discussions elsewhere in this book.

II

I begin with the category that Abrams calls the relation between the work and the world it tries to implicate or refer to. For this topic raises those issues where Modernism most emphatically sets itself against its predecessors, and thus it is here that by returning to our discussion of exemplification we can now fully evaluate its insistence that the new art must replace representational views of the content of art with constructivist views possessing at least equal power, but less complicit in the limitations of the prevailing social order. If we dealt only with the specific Modernist statements on this topic, it would be easy, and correct, to take the Modernists' arguments against representation as reductive and incomplete. Thought being what it is, and artists being unsystematic thinkers, these arguments prove much more specific and pointed about what they oppose than about what they want to put in its place. After all, theory need only clear the way, allowing the art itself to make the positive case. And so great was the revulsion, and the need, and the ambition, in the early years of this century, that subtle and careful argument would hardly serve. Consequently, many of the Modernist complaints about representation take the form of the large generalizations possible only when one deals with straw men or inferior writers, and much of their rhetoric remains insensitive to the achievements of the best representational art. Yet, if we keep the Modernists' more precise, subsidiary claims in mind, and if we develop a more defensible model of representation than the one they criticized, we will be in a position to appreciate the logic of their critique and the considerable sophistication and scope of their proposed alternative to mimetic ideals.

The primary reason why Modernist critiques of representational models of art were so crude was that they took on the impossibly general task of showing how the dominant mode of traditional art had reinforced the major social problems facing modern society. On the simplest level, representational art could be accused of submitting to the ideology of material progress that, in their view, dictated most of society's real values. Yet its humanistic heritage proved equally suspect, since the Modernists believed that this heritage provided moral and rhetorical masks allowing the culture self-congratulatory evasions of what it had in fact become. So representational art stands condemned of both excessive materialism and an excessively abstract rhetoric. On the most general social level, the prevailing mimetic ideal for art seemed inescapably tied to all that photography had come to represent: the authority of the scientific method; the empiricist concentration on conditions of practical life that excluded all spiritual concerns; and the rejection of all values based on historical inquiry, because they seemed incompatible with the ideal of progress. These allegiances, in turn, promised little relief from the modes of public judgment cultivated by the ideal of material progress. Representational writers might insist on the importance of the emotional life and the positive social role that virtues such as sympathy might play, but the work's commitment to reproducing its social world also reproduced the utilitarian ethic in fact governing that world. Consequently, rhetorical resistance to the prevailing values usually seemed merely an exercise in self-deception, substituting the old pieties for the cruelties of the new lucidity. The best nineteenth-century artists, therefore, could do little more than cultivate alternative forms of passivity, such as the self-defeating irony always lurking in the background of George Eliot's novels. In narrative and drama, paradigms for artistic exposition seemed to impose shapes on the action that made it difficult to locate, or to test, alternative powers: Realism breeds realists, as every practical political order keeps demonstrating. And realists seemed incapable of analyzing the ways in which the form of fiction is itself central in shaping the investments that govern a culture's self-representations. Representational artists and writers might test their interpretive ability in relation to the imaginative actions that they re-presented, but they could not fully reflect, within that mode, on the sources of their energies or on the possible contradictions embedded in the very logic of narrative judgment on which they relied. Even writers like Conrad and James, who tried to make some of these problems the subject for fictional analysis, seemed constrained, by their formal and epistemological commitments, to purely passive resistance, putting resignation in the place where a Modernist artist envisioned revolution. And when "the best lack all conviction," the average – those who in fact reinforce the audience's investments in the dominant cultural order – find themselves simultaneously arrogant and blind: convinced of the significance of their roles, but unable to understand the complicity that those roles involve. Representational ideals once profoundly caught up in the project of Enlightenment now seemed capable of sustaining only public values that reinforced a self-congratulatory bourgeois dispensation, which became more appalling as it achieved increasing power.

The virulence of these Modernist attacks could not be matched by their precision. Modernists were rarely clear on what representational writers had sought to do, nor did they attempt to make the necessary distinctions between the various arts, or between representational styles varying from Zola's naturalism to Byron's and Scott's heroic fantasies.

In fact, as Michael Levenson shows, these Modernist critiques did not even quite accurately reflect the prevailing fictional mode of their own time. For by 1900, what might be called a "public realism" had given way to the cultivation of subjective authority based on the intricate engagements of a complex recording psyche.[2] Representational claims were to be tested not so much by focusing on the pictorial features of the image as by emphasizing the qualities of the representing sensibility as it tries to make its experience testimony for its ability to interpret the events in general. Yet these oversimplifications do not disqualify the spirit of the Modernist critique. Once we recognize what the Modernists treated reductively in their polemical efforts to clear a ground for themselves, we can make a better case for their perceptions. Their blindness was not without insight, their oversimplifications not without an intriguing shift in the level of abstraction that may, in fact, allow us to connect their artistic methods with prevailing social values. For example, it is clear that in failing to distinguish between modes of representation in the different media, they ignored crucial differences. But they also thereby made it possible to shift the focus from the area of method, where we find those differences, to questions about the overall motives underlying the work. And it is there that we can locate significant common concerns and features among the different arts that have important parallels with the psychological and emotional economics prevailing in the marketplace.[3] Similarly, although in theory Modernist doctrine ignored the gradual subjectification of the representational arts, in practice Modernist art responded to that process in two important ways. First, it registered the increasing tension between what could and could not be expressed within an art purporting to be a "window" on the real. Second, it located, in its own contrary practice, an alternative form of testimony, capable of establishing semantic and social force for those constructive energies that the old model either had to ignore or appropriate under psychological narratives shaped by the old logic.

To understand that alternative testimony, we must first get clear on what is at stake when art is treated as representational; then we will be able to see how the relevant principles are transformed by the new dispensation. From a Modernist perspective, representational art had, by the nineteenth century, become a project of providing illusionary pictures that were presumed to serve as direct copies of specific scenic configurations. Art not only evoked phenomena; it literally "portrayed" them, so that it was conceivable to imagine how the image might be improved or altered in order to correspond better to some feature of the object for which it stood.[4] But that descriptive orientation is at best only part of the story. The traditional principle of mimesis continued to be a major influence on the way that most writers and painters conceived their task, and that principle leads far beyond the concept of copying. Mimesis entails idealization. Mimesis is the artistic rendering of appearances devoted to some latent, normative sense of what is potential within a scene or event, and it requires interpretive judgment on the part of the artist.

No theory of representation that does not handle both of these dimensions of the concept can suffice. To encompass both, however, we must shift from an essentially "documentary" model of the artistic image to one that emphasizes the rhetorical roles that the image can serve.[5] From this perspective, what motivates the art is not the desire to copy particulars, but the commitment to using art's likeness to the world of appearances in order to achieve a wide range of interpretive and performative effects that might have ethical consequences: Consider the contests, in the Renaissance, about who could best render appearances so that they seemed natural, and consider how often mimesis was invoked in the interest of Platonic theories of educating the spirit in underlying truths. We need not give up the claim that fictions clarify truths, but we must try to restate this claim, so that it is no longer dependent on pictorial theories of truth, but emerges from the relationship that authors try to establish with their audience.[6]

That relationship is quite complex, as is evident in the two, uneasily aligned, fundamental uses of the word "representation." In addition to the epistemological meaning, which stresses what a sign stands in the place of, there is of course a political meaning, which emphasizes the specific rights and obligations allowing a person to stand for other persons. A rhetorical theory entails reading the referential claims in terms of the political ones. Therefore the desire for fidelity to appearances is not an abstract truth condition, but a way of adapting one's discourse to the pragmatic expectations of one's audience, so that they will grant it the status of political representative. But that, too, is not a simple matter. Once again we encounter two uneasily aligned meanings. In one dimension, the political or rhetorical representative must be a fully *representative person,* so reflecting the values of a community that the audience can completely identify with the person. The representative is the one bound to divine the collective interest and to act accordingly: He or she in effect objectifies the collective *will,* just as science objectifies what can be taken as a collective reality. But the second dimension leads in a very different direction. For when constituencies select representatives, they often do not expect them simply to parrot what is normally seen as the interests of the group. They also envision the representative as taking the lead in formulating those interests. Representatives are expected to use the grounds for authority that they gain by their representativeness to project possible states where certain powers or certain interests, now blocked or murky, can be made available for the community. Representatives can alter the values that they represent, just as mimetic works of art can try to tease new understandings out of the communal understandings with which they work.

In order to show how these factors shape representation, we must treat its epistemological status as involving not two, but three, terms: a set of signs; a referent in some world that can be equated with the one we normally inhabit; and a set of interpretive procedures that justify the author's manipulation of those equations. Thus, instead of speaking in empiricist fashion about "accuracy to the facts," we must speak, in dramatistic terms, about the specific habits of "matching" that create a plausible theater implicating the audience in the representation. It is not specific properties of signs, but the logic linking them, that constructs this stage and binds the syntax of the work to the expectations about coherence informing the audience's sense of practical experience. By relying on the same interpretive principles that govern ordinary behavior, the artist can easily claim his or her fictions pertain directly to the world she shares with that community: first, because the principles directly implicate extraformal content; second, because the concrete detail can be said to provide essentially the same stimuli for all members of the audience, apparently by virtue of conditions that are objective, and not simply projections of the individual. Thus the audience can bring to the work all of the intensity of its beliefs and the concerns that they would bring to the same modes of action when they encountered them in life. And should the audience decide that the representation succeeds in portraying life, they can devote to it all of the conviction and compassion that they would give to actual events and commitments. The reward, for the artist who accepts representational constraints, is that she is accorded the power to manipulate and to interpret the most significant investments made by the community as it attempts to bring coherence to its experiences.

Nineteenth century representational artists seemed to fear that the artist can gain identifications with an audience only by appearing not to desire them. Desire must be subordinated to techniques of naturalizations as the work's ground for gaining individual authority. Recent criticism has been quick to leap upon this contradiction, for the good reason that it repeats the fundamental strategy used by bourgeois culture to secure its own dominance in society. By manipulating standard principles of social coherence, artists can create the illusion that the structure one gives to the actions is not simply a product of a specific culture's ideology, but captures deep truths that will be available to other cultures – as witnesses to one's own time, and as instruction for theirs. To stop with such criticism, however, is to miss the full range of possibilities, and perhaps even of obligations, that the politics of representation provides. Artists can use their power over conventions to make explicit the grounds of social life. They can even propose, from those grounds, ideal possibilities that the culture may be willing to accept as both desirable and attainable – or perhaps, indeed, shameful to ignore, once they have been pointed out (as has been the case with matters of race, for a good portion of Western society). Representational art, in other words, has the ability both to identify with a community and to project ideal roles for it. The greatest artists can simultaneously make an audience feel that its typical ideas and sympathies have been enhanced, and redirect these ideas and sympathies, so that they elicit identifications with the ideals that the author presents as compatible with them. *Middlemarch,* for example, succeeds to the extent that it makes an audience feel enlarged by, and committed to, the powers that Eliot's rendering makes available to them: not only to see as Eliot sees, but also to assume the moral attitudes that seem required by that angle of vision.

Representational art, then, involves a complex set of adjustments between the reinforcing of established values and the use of provisional identifications to alter the prevailing models of identity within the culture. This takes place in part through what the characters or scenes render, in part through the interpretation of characters and scenes that is suggested by the formal structure of the work. The effects are to be measured in part by the way that we, as audience, find our own interpretive abilities changing, and in part by our coming to project certain *alternative selves* upon that world. Representational art confers knowledge, not because of what it pictures, but because of the surrogate selves through whom audiences try out exalted states of thinking and feeling. Shared expectations about interpreting actions become the pretext for projective states that only the individual artistic performance can convince us are worth pursuing.[7]

Once we are forced to recognize that representational art can be as constructive and performative as the best of Modernist work, we must change the level of our argument about the differences that Modernism proposes. Rather than either simply asserting that representational art reduces its audience to conditions of passivity or celebrating Modernism's refusal of the forms of coherence provided by the eye and the story, we need to view each as manipulating different means to ends that have a good deal in common. The better we appreciate the role of identification and projection in traditional art, the better we are likely to understand what is involved in Modernist efforts to locate the authority of the work in the direct "testimony" it gives about powers made available in transpersonal states.

The Modernists were wrong to equate representation with empiricist principles; but they were not wrong to see that once a culture has strong empiricist criteria for knowledge, traditional ideals of mimesis become more difficult to state clearly and to defend. The easy transition between real and ideal is no longer so available, nor can one readily adapt those criteria for truth to the model of ethical agency upon which earlier thinkers, such as Philip Sidney and Samuel Johnson, could rely.[8] At one extreme, representational values seemed too dependent on external authority. At the other, they seemed not sufficiently responsive to the range, scope, and utility of the creative energies that could constitute internal sources of authority still capable of extraformal consequences. The very models of coherence that made quick and deep identifications possible seemed to impose forms within which the constructive intelligence could not take account of the sources of its energy, its own dependency upon the social order, or the contradictions that the tension between those two factors generated. Thus it is no wonder that the young Modernists found themselves tempted, on the one hand, by the desire to dispel such identifications in webs of infinite irony, and, on the other, by the possibility of negating their own need for imaginative identifications. Here the fascination with nothingness and pure textuality was born; and here we find one significant context for the paralyzed self-portraits of a Mauberly or an Ensor, or even an early Picasso.

Michael Levenson locates the crucial historical turn in the perspectival renderings emphasized by turn-of-the-century novelists like Conrad, Ford, and James. (See his *Genealogy of Modernism,* chapters 1 and 2.) He argues that rather than subordinate the narrating presence to some projected representative condition, these novelists made the condition of the rendering sensibility the only possible locus of truth – not for what it can project as a possible social agreement, but for what it can reveal about its own relation to the social world that the novel renders. So the performative energies of the narrators – and, by implication, of the author – pull against any common ground, leaving the desired testimony always on the verge of turning into ironies such as those in Ford's *Good Soldier.* Whereas earlier idealizations of mimesis could include both the performative and the loosely referential, this art demonstrates their incompatibility within modern culture. The performer could still try to submit to ideals of truth by proclaiming himself a privileged witness, but that insecure allegiance with the old order should never dispel the voice of ironic skepticism threatening to choke the art on its own effort to make self-consciousness do the work of epistemology.

So clear had the problems become, and so acute the consequences, that Modernist artists and writers had to explore very different imaginative orientations. By making the performance itself the locus of possible representativeness, they defined within their work models of agency and value capable of sustaining an alternative economics for negotiating issues of identification and authority. Rather than rely on the constraints that had seemed necessary to ground art's relationship to its audience, and rather than pose cognitive claims that would distinguish the artist from the designer or craftsperson, the art might make its own rhetorical needs and constructive efforts its means for establishing extraformal content. Representational art had already shown the way, in at least one respect: It made the authority of the work depend less on its "truth" than on the powers organized by imagining the illusionary world as intersecting one's actual situation. Suppose that this sense of congruence between powers and situations need not depend on the emotional and intellectual alignments produced by treating constructions as if they organized perceptual and dramatic fields that one reads by the same logic employed in those practical affairs. Suppose that we can begin to see how debilitating those logics are, how thoroughly they bind our deepest emotional energies to corrupt social, and even ontological, orders, only if we can find through art the means to get *beyond* representation. Perhaps then we could take the idea of the existence of an "other" side of representation as something more than a fantasy of those nostalgic for the old religious consolations. Perhaps we could rely on artworks to map that realm, by the energies and powers they articulate.

All of this was, and is, at stake in the Modernist effort to base its semantic claims on the direct representativeness of foregrounded authorial states. Kant had already laid the conceptual foundations for the values that could oppose empiricism when he claimed that the entire edifice of representation depends on the limited frameworks provided by the "understanding." Then idealist thought, along with myriad mystical movements from Steiner to Bergson, had followed Coleridge's lead in fleshing out a noumenal realm beyond representations, a realm that Kant thought the mind had to posit but could never say anything valid about. Those hopes, however, proved more a burden than a release for many of the Modernists, because they betrayed the depth of spiritual need that could as easily trap the imagination in nostalgic self-indulgence as it could establish secularly plausible alternatives to what the understanding governed. So Modernist authorial performances had somehow to marshal the mystical side of Kant against the positivism he also fostered, without succumbing to old versions of what constituted spiritual life.

Modernist art accomplished that task largely by replacing the logic of the window and the narrative account with what must be called the *logic of the imaginative site*. Whereas the logic of the "window" correlates scenic properties with forms of significance or types, that can be sustained by a mode of "telling," the logic of the "imaginative site" substitutes formal elements for those scenic features, and establishes their significance *by making the composing energies exemplify possible dispositions of mind with which an audience is invited to identify*. For example, as we saw in Chapter 1, instead of painting a social scene, Duchamp disposes line and tone to embody a mode of activity that can directly address the idea of chess. Matisse, instead of making his vehicle of representativeness the details of a woman's posture and relation to her surroundings, as Degas would, asks how the painterly energies can directly participate in understanding an aspect of sexuality. Similarly, the logic of the "site" requires treating authorial energies, not as *subjectively* oriented investments, but as a mode of *objective* expression. There is still an emphasis on a distinctive authorial performance, but its claims to provide a privileged interpretive position no longer rely on any autobiographical framework: Authorial power resides only in the work's direct exemplifying of what agency could be, if one tried to identify with it.

There are obviously as many exemplary sites for defining these possible modes of agency as there are constructivist works of art. However, the best brief way to understand the fundamental ideological structures sustained by these ideals of constructivist agency is to concentrate for a few moments on the two basic orientations of *will* that underlie this variety. Each mode is self-reflexive, but they offer very different versions of powers that the work carries in relation to the world: One mode is essentially a way of imagining the ways in which the mind engages what had been the province of representational art. The other is essentially concerned with how purely psychic powers can be articulated by dwelling on what formal energies can construct.[9] (Each mode may rely on transpersonal senses of what the agency makes available, or may dwell on powers that become representative only through the intensity of individual self-assertion.) For the first mode, the obvious avatar is Cézanne's effort to make the authorial energies exemplify forms of constructive activity capable of intensifying the perceptual energies we focus upon the world. Where description had been, there art must turn to a model of "realization" (*réalisation*) that defines attitudes it can take in order to understand its own contributions to the fullness of appearances. At the other pole, we have exemplary acts such as those of Stevens and Mondrian: These pursue a mode of *nobility,* or "monumentality," focused by self-reflexive energies that promise access to forces which cannot be contained within images bound to the logic of appearance.

In Cézanne and Williams, and more complexly in Pound and some of Picasso's work, art matters because of the ways it displays the mind disposing itself toward objective structures. The focus is not on what is represented, what stands before the eye, but on how the eye can move in the world. This is an art, not of the visible, but of the *conditions* of visibility (or, often in poetry, of the possible transparency of an eloquent use of

language that one finds in Stevens, Marianne Moore, and John Ashbery).
The art must take responsibility for *how* it makes the visible visible, so that
its subject becomes the alignment of *will* and *world,* accomplished without
any irritable reaching after symbols and stories. Full self-consciousness is
necessary for a full emotional attachment to things as they are. And the
only way not to have the will continually exceed perception is to have its
demands already factored into the stance one employs as one's means of
making those perceptions articulate. By keeping attention focused on the
constructive forces that allow the scene to appear as it does, and, for the
Impressionists, by transforming the role of light, so that light is inseparable from the compositional activity, this art projects itself as negating
habitual modes of seeing and telling, in order to allow the mind to
experience powers that have little to do with the limited range of subjective interests that usually occupies our attention. Just as Matisse's line
simultaneously creates and responds to his mistress's sexuality, Williams's
poet plays the role of a farmer, the composer-antagonist who with his
hands confined in his pockets nonetheless produces the structures which
give his field the possibility of assuming its potential fertility:

> The farmer in deep thought
> is pacing through the rain
> among his blank fields, with
> hands in pockets,
> in his head
> the harvest already planted.
>
> A cold wind ruffles the water
> among the browned weeds
> on all sides
> the world rolls coldly away:
> black orchards
> darkened by the March clouds –
> leaving room for thought.
> Down past the brushwood
> bristling by
> the rainsluiced wagonroad
> looms the artist figure of
> the farmer-composing
> – antagonist
>
> (*Imaginations* 98–9)

Such images of composition eventually lead far beyond a revitalized
landscape. At stake are the powers of mind that so define landscape,
through their antagonistic efforts to impose forms upon it. A fine discur-

sive account of those powers occurs in a remarkable passage in which Pound tries to show the implications of the Vorticist concern for constructive form.

> These new men have made me see form, have made me more conscious of the appearance of the sky where it juts down between houses, . . . of the great "Vs" of light that dart through the chinks over the curtain rings, all these are new chords, new keys of design. . . .
>
> All this is new life, it gives a new aroma, a new keenness for keeping awake. . . .
>
> "I have not repulsed God in his manifestation," says the old Egyptian poet. Today I see so many who could not say, or who could scarcely say it, for these manifestations at their intensest are the manifestation of men in the heat of their art, of men making instruments, for the best art is perhaps only the making of instruments.
>
> A clavicord or a statue or a poem, wrought out of ages of knowledge, out of fine perception and skill, that some other man, that a hundred other men, in moments of weariness can wake beautiful sound with little effort, that they can be carried out of the realm of annoyance into the calm realm of truth, into the world unchanging, the world of fine animal life, the world of pure form. (*Gaudier-Brzeska* 126–7)

Pound begins by focusing on the way form affects concrete vision. Then, without ever renouncing that concreteness, his third paragraph works a stunning transformation. It shifts from what one sees through artistic form to what one infers from the signs of its making, so that the final image of pure form moves fluidly between a sense of renewed animal life and the awareness of the mental energies making the renewal possible and transcending it. Now secular art can compete with traditional religious functions, because it has its own allegorical space. The dynamic qualities of form literally carry immanent energies so responsive to the deepest registers of our constructive concerns that we must see them as theophanic. And, from that realization, it is not a large step to Picasso, where all talk of "forms" and "gods" leads back to the drama of a will, able to produce on its own terms the very objective conditions that it needs, to satisfy its intense emotional demands on the objective world.

"Realizational" aesthetics treats form as a measure of possible ways the mind can be satisfied within the same world addressed by representational art. Stevens and Mondrian pursue a very different kind of visibility, committed to presenting forces or principles whose nobility becomes manifest in their resistance to that world. From this perspective, traditional works that invite the visual or hermeneutic logics central to representation subsume and displace precisely those energies that can give art its most distinctive extraformal roles. For it is not in the forms themselves, but in the energies of reflective concentration marshaled by art's synthetic activity that art provides the one model within secular life able to align us with what people once attributed to the gods. Rilke puts the alternative in terms as succinct as they are free of traditional spiritualist rhetoric:

> The perfect poem can only materialize on condition that the world, acted upon by all five levers simultaneously [i.e., the five senses], is seen, under a definite aspect, on the supernatural plane, which is in fact the plane of the poem. . . . [Thus the poet, like the lover,] is in such splendid danger just because he must depend upon the coordination of his senses, for he knows that they must meet in that unique and risky centre, in which, renouncing all extension, they come together and have no permanence. (*Selected Works* 54)

There are, in other words, two fundamental tasks that this model of constructivist abstraction attributes to the foregrounded authorial act. Rather than establish a mode of making the world visible, it puts such pressure on its sensuous surfaces that they provide an *alternative* physical medium, expressive in direct proportion to their success in undoing the forms of organization that create compelling images and stories. By recombining the senses, a new materiality is composed. Then, having produced a fully intensive form of imaginative participation in the real, the art must test its achievement. Since it cannot do that by any form of denotation – cannot turn back to see how the sky is transformed by form – it must base its claims on the states that it makes available for an audience willing to occupy Rilke's risky, extensionless center, where the intensive forces get coordinated as one structure.

History provides the best framework for locating this extensionless center. Whereas the realizational ideal transforms Impressionist claims to change how we see, Rilke wants to transform Symbolisme's effort to make us see the desires and forms that go into our seeing, in ways not contaminated by the analogical frameworks imposed by representational forms. Rilke shares the Symboliste war on extensional uses of language, but he thinks that success in that war entails replacing Symboliste versions of mystery with a model of concentration so pure that it makes the life of the senses the vehicle for attaining the "other side" of representation. Thus the old spiritualism, which Odillon Redon called "an expressive, suggestive, and indeterminate art" (*Theories of Modern Art* 120), provides the basis for a new model of agency. Without quite rejecting the subjectivist psychology informing the Symbolisme of Gauguin, and even of popularizers of Mallarmé such as Arthur Symons, Rilke seizes on the mobile aspects of subjectivity that those figures had elaborated, so that he can postulate psychic energies based on absolutely elemental, and transpersonal, principles.

This is *soul-making* in its most literal sense, as the arts of painting and poetry coalesce to form new models of the spirit out of Symboliste experiments. At first those experiments seemed part of the subjectivizing of reality that placed individual temperament at the core of the representational project. But attention to the complexities of the symbol had eventually produced the crucial idea of the artwork as itself the *equivalent* of certain psychic states. In that case, constructive energies themselves prove capable of defining transpersonal forms of spiritual life. Maurice Denis's 1909 statement of synthesist principles defined the new dispensation with admirable clarity:

> We have substituted for the idea of nature seen through a "temperament," the theory of equivalence or of the symbol; we asserted that the emotions or spiritual states caused by any spectacle bring to the imagination of the artist symbols or plastic equivalents. These are capable of reproducing emotions or states of the spirit without it being necessary to provide the copy of the initial spectacle; thus for each state of our sensibility there must be a corresponding objective harmony capable of expressing it.
>
> Art is no longer a visual sensation which we record. . . . Nor is it a creation of our spirit of which nature is only the occasion. Instead of "working with the eye, we search in the mysterious center of thought," as Gauguin said. ("Subjective and Objective Deformation" 105–6)

Equivalences are made – not found and reproduced. So art's goal is not to represent – but somehow to express and understand the nature, and grounds, of its power to represent. The mind becomes the *literal source* of the signs and forces that Romanticism thought of as mediated through nature, or through situations that dramatically call forth properties of the expressive psychological self. Realizational practice enables art to become its own subject, without thereby relying on either formalism or endlessly ironic metaartistic self-qualifications. Redefining Symboliste permissions makes it possible to replace the opposition between commentary and temperament with the more suggestive and substantial distinction between "reference" of all kinds and the process of exemplifying that "mysterious center of thought" in its power to make connections and produce synthetic relations. And this alternative establishes the necessary basis for the model of "participation" which, I argued, could replace the set of issues that enters when we try to speak of art's truth to experience. Now the work itself can be said to make directly available certain aspects of this mysterious center. And, if "the principles of art correspond to those of the soul . . . [so that] Art and the Soul are one,"[10] it becomes plausible to imagine, with Mondrian, that all of the arts share the task of treating their work as the literal testing ground for what we can predicate of spirit:

> Although each art uses its own means of expression, all of them . . . tend to represent balanced relations with ever greater exactness. The balanced relation is the purest representation of universality, of the harmony and unity which are inherent characteristics of the mind. . . .
>
> We find that in nature all relations are dominated by a single primordial relation, which is defined by the opposition of two extremes. Abstract plasticism represents this primordial relation in a precise manner by means of the two positions which form the right angle. . . . If we conceive these two extremes as manifestations of interiority and exteriority, we will find that in the New Plasticism the tie uniting mind and life is not broken; thus, far from considering it the negation of a truly living life we shall see a reconciliation of the matter–mind dualism. ("Natural Reality and Abstract Reality" 322–3)

III

In dealing with the Modernist ideals of the possible relations between the artwork and the world. I have had to invoke the concept of a disposition of *formal* energies that carries *extraformal* content. Now I must try to spell out, as clearly as I can, the specific understandings of "form" that enabled the painters and the poets to imagine plausible alternatives to the kind of coherence and allegorical scope that had created resonance and authority in representational art. This argument entails treating the syntactic patterning as if it allowed physical properties of the work to carry spiritual energies with which we may make projective identifications. Without such a case, we have no decent alternative either to Osborne's aestheticism or to the legion of critics and artists who consider Modernism the pursuit of autotelic, spatially composed formal entities, which try to make up in internal complexity what they thereby escape of the world, the flesh, and the devil. Even with these stakes, however, there is surprisingly little good Modernist commentary on questions of form, probably because the artists relied on their concrete work to demonstrate what the concept involved. Therefore I shall have to take some latitude with the statements we do have, in order to reconstruct from them the terms for a decent discursive account of the topic. I shall begin by relying on representative statements reflecting each of the two models of extraformal content that we have been considering, but I shall quickly try to abstract from their basic concerns to propose an ideal type: a form for form, perhaps.

T. E. Hulme offers a superb and influential summary of the realizationist perspective on the functions of form:

> Not only are the elements of an abstract art present in Cézanne, I should say also that there was an embryo of the creative activity which was later in Cubism to organize these elements. . . .
>
> Though the simplification of planes may appear passive and prosaic, entirely dictated by a desire to reproduce a certain solidity, and from one point of view almost fumbling, yet at the same time one may say that in this treatment of detail, there is an energy at work which is working towards abstraction and towards a feeling for structure. . . . In *Baigneuses* you get a use of distortion and an emphasis on form which is constructive. The pyramidal shape, moreover, cannot be compared to decoration, or to the composition found in the old masters. The shape is so hard, so geometrical in character, that it almost lifts the picture out of the realistic art which has lasted from the Renaissance . . .
>
> In Picasso, for example, there is much greater research into nature, so far as the relation of planes is concerned, than in any realist painting; he has isolated and emphasized relations previously not emphasized. All art may be said to be realism, then, in that it extracts from nature facts which have not been observed before. But insofar as the artist is creative, he is not bound down by the accidental relations of the elements actually found in nature, but extracts, distorts, and utilizes them as a means of expression, and not as a means of interpreting nature.[11]

This is not Romantic immanence. Art does not return us to a sacramentalized world, but creates another world in its place, which is poised between precise perception and the effort to define basic structures of desire that inform and flow from those perceptions. Thus Hulme suggests that form plays two fundamental roles, each with many variants. The first role is analytic, consisting in the practice of simplifying planes and volumes, so that the architectural building blocks out of which appearances are composed replace the scenic structures grounding representational art. Here it becomes possible to imagine an abstract referent for the work, as if, by purifying it of unnecessary detail, one could capture the enduring pattern that shapes the appearances. But, although this sense of abstraction as a distinctive level of reality does play an important part in Modernism, it serves primarily to set the stage for the second, synthetic role of form: Form becomes that foregrounding of the compositional energies which gives the composing power external expression and thus defines those capacities of spirit inviting the audience's provisional identifications. Taken together, these two aspects of form ultimately extend research into nature, until form becomes what Guy Davenport's Martyn Chalk calls "an intuitive grasp of how the world might be put together."[12] By grasping the abstract contours of the scene, one in effect gains a hold on the relation between natural and psychic constitutive energies that actually compose what we come to see.

However, this level of self-reflection does not fully capture what can be involved in lifting "the picture out of the realistic art which has lasted from the Renaissance." That will take versions of Mondrian's radically constructivist setting of art's architecture against those derived from observation, so that we must envision art's expressive activity as composing alternative sites of being, where form literally establishes a possible measure for the elemental harmonies of which the spirit is capable:

> Abstract art is therefore opposed to a natural representation of things. But it *is not opposed to nature* as is generally thought. It is opposed to the raw primitive animal nature of man, but it is one with true human nature. . . . Non figurative art demands . . . the destruction of particular form and the construction of a rhythm of mutual relations, of mutual forms or free lines. . . .
> . . . "The world is not separated from the spirit," but is on the contrary *put into a balanced opposition* with the spirit, since the one and the other are purified. This creates a perfect unity between the two opposites. . . . The execution of the work of art . . . must contribute to a revelation of the subjective and objective factors in mutual balance. ("Plastic Art and Pure Plastic Art" 122–3, 127)

Now the artist's form does not merely abstract from nature, or provide expressive metaphors for its own, parallel intensities. Art must oppose natural appearance, by destroying the seductions of particular forms. That demand, then, redefines form's relationship to the eye. The constructive desires that the painting articulates begin, not in seeing, but in thinking; not in abstracting from natural structures, but in the spirit's actually producing *another* nature, revealing some of its fundamental powers that are concealed by those appearances. This activity must negate the eye's desire for stasis, so that the experience of rhythm leads our visual energies to occupy a more dynamic site. There the spirit not only observes its own role in the architecture of appearances; it also finds itself actively involved in certain processes enabling it to envision new ways of understanding its relationship to objective forces. So we encounter, in its most radical manifestation, Modernism's challenge to criticism. A full account of form's extraformal content must be able to show how art's own disposition of physical and relational properties can directly embody crucial aspects of what the work refers to, as if the work literally possessed the capacity to carry meanings, without having to construct an illusionary realm.[13] Meaning resides in the capacity of form to make visible, and to establish value for, the syntax that the artist uses to align the architecture of elemental shapes underlying perception with the psychic architecture organizing the intensities of our looking.

We return once more to the matter of linking literal and figurative exemplification. But now we need to take up the question of how to describe form so that the conjunction seems a feasible one. This is not easy, so I beg the reader's indulgence for the remainder of this section as I first try to set the issue in terms of academic criticism and, next, turn to the necessary historical context provided by transformations of the concept of "symbol" in the nineteenth century. Let us begin with the critical concept of iconicity. This has become our vehicle for explaining the Modernist desire to create expressive force on the basis simply of the material disposition of painterly elements. Wendy Steiner's summary of her own very useful discussion of iconicity sets the necessary stage:

> Art was not to be conceived of once again as a copy – and hence inevitably an imperfect copy – of reality, but instead as an independent object with the same degree of "thingness" as objects in the world. . . . The true means of representing reality was not to represent at all, but to create a portion of reality itself. And the way to do so was to stress the properties of the aesthetic media in question, since these are palpable, thinglike.[14]

Once representational models lose currency, she continues, artists must turn from the rhetorician's ideal of *enargia,* the vividness of surface presentation that links poetry and painting, to the more profound analogy of art with *energeia,* the underlying creative force informing all expression. Then artists can treat form as capable of giving physical substantiality to "the dynamic and purposive life of nature" beneath appearances. At its most profound, this new "naturalness" makes for a rich tension "between the representational and non-representational features of the medium." The work is "both a sign of the thing world and part of the thing world" – both a part of the real, and about it.

But how do we explain the specific manner in which formal energies can integrate these aspects of the work as both a thing and a sign, both a reality and an embodied figure, so that we can provide a basis for attributing significant modes of representativeness to those energies? At this level of analysis, Steiner seems to me to get caught in troubles endemic to criticism, because her sense of the concept of "concreteness" is not capacious enough to take us much past Osborne. The problem is most evident, and most disturbing, in her claim that concrete poetry is the culmination of a distinctively Modernist writing, because the latter is the mode that most fully takes on a significant physical expressivity. Must the imperative to concreteness entail so literal a version of the physical? It ought not to take Heidegger to remind us that the very idea of a "thing" is part of what the new art calls in question. Yet, by equating iconicity with a rather narrow version of sheer visual presence, Steiner ends up an odd ally of empiricist thought: The form is the density of physical patterning central to Jakobson's theory, and the audience remains the distanced spectators of those patterns at work.

In my view, that materialist a reading of formal iconicity revives the old problem of how we correlate the subjective interpretive acts with the objective formal structure. And that is effectively to ignore the very originality of Modernism that I am attempting to describe. We do much better to remember how intent the Modernists were to link concreteness to abstraction, and to locate the power of the work in the self-reflexive states that it produced and interpreted. For in that case, form is a matter of constructing theaters, not of patterning signifiers, and we have a dynamic, participatory principle, which can carry the burden of connecting the icon to the performance bringing it into being. Recall that, although Hulme was not exactly eloquent on the need to combine a language of iconicity with traditional concerns for figural scope, his comments on "distortion" and "expression" insist on the importance of lifting the art object out of nature into a more self-reflexive domain. And Mondrian was quite eloquent, defining the physical dimension of the work as a mode of activity that, as act, has figural implications. When he speculates on a noniconic art that is "form and content at one and the same time" ("Plastic Art and Pure Plastic Art" 130), he means, not simply that form becomes overtly material, but also that the material content is substantially modified, by what I shall call the "virtual life" that form gives it. If a work of visual art can include within itself the life of the eye at its most intense, it cannot be treated simply as material substance. Rather, the work composes a site in which the nature of substance becomes mysterious, precisely because of its capacity at once to motivate and to express that participatory life. Form, for Mondrian, is iconic less as a mode of material presence than as a testimonial structure of physical forces, making possible intensities that can actually "purify" the subject. Artistic forms literally reveal subjective and objective factors in a perfect balance that destroys the hold of those particular forms tying us to a tragic existence. Form's concreteness depends on its capacity to balance those subjective and objective factors in a manner that actually composes the "site" of art as a mode of soul making: We find ourselves defined by the relationships we can sustain between extensive and intensive forces, as we surrender the need to impose our own tellings on the world.

These are large claims, obviously central to this book, because, if they can be defended, they provide a strong rationale for three major assertions I make about Modernist formal experiments: (1) Treatments of spatial form are dangerously reductive unless they elaborate the ability of those spatial relations to carry complex intensional forces. (2) These intensional forces involve forms of "virtual life," for the audience, that connects the ideas of Mondrian and Malevich to the foregrounding of the authorial will that one finds in Matisse, Pound, and Picasso. (3) This "virtuality" offers a useful model for the relational principles that can be shared by different media, so that what Matisse and Duchamp do with line parallels what Williams does with lineation and Stevens with the idea of literally composing a theater no longer bound to the old scripts.[15] But clearly, all of the claims depend on my elaborating the dynamic features of formal iconicity so that they account for this virtuality. To do that adequately, I must set the stage by making a brief historical digression into Romantic theories of the *symbol*. For those theories made clear the need to establish a model of nondiscursive semantic force in art, which could combine the concrete, material expressiveness of an "icon" with a dynamic principle incorporating a sense of the spiritual life that could pervade the object. But Romantic theory could secure those links only by relying on an opposition between "symbol" and "allegory" that simply does not stand up. Therefore the task of Modernism was to make its version of concrete immediacy incorporate the semantic force that allegory could carry. Only in that way could Modernism take responsibility for a fact that Romantic doctrines of the symbol kept evading: that for perceptions to become expressive in artworks, perceptions must be mediated by ideas. So, if the artwork is to carry a distinctive nondiscursive concreteness, it must do so, not by escaping ideas, but by incorporating them within the processes it composes for its audience.

Two definitions of "symbol" are common in Romantic thought, each relying on a contrast with allegory in order to sustain a version of iconic figuration. The first Romantic model concentrates on establishing a special relation between the concrete sign and the ideas it can convey. As Schelling defined it, the symbol is that which "does not merely signify the idea but is that idea itself."[16] Symbol, like myth (where Schelling finds his best examples), is neither the particular apprehended through the general and the schematic nor the general apprehended through allegorical particulars, but "the synthesis of the two, in which the general does not signify the particular nor does the particular signify the general, but in which the two are absolutely one." Rather than achieve unity with nature, the symbol allows us harmony with our own psyches, since there is no gap between what is experienced and the attributing of significance to experience. Symbols do not lead us to the noumenal; they flesh out the perfections of the active spirit, wrought to its uttermost in the effort to know who it is and where it stands. Such signs achieve concrete universality, because they address both intellect and sensation, without generating supplements that force the audience to seek the overall interpretive categories that allegory offers. Once those supplements become necessary, the mind loses the immediate energies of the prehensive moment and embarks on the endless self-regression of searching for an interpretive model, whose generality is necessarily at odds with the particular expressive act.

English Romantic theory often makes similar statements about immediacy. But when we examine them, we see that the immediacy is usually a means to justify attributing specific content claims to symbolic expression. The work is not merely a symbol as icon; it is also a symbol expressing, participating in, realizing, or making luminous one particular universal that can be regarded as some divine force immanent in experience. To theorists like Coleridge, there seemed to be little point in circumventing allegory and establishing the power of "signs" to embody meanings, unless one used that power to accomplish what allegory could no longer sustain. If the new semantics only proliferated symbols, it would lack any distinctive claim to cultural authority: Able to explain how myths signify, it would be unable to produce its own hierarchical model for values. What for Schelling is essentially a manner of signifying must become a specific means for mediating an otherwise inexpressible reality that underlies, and takes form in, the mental state evoked by the symbol. Then, so tied to a dynamic universal, the experience of what is expressed can flow beyond language into the unspeakable depths of full participation in Divine love (or, later, in the depths of full confusion posited by Freud's concept of the unconscious). Schelling's symbol makes complex experiences present; Coleridge's is primarily a lure for our attention, presenting traces of a dynamic life that extends far beyond the concrete image.

Neither strategy works. As Walter Benjamin and Paul de Man have reminded us, both models of immediacy end up deepening our reliance on the very allegory they try to banish, in large part because they still depend on referential principles of expression that enforce a conflict between the documentary and the figurative. This problem is clearest in

Schelling, because his sign theory can escape allegory, but only at the cost of a radical pluralism (like Goodman's). There is no need for allegory, so long as we can put ourselves within the same relation between the creative force and the signification that the symbol possesses, and so long as we share its cultural frame of reference. Then the representativeness exists simply in our grasp of the resonant particular. But there is nothing distinctive to the particular except the mode of apprehension that Schelling attributes to it, so there is no way to give that icon any scope.

Coleridge's symbol, on the other hand, appeals in principle to all understandings, but only because it is so vague that virtually any configuration can be said to express the same force. That vagueness in turn enables the artist to use a rhetoric of immediacy to conceal the work's reliance on an elaborate background of speaking, as shadow relies on light. Were there no implicit allegory, the dynamic presence would have no moral, and little affective, weight, because it would be indistinguishable from brute force, or perhaps even from the seductions of a lurking *malin genie*. As Hegel put it, we need not only spirit, but determinate spirit, which makes explicit demands upon us. And those demands require facing the problem of who has the authority to decide which manifestations of the universal are the important ones. The symbol as Coleridge defines it is, after all, a warrant for the most intense and exalted of psychological states; yet, without an implicit allegorical framework underlying the details, the symbol would be in the same position as purely documentary representation. All of its concreteness would be without significance, its dynamic energies mere force without any intelligible universality. Therefore, struggle as it would with paradox, the very ambition and intensity of Romantic thought kept forcing it back on the external supports for authority that it wanted to reject. What seemed to open a new future in fact led directly to Wordsworth's conservatism and to Coleridge on the cultural mediations that the clerisy must provide.

But suppose one could locate an aspect of artistic expression that preserved the semantic immediacy of the symbol, without the covert reliance on doctrine or priestly role, and with a means of taking responsibility for its own metaphoric expansiveness. Suppose that instead of distinguishing an internal iconic immediacy and an external attribution of significance, one could locate that figural significance directly in the processes necessary to bring the icon to a life that all participants in the work could share. This is exactly what Mondrian enables us to attribute to the foregrounding of formal syntax, and exactly what the case against representation needs for a positive alternative. Whereas the Romantic idea of symbol seeks a nondiscursive immediacy that must be supplemented by some interpretive framework, Modernist art conceives the iconic and the figural as inseparable, because the interpretation is simply the process of self-reflection that occurs as one brings the concrete object to life. There is no drama of finding meanings for perceptions; there is only an appeal to experience possible meanings as inseparable from either the constituting will or the audience's constitutive activity. In the first case, the symbol takes the form of self-interpreting expressive energy that parallels Schelling's definition; in the second, it requires for its meaning the concept of virtuality. *Virtuality* is the sense that the art object requires, for its completion, the audience carrying out a set of procedures for which the work provides the necessary guidelines. On this basis, Modernist art tries to forge a direct link between the concrete presentational energies and a direct, nondoctrinal principle of representativeness.[17] Rather than identify with some specific set of ideas and emotions that an author projects upon a given scenario, the audience is asked simply to reflect on the conditions of identity that emerge as it tries to constitute the work as a specific set of energies. Interpretation of the object is inseparable from self-reflection, so that any metaphoric extensions one makes derive from a literal test of empowerment.

The best way I know to understand how such distinctions clarify the uniquely Modernist project is to consider the various forms of *virtual identification* that artworks invite from an audience. Let us imagine four levels on which we can constitute the art object.

The first is simply a response to its material properties. One responds to the distinctness of a shade of red, or to the "weight" or aural lushness of a line of poetry. But there, significance is exhausted simply in the description we give of the material or illusionary configurations that they form.[18] There is only a distanced observation, without any virtual imaginative identification.

A second level emerges when some of the material properties take on metaphoric functions, because our response involves us in attaching emotive or psychological predicates to them, as if the material or illusionary particulars gave the properties a distinctive. twist or valence. Thus we see the brushwork in Cézanne's late paintings as transforming landscape into some kind of sublime struggle; or, more simply, we see the colors in a Kandinsky as actually constituting a mood, as actually expressing the architecture of the soul, because the expressive qualities can actually give the physical elements roles in spiritual life. Here the arts begin to take on an allegorical representativeness without needing any doctrinal base; the signs invoke a figural significance inseparable from the feeling that they are extensions of the audience's *virtual participation* in forces elicited by elemental relations of color, line, and spatial pattern. These relations are not merely structural; they elicit dynamic aspects of responding energies that lead us to imagine other people sharing the same emotional implications. Kant's constitutive mind becomes something like a constitutive force within physical life.

Traditionally this level of virtuality is connected to a third, which subordinates and naturalizes its effects. I refer to the response to signs that fleshes out an imaginary scenic or dramatic world for them. This response is not merely a matter of elaborating the implicit scenarios that the mind imposes in order to decode the signs. We speak of virtuality here, because the audience actually brings life to the scene, investing it with their own concerns, so that it becomes not merely a picture of the world but a fully engaging *virtual version* of the world. This is the mode of virtuality necessary for the full representativeness sought by mimetic art.

We enter the fourth level of constituting the art object when we shift that virtual identification from bringing a world to the work to aligning the psyche with the specific processes that constitute the work as a vital set of relational forces. This level of virtuality incorporates the activity of the two preceding ones. In addition to the life we give when we respond to material properties as metaphoric or expressive ones – a passionate red in one corner, a vigorous line or rhythm in another – we can also treat the synthetic force of the work as metaphorically expressive, because it too engages a virtual process of identification. Here the identification has the scope that parallels the sense of engagement created when we generate entire illusionary worlds. Only now the source of that scope is not the world we bring to the text, but the sense of the self that we elaborate as we reflect on how we participate in, and complete, the work's internal energies.

In Masaccio's *Holy Trinity*, for example, the thematic force of the new perspectival style depends on its ability to lead the viewer to grant the work two distinct levels of virtual presence. First the viewer must bring life to the perspectival relations that link the three persons of God, represented within a single coherent space; then she must give full imaginative intensity to where she stands. The deep truth of perspective, for Masaccio, is not only that the world assumes depth, but that this depth is coherent only from one particular position. Our occupying that position is not merely a physical fact, but a profound emblem of how the Trinity becomes real for us, if we stand in the proper relation toward it. When we turn to works by Mondrian, we do not encounter so elaborate a doctrine, or so metaphorically expansive a set of physical properties. Nonetheless, similar processes lead us to treat his intensive balances as considerably more than simply another metaphorically expressive property. Instead, that balance establishes what had been sought in the symbol: It directly implicates spiritual force that dwells within the activities that we undertake in order to bring the details to pictorial life. As we literally produce those balances, we also put ourselves in position to see our containing act as a distinctive mode of intentionality, whose elemental features establish the grounds for possible transpersonal identifications.[19] Virtual properties produce real equations – which become metaphoric in the very process of being realized, because we recognize the changes in who we become, and because we get to appreciate the ways in which those changes are articulated by a structure available to all subjects. The more elemental the structural relations, the more our participation seems to align us directly with fundamental energies shared by the entire audience, as if two emotions could become one. An art that had depended on the old stories now becomes a vital source, demanding new ways of accounting for the infinite incantations of itself that it makes available. In the process, ironically, this art recovers for secular culture Dante's vision of allegorical forces so concrete that they provide us a form of spiritual awareness which must be its own reality. All the rest is mere belief.

IV

Iconic formal properties define the basic relationships that must take the place of representational models for giving art coherence and representativeness. But although they explain how Modernist art establishes a distinctive content with special demands on our ability to make provisional identifications, these iconic formal properties do not, in themselves, provide a language of needs, motives, and projected values sufficient for understanding what the art proposes to make of the site it composes or what the identifications are capable of establishing. For the essential constituents of that language, we must shift to the focus provided by my third topic: the authorial roles that Modernist art emphasizes. Here our consideration of extraformal content necessarily involves speculations about modes of intentionality dramatized and models of agency projected, and here we locate the domain where poets can most elaborately respond to the challenge of the visual arts. Unable to match its range of iconic properties and virtual effects, poets could nonetheless claim to be at least the artist's equals in articulating what is at stake for our self-understanding in the new ways these works foreground an authorial presence.

Ironically, Paul Klee's *On Modern Art* provides one of the best analyses of the roles that words may play in these redefinitions of agency. The book takes its departure from the painter's desire to make words his medium for trying to "relieve the formal element of some of the conscious emphasis which is given and place more emphasis on content" (9). By playing the words in his book against a chronological arrangement of reproductions of his artworks, Klee shows how each formal "dimension" comes together to forge a complex "interrelational content" (see especially *On Modern Art* 37–45). Those relations, in turn, construct a final dimension that, he claims, can resist the "pathetic phase" of Romantic flights into infinity, by putting in its place the experience of "the life force itself," warranting a new "Romanticism that is one with the universe" (41–3). Where formal balances had been, the spectator now can realize that "these final forms are not the real stuff of the process of natural creation. For [the artist] places more value on the powers which do the forming than on the final forms themselves" (45).

Poets have always had a kind of custody over such self-reflexive versions of forming powers, so it should be no surprise to see William Carlos Williams locating in such painterly values the principles by which writing can claim to restore its ancient authority:

> What I conceive is writing as an actual creation. It is the birth of another cycle.
>
> In the past the excellence of literature has been conceived upon a borrowed basis. In this you have no existence. I am broken apart, not so much with various desire – but with the inability to conceive desire upon a basis that is satisfactory to either.
>
> The common resort is to divorce. What is that? It is for the police.
>
> But to me it has always been that until a new plane of understanding has been established – or discovered, all the values which we attempt are worthless. . . .
>
> Such then is this novel [Williams's "Novelette"]. You willing by an original force of understanding which by fierce singleness liberates on a fresh plane to perform in a new way that will include the world. (*Imaginations* 293, 296)

The "new plane of understanding" is inseparable from the mode of intelligence and desire that can be played out upon it. Only through that performative space does it become possible to include the world in a way that allows connection to take the place of "divorce." Creative activity literally gives a substance to spirit, by exemplifying modes of intentionality no longer bound by the authorial roles sanctioned by Christian thought or by the idealist metaphysics behind Coleridge's fascination with the "I am." As forms take hold, they build possible models of character.

Lyric poetry is probably the most economical and definitive artistic medium for exploring various approaches to authorial agency, because it emphatically establishes a relational syntax that serves as a direct surrogate for intense emotional states, while, simultaneously, trying to interpret what it makes manifest. So it should come as no surprise that we can best locate the crucial differences that separate Modernist experiments from the prevailing Romantic models of artistic agency by contrasting basic lyric modes. An easy way to do that is to focus on the difficulties that arise when very good critics make the case for a fundamental continuity between Romantic and Modernist poetry. George Bornstein, for example, uses Stevens's "Of Modern Poetry" as a model of the Modernists' fealty to a Romantic heritage of poetry devoted to acts of mind that seek to articulate human "powers, to which nature often stands as adversary."[20] In order to sustain that case, Bornstein's readings must posit dramatic personae engaged in this struggle with nature. We must read "Of Modern Poetry" as an utterance that we place in an imagined setting, where "language reveals to us the movements of the poet's mind." So situated, the act of mind becomes "provisional," a cautious groping through the nontransitive syntax of the opening lines into an increasing sense of urgency and a final, hesitant affirmation. This reading gives the poem the same kind of imaginative site that we project for nineteenth-century novels or dramatic lyrics, where we track a specific speaker's reaction to a single imaginary state of affairs. But can the poem's oratorical bravado really be seen as "provisional" or "tentative"? Can composition as elegant as those concluding lines be characterized as "urgent"? In fact, must those lines be characterized at all, in the dramatic sense of locating a particular disposition that speaks them? In searching for the needs and hesitations of character, Bornstein risks losing the powers that the poem does make available – powers of pure constructive intelligence, able to maintain a scope, and build structural supports, for a kind of monumentality that no poetics confined to character can produce for the modern world.

We do a much better job of seeing how Stevens creates a counterpressure to the pressure of reality if we treat the poem simply as a construct, creating in a linguistic structure a mode of thinking that can realize what motivates self-reflexive desires and can satisfy an enormous range of them. Stevens's poem is not a picture of a mind brooding over a specific situation but a performance, composing a *trans*personal form through which we can contemplate what any modern mind must do in its quest for value. The poet is not a sensitive maker of dramatic events. Rather, Stevens is closer to Mondrian and Picasso than to Whitman or Wordsworth. Expression is less the defining of a subject's emotional state than the creation of objective relations that make formal energies an invitation to reflect on what is available to particular modes of thinking. The aim is not to dramatize character, but to compose forces that can contain the personal within the more general site that the abstract action establishes. Thus the poem can hope to replace the failure of particular myths about the spirit with a monumental art testifying to the productive processes out of which myths are born and are destroyed. Whereas the Romantic lyric tries to revive certain forms of belief (often stopping with the ironies that attend on such a project), the Modernist lyric envisions the conditions of agency as more important than any particular belief that may put them into motion.

Duchamp makes this alternative to the expressivist subject so radical that he tempts us with the opposite possibility: that any attribution of personal agency to these imaginative sites threatens to dispel their challenge to conventional humanist assumptions. For once we are faced with such strange, mechanical, and impersonal energies, we are dealing with conditions so elemental that we find ourselves caught up in imaginative stances difficult to reconcile with the principles of understanding that govern our practical lives. Perhaps, then, Modernist compositional practices entail a complete repudiation of the Romantic desire to base the semantic content of works on the quality of the acts of mind they embody. Perhaps the imaginative leap of Modernism entails simply recognizing how texts speak, or how colors and shapes constitute feelings, in their own right.

Indeed, there are variants of Modernism – from Surrealism and Dada to much of Minimalism – for which this more radical formulation is necessary. But it does not quite fit the ambitions we have been tracing, because it entails surrendering the possibility that we can discursively recuperate the force of the energies performed. In order to assess the appeal that this radical critical stance continues to hold, I propose turning for a moment to the effects it manifests in Edward Said's important *Beginnings*. On the one hand, Said provides the best account we have of the experimental willfulness that allowed the Modernists to dream of their work as inaugurating profound cultural beginnings.[21] However, when he tries to characterize those beginnings in terms of a model of textuality derived from Derrida, Said runs into severe problems. Because of his commitments, he must insist on a radical opposition between Modernist works as statements or imitations and Modernist works as pure texts – that is, works whose writerliness precludes any translation into ethical terms. Whereas traditional art intends a meaning, Modernist art intends to call attention to itself as a "writing," continually producing *meanings,* but never resolvable into *a meaning.* Its formal mode is adjacency, not structure by sequence or dynastic hierarchy: "A text here has no central point or central trajectory; it imitates no spatial or temporal object; and its voice is more likely to be a doodling pen rather than a narrating persona." Such doodling, however, need not issue in indeterminacy. That would prove too easy a victory of modern social conditions over the resources available to writerly energies. One needs instead a Nietzschean model: These writerly texts are virtually pure triumphs of will, or of what Said calls "intention," precisely because they insist on the significance of the activity that prevents their being subsumed under any practical, perceptual, or intellectual category. Theme and structure are forceful because they retain the power to produce an eccentric order that approximates becoming a reality of its own, while remaining tied closely enough to concrete experience that we cannot dismiss the writing as mere play.

The example of Duchamp makes it clear that Said is not wrong. But his analysis may be quite limited, especially since, as a result of this version of Modernism, Said must return to eighteenth-century sources for models of a Western art that can have significant social consequences. Having internalized the Modernist mistrust of self-congratulatorily dialectical thinking, Said ends up denying that what he calls "intentions" have the capacity to establish their own kind of content, their own structure of authorial energies that invites identifications, even though these intentions cannot be consistently interpreted. That denial, however, seems to me to depend on a reductive sense of agency, which considers only the articulation of thematic or narrative unity. Many more other performative states are possible that, nonetheless, do not lead back to subjective expressionism. *The Waste Land,* for example, does not produce a clear unity as a narrative or an argument, yet it clearly poses itself the challenge of defining a model of intentionality that can capture both the malaise of its culture and the trace of resources remaining on which a new spiritual life might be constructed. Eliot uses the writing as a means for testing the capacity of the imagination to stage the self as poised between personal obsession and transpersonal participation in the very energies from which myths are born. Thus, although there is no clear authorial presence in *The Waste Land,* there is an inescapable drama of the cultural mind trying to come to terms with its own constant struggle between the synthesizing functions of the self-conscious ego and the forces of the "it" that disrupt psychic continuity.[22] By participating in the site from which the poem's voices speak, we enter a mode of divided agency, whose plights and whose powers cannot be represented in the old stories – and ought not be displaced into the new critical shibboleths.

The Modernists' preoccupations with impersonality provide a good index of the significant place these questions of agency occupied in their poetics. Forced by their revulsion at Wagnerian and at bourgeois values to reject the demands of the imaginary ego so central to Romantic expressionism, the poets made impersonality their vehicle for testing alternative models of intentionality to which values could be attributed. Since Eliot's doctrine is well known, I turn here to William Carlos Williams, so often Eliot's antagonist. Yet when the conditions of agency are at stake, we find Williams exploring parallel lines of balancing the demands of the inner life with the configurations available through formal structures. He argues that only when this "fixation by the imagination of the external as well as the internal means of expression . . . is reached can life proper be said to begin since only then can a value be fixed to the forms and activities of which it consists" (*Spring and All* 105–6).[23] Thus the most compelling models of agency prove to be those that can articulate their energies in terms sufficiently impersonal to allow the self to escape its own alienating individuality, as well as the vagaries of exalted lyric moments, with their inevitable fall back to ordinary consciousness. The *so-ness* basic to his rendering of Matisse now comes to define poetry's capacity to challenge our assumed dramatic psychology. For he imagines the intentional structure established within the work inviting us to ask whether our hesitations before the new may be the fault of our having too readily accepted a model of reality that greatly reduces what human agents are in fact capable of. We cannot rest with Hugh Kenner's helpful suggestion that in modern art the mind's choices are a main part of the plot (*The Pound Era* 186): We need to realize that the point of the plot is often to redefine our sense of what choice involves.

V

Everything I have said so far remains pure idealism unless I can explain how those works propose demands that we change our lives – or, more modestly, that we pursue forms of pleasure that are valuable for helping us to live our old lives decently. Therefore we need to turn now to Abrams's last category, the relation between the work and its audiences. Mimetic theory had several plausible ways to handle this issue: It could claim that art organizes or purges emotions; that it instructs and delights; that it provides forms of nondiscursive knowledge unavailable to the reason; or that it connects particulars to moral types capable of influencing behavior. But to the Modernists each answer seemed to be implicated in an idealistic humanism that they both feared and envied. So they had to try more abstract ways of understanding the two fundamental questions that haunt any effort to give art a social role: (1) How do we decide where the images that art creates "fit" into the framework of values and judgments that an audience adapts in nonartistic matters? (2) How do we decide on the value of that fit itself?

We have already examined various aspects of these questions, so I can be fairly brief on the subject of audience. At this point, we have to translate what we have been attributing to the work's "authorial energies" into a psychological language of conferred powers and modified interests. And for this purpose, we can concentrate on a single representative passage from Pound's early efforts to adapt his Romantic sensibility and his classical learning to the demands of modernity. The passage begins with Pound trying to imagine how to address a thoughtful man who is "ignorant of painting" and who thus falls into confusion when faced with a room full of many masterpieces by different artists:

> These things obey no common apparent law. . . . If however he is a specialist, a man thoroughly trained in some other branch of knowledge, his feelings are not unlike mine when I am taken into the engineering laboratory. . . . I realize that there are a number of devices, all designed for more or less the same end. . . . They all "produce power" – that is, they gather the latent energy of Nature and focus it on a certain resistance. The latent energy is made on a certain dynamic or revealed to the engineer in control, and placed at his disposal. (*Selected Prose* 24–5)

Then Pound goes on to interpret the implications of the powers so discovered:

> The soul of each man is compounded of all the elements of the cosmos of souls, but in each soul there is some one element which predominates, which is in some peculiar and intense way the quality or *virtù* of the individual. . . .
>
> This virtue is not a "point of view," nor an "attitude toward life," nor is it the mental calibre or "a way of thinking"; but something more substantial which influences all these. (28)

There is no clearer Modernist realization that the use value of art is not a matter of its adequacy to facts, but of its relation to needs and desires. Because Pound elegantly replaces the idea of art as picture with the metaphor of artworks as instruments designed to produce certain kinds of "power," he makes it possible to answer the first of my questions about audience engagement by simply, once again, invoking Nelson Goodman on exemplification. Audiences use works as labels. But for Pound, it is less important to note the range of possible labels than to focus attention on the authorial *act* – the most intense, and most evocative, of the work's exemplary properties. In the authorial acts, *virtù* is defined and tested, and there the work clearly organizes the kind of energies that one can imagine putting "powers" at the disposal of a society, as it turns back to existential situations.

When we ask how that potential power can actually be put to use, we move from Goodman's epistemological concerns to the more complex and vague issue of having to describe the judgments that we make about, and through, works of art. Here too we have already encountered the necessary principles, those of *identification* and *participation,* but I have had to postpone until now my detailed discussion of how the principles work. Pound's sense of *multiple selves* provides a superb context for reasoning the need that makes these principles central for Modernism. The narrower and more determinate the sense of self a poetics has – for example, in Neoclassical theory or in contemporary reader-response the-ory – the less emphasis the theory puts on the complexities of judgment. For, in such theories, we judge only whether the work appeals to a fixed set of interests. Rather than proposing new selves, the work can do little more than satisfy or deepen those interests, on the one hand, or reveal the presumed inadequacy or vulnerability of opposing stances, on the other. But with Pound's psychology – with the flexibility that Modernism must attribute to a self so obviously distributed across quite a variety of desires and emotional formations – the *so-ness* of exemplification yields a great deal more than affective and cognitive uses of art. As we learn what a label entails, we put ourselves in a position to test who we become by virtue of our connecting that label to the activity of a possible self.

A fortuitous conjunction of ideas gives Modernism a rich opportunity to extend the traditional values of sympathy and empathy into more radical, and more fluid, models of provisional identification. Sympathy and empathy are emotional states congruent with the logics of scene and narrative. These emotions align us to agents who share pretty much the same conditions and needs that we experience within practical life. Dif-ferent principles of alignment are called for when, rather than imitating that life, artworks insist on the independent reality enabling them to compose a distinctive site: not one that intensifies practical judgments, but one that challenges its audience to participate in the relational forces it composes, as though they could comprise their own world. With such an artwork, as Leo Steinberg put it in speaking of Picasso, we make our judgments about the work less by comparing it to what we already know than by watching what happens to *us,* as we extend ourselves within it (*Other Criteria* 222–3, 238–9). Pound adds the insistence that what hap-pens is not the separating of art from life, but the process of separating ourselves from our habitual selves, the better to envision new identities in which we can participate. Such participation, in turn, demands a practical judgment in which where we stand, and who we become, must be treated as correlates of one another – a principle that develops into a full ontology in Stevens.

Finally Pound poses a rather odd measure of the value of such powers: We evaluate them, he suggests, in terms of how deeply and how intense-ly they create forms of resistance and then set themselves to overcoming them. It is crucial to keep in mind the fact that there are many forms of resistance. Not every Modernist need accept the political and ethical ramifications of Pound's formulation. In Mondrian, for example, resistance is essentially the setting of intensional against extensional forces, whereas Matisse and Williams concentrate on the very particular resistance to certain ways of telling imposed upon the woman's body. Nonetheless, this ideal of resistance is useful for defining the position in which much of that art put its audience. If the power of art is to enable us to try on possible identities, and if these powers are conceived as conferred independently of the doctrinal content that shapes ideologies, that power will be most clearly in evidence when the audience cultivates alternatives to the given orders of fact and of value. Authenticity will be inseparable from rebellion – minimally, rebellion against the versions of self and value that the society cultivates; more radically, rebellion against both the ethical and the metaphysical senses of limit that define mature social behavior. This metaphysical temptation leads to what I call Modernism's "flirtation with the unlivable": Once value resides in resistance, there is constant pressure to measure the self's commitments by the degree to which they refuse to be coopted by any practical concerns. That art teaches best that least ties itself to specific social filiations. Similarly, that art provides the noblest ethical models that can most fully honor the struggle of each individual to resist conformity. Constructivist art therefore either pursues a radical individualism or so remakes agency that the struggle is against the very forms of understanding that define what we mean by "individual."

We have already seen Mondrian's case for that second alternative. To counter that, we need to register Pound's individualist reading of the powers that art proposes and measures. His subject is Jacob Epstein: "The test of a man is not the phrases of his critics; the test lies in the work, in its 'certitude.' What answer is to be made to the 'Flenites'? With what sophistry will you be able to escape their assertion?" (*Gaudier-Brzeska* 102). Art is conflict intensified, for only in such situations are people sufficiently challenged, not simply to adapt exemplars, but to struggle with them. Art makes freedom available by simultaneously teaching us to take on certain exemplars, and driving us to test our capacity to resist them through our efforts to compose our own responding certitudes. The audience must replicate tensions in the work between its sense of what the past provides and its desire to take full responsibility for having engaged those energies.

VI

No wonder Modernism had to present itself as so difficult and challenging an artistic movement. All four of its basic poetic categories had, as their ultimate goals, focusing such powers of resistance and using those powers to win a measure of imaginative responsibility for the energies and values that the artists set in the place of those dominating the marketplace. This is not the occasion to dwell on the successes and failures inherent in that enterprise; I attempt that in my concluding chapter. But no discussion of the underlying grammar of Modernism can conclude without commenting on the general relation of art to society that followed from those commitments.

Clearly, Modernist values are idealist. They locate all value in states of mind, and they place the burden of social change on imaginative constructs rather than on specific modifications in institutional structures. In their scheme of motives, how one represents oneself is more important than the material allegiances making such representations possible. In our schemes, it is very difficult not to treat these hopes as self-evasive means for continuing the status quo, or even for crushing more radical models that might be able to produce social change. But, as I have already said in a variety of ways, our prevailing assumptions generate scenarios that prove too simple for judging their models of judgment. Rather than leap to criticize the politics of Modernism, we must try to understand the combination of bitterness, utopian hope, and frustration over failed attempts to produce change that eventually shaped Modernist attitudes toward the relation of art to society.

The fundamental source of the Modernists' achievements in art, and of their limitations in politics, was their dream that in order to produce the necessary states of resistance to the status quo significant change had to come from the top down. If there was to be "a cure of the ground," it would have to be based on a shaping force capable of setting powers elicited for individuals against social conventions and prevailing psychological formations, which seemed to endure despite changes in specific political structures. But the route to change, ironically, separated the artists from those whom they professed to help. This idea of transforming the individual's sense of human agency could not establish principles that aligned the artist's vision with the social good. For that was like hoping a self-proclaimed physician could cure a patient who refuses to believe he is sick, and whose denial is indeed reinforced by the "odd" behavior of the physician. In fact, the desire to produce change by example had the disastrous consequence of tempting the poets to seek alliances with those like Mussolini and General O'Duffy, who promised to wield social power, and who got to that position in part because they were much better at using the artists than at using their art.

Ultimately, this gulf between artists and populace required a final twist to the dream of resistance: One had not only to resist the tyranny of the past, but also to set oneself against the dream that one's own work could help produce significant political change. On the personal level, virtually every poet and artist had to grapple with his or her version of the misanthropy engendered by that failed dream. Those individual stories we cannot take up now. We must, though, understand how that general condition put enormous pressure on Modernist hopes for creating alternatives to representational art. For only work capable of resisting representation could also claim to compose a site providing realities not undermined by the empirical conditions that undermine revolutionary dreams. For political thinkers like Frederic Jameson, that resistance becomes itself a significant form of utopian thinking. But with the exception of the Russian constructivists, the Modernist artists were too aware of the etymology of "utopia" to place their hopes in anything more definite than the effort to establish imaginative sites and alternative imaginative identifications at a considerable distance from any operable political values. Driven by bitterness, much of Modernist speculation tries to construct sites that are unassimilable to any social order, or even to any practical psychology. All that matters is giving expression to the intensity of their resistance to the prevailing social conditions and finding through that intensity means of surviving their own alienation.

This is not to say that Modernism cultivated only powers that are entirely discontinuous with virtues that can be extended into the practical world. But to keep the whole in perspective, we must also acknowledge the terms of the misanthropic and tragic sense of social life that came to accompany their radical ideals. Then we can appreciate the significance of two features of the Modernist poetic that complemented and sustained this deeply pessimistic strain of their imaginative work. First of all, once Modernism denies representational modes of coherence, there is little within its disposition of artistic energies to reinforce the demands of the practical world, either in theory or in practice. That a configuration of energies will not "play in Peoria" is not, for a Modernist, a significant critique of it. Quite the opposite, in fact: If art opposes representation, its power in large part depends on staging its resistance to those human virtues that help us adjust to that practical world. One thinks of Wyndham Lewis; of Pound's visionary states; of Picasso, at his most willful and satyrlike; of Duchamp's increasing aloofness; of Mondrian's refusal even to look at natural scenery; of Yeats's cry for god to send war in his time. From the point of view of those creating such states, the charge that they were insane or unfeeling applied better to the accuser than to the work. Such visions were, in many respects, the logical and emotional extension of a poetics that fed on resistance and that set power against truth, construction against compromise. The artists' romance with the "other side" of representation gained much of its erotic energy from the continual effort to imagine what cannot be reconciled to the orders that representation enforces. So, whereas most art tests itself against specific problems within the "real," this effort to establish new models of thinking was driven to test those models against everything that argued for common sense – and that therefore (to the radical mind) made a pretty good case against it.

Modernism is by no means the only movement whose ambition led it, at times, to rage against everything that makes social life worth living. Most lyric art is tempted to set its own intensity against the imperatives of practical li.c: This is the stuff that Geoffrey Hartman's and Harold Bloom's romanticism is made on, the stuff too of Spenser's and Donne's interest in Neoplatonism. But for those classical authors, that resistance to the empirical order had the sanction of religion. The extreme ambition of what may be the purest Modernist work shares the same critical perspective as the apocalyptic consciousness, but it lacks its consolations. The one consolation left is the coldness of Stevens's "Auroras of Autumn," the bleak playfulness of Picasso's pathetic satyr, or the incredibly distant yet intimate, elemental cry of Anna Livia Plurabelle's concluding monologue.

Whose act disposes these energies it becomes increasingly, and exhilaratingly, difficult to know. For at its most intense, constructivist energy so unites subject and object that the resulting experience borders on a purely intransitive state, which possesses its expressive power largely because it has no possible social sanction or use. That cold refusal to accommodate itself to practical judgment exacted a substantial social price: It drew the art, and the artists, into alliance with political systems that shared their impatience with human imperfection. This very danger, however, ultimately deepened the artists' need to make the art unrecuperable by any social vision. Although the artists still cared about society, they found most of their energy devoted to avoiding the trap of caring too much for social conditions that the individual cannot control. If Modernist art had pursued only formal energies that sustained "aesthetic emotions," it would deserve its marginalized place in modern society. The tragedy, and the sublimity, of Modernist artists consists in their having chosen that marginality as the only site where they could generate sufficient resistance to define and dignify the role of antagonist-composer.

Notes

Introduction

1 Complete information on the works cited in short form in these notes and in the text is given in the bibliography, "Works Consulted," at the end of this volume.

2 Two contemporary critical stances emphasize these ironic conditions as the fundamental values articulated in Modernist writing. The first is deconstruction, which I think continues on very different philosophical assumptions the fundamental claims about the unrecuperability of poetic language developed within New Criticism. For in both cases we find the intricacy and unparaphrasability of poetic language asked to establish an alternative to empiricism. For the New Critics the ironic overdeterminations served complex religious reasons (even for secular thinkers like Blackmur). Once ironic consciousness could undermine the authority of prevailing cultural values, it could also insist that our lack of power over our cultural plight required our turning to some form of faith and accepting a quiescent attitude toward social change. And with power so circumscribed, the New Critics had to locate their central terms for spirit in the activity by which consciousness managed to resist the very determining forces of history that made it impotent in the social world. Hence their emphasis on the poet's ability to weave complex, self-defining structures. But these structures ironically turn out to serve mimetic ends by becoming testimony to a historical fragmentation that mind could register but not transform. (Consult in this regard especially Cleanth Brooks, *Modern Poetry and the Tradition,* and F. R. Leavis's essay on Eliot's *Waste Land* in his *New Bearings in English Poetry*.) Deconstruction locates the fragmentation in the logic of nonidentity everywhere setting language against itself, and it replaces the ideal of organic unity by one of infinite free play or self referring indeterminacy. Yet there remains the insistence that constructive activity places us in an ironic relation to the kind of thinking that involves us in social activity. Therefore the art produces a constant awareness of a

complexity that the practical mind must simplify, and it idealizes a theoretical reflection that renders problematic and thematic desires within the text.

The second tradition of ironic reading is political. Here, constructive activity is subsumed under a mimetic model that treats the texts' experiments with juxtapositional structures as images of social fragmentation (even though it is at least as plausible to see Modernists as rebelling against what they thought was an all too seamless and confident bourgeois order). I call the model "mimetic" because it reads poetry in much the same way that one reads most novels, focusing on the dramatic terms that link clearly defined characters to social situations and concentrating on the contradictions inherent in those situations as emblems of the debilitating forces released by modern capitalism (without distinguishing the capitalist mode of economic organization from the other social organizations that also suffer the conditions of Modernity). For the best classical critical works on Modernism in this vein, see Irving Howe's introduction to his anthology on Modernism, *The Idea of the Modern in Literature and the Arts,* and George Lukács's famous discussion of the replacing of the nineteenth-century "concrete universal" with Modernism's "abstract particularity," in his "Ideology of Modernism." For more general, less ideologically insistent versions of Modernism that nevertheless reflect the same biases, see the first two chapters of Malcolm Bradbury and James MacFarlane's collection, *Modernism.*

The best theoretical effort to place Modernism in its social context without reducing it to realistic principles is Frederic Jameson's, especially in his *Political Unconscious.* But the difficulty of that enterprise leads Jameson to at least two serious problems. First, although he does focus attention on the artistic energies, he tends to interpret those energies along much the same lines that other social critics pursue in interpreting the dramatic action. Thus all of Modernism becomes linked with an idealism that puts the isolated subject in the place of historical reality; lived history gives way to an emphasis on abstract spatial relations; and the primary energies of the authors are devoted not to engaging reality but to containing fragmented, reified, and alienating social relations within a set of stylistic strategies that is in fact little more than a displacing of real historical forces. Second, when he does locate radical new energies in author's like Conrad and Lewis, he immediately casts those energies in terms of contemporary theorists like Deleuze, without recognizing their relations to those heroic fantasies of Nietzsche that do not fit Poststructuralist themes, and without fully confronting why these efforts to redefine agency seem to the artists so consistent with their conservative individualist politics. Thus for Jameson there is only one history, a process of increasing reification and domination by the structures of monopoly capital. Either art addresses that directly, or it is mere evasion and containment. But suppose instead that we imagine different domains of history. Some of these art can only reflect; others it can effect directly so long as it casts issues so that the energies distinctive to artistic composition can be seen as serving potentially productive roles in the psychic economies people develop or the self-images that influence their action. Then the Modernist interest in movements like Impressionism, which stress the dependence of phenomena on mental states, are not simple evasions of social reality, but attempts to understand how those dispositions affected by art also modify the stances we can take toward cultural contradiction. Perhaps the conditions of capitalism make subjectivism a necessary phase that we must go through to understand how realities are constituted, so that then we can examine the nonsubjective factors that appear only within those subjective emphases. And then we begin to see how Modernism both responds to and actively creates a version of the history it inherits as it tries to work beyond Impressionism to new models of agency. But we cannot understand these models if we are busy criticizing the artist's thinking because it is not constantly mirroring social conditions that it hardly takes the art to recognize.

I offer further discussion of these questions concerning political critiques of Modernism in my last chapter. For now, let this be seen as an initial attempt to project goals of historical identification that ought not be dismissed out of hand as reactionary. I prefer to consider this work as an effort to define historical and conceptual terms that can show the continuing relevance of those rich and complex attitudes toward literary value proposed by critics who concentrate on individual poets or schools: Richard Poirier on Robert Frost; Helen Vendler and Harold Bloom on Wallace Stevens; and Hugh Kenner on Ezra Pound, and even on the entire tradition of poets who construct homemade worlds. But these are not posed as general accounts of Modernism, and in most cases they depend on invidious comparisons that cannot take all of the major poets seriously, so they have had little influence upon the culture's overall attitudes toward Modernism. For a lively analysis of the basic terms that go into those invidious comparisons, see Marjorie Perloff's essay "Pound / Stevens: Whose Era?" in her *Dance of Intellect: Studies in the Poetry of the Pound Tradition.*

3   I feel uncomfortable with two key terms that I must use to deal with what Modernist art makes of the rhetorical category of "ethos," so I want to briefly discuss the reasons for my choice. First, I shall use the concept of *human agency* to refer to an amalgam of psychological features that can be said to be defined, and tested, by the energies that Modernist art foregrounds and distributes. "Agency" comprises the ways in which sensibility is envisioned, judgment articulated, the psyche's capacity for intensity dramatized, its access to other people understood, and its overall emotional economy organized and managed. As we shall see, the more concentrated the art, the more we are led from the public categories of ethos that are maintained in our social intercourse to the more intimate and complex constituents that seem to account for the agent's individual sense of its own needs and powers. And, correspondingly, the greater the danger that criticism will be forced to use expressions such as "integrated selves" (Quiñones 247), which smack of pop psychology, rather than let the work's energies elaborate the specific powers in question. (I am aware that this is a critical game in which there are no winners, since every generalization can be accused of belying the specific model of agency at work in the text. But even if there are no winners, there can be critics who recognize the difficulties and try to make critical generalization at least point in the right direction.)

My second terminological problem arises because one must use a single name for that sense of needs and powers that does not limit them to practical situations, but grants them a full range of self-reflexive situations. Providing such names had been the task of religion, the discipline devoted to describing the mind's needs and desires without displacing them into practical contexts. But now that one cannot use a religious vocabulary for the psyche when addressing a secular audience, and since English has no word comparable to the German word *Geist,* I find myself in the embarrassing situation of having to borrow the term *spirit,* in order to discuss the modes of self-consciousness that the arts foster. I know of no other word that captures the appropriate blend of sensibility and self-reflexive activity that constitutes the relevant emotional and intellectual properties. So I give myself that permission, secure at least that a term so bound to both Greek and Christian sources can be kept separate from any specifically religious context. And I allow myself the somewhat perverse pleasure of making all of this explicit, because the effort shows that even at the level of criticism we cannot escape the problems that go into positing the appropriate terms for agency. Thus there are crucial dimensions of this book – perhaps of any text in the humanities – that are thoroughly circular: The book seeks to demonstrate the significance of its concerns by showing how the values on which it concentrates can be central to an audience's reflections on the good life. The only test is the reading, so there arises the further circular process of trying to demonstrate that the kind of close reading that the arts invite have philosophical force, because they align us with powers that, we can then insist, can be central in any account of human needs, motives, and desires. As one might expect, I will have to return to these issues in my concluding chapter.

4   Richard Quiñones, in *Mapping Literary Modernness* (256–7), makes a very good statement on Modernist resistance to history. Jeffrey Perl, *The Tradition of Return,* provides a good background of relevant ideas.

5   One can, however, demonstrate in particular cases why contemporary theoretical assumptions lead one into trouble in simply trying to formulate what the Modernists were attempting. And then one can use those cases as examples of the need to avoid the specific conceptual structures proposed by contemporary theory, even though it is obviously necessary to be aware of what its general thematic and methodological orientations can provide. Let the following example suffice to justify my bid for independence. At first it seems perfectly plausible to interpret the critiques of representation on which Modernist art is based in terms of contemporary discussions of the dangers of specularity and the epistemological problems that dog representational models of "truth." Thus, in somewhat different ways, J. F. Lyotard, *The Postmodern Condition,* and Alice Jardine, *Gynesis,* make attractive cases for treating Modernism as the exploration of the modes of sublimity that arose as western culture lost faith in the mimetic principles that had shaped both its art and its philosophy. For Lyotard, Modernity in art becomes the use of technical expertise "to present the fact that the unrepresentable exists" and to evoke, through the "withdrawal of the real . . . the sublime relation between the presentable and the conceivable" (78–9). Jardine spells out the relevant

epistemological principles by treating representational ideals as the effort to confirm "the possibility of an imitation (mimesis) based on the dichotomy of presence and absence, and, more generally, on the dichotomies of dialectical thinking (negativity)" (118). Representation occurs whenever there is an attempt to put one sign in the place of another, then to take that sign as standing for what it in fact displaces. A dialectic would successfully recuperate what is negated. Poststructuralist theory opposes to that an emphasis on signs as chains of displacements and traces that occur because the recuperation is at best partial and internally divided. Then she draws the appropriate consequences. It is art's role and privilege to foster this displacement in such a way that one glimpses there what cannot take determinate form:

> The displacement and indeed destructuration of the dialectic in France are, for our purposes here, where the process of gynesis and its relationship to Modernity and to feminist theory become clearest. For as with the Cartesian ego, that which is beyond the Father, overflowing the dialectics of representation, unrepresentable, will be gendered as feminine. . . . It is no accident that the interrogative return to our sources of knowledge must also be a return to the mother's body. (138–9)

> The true, then, is to be thought strangely by Modernity, outside of the metaphysical categories of opposition – or between them. This approach involves first and foremost a relinquishing of mastery, indeed a valorization of non-mastery. Secondly, the *true,* to be isolated in those processes anterior to or, in some cases, beyond the Truth as produced by the *techné,* is that which can never be seen, which never presents itself as such but rather captures, points, withdraws, hides itself in its veils: and that *true* is seen as being "woman" – the "non-truth" or "partial true" of Truth. (154)

The problem is that, for most Modernists, the pursuit of alternatives to representation did not entail this rhetoric of antitechnique and antimastery. They thought the commitment to technique and the desire for mastery would enable them to cast their work as research that might undo the hold of representation by making present deeper, more universal, and hence more representative truths. Jardine's "non-truth of truth" is often a Symboliste, and later a Surrealist, ideal, but I hope to show it has little to do with the Modernist figures we shall study. Those Modernists did not treat the resistance to representation as primarily an epistemological issue involving claims on truth or the opposition between the presentable and the conceivable. For most of them the quarrel was not with "truth," but with one particular technique for constructing truths, which they felt confined art to the domain of appearances. Representation was not the equivalent of any logic of identity or model of knowledge, but only a specific historical model of artistic rendering, based on empiricist principles. In the visual arts, representation was the ideal of presenting the world as if one had to be able to view it through an illusionistic window, and in verbal arts it was conceived as relying on the same logic of interpretation that one would use if one were analyzing a historical event. Therefore the Modernists could hope to complement their critique of inherited principles by modes of rendering that relocated the domain of truth. That, in turn, required actually reinforcing demands on technique and determinacy, since only such means could enable one to resist the seductive appeal of appearances and make present states so compelling that they could take the place of the old values. From this perspective, Lyotard and Jardine are in bad faith, because they want both to speak confidently about the limits of reason and also to base a comprehensive set of value claims on what there is, by definition, no way to talk about. Where they rely on a fundamental and, on their own terms, undemonstrable absolute opposition confining all determinate content to the forbidden domain of presence, the Modernist can distinguish among kinds and degrees of presence, banishing only those that rely on illusionism or a copy model of truth.

The issue involves more than simple accuracy to Modernist beliefs. For if we put the Lyotard-Jardine case in historical perspective, we shall see that it is very close to a tradition that Modernism had to reject and, more important, that required the Modernists to foster the specific ideals of technique and of mastery that they did, as their means for rejecting it. Clearly, all of these concerns about the limits of representation and the alternatives to it go back to Kant's struggles with an imperious empiricism and must be read in the light of the discourses that Kant generated. There we see Lyotard and Jardine repeating an old temptation: to use Kant's effort to save rationality and notions of "nonsensible intuition" as the ground for asserting some version of pietist mysticism. If one can "know" only what one can represent, and if one's representations can produce only phenomena, there can be no possible rational access to the really real; the infinite is what faith or intuition grasp as they try to negate, and see beyond, what is limited about our representations. Hegel, in the "Preface" to his *Phenomenology,* called this the "bad infinite," since he thought that all it did was tautologically equate mystery with the unknowable, then let fantasy and need project contents upon it that were by definition untestable. If one were to speak responsibly about the infinite, Hegel added, one had to imagine a rigorous logic that could explain how a given mode of thinking might attribute to itself the power to surpass what had previously been determined as the bounds of finite knowledge. Such claims could be tested, first by their ability to explain the limitations of the old knowledge, second by a more complete account of how that knowledge can synthesize the energies that spirit had articulated within history. Spirit had claims to be infinite, to the degree that its internal organization of its own activities established forms for self-knowledge that were not available to pure description.

In this context, it becomes clear that most significant Modernist poetry and painting accepted Hegel's challenge, but primarily by attempting to turn him on his head. The poets and painters realized that neither Hegel's logic nor his sense of history had stood the test of time. But perhaps the problems arose because of his means, not because of his ends. Philosophy may be too

tied to discursive methods, and hence to the model of teleogical development, to be able to make good on Hegel's idea of spiritual power manifest in
its capacity to interpret its own sources and reflective processes. So it might
require the presentational strategies of art in order to capture his vision of
spirit able to display and interpret its own productive energies as it tries to
free them from the merely descriptive categories that the understanding
imposes. Art foregrounds the *techné* that can free *Geist* from the veils that it
weaves for itself. The specific demands of that *techné* then require the assertion that Modernist art could turn from representational to presentational
strategies, while still sustaining clear semantic force. The logic of mimesis is
not the only model for making, and unmaking, meanings. There is an
equally ancient tradition of artistic knowledge derived from modes of participation that the work makes available. What cannot be re-presented, except by a chain of displacing mediations, might nonetheless be effectively
and definitively presented as a concrete demonstration of powers in which
an audience is invited to participate self-reflexively. In this dispensation, one
simply finesses questions of reference and the ironies they generate, in order
to test the ways that works exemplify certain dispositions of our energies
and invite us to reflect upon who we become as we try to identify with
them. The emphasis on exemplification cultivates differences, but it also
allows them simultaneously to take determinate form and to provide provisional identities or "selves" that agents in society can share.

Poststructuralist thought, in both its textualist and its various historicist
forms, is very useful in showing how these differences take form, but it is
quite dangerous in its reductive accounts of why they matter, especially with
respect to the fundamentally ethical stakes that I see Modernism pursuing.
Therefore rather than continually argue with various thinkers in order to
specify how I differ, I shall simply work with the materials that I find more
congenial, and shall allude to Poststructuralist theories only when the specific dispute or dependency helps to clarify my positive claim.

6   Among the best instances of such work are John Cook, *Vorticism and Abstract
Art in the First Machine Age;* Timothy Matterer, *Vortex;* Reed Way Dasenbrock, *The Literary Vorticism of Pound and Lewis;* the essays by art historians
on abstraction, in Alan Bowness, ed., *Towards a New Art,* and Maurice
Tuchman, *The Spiritual in Art;* Harold Osborne, *Abstraction and Artifice;*
Wendy Steiner's two books, *The Colors of Rhetoric* and *Exact Resemblance to
Exact Resemblance;* Mike Weaver, *William Carlos Williams: The American Back-
ground;* Dickran Tashjian, *William Carlos Williams and the American Scene,
1920–40;* Henry Sayre, *The Visual Text of William Carlos Williams;*
Christopher Mcgowan, *William Carlos Williams' Early Poetry: The Visual Arts
Background;* Michael North, *The Final Sculpture: Public Monuments and Modern
Poets;* Charles Russel, *Poets, Prophets and Revolutionaries: The Literary Avant-
garde from Rimbaud through PostModernism;* Marjorie Perloff, *The Futurist Moment;* Bonnie Costello, "Affects of an Analogy: Wallace Stevens and Painting"; Richard Shiff, *Cézanne and the End of Impressionism;* Sanford Schwartz,
Matrix of Modernism; Marshall Berman, *All That Is Solid Melts into Air,* and,
above all, the two general histories of Modernist thinking by Alan Robinson

and Michael Levenson. I should also say that I find Albert Cook's *Figural Choice in Poetry and Art* the critical work closest to my own desires, because it tries to show how the art itself manages distinctive interpretations of those background ideas. I should also mention two very impressive works that I came upon too late to include in my arguments, Yves-Alain Bois, "Kahnweiler's Lesson," and Mark Roskill, *The Interpretation of Cubism.* And finally one must acknowledge that there is considerable controversy over the degree of influence that the painters exercised over the poets. For the best summary, see the last chapter of Steiner's *Colors of Rhetoric.* But in my view, no amount of general theorizing will resolve the issue. What matters is trying to specify on what level, and in relation to what purposes, it becomes more important to stress what poetry shares with those arts than what differentiates it.

1. It Must Be Abstract

1   For a discussion of representative examples of the two basic attitudes toward Modernism in the enabling rhetorics for a Postmodernist poetry, see Appendix 1.

2   The 1909 painting was the last Duchamp made in a representational mode. During the subsequent two years, he used the game of chess motif for a variety of paintings exploring different Modernist styles. Sarane Alexandrian, *Marcel Duchamp* (19), sees many of the same features that I do in those paintings, but he insists on strictly mimetic, psychological interpretive terms, so he can do nothing with the bare, elemental properties of the work or connect the literal testimony of the painting to the metaphoric scope projected by the authorial act: "The picture gives concrete form to [the chess players'] mental exertions as they concentrate on their next moves; this is why their silhouettes are of a ghostly vagueness and the intensity of their thought processes have almost eradicated any individual peculiarities. In the final version each of the players is cut in two, which indicates what his intentions are and also that, as he projects what his opponent is going to do, he is at once himself and the other man." One could note a similar change in the theorizing of T. E. Hulme, when he shifted, in 1910, from Conradian ideals of rendering to a full sense of abstraction. Alan Robinson notes the change (Chapter 4), but is so bound to his own sense of the influence of nineteenth-century ideals that he fails to see that it is in fact a very sharp response to changes taking place in the art world (*Poetry, Painting and Ideas, 1885–1914*).

3   For what Duchamp makes of this theme later, see Ottavio Paz, *Children of the Mire,* and for a superb general account of Duchamp, see David Antin, "Duchamp: The Meal and the Remainder."

4   In fact, the girl is Matisse's Algerian mistress, Bishkra. Apparently Williams missed the obvious signs that this grass is largely palm growing in an African sun, yet, ironically, his arguments about the transfer of sensations apply more richly when we know the actual situation.

5   The movement of this poem, from negation to plenitude, parallels what Pierre Descarques describes as the fundamental movement of Braque's

paintings. See his essay on the work of Braque in Francis Ponge, Descarques, and André Malraux, *Georges Braque*. Ponge's writings on Braque, here and in *Nouveaux Recueils,* also have striking similarities to Stevens's concern for permissions and secular nobility. For the gaps between such painterly remarks and even the best criticism on Stevens, see my remarks in Chapter 2 on George Bornstein's reading of this poem.

6 For a color reproduction that will prove very helpful in following my discussion, see no. 46 in Maria Grazia Ottolenghi, *L'Opera Completa di Mondrian*. I should add that the sequence of responses to the painting that I shall describe is probably typical, but it is not a necessary means for coming to agreement about the forces at work in the painting's formal structure. One could arrive by a wide variety of routes at a similar sense of the balances and modes of intensification that the painting exemplifies.

7 The strains that are so pronounced in the extreme claims the Modernists made in the prose they wrote on their art create substantial problems for criticism. For the prose seems to trap what promised to be radically new in terms that seem disappointingly caught up in the old spiritualism. As one might expect, such problems are most tellingly registered in the work of young Marxists such as Charles Harrison:

> The history of the ratification of abstract art is not so much explained as confused by the fact that theoretical . . . justifications were proposed to compensate for the absence of or to supersede representation in the artifacts of the artists concerned. . . . Documents such as *Ueber das Geistige in der Kunst* do not seem to have been treated at the time of their publications as if they were speculative and discursive, open to analysis and criticism. And in a sense they are not. They are generally assertive and dogmatic with little internal discursive detail. They seem nonetheless to have been accepted as if they were successful arguments in favor of those artifacts they purport to justify. This takes some explaining, given the patent logical and historical absurdity of much of what is asserted in these writings. ("Ratification of Abstract Art" 147)

The only way to handle this challenge is to recover, as fully as possible, the Modernist case for having formal principles play a central role in projecting extraformal content. No Modernist believed that these justificatory statements could substitute for the art (and not only because the prose put absurd ideas in an embarrassingly clear light). In fact, it was precisely the poets' sense of the limitations of discursive language that put such pressure on the testimonial dimension of their work. In discursive language, history emphatically asserts its problematic authority, forcing thinkers to cast new insights, or new ways of locating the force within old concerns, back into the very positivities that they are trying to resist. Wittgenstein provides a useful parallel: Faced with a similar problem, over the status of logic, he proposed taking the entire apparatus of descriptive prose as a ladder that one throws away, after one has climbed to the appropriate vantage point. In philosophy, this leaves only the mystical. The arts have a better use for their prose ladders, since they can conceive them as instruments leading back to the work, and then letting the work lead out to segments of possible worlds. The more frustrating the efforts to develop a justificatory language, the more one could insist on the expressive power of the specific nondiscursive force of the work.

An excellent example of art explicitly taking up the challenge posed by the gulf between prose about art and the actual state the work produces is the concluding passage of William Carlos Williams's *Spring and All* (in *Imaginations* 150–1). First he offers a murky and pompous piece of prose, celebrating the way a world is "liberated" when it becomes "accurately tuned to the fact which giving it reality, by its own reality establishes its own freedom from the necessity of a word, thus freeing it and dynamizing it at the same time." Next he shows, through the poem "Black-eyed Susan," how the name for the flower at once leads us to its sensuous richness and gives that a metaphoric resonance beyond the name.

For Mondrian's awareness of the same phenomenon one recalls the episode in which he was asked why he had done something against his theory and responded, "You must remember . . . that the paintings come first and the theory comes from the paintings." See Margit Rowell, "Interview with Charmion von Wiegand," in Thomas Messer, *Piet Mondrian* (82).

8 This is as good a place as any to insist that when I speak of "transparency" or "real equations that provide testimony for certain forces," I refer not to a metaphysician's dream of total transparency, but to an effectual transparency that makes present a set of relations which an audience could deny only by producing elaborate fabrications. Thus, although a Culler or Fish should be able to invent a counterexample of someone who reads Mondrian's internal relations in quite a different way, I suspect that the counterexample would be so remote from the experience of almost all those likely to read this book that it would demonstrate how much we do reenact the same structural forces. For similar reasons, I would argue that although there are good grounds in contemporary theory to say, as Richard Shiff did say in a 1988 correspondence, that now this reduction to elemental forces is seen simply as a "sign" or "figure" of naturalness, one cannot stop there. The question is whether the sign or figure in fact creates certain conditions that have particular transpersonal effects and predictable consequences. The "natural," or as I prefer to say, the sense of shared powers and connection to natural forces, can be nothing more than this contextual faith in the efficacy of certain signs and the willingness to rely on our sense of how other minds are likely to fill out the same virtual relations (a topic I elaborate in Appendix 2). Given the need to test claims, and even to formulate pragmatic rather than absolute versions that rely purely on theory, consider Stephen Bann's comment on the open-ended nature of the epistemological quest that Mondrian's art assumes:

> The concern to find a new "code" did not create the crisis of representation. On the contrary, it was a response to such a crisis which was already well under way in literature and portended a new epistemological configuration: a new way of prefiguring the map of knowledge and

the subject's relation to the external world. Abstract art, which achieves the break with mimesis in a particularly salient and polemical way, has for that reason become an obvious whipping boy, and indeed is still – from various quarters – under attack. To defend abstract art is, however, not to defend a genre or a movement. It is to accept responsibility for scrutinizing the relationship of art to knowledge in the modern world. ("Abstract Art – A Language" 145)

9 For a good discussion of some Modernist redefinitions of intentionality, see Gabrielle Schwab, "Genesis of the Subject, Imaginary Functions and Poetic Language." For the passage from Vico, see the section entitled "Poetic Logic," especially paragraph 402, in his *New Science*.

10 See Williams's letter to James Laughlin (September 8, 1942), reprinted in the *Literary Review*. When he puts the case in more general terms, Williams imagines abstraction as enabling art to capture "the pure effect of the force upon which science depends for its reality." See his *Spring and All* (in Webster Schott, ed., *Imaginations* 135, 138–9).

2. Self-subsuming Artifacts

1 I must emphasize that in attempting to speak of historical differences, one must concentrate on basic orientations of entire styles. As soon as one shifts the focus to talk about great artists or writers from any period, one finds that some dimension of their work corresponds to anything one might say about Modernism, especially if one tries, as I do, to dwell on traits that lead beyond description to interpretive issues. Thus, when I discuss the limits of representation later in this chapter, I do not claim that one can reduce the work of major representational artists to the limitations that Modernists attributed to the representational mode. Yet some aspects of their work remain so limited. However great the irony of a George Eliot or even of a Shakespeare, their art tends to support, or sometimes to reproduce, certain ways of thinking about social relations, because the entire casting of issues relies on notions of agency and ideals of readerly sympathy consistent with certain dominant cultural practices: At least, their audiences have found it difficult to read the work in accord with other practices. Thus it is no accident that Pound was perhaps the only person in his time who was responsive to James's concern for freedom and personality, because Pound could read the novels as authorial acts rather than as NET television dramas in the making.

2 The task is not made easier by the fact that both the Modernist poets and painters such as Picasso adapted concepts of abstraction for their work, while repeatedly insisting that they did not identify with the more radical forms of abstraction explored by their peers. But those disclaimers did not prevent their learning from or even competing with those artists. I think we are safe in generalizing, so long as we remember Michael Levenson's very reasonable description of the limits that one must accept if one deals with general concepts like Modernism (*A Genealogy of Modernism* 2). For good

discussions of the concept of Modernism, see, in addition to Levenson, the first two chapters of Malcolm Bradbury and James Macfarlane's *Modernism;* Irving Howe's introduction to his anthology, *The Idea of the Modern in Literature and the Arts,* and the bibliographical essay by Morris Beebe, "Introduction: What Modernism Was."

3   There are two very good critical analyses of how literary works engage these two poles of abstraction. The first is Wendy Steiner's elaborate and careful treatment of how abstraction shapes content in Modernist writing and painting, especially the chapter "Literary Cubism," in her *Exact Resemblance to Exact Resemblance: The Literary Portraiture of Gertrude Stein* (131–60). There she distinguishes two kinds of abstract works: those "with abstract subjects" and those "without" subjects. As an example of the first she offers Malevich's *Black Square on a White Ground,* which, she argues, has an "abstract subject" because the subject "does not occur within the sensible world" and because distinctions between objects and signs of objects, presentation and representation, become problematic. The second kind of abstract work, most evident in Abstract Expressionism, has no distinguishable subject, but makes its surface its content. Helpful as this is as a corrective to Osborne, however, Steiner does not give enough attention to how syntax defines the new content, even in her first form of abstraction. (In my view Malevich's subject is not squares, but particular relations between shapes and their grounds.) More important, Steiner's emphasis on iconicity leads her to concentrate only on the formal parallels between Stein and Cubism, without a sufficient sense of the themes thereby released for the imagination. Given her critical approach, there is no way the poet could escape the charge of too literal a borrowing that makes literary adaptations of Cubism "failed experiments" (160). What is needed is a willingness to flesh out Stein's comparison of her "elemental abstraction" to Picasso's, on a range of levels.

The second treatment, Alan Robinson's *Poetry, Painting and Ideas, 1885–1914,* does worry about such concepts. However, it pays little attention to concrete stylistic practices, so that what begins as a promising distinction between two modes of antimaterialist Modernist thought – the "empathetic" and the "Idealist" – ends up collapsing all of the poetry it deals with into the empathetic camp. That risks both underestimating the force of the Nietzschean factors in his major figure, Pound, and losing significant distinctions among Modernists. Yet resurrecting the second pole of his dichotomy would not provide the necessary term. Rather we need models with less rigid binary oppositions.

4   This is the first of many occasions where I shall have to struggle with a problem that I can resolve only by stating my own personal commitment, and my sense that the Modernist artists grappled with exactly the same issue: How does one identify provisionally with the mystical spiritualism central to much of Modernism and still show that the art remains relevant for a culture in which only the secularly defensible has a significant claim to authority? My most secure claim is that contemporary culture is becoming increasingly aware of the need to postulate secular alternatives to the versions of empiricism that were generated by the Enlightenment and that shaped the art and philosophy which Modernist abstraction opposed. One

finds versions of that claim in much of Continental philosophy (which perhaps never had a thorough empiricism) and in analytic philosophers such as Richard Rorty and Thomas Nagel. So at least the quest of the art can be relevant. This desire for new methods, however, still leaves open the question of the degree to which the resistance to empiricism sanctions our rejecting the more general criteria of rationality that constitute a somewhat looser, but decidely antimystical, model of conceptual consistency and experimental confirmation of ideas. Perhaps empiricism has blinded us to forces that require truly mystical stances in the arts. Although I cannot dismiss that possibility, I shall concentrate here on principles at work in the art (rather than in the statements about the art) which I think can be formulated so that they will be testable by an audience devoted to secular values. That audience, however, must be willing to grant a mode of assessment that consists simply in examining what takes place as an audience engages the work. Michael Philipson, *Painting, Language and Modernity,* provides a quite sophisticated deconstructionist argument to use in defending a version of the more mystical stance: namely, that much Modernist art leads us to suspend criteria of judgment, so that we come to see alternative modes of experience for which no possible language could be adequate. Yet, in my view, this form of "letting be" severely underestimates the artists' desires to make determinate structures that we can use to describe our capacities and our commitments.

5 Modernist statements claiming the concreteness of abstract art are legion. Perhaps the best may be found in Wassily Kandinsky, *Concerning the Spiritual in Art* (32–3). Subsequently, in his *Reminiscences,* Kandinsky provided one of the richest examples of what this involves by structuring that work in terms of a fundamental contrast between representational ideals and the forms of presence available from alternative ways of seeing. Also quite useful for the contrast between realistic representation and concrete abstraction is Williams's comment that "art is the pure effect of the force upon which science depends for its reality" (*Imaginations* 139). For here he recognizes art's commitment to a concreteness that representation cannot capture and that depends, for any description, on the relational fields created either by science or by art, which become allies in the new dispensation.

6 The quotation from Pound is from "Art Notes, May 8, 1919." See also "Art Notes, Sept. 12, 1918" (in *Pound and the Visual Arts* 128). For Wyndham Lewis on Fry in *Blast,* see Walter Michel and C. J. Fox, eds., *Wyndham Lewis on Art:* "The 'Decorative' artist (as examples, the sort of spirit that animates the Jugend, Rhythm, Mr. Roger Fry's little belated Morris movement) is he who substitutes a banal and obvious human logic for the coordination and architectures that the infinite forces of Nature bring about" (76). Also, for a fuller picture of Lewis's hatred of the class privileges and amateurism of Fry and his company, see "The Caliph's Design," in the same collection (178–81).

7 As parallels to Osborne's judgments, I offer the following quotations from Fry:

> The artist of the new movement is moving into a sphere more and more remote from that of the ordinary man. In proportion as the art becomes

purer the number of people to whom it appeals gets less. It cuts out all the Romantic overtones of life which are the usual bait by which men are induced to accept a work of art. It appeals only to the aesthetic sensibility, and that in most men is comparatively weak. (*Vision and Design* 22)

Most of the art seen here is neither naive nor primitive. It is the work of highly civilized and modern men trying to find a pictorial language appropriate to the sensibilities of the modern outlook. . . . Now these artists do not seek to give what can, after all, be but a pale reflex of actual appearance, but to arouse the conviction of a new and definite reality. They do not seek to imitate form, but to create form, not to imitate life, but to find an equivalent for life. By that I mean that they wish to make images which . . . shall appeal to our disinterested and contemplative imagination with something of the same vividness as the things of actual life appeal to our practical activities. (195)

Yet even Fry ends his book saying that this quality of reality that he is pointing to would, if he tried to explain it, "land me in the depths of mysticism" (244).

8   For Kandinsky, see "On the Problem of Form" (1912), in Herschel Chipp, ed., *Theories of Modern Art* (161); for Pound, see "Exhibition at Goupil Gallery" (1914). Later in this chapter I shall try to describe how Modernist artists tried to recuperate many of the functions of representation by modifying allegorical models. For now, though, it should suffice to point out that there are good critical treatments of Modernist allegorical space as serving radically presentational, nonmimetic functions, especially in the first chapter of Bert O. States, *The Shape of Paradox,* which discusses the relation of the mythical to the elemental in Beckett.

9   Rilke, letter of August 10, 1903, in *Letters on Cézanne,* where the passage was chosen by Clara Rilke as the epigraph. I should add here that the essentially Protestant treatment of allegory by Walter Benjamin's *Origin of German Tragic Drama* and Paul de Man's *Allegories of Reading* is another version of contemporary critical appropriation of historical terms that I think must be resisted, because it gives the term an import that is sharply at odds with both the ideas of allegory and the paradigms illustrating it that were central for the figures I am discussing. For a good discussion of the appeal of African art, as interpreted by Daniel Kahnweiler, the most neo-Kantian of early commentators on Cubism, see Yves-Alain Bois, "Kahnweiler's Lesson." And for the passage on Vico cited later, see the section on "Poetic Logic" in his *New Science,* especially paragraph 402.

10   The two basic modes of abstraction each have different ways of sustaining this version of concrete universality. When representational elements are used to set a thematic key, as in Duchamp's *Portrait of Chess Players,* the forces become direct extensions of the metaphoric referents set up by the image: We see what the elements of chess can be, or, in Picasso's *Bather,* we literally feel the body's sense of the expansiveness of sea air taking away any repressive inwardness. In noniconic abstraction, on the other hand, the ele-

ments and relations seem direct participants in, and expressions of, certain parallel natural and psychic energies.

11 I had written "art's significance for its culture." Then I realized that one of reasons that Gabo's optimism seems so naive now is Modernism's dream that its audience could be equated with its culture. Time has shown that in our world art is unlikely to have the kind of audience that makes cultures change. But since time has also shown that there is very little that can produce worthwhile changes in the quality of reflective lives on the scale of mass cultural change, I see little need to apologize for recasting their political hopes in educational and individualist terms. For more on Modernist individualism as a coherent ideology, see Sanford Schwartz, *The Matrix of Modernism,* and my concluding chapter.

12 Nelson Goodman's arguments are best developed in his *Languages of Art* (51–65, 85–95, and the last chapter). For the consequences of this position, see his *Ways of Worldmaking.* The best light to put on the critics' neglect of him is to admit that his parsimonious extensionalism causes serious problems when one tries to adapt it to the thematic concerns of literary criticism. For an effort to adapt them, and for a more thorough analysis and justification for my departures from his theses, see Chapter 8 of my *Act and Quality.* For other relevant commentary on Goodman, see Arthur Danto, *The Transfiguration of the Commonplace* (especially page 194).

13 I think the richest versions of these states occur when the idea of virtual exemplification functions as part of the work. For then we feel ourselves participating in an experiment, as we test the degree to which the beliefs can become compelling dimensions of our own actual experience. But securing this further leap would take us too far astray into abstractions, and it suffices here to see intentions simply as possible components of the ideas that we test. In Appendix 2, I try to clarify these considerations a bit further, by distinguishing between different types of virtuality, one involving the developing of illusionary contexts, and the other engaging the audience within the physical properties of the experience as if they could function metaphorically.

3. Knowledge Enormous Denies the God in Me

1 For a very good statement on the use of "instructive moments" as ways to get at the complexity of issues that engage the imagination, see Hazard Adams, *The Philosophy of the Literary Symbolic* (4, 28). Adams is also quite useful in explaining what Kant made available to nineteenth-century literary thought, the topic of the last part of this chapter.

2 I cannot become embroiled here in the critical disputes over the degree to which Modernism is a continuation of Romanticism or is the radical alternative to it that those like Hulme and Eliot envisioned themselves providing. As Marjorie Perloff suggests, in her "Pound / Stevens: Whose Era?", one's answer usually depends on whether one makes one's exemplar of Modernism Stevens or Pound. Aside from recommending George Bornstein's books on the subject and Albert Gelpi's *Coherent Splendor,* I have nothing to

add to the debate that I do not propose in discussing Bornstein on Stevens's "Of Modern Poetry" in Appendix 2 of this volume. In this study, I will be less concerned with whether Romanticism and Modernism are continuous or discontinuous – obviously there are levels on which each claim is correct – than with stating the problems in terms that are sufficiently general to allow us to see why we are tempted in individual cases to take one position or the other. Getting to that level of generality is one reason why I shall in a moment propose at the core of the development of Modernism a continuous conflict between principles of lucidity and desires to maintain the models of agency established within the culture's lyric traditions. At that level we can see how there are endless cycles of old solutions becoming new difficulties, and new difficulties ironically leading us back to versions of the old problems. One example of these patterns is the relation of Modernist ideals of form to Romantic thinking on the symbol that I take up in my Appendix 2.

3   I take up lucidity and lyricism most fully in my *Sense and Sensibility* (12–20). For a very good general account of similar tensions in contemporary culture, offered by an intellectual historian, see David Hollinger's distinction between the knower and the artificer, or cognitivism and Modernism, in his essay "The Knower and the Artificer." General criticism on the Romantics posits many similar dichotomies – most notably the "myths of freedom" and "myths of concern" described in Northrop Frye's *Study of English Romanticism;* Hazard Adams's "anti-allegory" and "allegory," in *The Philosophy of the Literary Symbolic;* and perhaps even de Man's "constative" and "performative," since those terms too are concerned primarily with distinguishing what can and cannot be handled by empiricist predicates. Finally I ought to note Stephen Knapp's very interesting *Personification and the Sublime: Milton to Coleridge,* which concentrates on the tension between literal and figurative in the eighteenth century and shows how literary thinkers developed a view of art as "epistemological leisure," enabling them to possess "the power of archaic belief" while avoiding "its absurd or violent consequences" (140–1). I prefer my terms because they point to the imaginary investments that are involved in each disposition of consciousness, yet, unlike Knapp's, do not reduce the figurative to archaic beliefs. Instead I try to understand the lyric as an enduring category that artists must keep attempting to recover, in conjunction with plausible models of lucidity. Broad concepts such as "lucidity" and "lyricism" also avoid the premature politicizing of Enlightenment dichotomies, as if they were primarily caused by, and alterable by, shifts in social relations. For example, J. M. Bernstein, *The Philosophy of the Novel,* uses something very close to the lucidity–lyricism distinction to support the kind of social claims that Lukács makes about reification in modern society. But to use these terms as principles for describing social relations seduces one into a rather shoddy moral melodrama, in which one's own version of lyricism takes on class consciousness, as it fights an all too identifiable and distanced enemy. What else is Frederic Jameson's "political unconscious" but a mythic version of lyricism given a social habitation and a name? For hypotheses about a political unconscious do not meet the standards of lucidity characteristic of modern political theory.

4   All quotations from Wordsworth's poetry are from *Selected Poems and Prefaces,* ed. Jack Stillinger (Boston: Houghton Mifflin, 1965). Numbers in parentheses at the end of the poetry extracts are line numbers.

5   I take the quotation from an excerpt in Richard Ellman and Charles Feidelson, eds., *The Modern Tradition* (662), where Schlegel actually uses the expression to refer to poetry. I adapt it as I do because, for Wordsworth, poetry becomes the paradigm for judgment. On the role of constitutive concreteness in Wordsworth's poetry, I find most helpful Frederic Garber, *Wordsworth and the Poetry of Encounter.* See also my essay "Wordsworth's 'Preface' as Literary Theory" for a defense of these terms against de Man.

6   Wordsworth, "Preface" to Lyrical Ballads, in *Selected Poems and Prefaces* (454–5).

7   Arthur Hallam's "On Some of the Characteristics of Modern Poetry" is accessible in Walter Houghton and Robert Stange, eds., *Victorian Poetry and Poetics,* 2d ed. (848–60). The importance of the essay can be measured by the fact that Yeats made it central to his definition of the options available to modern poetry.

8   It is impossible to know whether Keats played much of a part in the organization of the volume. But the title of the volume, and the fact that "Lamia" was put first although it was completed after all of the odes but "To Autumn," make it difficult to accept the central, even normative, role that Helen Vendler gives the odes (especially "To Autumn") in her *Odes of John Keats.* I shall return to her views of Keats later in this chapter. For Keats's poems I use *Poetical Works of John Keats,* here pp. 161–78.

9   In opting for that anima principle, Bruce Clarke, in "Fabulous Monsters of Conscience: Anthropomorphosis in Keats's *Lamia,*" gives a fine summary of the various interpretations. Walter Jackson Bate, *John Keats* (543–61), provides a parallel summary of earlier readings and is quite reasonable on the poem, until this conclusion: "Both [Apollonius and Lycius] are subjective in their approach to a reality – Lamia – far more complicated than either of them realizes," but although Apollonius sees part of the truth, "the approach of Lycius is vitiated from the beginning by the spirit of a more thoroughgoing and deliberate retreat" (560). Because he treats subjectivity as a moral category, Bate, ironically, cannot reconstruct the properties of radical subjectivity that prove so tempting in Lycius's actions. Lycius fails, but he may not have been wrong in his desires, which therefore must be understood both in more general cultural terms and in an imaginative specificity that is vitiated by moralizing criticism.

10 All quotations from Keats are from *The Poetical Works,* ed. H. W. Garrod (London: Oxford University Press, 1956).

11 Arnold, "Preface to Poems 1853."

12 It is an interesting irony that most critics who read from the Romantics to the Victorians, as Carol Christ does, stress the emerging imbalance and lack of confidence in the later writers, whereas those who concentrate mostly on the Modernists, as does Michael Levenson, stress the power of the Victorian synthesis that Modernism undoes. If I had to turn my historical analyses into so general a thesis, I would say that I want to show how the entire nineteenth century suffers from contradictions that only quite radical experiments in the

arts could hope to address adequately. Among the many other critical works on Victorian poetry that make useful comments on the relations between Victorian and Modernist poetry, I should mention J. Hillis Miller, *The Disappearance of God;* Gerald Bruns, "The Formal Nature of Victorian Thinking"; John D. Rosenberg, "The Two Kingdoms of *In Memoriam*"; Robert Langbaum's classic, *The Poetry of Experience;* Alan Sinfield, *The Language of Tennyson's "In Memoriam";* Jerome McGann, "The Religious Poetry of Christina Rossetti"; and Carol T. Christ, *The Finer Optic: The Aesthetic of Particularity in Victorian Poetry* and *Victorian and Modern Poetics.* The works most useful to me, because most aware of dialectical tensions in the age's thinking, are E. D. H. Johnson, *The Alien Vision of Victorian Poetry,* and Lionel Trilling, *Sincerity and Authenticity.*

13   Line 265. All quotations from Tennyson are from *Tennyson's Poetry,* ed. Robert W. Hill, Jr. (New York: Norton), 1971.

14   I think it is possible to claim that what Michael Levenson takes as essentially an early Modernist sense of the necessarily subjective grounds for assertions about truths is already present throughout Victorian poetry: One need only think of how Mill treats the lyric or how Langbaum talks about the dramatic monologue. Yet there is something distinctive in what Levenson sees: the dream, in the early twentieth century, that the highly sensitive subjective observer could somehow secure something that a community might take as significant truth about a scene. The Victorian lyric, on the other hand, has such a theatrical bent, and is so bound to the rhetorical aspects of language, that the subject it mediates tends to reveal its distance from any shareable sense of realities beyond the shared condition of being trapped in isolated and theatrical expressive egos.

15   In what I think is still the best book on Tennyson the poet, Christopher Ricks, *Tennyson,* there is a good discussion of the parallels in tone between "Ulysses" and "The Lotus-Eaters." One might also note that Tennyson's "Tithonus" is in many ways an even better example of how pervasive this self-evasive or intransitive lyricism is, because it uses the figure of Aurora to establish a version of the temporality of "To Autumn," only to make temporal flux serve as a contrast to the hero's plight. Trapped in his cold unresponsiveness to all that she offers, Tithonus must compensate for his distance from Aurora by performing his plight to himself in endless lyric lamentation, as if only Miltonic rhetoric can hope to give self-expression the energy and the dignity it cannot win in dramatic or philosophical terms.

I should add that in an essay where I devote a good deal more space to these matters, "Arnold and Tennyson: The Plight of Victorian Lyricism as a Context of Modernism," I argue that the point of my critical judgments is not to disparage the poetry, but to show how important pathos can be as a condition evoking deep sympathetic responses, even when we withhold intellectual assent.

16   I need at least to point out that Tennyson's awareness of these problems provides him an evocative context for developing the Christian alternative to such unchartered freedoms, a context I try to elaborate in the reading I give of "In Memoriam" in my "Arnold and Tennyson." My thesis there is

that "In Memoriam" elaborates a plausible way out of the trap of Tennyson's own lyricism that Eliot's early Modernism later tried to restate in non-Christian terms. If one cannot master lyric excess by subordinating it to reason, one can try to distinguish the two realms, then pursue a lyric stance so aware of its limitations that it can give voice to what it knows are only shadows of deeper needs and possible spiritual resources. The unmediated agonies of the cry mocking discursive language may lead to the transcendental immediacy of something like prayer. A voice from dramatic monologues may try to piece from its own fragments an abiding picture of need. Deprived of a dialectic with society, the lyric self can pursue a dialectic made of its own various voices as they loop through one another, forming a strange, but perhaps graspable, second nature. Even if the myth of lyric self-expression conceals the various symptomatic forces that permeate lyric cries (such as the negations in Ulysses' rhetoric), the symptoms themselves can eventually make available basic aspects of the self as an irreducible congery of needs masking as power, and of power hidden in the form of needs. Finally, even a poetry that cannot be read for what it masters produces what may be the more human, and more representative, state of true spiritual embarrassment before all that masters us. In the pathos of shattered consciousness, spirit may still reside.

17 All quotations from Arnold's poetry are from *Poems,* ed. Brander Matthews (New York: Collier, 1902). In this quotation the anaphoric "and" provides a superb illustration of the ways in which Derrida's concept of the supplement illuminates the Victorian desire for expression that continually displaces its own imperatives. For Derrida's most elaborate treatment of that concept, see his *Of Grammatology.*

18 The heirs I refer to are first Eliot, then Robert Lowell's use of the relation between mastery and pathos, and then the tendency in contemporaries to adapt Lowell's version of personalist poetry. For a good description of that vein of poetry, see Alan Williamson, *Introspection and Contemporary Poetry.* Williamson shows that the dominant trait of this poetry is the speaker's refusal to seek a disinterested stance by which to judge itself. For Modernism, of course, these very traits explain the need to reject scenic personal voices and to seek formal structures that are, simultaneously, expressive and sufficiently objective to provide the distance on which judgment depends.

19 The best summary of Kant's influence on nineteenth-century poetics is still Winfred Lehmann, *The Symbolist Aesthetic in France.* For a more philosophical treatment of the themes Kant makes available for artists and writers, see Hazard Adams's excellent chapter, in *The Philosophy of the Literary Symbolic.* For readings that try to relegate Kant to the junk heap of history, by treating him as essentially a formalist, see Frank Lentricchia's chapter, in *After the New Criticism,* and for a superbly careful antidote to such thinking, see Paul Guyer, *Kant and the Claims of Taste.* My own position is that although Kant's is a formalist theory of taste, Kant takes considerable pains to show that beauty is not simply a matter of taste; see especially the last sentences of section 17 of his *Critique of Judgment.*

20 *Fundamentals of the Metaphysics of Morals* (68–71).

21   I elaborate these possibilities for extending Kant's ethics in my essay "From Expressivist Aesthetics to Expressivist Ethics." And, in what follows, I ask the reader to indulge my effort to combine a plausible reading of Kant with terms that explain his influence. There are obviously many points of controversy that I must skip over.

22   If he is to show how purposiveness can have semantic force, Kant must elaborate a means of communication not bound to the categories of the understanding. His response is to propose the concept of "symbol," as a noncategorical, nonrational vehicle for the intuition. As the following passage makes clear, the result is to inaugurate a mode of thinking about signs that runs from Mallarmé to Goodman on "exemplification" (perhaps even sanctioning what I have tried to add to Goodman's nominalism):

> All intuitions which we supply to concepts a priori are . . . either schematic or symbolic, of which the former contain direct, the latter indirect, presentations of the concept. The former do this demonstratively; the latter by means of an analogy (for which we avail ourselves even of empirical intuitions) in which the judgment exercises a double function, first applying the concept to the object of a sensible intuition, and then applying the mere rule of the reflection made upon that intuition to a quite different object of which the first is only the symbol. Thus a monarchical state is represented by a living body if it is governed by national laws, and by a mere machine (like a hand mill) if governed by an individual absolute will; but in both cases only *symbolically*. For between a despotic state and a hand mill there is . . . no similarity; but there is a similarity in the rules according to which we reflect upon these two things and their causality. *Critique of Judgment* (197–8)

Purposiveness becomes cognitive precisely because its indirect presentation of the concept keeps analogical relations in focus. This, in turn, makes perfect sense of the concept of constitutive particularity, because we need the work as a whole in order to keep our attention on processes of reflection that get beyond categories to significant specific configurations proposing new models for experience. It is not a large jump to Mallarmé's appropriating the concept of symbol exclusively for the productive process, wherein the artist must "shun the materials of nature" in order to establish "a careful relationship between two images, from which a third element, clear and feasible will be distilled and caught by our imagination" (*Crisis of Verse* in *Selected Prose* 110).

4. Modernist Irony and the Kantian Heritage

1   I cite Mallarmé's poem and the translation from Anthony Hartley, ed. and trans., *Mallarmé* (Baltimore: Penguin Books, 1965) (91). When I come to Baudelaire's poetry, I will take poems and translations from Frances Scarfe, ed. and trans., *Baudelaire* (Baltimore: Penguin Books, 1961).

2   For a close reading of those final pages, and a more elaborate version of the points developed in this discussion, see my "Objective Image and Act of

Mind in Modern Poetry." For richer accounts of the aspects of desire that I discuss in Flaubert, see René Girard, *Deceit, Desire and the Novel*.

3 Indeed, it is Derrida on "*mimique*," in his "Double Seance of Mallarmé," who best defines the space that writing, as a foregrounded act, creates in literary constructs. But, as I keep insisting in various ways, that space is no more there primarily to articulate the consequences of writing than Cézanne's flattened perspective is there primarily to acknowledge the two-dimensionality of the canvas. The emphasis on the space of writing is not there as end, or even as an essentially epistemological concern for the status of discourse. Instead it is a means for using phenomena such as indeterminacy to display certain authorial powers for responding to what, in experience, becomes all too determinedly under the sway of the heterdox laws of nature. Not seeing their way beyond writing to such thematic forces is a serious weakness of the otherwise superb criticism in Jonathan Culler, *Flaubert: The Uses of Uncertainty*, and Ranier Waring, "Irony and the 'Order of Discourse' in Flaubert." I find Waring especially good on the mobile subjectivity that irony achieves for Flaubert, a point I shall take up later in this chapter.

4 For Auerbach, see his *Mimesis* (425–33). We need the French passage here, to see what Flaubert makes tense do:

> *Mais c'était surtout aux heures des repas qu'elle n'en pouvit plus, dans cette petite salle au rez-de chausseé, avec le poêle qui fumait, la porte qui criait, les murs qui suintaient, les pavés humides; toute l'amertume de l'existence lui semblait servie sur son assiette, et à la fumée du bouilli, il montait du fond de son âme commes du'autres bouffées d'affadissement. Charles était long à manger; elle grignotait quelques noisettes, ou bien, appuyée du coude, s'amusait, avec la pointe de son couteau, de faire des raies sur la toile cirée.*

5 In my essay "Objective Image and Act of Mind," I spend a great deal of time showing how such absorption in details sets the logic of metonymy against the Romantic desire for the kind of symbol that reinforces metaphoric structures. Later in this study I shall show how Eliot elaborates that logic as the perfect figure for his own despondent idealism, in which no dialectic is possible, even though the invitation to one seems always suggested.

6 Flaubert to Louise Colet, January 23, 1854, in *Correspondence* (126–33). The sense of irony as "plasticity" ought be remembered when we turn to the visual arts. See also Flaubert's letter of March 20–1, 1852: "The entire value of my book, if it has any, will consist of my having known how to walk straight ahead on a hair, balanced above the two abysses of lyricism and vulgarity (which I seek to fuse in analytical narrative)." Quoted from Paul de Man, ed., *Madame Bovary* (311).

7 For James, see his review of *Madame Bovary*, in his *French Poets and Novelists*, reprinted in Leon Edel, ed., *The Future of the Novel*. It is difficult now not to suspect that James assumed a disappointingly traditionalist attitude, condemning what he should have tried to understand. For the necessary corrective, see Auerbach, *Mimesis* (432), who makes this point about shifting distances very well.

8   I quote Baudelaire's writings on art from *Baudelaire: Selected Writings on Art and Artists* (248–9). For the longer quotations, I shall also provide a second set of page numbers referring to Baudelaire's *Oeuvres Complétes,* ed. Y. G. Le Dantec and Claude Pichois (here, 651–2).

9   It is important to realize that Baudelaire used Delacroix to develop a concept of beauty bound both to tradition, the realm where soul can become aware of its permanent qualities, and to the nervousness that constitutes Modernity (392–3). Eliot, writing about Dante ("Dante," in *Selected Essays* 199–240), makes very similar arguments in discussing the importance of the disciplined dream.

10   To illustrate the force of these ideas, see what Baudelaire's successors caught, and what they missed, when they made him their exemplar for new possibilities in European art. I quote from the Impressionist sculptor Medardo Rosso, "About Impressionism in Sculpture" (1902), as he succinctly defines the complex of themes that led directly from Baudelaire to Cubism:

> In his severe criticism of sculpture, could Baudelaire . . . have been wrong? Was he not right to treat sculpture as an inferior art when he saw sculptors make a being into a material entity in space, while in actuality every object is part of a totality and this totality is dominated by a tonality which extends into infinity just as light does?
> What is important for me in art is to make people forget matter. The sculptor must, through a summary of the impressions he receives, communicate everything that has touched his own feelings, so that, looking at his work, one can feel completely the emotion that he felt when he was observing nature. (Nochlin 78)

This is by no means silly. Its sense of antisculptural tonality and totality goes a long way toward accounting for both the Impressionist ideal of "atmosphere" and the poetics of "mood" that dominated the lyric styles of late nineteenth- and early twentieth-century poetry. But that very relation to nineteenth-century culture can blind us, as it does Rosso, to the rhetorical dimension that links Baudelaire on the one hand to the classical tradition still active in Delacroix, and on the other to the efforts of Modernists such as Jules Laforgue and Eliot to produce a more complex sense of agency than this literal version of a relational ontology allows. Baudelaire is ultimately an ethical poet – perhaps the first since the Romans to realize how important aesthetic experience is to that project, not because if reinforces public morality, but because it creates possible imaginative ideals worth imitating as modes of self-development. It is crucial, then, to recognize that Rosso's tonality is not the one Baudelaire sees in Delacroix. Rosso's lacks the dreamlike quality, and hence it misses the strange conjunction between temperament and texture that makes the visual a truly spiritual adventure. In missing that adventure, Rosso also misses the import of Baudelaire's response to his Romantic predecessors. Although Rosso is sophisticated about the changes in the nature of substance, of objects, that the concern for atmosphere entails, he continues to rely on a simple expressive model, in which the subject tries to recapture "the emotion that he felt when he was observing nature."

To Baudelaire, this merely continues the Romantic quest to define grounds outside the self that can produce and sanction exalted lyric states. But such a quest tries to posit for the subject the same kind of substance that it imagines for things, thereby reinforcing the terrifying dialectic of his predecessors, in which the constant effort to know the "I" keeps generating simulacra or supplements. And, in the frustration and fear that one's self will keep slipping away, agents become so obsessed with their own states that they make themselves extremely vulnerable to the opposite fear that one is an absolute solipsist.

11   This concern for building, rather than describing, psyches is also important for invoking the attitude that I think is necessary to appreciate fully Baudelaire's essays. Hazard Adams, in his chapter on Baudelaire's ideas in *The Philosophy of the Literary Symbolic,* quickly gets frustrated with Baudelaire's inability to specify grounds for his claims about correspondences: Adams charges Baudelaire with confusing symbolism as a model of correspondence with symbolism as a model of creativity (126) and argues that Baudelaire is not "systematic" and therefore lacks an idea of language that is "not hieroglyphic but creative and formative of nature" (134). But Baudelaire refuses to provide a theory of language because his sense of language and symbol is one that requires resisting theory, requires continually setting the performative imagination against any fixity of nature, even a claim about its creativity, which soon turns into allegory or lie. It is Ethos, not Logos, that obsesses Baudelaire, so that we must read him, not as a philosopher, but as a philosophical dandy. Person takes priority over the claims of system and of truth.

12   "*L'Incompatibilité*" provides a good example of how Baudelaire, in his early poems, builds mood reveries. He quickly brings the poem to a moment of silence that can be filled only by the spirit watching itself suffuse the scene it should be content to observe. Such attention allows the emerging incompatibility of mind and sky, stasis and moving cloud, to form a complex image of this spirit, as it broods over its own responsiveness to a sublime scene and transforms all indicatives into conditionals marking the nature of the poetic construct. Ultimately, the spatial relation of containing mind to containing sky modulates into an equation between the mind moving through the poem and the cloud moving through the sky. The movement then becomes a visual analog for what the mind has been doing all along to the landscape that it views, and thereby disrupts, while remaining a part. Thus shadow and substance, image and reflection, coalesce as reminders that the scene itself takes place for an observer against a backdrop of passing time that the mind can register, but not control. As poetry refuses the quest for an underlying symbolic order, leaving divine mysteries to the silence, it inaugurates a secular philosophical project of defining its own claims to be able to supplement that divinity, as it pursues its own analogical movements through an atmosphere inevitably of its own making.

13   Robert Viscusi, *Max Beerbohm, or the Dandy Dante,* provides a superb account of the dandy, but he does not see the connections to Kant's concept of autonomy.

14   I suspect that Baudelaire added the poem's third stanza in 1859 in order to stress the competing pressures on the conclusion – from sympathy with the victim and from the tendency to repeat the sins of the mime.

15   Leo Bersani, *Baudelaire and Freud,* chapters 11 and 12, thinks that Baudelaire's *Petits Poémes en Prose* evades the specular self who becomes the object of such pathos. I doubt that, if only because, however much the excess, there remains an investment in the mobility still caught in the circuit leading from self-disgust, to projected self-pity, to self-disgust again at allowing oneself to try to seduce an audience through pathos. The turn to prose does make it possible to reduce the pressure to make that theater a mode of sublimity. But that gesture also runs the risk of attempting to accommodate to modern cultural conditions by lowering the demand that one makes for "recommendation." Arthur Symons and the Georgians did invoke Baudelaire for such an enterprise, only to produce a poetry of mood that the Modernist poets thought far too self-protective to make the changes necessary for an art as assertively modern as Baudelaire had dreamed.

5. Eliot's Symboliste Subject as End and Beginning

1   T. S. Eliot, *Selected Essays,* "New Edition" (New York: Harcourt, Brace, 1950), 377. All quotations from Eliot's essays are from this source. Hereafter page numbers are given in parentheses after the quotations.

2   One of the advantages of reading Eliot in terms of his using Baudelaire against the Victorians is that it forces us to recognize how much more complex and powerful Symboliste models are than they appear in the influential account of them proposed by Hugh Kenner, especially in "The Possum in the Cave." Kenner concedes Symbolisme the honor of having introduced a "scientific Romanticism" that enabled poetry to rely on the expressive force of language without having to rely on mythological and argumentative supports. But his version of it exacts the enormous price of demanding that the poet look no farther than the words. So, whereas the Symboliste Eliot withdrew into the role of impersonal catalyst, mixing a complex but ungroundable set of connotative resonances (beyond which "there is frequently nothing to restore," *Pound Era* 133) Pound increasingly concentrated on a very different kind of construction, devoted above all to a "clean perception [that] sets realities before the mind" (141). In my view this analysis lets limited notions of the "real" foreclose the imaginative domain that poems can establish; loses the force of an emphasis on formal relations that enabled poets to adapt the work of Modernist visual artists; and runs the risk of blinding us to the imaginative energies that permitted Eliot's early poems to exert such influence on other American writers.

The stakes are clear in Eliot's own essay "Baudelaire," where we see him grappling with what he took to be the age's most pronounced version of the imperative to be absolutely modern. Only a spirit as flexible and self-absorbed as Baudelaire's seemed capable of transforming formal experiment into a fully human challenge to the psychic models that dominated an increasingly secular and therapeutic culture; only his self-theatricalizing bent seemed capable of rendering the intensity of psychic suffering that would make this revolution seem worth the effort; and only his insistently over-determined world would reveal the poet's own view of life as "objectively apprehensible." The view of life that Baudelaire constructed "is one which has grandeur and which exhibits heroism; it was an evangel to his time and to ours" (381). Therefore it was precisely this sensibility that a revisionary Modernism could employ as its release from Victorian self-evasions:

> He was one of those who have great strength, but strength merely to *suffer*. He could not escape suffering and could not transcend it, so he *attracted* pain to himself. But what he could do with that immense passive strength and sensibilities which no pain could impair, was to study his suffering. . . . Now the true claim of Baudelaire as an artist is not that he found a superficial form, but that he was searching for a form of life. . . . It is not merely in the use of imagery of common life, not merely in the use of imagery of the sordid life of a great metropolis, but in the elevation of such imagery to the *first intensity* – presenting it as it is, and yet making it represent something much more than itself – that Baudelaire has created a mode of release and expression for other men. ("Baudelaire" 374, 375, 377)

For the best critical commentary on Eliot's relation to Baudelaire and Symbolisme, see Piers Gray, *T. S. Eliot's Intellectual and Poetic Development, 1909–1922.*

3   "The Love Song of J. Alfred Prufrock," in T. S. Eliot, *The Complete Poems and Plays* (New York: Harcourt, Brace, 1952). All other quotations from Eliot's poetry are from this source.

4   We know from Bernard Bergonzi, *T. S. Eliot* (23), that at the time when he was writing *The Waste Land* Eliot was tempted to convert to Buddhism, and we have a good picture of his religious obsessions during the previous decade from Lyndall Gordon, *Eliot's Early Years,* so I combine the two here. The temptations of Buddhism become more important for *The Waste Land,* because its promise of a radical alternative to the ills of the West required Eliot to develop methods of abstraction that could put a whole culture on trial.

5   There is also a very elaborate, purely formal distance that I think reinforces the bid for independence from Prufrock's plight. The poem seems to have a carefully balanced mathematical structure, based on groups of three stanzas. There are, before the first ellipsis, three groups of three stanzas each: The first two of these, shaped around the Michelangelo refrains "How should I presume" and "known them all," generalizes his plight and brings it to its first dramatic climax. Then, between the ellipses, there are two short summary stanzas where his plight is rendered in terms of his recurrent fantasies. The next group of three stanzas has at its center Prufrock's ironic discovery that, despite his reflections, his decision has been made for him. Finally, the last six stanzas can be seen in a variety of relationships between groupings of

two and three stanzas. I develop this point, and give more elaborate versions of many of the themes in this chapter (including the discussion of metonymy), in my "Steps of the Mind in T. S. Eliot's Poetry."

6 David Lodge makes a very good summary of several ways that the metaphor–metonymy distinction could be used with respect to Modernism, in *The Modes of Modern Writing*. But he does not stress the underlying philosophical issues, and what he does recognize has not been taken up by other critics. Gregory Jay, *T. S. Eliot and the Poetics of Literary History*, does elaborate the philosophical issues, but he takes them directly from Lacan, without considering their relation to the actual rhetorical use of metonymy. Jay's concern with Lacan's ideas does draw him to the problems of identity and of universalization as they lead from the Victorians to Eliot. However, although he is very good on many facets of those problems, he pays a substantial price for interpreting Eliot's sense of historicity on a Bloomian model of struggling with particular predecessors. This prevents Jay from seeing that the more general tension between historicity and mythic orders shapes Eliot's concept of what it means to be modern.

In order to develop these philosophical implications, and to appreciate how deeply Eliot's use of metonymic details captures this law of heteronomy at the very core of Romantic and idealist experience, we shall have to spend a few moments tracing the ways in which contemporary thought has elaborated the basic metonymy–metaphor contrast. Ironically, this anachronistic move turns out to be historically revealing, because the logic underlying those speculations is essentially that of the Hegelian and Bradleyan idealism that shaped Eliot's philosophical work and that here reveals its continuing vitality.

Roman Jakobson first developed the concept of metonymy, in the hope that such recurrent figural structures might yield evidence for positing fundamental patterns of mental organization. In his view, metonymic functions comprise the "contiguity" axis of our linguistic usage; metaphoric functions comprise the other basic structure, an axis making possible relations of "similitude." Thus, when metonymies dominate, the brain processes information in terms of how the various associations in space or time compose sufficient contiguity to allow our grasping the whole. For example, by looking at various details like chairs and windows, we come to associate them in the form of a room, or by thinking of possible associations among words – for example, "hut" and "grass" – we compose an appropriate sense of place. Metaphoric functions, on the other hand, carry the burden of projecting similitude. They dominate when we operate in terms of how details or expressions might substitute for one another. When we are given the expression "hut," for example, we think of equivalent terms such as "home" or "building," or we imagine different objects that might satisfy the controlling semantic logic.

We need not dwell on the particulars of Jakobson's case. For my purposes, the important materials emerge in one of his subsidiary claims and in the metaphoric uses that Claude Lévi-Strauss elaborated for the concepts. At one point in his essay, Jakobson tried to use the metaphor–metonymy distinction to make generalizations about literary history. Romantic writing can be said to emphasize metaphoric relations, he asserts, because its primary concern is to link details in patterns of symbolic equivalence. Wordsworth's trees and stones and years all participate in one single underlying system of natural relations. Learning to read the metaphoric equations as emblems of natural law is the point of the poem. Metonymic relations, on the other hand, dominate the associational investments characteristic of the realistic novel, where we read, not to locate symbolic orders, but to appreciate the dense texture of any given social phenomenon. In these works, meaning is primarily a matter of contiguity, of the combination of discrete and otherwise discontinuous details.

More recent theorists like Lodge have been quick to point out that these dichotomies are oversimplified. The best Romantic art tends to foreground the pressure of temporal contiguities and subjective differences on the proposed metaphoric structures, and most realistic description will serve more or less covert allegorical intentions. Oversimplification, however, is no reason to dismiss terms that might prove useful if their provenance could be more carefully mapped. So, instead of relying on Jakobson's terms as accurate accounts of either general functions of language or historical distinctions among fictional styles, I propose to employ them as descriptions of particular forms of desire codified in language. We need only ask ourselves why we feel that temporality is so problematic in Romanticism, or why allegory is so disturbing when we recognize it lurking beneath realist surfaces. Then it seems plausible to assert that Jakobson has shown how particular figural structures can emphasize certain fundamental structures of human desire, thereby doing for historical styles what a somewhat chastened version of Northrop Frye can do for genre.

It is precisely this fusion of compositional structure and the forms of desire that made Jakobson's terms so influential for Claude Lévi-Strauss and Jacques Lacan, the two thinkers who established the full resonance for the concepts (and who thus lead us back to Eliot). The poles of metaphor and metonymy make it possible for these thinkers to show how even our basic modes of desire can be understood as being structured in the same way that language is structured. For Lévi-Strauss, metaphor is the dynamic operator that explains how myths organize social life. Societies that operate in accord with *"la pensée sauvage"* do not emphasize time as a continuous flow, but define change so that it is contained by the forms of repetition that social categories can provide. One does not merely succeed one's ancestors; rather, one repeats the structural and totemic roles that they played. Such performances are metaphoric because they are charged with meaning and significance: Particulars come into being explained by, and demonstrating, the power of timeless patterns.

Metonymic operations, on the other hand, seem to be marked by an inevitable sense of lack or displacement, when one considers their relations to those same cultural patterns. Once contiguity reigns, the past cannot be treated as a set of variations on established structures. Rather, the chain of particulars serves primarily to establish "a difference as a difference" (*Savage*

Mind 231; the entire discussion occupies 224–44). Persons, beliefs, and roles all lie next to one another, and their relation to the present is problematic enough to warrant Hegel's vision of history as a vast mausoleum. What exists in the present seems to have its sanction only by the force of its claim to be different from what preceded it. Historicism and realism enter into a strong alliance. Since both positions stress the relativity of historical phenomena, they force all claims about underlying structures or latent values to justify themselves by what they make available for empirical interests. Then there can be no shared telos for society; there is only the effort to allow expression for a variety of different interests. All abstract bonds or imperatives, all that Kant had tried to preserve under the rubric of reason, yield to the demands of a Mill or a Nietzsche that the thinker spell out specific configurations of force and consequence.

Lacan's stroke of genius was to see that this model of social differences, this sense of a social order where all that we have in common is a sense of how differently our values substitute for something none of us seems able to possess, might also provide very suggestive images for psychic life. If one begins by trying to understand how individuality is constituted, Lévi-Strauss's mythic order seems a purely imaginary construct, somehow necessary both to establish and to mask the dream of individual differences. Rather than seek that metaphoric structure in the social order, one must turn to the developmental patterns that lead us to project it. Then we see that the ideal of mythic substitutions is essentially a fantasy, born of the desire to repeat, in adult terms, the feeling of grounded personal identity that is provided by the mother's linking her infant's name to the process of nourishing it at her breast. The name then serves the problematic role of reflecting for the child an ideal ego and an ego-ideal. Simply by holding up, through the name, what comes to be a reflecting mirror, the mother creates a feeling of deep identity, ironically bound to the mirror's fragile surface. Given such contradictions, the working of desire turns out to be tragically metonymic. One's love objects turn out to be inadequate substitutes for projected states of fusion with the image that the mother created. All of the objects of desire that promise to secure one's identity arrive marked with a lack, precisely because they can offer only the specific configuration of a present moment to a psyche formed on typological demands that no longer correlate with any object. (I take these formulations mostly from Chapters 1 and 9 of Lacan's *Ecrits: A Selection*.)

From a Postmodernist perspective, one can avoid the Lacanian problematic if one learns also to set Nietzsche against Hegel, so that one eliminates the idea of "lack" from one's economy of desire. But in thinkers such as Giles Deleuze and Felix Guattari, the consequences are so extreme, and so frightening, that they make one nostalgic for nineteenth-century neuroses. Therefore, even if we could in fact overcome the pressure of lack, I do not see a good overall case for taking the risk. When Modernist poetry turns against Eliot, it does so, not by rejecting all lack, but by showing how art can break through the usual dualisms by freeing the will from categorical frames and "tellings," so that it can realize its power to transform shadowy absences into resonant metaphoric frameworks.

7   I devote a good part of my essay on Victorian poetry, "Arnold and Ten-
    nyson," to discussing how *In Memoriam* elaborates both the metonymic
    condition that was to haunt Eliot and the sense that somehow, by occupying
    the shadows created by grief, the spirit could find a compensatory strength.
    And in my "Steps of the Mind in T. S. Eliot's Poetry," I extend the discus-
    sion to show how "Ash Wednesday" tries to elaborate a new metaphoric
    principle out of this awareness of the problems that metonymy defines.

8   Carol T. Christ, *Victorian and Modern Poetry,* makes clear precisely what is at
    stake in insisting on the heritage from Baudelaire in Eliot. Christ's book
    provides the best account we have on the ways in which Victorian concerns
    about masks, about the capacity of image and symbol to capture objective
    grounds for emotion, and about the possibility of accounting for historical
    situations, carry over into Modernist poetry. But she does not provide a
    very rich motive for that continuity, nor does she see that Eliot is distinctive
    precisely because he tries to imagine modes of lyric agency that are relatively
    free of the moral blinders of that Victorian tradition. One result is that for
    her, "Preludes" is little more than an exercise in making "sensation the
    sufficient carrier of meaning." That is, she treats the speaking voice as
    Kenner's Symboliste, devoted to "a poetry whose organizing principle is
    often so ambiguous that it frees words and images to become not objective
    correlatives but indefinite emotions for which the reader had remarkable
    license 'to find a scheme into which, whatever they are, they will fit, if they
    exist'" (86–7). This view treats the poem's sensualism as an end, ignoring
    both the force that it has as a vehicle for breaking up the psyche into constit-
    uent units, and the roles that it plays in a more comprehensive meditation on
    metonymic features of mind–body relations. Christ cannot distinguish be-
    tween indefinite emotions and quite definite renderings of a condition in
    which an authorial act simultaneously articulates and resists what it sees as its
    relationship to a mode of knowing made dominant by nineteenth-century
    concerns. In other words, Eliot the poet is concerned not only to break from
    Victorian poetry, but to have his own poetry establish a site in which he can
    interpret and justify that break.

9   I take this occasion to quarrel with Ronald Bush's learned and helpful psy-
    chological analyses of Eliot's poems, in his *T. S. Eliot: A Study in Character
    and Style.* For "Preludes" seems to me an especially clear illustration that
    Eliot is concerned less to express a personal psyche than to compose relations
    that will enable other psyches to have a certain kind of reflective experience
    (a process that will also express the author's psyche, but by very devious
    routes). Using a language of personal psychology to interpret the poem
    deprives it of all of its strangeness and most of its keen intelligence, while
    ignoring the ways in which it can establish testimony for a particular sense of
    the deep lyric subject. When I discuss *The Waste Land,* I shall have further
    occasion to insist on the difference between reading the poem as the act of an
    empirical self and as the effort to compose a version of agency inviting
    empirical selves to try on new identities.

10 I give extended attention to those years in Eliot's career in my essay "Steps
    of the Mind in T. S. Eliot's Poetry." In preparing that, I found most helpful,
    of the many essays on Eliot and Bradley, Richard Wollheim, "Eliot and F.

H. Bradley: An Account," and George Whiteside, "T. S. Eliot's Dissertation." J. Hillis Miller, *Poets of Reality,* makes interesting use of Bradley to read the poetry, but he ignores the fact that "Prufrock" was essentially finished by 1911, before Eliot had begun serious work on Bradley, and he overstresses the solipsistic dimensions of Bradley's thought, particularly when he argues that time and objectivity do not exist for Bradley. Very good on Miller's errors is Michael D. Riley, "T. S. Eliot, F. H. Bradley, and J. Hillis Miller: The Metaphysical Context." Levenson is quite helpful on the relation between Eliot's *Poems 1920* and Pound's work of the same period.

11   The difference stems from the fact that Bradley shifts the terms within which Eliot thinks about the relationship of words to the world. The conflict between consciousness and sheer objects, which dominates "Preludes," gives way to the more capacious but more slippery realm of conflicts between particulars and cultural frameworks. For Bradley's idealism restores Hegel's insistence that the cause of lack is not the concreteness of the object, but its abstractness – that is, its lack of sufficient ties within a structure giving it a concrete role to play: "One object is more real than another – more of an object – by virtue of non-object relations" (*Knowledge and Experience in the Philosophy of F. H. Bradley* 131). Degrees of reality depend on the density of the relations that can be sustained by the attitude that one maintains in dealing with the objects; so empiricism fails, not because it is a false picture of the world, but because it is too limited in its refusal to attend to the various structures that influence what we ask descriptions to do. Metonymy, then, need not be simply a matter of lack, which attends to the distance between a description and some informing symbolic resonance. Rather, the gulf between particular and universal has a much more practical and social cast: It betokens either the failure of the social order to provide an appropriate framework, or the failure of the individual to align himself properly with what the social order offers. When we reflect on both kinds of failure, we see that a fully adequate knowledge would take the form of what Bradley calls an "absolute." First there is immediate experience; then the domain of individual interpretations; then the absolute, which allows each individual to see her own interpretations as placed coherently within an encompassing whole, giving meaning to all of its parts. The absolute, therefore, is an ideal metaphoric structure. It invites differences, then gathers them into relations even richer than any simple measure of similitude. But if one does not accept the absolute, the corresponding sense of metonymic lack is as devasting as the alternative is satisfying. For in that case one deals, not only with the isolation of the object, but also with that of the perceiving subject, whose interpretive gestures only confirm the solipsist's prison. And everything that Idealism tried to posit as metaphoric alternative to empiricist metonymies must itself be exposed as metonymic – a perfect inversion of Western aesthetics, and a perfect occasion for invoking the power and pathos of the intricate, and irreducible, mobility of the Baudelairean subject who opens *The Waste Land.* Were there an absolute, one could envision cultural history as a grand process of subsuming individual sensibilities within a comprehensive paradigm. If, however, there is no absolute, there is only the endless production of meanings that deepen

the isolation of the expressive agents trying to break out of their prisons. The effort to escape the prison confirms it, because we introduce differences into a world that traps "centers of feeling" at its margins.

12   For useful readings of the role that Tiresias plays as an emblem for the possibility of synthesizing the various strands of possible coherence in the poem, see Robert Langbaum, "New Modes of Characterization in *The Waste Land*"; Milton Miller, "What the Thunder Meant"; and Grover Smith, *The Waste Land*. Also relevant on the theme of inclusive consciousness is F. R. Leavis's discussion of the poem in *New Bearings in English Poetry* (90–114). Gregory Jay, *T. S. Eliot,* provides a rich sense of how that failure of metaphor opens the possibility of encountering some significant, but unstable, human core. For the alternative position, claiming that the poem's deliberate failure to recreate Tiresias's knowledge is an indictment of Western civilization, see William Spanos, and for useful commentary on the resolution, or lack of it, in the concluding passages, see Elizabeth Schneider, "Prufrock and After: The Theme of Change" (109); Milton Miller, "What the Thunder Meant" (447–52); and Leavis, *New Bearings* (105).

13   William Spanos does make an eloquent case for this indeterminacy as a critique of logocentric faiths, and Marjorie Perloff (in *The Poetics of Indeterminacy*) is as eloquent in arguing that Eliot is a severely limited poet, because he is too Symboliste and allegorical to explore the virtues of indeterminacy. Each critic, of course, means something different by indeterminacy: he the lack of overall coherence, she the refusal to submit details to allegorical pattern. Yet in each case, their concentrating on what cannot be determined leads the critic to underestimate both the intelligence that does forge specific poetic structures and the complex feelings that those determinate structures can sustain. I should add that in what follows, I assume that the determinate cause of Eliot's indeterminacies is his sense of the contradictions that stem from his attempt to correlate his essentially religious demands on the world with the secular humanism of his teachers. This passage on Irving Babbitt succinctly defines the metonymic terrors in humanism's metaphoric ambitions: "I mean that he knows too many religions and philosophies, has assimilated their spirit too thoroughly (there is probably no one in England or America who understood early Buddhism better than he) to be able to give himself to any. The result is humanism" (*Selected Essays* 428).

6. "The Abstraction of the Artist"

1   As I point out in note 1 to Chapter 5, Hugh Kenner has made versions of this distinction on several occasions. (Herbert Schneidau, *Ezra Pound,* also makes a good case for an objectivist Pound capable of resisting the floating signifiers cultivated by Symbolisme, and now made the center of metaphysical slippage in deconstruction.) It is important to add here that the limitations of this position provide one important reason why we cannot simply set Pound against Eliot, but instead must take the detour of seeing how the painters help us recast issues, and, in the process, alter the standard readings of Pound. Kenner's and Schneidau's Pound cannot, in fact, handle deconstruc-

tive versions of infinite regress, because the assertion of ideals of objectivity is a long way from demonstrating how such ideals are in fact feasible. My arguments here are based on the assumption that we can handle deconstructive claims only if we stop positing some objective world and instead examine ways in which the will or performative dimension, which displaces simple references, can take testimonial forms enabling audiences to agree about what becomes present in the experience.

2   Paul Signac provides a succinct example of avant-garde belief in the nineties: "The Impressionists were wrong in giving up the search for composition. Corot created pictures; except for Renoir they made nothing but studies" ("Excerpts from Paul Signac's Journal," in Nochlin 131). Gauguin neatly makes the rest of the case: "They heed only the eye and neglect the mysterious centers of thought, so falling into merely scientific reasoning" ("The Impressionists," in Chipp 65). When we turn to writers influenced by Impressionism, on the other hand, we find them celebrated for their example of a fluid antimaterialism. There are good summaries of that influence in H. Peter Stowell, *Literary Impressionism: James and Chekhov,* and in Suzanne Ferguson, "Defining the Short Story: Impressionism and Form." Finally, Clive Scott, "Symbolism, Decadence and Impressionism" (in *Modernism* 206–27), provides an excellent treatment of the influence that Impressionism had in shaping a literary ethos.

3   I should note that Clive Scott makes a very good general case for the way that both Impressionism and Symbolisme "disengage quality from object" (*Modernism* 219).

4   If we look at Valéry's entire account, we see him poking gentle fun at the struggle for appropriation in which both figures indulge. Degas, he tells us, used to love to talk about painting, but would not allow writers to talk about painting at all. Therefore, when Degas made statements to Valéry, such as his celebrated axiom "Drawing is not the same as form, it is a way of seeing form," Valéry pretended not to understand, as if painters, without writers, could not make verbal sense. Then, since it is Valéry's text, Valéry goes on to project modes of thematic significance for the paintings that Degas would not, or could not, assert:

> He meant to distinguish what he called the *mise en place,* or the conventional representation of objects, from what he called the "drawing," or the alteration which this exact representation – for example that of a camera lucida – undergoes from a particular artist's way of seeing and working. . . . The camera lucida . . . would enable us to begin work at any point, dispensing us from so much as taking a view of the whole, from any effort to find the relationships between lines and surfaces, and so from transforming the thing *seen* into the thing *experienced* – that is into a *personal* act. . . . What Degas called a "way of seeing" must consequently bear a wide enough interpretation to include *way of being, power, knowledge, and will.* (*Degas, Manet, Morisot* 82–3)

5   For the best treatment of why modern writers project an immediacy for painting, see Wendy Steiner's *Colors of Rhetoric,* and for a more general

theoretical account of the inescapable relation between image and story, see W. J. T. Mitchell, *Iconology: Image, Text, Ideology*.

6 There is one superb work in art history that does a much more thorough job than I do of examining the discourse generated by Impressionist painting, in order to establish a conceptual framework for the art: Richard Shiff, *Cézanne and the End of Impressionism*. (The core of Shiff's argument is also available in his essay "The End of Impressionism.") If there were time, I could engage this work on virtually every page of the next few sections of my book, but I shall try to confine myself to stating here my three fundamental differences with it. First, although Shiff and I both see several complex interrelations between Impressionist and Symboliste understandings of art, especially with regard to the competing claims of what he calls "making" and "finding," I think he is not sufficiently attentive to the pressures that these differences create for the artists. Shiff argues that "while the two styles may be opposed in some senses, the extent of their commonly defined ground may be of equal or greater import" (12). He proceeds to give a list of those common properties, the most important of which is the need to see in Impressionism a substantial concern for "its own subjectivity." On this claim I think he is absolutely right, but there remain very different ways of understanding that subjectivity – as I shall try to show later in this chapter. Moreover, in drawing these links Shiff is unclear on the crucial matter of whether our grasp of those similarities depends on hindsight or responds to the contemporary terms of understanding employed by the historical agents. Thus he says that Cézanne's "painting corresponds to an Impressionist mode of theory and practice, which I associate with the artist's self-image and intentions, . . . [while] it simultaneously appeared in agreement with a Symboliste mode of theory and practice, which I link to Cézanne's appreciative critics and to subsequent art historians" (xvii). But by settling for hindsight, he ignores the possibility that the perceived differences between the positions might have put certain pressures on Cézanne, or that Cézanne might have worked out unique ways of adapting Impressionist themes to the interpretive demands fostered by Symboliste critiques of that art. (For a different, more representative account of similarities between these two movements, see Pound's discussion of them in his *Gaudier-Brzeska*, which projects Symbolism as a plausible model for the permanent energies that art seeks as its content, but makes Impressionism the exemplary "method of presentation" for achieving such energies [82–5].)

My other two quarrels focus on the somewhat different casts that Shiff and I give to observations that are otherwise similar – yet there are important consequences to the differences. For example, Shiff treats what I call the poles of "disclosure" and "presentation" in terms of a dichotomy between "finding" and "making." Both of our perspectives set claims to reference against some condition of artistic will. Yet I fear that his contrast admits of no resolution: Once traces of making emerge, art's claims to truth grow problematic. (Even Shiff's more recent version of these poles as a tension between the "iconic" and "indexical" runs into the kinds of problems that de Man insisted upon. In my model, on the other hand, the presentational pole can be cast as "literal" and "metaphoric" exemplification that has a clear semantic claim on the world, precisely because of how the making displays itself. The basis for a constructivist aesthetic is finding that "finding" is not the only way to truth.

Shiff is too good a critic not to realize that the efforts of Modernist art require him to modify his dichotomy, so he too tries to find a way of postulating the making self as the focus of the artwork. But since he has only a language of reference as his model for public meaning, he seems to be stuck with what he calls a "position" that he does not argue for, but simply presents for study, namely, the hypothesis that Modernist art learns that it must refer to the making self: "What may distinguish the 'artist' from 'craftsman' is the incorporation in his making, of an originality which he can only *find*. His orginality is not made as the fabrications of its culture are; it is found only within himself, in his self-expression" (228). Now, however, Shiff is stuck with an expressivist view of Modernism that is dangerously close to that of Roger Fry. Shiff sees Modernism as the commitment to locating originality within the expressive self. That view is not incompatible with French Modernism, although I do not think that positing a referent for Picasso's willfulness is the best way to understand his sense of self. And very serious trouble arises when one turns to Mondrian or to the Russian Constructivists. Moreover, relying on that ideal of "finding" a self – even a "making" self – deprives the art of the adventure of trying to redefine our ideas of what human agency is and can be. In my view, a major motive within the art is, in fact, learning to replace the kind of "original" self that one must try to express as one's only claim to originality. Within his model, Shiff cannot give any positive content to that self: At best, its power emerges in denying the hold of convention. That is simply not enough reward for the difficulty of the enterprise.

7 This Mallarmé text is given a great deal of attention in Charles Moffett et al., eds., *The New Painting: Impressionism, 1874–1886,* almost all of it in the spirit of the new political criticism, and therefore blind to the idealizing project that Mallarmé is embarked upon.

8 It is important to see the political pressures that also seem to be successfully negotiated by this model of will. For it promises an individualism that is not disruptive, and an aristocracy compatible with democracy. In addition, it combines a sublimity of perception with an ethic of existential seriousness, because who one really is becomes inseparable from the artistic work of defining, as fully possible, what one gains access to from one's own angle of vision. Both Picasso and Maurice Merleau-Ponty make Cézanne the exemplar of what I call an "expressivist ethic," but even Monet would cry, "I am more and more maddened by the need to convey what I experience" ("Letters to Gustave Geffroy," in Nochlin 34). For a good Marxist account of the political pressures of the age, and for a skeptical attitude toward the individualism that I praise, see T. J. Clark, *The Painting of Modern Life: Paris in the Art of Manet and His Followers.* For more on Clark, see my Chapter 10.

9 Gustave Kahn, "*Réponse des Symbolistes*," *L'Evénement* (September 28, 1886), is quoted in John Rewald, *Post-Impressionism* (48). The best example

of Gauguin's expressivist commitments can be found in his *Intimate Journals* (70). This is a good example, contra Shiff, *Cézanne and the End of Impressionism* (especially 61–9), of the very different versions of subjectivity that some versions of Symbolisme set against the Impressionist emphasis on individual temperament.

10   The conflict between those who treat Cézanne as realist and those who insist on the primacy of his painterly qualities is fundamental to art history. But rather than show, as Shiff does, that each of the competing claims can be understood in its context, I think it is important to emphasize the degree to which Cézanne himself seemed compelled to attempt to reconcile them. For the best treatment of that enterprise, we must turn from art history to Merleau-Ponty's famous "Cézanne's Doubt." Recently, Robert Nozick's *Philosophical Explanations* has elaborated an independent philosophical case for what he calls an "ideal of realization."

11   Comparisons such as these are greatly facilitated by the very helpful catalog to the 1986 exhibition, Charles Moffett et al. eds., *The New Painting: Impressionism, 1874–1886,* which is organized in terms of the first eight Impressionist exhibitions. Cézanne's painting is reproduced there.

12   Rather than attempt my own extended discussion of technical matters, I refer the reader to the following books. On color modeling, see Shiff, *Cézanne and the End of Impressionism* (121–4); on the structure of surface tensions, see Earle Loran, *Cézanne's Composition;* and for good close readings of individual paintings as aesthetic artifacts, see Meyer Schapiro, *Paul Cézanne.* Also significant for Cézanne's critique of overall harmony as an immediate end is Hugh Kenner's discussion of the ways in which Modernist poetry tries to replace symphonic sound effects with fugal ones (*The Pound Era* 60–86).

13   Ultimately I shall connect this redefinition of the site of perception with the Cubists' quest for freedom from the very laws of gravity fundamental to the sculptural imagination. And we should note that that quest has as its intellectual context the close connection between empiricism and idealism involved in Impressionism's locating of spirit in the subtilizing of matter. Both Novotny and Shiff remark on that close connection, but neither sees its relationship to the desire to have compositional powers open a way beyond sculptural perspective. However, once we note this conjunction, we can also see why poets like Pound, who, Ian Bell shows, took such possible links between spirit and matter quite literally, found Modernist painting an important source of analogies for what they thought they had to realize. In order to complete the circuit, we ought also to remember that Edmund Husserl and Bertrand Russell, in very different registers, dreamed of an immediacy to "the here and now" that made it difficult to distinguish between mind and world as the location of that immediacy. Perhaps the best way to see Cézanne, in this regard, is to envision him trying to paint, not realism, but the activity of realizing what the imperative to realism makes possible for the mind. Then we see how real and ideal can be woven together on several levels. And we understand why, by taking that stance, he freed himself from a problem that Impressionism encountered as it tried to recon-

cile the old laws of perspective with its ideals of immediacy: On the one hand, its stress on the event of seeing encouraged radical experiments in maintaining the distinctiveness of the point of view giving access to a certain relational field; yet the complexity of that field as a single, present moment led to such diffuse harmonies that the idea of a single point of view came to seem far too substance bound: Where, in all the motion, would the organizing perspective be able to stand sufficiently still to know itself? So we are led back to the concerns about subjectivism so ably traced by Levenson, and we see how those concerns could generate the very different structures for multiple perspectives that Cubism inaugurated.

14   Meyer Schapiro, "The Apples of Cézanne: An Essay on the Meaning of Still Life," in *Modern Art* (1–38). Even more incongruous is Peter Gay's effort to psychoanalyze Mondrian by concentrating on his dislike of organic form (*Art and Act: On Causes of History*). Mondrian's work does not expose that dislike as a symptom, but sets it forth as a hypothesis that both the visual and the discursive materials attempt to explore as a route to alternative values. It is simply no news to remind us that if we take conventional therapeutic attitudes we can suggest conventional cures.

15   In *Working Space,* Frank Stella argues that this painterly war on illusionistic mass and the related force of gravity is not a resistance to Renaissance modeling, but a way of recovering its sense of the painting as a structure of real forces that are not subordinate to the logic of appearances. For Stella, architecture, not sculpture, is the enemy. But if we follow his somewhat anachronistic account (which deals only with the sculptural Cézanne of the *Grandes Baigneuses*), we lose the connection between painterly form and the actual logic of seeing that was crucial to Cézanne and to Picasso.

16   For good art-historical treatments of Cubist stylistic principles, see the now standard books by John Golding, *Cubism;* Robert Rosenblum, *Cubism and Twentieth-century Art;* and Max Kozloff, *Cubism and Futurism.* Also very helpful is Winthrup Judkins, "Towards a Reinterpretation of Cubism"; Pierre Daix, *Picasso;* Josep Paulu i Fabré, *Picasso, The Early Years;* and Daniel Kahnweiler, *Juan Gris.*

17   This use of the eye figure is common in several of Braque's paintings at this time: for example, in *Trees at Estaque* and *Road from Estaque.*

18   For a more complex and more interesting case of unpopulating a scene, consider what Picasso accomplished by removing the male figure who sat before the ladies in the early drafts of *Les Demoiselles d'Avignon.* As Leo Steinberg points out, in "The Philosophical Brothel," that had the effect of turning a scenic painting into a direct confrontation with the painter and the audience, thereby radically foregrounding the authorial act as a direct confrontation with the very image he is compelled to produce.

19   It is easy at this point to dismiss Picasso on political grounds, arguing, as John Berger does, in *Success and Failure of Picasso,* that he projects on the object the coldness that authorizes his proposing his own willfulness as the only plausible alternative. And that charge may be true. But one cannot base this criticism on some ideal of the "dialogical" or the "tribal," such as those we find in Mikhail Bakthin, *The Dialogic Imagination,* or Francois Lyotard,

The Postmodern Condition, because Picasso wants us to see just how absolute are the differences that such social models must negotiate. In this painting, really to understand the presence of the other is to realize how intractable one must be in asserting one's own willfulness. Individualism can no longer be contained within the Victorian expectations that allowed Mill to optimistically assume that society could accommodate the range of possibilities that liberalism was creating. So the moral of this note is that we must beware of theoretical idealizations that both insist on the absoluteness of differences and project worlds in which we are to let the other be other. For the other's being other will involve threats to the self, threats, I add, that can be productive, so long as social order is maintained on other than vague moral terms.

20 I do not think Picasso was quite this clear about his willfulness in 1909. But it is clear from her book *Picasso* that Stein understood the Nietzschean aspect of his work, as did Huntley Carter, later to be the regular art critic of the *Egoist,* writing about Picasso in a London journal in 1911: "Thus the study submitted to the readers of this journal and chosen for the purpose by M. Picasso . . . [*The Mandolin and the Pernod*] demonstrates that painting has arrived at the point when, by extreme concentration, the artist attains an abstraction which to him is the soul of the subject, though this subject be composed only of ordinary objects – mandolin, wine-glass and table, as in the present instance. It indicates too, that painting is at the point of its greatest development. It is on the threshold of the will, and not at the halting-place of men sick with inertia" ("The Plato-Picasso Idea," in Marilyn McCully, *A Picasso Anthology* 82). For other contemporary comments on Picasso's painting as willful heroism, see André Salmon, "On *Les Demoiselles d'Avignon,* in McCully (55–8); Kahnweiler, quoted in Palau i Fabré (517), and, for almost a parody of Picasso as a cultural myth, Gelett Burgess, "Picasso Is a Devil" (1912), reprinted in Gert Schiff, ed., *Picasso in Perspective.*

21 The easiest place to find reproductions of the Picasso paintings I refer to here is William Rubin, ed. *Pablo Picasso: A Retrospect.* In the particular case of the *Portrait of Kahnweiler,* it is worth noting that the Chicago Art Institute, before its recent remodeling, used to hang the painting next to Gris's portrait of Picasso, a pairing that made clear the difference between a design sense of Cubism and the forms of vital intelligence that, Picasso saw, the fragmenting of the canvas could allow. For a critical commentary on that willful intelligence as it appeared in 1912, see the essay by Picasso's friend Josep Junoy, "Picasso's Art," in McCully, ed., *A Picasso Anthology* (87–90). Such emphases are necessary, I think, because as soon as art rejects the transcendental energies of symbolism, its power depends on demonstrating intense conjunctions among forces within the world that we rarely recognize, under nonaesthetic modes of attention, or without the compositional activity of the artist. Symbolist mystery remains, but as testimony to secular human powers.

22 I am willing to generalize here, because I have worked out the specific stages of Picasso's Cubist experiments that pertain to my case in my essay "Picasso's Collages and the Force of Cubism." My version of those Cubist years

begins with his 1906 *Boy with a Pipe*. There we find him adapting his earlier Symboliste dualism between inner and outer reality, and his concerns with sexual inadequacy, to the formal tensions created by the effete lines that separate head from body and transform the pipe into a figure of impotence. The Renaissance balances of his portrait of Stein show the self-possession he desires, but they remain a far cry from the contradictions in his own 1907 self-portrait Before Picasso can earn Stein's centered intensity, he must first face the challenge of the stares that confront the painter in *Les Demoiselles d'Avignon*. By taking out the youth that earlier versions had put inside the bordello, Picasso makes those staring women directly confront his own complicity in a history that had oppressed them by systematically replacing nakedness with nudity (to use John Berger's distinction, *Ways of Seeing* 45–64). Yet Picasso is no feminist. By making those stares direct confrontations, he stages his own willfulness as capable of scavenging through historically incompatible styles in order to define, and thereby face up to, the intensity of their hatred. But his form of willfulness could not compete with Cézanne. It rapidly generated melodrama and sought a specular theater for expressionist effects. A more complete willfulness would have taken on the very logic of perception and the models of painterly representation that had bound themselves to it. So Picasso turned to more traditional painterly subjects, and far more subtle, synthesizing, authorial presences.

We need also to reflect on the fact that commentary on Picasso usually treats the works in terms of their place in his career. For his is an extreme version of what Edward Said has shown (in his *Beginnings*) to be the central role that the concept of "career" played in Modernist efforts to give authority to the selves that they invented. Picasso transformed the Cézannean model of "career" as a continuous course of research into "career" as something much closer to a continuous process of soul making. Then, like Yeats, Picasso defined and valued those states of soul by shaping his own dialectical framework that, in effect, becomes a form of warfare on the contingency of history. Where chance usually reigns, the Cubist Picasso sought a deliberately contoured constitutive particularity. Casting one's life in the form of a career makes art and life the continual testing and reappropriating of the long-term consequences of one's inventions. Over time, this continuity measures the powers that derive from exploring certain imaginative sites – giving a substance to the enticing idea of being Picasso.

23 I distinguish this American sense of absence in deconstruction, because Derrida seems increasingly interested in the qualities of event or apocalypse made available by the actual work of dissemination. There is a Derrida of lack and a Derrida of the excess that becomes lack when we try to recuperate it.

24 Krauss also demonstrates, by contrast, the critical acumen of Ludwig Coellen, a commentator writing on Picasso in 1912:

> This essential reality had to be discovered through the states and the values in which it is visible in objects: in other words, as a realm of feeling which serves as the vehicle for the object. . . . For Matisse,

colors had furnished the means for the presentation of pure feeling; Picasso's sphere was pure space and its differentiation. Space creates the colors which express states of feeling; only the creation of spatial form articulates the law which governs the origin of matter. . . . It remained for Picasso to press onward to the *pure* perception of space as a function of the human mind. . . .

Through the creation of Cubism he has provided an entirely new formal method of attaining, with the stylistic preconditions set by the present age, an appropriate embodiment of pictorial space; *he has replaced mechanical spatial perspective with a dynamic principle whereby a mental space is created within the picture.* . . . Picasso has arrived at his new principle through a one-sided emphasis on the dissolution of objective materiality, through an essentially romantic process of abstraction. ("Romanticism in Picasso" 97)

For other useful accounts of the roles that collage plays in Modernism, see David Antin, "Modernism and PostModernism: Approaching the Present in American Poetry," and Marjorie Perloff, "The Portrait of the Artist as Collage Text: Pound's *Gaudier-Brzeska* and the *Italic* texts of John Cage," in her *Dance of the Intellect* (33–76).

25 The pun turns out to be the best analog I know for the plays on irony and affirmation that Picasso uses for his weaving together of mental and physical energies. Take, for example, Yeats's "Nothing can be sole or whole that has not been rent." By Krauss's deconstructive logic, the puns unmake any coherent single sense of language, thus revealing the duplicity inherent in linguistic codes. The "rent" between world and words means that nothing can be sole or whole. But the puns work: that is, they force us to take language apart into its elements, and they lead us to a shared synthesis. With Yeats's poem, the act of decoding becomes in itself proof of the assertion. Only after the puns on "sole" and "whole" are rent, do we recognize their deeper unity and the spirit at work in flesh. It is no wonder, then, that Yeats has these lines uttered by Crazy Jane in her effort to supplant the bishop's transcendental religion. For her, desire itself confers on body the power of soul, because desire is a spirit of synthesis, a rendering in pursuit of whole and soul. Picasso is subtler and more elemental yet, because in his collage desire requires no human theater at all; it presents the most elemental of all forces, active as matter, in a process of producing coherent form and possessing the energy to reward any act that responds in kind. Such subtlety, I might add, did not go unnoticed by his peers. See, for example, the Coellen passage cited in note 24, and Max Raphael, connecting the constructivist image to the interplay of substance and spirit: By treating "pure blue and red as the pure matter of painting . . . pure matter in its full force," Picasso masters "the turmoil of inner experience . . . by drawing within the turmoil itself the laws by which we master it." To recognize the force of these paintings is to see that there must be "a new aesthetics and a new attitude to life" ("Open Letter to Herr Pechstein" 93). And for the general cultural concern for such issues, see Bell, *Critic as Scientist;* Linda D. Henderson, *The*

Fourth Dimension; and Stephen Kern, *The Culture of Time and Space: 1880–1918.*

26   I hope that this single quotation from Malevich, *Essays* (2:138–9), will suffice to indicate the general nature of his ideas about nonobjectivity:

> In the case of Suprematist contrast it is the different scales of the form, i.e., the sizes (dimensions) of Suprematist Elements in their mutual interrelations that have the greatest significance. In this case color in no way corresponds to form like form to color, but it is only combined by means of the dimensions and scales of space. . . . The creation of these sensations may really be an expression of the essence of phenomena in the non-objective functions of the universe.
>
> This essence of phenomena is sensed non-objectively, since that is the nature of its reality. This reality will never be consciously realized, since the consciousness of form is contained in the object, in something concrete, and man strives to understand it . . .
>
> Thus the investigation of phenomena by purely formal method brings us to forms . . . , but after that we must rely on sensation which should complete that which cannot be shown by the formal method. . . .
>
> Only the formal approach to the universe still does allow complete fusion between man and the universe.
>
> The formal method discovers the forms of phenomena, but not their reality or spirit. . . . For form, colour and spirit are phenomena with different states of energy. The total combination of their states in the universe in which my life is determined is a constant link with or in constant sensation of the spiritual aspect of the forces of the universe, both with and without image. This link in its turn, calls for the activity from one which is expressed in the creation of a new phenomena; the creation of these phenomena will depend on the quality, or capacity to conceive the image, its stableness will depend on the power of the imagination. Thanks to this striving there arises a mass of things that ought to determine my ideas.

27   For example, his roughly contemporaneous *White on White* elaborates the same principle of the tilt, but in a much quieter mode that emphasizes what might be called the "crossing of ontological planes." It is only in *Red Square Black Square* that he combines this level of simplicity with colors that have deep traditional associations – associations, I might add, that his prose insists have a great deal of significance for him. Such bondage to associations would immediately have earned the disdain of Mondrian, who is reported to have stopped talking to Theodor Van Doesburg when he introduced a diagonal line into a painting.

28   I take the idea of invoking Kant's schema from Alexander Gelley, "Metonymy, Schematism, and the Space of Literature." Gelley's essay is particularly useful, because it uses the idea of "schema" for mimetic representations, and thus makes it easy to see how Malevich's level of abstraction is simply a large step within already established ambitions for art.

29   Perry's most detailed statement of his case is in John Perry and John Bar-

wise, *Situations and Attitudes.* I take the anecdote from a lecture he gave at Stanford in 1983.

7. Modes of Abstraction in Modernist Poetry

1 For J. Hillis Miller, see *Poets of Reality* (287–9), and notice how close this position is, in its essentials, to the very different tones of Hugh Kenner's praise of Williams, in Kenner's *Homemade World,* as our paradigmatic American *"bricoleur."* For Joseph Riddel, see *The Inverted Bell: Modernism and the Counterpoetics of William Carlos Williams,* and for Carl Rapp, see *William Carlos Williams and Romantic Idealism.* I defend my criticism of Riddel in my "Presence and Reference in a Literary Text: The Example of Williams." Finally, I should note a fine book, Bernard Duffey, *A Poetry of Presence,* which I came upon too late to use in this chapter. Nonetheless I must mention his concern for ethos defined by poetic activity, which he treats as agency, following Kenneth Burke, and his compelling overall view of Williams's poems as seeking the kind of distinctive equilibriums that can truly define an individual life.

2 To be fair to Albert Cook and to Henry Sayre, I should note that my quarrels with them stem largely from limits inherent in the project each has set himself. Cook, *Figural Choice in Poetry and in Art,* concentrates on the physical aspects of Williams's constructivist sense of the line, because his critical book has as its basic concern the transformations of the very idea of imagery that the new art gave poets. Sayre, *The Visual Text of William Carlos Williams,* on the other hand, stresses formal design and the influence of Juan Gris on Williams, because Sayre's subject is the centrality of visual form in Williams's later work. I suspect that Sayre would agree to my using more thematic and Cézannean notions for the early Modernist poetry, and he might accept the transition I shall soon make to Williams's use of Gris. I should also note here that Sayre (13–14 and 41) gives an account of previous work on the subject to which I subscribe completely. I hope here to combine what Sayre shows about the power of artistic composition with what Rapp shows remain the pressures of the ego on Williams's imagination. For, if one can combine those domains, one can demonstrate how the site of art allows new modes of agency for realizing desires that carry over from nineteenth-century idealism: and in that case, one is reading a Williams who may not be so easily subject to the strictures that criticism now wields very glibly.

3 For a superb illustration of how Williams struggled to embed those abstractions in the dynamics of vision, compare the version of "Flowers by the Sea" that I give in the text to the first one, published five years earlier:

Over the flowery, sharp pasture's edge
unseen, the salt ocean lifts its form

flowers and sea
bring each to each a change

Chickory and daisies, tied, yet released
seem no longer flowers alone

but color and the movement – or perhaps the shapes
of quietness, whereas

the thought of the sea is circled and
sways peacefully upon its plantlike stem.
(*Collected Poems* 352)

The later version trusts the gathering power of the sentence to carry abstractions such as "the thought of the sea" without separating them from the material relations that it brings into focus. The contrast also shows that although David Walker's discussion, in his *Transparent Lyric* (148–9), is very good on the dynamic qualities of the sentence, his commitment to the powers of imagination leads him to underplay the importance of the sentence as a materializing force.

4   The question of precisely how Williams transforms traditional uses of metaphor is a thorny one. Sayre does an excellent job of refuting the standard claim that Williams strives to "rid his work of metaphor," but his counterargument creates problems. I think it is quite useful to suggest that Williams has "turned the function of metaphor around on itself: where metaphor is generally considered to be a means of evoking and defining the image – pinning down the flower in this case – the image now becomes at once the nexus and generator of a whole range of metaphors" (21–2). But a good deal depends on getting the nature of this exemplary generation right. For Sayre, the generation is a form of dissemination, introducing an extravagance that in turn produces a playfulness, with substantial parallels to Surrealist metaphor. In my view, on the other hand, Sayre's equation of composition with extravagance draws Williams much closer to Surrealism than he ever was. Sayre reads Williams's handling of metaphor through a theory of "excess" that Surrealist metaphors have produced within contemporary French thought. But the two levels of metaphor we have noted in this poem – the local embeddings that give force to the contrasts, and the more global sense of the sentence as figure – treat the exuberance of metaphor, freed from the task of higher-order denotation basic to Romantic theory, not as dissemination, but as the elaborating of a single process of focused desire. The metaphor here is all in the framing, all in the play of language that goes through its own process of releasing the phenomena from gravity, then circling it to sway on its plantlike stem. In fact, it is precisely this temptation to make metapoetic use of the poem's own language that best defines its metaphoricity – not because we can work out allegorical parallels, but because we can glimpse parallel structures of containment, by which artifice, in acknowledging its own workings, tracks its ability to align will and world. Metaphor does not make attributions about the objects, but shapes the frames in which they are allowed to appear, and thereby leads us back to the nature of the conceptual factors that allow sight its transforming power.

5   Usually this poem is read as the purest statement of Williams the objectivist (for example, in Kenner's *Homemade World*) and, in accord with a painterly model (in a talk that Michael Rifaterre gave at Georgetown University in 1983). These critics recognize the role of foregrounded artifice, but not its

self-reflexive functions. Yet the prose surrounding the poem dwells on abstract features of the creative imagination; for example, with assertions like this: "And what is the fourth dimension? It is the endlessness of knowledge– / It is the imagination on which reality rides. . . . Art is the pure effect of the force on which science depends for its reality – Poetry" (*Spring and All 139*).

6 For another treatment of Williams's use of the sentence as a model of mind made palpable, see my essay "What Modernism Offers the Contemporary Poet," which discusses the equivalence between cats and sentences in Williams's "Poem." Seen in terms of Modernist art, this title provides a resonant tension that plays abstraction against the literal poem that the movement realizes.

7 I obviously could cite more ways of envisioning the "there exists" than I take up in this book. In particular, the concept of expanding the implications of "there exists" set against the dialogical model of addressing another subject seems to me a fine introduction to the imaginative impulses behind much of Dada and Surrealism. But I ignore these, in part on the historical ground that they had little influence on the first generation of American Modernists, and in part on the conceptual grounds that their versions of agency involve relations to Modernist ideals of lucidity that are quite unlike those discussed in this study.

8 For good treatments of the stylistic traits of Cubist painting that influenced the poets, see Jacob Korg, *Language in Modern Literature;* Gerald Kamber, *Max Jacob and the Poetics of Cubism* (43–54); and especially Wendy Steiner, *Exact Resemblance* (Chapter 4). And for the best summary of those traits, see Gérard Bertrand, *L'Illustration de la Poesie à L'Epoque du Cubisme, 1909–1914* (68–9). Bertrand emphasizes four fundamental principles that the poets adapted from the painters: They accepted the challenge to reject tradition, in the name of a purified model of thinking and a new relation to temporality; they were led to treat language as a plastic medium; they sought a thematics based on various aspects of simultaneity that the atmosphere of the work can carry; and they sought conceptual, rather than illusionary, dramatic models of content, based on the reality that the work itself can be said to constitute. Steiner's *Exact Resemblance* elaborates the rationale for such influences, but her *Colors of Rhetoric* gives a sharp warning on the limits of the analogy.

9 The Gris collage mentioned in the poem was thought to be his *Roses* (1914). However, Sayre, *Visual Text* (41), argues that there is no record of that work being printed before 1930, whereas Gris's *Open Window* was published in *Broom* 1 (1922). Yet *Roses* has a much closer iconographic relation to the poem.

10 The one Modernist poet I know who truly realizes possible verbal analogs to collage decomposition and recomposition is Guillaume Apollinaire, especially in his "*Coeur, Couronne et Miroir.*" I provide a reading of the authorial action of two segments of that poem in my essay "Abstraction as Act: Modernist Poetry in Relation to Painting."

11 For the subsequent course of Stein's portraits, see Steiner's *Exact Resemblance*. Because I have concentrated on the Picasso paintings congruent with his early Cubist portraits – for example, Kahnweiler and Uhde – not those, such as *The Accordionist* or *Ma Jolie*, that try to reduce all semantic

markers to design facets attached to a two-dimensional surface – I think it most useful to concentrate on similar stylistic commitments in Stein.

12   I am aware that I give special thematic significance here to devices that Stein uses in other thematic complexes. I plead only that they fit, and that one would expect her to be at her most self-consciously testimonial about formal matters, when she is reflecting on Picasso.

13   See especially Lynn Hejinian, "Two Stein Talks," and on Stein's poetry see Marjorie Perloff's essay in her *Poetics of Indeterminacy* "Poetry as Word-system: The Art of Gertrude Stein."

14   For an excellent analysis of what this distinction entails for interpreting the relation of painting to Stevens's poems, see Bonnie Costello, "Affects of an Analogy: Wallace Stevens and Painting." And for Stevens himself on the issue, consider his angry, yet rueful, remark on the purchase by the Museum of Modern Art of a painting by William Baziotes: "After all, modern art is a technical interest. One has to know the progress of the thing as Sweeney knows it . . . to see it as it should be seen. I don't see it that way. I still feel that some painters are better than others: that they are more intelligent, more sensitive, more practiced" (*Letters* 579).

15   I have chosen to use the translation provided by Bradford Cook, *Mallarmé: Selected Prose, Poems, Essays and Letters* (4–7), because the points I shall be making do not rely on specific syntactic or semantic features that translation cannot capture.

16   Both John M. Slatin and Bonnie Costello begin their excellent books on Moore with the thesis that questions of defining poetry in conjunction with models of identity are central to her enterprise. But whereas Slatin, *The Savage's Romance,* emphasizes the contexts that Moore manipulates, Costello focuses on matters of building a poetic ethos. Thus Costello's *Imaginary Possessions* argues that the terms that Moore uses for poetry all try to combine "moral and aesthetic or intentional and expressive categories: feeling and precision, idiosyncracy and technique" (2). Costello does a superb job of showing how Moore's mobile intelligence gathers and disperses energies as it resists making imagistic effigies of itself, and Costello adds a highly informative and intelligent chapter on Moore's relation to the visual arts of her time. But although she is clear on how Moore's use of her medium is Modernist, Costello seems to me to stay essentially within a realizational aesthetic that cannot take account of either the powers or the sense of mystery that Moore tries to evoke for the conditions of agency that her poems establish. For example, Moore is simply too abstract for this formulation: "Moore's poems are not, finally, representations of things or statements of opinions. They are imaginative acts, efforts to reconstruct the world in language, and thus in relation to the self, to render the world harmless and to give the self objectivity" (65). If I am right, it is not so easy to talk about "self," or even about "objectivity" – these are indeed concerns of Moore's reconstructions, but Moore succeeds, at times, all too well, to allow so traditional a recuperative language. And without an adequate model of the forms of agency that Moore does compose, one cannot thoroughly handle the degree to which agency becomes gendered within Moore's imaginative universe. Therefore, we need to take a critical tack that emphasizes the actual

forces that Moore's compositional activity establishes. For that, the best analogs are those painterly models that eschew realization entirely, to focus attention on relational powers. In relying on those analogs, I need not deny that the visual Modernism most interesting to Moore consisted mostly in Cubist works. I claim only that she learned from them much the same lessons that Mondrian and Malevich did, both of whom continually cited Cézanne and Picasso. It is those painters who most clearly capture what Moore makes even of that Cubist work (for example, Picasso's collages) most dependent on virtuality. As a good test case for the differences I am trying to indicate, compare my treatment, in this chapter, of the last version of Moore's "Poetry" with Costello's. As in Slatin's fine reading of the poem's various stages, she sees all of the intricacy of the pronouns, but concludes that "reducing the poem to three lines may be Moore's attempt to uncover the genuine, but a short poem is no more genuine than an expansive one" (26). True enough, but *this* short poem's negation of the image introduces a quite different poetic theater. Pound succinctly caught the special quality of this kind of reading when he compared Moore to Williams: "Williams is simple by comparison – not so thoughtful. [Moore's poem] has a larger audience because of its apparent simplicity. It is the lyric of an aptitude. Aptitude, not attitude" (*Selected Prose* 399).

17 The best way to see the prevalence of the problem is to focus on critical work like Alicia Ostriker's *Stealing the Language,* which celebrates the expressive ego's efforts to steal and remake a patriarchal language. I cannot quarrel with the ideal of remaking the language, but I find it problematic to base poetic judgments primarily on whether or not the poems give full expression to specific subjective positions. As I suggested in my remarks on Alice Jardine, so long as new feminism stays in this vein, it is but old late Romanticism writ large, and both the critical force and imaginative resources of Modernism simply get relegated to ancient history. For a good critique of those tendencies, as well as of the attendant language of victimage that would have appalled Moore, see Susan Howe, *My Emily Dickinson.*

18 Moore's use of abstract testimonial principles, and her blend of the personal and the impersonal, also make it possible to claim that little is lost even if my thesis is wrong, or if the specifically gendered poems that I shall deal with do not prove sufficiently representative. The central point is that she insists on producing an ethos out of foregrounded authorial energies, so that they define a fully ethical presence, able to understand what its loves make possible. I think there is sufficient evidence to treat that ethos as gendered, and sufficient cultural reason to insist on that argument. But, for the general purposes of this book, we can take the gender claims as simply an index of her capacity to wrest complex twists on virtuality and transpersonality, which distinguish her work from the more painterly and perceptual versions of abstraction pursued by Williams and Stevens, especially during the decade after the First World War, when Moore was clearly embarked on a more radical rethinking of language than they were.

19 Quoted from *The Complete Poems of Marianne Moore* (New York: Viking, 1981), 83. All quotations of Moore's poetry are taken from this source.

20 It is crucial to note that Yeats's turn, in his last poems, against the personal

enabled him to incorporate the most radical lessons of Modernism. From the time of his work in the Abbey Theater, Yeats had made the artistic act the test of ethos: The man is the style he can wield. But in the last poems, style is not continuous with personality. In fact, it is precisely the intensity of formal energies that enables the art to explore modes of ethos that cannot take the form of self-dramatizing speakers. Among Yeats's critics, the best treatments of this turn against the personal are, first, the classical discussion of affirmative capability in Richard Ellmann, *The Identity of Yeats,* and then Bernard Levine, *The Dissolving Image,* on the implications of Yeats's distrust of the image and pursuit of the kind of spiritual intensity described in Yeats's late prose pieces, such as "The Holy Mountain." As much as I admire Levine's generalizations, however, I find myself unable to agree with any of his readings.

21   Quoted from *The Poems of W. B. Yeats,* ed. Richard J. Finneran (New York: Macmillan, 1983) 339. All other quotations of Yeats's poetry are taken from this source.

22   To appreciate how much Yeats shares with noniconic painting, observe how thoroughly this poem fits the language of "praise" developed by Clement Greenberg and Michael Fried, which I discuss at length in Chapter 10. Both critics celebrate an antitheatrical and self-critical reduction to the elements of form. Fried makes that reduction the vehicle for the work testing its ability to resist its own "thingness" by modes of concentration producing a sense of "presentness that is grace." See especially his "Art and Objecthood," and his introduction to *Morris Louis,* which concludes with an elaborate comparison of the kind of substance Louis creates and the site of art envisioned by Mallarmé.

8. Modernist Abstraction and Pound's First Cantos

1   Bonnie Costello, "Affects of an Analogy: Wallace Stevens and Painting," provides an excellent example of how to read Stevens's relation to paintings as the exploring of principles rather than the imitating of styles. Unfortunately, she nonetheless still confines her readings to poems on visual motifs, so she does not completely realize what exploring those principles involved.

2   We feel the pathos of this aspect of Pound's ambitions when we see his vulnerability before the snotty British establishment that he desperately wanted to crack. Thus Ford Madox Hueffer, descending from the lofty perch as editor of the *English Review,* wrote, in Pound's *New Freewoman,* that Pound should be included among the interesting young poets because there is "a suggestion of power in Mr. Pound's derivations from Romance writers."

3   There are two ways to illustrate the problematic role that the concept of form plays in Pound studies. One can analyze the specific blind spots that it creates in otherwise superb scholarship, and one can trace the general effects that it has had in shaping the interests and conflicts that occupy, and divide, Pound scholars (at least when they are not so intent on convicting every phase of his career of fascism that they are able to attend to the nature or

quality of thinking projected in his best poetry). As my example of the first kind of blind spot, I want to comment briefly on Reed Way Dasenbrock, *The Literary Vorticism of Pound and Lewis: Towards the Condition of Painting.* Dasenbrock's book on Vorticism seems to me most sensitive to its place in Pound's poetic career, yet still misses the most important feature of that influence, because he sees Vorticism only as an aesthetic stance, devoted to matters of form. Dasenbrock is superb in his claim that Vorticism is not primarily an art of abstraction, but an art that seeks, by abstraction, to refer to certain dynamic formal principles within the world (e.g., 73), and he is quite convincing when he argues that the major importance of Vorticism consists in its influence on the writing of Pound and Lewis. Finally, he makes a compelling case for interpreting the changes that occur in the *Cantos* during the thirties as the effect of a shift from the ideal of a vortex, based on holding perceptions in juxtaposition, to an emphasis on the ideogrammic method because the latter offers a means of arranging "his particulars so as to define generalities" (211).

All of these observations, however, confine Vorticism to the exploration of formal principles, ignoring both Pound's interest in Nietzsche's question of who one becomes by virtue of composing formal objects, and the desire of flesh out the obsessive sense of the artist as exemplary hero that Pound shared with Lewis. Therefore Dasenbrock has little choice but to treat the early *Cantos* almost exclusively as the exploration of perceptual juxtapositions – an imagism with dynamic force – that clearly must be inadequate to Pound's epic ambitions. Although he is very good on how the middle *Cantos* expand their scope, he cannot see the continuity of their Confucian orientation with Pound's earlier individualism. And Dasenbrock is satisfied only with the *Pisan Cantos,* because there he can assimilate the poetry to a Taoist perspective: Shorn of his political illusions, the poet can adopt a contemplative "counsel of patience and acceptance," reflecting the realization that the disorder of the world is at one with the desire to order it (220–3). That contemplative counsel, however, is not the stuff of the epic imagination, nor is it quite appropriate to either the poet's plaintive cry for a quick death, which pervades those *Cantos* (e.g., the end of numbers 83 and 84) or his rich, expressivist pride in the belief that "error is all in the not done, all in the diffidence that faltered" (*Cantos* 552).

Pound's critique of the "not done" could have been directed at this kind of criticism. For it seeks an essentially religious contemplative stance, because that allows us to enjoy Pound, even to identify with the intense moments he creates, without having to worry about the connection between one's interests and the forces that led him to his Fascist sympathies. If, on the other hand, we concern ourselves overtly with his ethics, or more generally with his efforts to imagine a humanity that can sustain so epideictic a mode as an epic, there is the constant pressure of having to distinguish what one praises, and one's own praising, from the results that such values produced for Pound. Yet until we face those problems, we will continue to go round in the same narrow Pound. There will remain room for the superb close readings of a Kenner, but as long as we treat the concern for formal intensity as the central motive of the *Cantos,* we shall remain torn between seeing the poem as an effort to glimpse the paradisiacal within the secular, and treating the poem as sustaining the vision of an ideal city safely out of time. (For good examples of the first, see the critical books by Christine Froula or Leon Surette; for the second, see Guy Davenport, *Cities on Hills.*) It remains impossible to decide whether Pound conceives form as an alternative to the city or a means of demonstrating models of possible political orders. And that leaves the way open to the host of Pound debunkers or deconstructors who are all too eager to elaborate, and provide psychoanalytic contexts, for the problems posed by Michael André Bernstein, who asks to what degree so aesthetically based a model of politics can address real-world situations without projecting fantasies that distort the very nature of the political order. (For more extensive commentary on Bernstein and the debunkers, see my note 8, this chapter.)

If we are to handle these questions, we must be able to provide a dramatic motive for the formal energies that casts them as elements manipulated by a purposive agent who is trying to balance the aesthetic, the utopian, and the practical. But when Pound critics speculate on agency, they tend to develop their concerns by opposing the personal to the formal, at one pole, and at the other by completely subordinating all question of self and purpose to the dynamics of writing. (The only exceptions I know are the treatments of Pound's individualism in the critical commentaries by Donald Davie, *Ezra Pound,* and Thomas Jackson, "Pound and Herder.") The best example of the first orientation is Wendy Flory's effort to show how much of the *Cantos* is a record of personal struggle. She does a fine job of spelling out what underlies the text. Unfortunately, she finds herself in such sharp opposition to critics who use form to deny biography that her version of the life is kept distinct from the poet's efforts to make the authorial activity within the text itself a means of addressing and incorporating those struggles. The result is an analysis of the sense of struggle that one would expect of a nineteenth-century author – precisely what Pound sought to overcome by treating formal energies as means for creating a model of agency that can translate the personal into a more public model of needs, resources, and modes of taking responsibility. Flory's dichotomy between existential and formal agency takes exactly the opposite form in deconstructive approaches to Pound such as that of Joseph Riddel, "The Anomalies of Literary (Post) Modernism," where the text itself becomes a kind of agency, a force of writing that disseminates an irreducible texture of permutations, absorbing all aspects of the real into the dizzying folds of textuality. Riddel then can easily subsume Pound's Nietzsche under Derrida's. But so unhistorical a gesture is possible only because, having surrendered any concern for the embodied author, the dominant formalism cannot absorb the actual historical role that Nietzsche played for Pound: as a model, not of infinite textuality, but of the kind of personal powers that could be elaborated through textual means. (For that historical Nietzsche as envisioned by other writers of Pound's age, see John Burt Foster, *Heirs to Dionysus;* for Pound's use of Nietzsche in his own reading, see Kathryne Lindberg, *Reading Pound Reading.* It is also useful to recall Charles Olson's Pound, in his essay "This Is Yeats Speaking," in *Human Universe* [99–104], a figure lost to our fear of the Fascist thematics connected with that model of self.)

4 Dasenbrock, *Literary Vorticism,* puts the negative case well: "'Dogmatic Statement' tries to do in words what a Vorticist painting could do much more easily. For that reason, though trying hard to be Vorticist, it is neither Vorticist nor a good poem" (89). There is, nonetheless, something to be said for the intelligence that Pound brings to his task.

5 For good accounts of Vorticism per se, see, in addition to Dasenbrock, *Literary Vorticism:* Timothy Materer, *Vortex: Pound, Eliot and Lewis;* Kenner, *The Pound Era* (145–261); and Ronald Bush, *T. S. Eliot* (39–55). The most interesting of these accounts, for the purposes of this chapter, however, is Ian Bell, "Pound's Vortex," which presents a position at the opposite pole from mine. Through a useful critique of Materer, Bell shows how dense and peculiar was Pound's version of Vorticism, because it relied on numerous transcendentalist and spiritualist echoes totally foreign to Lewis. From my point of view, this is all the more evidence of how much Pound still had to overcome before he could arrive at a vision of spiritual energies sufficient for a constructivism that could carry a modern, secular epic. But even these initial efforts to treat Vorticism as requiring a language of acts and powers indicates the inadequacy of those quasi-Lacanian accounts that link the Pound of imagism with the Pound obsessed by economics, casting him as an anal fetishist who desperately resisted productive energies. Take, for example, the following statements by Richard Sieburth, "In Pound We Trust":

> Against this slippery deconstructive "logic of the supplement," Pound's Imagism attempts to institute a poetics free from mediation, free from metaphor, free from temporality and, ideally, free from language altogether – a poetics of silence finally achieved, at great cost, only at the end of *The Cantos.* (151)

> Pound's antinomian and apocalyptic desire to move beyond metaphor, beyond mediacy, indeed, beyond language altogether into the "unnamed" and unnameable, finds its traditional utopian expression in his vision of an economy which, if not actually abolishing money as a middle term, would at least considerably diminish its material or symbolic significance. . . . Accordingly one of Pound's favorite nostrums from 1934 on involved the "stamp scrip" currency proposed by the German monetarist Silvio Gesell. . . . The attraction of a self-liquidating or self-castrating currency (stamp scrip, Pound noted, was money that eats up its own tail) indicates the extent to which he desires to dematerialize or disembody the medium of exchange, to reduce it to an evanescent mark or trace. (153)

> If Pound dismisses production as an economic problem in order to concentrate on distribution and circulation, so this theory of language tends to ignore the production of meaning in favor of a strictly instrumental attitude toward discourse. (167)

I quote at length because it seems to me crucial that we indicate the limits of this new metaphoric criticism, so intent on its ability to dispel the idealized author that it simply ignores what might be worth idealizing. I shall try to show that once Pound turned to Vorticism, his paramount concern, for at least a decade, became the power by which agents establish distinctive verbal identities and, through their expressions, take responsibility for their value commitments. If this is correct, generalizations about the *Cantos* as a whole are likely to ignore the different Pounds responsible for different parts of them. And generalizations from Pound's economics are especially likely to misrepresent the Vorticist individualist of the *Draft of Thirty Cantos,* because they impose a later obsession for understanding how an entire social order can take such responsibility for itself. In addition, the line of thinking pursued by Sieburth traps itself in a two-term model of language: There are only names and referents, with no distinction for the quality by which names are proposed and embodied, and hence no way to make sense of why Pound's quotations seek to render the tone of things as agents engage them. This is to trivialize the poet who said that there are no ideas, only ways of holding them, and it is to force poetry to choose between the banalities of public language or the unmediated ecstasies of silence. But for Pound, as for most poets, it is crucial to distinguish between mediations that interfere with what enables an agent to take clear responsibility for a position and those that make certain ecstasies possible. When these poets idealize silence, that silence is not opposed to all language, but only to various versions of idle talk, so that silence is the reward that comes from learning to handle the instrument of mediation. In the same vein, it is important to realize that Pound did not take Gesell's stamp scrip as abolishing or self-castrating the mediation of money, but as encouraging people to make money produce by using it rather than hoarding it. So here Pound does not oppose excess, but the hoarding that denies the possible enjoyment of the goods a society has available to it. In fact the language of excess, set against use value, is inappropriate to Pound, because his major concern is instead the clearer and less ideologically driven distinction between using and abusing resources. Pound turns to economics, not with the end of having unmediated currency, but with the hope that the less abstract and self-contained the monetary apparatus, the clearer the productive relations among human beings.

It should be obvious that if one cannot even be faithful to the intent of Pound's discourse, one is going to get into a lot of trouble when one freely spins metaphors out of the proposed economics. Perhaps the most severe problem arises in the cast that such critical thinking gives to the concept of metaphor. Seen in terms of the opposition between excess and reference, metaphor clearly becomes a scandalous disseminating force, to be resisted. But Pound does not eliminate metaphor, although he does often achieve metaphoric results by having particular descriptions spread an encompassing emotional tone or work by analogy with other descriptions (for example the concluding sections of Canto 2). Rather than fearing the excess of metaphor, Pound makes that potential excess an important measure of the speaking act: The authority of the speakers depends on how they control metaphor, as part of the overall tone they establish for engaging the real. Metaphor, then, need not be opposed to the clarity of language. Even at its most resonant, metaphor can be a clear instrument for producing a stance attuned to complex historical situations.

In rejecting the referential aspect of Imagism (an act that Sieburth ignores), Pound set himself the task of understanding how language can "produce" in the same way that analytic geometry can generate formulas that make realities intelligible. This entailed exploring ways to escape the very oppositions that warrant Sieburth's patronizing attitudes. But so long as criticism operates within those oppositions, it cannot even properly value its own misgivings about its procrustean terms. At one point, Sieburth tries to criticize those who too hastily "reduce Pound's work to a closed, phallo- or logocentric Fascist discourse" (165), and at another he admits that the *Cantos* do not seem to rely on the same fear of production that he teases out of the early and the late prose. Yet he can muster only two thin positive attributions: that there is a sense of "dynamic ambivalence" about Pound's treatment of production, which helps us understand how conservative economic positions like Pound's subordinate production to matters of distribution; and that the *Cantos* offer a mode of excess by indulging in puns (167). Perhaps nothing more need be said about a stance that depends on the pun as the main productive element in Pound's poetry. However, it may be instructive to notice just how Sieburth's own excess with metaphor leads him to this embarrassing position. Sieburth thinks that one can take excess in economics and in language as parallel, because both sustain a language of surplus value. He never asks what relational scheme determines a particular as "excess," or what interests the various kinds of surpluses might serve. But for Pound, as for most Modernists, there are crucial distinctions between the kinds of excess that art seeks and those created within a capitalist economy. In the case of art, excess is not incompatible with the most extreme efforts at economy, because the point of the art is to open areas of reflective plenitude. Mondrian, for example, uses the most severe means to elicit an extremely lush metaphysics, and Pound himself makes his efforts at precision the means for what many readers have found an unbearable plenitude of internal relations. At the other pole, it is feasible to conceive of excess that merely intensifies imaginative and emotional poverty. One thinks immediately of Orange County. But W. S. Merwin provides a more telling model, which is also more apposite for contemporary criticism, in his figure of American society as a bee that has lost its intestines, but continues to suck greedily at every promise of honey.

6 Pound's richest single treatment of expression is his "Affirmations: Vorticism," in *Ezra Pound and the Visual Arts* (5–10).

7 Although critics often comment on Pound's influence on Yeats's style, we ignore the more important current of influence from Yeats (via Allen Upward) to Pound, on the notions of individuality and personality. Pound cites Yeats's brother Jack as his model for the concept of certitude (*Literary Essays* 184), and his claims about Renaissance personality obviously parallel those made by William. See also Albert Gelpi's account of the Jungian dimension

of the *Cantos*, in *A Coherent Splendor*, which shows in another way how much Pound learned from Yeats and how actively he sought an alternative to the objectivity that critics such as Kenner and Herbert Schneidau attribute to him.

8   In making this case, the critic on the *Cantos* whom I am most concerned to address is Michael Bernstein, "Identification and Its Vicissitudes." First, he is the only one I know who sees how much questions of personal identity are at stake in the poem. He provides a sensitive and powerful account of the problems resulting from Pound's Keatsian capacity to make identifications: How can the "real" Ezra Pound stand up, or how can the *Cantos* be given a unifying voice and unifying quest? Under such pressure, Pound sought to make, out of his "desperate struggle with the process of assuming another's character, of discovering the necessary limits of identification and distancing," a quest "for the proper relationship to the objects of one's own desire" (541). But Bernstein argues that Pound's solution for developing a narrative stance not burdened by excessive identification was to establish through the narrative a self-abnegating "detachment from what he sees and an obligation to let the personae speak for themselves" (545). Bernstein goes on to praise the method of "silent arrangement, juxtaposition, and selection of the historical exempla," but all with emphasis on letting the others speak, rather than on Pound's earning his own space in which to construct a self out of the relations it can muster. I hope that I offer a decent countercase, in part because Bernstein's argument repeats the weaknesses in his important book *The Tale of the Tribe*. There ethos in Pound is analyzed primarily in moral terms, with the result that Bernstein ultimately ignores what is original in Pound's constructivist concerns. Instead, Pound's project is found wanting by being measured against the very categorical models Pound set himself against (see especially pages 47–50). Bernstein brings assumptions about the psyche to the poem and, in relying on them, he evades an encounter with the possible force of Pound's critique of our conventional humanism and empirical historiography. Also, Bernstein's relying on the idea of an epic leads him to treat Pound's tale as if it described a tribe familiar to us, rather than, in large part, projecting an idealized model of agency, through which some new tribe might be created out of our history. Blindness to the constructive dimension traps the critic in the entire complex of evils Pound thought inevitable within mimetic aesthetics.

9   True to the spirit of this remark, Pound's point deserves extensive quotation:

> [De Gourmont] was an intelligence almost more than an artist; when he portrays, he is concerned with hardly more than the permanent human elements. His people are only by accident of any particular era. He is poet, more by possessing a certain quality of mind than by virtue of having written fine poems; you could scarcely contend that he was a novelist. . . . He was intensely aware of the differences of emotional timbre; and as a man's message is precisely his *Facon de voir*, his modality of perception, this particular awareness was his "message." . . . Where

James is concerned with the social tone of his subjects, . . . with their *superstes* of dogmatized "form," ethic, etc., Gourmont is concerned with their modality and resonance in emotion. (*Literary Essays* 340)

"*Il est très difficile de persuader à de certains viellards – vieux ou jeunes – qu'il n'y a pas de sujets; il n'y a en littérature qu'un sujet, celui qui écrit, et toute la littérature, c'est-à-dire toute la philosophie, peut surgir aussi bien à l'appel d'un chien écrasé qu' aux acclamations de Faust interpellant la Nature. . .* (349) *La vie est un dépouillement. Le but de l'activité propre d'un homme est de nettoyer sa personnalité, de la laver de toutes les souillures qu'y déposa l'education, de la dégager de toutes les empreintes qu'y laissèrent nos admirations adolescentes.*" (354)

[It is very difficult to persuade certain greybeards – old or young – that there are not subjects; there is in literature only one subject, the one who writes, and all literature, that is to say all philosophy, is able to take the stage as well at the call of a dog that has been run over as at the acclamations of a Faust calling upon nature. . . .
Life is a dissection. The end of the activity proper for a man is to cleanse his personality, to wash it of all the stains that education deposits, to disengage all the imprints that our adolescent admirations leave there.]

10 According to Ronald Bush, to whom I am greatly indebted in my reading of these *Ur-Cantos*, Pound had dropped the metacommentary by 1918, in a version published in the *Futurist*. But only in the final version did he make the changes needed to stress the personal strength required to face the challenge that Tiresias poses.

This is also a good occasion to note my general differences with Ronald Bush's account, in his *Genesis of Ezra Pound's Cantos*, of how Pound finally overcame his self-defensive ironies. Bush attributes Pound's development past Vorticism and the "method" of the *Ur-Cantos* to three basic factors: his learning to adapt a Jamesian model of rendering (203); his coming to pursue de Gourmont's model of civilized intelligence; and his increasing faith in a principle of "eye witnessing" (187). None of these is wrong: But neither do they take us very far toward appreciating the significance of Pound's achievement. Thus, I shall argue that Bush subordinates what he correctly sees is the importance of Vorticism – its emphasis on constructive acts – to what remains a Jamesian ideal of mimesis. The result is a Pound as trapped in the discriminating, balancing, civilized mind as Kenner's Pound is in the appreciation of pattern and form. Moreover, Bush's awareness of the constructivist Pound melds, all too easily, into praise of Pound the poet of objective perceptions: "Unexplained fragments had no terror for him. Discontinuity was a normal and real part of perception" (226); and "Pound's 'reflector' registers images, and often the images are so vivid that they make us forget there is a consciousness behind them" (229). In what follows, I shall argue that the objectifying strategies in Pound are intended to be subordinate to the constructive act and the sense of individual power made available by that act. Both James and de Gourmont are not so much models as challenges forcing Pound to appropriate their strengths within a different dynamic, made possible by a poetry written to paint and not to music.

11 Quotations from the *Cantos* are given by line number from *The Cantos of Ezra Pound,* ed. T. S. Eliot (New York: New Directions, 1981).

12 This is the original version, from *Poetry* (September 10, 1917): 250–1:

> Justinopolitan
> Uncatalogued Andreas Divus
> Gave him in Latin, 1538 in my edition, the rest uncertain,
> Caught up his cadence, word and syllable:
> "Down to the ships we went, set mast and sail,
> Black keel and beasts for bloody sacrifice,
> Weeping we went."
> I've strained my ear for *-ensa, -ombra,* and *-ensa*
> And cracked my wit on delicate canzoni –
>   Here's but rough meaning:
> "And then went down to the ship, set keel to breakers,
> Forth on the godly sea."

13 In reading my manuscript, Albert Gelpi proposed instead that the acts of structuring depend upon the god. I am not sure how to handle our difference, except to point out that whatever the gods are for Pound, they are inseparable from the forms of self-consciousness that emerge as we realize our own creative powers.

14 In reading a draft of this chapter, Evan Watkins made a comment I think worth passing on: "As Pound assessed the political consequences of his schema of values, they led to political sympathies repugnant to most of us. But that does not mean we have to assess them the same way. If an authority names the difference, that has consequences, but it does not mean that it dictates what those consequences must be." Watkins hoped, by this remark, to make me see that one need not divide the realms of poetry and politics, since they both "originate in that difficult moment when 'significance' emerging as an idealizing form begins to have material consequences and as material production begins to be idealized in specific ways." However, I still think that one can distinguish consequences for individuals, where it makes sense to hope that art can provide idealizations, and consequences for politics, where idealizations often are either obvious (i.e., nuclear proliferation is a bad thing) or dangerous in their abstraction from the actual range of interests at stake in a given situation.

15 I take that "diffidence" to have included his need to rely on political authorities to sustain his personal values.

9. Why Stevens Must Be Abstract

1 *The Collected Poems of Wallace Stevens* (New York: Knopf, 1964) (280). Unless otherwise stated, all quotations from Stevens's poetry are from this edition; page numbers are given in parentheses.

2 Helen Vendler puts the distinguishing intellectual quality of Stevens's poetry

well in her "Hunting of Wallace Stevens." However, in my view this sense of his continual second-order relation to experience requires more attention to what those ideas make of the personal than Vendler brings to bear in her recent writing on Stevens. There she seems to share with the new historicists the desire to identify with the august imagination only when it is "checked, baffled, frustrated, and reproved" (*Part of Nature, Part of Us,* 41–2). There are two other basic theoretical directions in Stevens criticism, but neither seems to me to capture the kind of life that ideas held for him. Harold Bloom's Nietzschean Stevens focuses his energies on psychological drama that is impossible to socialize or participate in, whereas Joseph Riddel's deconstructionist Stevens, who seeks "a writing that kills" by constantly disclosing the artifice in our fictions (335), never ceases from decreation long enough to have a stance that one can demystify or, one must add, that society can accept as a fiction. For Bloom and Riddel, see, respectively, *Wallace Stevens: The Poems of Our Climate,* and "Metaphoric Staging: Stevens Beginning Again of the 'End of the Book.'"

More scholarly work on Stevens has not succumbed entirely to these theoretical blinders. Most pertinent for this book are Jacqueline Vaught Brogan, *Stevens and Simile,* and B. J. Leggett, *Wallace Stevens and Poetic Theory.* Brogan pays intelligent, careful attention to the force of simile in Stevens, and to the roles it plays, in reconciling deconstructive and metaphoric views of language, so that in separating language from the world Stevens nonetheless manages to bring "the thing in itself" into momentary being. However, she tends to rely on oppositions that I think simply dissolve, when one employs a more act-oriented sense of what language does, and she has no way of discussing the value of such achievements, because she cannot move easily from language into states of agency. Leggett offers a careful historical account of how Stevens's reading may have shaped the import that particular ideas had for him. He is especially good on the concept of abstraction, so I can only hope that here I extend his work by showing how the idea can take on compelling force in the poetry. And finally I must cite two critics whose work most clearly shapes the challenges I felt in this chapter. First is Bonnie Costello's exemplary abstracting of Stevens on paintings, so that we must deal with principles rather than simple visual analog ("Affects of an Analogy"). Marjorie Perloff, "Pound / Stevens, Whose Era?," does a fine job of challenging Stevens criticism to address the question of his Modernity, largely by using contrasts to Pound quite unlike the one I shall develop.

3   Bruns does not provide quite the social analysis one would expect from his description of the hermeneutical turn, since he does little to set Stevens in the discourses constituting a given social moment. Instead Bruns deals with general patterns of ideas, using the social as essentially a moral category. This, though, is quite typical of non-Marxist critical claims about the social. Nonetheless, the historical categories Bruns uses prove quite useful for distinguishing those critical traditions that emphasize the epistemological Stevens, like the Joseph Riddel of *The Clairvoyant Eye* and Frank Doggett, *Wallace Stevens: The Making of a Poem,* from those such as the Riddel of "Metaphoric Staging," Charles Berger, *Forms of Farewell: The Late Poetry of*

Wallace Stevens, and J. Hillis Miller, "Stevens' *Rock* and Criticism as Cure," who, in various ways, make Stevens a major poet of "the linguistic turn."

4   That "and so on" speaks depressing volumes about how philosophy tends to be employed in literary criticism, as does Bruns's effort to reverse Derrida on writing and voice, so that all of the contemporary idols can line up against a Stevens transformed into an archi-rationalist. Bruns ignores the fact, important to Derrida (and to Stevens), that although on one level writing absorbs all phenomena into a single surface or texture, it is precisely that single material that then "folds," in infinite ways. Voice, on the other hand, seems to generate differences, since it seems to originate in different persons and places, but in fact all of the voices end up requiring the same logic of identity: Each voice has a speaker, and then all of the other conventional moral ideals that permeate Bruns's hymn to otherness fall into place. One can see the deeper problems of difference that he ignores, or represses, or just plain misses, if one notices his need to equivocate between two quite different models of dialogue that he must work with – one essentially social and textual, where otherness is a matter of incompatible discourses and actual conflict of powers; the other Emmanuel Levinas's vulnerable sharing of traumas, where otherness seems something that the right therapist can adapt to. Given such slippage, I fear that notions such as "writing," "voice," and the "dialogical" are far too internally heterodox – that is vague – to propose as the building blocks for hypotheses attempting to describe actual historical or social conditions.

5   One could, of course, say that it suffices to revel in those differences as socially productive. There is some truth in this: I do not want to endorse Stevens's or Eliot's conservatism. Yet we should also note that it is very difficult for us simply to celebrate the differences, without turning them into something dialogical and conversational – that is, without re-idealizing a common abstract ground, however unstable as such, that the different languages share, and imaginatively recognize themselves as sharing. Rather than rest with differences, the imagination transforms them into means to an end, and we return to the liberal version of what Stevens tried to imagine. That is, we seek an abstract commonness that, at the least, will allow people to appreciate the terms that make a politics possible that is something more than the game of pursuing self-interest within the manipulable limits of the law.

6   For good general commentary on Stevens's reaction to the pressures of the thirties, see A. Walton Litz, *Introspective Voyager,* and Milton Bates, *Wallace Stevens: A Mythology of Self.* It is also important to see that critics like Riddel, and even Miller, in his early criticism, who stress the radical "process" aspects of Stevens's later poetry, especially the long poems, are responding to the need to reconcile change and abstraction, but they do so largely by ignoring Stevens's efforts to make those processes testimony to certain conditions of agency that can use poetry as a transparent medium – that is, a medium whose self-occluding properties are part of its means of extending itself into a world beyond the word.

7   The best evidence of these doubts is the degree to which Stevens's letters (e.g., *Letters* 369–70) and his revisions of poems such as "Examination of the Hero in a Time of War" show him worried that these assertions are too vague to locate an actual shared source of energies generating our supreme fictions. Therefore we see his poetry immediately following *Owl's Clover* trying new solutions. First he turns, in "Man with a Blue Guitar," to the possibility of a fully painterly notational style, in order to test the capacity of Modernist juxtaposition to reconcile change and scope. Next he has "A Thought Revolved" exercise on his own myth the bitter, satiric vein to which Joan Richardson, *Wallace Stevens,* has called our attention:

> Behold the moralist hidalgo
> Whose whore is morning star
> ....
>
> He liked the nobler works of man,
> The gold facade round early squares,
> the bronzes liquid through gay light.
> He hummed to himself at such a plan.
>
> He sat among beggars wet with dew,
> Heard the dogs howl at barren bone,
> Sat alone his great toe like a horn,
> The central flaw in the solar morn.
>   (*Collected Poems* 186–7)

8   It is at least amusing to note that Stevens made a point of telling Hi Simons that after he had jotted this thought down he found a statement by George Seurat echoing his own sense of harmony achieved simply through contrast. And it may be necessary to point out that in claiming that Stevens's work shows him dissatisfied with a pure sense of fixed contrasts, I am not insisting that he pursued a Hegelian version of dialectic. I claim only that as he thought about his polarities in relation to the question of what Modernity entails for the visual arts, he saw ways of producing a poetic voice that could get both forces working within the same poetic space. A sense of his own contradictions led him to try new imaginative possibilities, although he never claimed that these possibilities resulted in a single synthesis. Instead he was content to show that one could reconcile a sense of flux with a sense of abiding transpersonal forces, simply by focusing attention on how changing personal energies manifested recurrent principles.

9   I should also mention here than any general account of Stevens's relation to painting must confront the presence of two poets – one a sensualist epicure, perhaps closest to the Fauves, and the other an epicure's reflective mind, working at the limits of sensation. Here I shall deal only with the second Stevens, for reasons in large part suggested by the appropriateness of the Fauve comparison for the other one. The Fauves were the great materialists of early Modernist painting, managing to blend Impressionist and Postimpressionist elements, without invoking the expressionist psychological

melodramas that one finds in other branches of Postimpressionism, and without reaching for the conceptual realities that would soon beckon Braque. Modernism was style, so the brushstroke could become a vehicle of exuberant materialism, lushly paralleled in poetry, thematically and stylistically, in poems such as "Sea Surface Full of Clouds" and "Six Significant Landscapes." Stevens learned his lessons well enough to make painterly emphases on the composition of visual relations and atmospheric properties become the basis for a radical critique of humanism. If "the soil is man's intelligence" (*Collected Poems* 36), then the most comprehensive artistic realization of that intelligence is not in the displacements brought by ideas, but in the capacity to suffuse what in the flesh is immortal with a consciousness become virtually a part of the weather. "I am what is around me" (86): not the interpreter of the scene, but an instrument for rendering anew, in an aural medium, an atmosphere that intensifies the scene's sensual effects and shows the spirit how completely it can live a physical life. That life, however, is not an abstract one. Rather, abstraction is, like philosophy, the horny breath of the elders, so that poetry must pursue modes of thinking best exemplified in Peter Quince's improvisational elegance, as he tries to negotiate Susannah's masturbatory fullness.

Fortunately, there is good criticism on the relation of Stevens's early poetry to painting, among which I still find most helpful Michel Benamou, "Wallace Stevens: Some Relations between Poetry and Painting," especially page 49. So we can focus our attention on the elements that go into allowing the second Stevens to make this sensualist his dramatic foil. This Stevens still distrusts thematic interpretation and still seeks versions of Symboliste "atmosphere." But, like Mondrian's, his new atmosphere has little to do with visual appearances or with the play of artifice as an alternative physical space. In the years before he wrote the examples I shall take up, he began to make that new atmosphere possible by exploring two concerns, clearly expressed in "The Idea of Order at Key West." The solipsist speaker of *Harmonium* now seeks a "we" enabling him to fuse with the singer and with Ramon Fernandez. That, in turn, requires achieving sufficient distance from the sensations within a scene to concentrate on how these different consciousnesses can all participate in the same framework. The form of "we" depends on shareable structures for processing and assessing information. Second, the basic process becomes an act of interpretation; what matters is how the scene leads one to reflect. Just as the early poetry defines a model of agency attuned to the unfolding of scenes or metaphors, the new poetry must locate "you as you are," by learning to "throw away the lights, the definitions, / and say of what you see in the dark / That it is this or that it is that" (*Collected Poems* 183). Destroying reference (279) allows one to refuse the rotted names and concentrate on the form of our knowings:

Nothing must stand
Between you and the shapes you take
When the crust of shape has been destroyed.
(183)

10 I base my claims about these four principles on the following composite of
quotations:

> He will wonder at those huge imaginations, in which what is remote
> becomes near, and what is dead lives with an intensity beyond any
> experience of life. He will consider that although he has himself wit-
> nessed, during the long period of his life, a general transition to reality,
> his own measure as a poet, in spite of all the passions of all the lovers of
> truth, is the measure of his power to abstract himself, and to withdraw
> with him into his abstraction the reality on which the lovers of truth
> insist. He must be able to abstract himself and also to abstract reality,
> which he does by placing it in his imagination. . . . [By this process
> we come to see] the imagination and reality equal and inseparable.
> (*Necessary Angel* 22–3)

> The subject matter of poetry is not that "collection of solid static objects
> extended in space" but the life that is lived in the scene that it composes;
> and so reality is not that external scene but the life that is lived in it.
> Reality is things as they are. (25)

> The imagination gives to everything that it touches a peculiarity, and it
> seems to me that the peculiarity of the imagination is nobility, of which
> there are many degrees. . . . I mean that nobility which is our spiritual
> height and depth. (33)

> There is no element more conspicuously absent from contemporary
> poetry than nobility. . . . The nobility of rhetoric is of course, a lifeless
> nobility. Pareto's epigram that history is a cemetery of aristocracies
> easily becomes another: that poetry is a cemetery of nobilities. For the
> sensitive poet, conscious of negations, nothing is more difficult than the
> affirmations of nobility and yet there is nothing that he requires of
> himself more persistently. (35)

> As a wave is a force and not the water of which it is composed, which is
> never the same, so nobility is a force and not the manifestation of which
> it is composed. . . . It is not artifice that the mind has added to human
> nature. . . . It is the imagination pressing back against the pressure of
> reality. (37)

11 I try to work out the theory of metaphor that Stevens uses to explain how
those enclosures reveal the basic forms of desire in my "Wallace Stevens'
Metaphors of Metaphor: Poetry as Theory."

12 In writing on Gromaire, Stevens is also careful to posit the limitations of the
paint medium, so that he can better define the poet's task. Because painting
has so readily available an elemental architecture for spirit, with such obvious claims to be relatively free of ideological baggage, it all too easily
becomes formalist absorption in design. Gromaire, on the other hand, never
loses "the intensity, the passion of this search" (*Opus Posthumus* 291) for
portents of our powers. Such models remind the poet that he must be wary
of strict imitation. What matters is not the grammar, but the spirit it liber-

ates. So the poet's lack of obvious transpersonal architectural elements becomes his greatest opportunity. If he accepts the challenge of abstraction, he
must not only exhibit the life of spirit; he must make the very effort to name
that life part of his engagement in it.

13   Pach, *Masters of Modern Art* (11). Pach's book, a copy of which he gave to
Stevens (now at the Huntington Library), makes evident the early Modernist sense of abstract art as an art of the mind's power, or, as the dust-jacket
statement by Elie Faure puts it, of how "the spiritual plane has progressively
replaced the plane of nature." Stevens's own sense of how a theory behind
nonobjective painting might be formulated may be found in his remarks on
Dufy and on Gromaire, "Raoul Dufy" and "Marcel Gromaire," in *Opus
Posthumus* (286–92).

14   It is typical of Stevens, in his late poems, to emphasize self-referential uses of
indices, as his means of defining the authority on which a poem's conclusion
is based. See, for example, "Ordinary Evening in New Haven" and "A
Primitive Like an Orb."

15   Stevens's closest parallel to the method, as well as message, in Wittgenstein's
late reflections on the "as" takes place in a prose passage on how the imagination transforms the site of a homecoming ("Effects of Analogy," in
Necessary Angel 129–30). And for one philosophical essay providing a rich
poetic sense of the "as" in Wittgenstein, see Francis Sparshott, "'As' or the
Limits of Metaphor."

16   Quoted from Ludwig Wittgenstein, *Tractatus Logico-Philosophicus,* trans.
D. F. Pears and B. F. McGuinness (London: Routledge and Kegan Paul,
1961). Section and paragraph references for subsequent quotations are given
in parentheses.

17   Quoted from Ludwig Wittgenstein, *Philosophical Investigations,* trans. G. E.
M. Anscombe (New York: Macmillan, 1958), 193. Page numbers or section
numbers for subsequent quotations are given in parentheses.

10. Afterword: The End(s) of Modernism

1   For the past five years I have been trying versions of this task in a series of
essays too complex and diverse to take up here. But, since I intend to be
brief, it is prudent that I cite these more elaborate treatments of the issues.
The relevant essays of mine are the ones listed in the bibliography on the
canon, on Plato and the performative sublime, on Lyotard and Rawls, and
on expressivist ethics.

2   As a concrete example of such limitations in political criticism, I would like
to consider at some length the critical work that I consider the best Marxist
treatment of Modernist art, T. J. Clark's two essays, "More on the Differences with Comrade Greenberg and Ourselves" and "Arguments against
Modernism: A Reply to Michael Fried." Refusing to be satisfied by a politics
of demystification that does not propose positive values, and avoiding the
ambivalent idealism of those more influenced by Poststructuralist theory,
like Hal Foster and Frederic Jameson, Clark manages an impressive synthesis

of George Lukàcs and Bertolt Brecht. Clark argues that the Modernist emphasis on formal principles derives from the belief

> that art can substitute itself for the values that capitalism has made valueless. A refusal to share that belief – and that is finally what I am urging – would have its basis in the following three observations. First . . . that negation is inscribed in the very practice of modernism, as the form in which art appears to itself as a value. Second, that that negativity does not appear as a practice which *guarantees* meaning or opens out a space for free play and fantasy . . . but rather negation appears as an absolute and all-encompassing fact, . . . a fact which swallows meaning altogether. . . . [Third] there is a way – and this again is something that happens within modernism, or at its limits – in which that empty negation is in turn negated. . . . There is an art – Brecht's is only the most doctrinaire example – which says that we live not simply in a period of cultural decline, when meanings have become muddy and stale, but rather when one set of meanings – those of the cultivated classes – is fitfully contested by those who stand to gain from their collapse. There is a difference, in other words, between Alexandrianism and class struggle. ("More on the Differences" 184–5)

Once we see the consequences of Modernist experimentalism's willingness to annihilate "the normal repertoire of likeness," criticism must ask whether it is worth the price to indulge such violence, without seeing "if any other ground for representation had been secured, or could possibly be secured in the process" ("Arguments" 84). Such grounding need not entail a return to the old realism, but could derive from specific practices of "representation, which would be linked in turn to other social practices – embedded in them, constrained by them" ("Differences" 187). The only other option is to continue the bourgeois need to cultivate transcendental states of consciousness and freedom, "detached from the pressures and deformities of history" ("Arguments" 86).

Since I too rely rather heavily on this metaphor of "pressures," and since I have substantial affinities with Fried, this model of resistance and redefiniton ought to make it easy to weigh the different implications of our approaches. From my perspective, Clark's accusing Fried of ignoring the "violence" of those Modernist critiques of representation reveals Clark to be the one who ignores precisely their sense of the pressure requiring such experiments. For, to the Modernists, it was the focus on descriptive work and a particular novelistic reading of social engagement that distorted what had previously given most Western art its raison d'être. They dreamed of recovering, in new terms, older rhetorical ideals for art's representativeness that had been displaced by the narrow mimetic ideals making the realistic novel the dominant literary form for bourgeois culture. Thus, even if one modifies that realist aesthetic to speak of the ends of representation rather then specific means, as Clark does, one has the problem of locating specific principles for resisting the temptation to specular narcissistic selves, which seem the birthright of every class that turns for its representations to the imaginary worlds sustained by the arts, and one has difficulty rationalizing the roles that the romance states idealized by Jameson offer art as a form of social practice. There is no way to have a working-class art without representing a specular ideal. That is why critics like Foster speak only of resistance and avoid specific filiations. Second, Clark is less than generous in reducing Fried's positive claims to a thesis about the "priority of perception," while implying that a more descriptive art would engage a fuller, more reflective sense of mental powers. Fried's Modernism is an art of states, rather than of ideas – of particular configurations, rather than of generalizable principles. But these are by no means reducible to some simple model of perception. Indeed, Fried emphasizes optical relations in order to separate art from any simple perceptual process and to point out that its relational field requires a full intellectual engagement in a specific structure of energies. One could even argue that such a concern with structure is profoundly historical, in the sense that one must understand the art's refusals in order to appreciate its affirmations. Rather than being negative, Fried imagines art actively engaging a history within which dreams of revolution themselves seem escapist.

Because there is probably no resolving those competing views of history, the burden of the dispute comes down to Clark's argument that Fried's particular values are no longer of much historical interest or use, since they echo religious vocabularies and have their only support in the need of the bourgeois to conceal its own anachronism in transcendental myths of freedom and consciousness. Here I share the concern. But if we bracket overall Marxist rejections of religion and remember that we are dealing with analogies, we must try to look concretely at whether the variety of states Fried discusses can be dismissed so easily, especially when we adapt them to the model of "exemplary powers" that I have been working with. For, in that case, the art provides not only conditions of intense experience, but an art trying to focus reflection on who we become by virtue of those experiences. On that basis, I think there are good grounds for resisting Clark's claim that Modernism cultivates "consciousness and freedom." His claim is not wrong, but it is put so abstractly that it trivializes the nature of the concrete forces made available to consciousness as operating instruments (forces that further freedom, simply by making us realize what certain tools afford us). Moreover, once we see the concrete basis for such claims, it gets a lot more difficult to argue that in pursuing such ends the artists become the allies or the dupes of capitalist interests, and it becomes a good deal easier to point out the limitations in his sense that all meaningful opposition to the dominant social order must take overt political form. For the first of these claims, it should suffice simply to note that the concepts of "consciousness" and "freedom" are not used in the same sense by apologists for capitalism and by Greenberg and Fried, or even by Pound and Stevens. As bourgeois propaganda, those terms refer primarily to private property, deregulation of markets, and the ability to manipulate symbolic structures for personal ends. Of course, one could then argue that when artists propose other meanings for the terms, they are doing little more than concealing the real interests they support or pursuing the favor of the cultivated classes. But there are considerable obstacles to such arguments, which lead us to Clark's second claim. It is by no means clear that the cultivated classes in fact rule (at least in America) – Reagan, not Rockefeller, won the presidency – nor is it obvious that Modernist values served the cultivated classes. For the art offers little comfort to the reductive materialism and commercial mentality fostered by both the dominant culture and the repressive morality of those cultivated classes, and the art was far less amenable to late monopoly capitalism than is most of anti-elitist Postmodernism. In fact, it was to ground their opposition against the dominant culture that the artists turned away from immediate social contexts to develop religious analogies. Finally, considerations like these make it possible to argue against Clark's deepest commitments. For we have grounds for insisting that an art devoted to describing or invoking social conditions, and a criticism supplying the explanatory contexts that expose or champion specific social visions, consign art to a minor role among social disciplines and thereby vitiate what capacity for effecting change it does possess. This is of course not the kind of claim I can fully defend here. But if Modernist critique has any force at all, it ought to remind us of how easy, how slippery, and how manipulable claims about the social good are. And also, there is at least the chance that the way to change society is to change the ways in which individuals understand the powers available to them as separate and self-defining agents.

3 This discussion of art and politics would have to get much more complicated, if it were to do even sketchy justice to feminist arguments on the subject. For, on the one hand, feminist theory provides the best terms for linking the two domains, because its politics is precisely a process of reconstructing modes of agency that have been marginalized by patriarchal interests and distorted by prevailing models of representation. Yet the insistence on a politics of difference has, so far, led both to the overgeneralized deconstructive tendencies of Alice Jardine's treatment of representation (discussed in the notes to my "Introduction") and to the suspicious refusal of all Modernist values, because they do not fit certain abstractions about "female experience." Although I find the latter claim difficult to engage (How can one accused of supporting male hegemony say that the accusers are wrong without simply reinforcing the point?) it seems to me clear that it tends to force its proponents into honoring fundamentally bourgeois poets, such as Louise Bogan and Edna St. Vincent Millay, who do little to expand anyone's sense of powers. For what seems to me a superb discussion of the limits of this feminist stance, see Ellen Bryant Voigt, "Poetry and Gender."

4 For a good example of how far Marxist theory is from such a case, see the mangled effort to use Donald Davidson's notions of causal meanings for developing a new materialist psychology, in the essay by Michael Baldwin, Charles Harrison, and Mel Ramsden in *Pollock and After* (191–221). The best Marxist theorists of art, such as Terence Eagleton, can do no more than argue that it is impossible, now, to know what this competing art would be like, since we have only isolated cases such as Brecht, and we live in a society so corrupt that it is difficult to carry on any extended thinking about values.

What matters is that the arts ground themselves in the appropriate structure of historical interests: The necessary work and the necessary values will follow. But the Marxist position itself, with its appeals to hope and to faith, ends up in a version of theology. Thus, no argument is possible. Yet that makes it even more important that some criticism be willing to belabor these obvious and unwieldy points, in order to remind us of how much we are being asked to give up for such hopes.

5   For a good discussion of Shelley's use of the concept of powers that is also aware of the range of Romantic discussions of the topic, see the treatment of "Mont Blanc" in Richard Isomaki's dissertation, "Shelley's Causal Themes." And for a very interesting analog to this use of the concept of powers, see Frederic Turner, *Natural Classicism,* which speaks of the powers in poetry as the enactment of certain pleasures connected to fundamental neurological brain states. This is the registering of power in its most literal sense, which of course I can treat only as a metaphor for the self-regarding states that accompany intense reflective experiences. Finally, it is important to note that Modernists with the values Fried represents resist talk of powers, because they fear that any appeal to discursive principles as one's means of establishing representativeness threatens to displace the specific art energies into theatrical appeals for approval under some general category. This is not an unwarranted fear. But I think we must take the risk, if we are to appreciate what the Modernists intended, and if we are to give the fullest account of those, such as Frank Stella, who are fundamental to Fried's case. We have seen that for Mondrian and Picasso, the life of the work is not simply its structure of internal relations, but depends on forces that extend beyond the frame – both into what Mondrian thought were relations basic to nature, and into the responding energies of the audience. When we turn to the forms of painterly abstraction pursued by Morris Louis and Stella, the anthropomorphic case is more difficult to make, since neither of these paint-ers (unlike Mark Rothko or Barnett Newman) shares Mondrian's sense of the mystical forces that art mediates or promises any metaphoric function for his work. But even here, accepting a language of pure presence for the work exacts a substantial price, which I do not think we need to pay. If we treat their work as autonomous, in its self-enclosed presence, we also make it vulnerable to claims that it is only beautiful or only optical. But in Louis we see not just color relations, but color relations exemplifying an intel-ligence that plays on its control of gravity and its exquisite sense of spatial tensions and releases. And if we treat individual works in the context of an overall career, we see an intelligence constantly playing against its previous achievements, to push itself to the new states of responsibility that make his *Unfurleds* so stunning a transformation. Such responsibility becomes the dominant theme in Stella's work, which rivals Picasso's sense of the artist's career as the measure of the powers of a self-reflexive and self-generating intelligence. In Stella, what Fried calls "opticality" is less an end in itself than the deliberate, willful mark of a painterly decision to drive out everything from the canvas that is not subject to the consequences of an invented structural logic, all of whose permutations then are set free to hover between

the domain of pure system and the discovery of evocative mystery by purely transparent means. Thus we find Stella describing the project of his early work as seeking an independence in painting that could resist a "hesitancy, a doubt of some vague dimension" which made the work of Pollock and De Kooning "touching, but to me somehow too vulnerable" (*Working Space* 158).

6 I borrow the idea of legitimation from Jürgen Habermas, who argues that "the *claim to legitimacy* is related to the social-integrative preservation of a normatively determined social identity. *Legitimations* serve to make good this claim, that is to show how and why existing (or recommended) institutions are fit to employ political power in such a way that the values constitutive for the identity of the society will be realized" (*Communication and the Evolution of Society* 182–3).

7 As Evan Watkins has repeatedly pointed out to me (personal communication), there is no way to deny the fact that Modernism was born of and devoted to specific bourgeois conditions that are significantly removed from the situations, and the values, of people who have to resist serious oppression. Watkins calls Modernism the art of that class fraction that is free to challenge capitalist values, because it is at once isolated from the exercise of capitalist power and the beneficiary of the securities that capitalism can produce. Thus "it has little to offer to groups of the population who cannot afford to make a virtue of powerlessness," but who must directly engage the hegemony of capitalist interests within a specifically sociopolitical arena. Modernism can never be extended to the entire populace, so long as such struggles are necessary against massive exploitation. Thus, although Clark is wrong to deny that Modernism resists capitalism, he is not wrong to worry about how limited are the possible political consequences of Modernist values. I cannot disagree with this social picture. But there are increasingly large populations that share the class position fostering Modernism and are thus capable of living the life of bourgeois intellectuals, which is the one addressed by the art. Moreover, it seems at least arguable that all classes have a strong stake in preserving images of what such a freedom can make possible, since there seem few social options that allow this degree of reflection or this range to explore one's own capacity to define one's own claims to recommendation. So long as classes must struggle against oppression, the best they can hope from art is certain reinforcements or tactical measures, which apply only to the present, not to the world they want to bring about. But it may be shortsighted not also to keep in mind what the struggle might make it possible for more individuals to enjoy. Finally, even if not all can profit from the art, the oppressed can profit from the values that the art promulgates, so long as one stresses the intense imaginative experience of transpersonal states. For these establish a concrete basis for universal rights, rights that include the possibility of so constructing society that people do not have to imagine their art as useful only for political struggle. There seems to me no alternative but to cultivate at least some stances and forces that have strong claims to establish values that are good simply because of the human states they make available, however much the society fails to

provide access to such experiences. To lose sight of those, in our eagerness for social justice, is to risk eventually thinning out that which makes a liberal society worth pursuing.

8   Actually one can perhaps make better claims for Hegel as the source of a third model, since Hegel refuses the individual solutions worked out by Kant and insists on a redefined political order that can reconcile Romantic individualism with a sense of communal life. Or so Charles Taylor has argued, in his *Hegel and Modern Society,* a book I consider very important for our subject: first, because his account of the cultural contradictions of nineteenth-century life proves extremely useful in understanding why the Modernists were in such despair over liberal politics, and second because his terms allow us to work out the competing claims of Kantian individualism and Hegelian models of social integration. Taylor insists that Hegel provides a critique still relevant today "of the illusions and distortions of perspective that spring from the atomistic, utilitarian, instrumental conceptions of man and nature" basic to the culture's public life, while "at the same time puncturing the Romantic counterillusions they continuously generate" of a significant private autonomy (72). Instead, Hegel tries to show how individual identity can be seen as definable only in terms of "the public experience of the society" (91). Thus we see how leftist and rightist critiques of bourgeois politics have essentially the same critical relation to hegemonic cultural values. But at the same time, I think Taylor's problems in defending a Hegel whose actual structure for aligning public and private he must reject indicate how difficult it remains to develop the necessary politics. Therefore I feel justified in claiming that, although the Kantian line I pursue cannot project the Hegelian synthetic alternative, it can at least temper both individualism and utilitarianism, by defining, in defensible ways, both a structure of transpersonal values and a model of moral thinking that can be adapted to communal criteria. So, although Kant's thinking is not at present an active political force, it does define and sustain a general egalitarian politics that may be the best formulation of political protections, if not political ideals, that our philosophical resources allow us to articulate.

9   One might say that by concentrating the subject into a solipsistic point, Thomas Nagel, in *Mortal Questions,* greatly expands the field for an objective realism. However, it then becomes necessary also to redefine the rubric of objectivity, because the objective is no longer aligned with what empiricist science can describe. The range of emotional colorings and intricate personal beliefs that science had dismissed in the name of objectivity turn out to be potentially transpersonal – as responsive to interpersonal testing as any other observable phenomena. Moreover, as Nagel suggests, but does not develop, it may also become possible to imagine the very activity that characterizes subjectivity as, in principle, a common one. Although each person's sense of an "I" is incommunicable, we have good reason to believe that human beings in a fairly diverse range of cultural formations all experience that sense of difference in the same way. For a fascinating extension of that possibility into the nature of meaning, and the dynamics of passion, see Mary Bittner Wiseman, "Review of Annette Lavers's *Roland Barthes: Struc-*

turalism and After." And for its historical connections to Modernism, compare Josiah Royce, on Kant's absolute subject; Husserl, on transcendental subjectivity; and Wittgenstein's critique of private language, especially as developed in Saul Kripke's *Wittgenstein on Rules and Private Language.* Most continental philosophy has continued to insist on the primacy of subjectivity as a process of imposing individualizing contents on experience, but even here, very good Cartesians such as Sartre, and perhaps Derrida, take seriously Descartes's sense of how the *cogito* is ultimately so elemental as to be impossible to capture in any description. Wittgenstein and Nagel try to show why that is the case without positing any metaphysical mysteries.

10 It is important to realize that such transcendental states can include political commitments, but they cannot guide political action or even idealize the kinds of compromises necessary for political life. That is one reason why these ideals seemed most comfortable within extremist politics, which might in fact be as unlivable as the art.

11 As I was grappling with the task of final preparation of this book for publication, I realized that I could not leave it without returning to two matters that I think I did not sufficiently discuss. The first consists in a form of Modernism that I did not deal with, indeed that I still do not know how to appreciate. The terms of that Modernism became clear to me as I was listening to a paper on late Heidegger, given by Gerald Bruns. For Bruns, the great appeal of late Heidegger is that he finally separates thinking from *Dasein:* rather than continue to weave metaphors for presence, Heidegger accepts thinking as simply a mode of "throwness," so that the most radical forms of thinking are those that expect no return or payoff but simply explore the possibilities opened by the desires that become visible within the very process of attempting to express where one comes to inhabit as one continues to think. Then I realized that Julia Kristeva's *Revolution in Poetic Language* sought to clarify another version of this model of radical thinking within art. She makes the great achievement of Modernism the freeing of the *chora,* the patterns created in excess of sense, from domination by semantic concerns, so that we begin to explore a logic within physical processes and their expressive resources richer than any structure of connections relying on the understanding. And these semantics then come to carry an ethic like that developed by Georges Bataille, in which the primary value is the pure expenditure refusing to yield to the forms of sovereignty that the society uses to distinguish between the rational and the irrational.

My discussions of the work of art as a site in which we come to know who we can become provide terms that can be compatible with their insights. But whenever I describe those sites, I tend to deny them their radical otherness. In my discussions, these sites can be recuperated for more traditional modes of reflection because they provide experiments in agency. Although the works are unique to their media, the terms of agency explored allow me to appropriate the art within a loosely philosophical language and to claim that it offers us resources for thinking about ethical concerns. However radical the work, I treat the artist as intending to make the radical gestures continuous with problems about value that we can formulate on other terms. That is, in my accounts the radical thinking giving the art its distinctive reality gets cast as an effort to establish testimonial states that can address an audience who must rely on public languages for their reflective understanding. It is no wonder, then, that I am uncomfortable with Surrealist and dadaist work, where the principles of radical thinking are most central. On the other hand, I think I can say in my own defense that the conservative bent of Anglo-American writing keeps at least the poets I do deal with concerned with those metaphoric dimensions of agency. And insofar as the early Modernist poets and painters sought the explanatory and evaluative contexts that their prose argues for, they seem to me to be working within my more conservative version of Modernist sites. So, although I need not apologize for my descriptions, I must acknowledge more fully the presence of other aspects of Modernism that require very different languages. And this means, among other things, that I must apologize to Marjorie Perloff for all these years in which I have not seen the full force of her argument about a second Modernist tradition devoted to something I still refuse to call "indeterminacy."

The second matter that needs more discussion requires returning once more to the question of the politics of Modernism, and especially the politics possible for the idealist principles governing my relationship to Modernist poetry. Here the stimulus to my rethinking was a conversation at an academic conference: "Suppose," my respondent said, "that I grant you all of your descriptive claims about Modernism, and even grant you their relation to an individualist ethic; why should I accept that ethic as an alternative to Postmodernist values, especially to those versions of Postmodernism attempting to establish plausible political frameworks for interpreting and producing works of art? Of course there are problems with these new formulations, but at least they are not complicit in outdated or immoral institutionalized political positions. Moreover, they do a much better job than my individualism does of showing why we need new models of agency and how a person's social filiations must be central to such models. Although it is true that Modernism proves far more subtle and rigorous than contemporary critics grant, those virtues remain in the service of misanthropic or solipsistic projects that cannot generate the hope necessary if lives devoted to the arts are to be anything more than self-indulgent escapes from the social consequences of monopoly capitalism. These dangers are most evident in your claims about a testimonial art, since you imagine testimonial modes that simply ignore questions of how we test the social genesis and consequences of these self-referring stances. How can you be content to speak of powers whose only criteria is the story we tell ourselves about ourselves, since you insist that it was precisely such subjective criteria that the Modernists turned on with contempt as fundamentally bourgeois modes of self-congratulation? Think, for example, of Flaubert's Homais or Henry James's scathing portrait of Walter Besant. Do we not have to speak of powers as demonstrable means through which individuals can take on necessary roles or positions within social life?"

Once again, I do not think I have ignored these issues. But I see now that there is a social context for Modernist work that may make it possible to understand how the modes of agency and the specific values they cultivated may still play significant public roles. And if that proves true, then I can claim it is possible to extend my essentially phenomenological concern for a history faithful to the continuing power of the terms in which the agents themselves thought, so that it is compatible with more current emphases on historical contradictions and the unstable nature of those values that artists project as means for engaging such conditions. The key is locating those contradictions most fundamental to the Modernist enterprise, so that we can ask in what ways their grappling with those conditions remains a means of our engaging our own social circumstances. In the body of this book, I treat those conditions in abstract terms, as tensions between lucidity and lyricism. Now I want to suggest that the social basis for those tensions, and for many of the fundamental problems one might find with Modernist values, consist in their having at once to face and to repress some of the fundamental contradictions involved in the bourgeois heritage they are so anxious to reject, yet cannot avoid depending upon. Then the social force of Modernism consists in how and what it makes visible for us, as we continue to face contradictions between the need for individualist values and the complicities they create with retrograde social practices.

The best way to set the stage is to ask what seems to be repressed or evaded or reductively negotiated by the ferocity with which the Modernists engaged in their rather sloppy critiques of representation. Two social factors seem fundamental here: First, there is the inordinate pressure to separate themselves from a world of getting and spending, and thus to preserve the arts as a world where different modes of identity can be maintained, modes that maintain ties both to religion and to aristocratic ideals of individual responsibility; and, second, there is the Modernists' nagging realization that all of their desires for difference depend on the Enlightenment social forces that liberated the arts from a patronage system (if not from patronage) and gave them the role of competing for intellectual dominance in a free market of ideas. The Modernists had to be bourgeois against themselves. They had to use all of the freedoms of the bourgeois revolution to criticize the meanings that their society was giving to freedom, and they had to see their own complicity in that system as bondage to a history that they could escape only by the reconstitutive powers of art. But then they were dogged by the possibility that art might be only a fantasized escape, a means of evading their own true position, unless they made it sufficiently rigorous in its testimonies to take responsibility for the differences they wanted to assert. Yet to succeed in defining those differences might also lead to so separating themselves from their bonds to real history that they would have completely sacrificed life to art, social care to the narcissistic impersonality of the self-referring artifact.

I think these contradictions have not grown any less pressing. Indeed, as we grapple with attempting to draw a politics from art, we find ourselves faced once again with Adorno's dilemma: We can easily treat Modernist art as a powerful critique of bourgeois institutions and the psychic economies

engendered by those institutions, but how do we also adapt ourselves to
what the artists thought were positive alternatives to those economies? If we
dismiss those ideals as escapist fantasies, we trivialize the art, and, more
important for this discussion, we leave ourselves only a negative freedom
that, ironically, only more deeply replicates the isolated, unsocialized freedoms cultivated by capitalist market principles. And if we turn to Postmodernist alternatives, I suspect that we only buy more blindly into another
feature of those bourgeois values. For, in their efforts to undermine or
escape the forms of individualist testimonial heroism projected by Modernist artists, Postmodernist thinkers may trap themselves into a simple binary
system. These refusals may force Postmodernism, despite its abstract pro-
tests, to accommodate itself completely to bourgeois domesticities, fears of
self-projection, and fidelity to an economy of exchange values, as if these
were the fullest imaginative possibilities left to a chastened Western mind.
Such accommodations are evident with respect to what Foster calls "neo-
conservative" Postmodernism, and they apply all too easily to the modes of
consumption that Gerald Graff shows are basic to the rhetoric of transgression. But even the aesthetics of an oppositional politics runs the severe risk
of trapping expressive energies within the play of simulacra to be consumed
as part of the exchange values involved in "making it" within the art world.
For so long as the opposition refuses any alliance with Foster's "presentational politics," it has no practical or concrete tests of political efficacy, and
thus there is no way to distinguish gestures at being seen as political from
genuine political commitment. This is not to impugn the motives of those
who profess an oppositional politics, but it is to suggest that Postmodernist
principles afford no strong terms for identity, and hence continually risk
being subsumed within the culture of consumption that they would oppose.
Where Modernism risks alienating itself from all connection by its pursuit of
purity of form and motive, Postmodernism risks surrendering all modes of
dramatic integrity in order to avoid the appearance of cultivating a transcendental authority or self-righteous denial of one's own historicity. How can
we not deny those aspects of our history that constitute us as bourgeois
subjects – yet how can we not rely on that very constitution in formulating
our grounds for and rights to resist those cultural traditions?

So we return to the social tension between complicity and the effort to
construct alternative modes of agency that one finds working on every level
of Modernist art. But now, in order to understand the scope of the problem,
and the continuing force of their efforts to engage that problem, we must be
willing to hazard a very large generalization. The poets may be so caught up,
so mastered by these dilemmas, because in fact they have imagined their way
to the central paradox of twentieth-century social life, a paradox that we
have yet to explore thoroughly, and a condition that we travesty when we
rush to judge Modernist politics in moral terms or even to insist on more
fashionable, but less central, dramas of repression in their work. The problem is as simple as it is perplexing. Capitalism's shaping of bourgeois values
establishes at the same time perhaps the most debased political structure we
know and the most humane political forms of life that have so far proved

possible within our traditions. On the one hand, the great majority of individual subjects in our culture define themselves in large part by the dream that they too are free to pursue the corrupt pleasures and practices characterizing the upper levels of the social hierarchy; on the other hand, that dream is inseparable from the remarkable degree to which the society does in fact guarantee the freedoms and material conditions enabling persons to carry on the kinds of pleasures and actions making such ambitions possible. So the dreams that shape our considerable freedoms increasingly become dreams that have little sanction or use within any of the high-culture traditions also basic to the poets' self-definitions. To accept the dominant culture is to be trivialized within it; to dream of escape is to have to confront the twin demons of having no real social alternative and of knowing that one wants one's escape rewarded by the very privileges that one rejects when one sees how others handle them.

I cannot claim that Modernist poets and painters successfully handled these dilemmas. I think I can claim that as long as we continue to suffer from such conditions, we will find their art both moving in its registering of contradictions, and rewarding in the degree to which it does carve out imaginative sites where we can, as individuals, find alternative modes of self-identification. At one pole, we come to understand that many of the failures of the Modernists stem from their attempting to evade their own complicity in bourgeois values. Painters such as Cézanne and Braque developed a model of art as work requiring them to make accepting the limitations of bourgeois life a fundamental condition of the agency their art exemplified. The poets, however, almost without exception, saw themselves as aristocrats, tormented, like Baudelaire's albatross, by the demands of living within bourgeois forms. Consequently they imagined themselves far more free of class identifications than they were. Such imaginings made it far too easy to justify actions primarily because they offered alternatives to bourgeois ways – whether that took the form of Pound's treatment of his children or Stevens's need to mark himself as a connoisseur. And, lurking in the background, are the larger political identifications with visionary leaders and ruthless methods that seem much more acceptable when one has pure contempt for the ways of getting and spending (or, better, when one is so anxious to cast the self as one who cannot be reduced to bourgeois interests, for then the fact of difference tends to occlude just what the terms are by which one sanctions one's special status). Ultimately, what Carl Dennis called the "preference for monumentality over mortality" has its social roots here. So eager to expel the bourgeois within themselves, these poets could not abide its trappings in others; they therefore had no alternative but to devote their energies to elaborating ideals enabling them to sustain a misanthropy while projecting elitist fantasies. It is perhaps no wonder that Colleone's anachronistic heroism looms over every imaginative effort to establish a new heroism.

And yet the effort to find new heroic poses continued to make sense for them, and I think must for us. Here individualism still matters, and here we arrive at two plausible claims for the social significance of the powers that the Modernists saw themselves cultivating. Minimally, they keep us confronted by the pressure of who we become if we do not seek some mode of self-defining agency and some determinate relation to a community or set of historical energies. They force us to see what it means to succumb to the venal dimensions of bourgeois values, and their long struggle with the limits of ironic stances makes it difficult for their audience to be content with oppositional stances that base their freedom primarily on what they are not, rather than on what they can establish as positive principles. On one level, we find the Modernists demonstrating the traps that occur by defining oneself simply against prevailing mores, since their worst moments consist in their so responding to bourgeois values; on another level, I, at least, find the efforts at concrete self-definition (without any claims to being faithful to some latent original self) the one viable option to a world of simulacra.

The second claim is somewhat more grandiose. Once we see how Modernism is politically situated, I think it becomes possible to attempt separating its more doctrinal assertions – on art as well as on politics – from its technical and strategic inventions that spell out ways to elaborate forms of attention and psychic economies that are not readily accessible through representational art. We can distinguish between Modernist macroeconomics – its dreams of cultural revolution by imposing large-scale imaginative changes – and its microeconomics of the psyche, where it elaborates possible strategies by which individuals come to terms with their capacities to take at least imaginative control over their lives. These microeconomic adjustments do not entail direct social change: in fact, by relinquishing Modernist macroeconomic doctrines, the art becomes quite compatible with bourgeois culture. Yet compatibility is not necessary subsumption within bourgeois mores. Through the expressive devices cultivated by Modernist art, we gain the experience of knowing ourselves as active agents, without having to consume ourselves in getting and spending; we come to understand what it means to take responsibility for that activity; and we encounter remarkable processes by which we find our sense of ourselves as agents capable of being recast and redefined. These experiences provide the basis for a politics of individualism – not as a social doctrine, but as a living component of the necessary new social doctrine we ought not to pretend to have found. Modernist abstraction, at its best, offers individuals the power to experience, and to know, how our cognitive and affective energies can become themselves conditions of will. In Cézanne and in Stevens, for example, the most casual of details turns out to sustain the most intricate, intimate, and intense states of reflection of which we are capable: To observe ourselves thus absorbed is also to be able to will those states, and those powers, as conditions in which simply being in the world intelligently can suffice. Such states do not yet make a politics, or even an ethics. But they do give us the sense of personal worth that can provide reasons for caring about those far more painful domains, and they show us how, in many respects, aesthetics and ethics are one, because those two domains simply cannot be reconciled to a world of simulacra, or to a politics of resistance that thrives on what Postmodernism all too easily turns into a new aesthetic principle. In this regard, at least,

Modernism offers an alternative politics of resistance,: one can only combat the prevailing mores if one begins with constant refusal of the self's lazier, more accommodating impulses, and one can only trust one's accomplishment when the product carries full, articulate responsibility for the mode of thinking, feeling, and engaging others that it projects. This, to paraphrase Pound, is not vanity: Here error is all in the not done, all in the diffidence that faltered (*Cantos,* 522).

Appendix 1. Postmodernist Poetics Unfair to Modernist Poetry

1   I choose these statements, rather than more carefully balanced critical accounts, because they best exemplify the passions that govern most contemporary generalizations about Modernism in art and in literature. One also finds these passions in academic criticism, but usually in more complicated, and more circumscribed, treatments of individual authors: An analysis of these would require so much work that the poetry might get lost in the process. By the end of this study, we shall have considered enough representative academic criticism to test the degree to which what I isolate here is widely representative, even of the academy.

2   Perloff's essay, "Pound / Stevens: Whose Era?," argues in effect that we do not find better accounts in academic criticism because we have yet to develop a single perspective that can encompass an essentially romantic desire for a Stevensian meditative poetry and an essentially constructivist interest in poetry based on the logic of collage. Obviously, I think I can provide that language, but only if we are willing to accept two constraints. First it is necessary to deal with "Modernism" in poetry as a term that applies to a distinctive historical epoch, probably bound by Baudelaire and Mallarmé at one pole and by the emergence of political poetry in the thirties at the other. Not all of the poetry written during that time need fit the description, as would be the case if one spoke simply of "modern" poetry, but we should try to understand what it was that led the Modernists to see one another as contenders within a single contest. Conversely, we simply guarantee confusion if we allow ourselves to speak of a Postmodern that preceded the modern (as Francois Lyotard does in his *Postmodern Condition*), or if we develop categories based on terms not intelligible to the agents – at least until we do understand their possible shared sense of the Modern. Second, we must honor some version of the distinction Gregory Ulmer ("Of a Parodic Tone Recently Adopted in Criticism") proposes, drawing on Andreas Huyssen, between "Modernist" and "avant-garde." Ulmer defines "Modernist" as constructivist insistence on "the dignity and autonomy of literature," and "avant-garde" as an essentially European "iconoclastic and anti-aesthetic ethos . . . which attempted to break the political bondage of high culture through a fusion with high culture and to integrate art into life" (554). As will become apparent, I shall concentrate on the "Modernist" half of his polarity, in the hope that one can then appreciate alternative ways to imagine how art can be integrated into life. I also hope thereby to avoid the central problem of the avant-garde: that once it begins to be integrated into

society (or perhaps only to be understood by society), it must turn on itself.
This means that avant-garde art cannot fully reflect on the changes that its
own innovations make possible, without itself becoming in some respects
the establishment. Under that fear, art may continue to suggest significant
changes, but, as Duchamp's work illustrates, artists cannot successfully devote entire careers to exploring the full implications of these changes or to
building from them certain ways in which the art becomes a full philosophical enterprise. Moreover, honoring that distinction enables us to avoid the
difficult problem of wondering whether, when artists such as Picasso and
Eliot cease to be avant-garde, they cease to be modern. And one can then
honor the sense of avant-garde as a politics, proposed by Peter Bürger's
Theory of the Avant-Garde, without assuming that such gestures are the only
means by which art can have social significance. If one does not make the
necessary distinction, one ends up in Frederic Jameson's strange fusion of an
effort to share Perloff's praise for the disruptive force of collage experiment
with a ludicrously conservative lament for the loss of organicist values. (See
especially his "Postmodernism, or the Cultural Logic of Late Capitalism.")

3   The quotation in this sentence is from an influential statement about
Postmodernism in the visual arts, from the catalog for the Hirshhorn Museum exhibition, *Content: A Contemporary Focus, 1974–1984,* written by
Howard Fox. I use this source for two reasons: to show that both literary
positions are outgrowths of more general cultural attitudes, and to demonstrate the continuing importance of the visual arts in both shaping and
illustrating the force of our comments about twentieth-century poetry.
Most important in this context is the problematic ease with which charges of
formalism can then be leveled against Modernism. For the visual arts have,
in the work of Clement Greenberg, a distinct and powerful rationale that
equates Modernism with formalism, thus making it easy to propose against
him the kind of charges that Perloff echoes. Greenberg argues that Modernist artists responded to the dangers of illusory representationalism by attempting to locate the artwork's expressive properties within the purely
visual aspects of the medium and thereby expel all "extraformal content."
That warrants, in response, the following self-congratulatory paean in
which Fox baldly lays out claims that one will find put in more sophisticated
terms in collections like Hal Foster, ed., *The Anti-Aesthetic:*

> The most profound artistic development of the last decade or so has
> been a marked shift in mainstream art from a primary concern with
> material and formal elements of the art object to a focus on the extra-
> formal content of the work of art. The term "extra-formal content" as
> used here refers to content in its traditional sense, denoting something
> that is signified, some idea to be conveyed, something intended to be
> interpreted, including any aspect that might come under the broad label
> of "subject matter": language and concept; narrative; social, political or
> cultural relevance; moral issues; psychological and metaphysical con-
> cerns – in short all those aspects traditional to visual art in the Western
> world that the Modernists discredited as "literary" or "thematic" val-

ues. Indeed the central issue of post-Modernism is the issue of content. (15–16)

In my view the best critiques of Greenberg are those like Leo Steinberg's, in *Other Criteria,* that show how Modernist principles are capable of using an emphasis on form as their vehicle for achieving significant extraformal content.

4   I cite Charles Newman in part simply to indicate that this list of shared assumptions covers a rather large and diverse sample, only moderately reformulated to fit my concerns. Parallels to Perloff can be found in the criticism of William Spanos and Michael Davidson, as well as in David Antin's seminal essay, "Modernism and PostModernism: Approaching the Present in American Poetry," and similar views by poets are expressed in the various organs of the language poets and in the issue of *Epoch* edited by David Lehman in 1983, "Ecstatic Occasions, Expedient Form." One finds arguments similar to Holden's in the work of critics as politically diverse as Frederic Jameson, Gerald Graff, Donald Davie, Charles Newman, Christopher Clausen, and Robert Pinsky. I address these issues more extensively in my essay, "What Modernism Offers Contemporary Poetry."

5   My colleague Doug Collins make a good case for treating Modernist formal experiments as the artists' deliberate attempts to present their art as always already embarrassed and hence free to explore modes of thinking that do not make aggressive and seductive demands on the audience. On the ethics of so bearing one's potential embarrassments, see Sabrina Lovibond, *Realism and Imagination in Ethics* (158).

6   Good illustrations of Eliot's affinity to certain Poststructuralist concerns are found in William Spanos's essay on *The Waste Land,* and especially in Gregory Jay, *T. S. Eliot and the Poetics of Literary History.* But Perloff's refusal to see the Symboliste sensibility as anything but spilt Romanticism runs deep. In fact, the limitations of her position are clearest when she discusses Mallarmé's ideal of a coherent book, because she ignores all of his speculation on writing and his experiments in what form reveals about agency, taking that statement as little more than an extension of Palgrave's *Golden Treasury.* For her, what matters is that both authors envision a book as an emblem of concentrated lyricism, in the service of the dream of a deep expressive self: "From where does the image of the 'Flower which is absent from all bouquets' come if not from the innermost recesses of self?" (48). But a close look at Mallarmé's statement reveals an understanding of those recesses very different from Romanticism's, so different that only form can define the relevant extraformal content:

> For what is the magic charm of art, if not this: that beyond the confines of a fistfull of dust or of all other reality, beyond the book itself, beyond the very text, it delivers up that volatile scattering which we call the Spirit who cares for nothing save universal musicality. . . . If the poem is to be pure, the poet's voice must be stilled and the initiative taken by the words themselves. . . . In an exchange of gleams they will flame out like some glittering swath of fire sweeping over precious stones,

and there replace the audible breathing in lyric poetry of old – replace the poet's own personal and passionate control of verse. The inner structure of a book of verse must be inborn." ("Crisis of Verse," 111)

Appendix 2. A Conceptual Grammar for Constructivist Abstraction

1   Meyer Abrams, *The Mirror and the Lamp*, Chapter 1. It will be clear in the following discussion that I read Abrams through the logological model of Kenneth Burke, *The Rhetoric of Religion*. A good similar effort to establish a grammar of related concepts that form a poetic ideology is Ralph Cohen, *The Art of Discrimination*.

2   Michael Levenson's broad picture of the development of Modernism, in *A Genealogy of Modernism: A Study of English Literary Doctrine*, is worth summarizing, in part because it treats (a little more broadly and sensitively) the same concerns as Alan Robinson, *Poetry, Painting, and Ideas* (1885–1914), and Sanford Schwartz, *The Matrix of Modernism*. Levenson argues that George Eliot could so imagine secularism and subjectivism that neither was "conceived as an abandonment of perennially valued human activity" (14). With Conrad and Ford there arises a desire to correlate objective aspects of an event with the primacy of an individual reflective consciousness, so that there emerges a "dissociation of fact and subjectivity" (45), for which the most appealing solutions seemed at first to involve an emphasis on the intuiting and expressive "subject" offered by Bergson. Modernist impersonality, in Levenson's view, opposes not so much Victorian writing as an earlier phase of its own effort to combat Postvictorian problems. And it never quite overcomes the desire to have it both ways: to reconcile "the desire for the autonomy of form and the claim that the root source and justification for art is individual expression. . . . Pure form was a goal; individual will was its underpinning" (135). My only quarrel with this superb book concerns how one characterizes that sense of will, and that sense of form, to show how the two can be correlated. In my view, doing that entails a good deal more close reading of poems and paintings than Levenson offers. Such close reading is necessary, both to understand the complexity of what the individual agent becomes through the nineteenth century and to elaborate a stronger sense of abstraction than Levenson's use of Eliot as his central figure allows him. For Levenson, that centrality stems from Eliot's ability to achieve "a *rapprochement* between Modernist literature and traditional authority" (219). However, in my view, although that position does make Eliot central to the academic codifying of Modernism, it is also precisely the reason that most contemporary poets have had to look elsewhere. Poets are less in need of rapprochement than they are of new ways to understand how to use and value that heritage.

3   In lieu of any theory about how the arts interrelate, I want to claim only that any two phenomena can be compared on certain levels. The important question is not how the comparisons are possible, but how one elaborates the comparisons that one makes so that an audience can be convinced of their utility for the author's purpose – in my case, proposing a plausible language

for certain kinds of significance for the poetry. That is a matter of trying specific cases, not of providing a generalizable rationale.

4 I take this formulation of a picture theory of representation from Monroe Beardsley's discussion, in *Aesthetics: Problems in the Philosophy of Criticism,* section 16. Beardsley is discussing the visual arts and is quite aware that this theory does not account for all the ways that art can be said to represent. The theory does, though, distinguish representation from abstraction, which cannot be said to "portray."

5 This realization governs some of the best contemporary attempts to rationalize representation, beginning with Wayne Booth's *Rhetoric of Fiction.* But in practice, criticism is still dominated by the tendency, in E. H. Gombrich's idea of "matching," to stress the "documentary," or representational, features over the "ethical," or representativeness, features. (See *Art and Illusion,* Chapter 1.) For example, although David Lodge's *Modes of Modern Writing* offers an excellent rationale for a rhetorically based version of representation, which links the practice to the logic of historical inquiry, the book still subordinates the ends of the rhetoric to descriptive ideals, and thus evades the ethical implications of the rhetoric that explain why an artist would accept, or modify, the constraints imposed by the analogy with history. The most promising work attempting to provide a fully ethical account can be found in some recent essays by Robert Caserio; for example, "*The Rescue* and the Ring of Meaning." Also important in this regard is the reconstruction of Aristotle's theory of mimesis developed by Wesley Trimpi, *Muses of One Mind.*

Finally, I want to return to the comments I made in the preface about the limitations of the idea of representation that governs the versions of rhetorical theory brought to bear by certain Poststructuralists. Here it is important to note the inadequacies of the return by feminist film theory to Modernist critiques of representation, as well as treatments of the subject that derive from Paul de Man's insistence that the constative and the performative are inseparable. In de Man's case, one wants to say only, "Of course they are; negotiating that conflict is what the rhetorical search for acceptable representatives is all about." The feminist theory proposed in essays such as Kadja Silverman's "Film Theory's Structuring Lack" seems to me more ambitious, and more problematic. Here the epistemological version of representation links the claim that representation seeks a descriptive presence, or "pure truth," with a psychoanalytically inspired tale of castration resulting from the inevitable failure of the epistemological enterprise. I do not think that most representational artists were so stupid as to believe that they could reproduce the real, rather than select from it to create representational effects, and I see no reason to assume that epistemology has such lurid consequences. Finally, the feminist account reduces its useful attention to the position of the spectator to the banal, and reductive, role of the voyeur. As we shall see, rhetorical approaches to the theory of representation show how the audience are intended to be active participants in the imaginary world the work sets up: This is the whole point of the illusionism. The danger of representation, therefore, is not so much passive voyeurism as the audience's taking such pride in its ability to interpret the hidden interests of others that they tend not to turn sufficiently to examine themselves.

6   Let us take the time here to understand the similarities and differences between representation in the sciences and in the arts. This will help us see why representational art invites interpretation using empiricist criteria, and why these criteria cannot suffice, but require a rhetorical theory to capture the additional considerations. Both science and art rely on the same criteria of truth, although in somewhat different proportions: First, a set of correlates linking names to objects and events; then, a means for showing how one can arrange those correlates so as to make hypotheses that, if confirmed, support some general expectation about regularities or types, and thus establish for them a kind of form or lawfulness. A theory of representation must account for its denotational, or documentary, powers to stand for something "real." It must also account for its capacity to organize those details in relation to types or principles that confer significance on the surrogate. This means that no theorist of science could be content with the Modernist theory of the influence of science on the principles of artistic representation. No science is photographic. Insofar as we make photography a model for truth, we have only a model of documentation, not of heuristic procedure. The commitment of realism, to treating art as a "window," bound to the same observational criteria as a picture, is at best a means and not an end. One must also be able to account for those elements of the work that give the specific documentation exemplary status in a more comprehensive practice, concerned with discovering general principles and fostering further experiment. Whether or not the elements "represent," in a pictorial sense, they must prove "representative," in a methodological procedure.

Representation in art differs from representation in science on the ways in which this exemplary status is achieved. Science is, in principle, empiricodeductive: However one arrives at conclusions, one offers them as if one had isolated a set of regularities that hold, for certain relationships among particulars, in all situations where no additional variables enter. Certain elements, at certain temperatures, in controlled environments, always react in certain regular and predictable ways; other reactions can be predicted in terms of statistical measures. Exemplarity for artistic experiments also involves prediction, but not quite with the empiricodeductive apparatus of drawing one's conclusion from the principle of repeated testing. Rather than deriving the type from experiment, representational art derives the type from what many theorists have called "concrete universals" – whether the universal be Sidney's Platonic types, Zola's laws of behavior, the moral exemplars of Victorian fiction, or the representative social types proposed by George Lukacs. All of these variants share the belief that a controlled imaginative experiment gets its exemplary power by appealing to a more direct version of representativeness than the scientific type – a version based, not on explicit tests for the laws it instantiates, but on how an audience can use the situation to make certain projections deriving from its interests. Hamlet is a representative character, not because he exhibits certain demonstrable regularities in human behavior, but because audiences have come to think that they can use Shakespeare's specific construction as a way of focusing attention on certain aspects of their own actions or those that they observe in other people. It is the image, the sense of particular psychic relations articulated in this one character, that one takes as universal. The test of universality is not exact repetition, but the possibility of projecting the image as a label that can enter into complex relations with other images. In science, the exemplarity is based on seeing how the particulars illustrate or typify a law. The experimental data cease to have any importance as particulars, once the law has been formulated. In the arts, the data somehow "contain" the law. One finds the experiment exemplary, not so much because of the generalizations it yields, as because of the generality that the particular configuration takes on. Hamlet does not provide a rule about melancholics; he provides something like a map of the melancholic's psyche.

7   I obviously base most of my remarks about literary representation on the novel and the theater because they offer the most pronounced versions of the logic of the window. The theory's application to lyric poetry is not direct, but secular poets had no other way to imagine how they might make cognitive claims for their work, as one sees most clearly in Arnold's theoretical writings and in what, in Chapters 3 and 4, I describe as the "scenic" orientation of Postromantic lyricism. We should also note the possible links between the ideal of enhancing capacities for action that governs representational theory and the ways in which lyrical poetry adapts the classical ideal of eloquence. For the pursuit of eloquence is precisely the means by which an intensely rhetorical art organizes powers that we can then see ourselves extending into life. In this vein, constructivist poetics must be seen as the effort to show how poetry can establish defensible grounds for its own eloquence.

8   For a good treatment of the increasing sense of crisis about the concept of representation in the last half of the nineteenth century, see John Mcgowan, *Representation and Revelation: Victorian Realism from Carlyle to Yeats*. Also, I want here to make sure that I call attention to what can be claimed to be distinctively Modernist in writerly recastings of representational principles. Virtually all art can be said to "realize" something, even to call attention to how it makes that realization available. Modernist work differs in the degree to which it puts the burden of the art on the powers that the formal energies confer, and in the degree to which it refuses to attribute any distinctive symbolic value to the scenic features that the art gives access to, so that all of the representativeness must reside in the way the world is pieced together. These traits are closely linked, because the only way to value the scene, when it has no symbolic attributes, is to stress the direct psychic energies that it fosters.

9   In my *Enlarging the Temple*, I distinguish these as traditions of "immanence" and of "symbolism." I still think the basic outlines of that distinction hold, but several refinements are necessary. I was too concerned with content, rather than problems of rhetoric, to face the difficulties inherent in the fact that both traditions depend on devices of art, so immanence is not a response to something in nature, but to the fullness of will that a scene or a statement

will sustain. And I ignored the range of possible immanences, from Cézanne's *réalisation* to Surrealist pursuits of latent harmonies between natural
and mental energies, to the improvisatory poetry which, as Marjorie Perloff
forcefully argues, constitutes a countertradition to that of Symboliste Modernism. (See her *Poetics of Indeterminacy: Rimbaud to Cage*.) But in order to
avoid all taints of symbolism, Perloff does not allow any self-reflexive integration in her "other" tradition. In my view, Stevens and Williams seek
different kinds of integrative frames – the former in concentration of mind,
the latter in the cohesion of forces produced by a dialectic among fragments
and whatever provides the measure composing them into a structure of
relationships. (For an excellent treatment of the differences between these
poets, see Allen Dunn, "The Self-authenticating Stance in Stevens and
Williams.") Therefore I shall treat the major differences in mode as differences in the nature of the authorial acts projected: At the Stevens pole, the
activity is devoted to getting beyond images to the forms of mind that
determine what we can feel about a variety of existential situations; at the
other pole, the writing seeks to so compose the mind's access to appearance
that the work of disclosure aligns the will to the flesh, and the rewards of
perception to the satisfactions of making objects just so.

10   Huntley Carter, "The Coming Age," *New Freewoman* (February 6, 1913): 3.
11   T. E. Hulme, *Further Speculations* (124–8). We get an interesting sense of
how interart parallels work if we compare Hulme to his probable source, in
Kandinsky, *Concerning the Spiritual in Art*, "Cézanne has given [the form of a
triangle in his *Baigneuses*] new life. He does not use it to harmonize his
groups, but for purely artistic purposes. He distorts the human figure with
perfect justification. Raphael's 'Holy Family' is an example of triangular
composition used only for the harmonizing of the group; and without any
mystical motive" (31n).
12   I take this quotation from a typescript of Marjorie Perloff, "The Poetics of
Collage" (different from the essay on collage in her *Dance of the Intellect*),
which makes this formulation the basis for a very informative historical
account of the collage principle as understood by Modernism. It is also
worth noting that Davenport's statement contains a rich ambiguity basic to
Modernism: "How the world might be put together" could refer either to
an underlying essence or to the productive accidents produced by the work
of artists.
13   The best treatment of this testimonial quality of art that becomes a thing in
the world is Michael Fried's in "Art and Objecthood." But for Fried the self-
sufficiency is an end in itself, rather than a testimony to certain powers of
mind and art, because it is crucial that the work need nothing, especially not
a responder. He may be right for artists such as Stella, who are the objects of
his analysis, although even there I still see a complex drama of the powers of
will literally taking place. However, Fried's account clearly will not hold for
painters such as Mondrian and Malevich, who imagine response as part of
the condition of achieving dynamic balance. (For Malevich on this point, see
his *Essays on Art, 1915–28* [138–9].) There we need a language of the powers
that such states afford and the ways in which such powers can influence the
models of agency that we employ in our self-representations. And once we

provide those, we are in a much better position than Fried is to respond to the plethora of criticism that his stance has evoked. In my last chapter, I shall return to this topic and take up at some length the best of those criticisms, as formulated by T. J. Clark.

For a good literary analysis that shares the concerns of this discussion, see David Walker, *The Transparent Lyric: Reading and Meaning in the Poetry of Stevens and Williams*. Walker defines the innovation of Williams and Stevens as the realization, largely under the influence of Modernist painting, that poetry need not present a dramatic speaker, but could instead seek the state of "transparent lyric," which may "be defined as a poem whose rhetoric establishes its own incompleteness; it is presented not as completed discourse but as a structure that invites the reader to project himself or herself into its world, and thus to verify it as contiguous with reality" (18). I do not think it only a quibble to argue that what is incomplete from one perspective can be more complete from another, because rather than being simply contiguous with reality, this transparency allows a lucid, self-reflective awareness of who one becomes as one completes the objective structure. Walker shares Levenson's concern for reconciling subjective and objective dimensions of form's relation to extraformal content, and therefore tends to keep too much of the old language about subjects and response. The only way to avoid that is to risk barbarities like concepts of agency and testimony, which leave open the boundaries between the subjective and the transpersonal. Finally, for a good historical account of the logic of self-interpreting structures and their relation to Schopenhauer on representation and will, a subject to which I have devoted a good deal of attention, see John Irwin, "Self-evidence and Self-reference: Nietzsche and Tragedy, Whitman and Opera."

14 Wendy Steiner, *The Colors of Rhetoric* (17). The comments that follow on *enargia* and "energeia" are from pages 10–11, and those on the "representational" and the "nonrepresentational" from page 183. For an argument that her semiotic stance is limited by its inability to handle foregrounded acts, see my review of *The Colors of Rhetoric*, "Modern Art and the Mind's I/eye." And for a different treatment of Modernist iconicity, setting it in tension with the indexical or performative, see Richard Shiff, "Performing an Appearance: On the Surface of Abstract Expressionism" (86–99). I see my claims for the "testimonial" dimension of Modernist art as an effort to resolve the poles that Shiff insists are contradictory; once one admits a way of locating activity within the material form, the performative becomes transpersonal and inseparable from the icon. But before I can spell out the theoretical issues, I must emphasize that when the Modernists use versions of Aristotle's theory of "energeia," they are careful to insist that the work is not simply an object, but a literal activity; an imitation not of things in nature, but of nature's processes of making things. For representative statements, see James Joyce's *Stephen Hero*, Williams's *Selected Essays* (303–4), and Cézanne's "Letter to Paul Aix, 13 Oct. 1906" (in *Theory of Modern Art* 23). Here I cite Paul Klee: "The deeper [the artist] looks[,] the more deeply he is impressed by the one essential image of creation itself, as Genesis, rather than by the image of nature, the finished product." See Klee, *On Modern Art*, page 45.

These modifications of "energeia" also entail modifying what one can mean by "icon." Steiner is very good at summarizing Charles Peirce's three kinds of "iconic signs" and showing how they can be applied to art (pp. 20–1 of *Colors*). But as W. J. Mitchell points out, almost everything can be assimilated to the icon, since literal similarity to the referent is always possible, by some route of reference (*Iconology* 56). Therefore I think it is necessary to stipulate that I use the term "icon" to signify those features of artworks that rely on nonillusionistic properties as their basic route to reference. Thus they can be said to directly embody what they refer to, so long as one understands that the embodiment must take place within certain conventions that are themselves generally accepted by the audience whom the artist addresses. In visual art, this means the physical possession of properties (as will be clarified later in this appendix). In the verbal arts, I take "direct possession of properties" to refer not to the words themselves, but to the speech acts. By an "iconic form," I mean one that leads the reader or speaker to enact certain properties, ranging from rhythmic patterns to semantic ones, that the expression can be said to demand from those who understand its place in a cultural grammar. An example is the way we find ourselves literally composing Stevens's figurative "theater," in the poem discussed in Chapter 1.

15   Albert Cook, *Figural Choice in Poetry and Art* (124–48), is superb on the expressive effects of the physical dimensions of Williams's lineation.

16   All of the quotations in this paragraph are from Tzvestan Todorov, *Theories of the Symbol* (208–9). Hazard Adams, *The Philosophy of the Literary Symbolic*, is more responsive than Todorov to the fact of there being two basic traditions for understanding the idea of the symbol in the nineteenth century, which we might call the "formal," or "autotelic," and the "transcendental," but he is so concerned to show that the hope for a transcendental content is mistaken that he does not see that both versions have a significant but partial claim. Adams also treats Todorov's autotelic symbol as fundamentally a vehicle for creativity. This preserves a clear value for the concept, but risks its historical specificity without gaining a corresponding theoretical power that can combine the two strands in the figures of a transpersonal author and a schema of the mind, as we find in noniconic painting.

If one desires a concrete example of what Schelling is after, one can imagine a token that also serves as a type, as, say, Hamlet does as an exemplar of melancholy or Zeus as a figure for divine power. Seen from the artist's point of view, the symbol consists in finding the single concrete vehicle capable of conveying the full intricacy of an experience – for example, by rendering the contradictory feelings of generosity and contempt that characterize an act of charity. Thus Schelling need not make any radical claims about specific forces that the symbol is privileged to mediate. What matters is simply that the representation carry a dynamic significance that any other form of expression would have to simplify or divide into sensual and interpretive properties. In place of a description that sets the mind against what it objectifies, the symbol captures the interplay of objective properties and the synthetic or prehensiveness force of a responding sensibility.

17   When I speak of "immediacy" and "directness," I rely on several assumptions that must be made explicit if I am to forestall predictable, and reasonable, objections. When I speak of direct participation in what the work makes available and when I distinguish Modernist literalness from art that requires allegorical supplements, I do not think that I am committed to some radically unmediated natural state. I am speaking about agents who already have cultural lives – that is, who know how to respond to works of art and who have the emotional range necessary to care about the metaphoric and thematic concerns that occupy the artists' prose statements (the Modernist version of allegorical supplements). But, once we acknowledge these attributes, this work does not demand our also invoking a set of predicates that we use to define and to evaluate the illusionary content that the work invites us to construct. Not all such content is bound to any local ideology. There are literary classics, and, in my view, there are long-term, canonical, imaginative energies that it is difficult to imagine are not relevant to a reader willing to perform the labor necessary to make the text come alive. But such content can be quite bound to a specific historical formation. For there remains a substantial leap between the action of the work, authorial and mimetic, and the interpretive frames one brings to bear in order to elaborate its significance. That gap is considerably smaller when we learn to respond to Modernist abstraction, because how we constitute the object becomes the concrete measure of what significance we can attribute to it: Again, to see Mondrian as art at all is to see oneself participating in certain complex balances, and to understand "Of Modern Poetry" at all is to see that the poem is trying to construct the theater that it refers to. Thus there is considerably less inference, and considerably less need to rely on ideas that are not directly connected to properties that the work physically possesses. And, to the degree that we can bring the work to life because of those properties, we have located its force in something that remains relatively constant across cultural change. I see no need to speak of "universals" or "naturals truths," but one can make a strong case that such work can retain its imaginative force for a wide range of ideologies and cultural frameworks. Indeed, I find it hard to imagine a culture that has the technological sophistication of any modern society not being able to share this art, and I think the denial of my claims would require that concrete possibility, and not some pious abstractness about the fact that the natural is always constituted differently by different cultures.

18   For examples of this level of signification, one might consider Northrop Frye's "literal level" of the text or Roland Barthes's "functions" (see his "Structural Study of Narrative," 93–7). As these examples make clear, any workable notion of the material properties of a semantic medium, visual or linguistic, must include not only properties that can be treated as purely material properties, but also those that are irreducibly connected to its working within a sign system. That the green is the green of a tree-picture, or that the sounds are connected to a particular semantic assertion, are fundamental to the kind of material existence that the medium actually has in human practices.

19   One could say that this form of virtuality is also invoked in any expressivist

art, even the subjective expressionism that we associate with Romanticism or with the painting of Pollock and DeKooning. For there we are also invited to identify with the constitutive energies of the work. However, the work is not so clearly an icon for that identification, precisely because the identifications cannot be simply with the work, but must be with a specific person whom we interpret through it and postulate beyond the specific forces that we do reconstitute.

20   George Bornstein, *Transformations of Romanticism* (11). For a better, more recent account of the relations between Modernist and Romantic poetry, see Albert Gelpi, *A Coherent Splendor.*

21   Edward Said, *Beginnings: Intention and Method,* especially pages 10–12, 225, from which I quote in this paragraph. This emphasis on writing per se harms what is otherwise by far the deepest account we have of the distinctive features of Modernist literature. But for a better account of the distinctively writerly qualities of Modernism I suggest Ann Banfield, *Unnatural Acts,* because Banfield takes a truly linguistic approach, rather than relying on Derridean oppositions. For those who want those oppositions, Derrida's best response to Modernism takes place in his "Double Seance of Mallarmé," in *Disseminations.* And for another version of the impossibility of translating deconstructive languages into any positive language of values able to do more than cultivate differences (without criteria), see Michael Philipson, *Painting, Language, and Modernity.*

22   I owe my awareness of the intricacies and resistances of the "it" to my colleague Gary Handwerk, whose influence helped me to elaborate this relation between agency and "it" in the best version of these forces, Joyce's *Finnegans Wake.* See my "*Finnegans Wake* as Modernist Historiography."

23   For very rich parallel statements by a visual artist on the objectifying of the personal, see Kasimir Malevich, *World as Non-objectivity* (56–7):

> The formation of elements begins in movement, and in the process of movement interrelationships develop among themselves, establishing between themselves functions of interchange by means of relationships they form an organism [sic]. The relationship will be the linking movement of two differences, it will be the law of their existence. . . . The element is not yet a form, the form only begins when the link of elements begins. . . . As, in the final reckoning, elements do not exist in "the world" as some part of a building whole in form, for such a building also does not exist either, they arise from our own intention, the material for which being what we call an organism, which serves for the realization of the intention and the intention can be nothing else but in the expression "of the world."

In Chapter 6, I show how all of this comes alive in his *Red Square, Black Square.* One might also notice that the reason we find it so difficult to describe Joyce's relation to Stephen Daedalus is that we lack a sufficient vocabulary to articulate modes of relating to the imaginary individual ego that do not ultimately idealize its powers.

Works Consulted

Abrams, Meyer. *The Mirror and the Lamp*. New York: Norton, 1958.

Adams, Hazard. *The Philosophy of the Literary Symbolic*. Tallahassee: University Presses of Florida, 1983.

Alexandrian, Sarane. *Marcel Duchamp,* trans. Alice Sachs. New York: Crown, 1977.

Alpers, Svetlana, and Paul Alpers. "*Ut Pictura Poesis:* Criticism in Literary Studies and Art History." *New Literary History* 3 (1972): 437–58.

Altieri, Charles. "Abstraction as Act: Modernist Poetry in Relation to Painting." *Dada / Surrealism* 10–11 (1982): 106–34.

Act and Quality. Amherst: University of Massachusetts Press, 1981.

"Arnold and Tennyson: The Plight of Victorian Lyricism as a Context of Modernism." *Criticism* 20 (1978): 281–306.

Enlarging the Temple: New Directions in American Poetry of the 1960s. Lewisburg, Pa.: Bucknell University Press, 1979.

"*Finnegan's Wake* as Modernist Historiography." *Novel* 21 (1988): 238–50.

"From Expressivist Aesthetics to Expressivist Ethics." In Anthony Cascardi, ed., *Literature and the Question of Philosophy*. Baltimore: Johns Hopkins Press, 1986, 132–66.

"The Idea and Ideal of a Canon." *Critical Inquiry* 10 (1983): 37–60.

"John Ashbery and the Challenge of Postmodern Visual Art." *Critical Inquiry* 14 (1988): 805–30.

"Modern Art and the Mind's I/Eye." *Michigan Quarterly Review* 23 (1964): 587–95.

"Objective Image and Act of Mind in Modern Poetry." *PMLA* 91 (1976): 101–14.

"Picasso's Collages and the Force of Cubism." *Kenyon Review* 6 (1984): 8–33.

"Plato and the Performative Sublime." *New Literary History* 16 (1985): 285–74.

"The Poem as Act: An Attempt to Reconcile Presentational and Mimetic Theories." *Iowa Review* 6 (1975): 114–24.

"Judgment and Justice Under Postmodern Conditions: How Lyotard Teaches Us to Read Rawls." In Reed Way Dasenbrock, ed., *Redrawing the Lines: Analytic Philosophy, Deconstruction and Literary Theory,* Minneapolis: University of Minnesota Press, 1989, 61–91.

"Presence and Reference in a Literary Text: The Example of Williams." *Critical Inquiry* 5 (1979): 489–510.

"Reach without a Grasp." Review of Paul Fry, *The Reach of Criticism: Method and Perception in Literary Theory. Diacritics* 14 (1984): 58–66.

"Representation, Representativeness and 'Non-Representational' Art." *Journal of Comparative Literature and Aesthetics* 5 (1982): 1–23.

Sense and Sensibility in Contemporary American Poetry. New York: Cambridge University Press, 1984.

"Steps of the Mind in T. S. Eliot's Poetry." In *Twentieth Century Poetry, Fiction, Theory.* Special issue, *Bucknell Review* 22 (1976): 180–207.

"Wallace Stevens' Metaphors of Metaphor: Poetry as Theory." *American Poetry* 1 (1983): 27–48.

"What Modernism Offers Contemporary Poetry." In Hank Lazer, ed., *What Is a Poet?* Huntsville: University of Alabama Press, 1987, 31–55.

"Wordsworth's 'Preface' as Literary Theory." *Criticism* 18 (1976): 122–46.

Antin, David. "Duchamp: The Meal and the Remainder." *Art News* 71 (1972): 66–71.

"Modernism and Postmodernism: Approaching the Present in American Poetry." *Boundary* 2 (1972): 98–133.

Tuning. New York: New Directions, 1984.

Apollinaire, Guillaume. *The Cubist Painters.* Reprinted in Herschel Chipp, ed., *Theories of Modern Art.* Berkeley and Los Angeles: University of California Press, 1968.

Arnold, Matthew. *Poems of Matthew Arnold,* ed. Brander Matthews. New York: Collier, 1902.

"Preface to Poems, 1853." In R. H. Super, ed., *Complete Prose Works.* Ann Arbor: University of Michigan Press, 1977, 1:1–16.

Ashton, Dore, ed. *Picasso on Art: A Selection of Views.* New York: Penguin Books, 1977.

Auerbach, Erich. *Mimesis: The Representation of Reality in Western Literature.* Garden City, N.Y.: Doubleday (Anchor Books), 1957.

Baird, James. *The Dome and the Rock: Structure in the Poetry of Wallace Stevens.* Baltimore: Johns Hopkins Press, 1968.

Bakhtin, M. M. *The Dialogic Imagination,* ed. Michael Holquist. Austin: University of Texas, 1981.

Banfield, Ann. *Unspeakable Sentences: Narration and Representation in the Language of Fiction.* London: Routledge and Kegan Paul, 1982.

Bann, Stephen. "Abstract Art – A Language." In Alan Bowness, ed., *Abstraction: Towards a New Art.* London: Tate Gallery, 1980, 125–45.

Barthes, Roland. "Structural Study of Narrative." In Barthes, *Images, Music Text,* trans. Stephen Heath. New York: Hill and Wang, 1977, 79–124.

Writing Degree Zero, trans. Annette Lavers and Colin Smith. New York: Hill and Wang, 1968.

Bate, Walter Jackson. *John Keats*. Cambridge, Mass.: Harvard University Press (Belknap Press), 1964.

Bates, Milton J. *Wallace Stevens: A Mythology of Self*. Berkeley and Los Angeles: University of California Press, 1985.

Baudelaire, Charles Pierre. *Baudelaire: Selected Verse*, ed. and trans. Francis Scarfe. Baltimore: Penguin Books, 1961.

Baudelaire: Selected Writings on Art and Artists, trans. P. E. Charvet. Baltimore: Penguin Books, 1972.

Oeuvres Complétes, ed. Y. G. Le Dantec and Claude Pichois. Paris: Gallimard, 1968.

Beardsley, Monroe. *Aesthetics: Problems in the Philosophy of Criticism*. New York: Harcourt, Brace and World, 1958.

Beebe, Maurice. "Introduction: What Modernism Was." *Journal of Modern Literature* 3 (1974): 1065–84.

Beebe, Maurice, ed. "1980–1981, Annual Review." *Journal of Modern Literature* 8 (1980–1): 339–684.

Bell, Ian. *Critic as Scientist: The Modernist Poetics of Ezra Pound*. New York: Methuen, 1981.

"Pound's Vortex: Shapes Ancient and Modern." *Paideuma* 10 (1981): 243–71.

Benamou, Michel. "Wallace Stevens: Some Relations between Poetry and Painting." *Comparative Literature* 11 (1959): 47–60.

Benjamin, Walter. *The Origin of German Tragic Drama*, trans. John Osborne. London: New Left Books, 1977.

Berger, Charles. *Forms of Farewell: The Late Poetry of Wallace Stevens*. Madison: University of Wisconsin Press, 1985.

Berger, John. *Success and Failure of Picasso*. Baltimore: Penguin Books, 1965.

Ways of Seeing: A Book Made by John Berger [and Others]. Harmondsworth: Penguin Books, 1978.

Bergonzi, Bernard. *T. S. Eliot*. New York: Macmillan, 1972.

Berman, Marshall. *All That Is Solid Melts into Air: The Experience of Modernity*. New York: Simon and Schuster, 1982.

Bernstein, J. M. *The Philosophy of the Novel: Lukàcs, Marxism and the Dialectics of Form*. Brighton: Harvester Press, 1984.

Bernstein, Michael André. "Identification and Its Vicissitudes: The Narrative Structure of Ezra Pound's Cantos." *Yale Review* 69 (1980): 540–56.

The Tale of the Tribe. Princeton: Princeton University Press, 1980.

Bersani, Leo. *Baudelaire and Freud*. Berkeley and Los Angeles: University of California Press, 1977.

The Death of Stephane Mallarmé. New York: Cambridge University Press, 1982.

Bertrand, Gérard. *L'Illustration de la Poesie à l'Epoque du Cubisme, 1909–1914*. Paris: Klinchreich, 1971.

Bloom, Harold. *Wallace Stevens: The Poems of Our Climate*. Ithaca, N.Y.: Cornell University Press, 1977.

Blumenberg, Hans. *The Legitimacy of the Modern Age*, trans. Robert M. Wallace. Cambridge, Mass.: MIT Press, 1983.

Bois, Yves-Alain. "Kahnweiler's Lesson." *Representations* 18 (1987): 33–68.

Booth, Wayne C. *The Rhetoric of Fiction.* Chicago: University of Chicago, 1983.

Bornstein, George. *The Postromantic Consciousness of Ezra Pound.* Victoria: University of Victoria Press, 1977.

Transformations of Romanticism in Yeats, Eliot and Stevens. Chicago: University of Chicago Press, 1976.

Bowness, Alan, ed. *Towards a New Art: Essay on the Background to Abstract Art, 1910–20.* London: Tate Gallery, 1980.

Bradbury, Malcolm, and James McFarlane, eds. *Modernism.* Harmondsworth: Penguin Books, 1976.

Brogan, Jacqueline Vaught. *Stevens and Simile: A Theory of Language.* Princeton, N.J.: Princeton University Press, 1986.

Brooker, Jewel Spears. "Common Ground and Collaboration in T. S. Eliot." *Centennial Review* 25 (1981): 225–38.

"The Dispensations of Art: Mallarmé and the Fallen Reader." *Southern Review* 19 (1983): 17–38.

Brooks, Cleanth. *Modern Poetry and the Tradition.* Chapel Hill: University of North Carolina Press, 1939.

Bruns, Gerald. "The Formal Nature of Victorian Thinking." *PLMA* 90 (1975): 904–18.

"Stevens without Epistemology." In Albert Gelpi, ed., *Wallace Stevens: The Poetics of Modernism.* New York: Cambridge University Press, 1985.

Bürger, Peter. *Theory of the Avant-Garde,* trans. Michael Shaw. Minneapolis: University of Minnesota Press, 1984.

Burgess, Gelett. "Picasso Is a Devil" (1912). Reprinted in Gert Schiff, ed., *Picasso in Perspective.* Englewood Cliffs, N.J.: Prentice Hall, 1976, 30–1.

Burke, Kenneth. *The Rhetoric of Religion.* Berkeley and Los Angeles: University of California Press, 1970.

Bush, Ronald. *The Genesis of Ezra Pound's Cantos.* Princeton, N.J.: Princeton University Press, 1976.

T. S. Eliot: A Study in Character and Style. New York: Oxford University Press, 1983.

Cachin, Francois. "The Impressionists on Trial." Review of T. J. Clark, *The Painting of Modern Life: Paris in the Art of Manet and His Followers,* in *New York Review* 32 (May 30, 1985): 24–30.

Carter, Huntley. "The Coming Age." *New Freewoman* (1913): 16–17.

Caserio, Robert. "*The Rescue* and the Ring of Meaning." In Ross C. Murfin, ed., *Conrad Revisited: Essays for the Eighties,* 125–50.

Cézanne, Paul. *Paul Cézanne. Letters,* ed. John Rewald, trans. Marguerite Kay. Oxford: Cassirer, 1976.

Chase, Cynthia. "The Ring of Gyges and the Coat of Darkness: Reading Rousseau with Wordsworth." In Arden Reed, ed., *Romanticism and Language,* Ithaca, N.Y.: Cornell University Press, 1984, 22–49.

Chipp, Herschel, ed. *Theories of Modern Art.* Berkeley and Los Angeles: University of California Press, 1968.

Christ, Carol T. *The Finer Optic: The Aesthetic of Particularity in Victorian Poetry.* New Haven, Conn.: Yale University Press, 1975.

Victorian and Modern Poetics. Chicago: University of Chicago Press, 1984.

Clark, T. J. "Arguments about Modernism: A Reply to Michael Fried." In Francis Frascina, *Pollock and After: The Critical Debate,* 81–8.

"More on the Differences between Comrade Greenberg and Ourselves." In Benjamin H. D. Buchloh, Serge Guilbaut, David Solkin et al., *Modernism and Modernity.* Halifax: Press of the Nova Scotia College of Art and Design, 1983, 169–94.

The Painting of Modern Life: Paris in the Art of Manet and His Followers. New York: Knopf, 1985.

Clarke, Bruce. "Fabulous Monsters of Conscience: Anthropomorphosis in Keats's *Lamia.*" *Studies in Romanticism* 24 (1985): 555–79.

Clausen, Christopher. *The Place of Poetry: Two Centuries of an Art in Crisis.* Lexington: University Press of Kentucky, 1981.

Coellen, Ludwig. "Romanticism in Picasso." In Marilyn McCully, *A Picasso Anthology,* 94–7.

Cohen, Ralph. *The Art of Discrimination.* London: Routledge and Kegan Paul, 1964.

Coleridge, Samuel. "Appendix A" to *The Statesman's Manual.* In J. Shawcross, ed., *Biographia Literaria, Aesthetical Essays.* London: Oxford University Press, 1954, 308–48.

Cook, Albert. *Figural Choice in Poetry and Art.* Hanover, N.H.: University Press of New England, 1985.

Cook, John. *Vorticism and Abstract Art in the First Machine Age.* Berkeley and Los Angeles: University of California Press, 1976.

Costello, Bonnie. "Affects of an Analogy: Wallace Stevens and Painting." In Albert Gelpi, ed., *Wallace Stevens: The Poetics of Modernism,* 65–85.

Marianne Moore: Imaginary Possessions. Cambridge, Mass.: Harvard University Press, 1981.

Culler, Jonathan. *Flaubert: The Uses of Uncertainty.* Ithaca, N.Y.: Cornell University Press, 1974.

Daix, Pierre. *Picasso: The Cubist Years, 1907–1916.* Boston: New York Graphic Society, 1979.

Danto, Arthur. *The Transfiguration of the Commonplace.* Cambridge, Mass.: Harvard University Press, 1981.

Dasenbrock, Reed Way, ed. *The Literary Vorticism of Pound and Lewis: Towards the Condition of Painting.* Baltimore: Johns Hopkins Press, 1985.

Davenport, Guy. *Cities on Hills: A Study of I–XXX of Ezra Pound's Cantos.* Ann Arbor, Mich.: UMI Research Press, 1983.

Davidson, Michael. "Notes beyond the *Notes:* Wallace Stevens and Contemporary Poetics." In Gelpi, *Wallace Stevens,* 141–60.

Davie, Donald. *Ezra Pound.* Harmondsworth: Penguin Books, 1975.

de Man, Paul. *Allegories of Reading.* New Haven, Conn.: Yale University Press, 1979.

Blindness and Insight: Essays in the Rhetoric of Contemporary Criticism. New York: Oxford University Press, 1971.

Denis, Maurice. "Subjective and Objective Deformation." (1909). Reprinted in Herschel Chipp, ed., *Theories of Modern Art,* University of California Press 1968, 105–7.

Derrida, Jacques. "The Double Seance of Mallarmé." In Derrida, *Disseminations,* trans. Barbara Johnson. Chicago: University of Chicago Press, 1981, 173–216.

Of Grammatology, Trans. Gayatri Spivak. Baltimore: Johns Hopkins Press, 1976.

Descargues, Pierre. "The Work of Georges Braque." In Francis Ponge, Pierre Descargues, and André Malraux, *Georges Braque.* New York: Abrams, 1971, 77–240.

Descombes, Vincent. "An Essay in Philosophical Observation." In Alan Montefiore, ed., *Philosophy in France Today.* Cambridge, Eng.: Cambridge University Press, 1983, 67–81.

Dijkstra, Bram. *The Hieroglyphics of a New Speech: Cubism, Stieglitz and the Early Poetry of William Carlos Williams.* Princeton, N.J.: Princeton University Press, 1969.

Duffey, Bernard. *A Poetry of Presence.* Madison: University of Wisconsin Press, 1986.

Dunn, Allen. "The Self-authenticating Stance in Stevens and Williams." Ph.D. diss., University of Washington, 1981.

Eagleton, Terence. *Criticism and Ideology.* London: Verso Editions, 1976.

Eddy, Arthur Jerome. *Cubists and Post-Impressionism.* (1914) Chicago: McClung, 1919.

Edson, Laurie. "Henri Michaux: Artist and Writer of Movement." *Modern Language Review* 78 (1983): 46–60.

Eliot, T. S. *The Complete Poems and Plays.* New York: Harcourt, Brace, 1952.

Knowledge and Experience in the Philosophy of F. H. Bradley. London: Faber and Faber, 1964.

Selected Essays: New Edition. New York: Harcourt, Brace, 1950.

Selected Essays, 1917–1932. New York: Harcourt, Brace, 1932.

Ellman, Richard. *The Identity of Yeats.* New York: Oxford University Press, 1964.

Ellman, Richard, and Charles Feidelson, eds. *The Modern Tradition.* New York: Oxford University Press, 1965.

Ferguson, Suzanne. "Defining the Short Story: Impressionism and Form." *Modern Fiction Studies* 28 (1982): 13–24.

Flaubert, Gustave. *Correspondence.* Paris: Flammarion, 1926–32.

Madame Bovary, ed. and trans. Paul de Man. New York: Norton, 1965.

Flory, Wendy Stallard. *Ezra Pound and "The Cantos": A Record of Struggle.* New Haven, Conn.: Yale University Press, 1980.

Foster, Hal. *Recodings.* Port Townsend, Washington: Bay Press, 1986.

Foster, Hal, ed. *The Anti-aesthetic: Essays on Postmodern Culture.* Port Townsend, Washington: Bay Press, 1983.

Foster, John Burt. *Heirs to Dionysus: A Nietzschean Current in Literary Modernism.* Princeton, N.J.: Princeton University Press, 1981.

Fox, Howard, ed. *Content: A Contemporary Forum, 1974–84.* Washington, D.C.: Smithsonian Institute Press, 1984.

Frascina, Francis, ed. *Pollock and After: The Critical Debate.* London: Harper and Row, 1985.

Frascina, Francis, and Charles Harrison, eds. *Modern Art and Modernism: A Critical Anthology*. London: Harper and Row, 1982.

Fried, Michael. *Absorption and Theatricality: Painting and Theatricality in the Age of Diderot*. Baltimore: Johns Hopkins Press, 1980.

———. "Art and Objecthood." In Gregory Batcock, ed., *Minimal Art: A Critical Anthology*. New York: Dutton, 1968, 116–47.

———. *Morris Louis*. New York: Abrams, 1970.

Froula, Christine. *To Write Paradise: Style and Error in Pound's Cantos*. New Haven, Conn.: Yale University, 1984.

Fry, Roger. *Vision and Design*. London: Pelican, 1940.

Frye, Northrop. *A Study of English Romanticism*. New York: Random House, 1968.

Frye, Paul. *The Reach of Method*. New Haven, Conn.: Yale University Press, 1983.

Gabo, Naum. "The Constructive Idea in Art." In Robert L. Herbert, ed., *Modern Artists on Art*, 103–13.

Gadamer, Hans Georg. *Truth and Method*. New York: Seabury Press, 1975.

Garber, Frederic. *Wordsworth and the Poetry of Encounter*. Urbana: University of Illinois Press, 1971.

Gauguin, Paul. *The Intimate Journals of Paul Gauguin*. London: KPI, 1985.

Gay, Peter. "The Apples of Cézanne: An Essay on the Meaning of Still Life." In *Modern Art: 19th and 20th Centuries*. New York: Braziller, 1982.

———. *Art and Act: On Causes in History: Manet, Gropius, Mondrian*. New York: Harper and Row, 1976.

Geertz, Clifford. *The Interpretations of Culture*. New York: Basic Books, 1973.

Gelley, Alexander. "Metonymy, Schematism, and the Space of Literature." *NLH* 8 (1980): 469–88.

Gelpi, Albert. *A Coherent Splendor: The American Poetic Renaissance, 1910–1950*. New York: Cambridge University Press, 1987.

Gelpi, Albert, ed. *Wallace Stevens, The Poetics of Modernism*. New York: Cambridge University Press, 1985.

Gerhardus, Maly. *Cubism and Futurism*, trans. John Griffiths. New York: Dutton, 1977.

Girard, René. *Deceit, Desire and the Novel: Self and Other in Literary Structure*, trans. Yvone Freccero. Baltimore: Johns Hopkins Press, 1965.

Golding, John. *Cubism: A History and an Analysis, 1907–1914*. Boston Book and Art Shop, 1961.

Gombrich, Ernst. *Art and Illusion: A Study in the Psychology of Pictorial Representation*. Oxford: Phaidon, 1977.

Goodman, Nelson. *Languages of Art*. New York: Bobbs-Merrill, 1968.

———. *The Ways of Worldmaking*. Indianapolis: Hackett, 1978.

Gordon, Lyndall. *Eliot's Early Years*. Oxford: Oxford University Press, 1977.

Goux, Jean-Joseph. *Les Iconoclastes*. Paris: Du Seuil, 1978.

Graff, Gerald. *Literature against Itself: Literary Ideas in Modern Society*. Chicago: University of Chicago Press, 1979.

Gray, Christopher. *Cubist Aesthetic Theories*. Baltimore: Johns Hopkins Press, 1953.

Gray, Piers. *T. S. Eliot's Intellectual and Poetic Development, 1909–1922*. Brighton: Harvester Press, 1982.

Greenberg, Clement. *Art and Culture: Critical Essays*. Boston: Beacon Press, 1981.

Greenblatt, Stephen. "Loudun and London." *Critical Inquiry* 12 (1986): 326–46.

Guyer, Paul. *Kant and the Claims of Taste*. Cambridge, Mass.: Harvard University Press, 1979.

Habermas, Jürgen. *Communication and the Evolution of Society,* trans. Thomas McCarthy. Boston: Beacon Press, 1979.

Hallam, Arthur Henry. "On Some of the Characteristics of Modern Poetry." In Walter Houghton and Robert Stange, eds., *Victorian Poetry and Poetics,* 2nd ed. Boston: Houghton Mifflin, 1968, 848–60.

Hamilton, Ian. *"The Waste Land."* In Graham Martin, ed., *Eliot in Perspective*. New York: Humanities Press, 1970, 102–11.

Hampshire, Stuart. "Breaking Away." Review of Roger Shattuck, *The Innocent Eye,* in *New York Review* 32 (May 9, 1985): 18–20.

Harrison, Charles. "The Ratification of Abstract Art." In Alan Bowness, *Abstraction,* 146–55.

Hartman, Geoffrey. *Criticism in the Wilderness: The Study of Literature Today*. New Haven: Yale University Press, 1980.

Hejinian, Lynn. "Two Stein Talks." *Temblor* 3 (1986): 128–39.

Henderson, Linda D. *The Fourth Dimension and Non-euclidean Geometry in Modern Art*. Princeton, N.J.: Princeton University Press, 1983.

 "Mabel Dodge, Gertrude Stein, and Max Weber: A Four-dimensional Trio." *Arts* 57 (1982): 106–11.

Henley, William Ernest. *Poems*. New York: Scribner, 1919.

Herbert, Robert L., ed. *Modern Artists on Art*. Englewood Cliffs, N.J.: Prentice-Hall, 1964.

Holden, Jonathan. "Postmodern Poetic Form: A Theory." *New England Review* 6 (1983): 1–22.

Hollinger, David. "The Knower and the Artificer." *American Quarterly* 39 (1987): 37–55.

Holquist, Michael, and Walter Reed. "Six Theses on the Novel – and Some Metaphors." *New Literary History* 11 (1980): 413–24.

Howe, Irving, ed. *The Idea of the Modern in Literature and the Arts*. New York: Horizon, 1968.

Howe, Susan. *My Emily Dickinson*. Berkeley: North Atlantic Books, 1985.

Hueffer, Ford Madox. "The Poet's Eye." *New Freewoman* 1 (September 15, 1913): 166–7.

Hulme, T. E., *Further Speculations,* ed. Samuel Hynes. Lincoln: University of Nebraska Press, 1962.

Husserl, Edmund. *Logical Investigations,* trans. J. N. Findlay. London: Routledge and Kegan Paul, 1970.

Irwin, John. "Self-evidence and Self-reference: Nietzsche and Tragedy, Whitman and Opera." *NLH* 11 (1979): 177–92.

Isomaki, Richard. "Shelley's Causal Themes." Ph.D. diss., University of Washington, 1986.

Jackson, Thomas. "Pound and Herder and the Concept of Expression." *MLQ* 44 (1983): 374–93.

James, Henry. *The Future of the Novel: Essays on the Art of Fiction,* ed. Leon Edel. New York: Vintage Books, 1956.

Jameson, Frederic. *Fables of Aggression: Wyndham Lewis: The Modernist as Fascist.* Berkeley and Los Angeles: University of California Press, 1979.

The Political Unconscious. Ithaca, N.Y.: Cornell University Press, 1981.

"Postmodernism, or the Cultural Logic of Late Capitalism." *New Left Review* 146 (1984): 53–93.

Jardine, Alice. *Gynesis: Configurations of Woman and Modernity.* Ithaca, N.Y.: Cornell University Press, 1985.

Jay, Gregory S. "America the Scrivener: Economy and Literary History." *Diacritics* 14 (1984): 36–51.

T. S. Eliot and the Poetics of Literary History. Baton Rouge: Louisiana State University Press, 1982.

Johnson, E. D. H. *The Alien Vision of Victorian Poetry: Sources of the Poetic Imagination in Tennyson, Browning, and Arnold.* Princeton: Princeton University Press, 1952.

Johnston, Kenneth G. "Hemingway and Cézanne: Doing the Country." *American Literature* 56 (1984): 28–37.

Joyce, James. *Stephen Hero.* New York: New Directions, 1944.

Judkins, Winthrup. "Towards a Reinterpretation of Cubism." *Art Bulletin* 30 (1948): 275–6.

Kahnweiler, Daniel Henry. *Juan Gris: His Life and Work,* rev. ed. New York: Abrams, 1969.

Kamber, Gerald. *Max Jacob and the Poetics of Cubism.* Baltimore: Johns Hopkins Press, 1971.

Kandinsky, Wassily. *Concerning the Spiritual in Art, and Painting in Particular* (1912). New York: Wittenborn, Schulz, 1947.

"On the Problem of Form." In Herschel Chipp, *Theories of Modern Art,* 155–70.

"Reminiscences." In Robert L. Herbert, *Modern Artists on Art,* 19–44.

Kant, Immanuel. *The Critique of Judgment,* trans. Jo Meredith. Oxford: Oxford University Press (Clarendon Press), 1952.

Foundations of the Metaphysics of Morals, trans. Lewis White Beck. New York: Liberal Arts Press, 1959.

Keats, John. *The Poetical Works of John Keats,* ed. H. W. Garrod. London: Oxford University Press, 1956.

Kenner, Hugh. *A Homemade World: The American Modernist Writers.* New York: Knopf, 1975.

"The Possum in the Cave." In Stephen J. Greenblatt, ed., *Allegory and Representation.* Baltimore: Johns Hopkins Press, 1981, 120–44.

The Pound Era. Berkeley and Los Angeles: University of California Press, 1971.

"Some Post-symbolist Structures." In Frank Brady, John Palmer, and Martin Price, eds., *Literary Theory and Structure.* New Haven, Conn.: Yale University Press, 1973, 379–93.

Kern, Stephen. *The Culture of Time and Space: 1880–1918.* Cambridge, Mass.: Harvard University Press, 1983.

Klee, Paul. *On Modern Art,* trans. Paul Findlay. London: Faber and Faber, n.d.

Knapp, Stephen. *Personification and the Sublime: Milton to Coleridge.* Cambridge, Mass.: Harvard University Press, 1985.

Korg, Jacob. *Language in Modern Literature: Innovation and Experience.* New York: Barnes and Noble, 1979.

Kozloff, Max. *Cubism and Futurism.* New York: Harper and Row, 1973.

Krauss, Rosalind. "Re-presenting Picasso." *Art in America* 68 (1980): 90–6.

Kripke, Saul. *Wittgenstein on Rules and Private Language.* Cambridge, Mass.: Harvard University Press, 1982.

Lacan, Jacques. *Ecrits: A Selection,* trans. Alan Sheridan. New York: Norton, 1977.

Langbaum, Robert. "New Modes of Characterization in *The Waste Land.*" In Litz, *Eliot in His Time.* Princeton, N.J.: Princeton University Press, 1973, 95–128.

The Poetry of Experience. New York: Random House, 1957.

Leavis, F. R. *New Bearings in English Poetry.* London: Chatto and Windus, 1950.

Legget, B. J. *Wallace Stevens and Poetic Theory: Conceiving the Supreme Fiction.* Chapel Hill: University of North Carolina Press, 1986.

Lehman, David. "Ecstatic Occasions, Expedient Forms." *Epoch* 23 (1983): 31–97.

Lehman, Winfred. *The Symbolist Aesthetic in France, 1885–1895.* Oxford: Blackwell Publisher, 1950.

Lentricchia, Frank. *After the New Criticism.* Chicago: University of Chicago Press, 1980.

"Patriarchy against Itself: The Young Manhood of Wallace Stevens." *Critical Inquiry* 13 (1987): 742–86.

Levenson, Michael H. *A Genealogy of Modernism: A Study of English Literary Doctrine, 1908–22.* New York: Cambridge University Press, 1984.

Levin, Gail. "Wassily Kandinsky and the American Literary Avant-garde." *Criticism* 21 (1979): 347–61.

Levinas, Emmanuel. *Otherwise than Being or Beyond Essence,* trans. Alphonse Lingis. The Hague: Nijhoff, 1981.

Levine, Bernard. *The Dissolving Image: The Spiritual-esthetic Development of W. B. Yeats,* Detroit: Wayne State University Press, 1970.

Lewis, Wyndham. *Tarr.* New York: Knopf, 1926.

Wyndham Lewis on Art, ed. Walter Michel and C. J. Fox. New York: Funk and Wagnalls, 1969.

Lindberg, Kathryne. *Reading Pound Reading: Modernism after Nietzsche.* New York: Oxford University Press, 1987.

Litz, A. Walton. *Introspective Voyager: The Poetic Development of Wallace Stevens.* New York: Oxford University Press, 1972.

"*The Waste Land* Fifty Years After." In Litz, *Eliot in His Time.* Princeton, N.J.: Princeton University Press, 1973, 3–22.

Lodge, David. *The Modes of Modern Writings: Metaphor, Metonymy, and the Typology of Modern Literature.* London: Arnold, 1977.

Loran, Erle. *Cézanne's Composition: Analysis of His Form with Diagrams and Photographs of His Motifs.* Berkeley and Los Angeles: University of California Press, 1970.

Lovibond, Sabina. *Realism and Imagination in Ethics.* Minneapolis: University of Minnesota Press, 1983.

Lukàcs, George. "The Ideology of Modernism." In Epifanio San Juan, ed., *Marxism and Human Liberation: Essays on History, Culture and Human Liberation.* New York: Delta, 1973, 277–387.

Lynton, Norbert. "The New Age: Primal Work and Mystic Nights." In Alan Bowness, *Abstractness,* 9–21.

Lyotard, Francois. *The Postmodern Condition: A Report on Knowledge,* trans. Geoff Bennington and Brian Massumi. Minneapolis: University of Minnesota Press, 1984.

McCully, Marilyn, ed. *A Picasso Anthology: Documents, Criticism, Reminiscences.* Princeton, N.J.: Princeton University Press, 1982.

McGann, Jerome. "The Meaning of the Ancient Mariner." *Critical Inquiry* 8 (1981): 67.

"The Religious Poetry of Christina Rossetti." In Robert von Hallberg, ed., *Canons.* Chicago: University of Chicago Press, 1984, 261–78.

McGowan, Christopher. *William Carlos Williams' Early Poetry: The Visual Arts Background.* Ann Arbor, Mich.: UMI Research Press, 1984.

"William Carlos Williams' *The Great Figure* and Marsden Hartley." *American Literature* 53 (1981): 302–5.

McGowan, John P. *Representation and Revelation: Victorian Realism from Carlyle to Keats.* Columbia: University of Missouri Press, 1986.

MacIntyre, Alasdair. *After Virtue: A Study in Moral Theory.* South Bend, Ind.: University of Notre Dame Press, 1984.

Secularization and Moral Change. New York: Oxford University Press, 1967.

Malevich, Kasimir. *Essays on Art, 1915–28,* ed. Troels Andersen. Copenhagen: Borgen, 1968.

World as Non-objectivity: Unpublished Writing, 1922–25, ed. and trans. Xenia Glowacki-Prus and Edmund Little. Copenhagen: Borgen, 1976.

Mallarmé, Stephane. *Mallarmé* [Selected poems], ed. and trans. Anthony Hartley. Baltimore: Penguin Books, 1965.

Mallarmé: Selected Prose, Poems, Essays and Letters, ed. and trans. Bradford Cook. Baltimore: Johns Hopkins Press, 1956.

Materer, Timothy. *Vortex: Pound, Eliot and Lewis.* Ithaca, N.Y.: Cornell University Press, 1979.

Merrill, James. *Changing Light at Sandover.* New York: Atheneum, 1983.

Miller, J. Hillis. *The Disappearance of God.* Cambridge, Mass.: Harvard University Press, 1963.

Poets of Reality. Cambridge, Mass.: Harvard University Press, 1965.

"Presidential Address, 1986." *PMLA* 102 (1987): 281–91.

"Stevens' *Rock* and Criticism as Cure." *Georgia Review* 30 (1976): 5–31, 330–48.

Miller, Milton. "What the Thunder Meant." *ELH* 36 (1969): 440–54.

Mitchell, W. J. Thomas, *Iconology: Image, Text, Ideology*. Chicago: University of Chicago Press, 1986.

Moffett, Charles, Ruth Benson, Barbara Lee Williams et al., *The New Painting: Impressionism, 1874–1886*. San Francisco: Fine Arts Museum, 1986.

Mondrian, Piet. "Natural Reality and Abstract Reality," trans. Michel Seuphor. In Michel Seuphor, *Piet Mondrian, 49–59*.

   L'Opera Completa di Piet Mondrian, ed. Maria Grazia Ottolenghi. Milan: Rizzoli, 1974, 301–52.

   "Plastic Art." In Michel Seuphor, *Piet Mondrian*, 114–30.

   "Principles of Neo-Plasticism." In Michel Seuphor, *Piet Mondrian*, 166–8.

Moore, Marianne. *The Complete Poems of Marianne Moore*. New York: Viking, 1981.

   The Complete Prose of Marianne Moore. New York: Penguin Books, 1986.

Murfin, Ross C., ed. *Conrad Revisited: Essays for the Eighties*. University: University of Alabama Press, 1985.

Nagel, Thomas. *Mortal Questions*. New York: Cambridge University Press, 1979.

Newman, Charles. "The Post-Modern Aura." *Salmagundi* 64, 66–7 (1984): 1–218, 5–199.

Nielsen, A. L. "Imagining Space." *Literary Review* 24 (1981): 333–47.

Nietzsche, Friedrich. *Beyond Good and Evil,* ed. and trans. Walter Kaufman. New York: Random House, 1966.

Nochlin, Linda, ed. *Impressionism and Post-Impressionism, 1874–1904: Sources and Documents*. Englewood Cliffs, N.J.: Prentice-Hall, 1966.

North, Michael. *The Final Sculpture: Public Monuments and Modern Poets*. Ithaca, N.Y.: Cornell University Press, 1985.

Novotny, Fritz. *Painting and Sculpture in Europe, 1780–1880*. Baltimore: Penguin Books, 1960.

Nozick, Robert. *Philosophical Explanations*. Cambridge, Mass.: Harvard University Press (Belknap Press), 1981.

Olson, Charles. *Human Universe and Other Essays,* ed. Donald Allen. New York: Grove, 1967.

Oren, Michael. "Williams and Gris: A Borrowed Aesthetic." *Contemporary Literature* 26 (1985): 197–211.

Osborne, Harold. *Abstraction and Artifice*. New York: Oxford University Press, 1979.

Ostriker, Alicia. *Stealing the Language: The Emergence of Women's Poetry in America*. Boston: Beacon Press, 1986.

Pach, Walter. *The Masters of Modern Art*. New York: Huebsch, 1924.

Palgrave, Francis Turner, ed. *The Golden Treasury*. New York: Macmillan, 1983.

Pater, Walter. *Marius the Epicurean*. New York: Dutton, 1951.

   "Conclusion" to *Studies in the Renaissance*. In W. B. Yeats, ed., *Oxford Book of Modern Verse*. Oxford: Oxford University Press, 1936.

Paulu i Fabre, Josep. *Picasso: The Early Years 1881–1907*. New York: Rizzoli, 1981.

Paz, Ottavio. *Children of the Mire: Modern Poetry from Romanticism to the Avant-*

garde, trans. Rachel Phillips. Cambridge, Mass.: Harvard University Press, 1974.

Pecorino, Jessica Prinz. "Resurgent Icons: Pound's First Pisan Canto and the Visual Arts." *Journal of Modern Literature* 9 (1982): 159–74.

Perl, Jeffrey M. *The Tradition of Return: The Implicit History of Modern Literature.* Princeton, N.J.: Princeton University Press, 1984.

Perloff, Marjorie. *Dance of the Intellect: Studies in the Poetry of the Pound Tradition.* New York: Cambridge University Press, 1985.

The Futurist Moment. Chicago: University of Chicago Press, 1986.

"The Invention of Collage." *New York Literary Forum* 10–11 (1983): 5–47.

The Poetics of Indeterminacy: Rimbaud to Cage. Princeton, N.J.: Princeton University Press, 1981.

"Postmodernism and the Impasse of Lyric." In *Dance of the Intellect,* 172–200.

"Postmodernism and the Lyric Impulse." *Formations,* 1 (1984): 43–63.

"Pound / Stevens: Whose Era?" *New Literary History* 13 (1982): 485–514.

Perry, John, and John Barwise. *Situations and Attitudes.* Cambridge, Mass.: MIT Press, 1985.

Philipson, Michael. *Painting, Language and Modernity.* Boston: Routledge and Kegan Paul, 1985.

Pinsky, Robert. *The Situation of Poetry.* Princeton, N.J.: Princeton University Press, 1976.

Pleynet, Marcelin. *Systeme de la Peinture.* Paris: Du Seuil, 1977.

Poirier, Richard. *Robert Frost: The Work of Knowing.* New York: Oxford University Press, 1977.

Ponge, Francis, Pierre Descarques, and André Malraux. *Georges Braque,* trans. Richard Howard. New York: Abrams, 1971.

Noveaux Recueils. Paris: Gallimard, 1967.

Pound, Ezra. *The Cantos of Ezra Pound,* ed. T. S. Eliot. New York: New Directions, 1970.

Ezra Pound and the Visual Arts, ed. Harriet Zinnes. New York: New Directions, 1980.

Gaudier-Brzeska. New York: New Directions, 1970.

Literary Essays of Ezra Pound, ed. T. S. Eliot. London: Faber and Faber, 1960.

Personae. London: Faber and Faber, 1952.

Selected Prose, 1909–65: Ezra Pound, ed. William Cookson. New York: New Directions, 1973.

"Three Cantos." *Poetry* 10 (1917): 113–21, 181–8, 248–54.

Quiñones, Richard J. *Mapping Literary Modernism: Time and Development.* Princeton, N.J.: Princeton University Press, 1985.

Raphael, Max. "Open Letter to Herr Pechstein." In Marilyn McCully, *A Picasso Anthology,* 92–3.

Rapp, Carl. *William Carlos Williams and Romantic Idealism.* Lebanon, N.H.: University Presses of New England, 1984.

Rawls, John. *A Theory of Justice.* Cambridge, Mass.: Harvard University Press, 1971.

Raymond, Marcel. *From Baudelaire to Surrealism.* London: Methuen, 1970.

Rewald, John. *Post-Impressionism: From Van Gogh to Gauguin.* New York: Museum of Modern Art, 1978.

Richardson, Joan. *Wallace Stevens: The Early Years, 1879–1923.* New York: Morrow, 1986.

Ricks, Christopher. *Tennyson.* New York: Macmillan, 1972.

Riddel, Joseph. "The Anomalies of Literary (Post) Modernism." *Arizona Quarterly* 44 (1988): 80–119.

   The Clairvoyant Eye. Baton Rouge: Louisiana State University Press, 1965.

   The Inverted Bell; Modernism and the Counterpoetics of William Carlos Williams. Baton Rouge: Louisiana State University Press, 1974.

   "Metaphoric Staging: Stevens Beginning Again of the 'End of the Book.'" In Frank Doggett and Robert Buttel, eds., *Wallace Stevens: A Celebration.* Princeton, N.J.: Princeton University Press, 1980.

Riley, Michael D. "T. S. Eliot, F. H. Bradley, and J. Hillis Miller: The Metaphysical Context." *Yeats Eliot Review* 8 (1986): 76–89.

Rilke, Rainer Maria. *Letters on Cézanne,* ed. Clara Rilke, New York: Fromm International, 1985.

   Selected Works. vol. 1: *Prose,* ed. J. B. Leishman, trans. G. Craig Houston. London: Hogarth Press, 1967.

Robinson, Alan. *Poetry, Painting and Ideas, 1885–1914.* London: Macmillan, 1985.

Rosen, Charles, and Henri Zerner. *Modern Painting and the Northern Tradition: Fredrich to Rothko.* New York: Harper and Row, 1975.

Rosenberg, John D. "The Two Kingdoms of *In Memoriam.*" *JEGP* 58 (1959): 228–40.

Rosenblum, Robert T. *Cubism and Twentieth Century Art.* New York: Abrams, 1961.

Roskill, Mark. *The Interpretation of Cubism.* Cranbury, N.J.: Associated University Presses, 1985.

Rowell, Margit. "Interview with Charmion von Wiegand." In Thomas Messer, ed., *Piet Mondrian.* New York: Guggenheim, 1971, 77–86.

Royce, Josiah. *Lectures on Modern Idealism.* New Haven, Conn.: Yale University Press, 1964.

Rubin, William, ed. *Pablo Picasso: A Retrospective.* New York: Museum of Modern Art, 1980.

Russell, Charles. *Poets, Prophets and Revolutionaries: The Literary Avant-garde from Rimbaud through Postmodernism.* New York: Oxford University Press, 1985.

Said, Edward. *Beginnings: Intention and Method.* New York: Basic Books, 1971.

Sayre, Henry M. "Ready-mades and Other Measures: The Poetics of Marcel Duchamp and William Carlos Williams." *Journal of Modern Literature* 8 (1980): 3–22.

   The Visual Text of William Carlos Williams. Urbana: University of Illinois Press, 1983.

Schapiro, Meyer. *Modern Art: 19th and 20th Centuries.* New York: Braziller, 1978.

   Paul Cézanne. New York: Abrams, 1952.

Schneidau, Herbert. *Ezra Pound: The Image and the Real*. Baton Rouge: Louisiana State University Press, 1969.

Schneider, Elizabeth. "Prufrock and After: The Theme of Change." *PLMA* 87 (1972): 1102–14.

Scholes, Robert. *Textual Power: Literary Theory and the Teaching of English*. New Haven, Conn.: Yale University Press, 1985.

Schwab, Gabrielle. "Genesis of the Subject, Imaginary Functions and Poetic Language." *New Literary History* 15 (1984): 453–74.

Schwartz, Sanford. *The Matrix of Modernism*. Princeton, N.J.: Princeton University Press, 1985.

Schwarz, Arturo. *Marcel Duchamp*. New York: Abrams, 1975.

Scott, Clive. "Symbolism, Decadence and Impressionism." In Malcolm Bradbury and James McFarlane, eds., *Modernism*, 206–27.

Seuphor, Michel. *Piet Mondrian: Life and Work*. New York: Abrams, n.d.

Shaviro, Steven. '"That Which Is Always Beginning': Stevens' Poetry of Affirmation." *PMLA* 100 (1985): 220–33.

Shiff, Richard. *Cézanne and the End of Impressionism: A Study of the Theory, Technique, and Critical Evaluation of Modern Art*. Chicago: University of Chicago Press, 1984.

"The End of Impressionism." In Charles S. Moffett, Ruth Berson, Barbara Lee Williams et al. *The New Painting*, 61–89.

"On Criticism Handling History." *Art Criticism* 3 (1986): 60–77.

"Performing an Appearance: On the Surface of Abstract Expressionism." Typescript, 86–99.

Sieburth, Richard. "In Pound We Trust: The Economy of Poetry / The Poetry of Economics." *Critical Inquiry* 14 (1987): 142–72.

Silverman, Kaja. "Lost Objects and Mistaken Subjects: Film Theory's Structuring Lack." *Wide Angle* 7 (1985), 14–29.

The Subject of Semiotics. New York: Oxford University Press, 1983.

Sinfield, Alan. *The Language of Tennyson's "In Memoriam."* Oxford: Blackwell Publisher, 1971.

Slatin, John M. *The Savage's Romance: The Poetry of Marianne Moore*. University Park: Pennsylvania State University Press, 1986.

Smith, Barbara Herrnstein. "Contingencies of Value." *Critical Inquiry* 10 (1983): 5–39.

Smith, Grover Cleveland. *The Waste Land*. Boston: Allen and Unwin, 1983.

Spanos, William. *Martin Heidegger and the Question of Literature: Towards a Postmodern Literary Hermeneutics*. Bloomington: Indiana University Press, 1979.

"Repetition in *The Waste Land*: A Phenomenological De-struction." *Boundary* 2 7 (1979): 225–85.

Sparshott, Francis. '"As' or the Limits of Metaphor." *New Literary History* 6 (1974): 75–94.

States, Bert O. *The Shape of Paradox*. Berkeley and Los Angeles: University of California Press, 1978.

Stein, Gertrude. *Picasso*. Boston: Beacon Press, 1959.

Steinberg, Leo. *Other Criteria*. New York: Oxford University Press, 1972.
 "The Philosophical Brothel." *Art News* 71 (1972): 20–29, and 71 (1972): 28–
 47.
Steiner, Wendy. *The Colors of Rhetoric*. Chicago: University of Chicago Press,
 1982.
 *Exact Resemblance to Exact Resemblance: The Literary Portraiture of Gertrude
 Stein*. New Haven, Conn.: Yale University Press, 1978.
 "Literary Cubism." In Steiner, *Exact Resemblance to Exact Resemblance*, 131–
 60.
Stella, Frank. *Working Space*. Cambridge, Mass.: Harvard University Press,
 1986.
Stevens, Wallace. *The Collected Poems of Wallace Stevens*. New York: Knopf,
 1964.
 The Letters of Wallace Stevens, ed. Holly Stevens. New York: Knopf, 1966.
 The Necessary Angel. New York: Random House, 1951.
 Opus Posthumus. New York: Knopf, 1957.
Stevenson, Michael H. *A Study of English Literary Doctrine, 1908–22*. Cambridge,
 Eng.: Cambridge University Press, 1984.
Stewart, Jack F. "Impressionism in the Early Novels of Virginia Woolf." *Journal
 of Modern Literature* 9 (1982): 237–66.
Stowell, H. Peter. *Literary Impressionism: James and Chekhov*. Athens: University
 of Georgia Press, 1980.
Surette, Leon. *A Light from Eleusis: A Study of Ezra Pound's Cantos*. New York:
 Oxford University Press, 1979.
Sypher, Wylie. *Rococo to Cubism in Art and Literature*. New York: Random
 House, 1960.
Tashjian, Dickran. *William Carlos Williams and the American Scene, 1920–40.
 Whitney Museum of American Art . . . Dec. 12, 1978–Feb. 4, 1979*. New
 York: Museum of Modern Art, 1978.
Taylor, Charles. *Hegel and Modern Society*. Cambridge, Eng. Cambridge Univer-
 sity Press, 1979.
Tennyson, Alfred. *Tennyson's Poetry*, ed. Robert W. Hill, Jr. New York: Nor-
 ton, 1971.
Todorov, Tzvestan. *Theories of the Symbol*. trans. Catherine Porter. Ithaca, N.Y.:
 Cornell University Press, 1982.
Tomlinson, David. "T. S. Eliot and the Cubists." *20th Century Literature* 26
 (1980): 64–81.
Trilling, Lionel. *Sincerity and Authenticity*. Cambridge, Mass.: Harvard Univer-
 sity Press, 1972.
Trimpi, Wesley. *Muses of One Mind: The Literary Analysis of Experience and Its
 Continuity*. Princeton, N.J.: Princeton University Press, 1983.
Tuchman, Maurice. *The Spiritual in Art: Abstract Painting, 1890–1985*. Los An-
 geles: Los Angeles County Museum, 1986.
Turim, Maureen Chern. *Abstraction in Avant-garde Films*. Ann Arbor, Mich.:
 UMI Research Press, 1985.
Turner, Frederick. *Natural Classicism: Essay on Literature and Science*. New York:
 Paragon House, 1985.

Ulmer, Gregory. *Applied Grammatology: Post-Pedagogy from Jacques Derrida to Joseph Beuys.* Baltimore: Johns Hopkins Press, 1985.

"Of a Parodic Tone Recently Adopted in Criticism." *New Literary History* 13 (1982): 543–60.

Valéry, Paul. *Collected Works.* Vol. 12: *Degas, Manet, Morisot,* ed. Jackson Mathews, trans. David Paul. New York: Bollingen Foundation, 1960.

Vendler, Helen. "The Hunting of Wallace Stevens." Review of three books on Stevens. *New York Review of Books* 33 (1986): 42–7.

Part of Nature, Part of Us. Cambridge, Mass.: Harvard University Press, 1980.

The Odes of John Keats. Cambridge, Mass.: Harvard University Press (Belknap Press), 1983.

Review of Marjorie Perloff, *Frank O'Hara: Poet among Painters. New York Review of Books* 24 (1977): 7–10.

Wallace Stevens: Words Chosen out of Desire. Knoxville: University of Tennessee, 1984.

Vico, Giambattista. *The New Science of Giambattista Vico,* trans. Thomas Godard Bergin and Max Harold Fisch. Abridged. Garden City, N.Y.: Doubleday, 1961.

Viscusi, Robert. *Max Beerbohm, or the Dandy Dante.* Baltimore: Johns Hopkins Press, 1986.

Voigt, Ellen Bryant. "Poetry and Gender." *Kenyon Review* 9 (1987): 127–39.

Waring, Ranier. "Irony and the 'Order of Discourse' in Flaubert." *New Literary History* 13 (1982): 253–86.

Walker, David. *The Transparent Lyric: Reading and Meaning in the Poetry of Stevens and Williams.* Princeton, N.J.: Princeton University Press, 1984.

Weaver, Mike. *William Carlos Williams: The American Background.* Cambridge, Eng.: Cambridge University Press, 1971.

Whiteside, George. "T. S. Eliot's Dissertation." *ELH* 34 (1967): 400–25.

Williams, William Carlos. *The Collected Poems of Williams Carlos Williams,* ed. A. Walton Litz and Christopher MacGowan. Vol. 1. New York: New Directions, 1986.

Imaginations, ed. Webster Schott. New York: New Directions, 1970.

Letter to James Laughlin, September 8, 1942. *Literary Review* 11 (1957): 16.

A Recognizable Image: William Carlos Williams on Art and Artists, ed. Bram Dijkstra. New York: New Directions, 1978.

Selected Essays of William Carlos Williams. New York: New Directions, 1954.

Spring and All. In William Carlos Williams, *Imaginations,* 85–154.

Williamson, Alan. *Introspection and Contemporary Poetry.* Cambridge, Mass.: Harvard University Press, 1984.

Wiseman, Mary Bittner. Review of Annette Lavers, *Roland Barthes: Structuralism and After. Philosophy and Literature* 7 (1983): 106–15.

Wittgenstein, Ludwig. *Lectures and Conversations on Aesthetics, Psychology, and Religious Belief,* compiled by Yorick Smythies, Rush Rhees, and James Taylor; ed. Cyril Barret. Oxford: Blackwell Publisher, 1966.

Notebooks: 1914–16, ed. and trans. G. E. M. Anscombe. New York: Harper and Row (Harper Torchbooks), 1969.

Philosophical Investigations, ed. and trans. G. E. M. Anscombe. New York: Macmillan, 1958.

Tractatus Logico-Philosophicus, ed. and trans. D. F. Pears and B. F. McGuinness. London: Routledge and Kegan Paul, 1961.

Wollheim, Richard. "Eliot and F. H. Bradley: An Account." In Graham Martin, ed., *Eliot in Perspective.* New York: Humanities Press, 1970, 169–93.

Wordsworth, William. *Selected Poems and Prefaces,* ed. Jack Stillinger. Boston: Houghton Mifflin, 1965.

Worringer, Wilhelm. *Abstraction and Empathy: A Contribution to the Psychology of Style.* New York: International University Press, 1953.

Yeats, William Butler. *Poems of W. B. Yeats,* ed. Richard J. Finneran. New York: Macmillan, 1983.

Index